Employment Tribunal Procedure

A user's guide to tribunals and appeals

Third edition

HIS HONOUR JUDGE JEREMY McMULLEN QC is a Judge of the Employment Appeal Tribunal, and Southwark Crown Court. He was formerly a part-time chairman of employment tribunals, member of the ACAS panel of equal pay experts, and chair of the ILO Joint Panel, the Industrial Law Society and the Employment Law Bar Association.
REBECCA TUCK and **BETSAN CRIDDLE** are barristers at Old Square Chambers, London and Bristol, specialising in employment and discrimination law.

The Legal Action Group is a national, independent charity which campaigns for equal access to justice for all members of society. Legal Action Group:

- provides support to the practice of lawyers and advisers
- inspires developments in that practice
- campaigns for improvements in the law and the administration of justice
- stimulates debate on how services should be delivered.

Employment Tribunal Procedure

A user's guide to tribunals
and appeals

THIRD EDITION

Jeremy McMullen, Rebecca Tuck and
Betsan Criddle

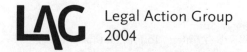

Legal Action Group
2004

This edition published in Great Britain 2004
by LAG Education and Service Trust Limited
242 Pentonville Road
London
N1 9UN
www.lag.org.uk

1st edition 1996: Jeremy McMullen and Jennifer Eady
Reprinted 1998: Jeremy McMullen and Jennifer Eady
2nd edition 2001: Jeremy McMullen, Jennifer Eady and Rebecca Tuck

While every effort has been made to ensure that the details in this text are correct, readers must be aware that the law changes and that the accuracy of the material cannot be guaranteed and the author and the publisher accept no responsibility for any losses or damage sustained.

The rights of the authors to be identified as authors of this work has been asserted by them in accordance with the Copyright, Designs and Patents Act 1988.

British Library Cataloguing in Publication Data
A CIP catalogue record for this book is available from the British Library

Crown copyright material is produced with the permission of the Controller of HMSO and the Queen's Printer for Scotland.

ISBN–10 1 903307 29 5
ISBN–13 978 1 903307 29 5

Typeset by RefineCatch Ltd, Bungay, Suffolk
Printed in Great Britain by Hobbs the Printers, Totton, Hampshire

Foreword to the First Edition

By LORD ARCHER OF SANDWELL QC
Chairman, Council on Tribunals

Industrial tribunals are the offspring of two historical processes. First was the stormy relationship between organised working people and the law. Where the common law had been left to develop according to the predilections of judges, employees in general, and trade unions in particular, found no greater understanding of their needs and aspirations among the judiciary than among their own employers. It is scarcely surprising, then, that employees felt greater confidence in a forum labelled 'tribunal' than they would have felt in a court.

Secondly, the rule of law had traditionally been declared to reside in the historic courts which dealt with disputes between individuals or between the individual and the executive. It was not until the Franks Report, in 1957, that specialist tribunals were accepted not as an exception to the rule of law, but as a constitutional part of it.

These two processes, then, converged in the mid-1960s, when newly-recognised rights to security in employment were enshrined in a succession of statutes. Since then successive governments have sought to reconcile the trade union movement to a system of adjudication without the unhappy associations of the courts, and in the last 30 years the jurisdiction of industrial tribunals has expanded to meet new forms of dispute and new needs. Unusually among tribunals, they deal largely, although by no means exclusively, with disputes not between citizen and government, but between citizen and citizen.

One consequence is that the jurisdiction is exercised in a relatively informal atmosphere, with a lawyer in the chair, and two colleagues whose contribution is not legal expertise, but some knowledge of the context in which industrial disputes arise. Yet the law administered in industrial tribunals is far from simple, and if it is to meet the varied situations found in a complicated world, it is likely to defy attempts at simplification. Even more confusing are the jurisdictional and procedural rules which are necessary to ensure that proceedings are heard in an orderly way, that everyone concerned understands the issues in the case, and that no-one is taken by surprise.

At the heart of such dispute resolution must be access to justice. Those who litigate in industrial tribunals are likely to need a guide through this labyrinth. *Employment Tribunal Procedure* will ensure that applicants throughout the country do not enter the process blind to the perils ahead. Those unfamiliar with this forum will benefit from its lucid guidance. The appendices are of particular value and the chronological approach of the text will help clarify and demystify tribunal procedure.

Few employees, and only a moderate proportion of smaller employers, are in a position to pay the fees of solicitors and counsel. If neither party has had access to advice, the tribunal is confronted with the dismaying task of extracting the essential issue from the evidence, while if one party enjoys competent representation and the other is denied it, we know from the research of Professor Hazel Genn and others that no tribunal, however competent and conscientious, can ensure a level playing field. If an issue is raised, or evidence is produced, at the hearing without previous warning, the tribunal is confronted with the options of excluding the new material, or of adjourning the hearing, with additional costs and delay to the parties, and the wasting of such time could have been allocated to other cases.

Everyone, then, has an interest in ensuring that litigants understand the jurisdiction which they are invoking, and take the proper procedural steps at the proper time. As yet, legal aid is not available for proceedings before industrial tribunals. Sometimes, competent help is obtainable from a trade union, a CAB, a law centre or the Free Representation Unit, but for many reasons, it is not always to hand at the necessary place and time. In this situation, there is an urgent need for a book setting out clearly in non-technical language the provisions which form the jurisdiction and procedure of industrial tribunals. This is such a book. It presents all the provisions clearly and accurately, and in a form which takes the reader quickly to the relevant information. While it comes to the aid of the puzzled litigant, it will also prove a blessing to trade union officials, personnel officers and others who help to prepare and present cases. For lawyers, too, it should provide a *vade mecum* which will spare much time-consuming research.

I venture to hope that it may inspire similar procedural guides to other systems of tribunals.

Preface

This book is written mainly to help advisers of people facing a tribunal hearing. We also hope it will be accessible to people bringing their own claims without the help of lawyers or specialist advisers. We have tried to show how working people can enforce their rights through the tribunal procedure; we take this commitment as being consistent with the legislation, which is about employment *rights* and anti-discrimination. What we say will be equally useful to employers and their advisers responding to claims.

It may seem odd that, as lawyers, we advocate using the tribunal procedures in the way we describe *only as a last resort*. Legal steps are no substitute for handling workplace problems at the workplace in accordance with agreed procedures. All parties will be better off if a dispute can be settled by negotiation without resort to a tribunal, or even to arbitration. Rights on union recognition introduced in 2002 and new procedures for workplace dispute resolution from October 2004 should assist this.

There have been many changes in legislation since the first edition – on working time, part-timers, race discrimination, sexual orientation, workplace representation, arbitration for unfair dismissal, giving a huge extension of rights to working people. The Human Rights Act 1998 has radically affected employment rights and the adjudication of them. New approaches to discrimination and other evils have been shaped by tribunals and courts in the UK and Europe. The programme of modernising tribunals which began with the 2001 regulations we described in the second edition has become more rigorous in the 2004 regulations. The Dispute Resolution Regulations 2004 give effect to new workplace procedures for grievances and discipline and there are new rules for tribunals and appeals to deal with them. These will make radical changes to the procedures for handling employment problems, without resort to tribunals.

They have also made it necessary for us to take a fresh look at the precedents and standard forms which were in the previous editions. The sheer number of kinds of cases which may be brought, and the many factual situations from which they arise, mean that it is more appropriate to put these in a different book. Fortunately, Naomi Cunningham's book *Employment Tribunal Claims: Tactics and Precedents* also published by LAG is designed to do just this. We have therefore included only the standard claim and response forms. For the substantive law on employment and discrimination, readers should look to other LAG publications: *Employment Law: an adviser's handbook* (Lewis, 2003) and *Discrimination Law Handbook* (Palmer, et al, 2002).

We are grateful to many legal, trade union and tribunal colleagues and clients who gave us ideas for this book and in particular Tony Pullen, Isabel Manley, Vereena Jones, Emma Smith, Alice Leonard and Colette Chesters for detailed comments on the original text. We also thank Adam Brett and Vice-President Mayo Price for their assistance on Northern Ireland law, and Vice-President Shona Simon for Scottish law, Mr Justice Burton, EAT President and Judge Goolam Meeran, ET President, for their invaluable comment on what we say about the latest rules which they both shaped, our clerks for their support and Katy McMullen for some editing. What appears is not their fault. We thank the Employment Tribunal Service, and the staff at London North West Region for earlier use of standard letters. Jennifer Eady, barrister, who co-wrote the first two editions but was unable to continue, has given us untold support and editorial comments and her work lives on in the text.

Throughout this book we have used 'chairman' to describe those who preside over employment tribunals. This is in accordance with the language of the legislation. References in statutes to *industrial* tribunals were replaced by statute in 1996.

We state the law as we see it on 1 October 2004 with the exception of the Employment Appeal Tribunal Practice Direction 2004 issued on 9 December 2004 and reproduced in appendix B.

Note on the law and tribunal procedure in Scotland and Northern Ireland

References to tribunals are to employment tribunals in England, Wales and Scotland, to industrial tribunals and the Fair Employment Tribunal in Northern Ireland, and to the Employment Appeal Tribunal. The written procedure in tribunals in England, Wales and Scotland is now the same and is set out in the same regulations, but the practical approach to certain issues in Scotland such as case management and witness evidence may differ. Scotland has its own chairmen, members and administration. The statutes containing employment rights apply across England, Wales and Scotland. Some aspects of the law of contract are different in Scotland, and some terms differ, and are preserved in the regulations, for example, sist (stay), expenses (costs), party litigant (litigant in person). Witnesses are usually excluded from the hearing until they give evidence.

The Employment Appeal Tribunal is a court of Great Britain and its judges and members may sit anywhere in England, Wales and Scotland, but certain aspects of the Practice Direction 2002 do not apply when it hears appeals in Scotland.

Employment and contract law in Northern Ireland are the same as in England and Wales, although it has its own set of statutes corresponding to those in England, Wales and Scotland, and is administered by industrial tribunals. These are the Equal Pay Act (NI) 1970; Sex Discrimination Orders 1976 SI No 1042 (NI 15) and 1988 SI No 1303 (NI 13); Industrial Relations (NI) Order 1992 SI No 807 (NI 5); Industrial Tribunals Order 1996 SI No 1921 (NI 18); Race Relations Order 1997 SI No 869 (NI 6); Employment Rights Order 1999 SI No 2790; Employment Rights (Dispute Resolution) Order 1998 SI No 1265 (NI 8); Employment Equality (Sexual Orientation) Regulations 2003 SR No 947, and regulations providing for fixed-term employees, part-time workers, parental rights and flexible working. The Labour Relations Agency performs the work of ACAS and the Industrial Court determines union recognition disputes.

Radical changes in tribunal procedure were introduced in April 2004 by the Industrial Tribunals Regulations 2004 SI No 165. These correspond to the rules which were in place in England, Wales and Scotland from 2001 until the further changes in October 2004 on which this book is based. Readers in Northern Ireland should look to the second edition of this book for a proper understanding of the equivalent of the 2004 NI rules. We understand that yet more change is coming and from April 2005 Northern Ireland will have regulations and rules which will in substance be the same throughout the UK. This third edition shows how employment tribunals and courts have interpreted concepts which continue to operate, for example, case management. We hope the book will be useful for all those involved in tribunals anywhere in the UK.

The Fair Employment and Treatment (NI) Order 1998 SI No 3162 (NI 21) outlaws discrimination on the ground of religious belief and political opinion. Cases are heard by the Fair Employment Tribunal under the Fair Employment Regulations 2004 SI No 164 which are similar to the industrial tribunal rules.

The Disability Discrimination Act 1995, the National Minimum Wage Act 1998 and TUPE Regulations apply throughout the UK.

J McM
Audit House, Victoria Embankment, London.

RT
BC
Old Square Chambers, Gray's Inn, London.

1 October 2004

Contents

Table of cases

Table of statutes

Table of statutory instruments

Table of European legislation

Abbreviations

2003 Regs	Equal Pay Act 1970 (Amendment) Regulations 2003
2004 Regs	Employment Tribunals (Constitution and Rules of Procedure) Regulations 2004
2004 Rules	Employment Tribunals Rules of Procedure (contained in 2004 Regs, Sch 1)
ACAS	Advisory, Conciliation and Arbitration Service
CBI	Confederation of British Industry
COET	Central Office of Employment Tribunals
CPR	Civil Procedure Rules
CRE	Commission for Racial Equality
DDA 1995	Disability Discrimination Act 1995
DRC	Disability Rights Commission
DTI	Department for Trade and Industry
EA 2002	Employment Act 2002
EADR 2004	Employment Act 2002 (Dispute Resolution) Regulations 2004
EAT	Employment Appeal Tribunal
ECHR	European Convention on Human Rights
ECJ	European Court of Justice
EDT	Effective date of termination
EERB Regs 2003	Employment Equality (Religion or Belief) Regulations 2003
EESO Regs 2003	Employment Equality (Sexual Orientation) Regulations 2003
EOC	Equal Opportunities Commission
EqPA 1970	Equal Pay Act 1970
ERA 1996	Employment Rights Act 1996
ET	Employment tribunal
ETA 1996	Employment Tribunals Act 1996
ETS	Employment Tribunal Service

FRU	Free Representation Unit
FTE Regs 2000	Fixed-term Employees (Prevention of Less Favourable Treatment) Regulations 2002
GMF	Genuine material factor
IE	Independent expert
JES	Job evaluation study
NIRC	National Industrial Relations Court
NMWA 1998	National Minimum Wage Act 1998
PTW Regs 2000	Part-time Workers (Prevention of Less Favourable Treatment) Regulations 2000
RFAT	Reserve Forces Appeal Tribunal
ROET	Regional Office of the Employment Tribunal
RRA 1976	Race Relations Act 1976
SDA 1975/1986	Sex Discrimination Act 1975/1986
TICE Regs 1999	Transnational Information and Consultation of Employees Regulations 1999
TUC	Trades Union Congress
TULRCA 1992	Trade Unions and Labour Relations (Consolidation) Act 1992
TUPE	Transfer of Undertakings (Protection of Employment) Regulations 1981
WT Regs 1998	Working Time Regulations 1998

CHAPTER 1

Constitution

General

1.1   Employment tribunals were first established by the Industrial Training Act 1964. Since that time, the role of employment tribunals has
changed dramatically and they now have jurisdiction to hear many
types of claim (see chapter 2), but the vast majority of cases involve
unfair dismissal or unlawful deductions from wages.[1]

1.2   In performing a judicial function, tribunals are creatures of statute. Unlike the courts, they have no inherent jurisdiction: if a tribunal
is to exercise a particular power, it is necessary to find out which
statute creates the power. There is no general power, except that a
tribunal is required to give effect to European Union law and European Convention on Human Rights (ECHR) rights incorporated by
the Human Rights Act 1998.[2]

1.3   The aim of employment tribunals has always been to provide 'an
easily accessible, speedy, informal and inexpensive procedure for the
settlement of . . . disputes . . . and to remove the . . . multiplicity of
actions.'[3] To some extent these goals have been achieved: tribunals
are not bound by the rules of evidence or procedure which govern
most courts. Instead they can moderate their own procedure as they
see fit.[4] In the 2004 Rules there has been a mission to present the
rules in a logical structure, using 'plain English', following the
recommendations of the Employment Tribunal System Taskforce
which reported in 2003.

1.4   The central provisions governing employment tribunal procedure
can be found in the Employment Tribunals Act (ETA) 1996, and in
the Employment Tribunals (Constitution and Rules of Procedure)
Regulations 2004 (the '2004 Regs'), schedule 1 to which contains the
'2004 Rules'.

1.5   There is no monopoly on rights of audience before tribunals,
which is another way of saying anyone can represent a party or can

---

1   In 2003/4 out of 115,042 applications to the tribunals in England, Wales and
    Scotland, about a third (37,644) were for unfair dismissal and about a quarter
    (approximately 30,000) were for unlawful deductions from wages, breach of
    contract and national minimum wage. Employment Tribunals Service annual
    report 2003–04.
2   *Secretary of State for Scotland v Wright* [1991] IRLR 187, EAT, applying *Pickstone v
    Freemans plc* [1987] ICR 867; [1987] IRLR 218, CA.
3   Royal Commission on Trade Unions and Employers' Associations under Lord
    Donovan 1968, Cmnd 3623, para 578.
4   Employment Tribunals (Constitution and Rules of Procedure) Regulations 2004
    SI No 1861 ('Rules') rr14(2) and 60(1).

choose to represent themselves, and no-one wears wigs or gowns. The tribunal, representatives and witnesses remain seated for the hearing and modes of address are relatively informal: 'Sir' or 'Madam' are acceptable and usual, without being too obsequious, or when referring to the tribunal: ' . . . as the Chairman pointed out' or to a member: ' . . . in answer to Ms A's question'; Mr, Ms for representatives, parties and witnesses. On the other hand, for most litigants in person and many lay representatives, tribunals will seem highly formal and legalistic. Evidence is given on oath or affirmation, witnesses are cross-examined, (2004 Rules r27(2), (3)) legal language is used and legal submissions are made. At times the issues before the tribunal will be complex and involve quite complicated legal analysis. Frequently parties will employ legal professionals who are trained in and used to the greater formality of the courts. All this increases the formality and costs of the proceedings, and sometimes causes delays.

1.6   In most cases the issues are quite simple ones of fact and there is no reason why the tribunal should not be able to adjudicate upon these cases without the 'assistance' of detailed rules of evidence and procedure and lawyers. In so doing, the tribunal will have regard to the overriding objective of the Rules, which is to enable it to deal with cases justly. That means, so far as practicable:

(a)   ensuring that the parties are on an equal footing;
(b)   ensuring that the case is dealt with expeditiously and fairly (see 2004 Regs reg 3);
(c)   dealing with the case in ways which are proportionate to the complexity or importance of the issues; and
(d)   saving expense.

This objective is similar, although not identical to that applied in the High Court and county court under the Civil Procedure Rules (CPR). The CPR refer to dealing with a case in a way proportionate not only to the complexity of the issues but also to the amount of money involved, the importance of the case and the financial position of each party. The CPR also require the court to allot to a case 'an appropriate share of the courts resources . . . taking into account the need to allot resources to other cases'. These omissions may provide a useful indication as to how it is intended that tribunals should approach their task in applying the overriding objective to the conduct of cases before them.

Position of employment tribunals in the legal system

1.7 Employment tribunals are the first stage in the legal process for enforcing most statutory employment rights. The decisions of one tribunal are not binding on any other tribunal or court, although they may be persuasive.

1.8 The next stage is the Employment Appeal Tribunal (EAT), to which an appeal lies from decisions of employment tribunals. There are divisions of the EAT in England and Wales (sitting in London) and in Scotland (sitting in Edinburgh); hearings can, and occasionally do take place in other parts of the country such as Cardiff. It has the status of a court of record, which means its decisions are binding on employment tribunals, and on county courts in England and Wales and sheriff courts in Scotland and create legal precedents which should be followed.[5]

1.9 Appeals from the EAT in England and Wales go to the Court of Appeal (Civil Division) and in Scotland they go to the Court of Session (Inner House). Appeals must be on points of law (not fact) and can only be made with the permission (leave) of the EAT or the Court of Appeal or Court of Session. In Northern Ireland the appeal process is by requisition to the tribunal to state a case on point(s) of law to the Court of Appeal. The requisition is drafted by the chairman and agreed with the members. From the Court of Appeal, appeals go to the House of Lords. Permission is required in England and Wales and Northern Ireland but not in Scotland.[6]

1.10 Since the Human Rights Act 1998 came into force, the tribunal must take into account any judgment or decision of the European Court of Human Rights when considering any matter in respect of which a human rights issue has arisen. Neither employment tribunals nor the EAT may make a declaration that a piece of legislation is incompatible with the European Convention on Human Rights, that power being limited to the House of Lords, Court of Appeal and High Court. It should be noted that employment tribunals do not have jurisdiction to hear a free standing complaint under the Human Rights Act.

---

5 Employment Tribunals Act (ETA) 1996 s20(3).
6 Court of Session Act 1988 s40.

Contempt

1.11   Although tribunals are not courts of record, for the purposes of the Contempt of Court Act 1981, they are inferior courts and any person acting in contempt of them can be punished by imprisonment. An order for committal for contempt may be made by the Queen's Bench Division of the High Court (under RSC Order 52 r1(2)(a)(iii) contained in CPR Sch 1). An example of the exercise of this power was seen in the case of *Peach Grey & Co (a firm) v Sommers*,[7] when the claimant to the tribunal proceedings had indirectly tried to persuade a witness to withdraw his evidence. The court held that it did have the power to commit the claimant to prison for that contempt of the proceedings of the tribunal as an inferior court.

Location and administration

1.12   The Employment Tribunal Service (ETS) has its head office in London.[8] The Public Register of judgments and written reasons for England and Wales is situated at the ETS Field Support Unit;[9] its role is administrative. There are also 13 Regional Offices of Employment Tribunals ('ROETs') and four offices in Scotland, with 34 hearing centres in Britain. The postal address of the claimant's workplace determines to which of the offices the claim is made and by which it is administered (see list of the Tribunals at appendix D) within one of the regions. The website tells you which office once you log in your postal code.[10] The head of all employment tribunals in England and Wales is the President of Employment Tribunals, who must have held a 'general qualification' for at least seven years.[11] This means a barrister or solicitor or advocate in England and Wales, Scotland or Northern Ireland, with rights of audience in part of the Supreme Court and the county courts, appointed by the Lord Chancellor. The appointment of the President may be revoked if the 'appointing office holder'[12] is satisfied that the President is 'incapacitated by infirmity of mind or body from discharging his/her duties of office', or 'is a

---

7   [1995] 2 All ER 513; [1995] ICR 549; [1995] IRLR 363, DC.
8   7th Floor, 19–29 Woburn Place, London WC1H 0LU.
9   1st Floor, 100 Southgate Street, Bury St Edmunds, IP33 2AQ.
10   www.ets.gov.uk.
11   2004 Regs reg 4(3) and Courts and Legal Services Act 1990 s71.
12   In England and Wales the Lord Chancellor and in Scotland the Lord President; 2004 Regs reg 2(1).

bankrupt.'[13] Recently the presidents in England and Wales have been circuit judges. The chief administrative officer of the ETS is the Secretary of Tribunals. The secretary is the named officer to whom all claims must be first presented at the address of the appropriate tribunal office. At each tribunal office there is a Regional Secretary, who may exercise any of the functions of the Secretary of Tribunals.

1.13　　There are 13 Regional Chairmen, one at each ROET, who take charge of the administration of cases by the tribunals in their regions and also hear cases.

1.14　　In Scotland there is a separate ETS[14] and three Offices of Tribunals (see addresses at appendix D). All claims in Scotland should be sent to the ETS. The President is appointed by the Lord President. The Vice President performs the functions of a Regional Chairman.

1.15　　The Industrial Tribunal and Fair Employment Tribunal in Northern Ireland hear cases equivalent to the jurisdiction in Britain.[15] An appeal goes to the Northern Ireland Court of Appeal.

Types of hearing

1.16　2004 Rules r14 sets out four types of hearing:

- Case management discussion under rule 17.
- Pre-hearing review under rule 18.
- A Hearing under rule 26 to consider procedural or substantive issues or determine the case, known in the rules as a r26 Hearing (see para 16.1 below).
- Review hearing under rules 33 or 36.

Each of these types of hearing will be discussed in more detail at paras 1.22–1.30.

Composition of tribunals

Chairman

1.17　A legally qualified chairman presides over the hearing and advises his/her lay colleagues on the tribunal on the relevant law and its application. The chairman must be a barrister or solicitor holding a

---

13　2004 Regs reg 4(5).
14　Based at Eagle Building, 215 Bothwell Street, Glasgow G2 7TS.
15　See the note after the Preface to this edition.

'general qualification' or an advocate solicitor or barrister qualified in Scotland or Northern Ireland, all of at least seven years' standing.[16] He or she is appointed by the Lord Chancellor or, in Scotland, by the Lord President. Part-time chairmen are also appointed who undertake to serve up to 30 days each year; in practice, they cover about one third of all tribunal sitting days.

1.18   It is the chairman's role to set out and sign the tribunal's judgment or order (2004 Rules r29) in any case and give the reasons for it. Chairmen do not, however, carry any more weight on the tribunal than their colleagues: they can be outvoted by the lay members of the tribunal and will then give the majority decision of the lay members and their own minority decision. The majority decision is binding.

Members

1.19   The general rule as set out in the Employment Tribunal Act 1996 is that the chairman of a tribunal usually sits with two 'other Members' universally known as lay members,[17] drawn from two panels of people following consultations with employers and employees. Lay members are appointed to serve on tribunals for a (renewable) period of three years, by the secretary of state after an element of competition as well as consultation with representative bodies such as the Confederation of British Industry and the Trades Union Congress.[18] They are entitled (and encouraged) to utilise their industrial knowledge and experience in assessing tribunal cases and are seen as forming (together with the chairman) the 'industrial jury'. Once appointed, they must act independently, and not as representatives.

1.20   If any member (including the chairman) of a tribunal has a personal or financial interest in a particular case, he or she should declare that interest to the parties and should not sit on that case. All those coming before tribunals should be able to have complete confidence in the independence and integrity of those hearing the case. Any direct interest in the case will automatically exclude a person from sitting.[19] The Human Rights Act 1998, by incorporating ECHR

---

16   2004 Regs reg 8(3).
17   ETA 1996 s4(1); see also 2004 Rules r26(2).
18   2004 Regs reg 8(3)(b) and (c).
19   *Porter v Magill* [2002] 2 AC 357, HL (and, in the employment law context, *Greenaway Harrison Ltd v Wiles* [1994] IRLR 380, EAT); *R v Bow Street Metropolitan Stipendiary Magistrate ex p Pinochet Ugarte (No 2)* [1999] 2 WLR 2272, HL; *Locabail v Bayfield Properties* [2000] IRLR 96, CA; *In Re Medicaments and Related Classes of Goods (No 2)* [2001] ICR, 564, CA.

art 6(1), provides that civil rights should be determined by an 'independent and impartial tribunal'. Until 1999 lay members were appointed and could be removed without notice by the Secretary of State for Trade and Industry. This led to challenges as to whether a sufficient degree of independence was achieved in cases involving that government department.[20] However, since 1999 lay members, although still appointed and paid by the secretary of state, have had an element of open competition in their appointment, and they are appointed for an automatically renewable period of three years, subject to 'conventional and appropriate' grounds of removal and non-renewal in respect of which there is a substantial measure of judicial control. This, according to the EAT, has provided sufficient guarantees of independence; *Scanfuture UK Ltd v Secretary of State for Trade and Industry*.[21] The occasions when the question of apparent bias might arise are considered in more detail in chapter 16 which also sets out guidance for parties who need to raise the question during the course of the hearing.

1.21   If one of the lay members is absent for any reason, and the parties both consent, the chairman may sit with just one lay member. While lay members are expected to give fair consideration to all cases whichever panel they are drawn from, the whole purpose of the composition of a tribunal is to try and ensure that both perspectives are present. Clearly this is not achieved if the chairman sits with just one lay member. In such circumstances, it is always a party's right to insist that a tribunal is fully constituted.

Chairman sitting alone

1.22   As set out above there are four types of hearing. Case management discussions[22] and pre-hearing reviews[23] are heard by Chairmen sitting alone. Hearings under rule 26 of the 2004 Rules of Procedure must be heard by 'a tribunal composed in accordance with section 4(1) and (2) of the Employment Tribunals Act'.[24] The ETA 1996 provides that the general rule, as set out above, is for proceedings before

---

20 See, eg, *Smith v Secretary of State for Trade and Industry* [2000] ICR 69; [2000] IRLR 6, EAT.
21 [2001] ICR 1096; [2001] IRLR 416, EAT.
22 2004 Rules r17.
23 2004 Rules r18.
24 The fourth type of hearing is a review which will be heard by the chairman or full tribunal which made the decision, see chapter 19.

employment tribunals to be before a chairman and two lay members (or one if the parties agree). However tribunal chairmen can make certain decisions alone. By ETA 1996 s4(2) – (4) (as amended by Employment Rights (Dispute Resolution) Act 1998 s3) the following proceedings 'shall' be heard by a chairman alone, subject only to the caveat in ETA 1996 s4(5) (see below):

(a) applications for interim relief in trade union membership, health and safety and other cases (Employment Rights Act (ERA) 1996 ss128, 131 and 132 and Trade Unions and Labour Relations (Consolidation) Act (TULRCA) 1992 ss161, 165 and 166);

(b) complaints concerning unauthorised deductions of union subscriptions (TULRCA 1992 s68A);

(c) claims for remuneration under protective award (TULRCA 1992 s192);

(d) complaints concerning failure to consult under Transfer of Undertakings (Protection of Employment) Regulations 1981[25] (TUPE) reg 11(5);

(e) complaints under Pension Schemes Act 1993 s126;

(f) applications under the insolvency provisions (ERA 1996 s182);

(g) applications for a redundancy payment from the secretary of state in the event of an employer's insolvency, or refusal/failure to make the payment (ERA 1996 s170);

(h) complaints relating to unlawful deductions from wages (ERA 1996 s23);

(i) applications for a written statement of particulars of employment, itemised pay statement, guarantee payments, or relating to claims for remuneration on suspension on medical grounds (ERA 1996 ss11, 34 and 64);

(j) claims for breach of the contract of employment (ETA 1996 s3);

(k) complaints concerning failure to keep records, appeals against enforcement notices and against penalty notices under the National Minimum Wage Act 1998 ss11, 19 and 22;

(l) proceedings where the complainant has given written notice withdrawing his/her claim;

(m) proceedings where the parties have given written consent to the case being heard by a chairman alone (even if they subsequently withdraw it);

(n) proceedings where the respondent no longer contests the case.

1.23 These cases are subject to the caveat in ETA 1996 s4(5) that they *may* be heard by a full tribunal following a decision by a chairman sitting alone, who must have regard to:

(a) the likelihood of a dispute arising on the facts which makes it desirable for the hearing to be in front of a full tribunal;

(b) whether there is a likelihood of an issue of law arising which would make it desirable for the case to be heard by a chairman alone;

(c) any views expressed by the parties; and

(d) whether there are other proceedings concurrently being heard which must be heard by a full tribunal.

1.24 In the past tribunals had regarded the statute as requiring chairmen to sit alone in those cases set out in ETA 1996 s4(2) – (4), unless a specific *exception* had been made, judicially, by a chairman. However, there are conflicting decisions of the EAT as to whether the discretion under ETA 1996 s4(5) must always be considered before a chairman may proceed to sit alone; in *Sogbetun v Hackney LBC*,[26] Morison P held that chairmen were under a mandatory duty to exercise their discretion under section 4(5), and always to explain why they had elected to sit alone. This reasoning was adopted by the EAT in Scotland in the case of *Harman v Town & Country Veterinary Group*[27] where the EAT held the tribunal to have been invalidly constituted in circumstances where the decision did not disclose that the chairman had even considered the issue of whether or not he should sit alone, let alone set out his reasons. A further division of the EAT held, in *Arriva Kent Thameside Ltd v Clarke*[28] that whether a failure to consider the section 4(5) discretion renders the decision a nullity or is merely an irregularity makes no real difference as the effect is the same; it is an error for a chairman to fail to explain the decision to sit alone.

1.25 However a different line of authority can be seen stemming from the case of *Post Office v Howell*[29] which expressly disagreed with *Sogbetun*, holding that even if there is such a mandatory duty, a chairman's failure to exercise it will neither raise a jurisdiction issue, nor render any judgment a nullity. The reasoning in *Howell*

---

26 [1998] IRLR 676; [1998] ICR1264, EAT.

27 EAT 71/01 30/5/01; available on the EAT website www.employmentappeals.gov.uk.

28 EAT 0341/00; 25 July 2001; available at www.employmentappeals.gov.uk.

29 [2000] IRLR 224, EAT.

was approved by Lindsay P in *Morgan v Brith Gof Cyf*[30] in which it was held that:

> ... it is no doubt desirable for a chairman to reflect upon subsection (5), even if he is not invited to do so ... Whenever there is real doubt on the question, it must always, in our view, be better for him to prefer a panel of three. But it is not, in our view, an error of law on a chairman's part, when dealing with a case which is in subsection (3) and the point is not raised by anyone, not to turn his mind to subsection (5).

1.26   None of these decisions lays down any requirement to consult the parties (note the requirement under section 4(5)(c), that regard is taken of '*any* views expressed by the parties'). However, it seems clear that if the parties are consulted, their representations must be considered. This might usefully be done at a case management discussion (see para 1.22). The notice of hearing indicates that the case will be heard by a chairman alone and if a party wants a hearing by a full tribunal, representations should be made at the time the notice is received.

1.27   Pre-hearing reviews under 2004 Rules r18, as set out above, are heard by a chairman sitting alone. At such a hearing the chairman may carry out a preliminary consideration of the proceedings and may also determine any interim or preliminary matter relating to the proceedings, including determination of whether a party is entitled to bring or contest proceedings.

1.28   Considering the question of preliminary hearings under the previous rules of procedure, the EAT in *Mobbs v Nuclear Electric plc*,[31] held that where it was necessary to hear evidence and reach a decision of fact in a preliminary hearing, it was not permissible for a chairman to sit alone. However, this decision was swiftly overturned by another division of the EAT in *Tsangocos v Amalgamated Chemicals Limited*[32] where it was held that a chairman sitting alone does have jurisdiction, without qualification, to determine jurisdictional points and to hear all other matters in connection with an originating application. The *Tsangocos* approach was adopted in *United Airlines v Bannigan and others*,[33] although it was emphasised in that case that a chairman should consider carefully the wisdom of sitting alone

30   [2001] ICR 978, EAT.
31   [1996] ICR 536, EAT.
32   [1997] IRLR 4; ICR 154, EAT.
33   EAT 192/97; 15 September 1997.

where there are disputes of fact, as the experience of lay members in such circumstances may be especially valuable. These sentiments were repeated in *Sutcliffe v Big C's Marine*,[34] ('the quality of justice must not be allowed to deteriorate because of resource implications').

1.29   The 2004 Rules use mandatory language at rule 18(1) which states that 'pre-hearing reviews shall be conducted by a chairman', but an exception is made if a party requests a fully constituted tribunal at least 10 days prior to the hearing and a Chairman considers it would de desirable because of likely determinations of fact.[35] Tribunals may, at a hearing, make any order or direction which a chairman has power to make under the rules (rule 60(2).) It therefore remains to be seen whether tribunals will continue to give effect to the warnings set out in *Bannigan* and *Sutcliffe*. Tribunals are likely to continue to heed these warnings bearing in mind the comments of the EAT in *Wellcome Foundation v Darby*,[36] that it is not every preliminary issue which will be suitable for a preliminary hearing, but rather that some cases will require a full hearing of evidence and argument. Consideration should be given to whether the issue is one which is properly to be taken in advance of a full hearing.

National security cases

1.30   The 2004 Regs introduce a requirement that a further panel be maintained, listing chairmen and lay members who are suitable persons to act in cases involving national security.[37]

Equal pay and sex, race and disability discrimination claims

1.31   There is no requirement that members of a particular gender or minority ethnic background, or with a particular interest in disability issues sit on tribunals considering these cases, nor that any member hearing such a case has any specialised knowledge. In these classes of case, however, selection of the tribunal will generally be made by the ROET so as to have at least one member with specialised knowledge or training. This is a particular concern in cases involving allegations of race discrimination following the government's undertaking at the time of passing the Race Relations Act 1976 to take

34 [1998] IRLR 428, EAT.
35 2004 Rules r18(3).
36 [1996] IRLR 538, EAT.
37 2004 Regs regs 10 and 11.

steps to appoint persons to the panels of lay members with specialised knowledge or experience of race relations matters. It remains,
however, a goal, not a legal requirement.[38] Specialist tribunals are
usually constituted for equal value claims (see para 22.30 below). As
the scope of protection from discrimination continues to expand
(sexual orientation, religion, belief or age), this goal can only be
achieved by increasing the diversity of people and chairmen
appointed to the tribunals.

Tribunal clerks

1.32   A tribunal clerk is appointed for each hearing. They will introduce
themselves to the representatives or parties and take details of witnesses (their full name, position, which oath or affirmation they will
take) and observers, and collect any additional documents and the
legal authorities which will be referred to during the course of the
hearing. If the claimant has been claiming jobseekers' allowance or
income support, the clerk will also take details of the benefit office
concerned. Any subsequent award of compensation will be notified
to that office should the recoupment provisions apply to an award of
compensation.[39]

1.33   The clerk to the tribunal also sits in at the beginning of most cases to
administer the oath/affirmation but tends not to stay throughout.
Limited assistance (though not legal advice) can be sought from
tribunal clerks before and during the course of a hearing but their
primary function is to assist the tribunal.

Tribunal consultative groups

1.34   Most ROETs now have consultative groups which meet about three
times a year and liaise with representatives of regular users of tribunals in the relevant area. An adviser with a general query on the
practices or procedures in a particular ROET may find it helpful to
ask the appropriate representative on the consultative group (for
example, the law centre/Citizens' Advice representative) to ask them
to raise the issue. If there appears to be no such representative,
advisers should contact the secretary to the relevant ROET with any
query. There is a National User Group.

38   *Habib v Elkington & Co* [1981] ICR 435.
39   Employment Protection (Recoupment of Jobseeker's Allowance and Income
Support) Regulations 1996 SI No 2349; ETA 1996 s16.

Jurisdiction and hearings

Jurisdiction: general

2.1 Tribunals are created by statute and have no powers other than those given them by parliament. If a case falls outside a tribunal's jurisdiction, it is not permitted to consider the matter.[1] Even if the parties do not raise the point, the tribunal must always be satisfied that it has the power to hear a particular case before it goes on to do so: ' . . . [it] cannot merely by silence confer upon [itself] a jurisdiction which [it does] not have'.[2] Furthermore, even if the point is not taken before the tribunal, lack of jurisdiction can always be raised on review or appeal.

2.2 Not all jurisdictional questions are dealt with in this book, as many give rise to questions of substantive law rather than procedure. Reference should be made to other texts (and the relevant Acts) to ensure that a particular claimant has the right to bring a complaint before a tribunal. Where the jurisdictional issue is of a procedural nature it is referred to in this chapter.

2.3 At the end of this chapter is a list of rights in which legislation provides that employment tribunals have jurisdiction in England and Wales, along with the time limits in which such claims must be presented; there is not room in this book for a complete list for Scotland, but the headings are roughly the same.

Territorial jurisdiction

2.4 A number of statutes deny protection to individuals who work outside Great Britain; for example Sex Discrimination Act 1975 ss6 and 10, Race Relations Act 1976 s8 and Trade Union and Law Reform (Consolidation) Act 1992.

2.5 The Court of Appeal in *Serco Ltd v Lawson*[3] held that the right not to be unfairly dismissed contrary to Employment Rights Act (ERA) 1996 s94 covers 'employment in Great Britain'. The Court stated that:

> . . . in most cases, it would not be difficult to determine whether the employment was in Great Britain. Borderline cases would have to be assessed in light of all the circumstances of the employment in each

---

1 See, for example, *Secretary of State for Scotland v Mann* [2001] ICR 1005, where the EAT held that employment tribunals have no jurisdiction in electoral matters and so could not hear a complaint of sex discrimination by a candidate in an election to the Scottish Parliament.

2 *British Midland Airways v Lewis* [1978] ICR 782, EAT.

3 [2004] EWCA Civ 12; [2004] IRLR 206.

particular case. Although the residence of the parties could be relevant to where the employment was, the emphasis was to be placed on the employment itself.

Regulation 11(5) of the 2001 Regs from which the appeal arose has now been revoked, and no corresponding provision has been enacted. However, as the Court of Appeal held, the relevant test is to examine the particular provisions of the statute being relied upon to determine whether the tribunal will have territorial jurisdiction. As the Court of Appeal recognised in *Serco*, different principles will apply when looking at territorial jurisdiction to contractual claims, claims of discrimination and claims of unfair dismissal. In *Saggar v Ministry of Defence*,[4] the EAT considered that the determination of whether work was done wholly outside Great Britain, so that a discrimination claim could not be brought before an employment tribunal[5] depended on consideration of the time period when it was alleged that the discrimination took place. If, during that time, the claimant did some work which was more than de minimis in Great Britain, that would be sufficient to found jurisdiction and to permit a claim of discrimination to be made. In a number of joined cases including *Croft v Cathay Pacific Airways Ltd*,[6] Peter Clark, giving judgment of the EAT applied *Serco* and went on to consider jurisdiction to entertain claims. While the tribunal had jurisdiction (they can consider any claim which a court in England or Wales could (see CPR Pt 6)) the doctrine of 'forum non conveniens' (most convenient forum, ie, country) applies to tribunals as it does to civil courts.

Acceptance of claims

2.6   Under rule 3(1) and (2) of the 2004 Rules of Procedure, a claim will not be accepted by the secretary to the tribunal if it is clear that one or more of the following applies:

(a)   (after 6 April 2005) the prescribed ET1 claim form is not used;

(b)   the claim does not include all the relevant required information as required under these rules;

(c)   the tribunal does not have power to consider the claim; or a relevant part of it; or if Employment Act (EA) 2002 s32 (com-

---

4   [2004] EAT 1385/01; LTL 13/7/2004.
5   See Race Relations Act 1976 s8(1) and Sex Discrimination Act 1975 s10(1).
6   UKEAT/0367/03DA, 26 June 2004, available on the EAT Website.

plaints about grievances) applies to the claim, the claim has been presented to the tribunal in breach of subsections (2) to (4) of section 32. (That is, setting out the grievance in writing and allowing time for a reply).

2.7 In these circumstances the secretary must refer the claim with a statement of reasons to a chairman who will decide whether the claim should be accepted and allowed to proceed.

2.8 If rejected in whole or in part the chairman must record that decision and give reasons. As soon as practicable, the decision and reasons will be sent to the claimant with information about how to apply for a review and to appeal to the Employment Appeal Tribunal. If a claim under EA 2002 s32 is rejected, the secretary will notify the claimant of the relevant time limits and the consequences of not complying with them (see para 3.3).

Types of hearing

2.9 A chairman or tribunal may hold any of four types of hearing described above at para 1.16.[7]

2.10 Provision is made for electronic hearings, except for r26 Hearings and reviews. The public must have access and be able to hear all parties, even if the hearing is to be conducted by means of electronic communication.[8] Proceedings may be held in private to hear evidence or representations which, in the opinion of the tribunal or chairman is likely to consist of information:

- which a person could not disclose without contravening a prohibition imposed by or by virtue of any enactment;
- which has been communicated to someone in confidence; or
- the disclosure of the information would cause substantial injury to an undertaking, other than an effect on negotiations in respect of collective bargaining.

National security proceedings

2.11 Different considerations apply to national security proceedings. Under 2004 Rules r54(1), a Minister of the Crown may, if he considers

---

7 2004 Rules r14(1).
8 2004 Rules r 15.

it expedient in the interests of national security, give notice to direct a tribunal or chairman to:

- conduct proceedings in private, wholly or in part;
- exclude the claimant from all or part of the proceedings;
- exclude the claimant's representative from all or part of the proceedings;
- take steps to conceal the identity of a particular witness in proceedings.

2.12   A tribunal or chairman likewise has the power to order any of these things to be done.[9] Further, it can order any person not to disclose documents or the contents of documents to persons excluded from the proceedings or even persons who *may* become excluded from proceedings. It can also take steps to keep secret all or part of the reasons for its judgment. If a Minister considers that any of these orders should be made, he has the right to appear before and address the tribunal or chairman on the matter. The tribunal or chairman must in the exercise of their functions ensure that information is not disclosed where to do so would be contrary to the interests of national security.

2.13   Further rules which apply to national security proceedings are contained in Schedule 2 to the 2004 Regs. A person who is excluded from proceedings or who *may* be excluded from proceedings when the Minister makes representation for their exclusion is not entitled to receive a copy of the response or grounds for the response to their claim.[10] If a tribunal or chairman is considering ordering disclosure of documents or the attendance of a witness before the tribunal, the Minister can make an application objecting to that requirement being imposed. The application will be heard and determined in private (see also paras 10.34–10.35 on disclosure and paras 22.53–22.54 on equal value claims).[11]

2.14   A claimant who is excluded from all or part of proceedings may, if the Attorney-General thinks it fit to do so, have a special advocate appointed to represent his or her interests.[12] He or she is also permitted to make a statement to the tribunal or chairman before the commencement of proceedings from which he or she stands to be excluded. The claimant is not permitted to gain knowledge of the

---

9   2004 Rules r54(2).
10   2004 Regs Sch 2 r4. See also 2004 Regs Sch 2 r3 which modifies the response procedure.
11   2004 Regs Sch 2 r6.
12   2004 Regs Sch 2 r8.

contents of the response to his or her claim or the proceedings in general through the special advocate, who is not permitted to communicate these matters. The special advocate may, however, apply for an order from the tribunal or chairman to allow this to happen.

2.15 A hearing in national security proceedings will, by default, take place in public, unless the Minister directs or the tribunal or chairman orders that the hearing should be in private.[13] Parties are permitted to give evidence, call witnesses, question witnesses and address the tribunal, unless, of course, they have been excluded from the hearing.

2.16 Reasons for a judgment or order will be sent in the first instance to the Minister. If he considers it expedient in the interests of national security, he may direct a tribunal or chairman either to prepare edited reasons for that decision or order or direct that the reasons should not be sent to specified persons, without edited reasons being sent instead.[14] If a direction is made preventing reasons from being sent, those reasons will not be entered in the Register. The effect of this provision is that the claimant can be prevented from receiving reasons, either full or edited, for having won or lost a case.

Forces jurisdiction

2.17 The Employment Tribunal Service (ETS) also has some involvement in cases involving members of the armed forces. The Reserve Forces Appeal Tribunal (RFAT) hears applications from individuals or employers wanting to contest call-up to service, and claims by reservists or employers to certain specified awards. This ETS provides hearing accommodation, tribunal clerks and support service for the RFAT. Chairmen and members who sit on the RFAT are drawn from the Employment Tribunal panels. In the year 2003–2004, there were 43 applications, 10 of which proceeded to hearing.[15]

2.18 The Tribunal also administers the Reinstatement Committee. Employers of reservists have a duty to re-employ them following service or to offer them the most favourable alternative employment which is reasonable and practical in his or her case.[16] If the reservist is unhappy with the response, an application can be made to the Reinstatement Committee. In the year 2003–2004, there were 17 cases, 11 of which proceeded to hearing.

13 2004 Regs Sch 2 r9
14 2004 Regs Sch 2 r10(3).
15 See ETS Annual Report 2003–2004.
16 See Reserve Forces (Safeguard of Employment) Act 1985.

EMPLOYMENT TRIBUNAL JURISDICTION AND TIME LIMITS

	Statutory right	Time limit
Equal Pay Act 1970		
s2 ##	breach of equality clause	6 *whole* months from termination of employment (s2(4))
s7A	complaint by member of armed forces regarding breach of term equivalent to equality clause.	9 *whole* months from the end of the service out of which the complaint arose. (s7A(8)).
Health and Safety at Work Act 1974		
s24	appeal against improvement or prohibition notice	As specified in the notice (s24(2))
s80	Safety Representatives and Safety Committee Regs 1977 SI No 500 reg 11(1): time off with pay for safety representative	3 *whole* months from failure to pay (reg11 (2))
Sex Discrimination Act 1975		
s63 ##	discrimination on the ground of sex or against a married person	3 months (s76(1))**
s68	appeal against non-discrimination notice	6 *whole* weeks from service of notice (s68(1))
s72(2) and s72(4)	application by EOC relating to discriminatory advertisement, etc	6 months or 5 years (s76(3))**
s73	preliminary action by EOC relating to persistent discrimination, advertisements, etc	6 months (s76(4))**
s77	complaint that contract, rule, collective agreement is void	none (SDA 1986 s64A)

Race Relations Act 1976		
s54 ##	discrimination on the ground of race	3 months (s68(1))
s59	appeal against non-discrimination notice	6 *whole* weeks from service of notice (s59(1))
s63(3)(a)	application by CRE relating to discriminatory advertisements, etc	6 months or 5 years (s68(4))
s64	preliminary action by CRE relating to persistent discrimination, advertisements, etc	6 months (s68(5))
Transfer of Undertakings (Protection of Employment) Regulations 1981, as amended 1987 and 1995		
reg 11(1)	failure to inform or consult appropriate representatives of employees of transfer of undertaking	3 months (reg 11(8)(a))
reg 11(5)	failure to pay compensation	3 months of order (reg 11(8)(a))
Industrial Training Act 1982		
s12	appeal by employer against assessment of industrial training levy	As specified by the relevant levy order
Sex Discrimination Act 1986		
s6(4A)	invalidity of discriminatory collective agreements and other rules	6 months (SDA 1975 ss63, 76(1), (5))**
Trade Union and Labour Relations (Consolidation) Act 1992 as amended 1993, 1996, 1998 and 1999		
s66(1)	union member not to be unjustifiably disciplined	3 months (s66(2))* (and extended where internal appeal)
s67(1) and (2)	compensation for unjustifiable discipline	4 weeks to 6 months from declaration (s67(3))
s68(A)	unauthorised or excessive union subscription deducted from wages	3 months (s68(1))*

EMPLOYMENT TRIBUNAL JURISDICTION AND TIME LIMITS

	Statutory right	Time limit
s70C	refusal to conduct collective bargaining re training	3 months (s70C(2))*
s87(1)	wrongful deduction of political fund contribution or employer's refusal to make deduction	3 months (s 87(2))*
s116(4)	trade union's secret ballot on employers' premises (repealed from 1 April 1996)	3 months (s116(5))*
s137(2)	refusal of employment on ground related to union membership or non-membership	3 months (s139(1))*
s138(2)	refusal of service by employment agency on ground related to union membership	3 months (s139(1))*
ss145A and 145B ##	inducements relating to union membership, activities or collective bargaining	3 months (s147)*
s146(5) ##	action short of dismissal relating to union membership and activities	3 months (s147)*
ss152 and 161(1)	interim relief in dismissal cases relating to union membership or non-membership	7 days following termination (s161(2))
s168(4)	time off for union duties	3 *whole* months (s171)*
s169(5)	time off with pay for union duties	3 *whole* months (s171)*
s170(4)	union member's time off for union activities	3 *whole* months (s171)*
s174(5)	exclusion or expulsion from union	6 months (s175)*
s176(2)	compensation for unlawful exclusion/ expulsion	4 weeks to 6 months from declaration (s176(3))

s189(1)	failure to consult or inform employee representative/union/employee on redundancies	Before the date of the last dismissal and 3 months thereafter (s189(5))*
s192(1)	remuneration under protective award	3 months (s192(2))*
s238	unfair dismissal during certain official industrial action (including maternity or health and safety grounds s238(2A))	6 months (s239(2))*
Sch A1 para 156(5)	detriment short of dismissal in cases concerning trade union recognition/bargaining arrangements	3 months (Sch A1 para 157(1))*

Pension Schemes Act 1993

s11(5)(e)	with Occupational Pension Schemes (Contracting-out) Regulations 1984 SI No 380 (amended by SI 1985 No 1323 and SI 1986 No 1716): contracting out	None
s113(1)	with Occupational Pension Schemes (Disclosure of Information) Regulations 1986 SI No 1046 reg 10: questions whether union is recognised	None
s126(1)	failure to pay contributions to scheme by the secretary of state	3 months from communication of decision (s126(2))*

Employment Tribunals (Extension of Jurisdiction) Orders 1994

*Art 7 # breach of contract 3 months from EDT **

EMPLOYMENT TRIBUNAL JURISDICTION AND TIME LIMITS

Statutory right	Time limit
Pensions Act 1995	
s62 with Occupational Pension Schemes (Equal Treatment) Regulations 1995 SI No 3183, equal treatment rules in pension schemes for people of different sex and family or marital status	6 *whole* months from termination of employment (Equal Pay Act 1970 s2(4) as amended by Pensions Act 1995 s63(4))
Disability Discrimination Act 1995	
s8 ## Discrimination/detriment on grounds of disability	3 months (Sch 3 para 3)**
Employment Rights Act 1996	
s11(1) – (2) reference of question relating to written statement of particulars of employment (s1) and itemised pay statement (s8)	While employed and 3 months beginning with termination of employment (s11(4))*
s23 ## unlawful deduction from wages	3 months from deduction or last in series (s23(2))*
s34 guarantee payment	3 months (s34(2))*
s48(1) detriment for taking paternity or adoption leave	3 months (s48(3))*
detriment in health and safety cases	
detriment in Sunday working for shop and betting workers	
detriment for being a trustee of occupational pension scheme	
detriment for being employee representative	

s48(1) *cont*	detriment for taking time off for study/training	
	detriment for taking leave for family/domestic reasons	
	detriment for making an application for flexible working	
s48[(1ZA)]	detriment in working time cases	3 months (s48(3))*
s48[(1A)]	detriment for making a protected disclosure	3 months (s48(3))*
s48[(1B)]	detriment for enforcing rights under Tax Credits Act 2002	3 months (s48(3))*
s51(1)	time off for public duties	3 months (s50(2))*
s54(1)	time off to look for work or make arrangements for training	3 months (s54(2))*
s57(1)	time off for ante-natal care	3 months (s57(2))*
s57(B)(1)	time off for dependants	3 months (s57B(2))*
s60(1)	time off for pension scheme trustees	3 months (from date failure occurred) (s60(2))*
s63(1)	time off for employee representatives	3 months (s63(2))*
s63C	time off for training	3 months (s63C(2))*
s64	remuneration on suspension on medical grounds	3 months (s70(2))*
s67	alternative work on maternity/medical grounds	3 months (s70(2))*
s80	complaints concerning parental leave under Maternity and Parental Leave etc Regulations 1999 SI No 3312	3 months (s80(2))*
s80H	rejecting application for flexible working	3 months (s80H(5))*
s92(1)	written statement of reasons for dismissal	3 months from EDT (s93, 111)
s94 ##	unfair dismissal	3 months from EDT (s111)*
s128	interim relief in dismissal cases relating to certain health and safety issues	7 days after EDT (s128(2))

EMPLOYMENT TRIBUNAL JURISDICTION AND TIME LIMITS

	Statutory right	Time limit
s163 ##	reference of question relating to failure by employer to make redundancy payment	6 months (s164)
s170	reference of question relating to payment equivalent to redundancy rebates in respect of civil servants, etc	None
s182	payment by secretary of state on insolvency of employer	3 months (s188(2))*
Employment Tribunal Act 1996 and Employment Tribunal (Extension of Jurisdiction Order) 1994		
s3 and reg 7	contract claims	3 months *
Employment Tribunal Act 1996 and Employment Appeal Tribunal Rules 1993 as amended by 2001 Regs and Rules of the Supreme Court Order 94 r8(3)		
s21 and EAT Rules r3(2)	appeal to EAT (or High Court)	42 days from promulgation of employment tribunal decision
Working Time Regulations 1998		
reg 30 ##	failure to permit exercise of rights or failure to pay annual leave	3 months (reg 30(2))* (6 months in armed forces cases)
Human Rights Act 1998		
s7	infringement of human rights (to a court; unless rules are made under s7(11))	1 year (s7(5))**

National Minimum Wage Act 1998

s11(1)	refusal to produce records	3 months from end of 14-day period within which records ought to have been produced (s11(2))*
S17	Right to NMW	3 months from underpayment (ERA 1996 ss13, 23)*
s19(5)	appeal against enforcement notice	4 weeks from date of service
s22(2)	appeal against penalty notice	4 weeks from date of service
S24	detriment in relation to NMW	3 months (ERA 1996 s48)*

Employment Relations Act 1999

s11(1)	refusal of right to be accompanied to disciplinary/grievance hearing	3 months (s11(2))*

Tax Credits Act 1999

Sch 3 para 2	detriment re tax credit rights	3 months (ERA 1996 s48)*

Disability Rights Commission Act 1999

Sch 3 para 10(2)	appeal against non-discrimination notice	6 weeks (para 10(1))

Transnational Information and Consultation of Employees Regulations 1999

reg 27	refusal of right to time off or to give information	3 months (reg 27(2))*
reg 32	complaints re detriment in respect of rights connected with European Works Councils	3 months (ERA 1996 s48)

Part Time Workers (Prevention of Less Favourable Treatment) Regulations 2000

reg 5	no less favourable treatment	3 months (reg 8(2))* (save for armed forces where the limit is 6 months)
reg 7	unfair dismissal/detriment on various grounds	3 months (reg 8(2))* (save for armed forces where the limit is 6 months)

EMPLOYMENT TRIBUNAL JURISDICTION AND TIME LIMITS

Statutory right		Time limit
reg 8	less favourable treatment/detriment	3 months (reg 8(2))* (6 months for the armed forces)
Fixed Term Employees (Prevention of Less Favourable Treatment) Regulations 2002 reg 7	unfair dismissal/detriment on various grounds	3 months (reg 7(2))*
Flexible Working (Procedural Requirement) Regulations 2002 reg 14	right to be accompanied at meeting	3 months (reg 15(2))*
Employment Equality (Religion or Belief) Regulations 2003 ## reg 28		3 months (reg 34(1))* (save for armed forces where the limit is 6 months)
Employment Equality (Sexual Orientation) Regulations 2003 ## reg 28		3 months (reg 34(1))* (save for armed forces where the limit is 6 months)

NOTES: Time limit extendable if * 'not reasonably practicable' or ** 'just and equitable'.

Employment Act 2002 s31 applies to reduce or increase awards and EA 2002 (Dispute Resolution) Regulations Reg15 applies to extend the time limit for 3 months after the normal deadline in certain circumstances.

Employment Act 2002 s31 applies to reduce or increase awards and also s32 applies to require step 1 statement of grievance to be submitted before a tribunal claim; and EA 2002 (Dispute Resolution) Regulations 2004 Reg15 applies to extend the time limit for 3 months after the normal deadline in certain circumstances

EDT: Effective date of termination

The right to consultation and information about collective redundancies and transfers is extended to 'appropriate representatives' of the employees

CHAPTER 3

Time limits

continued

General principles

3.1 The table at pages 22–30 sets out the time limits applicable to the initiation of all of the statutory claims which may be made before a tribunal. Different considerations apply to time limits for presenting a response, which are less strict, and for complying with interim orders. There are three general principles:

(1) There are time limits for most statutory claims.

(2) Most statutory claims are subject to an escape clause allowing the claim to be presented within a further time limit either because a relevant internal procedure is in operation or by the exercise of the tribunal's discretion.

(3) All time limits operate according to rigid rules based on a determination of the precise relevant date. These time limits are matters of jurisdiction, and not of discretion or procedure.

Time limits in general

3.2 Almost all statutory rights are subject to a time limit, but the following require particular attention:

Dismissal or disciplinary procedures and grievance procedures under Employment Act 2002 ss31 and 32

3.3 The Employment Act (EA) 2002 set up a regime for the resolution of disputes without recourse to the tribunals. The regime is implemented by the Employment Act 2002 (Dispute Resolution) Regulations (EADR) 2004.[1] The purpose is to channel disputes into a formal structure at workplace level. There are dismissal and disciplinary procedures, and grievance procedures. There are standard and modified procedures for both. The procedures are set out in EA 2002 Sch 2. In simple terms, an employer contemplating dismissal or disciplinary action must go through the procedure. An employee hoping to make a claim, must first go through step 1 of the grievance procedure. The regime has the following important aspects.

1. An employer contemplating dismissal for conduct or redundancy or certain forms of disciplinary action (but not suspension on full

1 SI No 752.

pay or a warning: EADR 2004 reg2(1)) must go through a three stage standard procedure.

2. An employee complaining about any matter in the statutes listed in EA 2002 Sch 4 must operate the first step in the procedure before presenting a complaint to a tribunal.
3. A complaint under one of the statutes listed in EA 2002 Sch 4 will not be accepted by the tribunal until the first step in the grievance procedure has been taken and 28 days have passed (to allow the employer to respond): EA 2002 s32.
4. Time may be extended for presenting a claim when procedures have or are believed to have been followed: EADR reg 15(1).
5. Failure *by an employee* to complete the steps in a dismissal and disciplinary procedure started by the employer or a grievance procedure started by the employee, or to exercise any right of appeal means that any award will be reduced by 10 per cent and may be further reduced by up to a total of 50 per cent: EA 2002 s31.
6. The mirror of this is that a failure *by an employer* to comply with the procedure will result in similar increases in the awards: EA 2002 s31.
7. Failure by an employer to follow the appropriate disciplinary procedure in a dismissal case will result in a dismissal being automatically unfair: Employment Rights Act (ERA) 1996 s98A.
8. Employers are required to include details in the statutory statement of particulars of employment of their disciplinary, grievance and dismissal procedures: ERA 1996 s1.
9. When EA 2002 s38 is brought into force, if the tribunal finds in favour of the employee and the employer was in breach of the duty to provide a written statement of terms of employment, the tribunal must also make an award of compensation for this breach too.
10. When EA 2002 s30 is brought into force, probably in 2006, every contract of employment has effect so as to require employees and employers to comply with a relevant statutory procedure.

3.4 Employment Act 2002 Sch 2 sets out general requirements, applicable to both the dismissal and disciplinary and grievance procedures. These include:

- Steps and action must be taken without unreasonable delay.
- The timing and location of meetings must be reasonable.
- Meetings must be conducted so as to enable each party to explain their case.

- If reasonably practicable, at appeals the employer should be represented by a more senior manager than attended the first meeting.

3.5 Once a party fails to carry out a required step, the other is released from further obligations to operate the steps in the procedure.[2]

3.6 The *standard procedure* applies in all cases where dismissal is contemplated, except when there is a mass dismissal, or the employees are on strike, or the business suddenly ceases to function because of an unforeseen event, or the employee is working illegally.[3] The *modified procedure* applies when the employer has dismissed an employee for reasons of conduct in circumstances where the employee could be dismissed without notice, and it was reasonable for the employer to move straight to dismissal before enquiring into the circumstances.

3.7 The *standard dismissal* and disciplinary procedure has three steps: statement of the alleged conduct, meeting and appeal. The modified procedure omits the middle step.

3.8 The standard grievance procedure is to be invoked in cases where a complaint could be made to a tribunal under one of the statutory rights listed in EA 2002 Schs 3 or 4. Broadly, these are dismissal, discrimination and disputes about pay. The standard grievance procedure has three steps: statement by the employee, meeting, appeal if the employee seeks it. The modified grievance procedure requires only a statement by the employee and the employer's response. It is used in certain cases when the employment has ceased. Neither procedure is required if the employment has ceased before one of the procedures has started and it is not reasonably practicable to start with step one.

3.9 Most significantly, it is not necessary *for the employee* to start a grievance procedure if the grievance is that the employer has dismissed or is contemplating dismissing the employee.[4]

3.10 EADR 2004 reg 15(1) states that the normal time limit for presenting the complaint, usually three months, will be extended for a period of three months in the following situations:

- The employee has not, by the normal expiry date, presented a claim but had reasonable grounds for believing that a dismissal

---

2   EADR 2004 reg 12.
3   EADR 2004 reg4.
4   EADR 2004 reg 6(5).

or disciplinary procedure, *statutory or otherwise*, was being followed. This will classically apply to dismissal cases.

- In cases *other than dismissal*, the employee presents a claim to the tribunal within the normal time limit but it is not accepted because EA 2002 s32 requires a step 1 statement in a grievance procedure to be made to the employer.
- In cases *other than dismissal*, the employee presents a claim to the tribunal after the normal time limit but having presented a step 1 grievance statement within the time limit.

3.11   It must first be borne in mind that under EA 2002 s32 a claim will not be accepted if it should have gone through step 1 of a grievance procedure. Once a step 1 statement is given to the employer, 28 days must elapse (waiting for a response) before the claim can be accepted by the tribunal. If the claim is nevertheless presented to the tribunal within the normal time limit, and is refused by the tribunal, the time is extended by three months. If the step 1 statement is sent to the employer within the normal time limit, but the claim is presented to the tribunal after that, the period is extended by three months.

3.12   If the step 1 statement is sent to the employer more than one month after the original time limit (for example, four months after the act complained of), the tribunal has no power to accept it.[5]

3.13   The time runs from the day after the expiry of the original time limit. The following example may help. The complaint is of a failure to promote on grounds of gender on 15 June. The original time limit expires on 14 September. The three month extension starts on 15 September and runs to 14 December.

3.14   It is therefore essential to use the grievance procedure before considering a claim to an employment tribunal in almost all types of cases. There are some circumstances in which it is necessary not to have had recourse to a grievance procedure. These are when the employee:[6]

- is no longer employed by the employer, and no grievance was put in writing before employment ended, and it was not reasonably practicable to enter a written grievance thereafter;
- has a grievance about disciplinary action which the employer says was wholly or mainly because of conduct. This does not include a warning or suspension on full pay. A written grievance must still

5   EA 2002 s32(4).
6   EADR 2004 reg11.

be submitted if the claimant alleges discrimination, or says that the action was taken because of conduct;

- has reasonable grounds to believe that putting a grievance in writing would result in a significant threat to them or to their property or to another person's property;
- has been harassed and has reasonable grounds to believe that putting a grievance in writing would result in further harassment;
- could not practicably have put in the grievance within a reasonable period (for example, because the employer is a sole trader and is on long-term sick leave);
- has had an appropriate representative put the grievance in writing;
- has had their grievance raised by an industry level grievance procedure;
- has chosen to raise their grievance as a 'protected disclosure' under ERA 1996 Part IVA (whistle blowing).

3.15 No definitions have been given for terms such as 'reasonably practicable' or guidance as to what might constitute 'reasonable belief' or 'reasonable grounds', and it is likely that case law will provide guidance in due course.

Failure by employer to make redundancy payment

3.16 Reference under ERA 1996 s163 of a question relating to a failure by an employer to make a redundancy payment. The reference is to the secretary of state, who may make a payment out of the National Insurance Fund. There is no time limit on this reference by a former employee.

Redundancy payments to public office holders

3.17 Reference of a question relating to payment of the equivalent of a redundancy payment to civil servants and other public office holders, under ERA 1996 s171. These are subject to the normal contractual limitation period of six years.[7] This is because the claim arises not under statute but under contract and the mechanism for resolving this particular contractual issue is referral of the question to a tribunal.

7   Limitation Act 1980 s5.

Discriminatory terms

3.18   A complaint under Sex Discrimination Act (SDA) 1975 s77(1) and SDA 1986 s6(4A) that a term in a contract, or a rule, or a collective agreement is void on the grounds that it is discriminatory. No time limit is prescribed.

UK claims affected by EU law

3.19   Claims based directly on the Treaty of Rome, for example, article 141 (equal pay), are not subject to any specific time limit under the Treaty. The European Court of Justice (ECJ) has held that such matters are for the member states' own jurisdictions to apply as matters of procedure.[8] This was followed in relation to time limits for enforcing claims under a directive which was intended to be directly effective (that is, not the Treaty itself) in *Emmott v Minister for Social* Welfare,[9] a case from the Irish Republic where the ECJ held:

> In the absence of Community rules on the subject, it is for the domestic legal system of each member state to determine the procedural conditions governing actions at law intended to ensure the protection of the rights which individuals derive from the direct effect of Community law, provided that such conditions are not less favourable than those relating to similar actions of a domestic nature nor framed so as to render virtually impossible the exercise of rights conferred by community law.[10]

3.20   In *Livingstone v Hepworth Refractories plc*[11] it was held that analogous time limits to those in domestic procedures should be applied to claims under article 141. In that case a time limit of three months was appropriate for a sex discrimination claim under article 141 as that is the time provided by the SDA 1975. This principle of equivalence as set out in *Emmott* was restated by the ECJ and the House of Lords in the joined cases of *Preston and others v Wolverhampton Healthcare Trust*.[12] In this case part-time employees brought claims under Equal Pay Act (EqPA) 1970 s2(4) and the Occupational Pension Schemes (Equal Access to Membership)

---

8   *Rewe-Zentralfinanz eG and Rewe-Zentral AG v Landwirtschaftskammer für das Saarland* (No 33/76) [1976] ECR 1989; [1977] CMLR 533, ECJ.
9   [1993] ICR 8; [1991] IRLR 387, ECJ.
10   See para 16 of the judgment.
11   [1992] ICR 287; [1992] IRLR 63, EAT.
12   [2001] IRLR 237; [2001] ICR 217, HL.

Regulations 1976,[13] complaining of having been denied access to occupational pension schemes. The ECJ held that the time limit in EqPA 1970 s2(4), requiring claims to be brought within six months of the termination of the claimant's contract of employment, was not contrary to European law. The House of Lords held that comparable claims in contract and for direct breach of article 141, were not more favourable taken as a whole. But they held that the EqPA 1970 s2(4) time limit for bringing a claim is unlawful in so far as it requires an employee who is engaged on a series of fixed-term contracts which forms a stable employment relationship to initiate tribunal proceedings within six months of the termination of each of those contracts; the six month period now runs from the end of the contract, or if a series of contracts which forms a stable employment relationship, the end of the last one in that series.[14]

3.21   In *Biggs v Somerset CC*[15] the Court of Appeal held that rights under the Treaty are not justiciable as free-standing claims in tribunals. Tribunals have jurisdiction only when given it by statute. Although they must apply EU law in the application and enforcement of domestic law, and even disapply domestic law inconsistent with it, they cannot hear cases founded solely on directly effective European provisions. The claim was made by a woman part-time teacher dismissed in 1976 who thought she must have a claim for unfair dismissal once she read of the judgment of the House of Lords in *R v Secretary of State for Employment ex p Equal Opportunities Commission*.[16] She argued that the exclusion of part-timers from the right to claim unfair dismissal was discriminatory (as had been held in that case) and that she should be entitled to bring a claim within three months of the Lords' judgment.

3.22   The Court of Appeal held that this was a matter of domestic law and procedure, as unfair dismissal was not within the Treaty, nor had the Equal Treatment Directive[17] then (that is, in 1976) become operative. There was no free-standing right of unfair dismissal in EU law which could be taken before a tribunal. Furthermore, it was possible for the claimant to have lodged a claim for unfair dismissal in 1976 and fought the battle then.

---

13 SI No 142.
14 Applied in *Preston v Wolverhamptons NHS Trust [No 3]* [2004] ICR 993; [2004] IRLR 96, EAT.
15 [1996] IRLR 203, CA.
16 [1994] ICR 317; [1994] IRLR 176, CA.
17 EEC/76/107.

3.23   In the light of the acceptance at many judicial levels of an individual's right to commence proceedings in the tribunal this judgment seems surprising. However, if the case is regarded as a decision on a non-EU matter such as unfair dismissal, the Court of Appeal was right to dismiss the right of individuals to bring claims in the tribunal based on EU law. It could be argued that, since the domestic procedures must not make it more difficult for individuals to enforce European rights than similar rights in domestic law, it cannot be right for an individual to have to use the courts rather than the more accessible tribunals for such enforcement.

3.24   If there is a right to bring a claim under directly effective EU provisions, the same principles apply to claims brought under relevant directives, for example, the Equal Treatment Directive, as to claims directly under the Treaty of Rome. There may be an exception that time runs only from the date when a directive is properly and fully transposed into UK law, but this *Emmott* principle is now thought to be limited to its facts, following the ECJ's judgment in *BP Supergas v Greece*,[18] to the effect that domestic time limits may prevail even when the state has not fully transposed its EU obligation.[19]

3.25   For claims based on the Treaty the date appears to run from 'the date upon which it could reasonably be said to be clear to any person affected . . . that such a claim could properly be made'.[20] One interpretation is to make time run for equality of redundancy pay (and arguably pensions) from the date of the judgment of the ECJ in *Barber v Guardian Royal Exchange Assurance Group*.[21] This was accepted by the EAT in *British Coal Corporation v Keeble*;[22] the same principle was also in play in *DPP v Marshall*[23] where a claim under the SDA 1975 by a transsexual was permitted where it was made within three months of the ECJ decision in *P v S*[24] when it had been stated that gender reassignment fell within the ambit of the Equal Treatment Directive. This seems to treat judgments of the ECJ in a different way from judgments of the High Court in the UK, where the principle is maintained that judgments of, for example, the House of

---

18   [1995] 1 All ER 684, ECJ, and see also *Marks & Spencer v HM Customs and Excise* [2003] 2 WLR 665 for direct effect.
19   See *Emmott v Minister for Social Welfare* [1993] ICR 8; [1991] IRLR 387, ECJ.
20   See *Rankin v British Coal Corporation* [1995] ICR 774; [1993] IRLR 69, EAT.
21   [1990] ICR 616; [1990] IRLR 240, ECJ.
22   [1997] IRLR 336, EAT.
23   [1998] ICR 518; [1998] IRLR 494, EAT.
24   C-13/94; [1996] ICR 795, ECJ.

Time limits 41

Lords do not change the law, but simply make clear what the law always was.

3.26 It is always necessary to apply domestic legislation with its own time limit and other procedural restrictions to cases where there is no directly effective EU right. According to the Court of Appeal, the existence of a statutory bar is not a good reason for contending that it was not reasonably practicable to present a claim, or that it is just and equitable to extend time.[25]

Human Rights Act 1998 claims

3.27 Claims under the Human Rights Act (HRA) 1998 must be made within one year of the act complained of, unless the complaint is raised by a victim in proceedings instigated by a public body.[26] (Employment tribunals do not have jurisdiction to hear free-standing complaints under HRA 1998. See para 1.10 above.)

Time limits and escape clauses

3.28 Most of the time limits are softened by words such as those relating to unfair dismissal complaints,[27] which introduce a secondary time limit:[28]

> . . . an employment tribunal shall not consider a complaint . . . unless it is presented to the tribunal –
> (a) before the end of the period of three months beginning with the effective date of termination, or
> (b) within such further period as the tribunal considers reasonable in a case where it is satisfied that it was not reasonably practicable for a complaint to be presented before the end of the period of three months.

3.29 A different formulation applies in relation, for example, to complaints of sex, race, disability, sexual orientation, religion or belief, part-timer or fixed-term contract employee discrimination:

25 See *Biggs v Somerset CC* [1996] IRLR 203, CA, (unfair dismissal claim refused to part-time worker 18 years late); *R v Secretary of State for Employment ex p Equal Opportunity Commission* [1994] ICR 317; [1994] IRLR 176, HL (the part-time workers' case).
26 HRA 1998 ss7 and 22.
27 ERA 1996 s94.
28 ERA 1996 s111(2).

A court or tribunal may nevertheless consider any such complaint . . . which is out of time if, in all the circumstances of the case, it considers that it is just and equitable to do so.[29]

3.30   These latter claims have only one limitation period. This escape clause does not carry with it a (secondary) limitation period, but the tribunal must consider the length of time since the end of the limitation period when deciding whether it is just and equitable to allow it.

3.31   Provisions which do not give the tribunal any flexibility are:

- claims under EqPA 1970 s2(4);
- a claim for time off with pay for a safety representative (Health and Safety at Work Act 1974 s80 and Safety Representatives and Safety Committees Regulations 1977[30] reg 11(2));
- appeals against non-discrimination notices under SDA 1975 s68 and Race Relations Act (RRA) 1976 s59;
- an application for interim relief (Trade Unions and Labour Relations (Consolidation) Act (TULRCA)1992 s161(2) and ERA 1996 s128);
- complaints by union members for a declaration following findings of unjustifiable discipline (TULRCA 1992 s66(3)) and expulsion/exclusion (TULRCA 1992 s176(3));
- applications for compensation following findings of unjustifiable discipline or unlawful expulsion/exclusion from a trade union (TULRCA 1992 ss67 and 174).

Jurisdiction

3.32   Almost all of the statutory rights which are subject to a time limit are affected by a jurisdictional bar. Tribunals have no jurisdiction to hear a case brought outside the time limit.[31] This means that the parties cannot waive a time limit, for example, by agreeing to have the case heard even though a complaint was not made within time. Parties can, however, agree to submit an unfair dismissal claim to ACAS[32]

---

29   SDA 1975 s76(5), Race Relations Act (RRA) 1976 s68(6), Disability Discrimination Act (DDA) 1995 Sch 3 para 3, Part-time Workers (Prevention of Less Favourable Treatment) Regulations (PTW Regs) 2000 SI No 1551 reg 8(3).
30   SI No 500.
31   *Biggs v Somerset CC* [1996] IRLR 203; [1996] ICR 364, CA.
32   Advisory, Conciliation and Arbitration Service.

Arbitration even if the complaint is out of time in the tribunal (see chapter 14). It also means that the tribunal itself can and should take the point if it is aware of it.[33] Furthermore, a new point relating to jurisdiction, even though not raised at the tribunal, may be taken on appeal to the Employment Appeal Tribunal (EAT), but the EAT is reluctant to hear even this kind of new point (see chapter 23).[34] The vast majority of statutory rights are qualified by words such as 'an employment tribunal shall not consider a complaint . . . unless it is presented . . . ' within the specified period.[35]

3.33   A similar bar in different words appears in EqPA 1970 s2(4) and ERA 1996 s11(4) (claims for written particulars). Although the National Industrial Relations Court (NIRC) in *Grimes v Sutton LBC*[36] felt the latter provision was not jurisdictional, the better view, it is submitted, is now found in *Rogers v Bodfari (Transport) Ltd*[37] and *Secretary of State for Employment v Atkins Auto Laundries Ltd*,[38] which related to the comparable provision on redundancy pay now in ERA 1996 s164(3).

3.34   Time limits, therefore, are rigid and jurisdictional.

When does time start running?

3.35   All the statutory rights depend on the identification of a relevant event from which time begins to run. Once that date is clear, the rules relating to the counting of time can be applied. The 'normal time limit' for various types of claim are discussed below; it must be borne in mind however that time limits will be extended in the circumstances set out in regulation 15 of the Employment Act 2002 (Dispute Resolution) Regulations 2004[39] where dismissal, disciplinary or grievance procedures have been, or ought to have been applied (see paras 3.3–3.15 and see the table at pages 22–30 above).

---

33 *Rogers v Bodfari (Transport) Ltd* [1973] ICR 325; [1973] IRLR 172, NIRC and *Dedman v British Building and Engineering Appliances Ltd* [1974] ICR 53; [1973] IRLR 379, CA.

34 *House v Emerson Electric Industrial Controls* [1980] ICR 795, EAT. *JF Knight (Roadworks) Ltd v Platfoot* [2001] ICR Part 3 p xvi.

35 ERA 1996 s104(2) (on unfair dismissal).

36 [1973] ICR 240, NIRC.

37 [1973] ICR 325; [1973] IRLR 172, NIRC.

38 [1972] ICR 76, NIRC.

39 SI No 752.

Unfair dismissal

3.36   The normal time limit runs from the effective date of termination (EDT) as defined in ERA 1996 s97(1). A specific exception is provided by ERA s104(3) so that a claimant can present a claim after notice has been given but before the EDT. The same goes for a claimant claiming constructive dismissal under ERA 1996 s95(1)(c) who, instead of terminating summarily (as he or she would be entitled to do), gives notice and between the giving of notice and the EDT lodges a complaint.[40]

3.37   Since the termination of a fixed term contract on its due date is not a termination by notice, a complaint presented before the due date does not fall within the exception in ERA 1996 s97(4).[41] If you know the contract is not going to be renewed, you must wait until after it has expired before presenting a claim.

Redundancy pay

3.38   A claim for redundancy pay must be made within six months of the 'relevant date'. This is defined by ERA 1996 s145 and is a slightly expanded version of that applying to unfair dismissal under ERA 1996 s97(1). A claim is in time if within the six months counting the EDT:[42]

- a redundancy payment has been agreed and paid;
- the employee has made a claim in writing to the employer for redundancy pay;
- a question has been referred to a tribunal by claim; or
- an unfair dismissal complaint has been presented in time, that is, within three months.

This means that the claimant need not present a claim to the tribunal but can stop time running by writing to the employer and claiming redundancy pay.

3.39   Extension of time can be granted by the tribunal if during a *further* limitation period of six months the employee takes the second, third or fourth step above *and* the tribunal considers it just and equitable in

---

40   *Presley v Llanelli BC* [1979] ICR 419; [1979] IRLR 381, EAT.
41   *Throsby v Imperial College of Science and Technology* [1978] ICR 357; [1977] IRLR 337, EAT.
42   ERA 1996 s164.

all the circumstances to allow the complaint to go ahead, having regard to the reason for the failure to take any of the above steps in the original six-month limitation period.

Equal pay

3.40 Claims under EqPA 1970 s2 for breach of an equality clause should be brought during the existence of the contract, or within six months of the employee leaving.[43] It should be noted that in *Preston v Wolverhampton*[44] the ECJ held that where a person is engaged on a series of fixed term contracts in a stable employment relationship, he or she is not required to initiate proceedings within six months of the termination of each of those contracts.

Written particulars

3.41 Claims under ERA 1996 s11(4) seeking written particulars of contractual terms, or an itemised pay statement, must be brought during the existence of the contract or within three months of the employee leaving.

Interim relief

3.42 Claims for interim relief (ERA 1996 s128) must be brought at any time up to seven days after the EDT. This right arises in cases of dismissal on the grounds of trade union activity or membership (TULRCA 1992 ss152 and 161), or health and safety complaints (ERA 1996 s100) or taking action as an elected employee representative (ERA ss101A(d) and 103) or making a protected disclosure under the whistle blowing jurisdiction of the Public Interest Disclosure Act 1998 (ERA 1996 s103A). A claim can be brought *before* the EDT, and the period of seven days runs from the day *after* the EDT, so a dismissal taking effect on a Tuesday would require presentation of a claim by the end of the following Tuesday.

3.43 None of these claims attracts an escape clause giving the tribunal discretion to extend the deadline.

---

43 EqPA 1970 s2(4) and 2ZA. See also paras 22.16–22.21.
44 [2001] IRLR 237; [2001] ICR 216, HL.

Discrimination

3.44   Special time limits apply to discrimination claims. These are generally where the act complained of extends over a period of time. Time runs from the date of the act complained of. But 'any act extending over a period shall be treated as done at the end of that period'.[45] Discrimination against someone on the grounds of raising health and safety issues, 'whistle blowing', working time issues or raising the issue of parental leave is complainable within three months of the act complained of, or ' . . . where that act . . . is part of a series of acts . . . the last of them'.[46] A similar provision applies in respect of action short of dismissal on trade union grounds.[47]

3.45   When a contractual term is unlawful by way of discrimination, it is treated as extending throughout the duration of the contract.[48] Where discrimination arises in respect of other matters than terms of the contract, it continues throughout the duration of the regime in which the discrimination is carried on. In *Barclays Bank plc v Kapur*[49] Asian workers, formerly employed by the bank in East Africa, who joined the bank's pension scheme in England in 1970 were denied recognition of their previous service in Africa, arguably on discriminatory grounds. This was held not to be a one-off act of discrimination but a continuing regime providing unfavourable pension rights as long as the employees remained in employment (although, having succeeded in the preliminary procedure, the employees lost at the hearing of the substantive claim).[50] Similarly, a failure to take proper remedial action following an act of discrimination has a continuing effect until that remedial action is taken.[51] The critical distinction is between a single act such as a decision on grading which may have consequences on pay but does not

---

45   SDA 1975 s76(6)(b), RRA 1976 s68(7)(b), DDA 1995 Sch 3 para 3(2)(b), Part-time Workers (Prevention of Less Favourable Treatment) Regulations (PTW Regs) 2000 SI No 1551, reg 8(2).
46   ERA 1996 s46(3)(a). Employment Equality (Religion or Belief) Regulations 2003 SI No 1660, reg 34(4)(b) and Employment Equality (Sexual Orientation) Regulations 2003 SI No 1661, reg 34(4)(b).
47   TULRCA 1992 s147(1)(a).
48   SDA 1975 s76(6)(b) and RRA 1976 s68(7)(a).
49   [1991] ICR 208; [1991] IRLR 136, HL.
50   [1995] IRLR 87, CA.
51   *Littlewoods Organisation plc v Traynor* [1993] IRLR 154, EAT.

in itself continue, and a general regime which has a continuing discriminatory effect.[52]

3.46 This distinction between single and continuing acts was considered in *Owusu v London Fire and Civil Defence Authority*[53] where the EAT held that a failure to promote or shortlist was a complaint of a one-off act, but a repeated failure to upgrade the claimant, or to allow him to act at a higher grade when the opportunity arose was considered to amount to a discriminatory practice, that is, a continuing act. In *Cast v Croydon College*[54] a series of refusals concerning a benefit was held by the Court of Appeal to amount to a continuing act if there was further consideration of each request, rather than merely a reference back to the earlier decision. Further guidance was given by the Court of Appeal in *Hendricks v Commissioner of Police of the Metropolis*[55] when it was held that:

> The question was whether that was an act extending over a period, as distinct from a succession of isolated or specific acts for which time would begin to run from the date when each act was committed.

3.47 When the act complained of is the refusal by employers to accept a grievance, time begins to run from the date on which the decision was communicated to the complainant, not the date on which the decision was made.[56] Where the employee invokes an internal appeal which is unsuccessful, the operative date depends on whether, as a matter of contract, the employment continues pending appeal.[57]

3.48 For deliberate omissions which are claimed to be discriminatory, time runs from the date on which a 'decision' is taken 'at a time and in circumstances when [the employer] was in a position to implement that decision'. So in *Swithland Motors plc v Clarke*[58] car dealers seeking to take over the assets of a dealership which went into receivership interviewed but refused to appoint male car salesmen, allegedly on discriminatory grounds. They made the 'decision' not at the time of the interview but at the time of the takeover when they were in a

---

52 *Sougrin v Haringey Health Authority* [1991] ICR 791; [1991] IRLR 447, EAT; *Owusu v London Fire and Civil Defence Authority* [1995] IRLR 574, EAT. See also *Lindsay v Ironsides, Ray and Vials* [1994] ICR 384; [1994] IRLR 318, EAT: preliminary issue should be tried as to whether a single discriminatory act is out of time.

53 [1995] IRLR 574, EAT.

54 [1998] IRLR 318; [1998] ICR 500, CA.

55 [2003] IRLR 96.

56 *Aniagwu v Hackney LBC* [1999] IRLR 303, EAT.

57 *Adekeye v Post Office (No 2)* [1997] IRLR 105; [1997] ICR 110, CA.

58 [1994] ICR 231; [1994] IRLR 275, EAT.

position to implement the decision. But where the discrimination takes the form of *dismissal*, the time runs from the date of the expiry of the notice (if given) and not the date of the decision to dismiss or the giving of the notice.[59]

3.49   Even if acts outside the three-month period do not constitute part of a series of discriminatory acts or a continuing regime, they may nevertheless be adduced as evidence of discrimination occurring within the time limit.[60] Similarly, acts which prove discrimination occurring *after* the presentation of a valid claim may also be adduced[61] (though not for the purpose of determining whether there was a continuing act according to the Court of Appeal in *Robertson v Bexley Community Center t/a Leisure Link*).[62]

Wages protection and Sunday trading cases

3.50   Claims relating to unlawful deductions from wages in respect of a series of deductions must be made within three months of the *last* deduction.[63]

3.51   Claims of detrimental treatment for refusing to do Sunday shop work following a series of acts must be brought within three months of the *last* of them.[64]

The rules on counting time

3.52   Having identified the date of the relevant event which triggers a claim, complaint, application or appeal to a tribunal, by reference to the appropriate statute or regulations, it is possible to determine the time limit for presentation of the claim. The rules for calculating time were comprehensively summarised in *Pruden v Cunard Ellerman Ltd*.[65] Following citation of relevant authorities and reference to the Interpretation Act 1978, Wood J said:

59 *Lupeti v Wrens Old House Ltd* [1984] ICR 348, EAT; *Coutts v Cure* [2004] UKEAT 0395/04.
60 *Eke v Customs and Excise Commissioners* [1981] IRLR 344, EAT.
61 *Chattopadhyay v Headmaster of Holloway School* [1982] ICR 132; [1981] IRLR 487, EAT.
62 [2003] IRLR 434., CA.
63 ERA 1996 s23(2) and (3).
64 ERA 1996 s48(3).
65 [1993] IRLR 317, EAT. See also *RJB Mining (UK) Ltd v National Union of Mineworkers* [1995] IRLR 556, CA.

Where time is specified to run from a particular date, the word 'date' means the whole of the period of 24 hours from midnight to midnight, and the law takes no account of a fraction of a day unless special reasons require it . . . Where a complaint is required to be presented within a specific period – 'from', 'after' or 'of ' – a particular date, that date is to be excluded from the calculation . . . However, where a complaint is required to be presented within a specified period beginning with 'a particular date' that date is to be *included* in the calculation . . . Those principles are well established.[66]

3.53   An expanded analysis appears in Civil Procedure Rules Part 2.8 and the accompanying notes, and the 2004 Regs add guidance on counting time in regulation 15. In the table at pages 22–30, the expression 'whole' weeks or months refers to time periods which begin from, after or on a particular date. For example, a dismissal for trade union activities occurring on a Tuesday triggers a limitation period of seven whole days so that a claim must be presented on or before the following Tuesday. A claim for equal pay by a woman who left her job on 15 June must be presented on or before 15 December.

3.54   However, most claims under employment protection legislation must be brought 'before the end of the period of three months beginning with' [the relevant event]. For example, an unfair dismissal claim must be brought within the period of three months beginning with the effective date of termination. In such a case a claim for a dismissal arising on 15 June must be presented on or before 14 September. The date of the relevant event, in this case dismissal, is day one of the limitation period.

3.55   The EAT in *Pruden*[67] resolved the problem which arises when the trigger event is the last day of a month, because months consist of different numbers of days, that is, 28, 29, 30 or 31. Only four months have the same number of days as the corresponding month three months later (May, June, July, October). For all other months, the approach in *Pruden* will produce the correct answer. In that case, a claim presented on 30 November in respect of a dismissal on 31 August was within time. If there is no corresponding date in the month in which limitation occurs, take the next earlier date. So a dismissal on 30 November must generate a claim by 28 February in the succeeding year (or 29 February in a leap year).

3.56   The only slight surprise in applying these rules is that a dismissal on the last day of the month of February (that is, 28) must generate a

66 [1995] IRLR 556 at para 6.
67 *Pruden v Cunard Ellerman Ltd* [1993] IRLR 317, EAT.

claim on 27 May, which is, of course, four days before the end of the month. However, a dismissal on the next day, 1 March, must generate a claim by 31 May, four days later.

Commencement of proceedings

3.57   Time ceases to run when proceedings are properly commenced. By 2004 Rules r1(1), a claim 'may be brought before an employment tribunal by the claimant presenting to an Employment Tribunal Office the details of the claim in writing . . . ' Some rare proceedings are commenced by an *appellant* with a notice of appeal, for example, those under the Health and Safety at Work Act 1974. Presentation is a unilateral act. It does not require any response by the tribunal office.[68] As long as the claim is physically or electronically delivered to the relevant office before midnight at the end of the last day in the limitation period, the application is validly presented. So if a letter box is available at the office, posting through it will be effective presentation. If there is no provision for postal delivery through a letter box at the relevant office, service can be effected on the next available date when the office is open.[69]

3.58   Presentation must be made to 'the Employment Tribunal Office. This means to any office in Great Britain which has been established for any area specified by the President and which is operated by the Employment Tribunals Service to carry out administrative functions in support of functions being carried out by a tribunal or chairman'.[70]

3.59   Presentation may be effected by electronic means: 2004 Rules r61(1). In such a case the ET1 expressly discourages following this up with a hard copy, but it would be prudent to do so with a covering letter as soon as practicable. There is of course always a risk that there may be a fax transmission problem, or some simple practical problem such as lack of paper, which means that the fax is not 'presented' at the tribunal. Arguably, a claim is validly presented if it is transmitted and stored electronically at the tribunal awaiting paper and printout. When e-mail presentation is available, that too will suffice.

3.60   If it is impossible to 'present' the claim within the time scale, for example because there is no letter box at the tribunal office available

---

68   *Hetton Victory Club Ltd v Swainstone* [1983] ICR 341; [1983] IRLR 164, CA.
69   *Ford v Stakis Hotels and Inns Ltd* [1987] ICR 943; [1988] IRLR 46, EAT.
70   2004 Regs reg 2(1).

for use when the office is closed, as on a weekend, or possibly when a fax machine malfunctions, *either* the deadline is extended until the next working day *or* it would be possible to argue that it was not 'reasonably practicable' to present the claim on time and to make use of the secondary limitation period (see below).

Extending the deadline

3.61 Extensions of time where disciplinary or grievance procedures are under way are discussed above in the context of rights under EA 2002 ss31 and 32. Extensions of normal time limits can be granted in the two categories of case; where it was 'not reasonably practicable' to have presented the compliant in time, or where it is 'just and equitable' to extend time. For those situations where power is given to the tribunal to extend the deadline on the grounds that 'it was not reasonably practicable' to present the claim on time, a *further,* secondary, limitation period applies which is itself subject to legal constraint. So, for unfair dismissal, the tribunal must make a finding in relation to the limitation period that it was not reasonably practicable to present the claim on time, and then go on to consider whether the claim was presented 'within such further period as the tribunal considers reasonable . . . '[71]

Failure to meet the deadline: 'not reasonably practicable'

3.62 The limitation period may be extended by reason of an escape clause in the legislation. The following general principles were laid down in *Walls Meat Co Ltd v Khan:*[72]

> The performance of an act . . . is not reasonably practicable if there is some impediment which reasonably prevents, or interferes with, or inhibits, such performance. The impediment may be physical, for instance the illness of the complainant or a postal strike; or the impediment may be mental, namely, the state of mind of the complainant in the form of ignorance of, or mistaken belief with regard to, essential matters. Such states of mind can, however, only be regarded as impediments making it not reasonably practicable to present a complaint within the period of three months, if the ignorance on the one hand or the mistaken belief on the other, is itself

71 ERA 1996 s111(2).
72 [1979] ICR 52 at 60 per Brandon LJ; [1978] IRLR 499, CA.

reasonable. Either state of mind will, further, not be reasonable if it arises from the fault of the complainant in not making such enquiries as he should reasonably in all the circumstances have made, or from the fault of his solicitors or other professional advisers . . .

Each of these triggers for the operation of the escape clause is considered below.

Burden of proof

3.63   Since the issue relates to jurisdiction, it is for the claimant to prove the facts necessary for establishing jurisdiction and for establishing that it was not reasonably practicable to comply with the deadline.[73]

Physical inability

3.64   Physical illness and mental depression may make it not reasonably practicable for the claimant to make a claim in time. But if the claimant is in touch with an adviser, it seems the claimant will be assumed to have passed the responsibility for ensuring the necessary steps are taken to the adviser and may not rely on his or her own incapacity.

3.65   The Court of Appeal in *Schultz v Esso Petroleum Ltd*[74] held that the question of reasonable practicability must be considered against the background of the surrounding circumstances and the aim to be achieved. Mr Schultz was dismissed due to long-term absence, caused by depression. He initially attempted to instigate an appeal procedure, and for the first seven weeks of the limitation period he was capable of giving instructions to his solicitor. Thereafter however he was too ill to do so. The Court of Appeal disagreed with the tribunal and the EAT which had both held that it was reasonably practicable to have presented the application in time; it was held not to have been fair to give the same weight to a period of disabling illness regardless of which part of the limitation period it falls within.

Postal delays

3.66   If the claim is correctly addressed but is either lost or delayed in the post, it may not be reasonably practicable to present it on time. Evidence must be produced by the claimant or his or her adviser to show

---

73   *Porter v Bandridge Ltd* [1978] ICR 943; [1978] IRLR 271, followed in *Walls Meat v Khan* [1979] ICR 52: ' . . . the burden of proof being on the employee . . . '
74   [1999] 3 All ER 338; [1999] IRLR 488, CA.

that the claim was posted and was correctly addressed. Evidence can be brought to show that a letter posted first class one day will be delivered to the same town the next. But in *St Basil's Centre v McCrossan*[75] it was suggested that the time scale set out in the practice direction applying in the High Court for the service of documents[76] should apply. CPR Part 6 r6.7 says that in the normal course of post documents are deemed to have been served (a) in the case of first class mail, on the second working day after posting. This approach was expressly approved by the Court of Appeal in the case of *Consignia Plc v Sealy*[77] where the respondent, (now again known as the Royal Mail) was unable to defeat the claimant's claim on the basis that it was out of time because, despite presentation being two days late, it had not been 'reasonably practicable' to have presented the claim within the time limit. In *Godwin v Swindon BC*[78] the Court of Appeal affirmed this approach. The claimant served the claim form by first class post on Thursday, it arrived on Friday, which was the last day to comply with the rule. But the deemed day was Monday (two days for first class post, not including weekends). The claim was struck out. May LJ explained that certainty was vital, so that deemed days should not be rebuttable by evidence of when a document actually arrived as this would give rise to more disputes.

3.67   This is a slightly odd approach to the meaning of 'practicable' and is more akin to 'feasible', the meaning attached to it by the Court of Appeal in *Palmer v Southend-on-Sea BC*.[79] It is likely that the time scale specified in the Rules and interpreted in the CPR will be held to be 'reasonable' as an expectation by the claimant and his or her advisers. A shorter period may also be reasonable in the circumstances. What is unlikely to be reasonable, however, is a delay between the preparation of the claim and its being taken to the post. A postal delay may excuse the presentation of the application within time, but will not excuse a failure to take the prepared claim to the post, since it cannot be said that it was 'not reasonably practicable' to present the claim within time. The lesson is: do not delay.

3.68   Objective circumstances which might provide justification may be affected by the claimant's actions during that time so as to defeat the

---

75   [1992] ICR 140; [1991] IRLR 455, EAT.
76   Practice Direction (post: first and second class mail) [1985] 1 All ER 889.
77   [2002] EWCA Civ 878; ICR 1193; IRLR 624.
78   [2001] EWCA Civ 1478.
79   [1984] ICR 372; [1984] IRLR 119, CA; followed in *London Underground v Noel* [2000] ICR 109, CA.

escape clause. In *Capital Foods Retail Ltd v Corrigan*[80] the EAT held that part and parcel of the reasonableness of the claimant complying with the deadline is a duty to follow up the presentation of a complaint which has been unacknowledged. Rule 2(2)(a) of the 2004 Rules requires the tribunal office to notify the parties (including the claimant) of the case number and address for further communications upon accepting a claim (or send it back it if it is not accepted: r2(1)). Failure to do anything about an unacknowledged claim may jeopardise the escape clause in the limitation period. In other words, if you post a claim which ought to arrive with one month to spare, hear nothing for two weeks and yet do nothing further until after the deadline, you cannot complain that it was not 'reasonably practicable' to present the claim on time, since with due diligence the failure to acknowledge could have been investigated and a new claim presented within time.[81]

Ignorance of rights and facts

3.69 This comes within the category of 'mental impediment – namely the state of mind of the complainant' as Brandon LJ put it:[82]

> . . . if . . . an employee was reasonably ignorant of either (a) his right to make a complaint for unfair dismissal at all, or (b) how to make it, or (c) that it was necessary for him to make it within a period of three months from the date of dismissal, an industrial tribunal could and should be satisfied that it was not reasonably practicable for his complaint to be presented within the period concerned.

3.70 In *Walls Meat* itself, the claimant was under the impression that his claim for unfair dismissal was being handled by the tribunal adjudicating his claim for unemployment benefit. His mistake was held to be reasonable. The escape clause will be more readily available to someone who was totally ignorant of all these factors, than to someone who knew of the right to claim unfair dismissal but was unclear about how and when to exercise it. In the latter case, the claimant would be on notice and would find it more difficult to make out the justification for a late claim.

---

80 [1993] IRLR 430, EAT.
81 In the context of appealing to the EAT within the prescribed time limit, see *Peters v Sat Katar Co Ltd* [2003] IRLR 574, where the CA held that it had been reasonable for a litigant in person to have assumed that her appeal had been received by the EAT.
82 *Walls Meat Co Ltd v Khan* [1979] ICR 52 at 61, CA.

3.72   In assessing the reasonableness of the claimant's belief, the tribunal will find such a claim more difficult to accept if it comes from a highly articulate claimant. In *Avon CC v Haywood-Hicks*[83] it was held that an intelligent and well-educated claimant ought to have investigated his rights within the time limit. Clearly, since compensation for unfair dismissal has been in existence since 1971, it is difficult to claim ignorance of the right to claim and of the need to seek advice.

3.73   To ignorance of rights can be added an extra category: ignorance of a material fact. In *Machine Tool Industry Research Association v Simpson*[84] an employee accepted her redundancy but after the deadline for claiming unfair dismissal had expired discovered some facts which led her to believe she had not been dismissed for redundancy and claimed unfair dismissal. Her claim was allowed to proceed. Purchas LJ said (at 564):

> . . . 'reasonably practicable' imports three stages, the proof of which rests on the employee. The first proposition . . . is that it was reasonable for the employee not to be aware of the factual basis on which she could bring an application to the tribunal during the currency of the three months limitation period . . . [I]f that is established, it cannot be reasonably practicable to expect a claimant to bring a case based on facts of which she is ignorant. Secondly, the claimant must establish that the knowledge which she gains has, in the circumstances, been reasonably gained by her and that that knowledge is either crucial, fundamental or important . . . to her change of belief . . . [T]hat concept . . . is an objective qualification of reasonableness, in the circumstances, to a subjective test of the claimant's state of mind. The third ground . . . is that the acquisition of this knowledge had to be crucial to the decision to bring a claim in any event.

3.74   So the discovery of facts which for the first time enable the claimant to put forward a claim justifies escape from the limitation period. Illustrations of this approach are found in:

- *James W Cook & Co (Wivenhoe) v Tipper*,[85] where employees made redundant were entitled to bring their claims for unfair dismissal when, after the deadline, they realised that all chances of getting their jobs back disappeared on the closure of the yard they were

---

83   [1978] ICR 646; [IRLR] 118, EAT.
84   [1988] ICR 558; [1988] IRLR 212, CA.
85   [1990] ICR 716; [1990] IRLR 386, CA.

working in. It was not reasonably practicable to bring proceedings during the relevant period.

- *Churchill v Yeates & Son Ltd,*[86] where it was held that it was not reasonably practicable for an employee to bring a complaint 'until he is aware of a fundamental fact which renders his dismissal unfair'. There was doubt about the correctness of the employer's reason for dismissal as being, among other things, redundancy.

3.75   In all cases of timing, the essential ingredient is the employee's reasonable and genuine belief. It is not necessary for the claimant to establish the truth of the new fact, only the reasonableness of a belief in it.[87]

Advisers: wrong advice or delay

3.76   The general rule is that you cannot use the escape clause where your advisers have been at fault. As Lord Denning MR said:

> If a man engages skilled advisers to act for him – and they mistake the time limit and present [the claim] too late – he is out. His remedy is against them.[88]

3.77   Since then, under the CPR, the Court of Appeal has held that the failure by a legal adviser to enter proceedings in time should not be visited upon the claimant for otherwise the defendant would be in receipt of a windfall: *Steeds v Peverel Management Services Ltd.*[89] This was followed and applied by the EAT in *Chohan v Derby Law Centre*[90] where a tribunal had wrongly focused on the fault of a solicitor without considering other matters in a discrimination (not unfair dismissal) case.

3.78   Within this category are solicitors, Citizens' Advice, trade union full-time and lay officers including shop stewards, and representatives of trade, employers' and professional associations.[91] In *Riley v Tesco Stores*[92] the claimant received incorrect advice from Citizens' Advice workers but was not excused.

---

86   [1983] ICR 380; [1983] IRLR 187, EAT, approved in *Marley (UK) Ltd v Anderson* [1996] IRLR 163, CA.
87   *Marley (UK) Ltd v Anderson* [1996] IRLR 163, CA.
88   *Dedman v British Building and Engineering Appliances Ltd* [1974] ICR 53; [1973] IRLR 379, CA.
89   [2001] EWCA Civ 419, pp38–40.
90   [2004] IRLR 365, EAT.
91   See *Hammond v Haigh Castle & Co Ltd* [1973] ICR 148; [1973] IRLR 91, NIRC.
92   [1980] ICR 323; [1980] IRLR 103, CA.

3.79 A different test is applied to employees of tribunals and job centres. In *Jean Sorelle Ltd v Rybak*[93] it was held that a tribunal could decide that information given by an employee of the tribunal office did not fall within the category of skilled advice, so that if it were incorrect and relied on by the claimant so that he or she missed the deadline, he or she would be saved by the escape clause. The distinction between advisers retained by the claimant and staff of official bodies was also drawn in *London International College Ltd v Sen*.[94] Here the claimant received advice from a solicitor and also contacted the tribunal office. It was held that the fact that the claimant had consulted a solicitor did not automatically make it reasonably practicable for the claimant to present a claim in time. The proper approach is to ask what was the substantial cause of the late application, and since in *Sen* this was the information given by the tribunal office, the escape clause was operated in favour of the claimant.

3.80 Of course, failure by a skilled adviser to ensure that the claim posted on time has been received in time remains inexcusable, and unreasonable conduct during the intervening time might exclude the operation of the escape clause.[95]

Delay caused by internal procedures

3.81 It is often thought by claimants, particularly those in jobs where there is sophisticated appeal and disciplinary machinery, that time does not begin to run against them until the exhaustion of the relevant appeal procedures. This is partly right and reflects the new regime in EA 2002 ss31 and 32 but the statutory procedures will not always generate extra time.

3.82 Where there is an appeal against a decision to dismiss, the date from which time will run depends on whether, during the period between the decision to dismiss and the outcome of the appeal, the employee stands dismissed with the possibility of reinstatement, or whether he or she is suspended with the possibility of the proposed dismissal not being confirmed.[96]

3.83 However, in most cases, the decision of management to dismiss causes an effective date of termination for the purposes of the commencement of a relevant limitation period, and is not affected by

93 [1991] ICR 127; [1991] IRLR 153, EAT.
94 [1993] IRLR 333, CA.
95 See *Capital Foods (Retail) Ltd v Corrigan* [1991] IRLR 430, EAT.
96 *Drage v Governors of Greenford High School* [2000] IRLR 314, CA.

any internal appeal machinery. To err on the side of caution, the earlier date should be taken as the one from which time will begin to run. Naturally, in such cases, if the claimant is successful at the internal appeal, reinstatement occurs and there has been no dismissal.[97] If the effective date of termination starts the limitation period running, however, an internal appeal can have no effect on it; nor is it a sufficient ground for finding that presentation of a complaint of unfair dismissal was not reasonably practicable.[98]

3.84   This approach was approved in *Palmer v Southend-on-Sea BC*.[99] There, two local government workers were convicted of stealing petrol and dismissed, but the council's appeal committee indicated that should their conviction be overturned, the dismissals might be reconsidered. The Court of Appeal did overturn their convictions but the council refused to reinstate them. The tribunal's decision that it had been reasonably practicable to present claims to the tribunal within three months was upheld.

3.85   The moral is that if there is an internal appeal procedure, a claim for unfair dismissal should still be lodged in any event. The tribunal hearing can always be postponed on the ground that an internal procedure is operating and will imminently decide the matter. Most employers would accept the lodging of a claim in such circumstances as simply a protective measure and not in any way an attempt to threaten them or short-circuit existing procedures.

3.86   The only clear case in which it is likely that the escape clause will be operated in favour of the claimant is when the employer itself encourages the claimant to forego making a claim in time. In *Owen v Crown House Engineering Ltd*,[100] negotiations took place with the claimants' union following redundancy notices. The employers invited the union official to 'hold his hand' in submitting claims to the tribunal so that the employers' board could consider the matter in more detail. The NIRC upheld the 'vital importance of attempting to settle all differences by amicable negotiation' and that had claims been made 'it would almost certainly have killed any hope of a fruitful outcome to the negotiations'.[101] So, action by employers causative of the claimant missing the deadline can give rise to the operation of the escape clause.

97 See *J Sainsbury Ltd v Savage* [1981] ICR 1; [1980] IRLR 109, CA.
98 *Bodha v Hampshire AHA* [1982] ICR 200.
99 [1984] ICR 372; [1984] IRLR 119, CA.
100 [1973] ICR 511; [1973] IRLR 233, NIRC.
101 [1973] ICR 511, per Sir Hugh Griffiths at 516.

3.86   Given that an appeal stage is part of the statutory dismissal and disciplinary procedures, if this is ongoing when the normal time limit for bringing a complaint expires, under regulation 15 of the Employment Act 2002 (Dispute Resolution) Regulations 2004,[102] an extension of time will be granted. However, for safety's sake, however, it is still advisable to present the claim within the time scale.

Criminal or other proceedings

3.87   It can sometimes be reasonable to misunderstand the nature of proceedings where a similar issue is being judged by social security and employment tribunals.[103] A safe rule is to make a claim in time. The existence of criminal proceedings will certainly affect many tribunal claims for unfair dismissal based on dishonesty, and the appropriate course is to present a claim to the tribunal within the statutory time limit, then to apply for a stay of the tribunal hearing. (Denning LJ in *Khan* (above)[104] held that the existence of criminal proceedings was not an acceptable reason for saying it was not 'reasonably practicable' to lodge a claim in time.) In such a case it is likely that the claimant will have access to legal advice. This should include advice on, at the very least, time limits for presenting an unfair dismissal claim. In these circumstances, it is unlikely that the escape clause would be operated in favour of the claimant if no claim were lodged at the employment tribunal (see also para 12.19 below).

Failure to meet the deadline: time limits on the escape clause

3.88   When the tribunal is satisfied that it was not reasonably practicable to present the claim during the limitation period (for example, three months), it must then go on to decide whether it was presented 'within such further period as the tribunal considers reasonable . . . '[105] A broader discretion is thus given to the tribunal than in respect of the original limitation period. The length of time permitted is a matter of fact for the tribunal to determine. In *Marley (UK) Ltd v Anderson*,[106] the EAT held that, although the Court of Appeal in *James*

---

102   SI No 752.
103   See *Riley v Tesco Stores* [1980] ICR 323; [1980] IRLR 103, CA.
104   *Walls Meat Co Ltd v Khan* [1979] ICR 52; [1978] IRLR 499, CA.
105   ERA 1996 s111(2).
106   [1994] IRLR 152.

W Cook[107]did express views about the timescales in that particular case (four to six weeks 'were simply too long'), there was an error of law when the tribunal felt itself *bound* by that approach. Similarly, the tribunal must not simply consider the length of the delay, but also the circumstances in which the delay occurred and the reasons for it extending beyond the limitation period.

Failure to meet the deadline: 'just and equitable'

Discrimination on grounds of sex, race, disability, part-time or fixed-term status, sexual orientation, religion or belief

3.89   Questions of reasonable practicability do not arise in relation to claims of discrimination on grounds of sex, race, disability, part-time or fixed-term status, religion or belief or sexual orientation, since the limitation period of three months may be set aside if 'in all the circumstances of the case [a tribunal] considers that it is just and equitable to do so'.[108] Because of the wide discretion given to tribunals, it is unlikely that a decision can successfully be appealed. The 'circumstances of the case' appear to be those related to the reason for the delay, and tribunals are not required to investigate them in full.

3.90   That different statutory considerations apply is apparent from *Trust House Forte (UK) Ltd v Halstead*,[109] where late claims were made in respect of unfair dismissal and racial discrimination. The tribunal gave the claimant the benefit of the escape clause in respect of both claims. On appeal, the EAT refused to uphold the unfair dismissal claim, but did not interfere with the exercise of discretion in relation to the discrimination claim. The breadth of discretion can be seen in the case of *Southwark LBC v Afolabi*[110] where a claim was lodged some nine years out of time, but because the claimant only realised his potential claim on seeing his personnel file some nine years after his failure to gain promotion, it was just and equitable to extend the time limit.

3.91   Given the breadth of the discretion, it would be appropriate to call evidence relating to the degree of prejudice should the tribunal

---

107 *James W Cook & Co (Wivenhoe) v Tipper* [1990] ICR 716; [1990] IRLR 386, CA.
108 SDA 1975 s76(5); RRA 1976 s68(6); DDA 1995 Sch 3 para 3; PTW Regs 2000 reg 8(3). Employment Equality (Religion or Belief) Regs 2003 reg 34(4)(b) and Employment Equality (Sexual Orientation) Regs 2003 reg 34(4)(b).
109 EAT 213/86, unreported.
110 [2003] EWCA Civ 15; [2003] ICR 800.

exercise its discretion, for example, whether the length of the delay and the circumstances attending it make it more difficult for the employer to defend the case, and whether the employer has in any way contributed to the delay or acquiesced in it. In general, though, the approach is that the tribunal can take account of anything it considers relevant.[111] This is reflected in the Court of Appeal judgment in the case of *Stott and others v Prison Service HMP Wakefield*[112] where Simon Brown LJ said that this discretion 'could not have been wider'.

3.92   It is worth recalling that time does not begin to run until the *end* of a period during which a continuing act of discrimination has occurred, or the last of a series of acts of discrimination, and may not have begun to run in respect of a continuing policy which is held to be discriminatory. A claim can be made at any time during its currency.

Redundancy pay

3.93   A *further* limitation period applies in respect of redundancy payments (see para 3.39 above).

---

111 *Hutchinson v Westwood Television Ltd* [1977] ICR 279; [1977] IRLR 69, EAT.
112 [2003] EWCA Civ 1513.

Stages before proceedings are commenced

Dismissal and grievance procedures: EA 2002 s32

4.1   As set out in paras 2.6 and 3.3–3.15, employees are not permitted to present certain complaints to the tribunal under a jurisdiction listed in Employment Act (EA) 2002 Schs 3 or 4 if either the standard or modified procedure applies. These include unfair dismissal, discrimination and equal pay, redundancy, unlawful deductions from wages and detriment in employment. Failure to comply with this requirement will result in the tribunal refusing to accept the claim.[1]

The correct respondent

4.2   After checking to make sure that the tribunal has jurisdiction to hear the case (see the table at pages 22–30 above), the claimant needs to consider who is the correct respondent to name on the claim form. This will generally be the employer but it may also be a fellow employee or other individuals in claims of discrimination or, it might be a trade union.

4.3   Sometimes it is unclear who the relevant employer is, for example, in cases arising out of transfer of a business or where there is a complicated arrangement of associated companies. Difficulties in naming the correct respondent may be resolved by a reply given to a letter before presenting a complaint.[2] If in doubt, the claimant should name all possible respondents and explain the reasons for doing so in the claim form.

4.4   When a purely technical error has been made in naming a respondent the tribunal may allow an amendment late on in the proceedings (see para 7.8 below).[3]

4.5   A tribunal is given a broad discretion to join a party to proceedings as a respondent 'at any time',[4] and can do so even after the time limit for presenting a claim against a new respondent has expired.[5] It can also be done after a decision on the merits of the case has been

---

1   Employment Tribunals Rules of Procedure 2004 (2004 Rules) r3(2)(c).
2   See para 4.12 below.
3   *Chapman v Goonvean and Rostowrack China Clay Co Ltd* [1973] ICR 50; [1972] IRLR 124, NIRC.
4   2004 Rules r10(1); at 10(2)(k) and (r).
5   *Drinkwater Sabey Ltd v Burnett* [1995] ICR 328; [1995] IRLR 238, EAT, following *Gillick v BP Chemicals Ltd* [1993] IRLR 437, EAT.

given: in *Linbourne v Constable*[6] the Employment Appeal Tribunal held that an amendment should be allowed to substitute a respondent even after a decision had been given. The guidelines to be taken into consideration by the tribunal in such cases were set out by the National Industrial Relations Court in *Cocking v Sandhurst (Stationers) Ltd:*[7]

- Did the unamended claim comply with the rules relating to the presentation of claims (see para 5.5) and was it presented within the relevant time limit? If not, there is no power to amend and a new claim must be presented within the relevant time limit.
- If it did comply with the rules on presentation, the tribunal has discretion to allow an amendment which would add or substitute a new party. It should do so only if the mistake corrected was a genuine mistake and was not misleading or such as to cause reasonable doubt about the identity of the person intending to claim or, as the case may be, to be claimed against.
- In deciding whether or not to exercise its discretion, the tribunal should have regard to all the circumstances of the case, including any injustice or hardship which may be caused to any of the parties or potential parties if the amendment were allowed or refused. If allowing the amendment might cause unnecessary additional cost to one party, the tribunal might properly conclude that this was an appropriate case for the amending party to be ordered to pay the additional costs caused by the late amendment (see chapter 18 on costs and preparation time orders).

4.6   When an amendment is allowed after a judgment has been given, as in the *Linbourne* case (above), the tribunal will give the new respondent an opportunity to be heard on the merits of the case unless there would be no prejudice by not doing so. Generally, see chapter 7 on amendments.

Unincorporated associations

4.7   One word of warning: proceedings must be commenced against some legal 'person' or body, whether that 'person' is an individual, a collection of individuals or a company. If the employer is an unincorporated association, the claim cannot be made against the

6   [1993] ICR 698, EAT.
7   [1974] ICR 650, NIRC.

association in the abstract, as it is not a legal body. The correct respondent in these cases is the individual or individuals with effective day to day control of the association, often the chairman or members of the management or executive committee.[8] Applicants can bring a claim against 'representative' respondents in such circumstances, as in *Affleck v Newcastle Mind*.[9] A trade union is an unincorporated association but it may sue and be sued in its own name.[10]

Insolvent employers and workers

4.8 As with court proceedings, tribunal proceedings may be commenced or continued against a company in administration only with the permission of the High Court or the administrator.[11] The administrator is an interested party and may be joined to the proceedings. However, failure to obtain the permission of the court does not make the claim a nullity. The proper course is for the tribunal to stay (*sist*, in Scotland) the proceedings while the leave of the court is obtained.[12] It is highly likely that a similar approach would be taken where the company is in compulsory liquidation under Insolvency Act 1986 s130(2).

4.9 If the administrator adopts the contracts of employment of a company's employees, he or she will be liable to be sued personally, so leave of the court is not required. The Insolvency Act 1986 limits the responsibilities of administrators once the administrator adopts or is deemed to adopt a contract of employment.[13]

4.10 If the respondent is bankrupt, their trustee in bankruptcy will have a clear interest in the outcome of the proceedings and would be entitled to apply to be joined as a party. In these cases a case management discussion may assist in clarifying the position of the insolvent party and the interests of others who may wish to be joined in the proceedings.

---

8 *Bradley Egg Farm v Clifford* [1943] 2 All ER 378.
9 [1999] IRLR 405, EAT.
10 TULRCA 1992 s 10(1)(b).
11 Insolvency Act 1986 s11(3), applied in *Carr v British International Helicopters Ltd (in administration)* [1994] ICR 18, EAT.
12 *Carr v British International Helicopters Ltd (in administration)* [1994] ICR 18, EAT.
13 Which was held to be unlimited in *Powdrill v Watson* [1995] 2 AC 394; [1995] ICR 1100; [1995] IRLR 269, HL, confirming [1994] ICR 395, CA (the *Paramount Airways* case).

4.11   The secretary of state is likely to be interested in most claims against insolvent employers, since there is likely to be a payment out of the National Insurance Fund under Employment Rights Act 1996 s182. The tribunal will notify the department of these claims and the secretary of state may be joined as a party.[14] Without reference to their trustee in bankruptcy, an insolvent (bankrupt) employee can claim unfair dismissal and discrimination (provided the remedy is limited to injury to feelings) but other claims must be approved by the trustee.[15]

Letter before proceedings

4.12   While claimants are under no obligation to notify their employers (or other potential respondents) of a claim before presenting it to a tribunal, a *letter before proceedings* can serve to resolve some of the issues between the prospective parties before tribunal proceedings are commenced. It may even render such proceedings unnecessary if the employer makes the payment or takes the action sought by the employee. If there is no risk of time limits being missed, it is generally worth writing a letter notifying the prospective respondent of the complaint which may be made.

4.13   This is particularly helpful when a claimant is unsure about the precise identity of the employer. An application can be made to change the name of the respondent after tribunal proceedings have been commenced (see para 7.3). The fact that the first named respondent took no steps to correct the mistake on receipt of the letter before proceedings, or that the correct respondent had already been put on notice by such a letter, will assist the employee in making the application and/or in applying for any costs incurred by the failure to clarify the position at an earlier stage.

4.14   The letter before proceedings should set out the broad nature of the complaint and indicate that the writer will commence proceedings in the tribunal unless steps are taken to remedy the situation within a specified period of time. Obviously, a prospective claimant should have in mind at this stage what he or she hopes to get out of the proceedings and the limitations on tribunal remedies. The letter

---

14   2004 Rules r51.
15   *Grady v HM Prison Service* [2003] ICR 129, CA and *Khan v Trident Safeguards* [2004] EWCA Civ 624.

should be 'open': it should express the full claim and not deal with proposals for settling the claim as a form of compromise. Such proposals, if made, should be contained in separate correspondence, specifically marked 'without prejudice'.[16]

4.15 It is not necessary to go into much detail at this stage and it would be unwise to do so without full instructions and advice. Be warned: respondents will often seek to cross-examine on the basis of any inconsistencies, however slight, between correspondence before proceedings and the case as stated in the course of the proceedings. On the other hand, if the claimant is confident that a full account can be given at this stage, the fact it has been given even before proceedings are commenced can make the case easier to sustain subsequently in the tribunal. This is especially true in constructive dismissal and discrimination cases, where the claimant's contemporary perception of events is very important.

4.16 Furthermore, if there is no reasonable defence to the complaint and the case is one where there is a real chance of the claimant obtaining an order for costs against the respondent (para 18.27), the fact that the nature of the complaint and the relief sought has been detailed before the commencement of tribunal proceedings will be a relevant factor in any application for costs against a respondent who failed to take that opportunity to resolve the matter.

Questionnaires

4.17 In discrimination cases (sex, race, disability, equal pay, sexual orientation and religion or belief), information can be requested from an employer or other respondent by use of a questionnaire *before* any claim is presented to a tribunal.[17] The forms are found in the schedules to relevant regulations.[18]

---

16 See para 10.39.
17 SDA 1975 s74(1); RRA 1976 s65(1); DDA 1995 s56; Equal Pay Act (EqPA) 1970 s7B(2); Employment Equality (Religion or Belief) Regulations 2003 SI No 1660 reg 33; Employment Equality (Sexual Orientation) Regulations 2003 SI No 1661 reg 33.
18 Sex Discrimination (Questions and Replies) Order 1975 SI No 2048, Race Relations (Questions and Replies) Order 1977 SI No 842, Disability Discrimination (Questions and Replies) Order 1996 SI No 2793, Employment Equality (both Religion and Sexual Orientation) Regulations 2003 SI Nos 1660 and 1661 and Equal Pay (Questions and Replies) Order 2003 SI No 722.

4.18   The questionnaire enables a prospective claimant to find out background information which may assist the claim, for example, the relative numbers of men and women or the racial background of employees in each grade within the workplace; and to question the prospective respondent on the reasons for the action which has led to the grievance. It may also lead to the provision of relevant statistical evidence, even if the employer has to create documentation in order to provide such information. As a respondent cannot be ordered to create documents which are not already in existence, this is an unusual and potentially very useful procedure.

Time limits on questionnaires

4.19   The Regulations each provide for time limits within which the questionnaire must be served if it is to be used as evidence before a tribunal.[20] These limits are as follows:

- If the questionnaire is served *before* the presentation of a claim: three months beginning with the date of the act complained of.
- If the questionnaire is served *after* the presentation of a claim: 21 days beginning with the day on which the claim was presented.

4.20   A questionnaire served outside these time limits (and once a tribunal claim has been commenced) must be served with the permission ('leave') of the tribunal if it is to be admissible as evidence. When permission is given by a tribunal, the time limit within which it must then be served will be specified by the tribunal itself. If a claimant wishes to serve a questionnaire out of time, the best course is to send a copy to the respondent, giving notice of the intention to apply to the tribunal for permission to serve out of time. At the same time an application to the tribunal should be made, including with the application a copy of the proposed questionnaire together with all relevant correspondence. The tribunal which considers whether or not to grant permission will consider matters such as the length of any delay, the reasons for it and the possible prejudice to the respondent, as well as the relevance or oppressiveness of the questions included within the questionnaire itself.[21]

20   SDA and RRA (Questions and Replies) Orders art 5, Equal Pay (Questions and Replies) Order art 4, DDA (Questions and Replies) Order art 3, Employment Equality (Religion or Belief) Regulations reg 33 and Employment Equality (Sexual Orientation)Regulations reg 33.
21   *Williams v Greater London Citizens Advice Bureaux Service* [1989] ICR 545, EAT.

4.21   The recipient of a questionnaire is not obliged to serve a reply nor can they be ordered to do so. If, however, the tribunal finds that a respondent has deliberately and without reasonable excuse omitted to reply to a properly presented questionnaire within a reasonable period of time (the various orders and regulations set an eight week deadline), or that the replies given are evasive or equivocal, it may draw any inference from that fact that it considers just and equitable to draw, including an inference that the respondent committed an unlawful act of discrimination. Any respondent on the receiving end of a questionnaire would be well-advised to answer clearly and promptly.

4.22   If on receipt of the reply to the original questionnaire it is apparent that further questions need to be asked, there is nothing to stop a claimant applying to the tribunal for permission to serve a further questionnaire, but you will be unable to ask for further particulars of the original questionnaire itself. Indeed, the service of further questionnaires is a practice which the Employment Appeal Tribunal has endorsed in appropriate circumstances as a 'sensible and necessary part of the procedure'.[22]

Financing a case and costs implications

4.23   Legal help is not available for representation at tribunals in England and Wales (see para 18.3 below). Legal aid is available in limited cases in Scotland, having been introduced in order to satisfy the Human Rights Act 1998 requirement that parties have a fair trial.[23] There are no moves to extend legal help to assist parties bringing claims in England and Wales. A prospective claimant may, however, be eligible to receive legal assistance (which may include representation) from the following sources:

• a trade union or professional association;
• in sex discrimination or equal pay cases, the Equal Opportunities Commission (EOC);
• in race discrimination cases, the Commission for Racial Equality (CRE);

---

22 *Carrington v Helix Lighting Ltd* [1990] ICR 125; [1990] IRLR 6, EAT.
23 For information on legal aid in Scotland, contact the Scottish Legal Aid Board (see address in appendix D) or on their website: www.slab.org.uk.

- in disability discrimination cases, the Disability Rights Commission (DRC);[24]
- law centres or Citizens' Advice;
- other free advisory bodies, such as the Free Representation Unit (FRU), the Bar Pro Bono Scheme,[25] and various other local and community-based projects;[26]
- solicitors who have a franchise under the 'legal help' scheme (for advice and all steps other than actual representation);
- under an insurance scheme – increasingly a feature of many household insurance policies;
- Advisory, Conciliation and Arbitration Service (ACAS) (basic, non-partisan advice only).

4.24   Respondents may also be eligible for assistance from the above sources, although corporate respondents are less likely to be in need of financial assistance in obtaining legal advice or representation. Respondents who are members of trade associations may be entitled to free advice and representation under the terms of their membership.

4.25   Both lay and professional advisers may also refer appropriate cases to the EOC, CRE or DRC, or act as a referral agency to FRU, which may be able to provide preliminary advice and representation at the hearing. Addresses for the above organisations are set out in appendix D.

4.26   Although anyone can appear at a tribunal, it stands to reason that the more and the better informed the advice and assistance that a party receives before or during the hearing, the better prepared he or she is likely to be.

4.27   The successful party in a tribunal case is, however, unlikely to be able to reclaim from the other side any legal costs incurred during the proceedings. The general rule in tribunals is that costs or preparation time orders will not be awarded unless a party has acted vexatiously, abusively, disruptively or otherwise unreasonably or the bringing or conduct of the proceedings is misconceived.[27] If one party believes that there may be a good argument for obtaining costs against the

24   At the date of writing a white paper proposes the establishment of a Commission for Equality and Human Rights, which would replace the EOC, CRE and DRC and would include issues relating to sexual orientation and religion or belief, although this proposal is opposed by the CRE.
25   See addresses in appendix D.
26   See the website of the Community Legal Service: www.clsdirect.org.uk.
27   2004 Rules rr38–47.

other, it is worth bringing this to the other side's attention in writing before making the application. If the other side continues to act in the same unreasonable, etc, manner, the letter will assist any application to the tribunal for costs. On the other hand, letters threatening applications for costs in tribunals are often made where there is really no ground for such an application. The recipient of such a letter should consider its contents seriously and take further advice if necessary, but should not be deterred from bringing or defending a claim by a groundless threat. Tribunals may also warn a claimant of the risk of a costs award in proper circumstances, although the Court of Appeal in the case of *Gee v Shell UK Ltd*[28] found that where a tribunal had warned a claimant that she was at real risk of a substantial costs order and might lose her house, unfair pressure had been placed on her as costs orders are exceptional in tribunals. This case did however involve consideration of the 1993 rules and the 2004 rules lower the threshold as to when costs can be ordered. The subject of costs orders is dealt with in more detail in chapter 18.

Checklist: Pre-proceedings considerations

- Is the claimant eligible for 'legal help' or any other financial aid in respect of the claim?
- Do questions of sex, race, or disability discrimination or of equal pay arise where advice and assistance might be obtained from the EOC, CRE or DRC?
- Is the complaint one which a tribunal can properly hear or should it be brought in some other court or tribunal?
- Does the claimant meet the jurisdictional conditions in relation to pursuing a particular claim in a tribunal?
- Is the correct respondent named?
- Are any of the parties insolvent?
- Has a letter before proceedings been sent to give the respondent the opportunity of meeting the claim without the necessity of tribunal proceedings?
- In discrimination, has the appropriate questionnaire been served?

28   [2003] IRLR 82, EAT.

CHAPTER 5

The claim

Introduction

5.1 From 6 April 2005 all claims presented to tribunals must be presented on a prescribed claim form, known as an ET1, an example of which can be seen at appendix A below. Although the claim form is the tribunal equivalent of a claim and statement of case in the civil courts, it has not been the practice to treat a claim in the same formal way as a document commencing proceedings in the civil courts. With the increased demand for detail at the earliest stage, the contents of the claim are likely to take on a more formal character.

5.2 Two or more claimants may present their claims in the same document if their claims arise out of the same set of facts and each gives the required information.[1] This is particularly useful where multi-claimant claims arise, for example, in a large-scale redundancy case where a number of dismissed employees claim to have been unfairly dismissed in like circumstances; or in an equal pay case involving a challenge to pay arrangements applicable to many female employees.

5.3 The time limits within which proceedings must be brought in the tribunal are dealt with in chapter 3 and any potential claimant should pay particular attention to these.

Minimum requirements and Form ET1

5.4 The Claim Form, or ET1, can be obtained from any local office of the Employment Service, including job centres, and from most advice centres, or from the tribunals website.[2] Guidance notes entitled 'How to apply to an Employment Tribunal' (and also 'What to do if taken to an Employment Tribunal') are an integral part of the booklets containing the claim form. They are available in large print, Braille and audio tape, and in 'alternative languages'.

5.5 Any claim made, (before 6 April 2005, whether by using form ET1 or by any other document), must, according to 2004 rules r1(4), contain the following details:

(a)   each claimant's full name;
(b)   each claimant's address;

---

1   See Employment Tribunals Rules of Procedure (2004 Rules) r1(7).
2   www.employmenttribunals.gov.uk.

(c)   the name of each person against who the claim is made (the respondent);

(d)   each respondent's address;

(e)   details of the claim;

(f)   whether or not the claimant is or was an employee of the respondent;

(g)   whether or not the claim includes a complaint that the respondent has dismissed the claimant or has contemplated doing so;

(h)   whether or not the claimant has raised the subject matter of the claim with the respondent in writing at least 28 days prior to presenting the claim to an Employment Tribunal Office;

(i)   if the claimant has not done as described in (h), why not.

5.6   Prior to the 2004 rules a fairly flexible approach was taken if claims were presented which failed to comply with requirements for giving essential information. That is not likely to be the case now. Rule 1(5) of the 2004 rules expressly sets out circumstances in which certain items of required information need not be given, namely:

(a)   if the claimant is not or was not an employee of the respondent the information in paragraphs (4)(g) to (i) is not required

(b)   if the claimant was an employee of and was dismissed by the respondent the information in paragraphs 4(h) and (i) is not required; and

(c)   if the claimant was an employee of and was not dismissed by the respondent, and the claimant has raised the subject matter of the claim with the respondent as described in paragraph 4(h), the information in paragraph 4(i) is not required.

5.7   If the claim does not contain all the required information it will not be accepted by the secretary to the tribunal.[3] It will be referred to a chairman, and if he or she considers that it ought not to be accepted he or she shall, as soon as is reasonably practicable, inform the claimant of that decision and the reasons for it in writing, and shall provide information on how that decision may be reviewed or appealed.

3   2004 Rules r3(2)(a).

Presentation of the claim

5.8   This subject is dealt with in full in chapter 3 on time limits. In England and Wales the claim should be 'presented' to the tribunal office in the postal district where the claimant is or was employed.[4] In Scotland, all claims should be presented to the Central Office in Glasgow.

5.9   The claim can be delivered by hand, sent by post, fax, completed online at www.employmenttribunals.gov.uk, or by other means of electronic communication such as e-mail,[5] but the time limits for presentation must be complied with. Claims which are sent to tribunal offices are accepted as having been duly 'presented'.

5.10   Those acting for claimants should take all steps to make sure that the claim has been received by the tribunal in time. If it is sent by post, the onus is on representatives to telephone the Central Office of Employment Tribunals (COET) to make sure that it has been received.[6]

5.11   Applications sent by fax are 'presented' when they arrive at the tribunal, not when sent, so when a solicitor was unaware of the change of telephone code such that the claim was not sent, the EAT held that it was reasonably practicable to have found out the correct code earlier, and to have presented it on time.[7]

Action on receipt of the claim

5.12   As soon as a claim is received at a tribunal office, it is date-stamped and kept with the envelope. As a matter of evidence, this will generally be taken to be the date on which the application was 'presented'. The relevant date is, however, not the date of 'receipt' but the date of actual 'presentation' and if there is evidence that the application was presented, for example, by the claimant putting it through the letter box of the tribunal office in person the day before, then this will be the crucial date in respect of any time limit.[8]

---

4   2004 Rules r1. See appendix D – where to send your application.
5   2004 Rules r63(1).
6   See *Capital Foods (Retail) Ltd v Corrigan* [1993] IRLR 430, EAT, and see para 3.68 above on time limits.
7   *Hartley v HFC Bank* EAT/1468/99, 17 March, 2001, unreported.
8   *Post Office v Moore* [1981] ICR 623, EAT.

Initial vetting procedure

5.13   Once a claim is received, the secretary to the tribunal must consider whether it ought to be accepted.

5.14   If a claim is accepted by the secretary he or she will:[9]

(a)   send a copy of it to each respondent and record in writing the date on which it was sent;

(b)   inform the parties in writing of the case number of the claim (which must from then on be referred to in all correspondence relating to the claim) and the address to which notices and other communications to the Employment Tribunal Office must be sent);

(c)   inform the respondent in writing about how to present a response to the claim, the time limit for so doing, what may happen if a response is not entered within the time limit and that the respondent has a right to receive a copy of any judgment disposing of the claim;

(d)   when any provision relevant to the claim provides for conciliation, notify the parties that the services of a conciliation officer are available to them;

(e)   where there is a fixed period for conciliation, notify the parties of the date on which ACAS's duty to conciliate ends, and that after that date the services of a conciliation officer shall be available to them only in limited circumstances; and

(f)   if only part of the claim has been accepted, inform the claimant and any respondent which parts of the claim have not been accepted and that the tribunal shall not proceed to deal with those parts unless they are accepted at a later date.

5.15   The secretary must not accept or register claims if one or more of the following circumstances apply:[10]

(a)   the claim does not include all the relevant required information;

(b)   the tribunal does not have power to consider the claim (or that relevant part of it);

(c)   Employment Act (EA) 2002 s32 (complaints about grievances) applies to the claim or part of it and the claim has been presented to the tribunal in breach of section 32(2)–(4).

---

9   2004 Rules r2(2).
10   2004 Rules r3(2).

5.16   As the secretary performs an administrative, not a judicial, function if he or she considers that a claim ought not to be accepted, it must be referred, together with a statement of reasons for not accepting it, to a chairman. The chairman must then decide whether, in his or her opinion, the claim should be accepted and should proceed. If the chairman decides the claim ought to be accepted, the secretary must proceed to deal with it in the ordinary way.[11] However, if the chairman decides it should not be accepted, he or she must record his or her decision and reasons for it in writing. As soon as is reasonably practicable, the secretary then informs the claimant of the decision and gives information on how the decision may be reviewed or appealed.[12]

5.17   If the reason for not accepting a claim relates to breach of the statutory grievance procedures (EA 2002 s32 see paras 3.3–3.15), the secretary must inform the claimant of the relevant time limit, and of the consequences of not complying with section 32.

The register

5.18   Employment Tribunals (Constitution and Rules of Procedure) Regulations 2004 (2004 Regs)[13] reg 17 and 2004 Rules r32 require the secretary to maintain a register at the office of the tribunals which are open to inspection by any person, without charge, at all reasonable hours. Unless the claim involves allegations of sexual offences[14] the register must contain documents recording the judgments of tribunals or chairmen and the reasons.

5.19   The register is often used by members of the press to obtain prior information on the nature of particular tribunal cases, and latterly has been used by people who wish to offer their services to parties to represent them. Following a large number of complaints from claimants and respondents who found advances from third parties unwelcome and intrusive, the government consulted on whether the information on the register should be altered, or abolished completely as the Employment Tribunals System Taskforce recommended in its 2002 Report. What is left are now the judgments and reasons only.

---

11   2004 Rules r3(4).
12   2004 Rules r3(5).
13   SI No 1861.
14   In relation to which see 2004 Rules r49.

Informing others of the claim

5.20   Often claimants will send a copy of their claim to the respondent or respondents at the same time as presenting it to the tribunal office. While this is good practice, it is not obligatory and once a claim is accepted the secretary will send a copy of it to the respondent, and give the information set out above at para 5.14.[15]

The contents of the claim form (ET1)

5.21   From 6 April 2005 all claims to tribunals must be made on the prescribed form. This ensures that all the required information is included, which is vitally important if the claimant is to have the claim accepted and/or avoid a pre-acceptance hearing. The claim identifies (by means of the symbols * and •) information which is mandatory *, and that which ought to be included if relevant •. It should be noted that it is no longer necessary for parties to identify the type of complaint that they are making in summary from at the outset of the form.

Box 1: Claimant's details

5.22   It is mandatory for the claimant to provide their first and surnames and address. A claimant is also asked to give their sex and date of birth (relevant for example, to check whether the claimant has reached normal retirement age, or to calculate statutory redundancy payments), their telephone number, and to specify their preferred method of communication. E-mail is an option, but ought only to be given if checked daily. If an address other than the claimant's home address is to be used for documents, this must be specified. A party may at any time change the address to which correspondence are to be sent, by giving notice to the employment tribunal office and to the other parties.[16]

---

15   See also 2004 Rules r2(2).
16   2004 Rules r61(5).

Box 2: Respondent's details

5.23   It is mandatory to give the name of the employer(s) or organisation(s) being complained about, along with their address. Their telephone number ought also to be included along with the address at which the claimant actually worked if this differs from the address already given.

5.24   More than one respondent can be named, for example, in a transfer of undertakings case against transferor and transferee, or where the allegation is one of discrimination and the complaint is made, for example, both against the individual discriminator and constructively against the employer.

5.25   If a claimant is unsure of the correct identity of the respondent (that is, where the employer is one of a group of companies or in a transfer of undertakings case), then all possible respondents should be identified and the reasons for doing so set out when giving the detail of the claim; a complaint against a particular respondent can always be withdrawn at a later date. Mistakes over the identity of the correct respondent should not be fatal, as an application to amend the identity of the respondent can be made at a later date (see chapter 7).

Box 3: Action before making a claim

5.26   This section of the claim is designed to identify whether the claimant, if an employee/former employee, has complied with the requirements of EA 2002 s32, to present a grievance before resorting to litigation (see paras 3.3–3.15). If the claimant is or was employed, and does not say that the respondent dismissed him or her, box three must answer questions as to whether their complaint was raised in writing, when, if not, why not. It must further say whether a 28 day period has been allowed between submitting the grievance and sending the claim to the tribunal. As to potentially permissible reasons for failing to raise a grievance, see para 3.14.

Box 4: Employment details

5.27   This part of the claim is not mandatory, but is clearly designed to allow the tribunal to have as full a picture as possible of not only the type of claim being made, but also its potential value. This part asks claimants to give information as to the dates of their employment, what their job was/is or what connection they have to the respondent, whether there was a notice period, paid or unpaid, how many hours each week the claimant worked, what their earnings (gross and net) were, whether he or she was in an employer's pension scheme, whether there were any other benefits, whether alternative employment has been secured, and if so when and how much is earned.

5.28   In relation to the dates of employment, the start date should be the date the claimant's continuous employment commenced (whether it was with a previous employer or under a different contract of employment). The date of termination will be the date on which notice expired or (if no notice was given or if the claimant was paid in lieu) the actual date on which the claimant left the employment. Regard should be had to the relevant statutory provisions applicable to a particular complaint where the start or end date of employment might be in issue. If the start or end date is likely to be in contention, a claimant might find it useful to give further particulars of such matters in the details of complaint, or in box 10, 'other information'.

5.29   Generally speaking the 'normal working hours' will be the contractual minimum hours the claimant was required to work, and this may include overtime where there is a contractual obligation to work it.[17]

5.30   The earnings details may be used in establishing, for example, any basic award or redundancy payment or compensatory award and should be given as accurately as possible, although a claimant will not be held to a mistaken weekly rate if he or she later seeks to amend these details unless a default judgment is given. It is up to the claimant whether to give weekly or monthly figures, but it helps if the information is given for a consistent period throughout. If the claimant's wage varied from week to week, the average amount for the last 12 calendar weeks of the employment should be taken.[18] Under 'other benefits', all additional 'perks' should be listed, including any bonuses, company cars, mobile telephones, etc. While these will not be included as part of a 'week's pay' for the purposes of a basic award or redundancy payment, they are part of the claimant's loss in terms of any compensatory award or equal pay order.

---

17   *Gascol Conversions v Mercer* [1974] ICR 420; [1974] IRLR 155, CA.
18   ERA 1996 s224(2).

Boxes 5, 6, 7, 8 and 9

5.31 Before examining each of these in turn, depending on the nature of the complaint being presented, the details of complaint must be set out in the appropriate part.

5.32 This is the claimant's opportunity to set out the nature of his or her case. It will generally be the first document the tribunal members hearing the case actually read. Care should therefore be taken to present the details to the claimant's best advantage (which may mean setting out the details on a separate sheet attached to the ET1 rather than trying to work within the confined space given on the form). While there may be some advantage in keeping certain matters open, for example, in an unfair dismissal case, in not admitting the reason given for dismissal straight away but putting the respondent to proof. The purpose of the claim is to set out the case the respondent has to meet and to make it clear what is and what is not in issue. It is often useful to give detailed particulars especially where the burden of proof is on the claimant, for instance in *constructive* unfair dismissal cases.

5.33 In cases where the claimant is relying on a number of different incidents (for example, where there has been on-going harassment or in a 'last straw' constructive dismissal case,[19] it is advisable to set out details of all incidents which are relied on; in this way the claimant cannot be accused of raising them for the first time at the hearing of the claim.

5.34 It is not necessary to set out the relevant law in the claim, although reference to the relevant sections can assist in making the nature of the claim clear to those reading the document (for example, in specifying that the claim is one of indirect sex discrimination under Sex Discrimination Act 1975 s1(2)(b), of unlawful racial discrimination on the grounds of victimisation under Race Relations Act 1976 s2, etc). Furthermore, the relevant law should be borne in mind when to ensure that important points are not left out, such as the size and administrative resources of the respondent in an unfair dismissal case.

5.35 It is not helpful to include background detail if this is not relevant to the type of claim being made: if the issue in a case of unfair dismissal by reason of redundancy is the fairness of the selection

---

19   For example, *Lewis v Motorworld* [1986] ICR 157; [1985] IRLR 465, CA.

procedure, details of the claimant's views on the need for redundancies, and the business decisions which led to the redundancy situation in the first place, are unlikely to assist the tribunal. On the other hand, when information is relevant and may later form the subject of a request for further particulars or for written answers, it will help to expedite the claimant's claim to provide the details from the start: where relevant, name names, give dates, set out the gist of conversations relied on and so on.

Box 5: Unfair dismissal and constructive dismissal

5.36   If the complaint is one of dismissal, either unfair or constructive, details of the complaint should be set out in box 5.1. As set out in the guidance notes to the ET1 a claimant should:

> . . . use the box provided to explain why you think the ending of your employment was unfair and give any other information which you think would be helpful to use. If you disagree with the reason the respondent gave for dismissing you, please say what you think the reason was. You should describe the events which led up to your employment ending and describe how the dismissal took place, including dates, times and the people involved. If you are claiming that the respondent's actions led you to resign and leave your job, please explain in detail the circumstances surrounding this.

5.37   Question 5.2 asks what the claimant wants should his or her case be successful; either reinstatement (to get the old job back and compensation), re-engagement (to get another job with the same employer and compensation) or compensation only. It is not a requirement of the 2004 Rules to give this information, and the box can be left blank. It does, however, give a clear indication to the respondent of the relief sought and, consequently, of its potential liability. This is all the more important given the large sums tribunals can (and do) now award and the need for respondents to ensure that the costs expended in defending a claim are proportionate to its ultimate value.

5.38   When reinstatement or re-engagement has been indicated as a remedy sought, it is of relevance when considering whether the employer was entitled to engage a permanent replacement. However, whatever the claimant states under this head will not be binding and the tribunal should address the question again if and when it considers remedies at the full hearing of the complaint.

Box 6: Discrimination

5.39   Details of the discrimination complained of and the dates on which it is said to have occurred must be set out under this heading. When considering dates, if a course of conduct or a continuing act is complained of, that should be made plain.

Box 7: Redundancy payments

5.40   As well as saying why the claimant is entitled to a redundancy payment, what steps have been taken to obtain this already should be set out. Again, the policy objective of ensuring that litigation is a last not a first resort can be seen.

Box 8: Other payments you are owed

5.41   This requires details of whether the complaint is for holiday pay, notice pay or other unpaid amounts as well as the precise amount being claimed, and whether this is before or after tax. Reasons as to why sums are due must be given.

Box 9: Other complaints

5.42   As its title suggests, this is a 'catch all'. Details of acts complained of, when and where should all be given. Complaints set out in box 9 might, for example, include failure to consult representatives before a TUPE transfer, or complaints in relation to refusal to allow flexible working.

Box 10: Other information

5.43   A covering letter is not to be submitted with the claim, and so any additional information which a party wishes to communicate must be contained or described in this form. For example, if the claim is out of time, an explanation should be given here. If internal disciplinary or grievance procedures are ongoing and a stay is sought, this is the relevant place to include the information/request.

Box 11: Details of the claimant's representative

5.44   If the claimant is represented, the address given here will be the one to which the tribunal will send all notices and other documents. E-mail should only be specified as the required method of communication if the account is checked daily. Any adviser who is 'on the record' on the ET1 must be prepared to keep their client properly informed as to the conduct of the proceedings and as to the times and dates of any hearings. Any changes to the named representative or to the contact address should be notified to the tribunal and all other relevant parties.[20]

20   2004 Rules r61(5).

The response

Introduction

6.1 The response is the respondent's defence to an application to the tribunal and provides the opportunity for the respondent to set out its case and to state where there are specific points of dispute or agreement. While the response should not be treated in precisely the same way as might a defence in civil court proceedings, there is some similarity in the tribunal rules to Civil Procedure Rules (CPR) Part 16 which specifies the requirements of a claim form and defence. The Employment Tribunals Rules of Procedure[1] (2004 Rules) see a more formal approach taken to the claim and response than has been the case previously. The response, together with the claim, will generally be the first documents read by the tribunal and is the starting point for any consideration of the respondent's case. It is, therefore, good practice (and from 6 April 2005, essential) to ensure that the response accurately sets out the case the respondent wishes to present.

Minimum requirements and Form ET3

6.2 A response must be in writing and should contain the respondent's full name and address and say whether or not the respondent wishes to resist the claim, and if so, on what grounds.[2] A respondent may enter a response by means other than the ET3 providing it meets the basic requirements. From 6 April 2005 it will be compulsory to ensure that the response takes the form of the Central Office of Employment Tribunals' Form ET3 (see example in appendix A). A copy will be sent to the respondent(s) with a copy of the claim.

6.3 A single document may include the response to more than one claim if the remedy claimed arises out of the same set of facts, provided that:

- the respondent intends to resist all the claims and the grounds for doing so are the same in relation to each claim; or
- the respondent does not intend to resist any of the claims.[3]

---

1 Contained in Sch 1 to the Employment Tribunals (Constitution and Rules of Procedure) Regulations 2004 SI No 1861.
2 2004 Rules r4(3).
3 See 2004 Rules r4(5).

6.4   Rule 6 of the 2004 Rules states that a response will not be accepted if it does not contain all the required information, and the compulsory form ET3 makes it clear that giving details of the grounds on which the claim is to be resisted is indeed 'required' information. It is therefore the view of the authors that a 'holding ET3' seeking to give details after further instructions or inquiries will no longer be permissible. If all necessary information is not available at the time of completing the ET3 a respondent should state this in Box 5 ('Other Information').

6.5   If the respondent believes that it is unable to answer the case set out in the claim because insufficient details have been presented, the proper course is to say that in the ET3 and apply for an order that additional information be given.

Time limits

6.6   The response must be submitted within 28 days after a copy of the claim was sent by the regional office, except where the claim made is against a foreign state, where the time limit is two months by virtue of the provisions of State Immunity Act 1978 s12(2). A response to a claim sent out on Wednesday must be received by the tribunal on the Wednesday four weeks later.[4]

6.7   Once the time limit for entering a response has passed and either no response has been presented, or a response has been presented out of time and it has not been decided whether or not to accept it, a chairman may issue a default judgment to determine the claim without a hearing.[5]

Acceptance of response

6.8   Rule 6(2)(b) states that a response will not be accepted if it is clear that it has not been presented within the relevant time limit. An extension of time for entering a response may be sought under 2004 Rules r11 (see also r5(4)) provided an application is presented to the tribunal within 28 days of the date on which the respondent was sent a copy of the claim. The respondent must explain why it is not possible to

4   Employment Tribunals (Constitution of Rules of Procedure) Regulations 2004 (2004 Regs) SI No 1861 reg 15(2).
5   2004 Rules r8.

comply with the time limit, and an extension will be granted if the chairman or tribunal is satisfied that it is 'just and equitable' to do so.[6] If an extension of time is granted, any prejudice suffered by the claimant by an unnecessary delay might result in a costs award against the respondent concerned.

6.9 If an application to extend time is made,[7] then in accordance with rule 11, where a party is legally represented that party or his representative must provide all other parties with the following information at the same time as the application is sent to the tribunal:

- details of the application and why it is sought;
- that any objection to the application must be sent to the Employment Tribunal office within 7 days of being informed in writing of the application;
- that any objection to the application must be copied to both the tribunal and all other parties.

6.10 If a party is not legally represented, this information will be provided by the secretary to the tribunal. It should also be noted that any application '*must* include an explanation of how the direction or order would assist the tribunal or chairman in dealing with the proceedings efficiently and fairly.' (emphasis added).[8]

6.11 Rule 10(2)(e) says time can be extended for anything – subject to rule 4(4) which is the rule saying that any application to extend time to submit an ET3 should be made within the 28 day time limit. Any application will then be considered in accordance with the principles set out in *Kwik Save v Swain*[9] in which Mummery J stated that the chairman in considering whether to extend time, must take account of all relevant factors and reach a conclusion which is 'objectively justified on the grounds of reason and justice'. If a postponement of the hearing is caused by the late acceptance of a response, the chairman may consider whether it is appropriate to make a costs or preparation time order against the respondent.

---

6   See para 3.89 above for the meaning given to 'just and equitable' as used in discrimination legislation.
7   See chapter 8 on application for orders.
8   2004 Rules r11(3).
9   [1997] ICR 49, EAT.

Failure to enter a response

6.12   When no response has been presented, and no application to extend
time has been made within the 28 day time limit and granted, any
response then presented to the tribunal will be declined by the
secretary to the tribunal.[10] In practice this is a case manager at the
tribunal office. The response together with the secretary's reasons
will then be given to a chairman who will decide whether it should be
accepted. The chairman may decide to accept the response[11] even
though it has been presented out of time. This is because the question of the time limit in relation to a response is a procedural not a
jurisdictional matter and in general, tribunals should be understanding in extending time for respondents, as the consequences of not
doing so are that a respondent would be debarred from defending the
claim. As noted above however, if no response has been received
within the 28 day time limit, or if a response has been presented but a
decision has not been made to accept it, a default judgment may be
issued under 2004 Rules r8.

6.13   A refusal by a chairman to accept a response must be given in
writing and accompanied by reasons. It may be subject to a review, or
can be challenged by way of appeal.[12]

6.14   2004 Rules r9 states that a respondent who has not presented a
response, or whose response has not been accepted shall not be
entitled to take any part in the proceedings except to:

- make an application under rule 33 (review of default
  judgments);
- make an application under rule 35 (preliminary consideration
  of application for review) in respect of rule 34(3)(a) and (b)
  (administrative errors and not receiving notice of hearing);
- be called as a witness by another person; or
- be sent a copy of a document or corrected entry in accordance with
  rules 8(4), 29(2) or 37.

6.15   Except for the actions specified in these rules, the respondent
concerned is no longer considered to be a 'party' to the
proceedings.[13]

---

10   2004 Rules r7(2)(b).
11   Rules 2004 r6(5).
12   EAT Practice Direction.
13   2004 Rules r9.

Action on receipt of a response

6.16 As the case will have been assigned to a tribunal office after the receipt and registration of the claim, the respondent will be asked to return the response to the secretary to that particular office. Once a response has been received, the secretary will consider whether the response should be accepted in accordance with 2004 Rules r5. If it is not accepted it will be returned to the respondent and the claim will be dealt with as if no response to the claim had been presented.[14] If the response is accepted, the secretary sends a copy of it to all the other parties to the proceedings.[15] Best practice would suggest that a respondent copy the response to all other parties at the same time as sending it to the tribunal but there is no obligation to do so.

Contents of the ET3 response

Box 1: The respondent's details

6.17 It is mandatory under the ET3 which parties must use after 6 April 2005, to give the name of the respondent organisation and its address. Ideally, the legal status of the respondent ought to be included as well (for example, charity). Other information sought is the phone number and preferred method of communication, whether post, fax or e-mail. E-mail ought not to be selected unless the mailbox is checked every day, and even if this is selected, some documents, for example those containing a company chairman's signature, may not be capable of transmission in this way. If the respondent is represented, the address of the representative should be given so that all future communication goes to them. Any changes to the contact address (including, for example, a change of representative) should be notified to the tribunal and all other relevant parties.[16]

Box 2: Action before a claim

6.18 While not a mandatory field, Box 2 asks:

(1) Was the claimant an employee?

---

14 2004 Rules r5(1).
15 2004 Rules r5(2).
16 2004 Rules r61(5).

(2) If the complaint is about dismissal, do you agree that the claimant was dismissed?

(3) If the complaint is about something other than dismissal, does it relate to an action you took on grounds of the claimant's conduct or capability?

(4) Has the substance of the complaint been raised in writing under a grievance procedure?

If the answer to questions (2) or (3) are positive the respondent is asked to go on to state what 'stage [they] have reached in the procedure'. This is a reference to a disciplinary or dismissal procedure, and details of all meetings which have taken place should be set out.

6.19   In relation to grievances, the respondent must either give details of the stage reached in the grievance procedure, or, if the claimant says they have raised a grievance and this is denied, details of whether it has been received, and if so why it has not been accepted as a proper grievance should be given.

Dismissal

6.20   In certain cases (most obviously claims of unfair dismissal), the claimant's case will depend on the tribunal first establishing that there was in fact a dismissal. If this is admitted by the respondent, as indicated by ticking the box under this part of the form, the tribunal will move to consider the reason for and fairness of that dismissal. If the reason given by the claimant is disputed, or dismissal is not admitted (for example, in a constructive dismissal claim or in a case where the meaning of the words taken by the claimant to terminate the employment is in dispute), this should be made clear on the face of the ET3. The tribunal can then go on either to consider the question of dismissal as a preliminary issue at a pre-hearing review under 2004 Rules r18 or, more likely, identify this as an issue to be determined as part of the substantive r26 Hearing into the whole claim. The latter course may be the more appropriate in a constructive unfair dismissal case where the issues relating to whether there was a dismissal are likely also to determine the question of the fairness of the dismissal if so found. Identifying this as an issue between the parties is, however, also likely to dictate which side goes first in the tribunal hearing: the claimant will bear the burden of proving dismissal if this is not accepted and will generally present his or her case first in such circumstances.

6.21   When dismissal is admitted, while it is not necessary for the respondent to state the reason for that dismissal, good practice would be to include this information in Box 4 when setting out the response.

Box 3: Employment details

6.22   Much more detail than has ever previously been requested ought now be given in Box 3 of the ET3. If the dates of employment given by the claimant are not agreed with, reasons are sought, respondents are asked for whether the claimant's job title/description are agreed with and if not why not and are asked whether the claimant's information about notice pay is correct and if not why not. Then a series of questions is asked concerning the claimant's hours of work, basic pay, other benefits and pension details.

The dates of the claimant's employment and notice pay

6.23   The dates given here may give rise to questions relating to the tribunal's jurisdiction to hear the complaint in question and may be used in any calculation of a basic award or redundancy payment and should therefore be completed as accurately as possible. The start date should be the date on which the claimant's period of continuous employment commenced (whether it was with a previous employer or under a different contract of employment) and the date of termination will be the date on which notice expired or (if no notice was given or if the claimant was 'paid in lieu') the actual date on which the claimant left the employment. Attention should be paid to the relevant statutory provisions applicable to a particular complaint when the start or end date of employment might be in issue. Where this might be a matter of contention between the parties, fuller particulars can be provided in the details of the response in Box 4.

Details of the claimant's earnings

6.24   This information may be used in establishing any basic award or redundancy payment or compensatory award. If the respondent disagrees with the information supplied by the claimant, this should be made clear by ticking the appropriate box and supplying the information the respondent believes to be correct. Often the respondent may be in a better position to supply details relating to net earnings, pension contributions, etc, and it is helpful to all concerned if the information is provided at this early stage. If it remains in dispute, at least all parties then know of the issue between them and can endeavour to find material (for example, actuarial evidence, etc) to support their particular position. The information should be given as accurately as possible, although a respondent will not be held to a mistaken weekly rate if it later seeks to amend these details.

6.25   If the claimant's wage varied from week to week, the average amount for the last 12 calendar weeks of the employment should be taken (see ERA 1996 s224(2)). Under 'bonuses/benefits', all additional 'perks' should be listed, such as bonuses or commission, and in the following box details of all pension benefit should be set out. While these will not be included as part of a 'week's pay' for the purposes of a basic award or redundancy payment, they are part of the claimant's loss in terms of any compensatory award.

Box 4: Response

6.26   A mandatory box is to tick whether or not the claim is resisted. Even if the respondent does not wish to contest all or part of the claim, it is still vital to complete a response, as adverse consequences arise for a respondent who has failed to enter a response (see above). If liability is not contested but the remedy is, the appropriate course is to tick the box indicating that the claim is not resisted, but making it clear in the box which follows that there remains a dispute as to remedy; the case will then be listed for a hearing before the tribunal on the question of remedy only.

6.27   This is the respondent's first opportunity to set out the nature of the defence. Care should therefore be taken to present the details to the respondent's best advantage, which may mean setting out the details on a separate sheet attached to the ET3 (in Scotland, a paper apart) rather than trying to work within the confined space given on the form.

6.28   The purpose of the response is to set out the respondent's case in answer to the allegations made by the claimant in the claim and to make it clear what is and what is not in issue.

6.29   Where the respondent bears the burden of proof, it is particularly important to make sure that the case set out in the response accurately reflects the way in which the respondent in fact wishes to present the case. In discrimination cases where the claimant has the burden of proof but it will transfer to the respondent if a prima facie case is made out, it is important to set out the explanation which will be offered if the circumstances call for it.

6.30   Sufficient details should be given to show how the respondent views the facts and matters which led to the decision to dismiss or take the other action complained of, for example, if there was a history of warnings and/or a number of disciplinary meetings, details should be provided here (as well as in Box 2) so that the claimant knows in advance the events on which the respondent intends to rely.

6.31   It is not mandatory to set out a reason for dismissal, but it is prudent to do so. The Employment Rights Act (ERA) 1996 s98(1) and (2) sets out the reasons for dismissal which will be found to be potentially fair and the respondent should consider that section before stating a reason for dismissal. In *Blue Star Ship Management Ltd v Williams*[17] it was held that an amendment to allege a different reason for a dismissal would generally not be allowed at a late stage in the proceedings unless 'it can genuinely be said that the amendment is no more than for the purpose of giving an appropriate label to a fully established set of facts'.

6.32   Where the facts and matters relied on for the dismissal are clearly put forward by the respondent, the tribunal may find that the dismissal was fair, although for a different reason under ERA 1996 s98 than the label given by the respondent, provided the grounds relied on are those set out by the respondent. A tribunal will not be entitled to find a dismissal fair on a ground not set out or argued for by the respondent where the difference in grounds goes to the facts or substance of the dismissal or where there might have been some difference in the way in which the claimant conducted the case in the light of the reason relied on. If, however, the different grounds are in fact just different labels and there was no basis for thinking that the claimant has been prejudiced in the presentation of his or her case, it will be open to a tribunal to find the dismissal fair for a different reason to that stated by the respondent. This can be seen for example in the case of *Hannan v TNT-IPEC (UK) Ltd*[18] where the tribunal held that the dismissal was not by reason of redundancy (as had been argued by the respondent), but was for some other substantial reason which was fair in all the circumstances of the case. As the grounds relied on by the tribunal for this conclusion were the same as those initially relied on by the respondent in seeking to claim that the

17 [1978] ICR 770; [1979] IRLR 16, EAT.
18 [1986] IRLR 165, EAT.

dismissal was by reason of redundancy and as there was no reason to think that the claimant's case would have been differently conducted had 'some other substantial reason' been the label used by the respondent on the ET3, the EAT refused to allow the employee's appeal against the tribunal's decision.

6.33   Alternative reasons should be given when appropriate, such as '(1) redundancy or (2) business reorganisation amounting to some other substantial reason of a kind such as to justify the dismissal of an employee holding the position which the claimant held'.

6.34   Even when dismissal is not admitted, if it is subsequently found that the claimant was in fact dismissed, the tribunal will go on to consider whether that dismissal was fair. In such cases the respondent should consider setting out the alternative grounds on which it might be considered that any dismissal found was in fact fair. In particular, if a respondent intends to continue to contest liability once it is found that there was a dismissal, a reason should be put forward for that dismissal as an alternative to the respondent's primary case as soon as possible. Although a respondent can subsequently apply to amend and put forward a reason for the dismissal, leave will not be given if this would require further evidence to be adduced and considered or an adjournment of the hearing.[19]

6.35   It is not necessary to set out the relevant law in the response, although reference to the relevant sections can assist in making the nature of the defence clear to those reading the document, for example, by specifying that a claim of indirect sex discrimination is contested on the basis of a defence of justification under Sex Discrimination Act 1975 s1(2)(b)(ii). Furthermore, the relevant law should be borne in mind when completing the response to ensure that important points are not left out, such as the size and administrative resources of the respondent's business in an unfair dismissal case.

6.36   It is not helpful to include background detail if this is not relevant to the type of claim being made, for example, if the issue in an unfair dismissal by reason of redundancy case is the fairness of the selection procedure, details of the claimant's capability will only be relevant if this formed part of the selection criteria. On the other hand, where information is relevant and may later form the subject of a request for additional information or for written answers to be given to questions put by a chairman, it will help to provide the details from the start and will avoid the possibility that the respondent will be accused of having

19   *Ready Case Ltd v Jackson* [1981] IRLR 312, EAT.

raised matters for the first time at the substantive hearing of the case. Whenever relevant, name names, give dates, set out the gist of conversations relied on and so on.

Box 5: Other information

6.37 No covering letters should be sent with ET3s, and therefore any additional information should be set out in this box. For example, any explanation as to why the response is out of time, or to inform the tribunal that informal grievance or disciplinary proceedings are ongoing.

Box 6: Your representative

6.38 If a representative has been instructed, their details, including preferred method of communication, should be set out in this section of form ET3.[20]

Incorrect identification of the respondent

6.39 If the body named as respondent by the claimant is in fact wrong (or, at least, it intends to argue that this is the case), this should be detailed as a preliminary matter in the body of the response, or else in box 5 which asks for any 'other information'. If identification of the correct respondent requires resolution of some preliminary legal or factual point (for example, when there might have been a transfer of an undertaking), the tribunal is likely to consider this at a pre-hearing review under 2004 Rules r18 (see chapter 11). The tribunal has a broad discretion to join other parties as respondents and/or to allow an amendment to the identification of the respondent in the claim (see para 7.8).

Jurisdictional points

6.40 If a jurisdictional point is apparent to a respondent on receipt of the claim (for example, the claim was presented out of time or the

---

20 See para 6.17 above in relation to selection of e-mail as preferred method of communication.

claimant fails to meet the qualifying requirements for the type of claim submitted), the best course is to raise this as a preliminary issue in the response, before going on to set out the details of the grounds on which the claim is resisted. If appropriate, the respondent should also apply for the jurisdictional issue to be determined at a pre-hearing review under 2004 Rules r18.

6.41   As a jurisdictional point cannot be waived by a party or by the tribunal, it would in fact be open to the respondent to raise the matter not in the response but at some subsequent stage in the proceedings, even as late as an appeal. If the respondent is aware of the point at the stage of completing the response however, there is no good reason why it should not be raised in that document, particularly if leaving it to some later stage (for example, just before the hearing) might take the claimant by surprise and lead to an adjournment or postponement of the case. If a respondent was intending to raise a jurisdictional issue at the time of completing the response and yet failed to raise it until shortly before the hearing, thereby necessitating an adjournment or postponement, it might well be open to the tribunal to conclude that such conduct was unreasonable and should result in the respondent being ordered to pay the costs or preparation time incurred by the claimant.

6.42   If liability is in dispute, a respondent should not seek to rely exclusively on a jurisdictional question but should look ahead to consider what might happen if the tribunal does have jurisdiction to hear the complaint. The substantive response to the claim should be put forward 'without prejudice' to the respondent's contention that the tribunal has no jurisdiction to hear the complaint.

Counterclaims and the claimant's response

6.43   A claimant is entitled to make a complaint of breach of contract in a tribunal claim.[21] The respondent may want to include a (counter)-claim in addition to the defence entered by way of the response. As the counterclaim is a positive claim by the respondent, it must include 'details'.[22] Once this is done a chairman may make a specific order under 2004 Rules r10 specifying the procedure to be followed by the respondent and the claimant making a response to it.

21   Employment Tribunals (Extension of Jurisdiction) Orders 1994 SI Nos 1623 and 1624 (Scotland).
22   2004 Rules r7(1).

Amendment

Introduction

7.1   Within its general power to regulate its own procedure under Employment Tribunals Rules of Procedure[1] (2004 Rules) r60(1), and its specific power under r10(2)(q), a tribunal may at any stage of the proceedings consider an application to amend the claim or response. The principal grounds on which a claim is to be brought or defended should be clear in the claim or response. If the initial document presented fails to set out the claim or defence properly, the party who wrote it should ask to amend it as soon as possible. Any application to amend should make clear the precise terms and intended effect of the amendment sought.[2] An application should be made as required by 2004 Rules r11 which means that it must include an explanation of how the order permitting the amendment will assist the tribunal in dealing with the proceedings efficiently and fairly.

7.2   The guidelines which will be considered by the tribunal when faced by an application to amend are set out below. Generally a tribunal will permit an amendment to be made provided the other side is not put at a disadvantage (prejudiced) by it. A late amendment, even shortly before the commencement of the substantive hearing, may well be allowed: any prejudice suffered by the other side may be remedied by granting an adjournment of the hearing with an order for costs or preparation time against the person applying to amend so late in the day.

Amendment of the claim

7.3   The guidelines which tribunals should follow when considering any application to amend a claim, whether to add or substitute respondents or to change the basis of the claim made, were set out by the National Industrial Relations Court (NIRC) in *Cocking v Sandhurst (Stationers) Ltd:*[3]

- Did the unamended claim comply with the rules relating to the presentation of claim forms (see chapter 5) and was it presented within the relevant time limit (see chapter 3 on time).

1   Contained in Sch 1 of Employment Tribunals (Constitution and Rules of Procedure) Regulations 2004 SI No 1861.
2   *Harvey v Port of Tilbury (London) Ltd* [2000] ICR 1030; [2000] IRLR 693, EAT.
3   [1974] ICR 650, NIRC.

- If not, there is no power to amend and a new claim must be presented within the relevant time limit if this is still possible.
- If it was, the tribunal has a discretion to allow an amendment which would add or substitute a new party but should only do so if satisfied that the mistake sought to be corrected was a genuine mistake and was not misleading or such as to cause reasonable doubt over the identity of the person intending to claim or to be claimed against.
- In deciding whether or not to exercise its discretion, the tribunal should have regard to all the circumstances of the case, including any injustice or hardship which may be caused to any of the parties if the amendment were allowed or refused. If allowing the amendment might cause unnecessary additional cost to one party, the tribunal might properly conclude that this was an appropriate case for the amending party to be ordered to pay the additional costs or preparation time of, or occasioned by, the amendment (see chapter 18).

7.4   The NIRC's decision in *Cocking* has since been approved by the Court of Appeal in *British Newspaper Printing Corporation (North) Ltd v Kelly*.[4] To the extent that *Kelly* suggests that no rules relating to time limits apply to amendments of claims before the employment tribunal, the Employment Appeal Tribunal (EAT) in *Harvey*[5] disagreed, giving clear reasons why the court in *Kelly* may not have appreciated all the issues involved.

7.5   A detailed review of the practice and procedure relating to applications to amend was undertaken by the EAT in *Selkent Bus Co Ltd v Moore*[6] and the *Cocking* guidance should be read in conjunction with this. It was stated in *Selkent* that the general guiding principle is that the tribunal's discretion should be exercised in a way which is consistent with the requirements of 'relevance, reason, justice and fairness inherent in all judicial discretions'.

7.6   If a party seeks to add or substitute a new right to complain, but one which is linked to or arises out of the same facts as the original claim, judicial discretion will usually permit the amendment. For example, in *Capek v Lincolnshire CC*[7] a claim for breach of contract to recover arrears of pay was held to have been made prematurely and

4   [1989] IRLR 222, CA.
5   *Harvey v Port of Tilbury (London) Ltd* [2000] ICR 1030; [2000] IRLR 693, EAT.
6   [1996] ICR 836, EAT.
7   [2000] IRLR 590, CA.

therefore the tribunal did not have jurisdiction to hear the claim, but in reaching this conclusion the Court of Appeal ordered that the matter be remitted to the tribunal to consider whether there had been an unlawful deduction of wages which the tribunal had jurisdiction to hear under Employment Rights Act (ERA) 1996 Part II. In substance the two claims were the same.

7.7   If the amendment sought relates to an entirely new claim unconnected with the original claim as set out and is otherwise out of time, it will not be permitted. In *Housing Corporation v Bryant*[8] the failure of a claimant to make any reference in her unfair dismissal claim to alleged victimisation defeated her subsequent application to amend to include a claim under the Sex Discrimination Act 1975.[9]

7.8   If a purely technical error is made in the naming of a respondent, *and* no prejudice has been caused, the tribunal may take a pragmatic approach, allowing an amendment late on in the proceedings, even after the issue of a consent order.[10] A tribunal is given a broad discretion to add ('join') a person to proceedings as a respondent and can do so at any time, even when the time limit for bringing a claim has expired by the time of the application to amend. This may be done at a case management discussion under 2004 Rules r10(2)(r). Usually, the person whom it is sought to join should be given the opportunity to be heard on the application at a pre-hearing review.[11] A new respondent may even be joined after a decision on the merits of the case has been given; although in that case, the new respondent must be afforded the opportunity to be heard, either by a rehearing after the presentation of an ET3 or by review.[12]

Amendment of the response

7.9   Similar principles apply to any application to amend the response. The later a respondent seeks to amend the basis of the defence relied on, the less likely it is that the tribunal will allow the amendment to be made. In particular, the tribunal will be reluctant to allow a

8   [1999] IRLR 123, CA.
9   See also *Harvey v Port of Tilbury (London) Ltd* [1999] ICR 1030; [1999] IRLR 693, EAT.
10 *Milestone School of English Ltd v Leakey* [1982] IRLR 3, EAT.
11 *Gillick v BP Chemicals Ltd* [1993] IRLR 437.
12 *Linbourne v Constable* [1993] ICR 698, EAT.

respondent to amend in order to claim a new reason for a dismissal,[13] or to put forward a reason for a constructive dismissal where previously none was claimed,[14] unless the *substance* of the case was already contained within the original response, that is, the amendment is no more than for the purpose of giving an appropriate label to a fully described set of facts.[15]

Amendment and striking out

7.10   By 2004 Rules r18(7)(b) a tribunal may (of its own initiative or on application) order any part of a claim or response to be amended or struck out on the grounds that it is scandalous, misconceived or vexatious. See also paras 11.17–11.26.

---

13   *Kapur v Shields* [1976] ICR 26, QBD.
14   *Ready Case Ltd v Jackson* [1981] IRLR 312, EAT.
15   *Blue Star Ship Management Ltd v Williams* [1978] ICR 770; [1979] IRLR 16, EAT. See paras 6.31–6.32 above.

Case management: orders

Tribunal's power to manage proceedings: giving orders

8.1 A tribunal may at any time, either on the application of a party or of its own initiative, give orders on any matter arising in connection with the proceedings before it 'as appear . . . appropriate'.[1] Examples of orders which may be made under rule 10(1) are set out in rule 10(2), and are orders:

(a) as the manner in which the proceedings are to be conducted including any time limit to be observed;

(b) that any party provide additional information;

(c) requiring persons to attend to give evidence or to produce documents;

(d) requiring any person in Great Britain to disclose documents or information to a party to allow a party to inspect such material as might be ordered by a County Court (or in Scotland, by a sheriff);

(e) extending any time limit, whether or not expired (subject to rules 4(4), 11(2), 25(5), 30(5), 33(1), 35(1), 38(7) and 42(5) of schedule 1, and to rule 3(4) of schedule 2);

(f) requiring the provision of written answers to questions put by the tribunal or chairman;

(g) that (subject to rule 22(8)) a short conciliation period be extended into a standard conciliation period;

(h) staying (in Scotland sisting) the whole or part of the proceedings;

(i) that part of the proceedings be dealt with separately;

(j) that different claims be considered together;

(k) that any person who the chairman or tribunal thinks may be liable for the remedy claimed should be made a respondent in the proceedings;

(l) dismissing the claim against a respondent who is no longer directly interested in the claim;

(m) postponing or adjourning any hearing;

(n) varying or revoking other direction;

(o) giving notice to the parties of a pre-hearing review or a hearing;

(p) giving notice under rule 19;

(q) giving leave to amend a claim or response;

---

1 Employment Tribunals Rules of Procedure (2004 Rules) r10(1).

(r)   that any person who the chairman or tribunal considers has an interest in the outcome of the proceedings may be joined as a party to the proceedings;

(s)   that a witness statement be prepared or exchanged; or

(t)   as to the use of experts or interpreters in the proceedings.

8.2   Orders, whether given in case management discussions (see 2004 Rules r17), pre-hearing reviews (2004 Rules r 18) or given in writing (applications to be made in writing under 2004 Rules r11), can be used by parties to deal with:

- defining the issues, discussed in chapter 9;
- disclosure discussed in chapter 10; and
- other interim issues discussed in chapter 12.

Need for case management discussions

8.3   Case management discussions, conducted by a chairman, may deal with matters of procedure and management of the proceedings, and they may be held in private. Determination of a person's civil rights or obligations cannot be dealt with in a case management discussion.[2] Such hearings are analogous to pre-trial reviews or case management conferences in the civil courts, for example, under CPR Parts 27, 28 and 29 for small claims, fast and multi-track cases. They are often useful in ensuring that the case proceeds to a final hearing in an orderly and coherent manner and the use of their forerunners, 'directions hearings' has been encouraged by the EAT in a number of cases.[3] As there are no automatic directions in tribunals (although some regions have adopted a practice of sending out directions), case management discussions can be helpful in ensuring that matters such as the answering of questions, disclosure and inspection take place in good time to allow the parties to prepare for the substantive hearing. Orders can be given not just as to the form of the hearing of the case (for example, the order in which the issues will be considered or the way in which combined applications will be

---

2   2004 Rules r17.

3   See *Brooks v British Telecommunications plc* [1991] ICR 286; [1991] IRLR 4, EAT; *Goodwin v Patent Office* [1999] ICR 302; [1999] IRLR 4, EAT; *Martins v Marks and Spencer plc* [1998] IRLR 326, CA.

heard), but also as to the time table for all further interim stages. In *Kuttapan v Croydon LBC*[4] the EAT held that the power to give directions includes a power to set aside or revoke a striking-out order: in that case the order was a mandatory one as the claimant had failed to comply with an order to pay a deposit.

8.4   Mummery LJ in the course of his judgment in *Martins v Marks and Spencer plc*[5] suggested that in race discrimination cases it would be good practice to hold a meeting for 'preliminary directions' so that the issues are identified before the hearing of a case commences. Similarly the need for clear directions in disability discrimination cases was emphasised by the EAT in *Goodwin v Patent Office*.[6] In these cases the EAT stated that it 'will generally be unsatisfactory for the disability issue to remain unclear and unspecific until the hearing itself', and if expert evidence is to be called, parties should be given advance notice, and the medical report disclosed. Appellate courts will be very slow to interfere with orders given (or not given). As the Court of Appeal in *X v Z Ltd*[7] emphasised that 'tribunals themselves are the best judges of case management decisions which crop up every day as they perform their function ... of trying to do justice with the maximum flexibility and the minimum of formality'.

Applying for orders

8.5   At any stage of the proceedings a party may apply for an order to be issued, varied or revoked, or for a case management discussion or a pre-hearing review to be held.[8] An application for an order must include an explanation as to how it would assist the tribunal or chairman in dealing with the proceedings efficiently and fairly,[9] it must be made not less than 10 days before the date of the hearing at which it is to be considered (if any) unless it is not reasonably practicable to do so, or the chairman or tribunal considers it to be in the interests of justice that shorter notice be allowed.[10] If a party is legally represented (except when the application is for a witness

---

4 [1999] IRLR 349, EAT.
5 [1999] IRLR 326, CA.
6 [1999] ICR 302; [1999] IRLR 4, EAT.
7 [1998] ICR 43, CA.
8 2004 Rules r11(1).
9 2004 Rules r11(3).
10 2004 Rules r11(2).

order), that party must provide to all other parties details of the application and the reasons why it is sought. The notice must state that any objection to the application must be sent to the tribunal office within seven days of being informed in writing of the application and that any objections must be copied to the tribunal and all other parties;[11] if a party is not legally represented, the secretary to the tribunal will inform other parties of these matters.[12]

8.6   Whereas under the old rules, parties would previously simply attend 'directions hearings' and state there what orders they sought, under the 2004 Rules of Procedure if any order is to be sought by a party, advance notice of it must be given (unless it is not reasonably practicable or it is in the interests of justice). Parties must therefore give careful thought to what orders will be sought. To make the best use of a case management discussion in the tribunal, the parties should be represented by those who have so far had conduct of the case and/or will be presenting the case. If agreement can be reached with the other side as to the directions to be made and the timetable to be observed, this should be set out in writing 10 days before the hearing, preferably in the form of a draft order (although it is likely that chairmen will continue the practice of considering any applications for orders on the day of case management discussions). If no agreement can be reached, the parties should at least try to identify the issues on which directions are required in advance of this hearing. The parties should bring their full files to the directions hearing, and those attending should be prepared to fix a date for the substantive hearing and so should attend with a clear, and preferably agreed, time estimate and with the dates when representatives, parties and witnesses are able to attend.

8.7   When a tribunal makes an order, it will usually state the time within which the answers must be supplied and a copy of the order will be sent to all other parties by the secretary.[13] An order may also impose conditions and it shall inform the parties of the potential consequences of non-compliance.[14] If a tribunal refuses to make an order, a further application can be made, but not on the same grounds.[14a]

---

11   2004 Rules r11(4).
12   2004 Rules r11(5).
13   2004 Rules r10(3).
14   Set out in 2004 Rules r13; and see para 8.10 below.
14a   *Goldman Sachs Services Ltd v Montali* [2002] ICR 1251. See also para 19.8.

Application to vary or set aside an order

8.8 Any order made by a tribunal at a case management discussion will be interim in nature and, therefore, not open to review (see para 19.8 below). Where, however, an interim order or direction is initially made either by a chairman on his/her own initiative without having given the parties any opportunity to make oral or written representations,[15] or after considering representations from only one party, the order is essentially provisional and may be reconsidered by the tribunal upon application by an absent party.[16]

8.9 Such an application must be made before the time at which, or the expiry of the period within which, the order was to be complied with.[17] It must also be in writing and must include the reasons for the application.[18] As with orders made under 2004 Rules r11, the right to make an objection within seven days must be communicated to all parties, either by the legal representative, or if there is none, by the secretary to the tribunal.

Failure to comply with an order

8.10 If a party does not comply with an order made under 2004 Rules r10, it is set out in rule 13 that the tribunal:

- may make an order in respect of costs or preparation time under 2004 Rules 38 to 47; *or*
- may (subject to rules 13(2) and 19) at a pre-hearing review or a r26 Hearing make an order to strike out the whole or part of the claim, or as the case may be, the response, and where appropriate direct that a respondent be debarred from responding to the claim altogether (see 2004 Rules r13(1)(b));
- may make an order to provide that unless the order is complied with, the claim, or, as the case may be, the response shall be struck out on the date of non-compliance without further consideration of the proceedings or the need to give notice under rule 19 or hold a pre-hearing review or a hearing.

---

15 2004 Rules r12.
16 *Reddington v Straker & Sons Ltd* [1994] ICR 172, EAT.
17 2004 Rules r12(2)(b) and (3).
18 2004 Rules r12(3).

8.11   It would seem that 2004 Rules r13(1) envisages that an order to strike out in these circumstances will not be accompanied by an order relating to costs (note the use of the word *or* above). There seems, however, to be no reason why the two orders should be mutually exclusive and nothing to prevent the tribunal from exercising its general jurisdiction to award costs or a preparation time order under 2004 Rules rr40(3) and 44(3) in any event. After all, if a party has conducted the proceedings in such an unreasonable way as to be struck out in these circumstances, why should the remaining party not be reimbursed for the costs or preparation time it has thereby incurred?

8.12   A tribunal cannot exercise its power under 2004 Rules r13(1)(a) to award costs without having sent notice to the party in default giving it an opportunity to show cause why the tribunal should not do so;[19] or its power under 2004 Rules r13(1)(b) to strike out without having sent notice to the party in default giving it an opportunity to show cause.[20] The notice cannot be sent out before expiry of the time limit ordered for the further particulars to be provided.[21]

19 2004 Rules r38(9).
20 2004 Rules r19(1).
21 *Beacard Property Management and Construction Co Ltd v Day* [1984] ICR 837, EAT.

CHAPTER 9

Case management: defining the issues

Defining the issues

9.1 Anyone contemplating or conducting tribunal proceedings needs to be able to make the best assessment possible of the prospects of success at all stages in the process. It is also necessary, before a full hearing, to learn as much as possible about the way in which the other side intends to conduct the case. Under Employment Act (EA) 2002 s32 and Schs 3 and 4 before the employment tribunal will have jurisdiction to hear the claims listed therein, a grievance will have to have been lodged and a period of 28 days allowed for an answer (see para 3.3). Further, the Employment Tribunals Rules of Procedure 2004[1] (2004 Rules) set out at rule 1(4) minimum information which must be given in the claim form, and from April 2005 standard claim forms must be used,[2] failing which the claim will not be accepted.[3] The purpose of these provisions is clearly to ensure that issues between the parties, and tribunal claims, are set out as fully as possibly, at an early stage. Whereas tribunals would previously accept a claim even if it had no particulars whatsoever, dealing with this by ordering additional information to be given, that is no longer the case. It remains the case, however, that parties will consider the case as set out by the other side to be inadequate, and orders for the provision of additional information or for written questions to be answered can assist in defining the issues. Parties can apply for an order in writing, or orders may be made by the tribunal at either case management discussions, or at pre-hearing reviews.

Additional information

9.2 A party to tribunal proceedings may ask the other party to provide additional information of the claim or response. Although there are no formal 'statements of case' in tribunal proceedings, the process is similar in many respects to requests for further information in High Court or county court cases under Civil Procedure Rules (CPR) Part 18 (although there is no requirement for a signed statement of truth in any such document before the tribunal).

---

1 Set out at Employment Tribunals (Constitution and Rules of Procedure) Regulations 2004 SI No 1861 Sch 1.
2 See chapter 5.
3 See 2004 Rules r3(1) and (2).

9.3   The purpose of a request for additional information is to ensure that a party is properly informed of the other side's case, so he or she can be prepared to meet it at hearing. For example, if an employer's response contains the allegation that the claimant was unable to perform his or her duties satisfactorily, the claimant would be entitled to additional information as to which duties are referred to and the manner in which it is alleged that their performance was unsatisfactory.[4] Or if a claimant claims he or she was treated in a way which was inconsistent with the treatment of other employees and with the general practice within that employment, the employer would be entitled to request additional information of the general practice alleged, and citation of instances involving other employees.[5]

9.4   As a general rule, a party should not be required to supply additional information in respect of an issue on which the other side bears the burden of proof.[6] Where a party puts forward a positive case, however, additional information may be ordered of the allegations made even though they do not bear the burden of proof. For instance, in a case where dismissal is admitted (where the employer will bear the burden of proving the reason for that dismissal), it has been held that a claimant who speculates on the real reason for the dismissal may be required to provide additional information of any positive assertion made.[7]

9.5   The necessity of requesting additional information arises when the other side has failed fully to particularise its case. If the replies given to a request are still not sufficiently particularised, a further request can be made: a request for additional information of the additional information. But requests should not develop into an attempt to carry out the trial of the issues on paper. Tribunals will not order additional information requested solely for the purpose of ascertaining who are the witnesses the other party is likely to call to give evidence.[8]

9.6   Tribunals have historically been reluctant to order that additional information be provided which goes solely to compensation when the issues on liability have not yet been determined,[9] even though this might be useful for an employer seeking to make a realistic offer of

4   *White v University of Manchester* [1976] ICR 419; [1976] IRLR 218, EAT.
5   *International Computers Ltd v Whitley* [1978] IRLR 318, EAT.
6   *James v Radnor CC* (1890) 6 TLR 240, QBD.
7   *Colonial Mutual Life Assurance Society Ltd v Clinch* [1981] ICR 752, EAT.
8   *P&O European Ferries (Dover) Ltd v Byrne* [1989] ICR 779; [1989] IRLR 254, CA.
9   *Colonial Mutual Life Assurance Society Ltd v Clinch* [1981] ICR 752, EAT.

settlement. Tribunals are, however, increasingly willing to order that proper particulars be provided of loss at an early stage, which may include directing that a full schedule of loss be prepared and that disclosure of documents relevant to loss and mitigation is given.[9a] While this practice is by no means automatic, it might be expected where:

- the claim is one of unlawful discrimination or is otherwise one where damages are at large or might be significant;
- the tribunal intends to consider the question of remedy concurrently with that of liability or has provisionally listed the issue of remedy to be considered immediately after the liability hearing;
- it is helpful to allow all concerned to direct a proportionate amount of resources to the case. In particular, this might allow a respondent to take a 'commercial view' as to the value of resisting the claim.

9.7   When responding to a request for additional information, a party is not obliged to supply information which has not been sought, although it may be advisable to expand the answer if it is not otherwise possible to answer the request properly. At the same time, parties should be wary of requests which require 'all facts and matters relied on in support of the allegation that . . . ' An incomplete answer to such a request may result in an objection to the subsequent introduction of further matters relied on in support of the allegation concerned but not specified in the reply. This is an attempt to use the additional information as a means of defining the limits of the opponent's case.

9.8   If, after responding to a request for additional information, new information comes to light which adds to the case a party wishes to put forward, or if it has left out certain matters by mistake, it is better to raise these points either by amendment or by voluntary additional information, rather than to wait until the hearing of the case.

9.9   In making a request for additional information, or in responding to such a request, the basic principles to be applied should be borne in mind, as summarised by Wood P in *Byrne v Financial Times Ltd*:[10]

> General principles affecting the ordering of further and better particulars include that the parties should not be taken by surprise at

---

9a   Also, claim forms which will be compulsory from 6 April 2005 require detailed information on income and any alternative work secured.

10   [1991] IRLR 417 at 419, EAT.

the last minute; that particulars should only be ordered when necessary in order to do justice in the case or to prevent adjournment; that the order should not be oppressive; that particulars are for the purpose of identifying the issues, not for the production of the evidence; and that complicated pleadings battles should not be encouraged.

The power to order additional information

9.10   A request for additional information should first be made directly to the other party without seeking an order from the tribunal. It is always better to try to obtain further details from the other side on a voluntary basis and this is certainly the practice encouraged by tribunals.

9.11   Rule 10(1) of the 2004 Rules provides that a chairman may at any time, either on the application of a party or on his or her own initiative, give orders on any matters which appear to the chairman to be appropriate. This includes providing additional information.[11]

Additional information of questionnaires

9.12   A tribunal will not order a respondent to provide additional information of a reply to a questionnaire. The proper course of action if a claimant wishes to ask further questions of the respondent in such cases, is to seek leave to serve a further questionnaire (see para 4.17). Alternatively a claimant can ask a tribunal to draw an adverse inference from incomplete or inadequate answers.

Equal pay cases

9.13   In an equal pay case, where the respondent seeks to rely on the genuine material factor defence provided by Equal Pay Act 1970 s1(3), a claimant can request precise details of the percentage pay differentials which are said to be explained by the material factor relied on; see *Enderby v Frenchay Health Authority and Secretary of State for Health*.[12] The arguments previously relied on by respondents to resist

---

11   2004 Rules r10(2)(b). See chapter 8 on how to make an order/apply to have it set aside/consequences of failing to comply.
12   [1994] ICR 112; [1993] IRLR 591, CA and ECJ.

any such request for additional information of this defence[13] would now be contrary to the decision of the European Court of Justice in *Enderby*.

Written answers

9.14 2004 Rules r10(2)(f) provides that tribunals may order a party to provide written answers to questions put by the tribunal or chairman. While there is no express provision for tribunals to order that written answers asked by parties be answered, the tribunal may still order that such questions be answered under its general power to manage proceedings and make such orders 'which appear to the chairman to be appropriate'.[14]

9.15 The difference between written answers and additional information is that written answers will be asked for in respect of relevant issues not referred to in the claim or response forms. Written answers are viewed in the same way as orders for further information in the High Court or county court and the same guidelines are likely to be applied. Indeed the earlier wording of the 1993 and 2001 Employment Tribunal Rules relating to written answers (rule 4(3) of both used language similar to that of the CPR, that is, that such an order may be made if the tribunal 'considers (a) that the answer of the party to that question may help to clarify any issue likely to arise for determination in the proceedings, and (b) that it would be likely to assist the progress of the proceedings for that answer to be available to the tribunal before the hearing'.

9.16 Like information given in court proceedings, written answers are unlikely to be ordered where other procedural processes would be more appropriate, for example, where the answer could be sought by way of a request for additional information or where it would be resolved on disclosure. Some tribunals have indicated that they will not be prepared to order written answers to questions in sex, race or disability discrimination[14a] cases where the information could be sought by using the questionnaire procedure (see para 4.17 below). Although where the time limit has already passed for the issue of

---

13 *Byrne and others v Financial Times Ltd* [1991] IRLR 417, EAT.
14 2004 Rules r10(1).
14a And now also claims under the sexual orientation or religion or belief regulations.

the questionnaire, such an application might be viewed more sympathetically. Further, a questionnaire may remain the best option for claimants given the formal way in which inferences can be drawn from a failure to answer or from an unsatisfactory or inadequate answer. As with additional information, tribunals will be reluctant to order that written answers be provided where the questions asked amount to an attempt to try the issues in the case on paper rather than at a hearing.

9.17   Written answers will be considered by the tribunal not as part of the 'claim and response' process but as representations made by the party concerned as part of its case.

9.18   See chapter 8 for how to apply for an order, how to have it varied or set aside and consequences of non-compliance.

9.19   A case involves many steps before it is heard. Important matters to be considered are whether there ought to be joinder or dismissal of any respondents; whether proceedings should be combined, whether test cases are appropriate and whether witness orders should be requested, and if so how.

Joining and dismissing respondents in the proceedings

9.20   A tribunal or chairman can order (generally in a case management discussion or at a pre-hearing review):

- that any person who the chairman or tribunal considers may be liable for the remedy claimed should be made a respondent in the proceedings (2004 Rules r10(2)(k));
- dismiss the claim against a respondent who is no longer directly interested in the claim (2004 Rules r10(2)(l)); or
- that any person who the chairman or tribunal considers has an interest in the outcome of the proceedings should be joined as a party to the proceedings (2004 Rules r10(2)(r)).

These orders may be made either by the tribunal or chairman, on their own initiative or on an application by a party usually to a chairman alone.[15]

---

15   2004 Rules r10(1); see chapter 8 on applying for orders generally.

9.21   There is no re-enactment in the 2004 Rules of the express provision in 2001 Rules r19(3) that where a number of persons who have the same interest in a claim one or more may be cited as the party against which relief is sought, or may be authorised by the tribunal to defend on behalf of all persons so interested. The right to so order is maintained under the *general* provision that tribunals may make such orders as they think fit.[16]

9.22   While the tribunal's powers were previously limited to the people against whom a remedy is sought,[17] it is now possible for any party which has an 'interest' in proceedings to be joined,[18] leaving it open to a tribunal to join a person even if the remedy sought cannot be ordered against that individual or organisation.

9.23   In practice however, it remains to be seen whether the test is likely to alter because the tribunal must always be satisfied that the joinder is appropriate, and if a party is not one against whom a remedy may be ordered it is not immediately apparent what their interest is likely to be or how the appropriateness test will be satisfied. The new rules do however make it clear that a chairman/tribunal can order joinder of their own accord, for example when it is apparent that an individual or a body should be joined in the proceedings, but the claimant has failed to include that person in the claim. The tribunal can now resolve the problem of its own accord. It is a power which might conveniently be exercised in a case involving the transfer of an undertaking, where the claimant might not be sure who the correct legal respondent is.

9.24   If the actions or advice of third parties are relevant to the issues in a claim, for example, an ACAS officer's involvement in a conciliated settlement, or an adviser's negligence in a claim made out of time, unless they can be said to have an interest in the proceedings the tribunal cannot order that they be joined as parties. However, the tribunal may be able to order that they attend as witnesses or to produce documents.[19]

---

16 2004 Rules r10(1).
17 See 2001 Rules r19(1); also *Sandhu v Department of Education and Science* [1978] IRLR 208, EAT, where an application to join a party against whom no remedy could be sought was refused.
18 2004 Rules r10(2)(r).
19 *Marshall v Alexander Sloan & Co Ltd* [1981] IRLR 264; and *Riley v Tesco Stores Ltd* [1980] ICR 323; [1980] IRLR 103, CA.

Industrial pressure from third parties

9.25   More specifically, the question of joinder of parties is raised by Trade Unions and Labour Relations (Consolidation) Act (TULRCA) 1992 ss150 and 160, which provide that where a dismissal[20] or action short of dismissal[21] takes place due to trade union or shop-floor pressure, an employer *or* the dismissed employee may request that the tribunal join the trade union or other people exerting the pressure as additional respondent(s) to the proceedings.

9.26   If this request is made before the hearing begins, the tribunal *must* allow it; if it is made later, the tribunal may refuse it. If it is made after the tribunal has given its determination as to the appropriate remedy, it must refuse it.[22] The person making the application for joinder does not even have to show an arguable case. Once joined, however, the trade union (or other individual concerned) has the right to seek an adjournment, to ask for a pre-hearing review, or to make any other appropriate application under the 2004 Rules, as if it had been a party from the outset.

Race and sex discrimination cases

9.27   Other instances where it may be appropriate to join an individual to tribunal proceedings include race and sex discrimination cases when an individual employee might be held to be personally responsible for discriminatory acts for which his or her employer is also liable.

National Insurance Fund

9.28   Claims can be made against the secretary of state for payments from the National Insurance Fund for redundancy or on an employer's insolvency. The secretary of state has rights under 2004 Rules r51 to appear as if he or she were a party, and to be heard at any hearing which may involve a payment out of the National Insurance Fund. In that event he or she is treated for the purposes of the rules as if he or she were a party. In addition, the tribunal may join the secretary of state as a party under the general provisions of 2004 Rules r10(2).

20   TULRCA 1992 s160.
21   TULRCA 1992 s150 – for claims brought under TULRCA 1992 s146.
22   TULRCA 1992 ss150(2) and 160(2).

Combined proceedings

9.29 On the application of a party or on its own initiative, a tribunal or chairman may order that different claims be considered together.[23] This order will not be given unless all relevant parties have been given notice that an order may be made and they have been given the opportunity to make oral or written representations as to why an order should not be made.[24] In considering whether to make an order the tribunal is likely to have regard to whether some common question of law or fact arises in two or more applications; whether the applications arise out of the same set of facts, or whether there is some other reason which makes it desirable that those cases are heard together.

9.30 This power might be exercised where there are several unfair dismissal claims arising out of a large-scale redundancy exercise, or a number of equal pay claims where there are common issues of law and fact; or where a claimant has made separate claims, for example, for unfair dismissal and race discrimination, arising out of substantially the same set of facts.

9.31 An order that cases be considered together is not the same as an order that there will be a test case (see para 9.36 below) where the tribunal is still hearing separate applications. Any decision should deal separately with points of difference in the cases, even if that means that separate judgments are given.[25] For instance, in a redundancy resulting in a number of unfair dismissal claims, while there may be common questions relating to the selection criteria and collective consultation, individual application of the selection criteria and consultation might vary considerably.

9.32 In many cases where there are multiple applications involving similar issues of fact or law, an order combining cases is in everyone's interest. It saves having to adduce evidence or to make legal submissions more than once. It can lead to a substantial saving in costs and time, particularly when many witnesses are involved.

9.33 Parties may, however, have genuine concerns about claims being considered together, particularly if this may prejudice one person's case. In *Dietmann and Wahlstrom v Brent LBC*,[26] a case arising out of

---

23 2004 Rules r10(2)(j).
24 2004 Rules r10(4).
25 *Paine & Moore v Grundy (Teddington) Ltd* [1981] IRLR 267, EAT.
26 [1987] IRLR 146, CA.

the public inquiry into the death of a child, Jasmine Beckford, two social workers, each claiming that she had been unfairly dismissed, argued against their cases being combined. Each said that her answers to the allegations against her might be used to cross-examine the other. Their appeals were rejected. The Court of Appeal held that justice could not be seen to be done if there were two separate hearings at which each claimant was exonerated by the tribunal and the blame laid at the feet of the other. The Court also emphasised the discretionary nature of the tribunal's decision in ordering that cases be combined. Once the tribunal has made its order, it will, therefore, be difficult to appeal against that exercise of its discretion.

9.34   When it has been ordered that claims be considered together, the tribunal can make further directions as to how it will go about hearing the different applications under its general powers in rule 10. In some cases, all the claimants' evidence will be heard together; in others the tribunal will hear each case in total, giving its reasons in one case before moving on to the next.

9.35   This latter procedure may be of assistance where cases involve identical issues of law; the finding in the first case might well be decisive for the parties in other cases (and see paras 9.36–9.40 below on test cases). Ultimately the tribunal hearing the cases which have been combined has the right to control its procedure as it sees fit, although a case management discussion is useful to canvass such questions with the parties in advance of the hearing.

Test cases

9.36   Tribunals do not have the same powers as the courts to order that representative claims be heard as 'test' cases which would bind all others bringing claims on the same grounds.[27] The only way of proceeding with a test case in the tribunal is to use the provision in rule 10(2)(j) to consider claims together. For example, a number of cases can be considered together and a few 'test' claims heard,[28] which are representative of all the other cases. Findings of the tribunal will be decisive in all other cases. This is particularly useful where there are numerous claimants with equal pay claims.[29]

---

27   CPR Part 19.
28   See para 9.39 below as to how 'test' cases are selected.
29   See *Ashmore v British Coal Corporation* [1990] ICR 485; [1990] IRLR 283, CA.

9.37   There is no power to allow representative proceedings to be brought and subsequently relied on by individuals who did not themselves bring claims within the specified time limit. This means that all potential claimants must still present their claims as individuals within the time limit. They cannot rely on claims brought by others. In redundancy cases, an employment tribunal may make a protective award which will apply to all 'employees of a description to which the award relates', and under TULRCA 1992 ss190–192 claimants can present a claim within three months of the date on which a protective award was made, if they are one of the employees of that description.

9.38   While test cases can be mutually advantageous for the parties in expediting matters and saving costs, it is often difficult to select lead cases which are truly representative of all classes of applications. In many multi-claimant cases arising out of the same facts or involving the same issues of law, it is not possible to carry out this exercise because the applications each raise individual issues which will need separate consideration; hence the need for individual hearings in the Ministry of Defence pregnancy discrimination claims in the early 1990s. Before ordering that cases be combined and test cases selected for initial consideration, the tribunal should be satisfied that similar issues arise to justify the same result in each case.

9.39   In selecting test cases, assistance may be derived from the provisions of CPR Part 19.10 and the relevant practice direction (CPR PD 19) which are concerned with Group Litigation Orders in the civil courts. In tribunals, as in civil courts, it is important that a sufficient number of lead cases should be chosen to obtain judgments on all the points required for the disposal of as many of the cases as possible. Equally, to achieve the greatest saving in interim costs, the selection of the lead cases should be made as soon as possible. On the other hand, some issues may not become apparent until fairly late in the preparations for trial. A measure of flexibility will usually be appropriate in group litigation.

9.40   A decision in a test case binds all the other cases which are being considered together in so far as the issues are similar. If a party to an application which has been combined seeks to pursue a tribunal case despite the test case decision, the tribunal may exercise its powers under 2004 Rules r18(7) to strike out the claim or response in that case.[30]

---

30 *Ashmore v British Coal Corporation* [1990] ICR 485; [1990] IRLR 283, CA.

Witness orders

9.41   By 2004 Rules r10(2)(c) and (d) a tribunal (which may be a chairman sitting alone)[32] may on application by any party or of its own initiative order any person within Great Britain, including a party, to attend the tribunal to give evidence or to produce documents; or to disclose documents and allow a party to inspect material. If attendance is required, the tribunal will specify the time and place at which the individual concerned is to attend. As with all orders[33] if an order is made against a person in their absence, whether a party or not, they may apply to the tribunal to vary or set aside that order. This should always be before the time for compliance with the order has expired.[34]

9.42   The power given to tribunals to order a witness to attend is analogous to the power of the civil courts under CPR Parts 31 and 34 to order the disclosure of documents and to summon a person to attend before it. A person who is subject to a tribunal witness order and who fails to comply with its terms is liable on summary conviction to a fine under Employment Tribunals Act 1996 s7(4).

9.43   The tribunal's power to order a witness to attend is discretionary in nature and it is therefore difficult to appeal against it. Since such an order is by its nature 'interim', there is no power to review it. It is, therefore, all the more important for anyone applying for a witness order to make sure that all the facts relied on are clearly set out. Similarly, an application to set aside or vary the order should be made as soon as possible (and in any event before the date on which attendance is required (2004 Rules r13(3))), clearly setting out the grounds relied on. If necessary, an oral hearing should be requested.

9.44   The relevant considerations to be borne in mind by tribunals before deciding whether or not to make a witness order were set out by Sir John Donaldson P in *Dada v Metal Box Co Ltd*:[35]

> The first is that the witness prima facie can give evidence which is relevant to the issues in dispute . . . We do not suggest that the tribunal should ask the claimant to give a full proof of his evidence but the claimant should indicate the subject-matter of his evidence and show the extent to which it is relevant. The second . . . is that it is necessary to issue a witness order . . . [W]itnesses should always be invited to attend by the claimant before he applies for witness orders.

32   2004 Rules rr17(1) and 18(1).
33   See chapter 8 above.
34   2004 Rules r12(2) and (3).
35   [1974] ICR 559; [1974] IRLR 251, NIRC.

If they agree to attend and the claimant is quite satisfied that they will attend, then it is unnecessary to issue witness orders . . . A witness may not reply to the request for an undertaking that he will attend. In those circumstances, it may be necessary to issue such an order. He may refuse, in which case . . . a witness order is clearly needed. Again, he may equivocate . . . In such circumstances it will . . . be a matter for the judgment of the tribunal . . . Finally, although not exclusively . . . there is the . . . witness who says, 'Certainly I will come and give evidence, but it would be very much easier for me to come if I had a witness order requiring me to come'. That situation can arise if an employer is unwilling to release a witness. Again that would be a reason for granting a witness order.

9.45　In *Noorani v Merseyside TEC Ltd*[36] the Court of Appeal emphasised that the tribunal has a broad discretion, and that it must inquire as to whether the evidence a witness could give is sufficiently relevant to justify the order. There is, however, no requirement that any evidence which might be relevant must be admitted. In practice, tribunals are generally prepared to grant witness orders subject to any subsequent application to vary or set aside.

9.46　In most cases, a witness order should not be necessary: those witnesses who will give evidence in your favour are unlikely to refuse to attend, although they may prefer to do so under a witness order for the reasons outlined in the *Dada* case. A potential witness who is reluctant to attend on your behalf is unlikely to co-operate before the hearing in the drafting of a witness statement. As a general rule, if you are unsure what a person may say when called to give evidence, it is unwise to call him or her. Applying for a witness order to require the attendance of someone who may be hostile to the client's case would be giving a hostage to fortune. It is far better to leave it to the other side to call a witness, so that there is the opportunity to cross-examine (see para 16.92).

9.47　In limited circumstances, if the witness displays no desire to tell the truth and is resistant to the party calling him or her, it is possible to ask the tribunal for permission to treat the witness as 'hostile'. If granted, the party calling the witness may cross-examine but cannot present evidence to show that the witness should not be believed. Such applications are rarely granted.

9.48　In some cases, a party may have little choice but to apply for a witness order to require the attendance of a person whose evidence may or may not be favourable. For instance, in a transfer of undertakings

36　[1999] IRLR 184, CA.

case, the respondent-transferee may apply for a witness order requiring the receiver who carried out the dismissals of the claimant employees to attend, although that receiver may not be prepared to provide a witness statement in advance.

9.49   When calling witnesses subject to a witness order, parties should bear in mind that the order may need to be amended to state a different date and time if the hearing goes part-heard before that witness's evidence is completed. When the witness has finished giving evidence, it is necessary to ask the tribunal if he or she may be 'released', so that the witness will not be in breach of the order by leaving the tribunal after having given evidence but before the expiry of the time period specified in the order.

Case management: disclosure of documents

continued

Disclosure of documents

10.1   The documentation relevant to a particular case will generally provide the best evidence to the issues in that case. It avoids the need to rely on selective recollection of events, and can provide a useful indication of the real view taken by a particular individual at the time an event occurred rather than that which he or she might adopt when giving evidence after proceedings have commenced. Finding out about the existence of those documents and gaining sight of them is effected by *disclosure* (*recovery* in Scotland) and *inspection*. It may well be the most crucial step taken by the parties. The documents available in a case will often be the best weapon available and the earlier inspection of the documents takes place, the earlier a party can use the weapon to its advantage, whether by way of requests for further disclosure, or further information, or for use in assessing the merits of the case generally and in settlement negotiations.

General principles

10.2   Unlike in High Court or county court proceedings (see Civil Procedure Rules (CPR) Part 31), there is no general duty to make disclosure in tribunal proceedings. Unless a party requests disclosure, the other side is not obliged to disclose any documents at all. Late production of documents, on the morning of the hearing, may, however, give good grounds for seeking an adjournment with an order for costs or preparation time to be made against the party with previously undisclosed documents. Where the late disclosure involves just one or two short documents, the tribunal may expect the hearing to go ahead after a short adjournment on the morning to enable the other party to read the new papers. The principle is that no party should be disadvantaged by late disclosure of documents.

10.3   Such difficulties can be overcome to a large extent by seeking disclosure before the hearing. As there is no general duty to disclose all documents, this can often be a very imprecise procedural instrument. As an employee will not know all the documents in the employer's possession, *specific* requests may miss the most important document in the case. The crown jewels may be a board minute or confidential memo referring to the employee as a dangerous militant who will have to be removed (in a union reasons case), or stating he or she they does not 'fit in' (in a discrimination case). General requests for disclosure of an employee's personnel file, or for all documents on which the other side intends to rely, may not produce the goods: damning policy documents, for instance, may not be specific to that employee. A request for all documents relevant to the issues in the case may be the best way to ensure at the hearing that all the cards are on the table. Assistance might also be derived from the wording of the CPR, which provide that 'standard disclosure' will include the following:

- the documents on which a party relies; and
- the documents which:
  - adversely affect that party's case;
  - adversely affect another party's case; or
  - support another party's case.[1]

10.4   Moreover, when giving disclosure, a party should not be selective as to the documents to be disclosed within a particular class and should not allow a misleading impression to be gained by partial disclosure. The principles were set out by Waite P in *Birds Eye Walls Ltd v Harrison:*[2]

> Once . . . a party has disclosed certain documents . . . it becomes his duty not to withhold . . . any further documents in his possession or power . . . if there is any risk that the effect . . . might be to convey to his opponent or to the tribunal a false or misleading impression as to the true nature, purport or effect of any disclosed document.
>
> . . . [T]wo principles [are] to be borne in mind if injustice is not to be suffered . . . the duty of every party not to withhold from disclosure any document whose suppression would render a disclosed document misleading is a high duty which the tribunals should interpret broadly and strictly . . . Tribunals should . . . ensure that if any party can be . . . at risk of having his claim or defence unfairly restricted by the denial of an opportunity to become aware of a document . . . material to the just prosecution of his case, he does not suffer any avoidable disadvantage as a result.

10.5   Part of a document may be disclosed if it is made clear that the document is not complete, and the whole of the document *must* be offered to the tribunal or the other side if it is requested.[3]

1   See CPR 31.6.
2   [1985] ICR 278; IRLR 47, EAT.
3   *C J O'Shea Construction Ltd v Bassi* [1998] ICR 1130, EAT.

10.6   *Disclosure* means providing a list of documents; *inspection*, which may include the taking of copies of documents, is what is required to see them. In practice, parties generally agree to conduct disclosure by mutual exchange of copies of relevant documentation. Rarely, a charge is made for copying and, if it is reasonable, it should be paid. Reliance on the more technical form of disclosure by list arises where the great majority of documents are with one party, usually the employer, the request is generalised, and providing extensive copies might be unduly burdensome. In these circumstances, or where the party in question is just being bloody-minded, disclosure may well be by list, the other party being expected to request inspection of specific items (usually at the other side's premises or at the offices of their solicitors) or to undertake the copying.

The power to order disclosure

10.7   The power to order disclosure is provided by Employment Tribunals Rules of Procedure[4] (2004 Rules) r10(2)(d). A tribunal may, on the application of a party or of its own motion, order one party to grant to another such disclosure or inspection of documents (including the taking of copies) as might be granted by a county court. The procedure of the county court is set out in CPR Part 31 (Disclosure and Inspection). The essence of the CPR is that orders for disclosure are now limited to 'standard disclosure' unless the court directs otherwise,[5] such that a party is only required to disclose those documents on which he relies, documents which adversely affect his own or another party's case, or which support another party's case, and documents which he is required to disclose by a relevant practice direction.[6] A party must make a reasonable search for documents,[7] but as in all aspects of the operation of the CPR, the principle of proportionality must be considered, and a party will not be compelled to do that which would be disproportionate in the circumstances of a particular case.

---

4   Contained in Employment Tribunals (Constitution and Rules of Procedure) Regulations 2004 SI No 1861 Sch 1.
5   CPR 31.5.
6   CPR 31.6 and 31.8.
7   CPR 31.7.

10.8   As under the old rules of 1993 and 2001, orders will not be granted if the request for disclosure amounts to a 'fishing expedition' (see further paras 10.22 and 10.67).

10.9   Tribunals encourage parties to avoid the need for formal applications for disclosure and inspection and, instead, to agree to the mutual exchange of documents and the creation of an 'agreed bundle' for use in any tribunal hearing. An agreed bundle does not mean that all parties agree on the relevance of the documents it contains or as to the truth of their contents. All it means is that there is no live dispute about the existence and authorship of the documents involved, so the writer need not be called as a witness simply to prove that he or she created the document. Of course, the writer should be called if there is dispute about the reasons for what is written. So a director who signed a disciplinary procedure agreement need not be called but the manager who wrote the dismissal letter under the procedure should be.

10.10   Although the tribunal's power in relation to disclosure and inspection is quite limited, the notice of hearing expressly suggests that mutual disclosure by list should take place voluntarily and that sufficient copies should be provided for other parties, before the hearing, and for the tribunal members and the witness table at the hearing.

10.11   A decision relating to disclosure may be made by a tribunal chairman sitting alone[8] and may arise from the tribunal acting of its own motion.[9] Before determining an application for disclosure, a tribunal will require a legally represented party making the application to give notice of it to all other parties, giving particulars of the application and explaining that any objections must be sent to the tribunal office within seven days of being informed of the application, any such objections being sent to the tribunal and any other party.[10] If a party is not legally represented information on how to object will be given by the secretary to the tribunal.[11]

10.12   If the tribunal determines an application for disclosure on the papers, or in the absence of any party, the absent party against whom any order is made may apply to the tribunal to vary or set aside the

---

8   2004 Rules r17 if it is a case management discussion, or rule 18 if it is a pre-hearing review.

9   2004 Rules r10(1).

10   2004 Rules r 11(4).

11   2004 Rules r11(5). See chapter 8 above on how to apply for orders generally.

requirement.[12] Any order for disclosure is an interim order and not a judgment. There is no power for the tribunal to review it (see para 19.8) but it can be appealed.[13] The order in any instance is, however, largely a matter for its discretion and it will be difficult for any party to appeal against it.

Failure to comply

10.13 If a party fails to comply with an order for disclosure, the tribunal may, under 2004 Rules r13(1), make an order for costs (expenses) or preparation time under rules 38–46, or strike out the whole or part of the claim or response, and debar a respondent from defending the proceedings altogether. The tribunal cannot, however, strike out or debar unless prior notice has been sent to the party concerned giving an opportunity to show cause why the tribunal should not do so.[14]

10.14 In considering whether to strike out or debar, the tribunal will take into account similar considerations to those applied in the High Court or county courts.[15] The main test is whether there is a real or substantial risk that, as a result of the default, a fair trial will no longer be possible.[16]

10.15 Failure to comply with an order for disclosure, without reasonable excuse, may also render the party concerned liable on summary conviction to a fine not exceeding level 3 on the standard scale.[17]

No duty to create documents

10.16 Disclosure applies only to existing documentation; there is no obligation under this procedure for a party to create a document. Where statistics are sought which will have to be created for that case, the questionnaire in discrimination cases, or the written answer procedure under 2004 Rules r10(2)(f), might provide the only means of obtaining such information (see paras 4.17 and 9.14).

---

12 2004 Rules r12.
13 *Science Research Council v Nasse* [1980] AC 1028; [1979] ICR 921; [1979] IRLR 465, HL.
14 2004 Rules r19.
15 *Landauer Ltd v Comins & Co* (1991) *Times* 7 August, CA.
16 *National Grid Co Ltd v Virdee* [1992] IRLR 555, EAT.
17 Employment Tribunals Act 1996 s7(4).

Disclosure and inspection: general principles

Documents

10.17   A 'document' is widely defined for the purposes of disclosure. It is not limited to writing or print on paper but includes anything on which information or evidence is recorded, for example, tape recordings,[18] photographs, videotapes, microfilms,[19] computer disks, e-mails and so on. Documents are defined in CPR Part 31.4.

10.18   In High Court and county court proceedings, the documents used at court hearings should be the originals whenever possible. This rule does not apply to tribunal proceedings, although the original should be available for inspection if any question is raised (or is likely to be raised) as to its authenticity, or its alteration.

Relevance

10.19   A document of which disclosure is sought must first be shown to be material and relevant to the issues in the proceedings. A document is 'relevant' when:

> . . . it is reasonable to suppose [it] contains information which *may*, not which *must*, either directly or indirectly enable the party [applying for disclosure] either to advance his own case or to damage the case of his adversary [including] a document which may fairly lead him to a train of enquiry which may have either of these two consequences . . .[20]

10.20   A document is not relevant if it is intended to be used merely to attack a witness's credibility;[21] nor if it is being sought to find out the names of the other side's witnesses.[22]

10.21   Relevance is not the only criterion. If the tribunal is satisfied that the documents are material and relevant to the case, it may still exercise its discretion to decide not to order disclosure. Relevant to the tribunal's exercise of discretion are the following questions:

- Will refusing disclosure hinder a fair hearing?
- Will refusing disclosure cause delay and thereby increase costs?

18   *Grant v Southwestern and County Properties Ltd* [1974] 2 All ER 465, Ch D.
19   Bankers' Books Evidence Act 1879.
20   *Compagnie Financière du Pacifique v Peruvian Guano Co* [1882] 11 QBD 55, CA.
21   *George Ballantine & Son Ltd v F E R Dixon & Son Ltd* [1974] 2 All ER 503, Ch D.
22   *Knapp v Harvey* [1911] 2 KB 725, CA.

- Is the request proportionate? Regard may be had to the number of documents involved, the nature and complexity of the proceedings, the ease and expense of retrieval and the significance of the document.
- Would an order for disclosure in the terms sought be oppressive or disproportionate?
- Are there any other relevant considerations, such as confidentiality or provisions of the Data Protection Act 1998, which need to be balanced against the question of relevance?

10.22 It is for the party applying for disclosure to show that the document is relevant to an issue or issues already clearly defined in the proceedings, that is, it is not a fishing expedition and disclosure is necessary at that stage in the proceedings.[23]

Privilege

10.23 *Privilege* protects a document from disclosure or inspection in the interests of the administration of justice. For public policy reasons, a party will not be obliged to hand over certain classes of documents. Privilege may arise in a number of instances which are considered below.

Confidentiality

10.24 General guidelines as to confidentiality of documents and disclosure in tribunal cases were set out by Lord Wilberforce in *Science Research Council v Nasse; Vyas v Leyland Cars*[24] and can be summarised as:

- If a tribunal is satisfied that disclosure of a document is necessary in order fairly to dispose of the proceedings, it must order disclosure of the document, even though the document is confidential. There is no principle in law by which documents are protected from disclosure by reason of confidentiality by itself.[25]

---

23 *Rolls Royce Motor Cars Ltd v Mair and others* EAT 794/92.
24 [1980] AC 1028; [1979] ICR 921; [1979] IRLR 465, HL.
25 *Alfred Crompton Amusement Machines Ltd v Customs and Excise Commissioners (No 2)* [1974] AC 405; [1973] 2 All ER 1169, HL. Although considerations of the right to privacy might now arise under European Convention on Human Rights art 8, incorporated under Human Rights Act 1998.

- There is no presumption against disclosure of confidential documents.
- Where there is an objection to disclosure of documents on the grounds of confidentiality, the tribunal should inspect the documents to decide whether disclosure is necessary for the fair disposal of the case or for saving expense.
- In exercising its discretion as to whether to order disclosure, the tribunal should have regard to the fact that documents are confidential and should consider whether the necessary information can be obtained by other means, not involving a breach of confidence.
- Confidentiality is a relevant factor in deciding whether to order disclosure: relevance is not the only factor and general orders for disclosure are not always appropriate in tribunal proceedings.

10.25 A party will not be able to claim privilege against disclosure solely on the ground that the document, or its contents, was supplied in confidence by a third party.[26]

10.26 It is for the tribunal in its discretion, rather than as a matter of strict entitlement by a party, to decide questions of confidentiality and disclosure. It can decide them at some interim stage or as they arise during the hearing.[27] Often the most appropriate course is to consider all arguments relating to disclosure and the confidentiality of documents at a separate case management discussion. This has been particularly encouraged by the Employment Appeal Tribunal (EAT) for complex cases.[28]

10.27 If the tribunal, at whatever stage, considers it appropriate that there should be an examination of the documents, it should consider how the facts in the documents can be disclosed without divulging the confidential parts. As a general rule, names and addresses of those against whom comparison is being made (for example, in a case alleging discrimination at interview for a job) should not be disclosed, although qualifications may well be, as might other factors necessary for the tribunal to make a proper assessment of the value of the evidence.

---

26 See note 25 above.
27 *British Railways Board v Natarajan* [1979] ICR 326; [1979] IRLR 45, EAT.
28 See *Brooks v British Telecommunications Plc* [1991] ICR 286; [1991] IRLR 4, EAT (affirmed [1992] ICR 414, [1992] IRLR 66, CA) and *Halford v Sharples* [1992] ICR 146, EAT (affirmed [1992] ICR 583, CA).

Public interest immunity

10.28   All claims of privilege rely on general principles of public policy. Public interest immunity goes further and asserts protection from disclosure on the ground that disclosure would be injurious to the public interest.[29] When public interest immunity is claimed, the tribunal will have to balance that claim against the importance of the documents to the proceedings, the extent of injustice caused by their non-disclosure and the public interest in fair administration of justice.[30] There is no 'right' to resist disclosure on such a ground but the party seeking to do so should be able to show some public duty which outweighs the public policy considerations in favour of disclosure.

10.29   The circumstances in which public interest immunity might arise have been identified as falling within two types: immunity extending to a whole class of documents and immunity simply in relation to the contents of a particular document. The distinction has been described by Lord Wilberforce as follows:

> . . . with a 'class' claim it is immaterial whether the disclosure of the particular contents of particular documents would be injurious to the public interest – the point being that it is the maintenance of the immunity of the 'class' from disclosure in litigation that is important; whereas in a contents claim, the protection is claimed for particular 'contents' in a particular document. A claim remains a 'class' even though something may be known about the contents; it remains a 'class' even if parts of the documents are revealed and parts disclosed.[31]

10.30   Where immunity is claimed on a 'class' basis, an order for inspection should be made with extreme care and should not be exercised before giving the party claiming the immunity the opportunity to appeal.[32]

10.31   If a claim of 'class' immunity is accepted and documents are excluded on that basis, no use whatever can be made of the documents and no reliance placed on anything contained in them by any of the parties to the proceedings.

10.32   Police complaints files containing documents prepared under the Police and Criminal Evidence Act 1984, and files compiled under the

29   See CPR Part 31.19.
30   *D v NSPCC* [1977] 1 All ER 589, HL.
31   *Burmah Oil Co Ltd v Bank of England* [1980] AC 1090, HL at 1111.
32   *Halford v Sharples* [1992] ICR 146, at 155–158, EAT and [1992] ICR 583, at 609–610, CA.

police disciplinary regulations, are discoverable as a 'class'. But immunity or other kinds of privilege may be claimed in respect of the contents of *particular* documents within those categories.[33]

10.33   'Class' immunity has also been held not to apply to files held by the Association of Chief Police Officers consisting of confidential reports kept on each individual chief officer[34] (subject to the exclusion of particular documents relating to positive vetting and the private lives of individual officers). Nor does it apply to statements made in the course of police grievance proceedings.[35]

National security

10.34   Where the disclosure of any information would, in the opinion of a minister, be contrary to the interests of national security, any disclosure of that information will be prohibited.[36] Even without this statutory prohibition, which could be applied in most proceedings before a tribunal, interests of national security, any disclosure of that information will be prohibited.[37] Whenever public interest immunity is claimed, courts and tribunals will generally not look behind that certificate to assess the likely danger themselves. In *Balfour v Foreign and Commonwealth Office*[38] the Court of Appeal held that while a tribunal should be vigilant to ensure that a claim of public interest immunity was raised only in appropriate circumstances, and was particularised, once a certificate of a minister demonstrated that the disclosure of documentary evidence posed an actual or potential risk to national security, the tribunal should not exercise its right to inspect that evidence.[39]

10.35   In any tribunal cases relevant to national security a minister may make an application to the tribunal objecting to an order for disclosure or inspection, or if such an order has been made, requesting that it be varied or set aside. Such applications will be heard in private.

---

33   *R v Chief Constable of West Midlands Police ex p Wiley* [1995] 1 AC 274; overruling *Neilson v Laugharne* [1981] QB 736, CA.
34   *Halford v Sharples* [1992] ICR 146, EAT (affirmed [1992] ICR 583, CA).
35   *Metropolitan Police Commissioner v Locker* [1993] ICR 440; [1993] IRLR 319, EAT.
36   Employment Rights Act 1996 s195.
37   Employment Rights Act 1996 s193(2).
38   [1994] ICR 277, CA.
39   See also *Conway v Rimmer* [1968] AC 910, HL.

Diplomatic privilege

10.36 Embassy documents are protected by absolute privilege.[40] See also para 10.51 below.

Legal privilege

10.37 Legal privilege falls under two heads:

- *Legal advice privilege*: communications between client and legal adviser which are confidential and made for the purpose of obtaining or providing legal advice. These include documents which come into being in contemplation of litigation, but are not limited to that classification. The basis of the privilege is the principle that any person should be entitled to seek and obtain legal advice at any time without fear that it might later be disclosed to another; the privilege is therefore owned by the client, not the lawyer, and continues indefinitely. This head of privilege will be construed broadly.[41]
- *Legal proceedings privilege*: communications between client, legal adviser and third parties which are made for the purpose of existing or contemplated legal proceedings. This privilege is more limited in nature and has a restricted life. It can no longer be relied on once the litigation concerned has come to an end.

10.38 'Legal adviser' is defined as a qualified lawyer: a barrister, advocate, solicitor or salaried legal executive, whether in independent practice or employed 'in-house'.[42] It does not extend to other professional advisers such as personnel consultants and, presumably, trade union officials and other advice workers even though the advice is clearly in the nature of legal advice.[43] The difficulty with this restriction in tribunal proceedings is that because of the open nature of the forum and the lack of legal aid, claimants (in particular) are often likely to have received advice from those who are not legal professionals. If that advice-giver is merely acting as the means of communication between the claimant and a professionally qualified legal adviser, the communication will still be privileged, but if the advice comes direct from a non-qualified source, no privilege will attach.

---

40 *Fayed v Al-Tajir* [1987] 2 All ER 396, CA.
41 *Balabel v Air India* [1988] 2 All ER 246, CA.
42 See *Halsbury's Laws of England* 4th edn (Butterworths), Vol 13 at paras 71 onwards.
43 *New Victoria Hospital v Ryan* [1993] ICR 201; [1993] IRLR 202, EAT.

Without prejudice communications

10.39   It is a rule of evidence that without prejudice communications between the parties should not be disclosed to a court.[44] This rule applies to tribunals, as confirmed in the case of *Independent Research Services Ltd v Catterall*.[45] In *Catterall* the public policy behind the rule was described: parties should be free to try and settle their differences without fear that anything they say in the course of negotiations will be used in evidence as a sign of weakness or lack of confidence in their case. On the assumption that negotiations are genuine and not a pretext to hide a threat, without prejudice correspondence – for example, describing an offer made by an employer to settle an claimant's case – will be excluded as inadmissible and cannot be ordered to be disclosed.

10.40   The tribunal must, in order to apply this rule and exclude evidence, be satisfied that there was an extant dispute between the parties, and that the communication in question was a genuine attempt to compromise that dispute. In *BNP Paribas v Mezzotero*[46] a woman who raised a grievance complaining that on her return from maternity leave she had been demoted, was invited to a meeting with her employers, which, upon her arrival, they expressed to be without prejudice. At the meeting the employers made an offer to terminate her employment; she did not accept. She brought proceedings complaining of sex discrimination, unequal pay and victimisation, and a dispute arose as to whether the contents of the meeting expressed to be without prejudice could be referred to. The tribunal found that it could, and Cox J giving judgment of the EAT found that decision to be without error, (at paragraphs 30–31):

> It is unrealistic in my judgment to refer to the parties as expressly agreeing at this meeting to speak without prejudice, given the unequal relationship of the parties, the vulnerable position of the applicant in such a meeting as this, and the fact that the suggestion was made by the respondents only once that meeting had begun.
>
> The chairman was not, therefore, obliged on the material before him to conclude that by the time of the meeting on 7 January there was an extant dispute between the parties *as to termination* and that the employer's statements were made in a genuine attempt at compromise of that dispute.' [emphasis added]

44   *Cutts v Head* [1984] Ch 290, CA.
45   [1993] ICR 1, EAT.
46   [2004] IRLR 508, EAT.

10.41 Usually correspondence which is intended to constitute an offer to compromise an extant dispute is headed 'without prejudice'. However, the presence or absence of these words is not conclusive. Material can be excluded if it forms part of a series of negotiations, some of which are properly headed 'without prejudice' and some are not.[47] In *Catterall*[48] the EAT held that an exception could be made to the rule excluding the without prejudice material only if excluding it would allow a dishonest case to be advanced.

10.42 On the other hand, just because a letter is headed 'without prejudice' does not mean to say it will be privileged; it will be the contents of the letter which matter. If these are written with a view to settlement, the communication will be privileged; if not, then the fact that it is so labelled will do nothing to create a privilege where none exists.[49]

Communications with ACAS conciliation officers

10.43 In tribunal proceedings, 'without prejudice privilege' extends to communications between a party and an Advisory, Conciliation and Arbitration Service (ACAS) conciliation officer unless the privilege is expressly waived by the party communicating with the conciliation officer.[50]

Medical reports

10.44 Medical reports will often be confidential documents. It is even possible that a claimant might be the subject of the report in question, but has never seen it before the tribunal proceedings and may be surprised and even distressed by its contents. Such considerations, however, should not outweigh the need to order disclosure and inspection to the claimant in an appropriate case.[51] Safeguards may, however, be employed, such as covering up irrelevant parts of the report or limiting disclosure to legal advisers.[52] Even where disclosure could be detrimental to a party's mental health, this

---

47 *South Shropshire DC v Amos* [1986] 1 WLR 1271, CA.
48 *Independent Research Services Ltd v Catterall* [1993] ICR 1, EAT.
49 *Chocoladefabriken Lindt & Sprungli AG v Nestle Co Ltd* [1978] RPC 287, Ch D.
50 Employment Tribunals Act (ETA) 1996 s18(7) and *M & W Grazebrook Ltd v Wallens* [1973] ICR 256; [1973] IRLR 139, NIRC.
51 *McIvor v Southern Health & Social Services Board* [1978] 1 WLR 757; [1978] 2 All ER 625, HL.
52 *Department of Health and Social Security v Sloan* [1981] ICR 313, EAT.

consideration may be outweighed by the need to ensure that he or she is not prejudiced in presenting his or her case.[53]

10.45　　Disclosure of medical reports obtained by an employer will rarely be refused in a case where the reason given for the claimant's dismissal is incapability due to ill-health,[54] or where an issue to be determined is whether a person is disabled within the definition of the Disability Discrimination Act 1995.

10.46　　Arguments that a person's right to privacy and family life under article 8 of the European Convention on Human Rights means that he or she should not therefore be obliged to undergo a medical examination or disclose his or her medical records even where he or she is claiming damages for personal injuries,[55] have received short shrift from the tribunal. This was seen in *De Keyser v Wilson*[56] where Lindsay P stated that a request for a medical report could not give rise to any actionable breach of article 8. Just as courts in personal injury cases may stay proceedings indefinitely in the event of a party refusing to give permission to disclosure of his or her medical records, employment tribunals too have this option open to them. However, *De Keyser* stopped short of considering whether there would be a breach of article 8 if there was a request for confidential medical records, limiting itself to the issue of requiring a person to attend a medical examination, in circumstances where the doctor carrying out the examination would be bound by conventional medical confidence.

Medical Reports Act 1988

10.47　This Act gives an employee a statutory right to access medical reports prepared for employment purposes by a medical practitioner with responsibility for the clinical care of the employee, that is, the employee's own general practitioner or hospital doctor or consultant or the company's doctor where the employee has been under his or her care and so the report is not the result of a one-off examination.

10.48　　The Act also protects the employee in the normal course of his or her employment as it places restrictions on the obtaining of medical information by the employer from the employee's own adviser.

53　*Department of Health and Social Security v Sloan (No 2)* (unreported) EAT 342/81.
54　*Ford Motor Co Ltd v Nawaz* [1987] ICR 434; [1987] IRLR 163, EAT.
55　See *Sherrif v Klyne Tugs* [1999] IRLR 418, CA.
56　[2001] IRLR 324, EAT.

Waiver of privilege

10.49 The privilege which attaches to certain documents can be lost if the party who could claim it chooses to 'waive' that protection. Where this occurs, the document becomes as any other and can no longer be claimed to be 'privileged' from disclosure or production.

10.50 In most cases, the privilege will be the property of the client and not the lawyer or other adviser; consequently, only the client can waive the privilege which attaches to a particular document. A lawyer or adviser can, however, waive privilege on his or her client's behalf. In the case of 'without prejudice' communications, the privilege belongs to both parties to the document and it can only be waived by them jointly; it is not capable of unilateral waiver.[57]

10.51 Diplomatic privilege can only be waived by the state to whom it belongs or by the ambassador on behalf of that state.[58]

10.52 In High Court and county court proceedings, a formal list is used for disclosure, which must accord with CPR 31.10. Documents which are privileged must be identified as such. While there is no standard form of list in tribunal proceedings, caution must still be taken not to list as available for inspection those documents in respect of which privilege may be claimed.

10.53 Privilege may be lost by reference to the document concerned during the course of a hearing. This may occur by the party owning the privilege giving evidence with reference to that document or by the party's representative mentioning it in the course of speeches or in questioning a witness. If it is not intended for privilege to be waived, then the party wishing to claim it should be careful not to rely on the document during the course of the proceedings.

Mistaken disclosure

10.54 When a privileged document is mistakenly included in a list of documents on disclosure, the privilege is not necessarily to be taken as having been 'waived': in such circumstances the party wishing to claim privilege should seek as soon as practicable to rectify the mistake by amending the list of documents. If, however, the other party is allowed to inspect the document concerned or is even supplied with a copy, it may be far more difficult subsequently to seek

---

57 *Walker v Wilsher* (1889) 23 QBD 335, CA.
58 *R v Madan* [1961] 2 QB 1, CA.

to assert privilege in respect of it. In such circumstances, the party wishing to claim privilege should seek to rectify the situation as soon as possible by notifying the other side of the mistake which has occurred and identifying the document as one in respect of which privilege is claimed. Whether or not privilege will still attach to the document will depend on the circumstances of the disclosure and the conduct of the parties. If the party to whom the document has been disclosed consciously took advantage of the opponent's mistake to obtain a copy, the tribunal may be persuaded to rectify that mistake so that the privilege may be reclaimed.[59]

Partly privileged documents

10.55   A party claiming privilege in respect of a document will not be permitted to rely on parts of that document on a self-selected basis.[60] Just as with other documents, a party is under a duty not to give partial disclosure:

> Where a party is deploying in court material which would otherwise be privileged, the opposite party and the court must have an opportunity of satisfying themselves that what the party has chosen to release from privilege represents the whole of the material relevant to the issue in question. To allow an individual item to be plucked out of context would be to risk an injustice through its real weight or meaning being misunderstood.[61]

10.56   Where a document deals with more than just one subject matter and privilege is claimed in respect of one distinct part, then it will be possible to disclose the other part or parts of the document without having been taken to have waived privilege in respect of the whole.[62] If the privileged part of the document is not so self-contained, however, part disclosure may be taken to be a waiver of the whole.

10.57   If there is any doubt, no part of the document should be disclosed but the guidance of the tribunal should be sought at an interim stage. If the tribunal then orders that part of the document can be

---

59 *Derby & Co Ltd v Weldon (No 8)* [1991] 1 WLR 73, CA.
60 See *C J O'Shea Construction Ltd v Bassi* [1998] ICR 1130, EAT.
61 *Nea Karteria Maritime Co Ltd v Atlantic and Great Lakes Steamship Corp* [1981] Com LR 139, QBD per Mustill J.
62 *Great Atlantic Insurance Co v Home Insurance Co* [1981] 1 WLR 529, CA.

edited out or 'redacted', there can be no doubt but that the party claiming the privilege has not thereby waived its right to protection from disclosure of the concealed part.

Documents from third parties

10.58 If disclosure is desired from another person who is not a party to the proceedings, and who is not prepared to produce the document(s) in question voluntarily, the tribunal is given the power by 2004 Rules r10(2)(c), either on the application of a party or of its own motion, to order the attendance of any person at an appointed time and place and to require that person 'to produce any document'.[63]

10.59 Such an order may be required in a number of cases, for example, cases involving a transfer of an undertaking where the previous employer (the transferor) or the receiver is reluctant to release certain documents on a voluntary basis.

10.60 Furthermore, as the tribunal's power is not limited merely to requiring a non-party to attend before a hearing of the tribunal, the order made can require the person concerned to produce the document before any substantive hearing in the case. This may be the best means of securing sight of the document before a full hearing, giving all parties prior knowledge of its contents and thus time to prepare their respective cases properly in the light of this, without the need to adjourn a full hearing.

10.61 In considering whether to order production of documents by someone who is not a party to the proceedings, the tribunal will apply the same tests of relevance and necessity as already outlined above. Furthermore, the person subject to such an order will also be able to rely on privilege from production in the circumstances already set out in this chapter. It should also be borne in mind that non-parties can only be ordered to attend and produce documents if they are present within Great Britain.

10.62 Any person who fails, without reasonable excuse, to comply with an order to attend and produce documents is liable on summary conviction to a fine not exceeding level 3 on the standard scale.[64]

---

63 See also CPR Part 31.17.
64 ETA 1996 s7(4).

Oppressive requests

10.63   In considering whether or not to order disclosure and inspection of documents, tribunals will also bear in mind the extent of the demand being made on the party who will have to produce the documents in question. This is particularly so given the overriding objective which requires the examination of proportionality.[65] Usually the respondent will hold most of the relevant documentation and where the evidence sought by the claimant relates (as it may in a discrimination or equal pay case) to a large number of people or a period of many years, the respondent may well have grounds for claiming that an order for full disclosure would be oppressive. In such a case, the order made may be limited to selective disclosure, as in *Perera v Civil Service Commission*,[66] where the application for disclosure would have involved the disclosure of documents relating to some 1,600 people.

10.64   Much will depend on the particular circumstances of the case and tribunals will be prepared to order quite wide-scale disclosure where necessary to determine the issues which arise in a particular case. In *Selvarajan v Inner London Education Authority*[67] the EAT held, in a race discrimination case, that documents which had come into existence over a period of some 15 years before the Race Relations Act 1976 would be the subject of an order for disclosure as they could be logically probative of subsequent discrimination.

10.65   Where an application is given for selective disclosure in such cases, it is always open to the tribunal to reconsider the matter subsequently and make a fuller order if appropriate. The proper course of action for the tribunal is first to isolate the issues to which disclosure is relevant and then make orders for disclosure which address those issues if necessary. If it subsequently turns out that the issues are broader than first appeared, or if further disclosure is required to meet those issues, this can be reconsidered by the tribunal later in the proceedings, as in *Rolls Royce Motor Cars Ltd v Mair and others*,[68] a case involving some 150 claims of unfair dismissal in a large-scale redundancy exercise over various divisions of the employing company.

---

65   See Employment Tribunals (Constitution and Rules of Procedure) Regulations 2004 (2004 Regs) reg 3(2)(b).
66   [1980] ICR 699; [1980] IRLR 233, EAT.
67   [1980] IRLR 313, EAT.
68   (unreported) EAT 794/92.

10.66 It has also been held that there is no general principle whereby claimants are entitled to gain disclosure of appraisal scores in a redundancy selection exercise.[69]

Equal pay and discrimination cases

10.67 In cases claiming equal pay, documentary evidence of previous wage-bargaining or of the background to a collective agreement may well be relevant and necessary to a determination of the issues between the parties, even though it requires consideration of matters which now appear to be ancient history. Disclosure may be sought to assist the claimant in identifying an appropriate comparator, although there should be some evidence that a prima facie case is made out so the application can be shown to be more than a mere fishing expedition.[70]

10.68 Where a claimant alleges discrimination, very often that claim will depend on documentary evidence relating to the treatment of other employees, including statistical and monitoring information. Guidance was given on the approach which should be taken in respect of disclosure in such proceedings in *West Midlands Passenger Transport Executive v Singh*.[71] In that case, the Court of Appeal held that, in determining whether information sought in a discrimination case was relevant, the special features of discrimination proceedings should be borne in mind, that is:

- The document(s) in question need not conclusively prove that the employer has discriminated; for the purposes of the disclosure application it need only be established that the document(s) *may tend to prove* that such discrimination has taken place.
- Direct discrimination means that the complainant has not been assessed according to individual merit but has been treated less favourably as a member of a particular group. Statistical information may establish a discernible pattern in the treatment of that particular group (for example, under-representation in certain jobs, lack of promotion) which may in turn give rise to an inference of discrimination against members of the group.

---

69 See *Eaton Ltd v King* [1995] IRLR 75, EAT, and *British Aerospace plc v Green and Others* [1995] IRLR 433, CA; however, a more generous view was taken in *FDR Ltd v Holloway* [1995] IRLR 400, EAT.
70 See *Clwyd CC v Leverton* [1985] IRLR 197, EAT.
71 [1988] ICR 614; [1988] IRLR 186, CA.

- If a practice is being operated against a group, then, in the absence of a satisfactory explanation, it will be reasonable to infer that the complainant, as a member of that group, has been treated less favourably on the grounds of race or sex.
- Evidence of discrimination against a group in relation to promotion may be more persuasive evidence of discrimination in the particular case than previous treatment of the claimant, which may be indicative of personal factors peculiar to the claimant.
- As suitability of candidates can rarely be measured solely by objective means but will generally involve subjective judgments, evidence relating to the success or failure of members of a particular group may indicate that the real reason for failure is a conscious or unconscious discriminatory attitude which involves stereotyped assumptions about members of that group.
- As employers are permitted to adduce evidence demonstrating that in practice they operate a policy of non-discrimination, the employee must be entitled to seek evidence to the contrary.

10.69   *West Midlands Passenger Transport Executive v Singh* involved allegations of race discrimination, but the principles set out by the Court of Appeal apply to complaints of discrimination generally.[72]

10.70   As disclosure in discrimination cases may include applications and assessments in relation to other candidates or employees, questions of confidentiality might well arise. Often these can be resolved by covering up references which name or otherwise identify the particular individual, but this should not be at the expense of obtaining the necessary information from the document, that is, relating to the sex or race and to the qualifications and experience of the person concerned.

---

72 These guidelines are now less relevant due to the reversal of the burden of proof in sex, race and disability discrimination cases, given that once a prima facie case of discrimination is raised it is for the respondent to show a non-discriminatory reason, and to do this it is likely disclosure will be volunteered.

Checklist: Disclosure

- Before making an application to the tribunal, ask the other side for voluntary disclosure of documents: if there are likely to be equal quantities of documents on both sides, propose mutual exchange of copy documents; if the other side holds the bulk of the documentation, be prepared to pay the reasonable photocopying charges for the documents to be provided in full or seek inspection so that copies of the actual documents (or parts) required can be sought specifically.
- If you are aware of the existence (or likely existence) of certain documents, be specific in your request. If you are unsure as to the documentation in the other side's possession, ask more generally for disclosure of documents relevant to the issues in the case. In any event, it is often useful to add a 'catch-all' request for all relevant documents: however certain you are as to the existence of particular documents, you are unlikely to have full knowledge of all documentation in the other side's possession.
- If necessary, make the appropriate application to the tribunal for disclosure of the documents, making the basis for the request clear and indicating that you have already sought voluntary disclosure but without success.
- If you are not satisfied with the disclosure given, keep the tribunal informed, making clear your reasons for dissatisfaction.
- If an order for disclosure has been made against you in your absence with which you are unhappy, apply to the tribunal as soon as possible (and certainly within the time period specified) for that order to be varied. If you feel it would assist, ask at the same time for an oral hearing on the question.
- When considering the documents you have to disclose, bear in mind the protection offered by the principles relating to confidentiality and privilege. Be careful not to waive privilege unless that is what you really want.
- If you realise that you have included a privileged document in a list sent to the other side without indicating that privilege is claimed, immediately amend that list to make the claim clear.
- If a privileged document has actually been sent to the other side by mistake, immediately seek the return of that document, making it clear that privilege is claimed in respect of the document concerned.

- If questions of confidentiality or privilege arise in relation to *part* of a document, consider whether it is possible to reach agreement with the other side on a means of presenting that document without disclosure of the confidential or privileged part. If you do reach agreement, make it clear that disclosure is being given on the basis of that agreement and that you do not waive privilege in respect of the document as a whole. If agreement cannot be reached and if in doubt as to the severability of that part of the document which you regard as privileged, do not disclose the document in part but refer the dispute to the tribunal.
- If a person who is not a party to the tribunal proceedings has relevant documents and is unwilling to give these up voluntarily, apply for an order for that person to attend and produce them.
- If at all possible, seek to 'agree' a bundle of documents for use before the tribunal. If agreement cannot be reached in relation to particular documents, put the rest into an agreed bundle and deal with the issues relating to the disputed documents at an interim hearing or as a preliminary issue or at some other appropriate time at the substantive hearing.

Pre-hearing review

Introduction

11.1   Pre-hearing reviews are conducted by a chairman sitting alone, and are generally held in public. At such a hearing a chairman may:[1]

(a) determine any interim or preliminary matter relating to the proceedings;
(b) issue any order in accordance with rule 10 or do anything else which may be done at a case management discussion;
(c) order that a deposit be paid in accordance with rule 20 without hearing evidence;
(d) consider any oral or written representations or evidence;
(e) deal with an application for interim relief made under section 161 of TULR(C)A or section 128 of the Employment Rights Act (see chapter 21).

11.2   According to 2004 Rules r18(3) pre-hearing reviews are to be conducted by a full tribunal if a party makes a request that it be heard by a full tribunal rather than a chairman sitting alone, such a request to be made not less than 10 days before the date of the hearing and in writing; or if a chairman considers that one or more substantive issues of fact are likely to be determined at the pre-hearing review, that it would be desirable for the pre-hearing review to be conducted by a tribunal, and he has issued an order that the hearing be conducted by a full tribunal.

11.3   It is made plain that notwithstanding the preliminary or interim nature of a pre-hearing review, a chairman (or the tribunal) may give judgment on any preliminary issue of substance relating to the proceedings. The following judgments or orders may be made at a pre-hearing review:[2]

(a) as to the entitlement of any party to bring or contest particular proceedings;
(b) striking out or amending all or part of any claim or response on the grounds that it is scandalous, or vexatious or has no reasonable prospects of success;
(c) striking out any claim or response (or part of one) on the grounds that the manner in which the proceedings have been conducted by or on behalf of the claimant or respondent (as the case may be) has been scandalous, unreasonable or vexatious;

---

1   Employment Tribunals Rules of Procedure 2004 (2004 Rules) r18(2), contained in Employment Tribunals (Constitution and Rules of Procedure) Regulations 2004 SI No 1861 Sch 1. See rule 18(2).
2   2004 Rules r18(7).

(d) striking out a claim which has not been actively pursued;

(e) striking out a claim or response (or part of one) for non-compliance with an order or practice direction;

(f) striking out a claim where the chairman or tribunal considers that it is no longer possible to have a fair Hearing in those proceedings;

(g) making a restricted reporting order (subject to rule 50).

11.4   Before making any such judgment or order, notice must be sent to the party against whom it is proposed to make the order, (or the party must be given an opportunity to give reasons orally) giving him or her the opportunity to give reasons as to why the order ought not to be made.[3] If a party does not request a pre-hearing review when told of the proposed order, it may be made in the absence of the parties.

11.5   Under 2004 Rules r30(1), reasons must be given for judgments, and may be given for orders. If a request is made before or at the time the order is made, reasons must be given.

Preliminary hearing on jurisdiction

11.6   Rule 18(2)(a) of the 2004 Rules is pre-eminently designed for issues of jurisdiction, for example, to determine whether a claim is brought within the relevant limitation period, or if not, if the time limit ought to be extended. If the claim is out of time and there is no power to extend the time limit, the matter may be dealt with by the tribunal refusing to accept the claim.[4] Otherwise the rule 18 pre-hearing review is available. At first sight, a dispute about whether a respondent is properly joined in a TUPE[5] case might be one about the entitlement of a party to contest proceedings. But here it would be necessary for the tribunal to make findings of fact clearly overlapping with the task of the tribunal hearing the substantive claim. It is for this reason that the EAT and the Court of Appeal have been keen to restrict the determination of preliminary points in employment law, reflecting the warnings against these procedures given in *Allen v Gulf Oil Refining Ltd*.[6] In *Secretary of State for Education v Birchall*[7] Mummery J said:

---

3   2004 Rules r19.

4   2004 Rules r3(2).

5   Transfer of Undertakings (Protection of Employment) Regulations 1981 SI No 1794.

6   [1981] AC 1001, HL: see *Munir v Jang Publications Ltd* [1989] ICR 1; [1989] IRLR 224, CA; *Post Office Counters Ltd v Malik* [1991] ICR 355.

7   [1994] IRLR 630, EAT.

> . . . there are . . . dangers in isolating an issue from the main dispute and ordering it to be determined as a preliminary point on the basis of assumed facts. It is often quicker and cheaper to find all the facts first and then to resolve the issues.

11.7 That statement arose in a case where issues of race discrimination, normal retirement age and fixed-term contracts were all raised. The wisdom of this approach can be seen, for example in constructive dismissal cases, where the entitlement of an employee to bring a claim depends on them proving a dismissal (and therefore that the tribunal has jurisdiction), but it is frequently counter-productive to hear evidence relating to a dismissal without consideration of all of the surrounding facts.

11.8 Sometimes preliminary points are taken to the highest level before the facts have been determined, only to frustrate or exhaust one of the parties. Preliminary points were taken to the House of Lords in, for example, *Barclays Bank plc v Kapur*,[8] where it was held that failure by the bank to give pension credit for previous service in East Africa was a continuing act and the claim was not time-barred. On trial of the merits of the claim, however, the EAT and Court of Appeal overturned the tribunal's finding that the action was based on race discrimination,[9] thus rendering pointless the findings in the preliminary hearings. Generally the tribunal will be unwilling to determine a discrimination claim as a preliminary issue under the pre-hearing review, since discrimination cases should go to a full hearing: *Khan v Trident Safeguards*.[10]

Order to pay a deposit

11.9 Pursuant to 2004 Rules r20, at a pre-hearing review if a chairman considers that the contentions put forward by any party in relation to a matter required to be determined by a tribunal have little prospect of success but are nevertheless arguable, the chairman may make an order against that party requiring them to pay a deposit. This requires the party to pay a deposit of an amount not exceeding £500 as a condition of being permitted to continue to take part in the proceedings relating to that matter. Before making the order, the tribunal

---

8 [1991] ICR 208; [1991] IRLR 136, HL.
9 [1995] IRLR 87, CA.
10 [2004] EWCA Civ 624; (2004) *Times* 28 May.

must take reasonable steps to ascertain the ability of the party to comply with such an order, and account has to be taken of any information so ascertained in determining the amount of the deposit.[11] A form is sent out by the tribunal requesting information as to means.

11.10   Payment must be made within the period of 21 days of the day on which the document recording the making of the order is sent, or within such further period, not exceeding 14 days, as the chairman may allow in light of representations made by that party within the period of 21 days. In default of payment the chairman *shall* (note mandatory language) strike out the claim or response (or the part to which the order relates). This is not a matter of discretion, so when an order has been made, it is a condition for continuing with the case, or with that part of the case covered by the order, that the deposit is paid.[12]

11.11   The deposit is refundable in full as a general rule.[13] It is refundable on withdrawal of the claim, since proceedings would then be at an end. (A costs application may however be made by the other party; see chapter 18.) The rules do not provide this, but the deposit ought to be refundable as soon as the party agrees to take out the offending part of the claim or response; or if at the pre-hearing review the tribunal in its discretion, could decline to order the deposit to be made if the document is amended.

11.12   The deposit is also refundable at the end of the proceedings *unless* 2004 Rules r47 applies. Rule 47 provides that when:

(a) a party has been ordered to pay a deposit, and
(b) in relation to that matter the tribunal or chairman has found against the party, and
(c) no award of costs or preparation time arising out of the proceedings on the matter,

the tribunal or chairman shall consider whether to make a costs or preparation time order on the grounds that he conducted the proceedings unreasonably in persisting in having the matter determined; but the tribunal or chairman shall not make a costs or preparation time order on that ground unless it has considered the document recording the order under rule 20 and is of the opinion that the grounds which caused the tribunal or chairman to find against the

---

11   2004 Rules r20(2).
12   2004 Rules r20(4).
13   2004 Rules r20(5).

party in its judgment were substantially the same as the grounds recorded in that document for considering that the contentions of the party had little reasonable prospect of success.

Costs (expenses) at the main hearing after a deposit order

11.13 As set out above, in a case where a deposit has been ordered, even if no order of costs or preparation time is made at the substantive r26 Hearing, the tribunal must still go on to consider whether to award costs or preparation time against the party 'on the ground that he conducted the proceedings relating to the matter unreasonably in persisting in having the matter determined by a tribunal'.[14] To determine whether a party behaved unreasonably by proceeding with an issue in relation to which a deposit had to be paid, the tribunal will consider the reasons set out by the first tribunal when it ordered a deposit, and decide whether the reasons for subsequently failing in relation to that issue were 'substantially the same'. If the reasons were substantially the same, a costs order 'shall be considered' but the tribunal still has discretion whether or not to make the order.

11.14 If a costs or preparation time order is made against a party who has paid a deposit, (whether or not the costs order is in relation to the same issue that the deposit was made), the deposit is paid in part or full settlement.[15]

11.15 The issue of costs/preparation time is in the discretion of the second tribunal and it does not follow automatically because a deposit order has been made, and an adverse finding has been reached for substantially the same reasons at the full hearing, that costs or preparation time must be awarded. If they are, the deposit is set off against and used to discharge any award of costs made by the tribunal, whether for the matters covered by the deposit or otherwise.[16] If the amount of the deposit exceeds the amount of the costs or preparation time order the balance shall be refunded to the party who paid it.

11.16 At the substantive hearing, no member of the tribunal who sat on the pre-hearing review may take part,[17] even if no order was made (it being sufficient that the issue was 'considered'). There is no rule

14 2004 Rules r47(1).
15 2004 Rules r47(2).
16 2004 Rules r49.
17 2004 Rules r18(9).

saying that the second tribunal should not know and have read the reasons of the first tribunal if it made an order, but in practice the decision recording the making of the order or refusing to make one is kept in a sealed envelope on the file and not read until the end of the substantive hearing.

Striking out

11.17   The Court of Appeal has held that the tribunal's general powers of case management do not however include any power to strike out cases in situations not covered by the rules.[18] 2004 Rules r18(8) makes it clear that the tribunal has the power to strike out only on the grounds stated in 2004 Rules r18(7)(b) to (f) (set out above at para 11.3). The ground at rule 18(7)(e) of non-compliance with an order must include not paying a deposit when it has been ordered as rule 20(4) states that a tribunal '*shall*' strike out the claim or response (or the part of it to which an order relates) if there has been non-payment of a deposit within 21 days of being sent the order, or within such further period, not exceeding 14 days, as the chairman may allow in the light of representations made by that party within the period of 21 days.

Claims or responses which are scandalous, vexatious or have no reasonable prospect of success, or which have been conducted in a scandalous, unreasonable or vexatious manner

11.18   At any stage of the proceedings, a tribunal may order that all or part of any claim or response be struck out or amended on the basis that it is 'scandalous or vexatious or has no reasonable prospect of success'.[19] Before exercising its power to strike out, the tribunal must either give the party against whom such an order is proposed the opportunity to give reasons orally why it should not be made or send notice to that

---

18   See *Care First Partnership Ltd v Roffey and others* [2001] IRLR 85, CA.
19   2004 Rules r18(7)(a), or that the manner in which proceedings have been conducted by or on behalf of the claimant or respondent has been 'scandalous, unreasonable or vexatious', 2004 Rules r18(7)(c).

party giving him or her an opportunity to give reasons orally or in writing.[20]

11.19   When considering whether the claim or response or a party's conduct offends this rule, the tribunal must adopt the same approach towards those expressions as it would towards an application for costs.[21] (See paras 18.12–18.19.) 'Vexatious' includes matters which constitute an abuse of process; a term which may be widely construed and is not limited to dishonest claims or defences, or to conduct which is in bad faith. In *Ashmore v British Coal Corporation*[22] Stuart-Smith LJ expressed the following view:

> A litigant has a right to have his claim litigated, provided it is not . . . vexatious or an abuse of the process. What may constitute such conduct must depend on all the circumstances of the case; the categories are not closed and considerations of public policy and the interests of justice may be very material.

11.20   In *Ashmore*, the originating application was struck out as an abuse of process; the claimant was one of 1,500 women canteen workers who brought equal pay claims against British Coal. The claims had been combined and 14 sample cases selected for consideration. While these were expressly stated not to be 'test' cases, all the other claims had been stayed. When the sample cases were determined against the claimants, Ms Ashmore applied to have the stay on her case lifted. British Coal's application to have her claim struck out on the ground that it was vexatious was upheld by the tribunal. It was held to be an abuse of the process to seek to relitigate an issue which had already been fully litigated in the sample cases which were representative of all the other claims. There were no material differences between the sample cases and hers, and her union (the Union of Democratic Mineworkers) had been present when the lead cases had been selected, yet had made no representations against this procedure.

11.21   In an application to strike out a claim on grounds similar to those in *Ashmore*, a prima facie burden lies with the party making the application. There is an entitlement to relitigate the same issues between different parties unless it can be shown that there are special reasons (such as those applying in *Ashmore*) which would render it an abuse of process.[23]

---

20 2004 Rules r19(1).
21 See *HM Prison Service v Dolby* [2003] IRLR 694.
22 [1990] ICR 485; IRLR 283, CA.
23 *Department of Education and Science v Taylor and Others* [1992] IRLR 308, QBD.

11.22   Tribunals have historically rarely exercised the power to strike out proceedings, even where there seems to be little left for the claimant to gain by pursuing a complaint. In *Telephone Information Services Ltd v Wilkinson*,[24] an employer had made an offer to pay to an employee bringing a claim of unfair dismissal the maximum statutory compensation which could be awarded for this kind of claim. The employee was not prepared, however, to withdraw the claim and the Employment Appeal Tribunal (EAT) upheld the tribunal's refusal to strike it out. The employee was entitled to pursue a claim in the expectation that a finding of unfair dismissal might be made regardless of any extra monetary compensation.

11.23   If a claimant withdraws a claim, the tribunal dismisses it, and the claimant then seeks to institute the same complaint within the time limit for commencing proceedings, the tribunal will strike out the second claim if it is wholly misconceived.[25] In these circumstances, however, the appropriate course of action is for the claimant to apply for a review of the tribunal's judgment to dismiss the first application on withdrawal by the claimant. When the remedy of review is still open to the claimant, the EAT has held that it *would* be appropriate to strike out the second application, as in *Acrow (Engineers) Ltd v Hathaway*,[26] a case from which the claimant withdrew on the grounds of ill-health. Claimants must however be aware that if a claim is withdrawn, and then further proceedings commenced, arguments as to whether cause of action estoppel prevents the subsequent proceedings may arise, as in *AKO v Rothschild Asset Management Ltd*.[27] In civil courts a 'discontinuance'[28] does not release or discharge the cause of action. It preserves the right to establish an untried claim on the merits in other proceedings. However, a withdrawal does not preserve such rights. Mummery LJ in *AKO* therefore gave guidance that:

> Unless and until the Employment Tribunal Regulations are amended to deal with this point, it would be advisable for tribunals, on being notified of the withdrawal of an originating application, to ask the applicant for a statement of the circumstances of the decision to withdraw before deciding whether to make an order dismissing the proceedings.

24 [1991] IRLR 148, EAT.
25 *Mulvaney v London Transport Executive* [1981] ICR 351, EAT.
26 [1981] ICR 510, EAT.
27 [2002] EWCA Civ 236; [2002] IRLR 348; see also *Barber v Staffordshire CC* [1996] IRLR 209, CA.
28 CPR Part 38.

11.24 All, or part of the claim or response may be struck out where the manner in which proceedings are conducted, by or on behalf of the claimant or respondent is 'scandalous, unreasonable or vexatious'.[29] When a respondent's representative assaulted the claimant's representative in the tribunal waiting room, this conduct led to the tribunal deciding that the notice of appearance (response) was to be struck out.[30] However, as the EAT made clear in *Bolch v Chipman*[31] while conduct outside a tribunal can be considered to be scandalous, unreasonable or vexatious, it must be conduct relating to the way in which the proceedings have been conducted, and furthermore that not all misbehaviour will automatically lead to a strike out. The tribunal must also determine that a fair trial is no longer possible and that striking out the response is a proportionate penalty. In *Bolch* the behaviour complained of was that the respondent threatened the claimant outside his house.

11.25 Consideration of a representative's conduct in 'conducting' proceedings, can not include consideration of whether a representative was unreasonable in 'bringing' proceedings.[32]

11.26 In *Bennett v Southwark LBC*,[33] the tribunal struck out a claimant's complaints where her representative, having been refused an adjournment said: 'If I were an Oxford educated white barrister with a plummy voice I would not be put in this position'. The tribunal considered that since there were no grounds for finding that the tribunal had been biased, this was 'scandalous conduct' and was also 'vexatious', and the claim was accordingly struck out. However, the Court of Appeal, by a majority, held that the tribunal had erred in striking out the claim.

> . . . the word 'scandalous' is not a synonym for 'shocking'. It embraces two somewhat narrower meanings; the misuse of the privilege of legal process in order to vilify others and giving gratuitous insult to the court in the course of such process. If the conduct of a party's case is shown to have been scandalous, it must also be such that striking out is a proportionate response to it.

Sedley LJ went on, however, to say that:

29 2004 Rules r18(7)(c).
30 *Harmony Healthcare plc v Drewery* (2000) *Independent* 20 November, EAT.
31 [2004] IRLR 140, EAT.
32 *Hosie v North Ayrshire Leisure Ltd* 2 October 2003; IDS 747, EAT.
33 [2002] IRLR 407, CA.

It is not every instance of misuse of the judicial process, albeit properly falling within the description of 'scandalous, frivolous or vexatious', which will be sufficient to justify the premature determination of a claim or of the defence to it. Firm case management may well afford a better solution . . . Our system of justice depends far more than is often realised on a level of courtesy and formality which ensures that hard things can be said without giving insult or offence. There is no reason in this respect to expect a lesser standard of unqualified representatives than is expected of professional lawyers.

The vexatious litigant

11.27   When an individual is persistently and unreasonably vexatious in making applications to the tribunal or in instituting appeals to the EAT, the EAT has the power (on application by the Attorney General or Lord Advocate), under Employment Tribunals Act (ETA) 1996 s33, by way of a restriction of proceedings order, to prevent proceedings by that person being instituted or continued, either in the tribunal or EAT, unless permission is given to do so. Where a restriction of proceedings order is made, the person concerned cannot, without the permission of the EAT, institute or continue proceedings before an employment tribunal or the EAT, or make an application in connection with such proceedings. Unless an order provides that it will cease to have effect at the end of a specified period, it remains in force indefinitely. Examples of where this power has considered include:

- *Attorney General v Wheen*[34] where Mr Wheen was found to have 'habitually and persistently and without any reasonable ground instituted vexatious proceedings in an employment tribunal or before the Appeal Tribunal'. Arguments that the power under ETA 1996 s33 were contrary to the European Convention on Human Rights article 6 right to a fair trial failed, and were said in fact to be 'unarguable'.
- *Attorney General v England*[35] where Mr England, who had brought numerous cases for failure to be appointed, swore an affidavit

34 [2001] IRLR 91, CA.
35 EAT/367/00.

undertaking not to lodge any more proceedings (he was then aged 64) and the parties agreed to a one year stay, at the end of which he would reach an age whereby he would not be entitled to bring such claims in any event.

• *Attorney General v D'Souza*[36] where the EAT confirmed that it is not permitted to examine the merits behind each of the underlying proceedings on which the Attorney General relied in support of the order. Indeed, the underlying proceedings relied upon are not limited to those which are frivolous, vexatious or an abuse of process. Using the words of Lord Bingham, the EAT found that Mr D'Souza 'keeps on and on litigating when earlier litigation has been unsuccessful and when on any rational and objective assessment the time has come to stop'. He is subject to an indefinite restriction of proceedings order.

Failure actively to pursue a claim

11.28 The tribunal has the power, on the application of a respondent or of its own initiative, to strike out a claim if it has not been actively pursued.[37] In exercising its discretion the tribunal will apply the same guidelines as apply under the CPR Part 3.4 and the Practice Direction thereto.[38] The House of Lords in *Birkett v James*[39] distinguished between two types of case; where there has been:

• 'intentional and contumelious' default by the claimant, that is, where the claimant has failed to comply with an order of the tribunal and it has been made clear that the claim would be struck out unless the claimant complied with the order within the time allowed;[40]
• (i) inordinate and inexcusable delay on the part of the claimant or his or her representatives *and* (ii) that delay will give rise to a substantial risk that it is not possible to have a fair trial of the issues in the action or is such as is likely to cause or to have caused serious prejudice to the respondent.

---

36 EAT/0139/04.
37 2004 Rules r18(7)(d).
38 *Evans v Metropolitan Police Authority* [1993] ICR 151; [1992] IRLR 570, CA.
39 [1978] AC 297, HL, and see Arbitration Act 1950 s13A(2).
40 For example under 2004 Rules r13(3).

11.29   In the first type of case, the normal rules for striking out will be followed where a party does not comply with orders or practice directions.[41]

11.30   Before the tribunal strikes out a claim for failing actively to pursue it, the claimant must be given the opportunity to give reasons orally why this order should not be made, or notice must be sent giving an opportunity to give reasons orally or in writing.[42]

41   2004 Rules r18(7)(e).
42   2004 Rules r19(1).

CHAPTER 12

Adjourning, postponing and staying proceedings

Adjournment and postponement

12.1 Under Employment Tribunal Rules of Procedure 2004[1] (2004 Rules) r10(2)(m) a tribunal may order that any hearing may be postponed or adjourned. There is also a specific power under 2004 Rules r40(1) to order costs or expenses to be paid when a party has sought a postponement or an adjournment of a hearing or pre-hearing review. There is a further specific duty to postpone any hearing until after the end of any conciliation period.[2]

12.2 Apart from these specific cases, the tribunal has a wide discretion to postpone or adjourn proceedings (and indeed to regulate its own proceedings: see 2004 Rules r60(1)). The breadth of the discretion was made clear in *Jacobs v Norsalta Ltd*,[3] a case when tribunal proceedings were stayed pending High Court proceedings involving complicated questions of compensation, where Phillips J stated that:

> ... the tribunal has a complete discretion, so long as it exercises it judicially, to postpone or adjourn any case provided there is good, reasonable ground for so doing.

12.3 An application for a postponement or adjournment should generally be made in writing and may lead to an oral hearing. While the tribunal has a very wide discretion; (a) the tribunal should not adjourn or postpone without giving all parties an opportunity to make representations;[4] and (b), an adjournment or postponement should not be granted dependent on payment of costs which have been ordered against a party.[5]

12.4 It is relevant to bear in mind who is making the application, since there are sometimes tactical advantages associated with delay. For example, postponement of a hearing on compensation following a finding on liability against an employer would have the beneficial effect (from the employer's point of view) of delaying the running of interest from an award of compensation. Generally, tribunals will be astute to look carefully at the reasons given in support of the application and to balance these against the possible prejudice to other parties.

1 Contained in Employment Tribunals (Constitution and Rules of Procedure) Regulations 2004 SI No 1861 Sch 1.
2 2004 Rules r22(3).
3 [1977] ICR 189, EAT.
4 *Bowater plc v Charlwood* [1991] ICR 798; [1991] IRLR 340, CA.
5 *Cooper v Weatherwise (Roofing and Walling) Limited* [1993] ICR 81, EAT.

Factors relevant to a decision

12.5   The following factors are relevant to the decision whether or not to grant an application to postpone or adjourn.

Ill-health or unavailability of parties and witnesses

12.6   In order to avoid uncertainty, an application based on the ill-health of a party or a witness should be accompanied by a doctor's certificate. In the case of *Teinaz v Wandsworth LBC*[6] an employment tribunal refused an application to adjourn on the basis of ill-health, despite that application being accompanied by a medical certificate, because it formed the view that the claimant had chosen not to attend, and criticised the adequacy of the medical certificate. However, this decision was overturned by the EAT and the Court of Appeal. Peter Gibson LJ held:

> Although an adjournment is a discretionary matter, some adjournments must be granted if not to do so amounts to a denial of justice. In order to comply with the right to a fair trial under article 6 of the European Convention on Human Rights, a litigant whose presence is needed for the fair trial of a case but who is unable to be present through no fault of his own will usually have to be granted an adjournment, however inconvenient it may be to the tribunal or court and to the other parties. However, the tribunal or court is entitled to be satisfied that the inability of the litigant to be present is genuine, and the onus is on the applicant for an adjournment to prove the need for such adjournment.

12.7   If a tribunal has doubts as to whether the medical evidence supporting such an application is genuine or sufficient, it, according to the Court of Appeal in *Teinaz*, has a discretion to direct that further evidence be promptly provided or to invite the party seeking the adjournment to authorise the legal representatives for the other side to have access to the doctor giving the advice in question. If, however, such further information is sought, and the question about ability to attend the tribunal is not properly answered, the tribunal will be acting appropriately if it then refuses an adjournment and concludes the case in the absence of that party, as in *Andreou v Lord Chancellors Department.*[7]

12.8   Unavailability of a witness, for example by being on holiday

6   [2002] IRLR 721, CA.
7   [2002] IRLR 728, CA.

abroad or working abroad, could also provide grounds for postponing or adjourning. On the other hand, proceedings could commence to some extent without a relevant witness and then adjourn unfinished (part-heard) in order to accommodate the witness's availability.

12.9 A last-minute change of representation might also justify an application. Plainly the interests of justice, as well as the provisions of article 6 of the European Convention on Human Rights, require a party to be represented properly. A sudden change of representation might frustrate this if the new representative was unprepared. On the other hand, the tribunal will need to balance this against the article 6 requirement to provide a fair hearing to all parties, a requirement which might be frustrated by delay.[8] Obviously the reason for any such change of representation at a late stage will be relevant.

12.10 No allowance is made in the rules for difficulties caused to advocates by a case being adjourned (part-heard) to another date when they are booked for another case. This common practical problem could be overcome with sympathetic and realistic exercise of discretion in relisting cases although for barristers, the Code of Conduct dictates that their obligation is to attend the part-heard hearing in preference to any other matter in their diary with which they have not had any dealing.

Staying (or sisting) proceedings in the tribunal

12.11 Under 2004 Rules r10(2)(h) proceedings in the employment tribunal may be put on hold until some other event occurs; the case will be stayed (or sisted in Scotland). The event may, for example, be part of the litigation between the same parties, such as proceedings going on in other jurisdictions.

Proceedings in other cases

12.12 Sometimes a case raises a legal issue which is waiting to be determined in another case by a higher UK court, or the European Court of Justice (ECJ), and this might affect the outcome of a given case. Although it could make sense and save costs to postpone a hearing which might become abortive as a result of the outcome of different proceedings in a different court, the parties and the tribunal have no

8 See *Somjee v United Kingdom* [2002] IRLR 886, ECHR.

control over those other proceedings. The tribunal will wish to consider whether the other case will really determine all relevant issues and whether it might be preferable to proceed to make findings of fact in the case before it in any event. It should not be assumed that the existence of a 'test case' raising similar issues will necessarily result in a general stay of proceedings: each case should be considered individually.

12.13 For example, in *Financial Times v Byrne (No 2)*[9] it was argued that the hearing of a preliminary point on equal pay should be stayed pending the determination by the ECJ of *Enderby v Frenchay Health Authority*.[10] The application was rejected partly because the *Enderby* case would not determine all of the relevant issues in the *Financial Times* case; but also because the claimants in that case had no control over the *Enderby* proceedings, which might have been settled without a hearing, have been further delayed or determined without reference to the issue relevant in the *Financial Times* case.

12.14 An example however, of when tribunals were ordered, by the President of the Employment Tribunals,[11] to stay applications pending the outcome of another case, was seen when ex p *Seymour-Smith*[12] was due to be heard in the ECJ. A possible outcome of the case was that those with one year's service could have been given the right to make a claim for unfair dismissal. Therefore, tribunals adjourned all applications in unfair dismissal cases where claimants had more than one year of service, but less than two (at that time the necessary qualifying service to bring an unfair dismissal claim) unless the case could be determined without reference to the question of qualifying service. In the event, the ECJ did not find the rule that a claimant needed two years' service to be discriminatory at the dates in question.

High Court proceedings

12.15 A tribunal is more likely to stay proceedings if a very similar issue between the same parties is to be determined in the High Court/ Court of Session (or the county/sheriff court) and it is likely to bring about a final conclusion to all or the major issues in the tribunal

---

9 [1992] IRLR 163, EAT (leave to appeal refused by CA).
10 [1994] ICR 112; [1993] IRLR 591.
11 [1998] IRLR 351, EAT.
12 *R v Secretary of State for Employment ex p Seymour-Smith* [1999] 2 AC 554; [1999] All ER (EC) 97; [1999] 3 WLR 460; [1999] ICR 447; [1999] IRLR 253, ECJ, applied [2000] 1 All ER 857; [2000] ICR 244; [2000] IRLR 263, HL.

proceedings. A claimant who claims unfair dismissal and wants to reserve the right to issue proceedings for wrongful dismissal in the High Court, should present an unfair dismissal claim in the usual way, but seek at the same time, a stay of tribunal proceedings.[13] A claimant would generally be well advised to do this if the wrongful dismissal claim is worth more than the limit on contract claims in the tribunal or if he or she is seeking remedies other than damages.[14]

12.16   When there is such a potential overlap between the facts to be determined in the tribunal and those raised in High Court proceedings, it is generally desirable for the same issues to be determined by the High Court rather than by a tribunal[15] – otherwise 'the judge would be put in a strait jacket'.[16] However, it is possible for tribunal hearings to be conducted first, as in *Sajid v Sussex Muslim Society*[17] where an unfair dismissal claim was conducted in the tribunal, and a breach of contract claim withdrawn in light of the limit of £25,000 as recoverable damages. When a breach of contract claim was later commenced in the High Court, it was found not to be in breach of the principle of cause of action estoppel, and the action therefore fell to be considered in the High Court.

12.17   Considerations which might point to waiting until after the High Court case has been decided generally relate to the more stringent procedural requirements of that forum, that is:

- the desirability for strict rules of evidence to be applied;[18]
- the use of more formal statements of case;[19]
- the total amount of damages which may be higher than a tribunal can award;
- complexity of the issues;[20]
- the availability of more stringent rules on disclosure;
- the power to award costs;
- better remedies, and the prospect of delay.[21]

---

13 *Warnock v Scarborough Football Club* [1989] ICR 489, EAT.
14 Employment Tribunals (Extension of Jurisdiction) Orders 1994 SI No 1623 (England and Wales) and SI No 1624 (Scotland) states that the limit for contract claims in tribunals is £25,000.
15 *Green v Hampshire CC* [1979] ICR 861, Ch D.
16 *Automatic Switching Ltd v Brunet* [1986] ICR 542, EAT per Sir R Kilner Brown.
17 [2002] IRLR 113, CA.
18 *Bowater plc v Charlwood* [1991] ICR 798; [1991] IRLR 340, EAT.
19 *Bowater*.
20 *Jacobs v Norsalta* [1977] ICR 189, EAT.
21 *Jacobs v Norsalta*.

If these are not important considerations, there is no reason to stay the tribunal proceedings.

Foreign proceedings

12.18   A postponement was granted pending the imminent issue of High Court proceedings in England coupled with the existence of other actions abroad in *JMCC Holdings Ltd v Conroy.*[22] Again, similarity of issues, together with convenience of location, are matters to be considered.

Criminal proceedings

12.19   In cases involving allegations of dishonesty, such as unfair dismissal for misconduct, and a concurrent prosecution in the Crown Court, it is desirable for tribunal proceedings to be stayed so as to allow complete flexibility for the claimant and their advisers in the criminal trial. Yet in *Bastick v James Lane (Turf Accountants) Ltd*[23] the EAT declined to interfere with a chairman's decision to refuse a stay sought by a claimant charged with theft in circumstances leading to a claim for unfair dismissal. The chairman decided that the issues were not sufficiently similar. Of course, the issues *are* different: whether there was sufficient material before the employer to justify a dismissal, compared with whether the employee committed theft beyond reasonable doubt. There are, however, very strong policy reasons for allowing criminal proceedings to go first. Given the very different tasks of the tribunal and the Crown Court, a claimant should not build up false hopes that an acquittal in the criminal proceedings will mean a finding of unfair dismissal in the tribunal. A very notable difference is of course that the standard of proof used in criminal proceedings is 'beyond reasonable doubt' whereas tribunals examine matters 'on the balance of probabilities'.

12.20   In Scotland, the practice is generally to sist (stay) the hearing of the tribunal application until the resolution of the criminal proceedings.

22 [1990] ICR 179, EAT.
23 [1979] ICR 778, EAT.

Appeal

12.21 There is no obligation on a tribunal to stay (sist) pending an appeal, for example, on a preliminary point or a ruling on procedure against a party (see para 23.39). Similarly, there is no obligation on a tribunal to stay a hearing on remedies pending an appeal by an employer on liability. It may be in the parties' interest to agree to stay further proceedings in order to save costs, but in the absence of agreement, there is no reason why a claimant's case should be held up. A solution might be to agree, subject to appeal, that time for computing interest on any award is deemed to run from the date a compensation hearing would have taken place. This would not, however, safeguard against the potential prejudice caused by delay should issues of fact have to be determined.

Internal procedures

12.22 The tribunal may not accept a claim if there has been a breach of Employment Act 2002 s32 (concerning presentation of grievances to employers),[24] (see paras 3.3–3.15). There is a clear legislative policy of wanting parties to exhaust internal routes before resorting to litigation, but, as set out in paras 3.81–3.86, waiting for the result of internal appeals will generally not be a good excuse for failing to file proceedings in time – proceedings should be issued and a stay sought.

Conciliation

12.23 The 2004 Rules make provision for a set conciliation period; seven weeks for the 'short' or thirteen weeks for the 'standard' period (see 2004 Rules rr21–24; and see paras 13.20–13.36. This period is to give the parties a limited opportunity to reach an ACAS[25] conciliated settlement and hearings will not take place during this period. Quite apart from this set period, the possibility of a settlement through conciliation (whether via internal appeals or otherwise) has long been a ground for exercising discretion in favour of a stay, since it is possible that a favourable result for the claimant would avoid the need to continue tribunal proceedings.

24 2004 Rules r3(2)(c). See chapter 3.
25 Advisory, Conciliation and Arbitration Service.

Costs/expenses on adjournment or postponement

12.24   Once the interests of justice have identified a reason for granting a stay, any resulting disadvantage to the other party can be compensated in costs or, for those not legally represented, expenses (there is no power to make an order for preparation time). There is no requirement that the pejorative terms of 2004 Rules r40(3), 'vexatiously, abusively, disruptively or otherwise unreasonably', etc, should be met with. Rather, 2004 Rules r40(1) is entirely neutral and allows the tribunal to exercise its discretion to award costs or expenses on the application of a party for a postponement or an adjournment without the need to attribute unreasonableness to a party. Costs can be awarded in favour of or against the party applying.

CHAPTER 13

Settlement, conciliation and withdrawal

General considerations

13.1 In tribunal proceedings, as in any litigation, there are often a number of advantages in settling the case before (or during) the full hearing. Settling a case means entering into an agreement with the other side, with both parties being bound by the terms of that agreement without having to have the issues in the case determined by the tribunal.

13.2 Concluding a claim by this means is often advantageous for both parties because:

- agreeing to settle a claim avoids the risk of losing as well as the unpleasantness of a hearing;
- the recoupment provisions[1] do not apply to settlements;
- both parties avoid the costs (expenses) of fighting the case to the end (apart from legal costs. There will generally be costs in preparing for and attending the tribunal, whether in terms of taking time off work or loss of management time);
- while the remedies open to the tribunal are limited by statute, the parties may agree to include in the agreement matters which are outside the tribunal's jurisdiction, such as an agreed form of reference or a confidentiality clause.

13.3 The advantages of resolving tribunal proceedings have long been recognised by parliament and a statutory conciliation procedure is available through the offices of the Advisory, Conciliation and Arbitration Service (ACAS). When a claim has been presented to an employment tribunal, and a party either requests the intervention of a conciliation officer, or that officer considers there to be a reasonable prospect of success in taking action, the officer has a duty to endeavour to promote a settlement of the proceedings without their being determined by the tribunal.[2]

Withdrawing a claim

13.4 A claimant may simply withdraw all or part of the claim at any time, either orally at a hearing or in writing. In order to withdraw a claim in writing, the claimant must inform the employment tribunal office of

1 Employment Protection (Recoupment of Jobseeker's Allowance and Income Support) Regulations 1996 SI No 2349.
2 Employment Tribunals Act (ETA) 1996 s18

the claim or parts which are to be withdrawn and against which respondents it is being withdrawn.[3]

13.5   The secretary to the tribunal informs the other parties to the proceedings of the withdrawal. Withdrawal takes effect on the date on which the tribunal office receives written notification or the tribunal receives oral notification. When the whole claim is withdrawn, proceedings against the relevant respondent are brought to an end on that date. The Employment Tribunals Rules of Procedure[4] (2004 Rules) specify that the withdrawal of proceedings does not affect proceedings as to costs, preparation time or wasted costs.[5]

13.6   When a claim is withdrawn, a respondent may make an application to have the proceedings against it dismissed. The application must be made in writing to the employment tribunal office within 28 days of the notice of withdrawal being sent to the respondent. The time limit may be extended by a chairman on a just and equitable basis. If the respondent's application is granted and the proceedings are dismissed, the proceedings cannot be continued by the claimant unless the decision to dismiss is reviewed or appealed.[6] There is nothing in the 2004 Rules to indicate the considerations which will be taken into account in determining whether or not to grant such an application. If the claimant intends to withdraw so as to pursue a claim in the civil courts (in effect to discontinue proceedings in the tribunal), an adviser should ensure that the other side and the tribunal are on notice of that fact or there is a considerable risk that the claimant will be prevented by law ('estopped') from pursuing the claim.

Withdrawal on terms

13.7   Settlements in tribunal proceedings are not without risk. Anyone entering into an agreement to settle a case should only do so if they understand and agree to the terms on which the case is to be compromised. The terms of the settlement create a binding contract between the parties which can be enforced in the ordinary courts. Those terms may include an agreement by the employee to waive certain legal rights arising out of the employment relationship. Care

3   2004 Rules r25(1) and (2).
4   Contained in Employment Tribunals (Constitution and Rules of Procedure) Regulations 2004 SI No 1861 Sch 1.
5   See *McPherson v BNP Paribas* [2004] IRLR 558 on the relevance of withdrawal to the making of a costs order.
6   2004 Rules r25(4).

should be taken not to surrender legal rights unintentionally. If it is not intended to compromise any future claims relating, for example, to accidents at work or to pension rights, then the agreement should make this clear. If a settlement includes terms relating to pension rights, then particular care should be taken to ensure that the agreement comes within the terms of the pension scheme.

13.8   Generally speaking, any attempt to contract out of an employee's statutory employment rights will be invalid.[7] An employee can only contract out of the right to bring tribunal proceedings in relation to statutory employment rights by:

- entering into a settlement through ACAS;
- entering into a compromise agreement after having been advised by a suitably qualified (and insured) relevant adviser; or
- entering into an agreement during the course of a hearing before a tribunal which forms the basis of a tribunal's decision by consent.

13.9   These protections do not apply to contract claims arising out of the employment relationship which can be brought in the tribunal. Such claims are founded on common law principles and are treated as they would be in any court: an agreement between the parties can effectively contract out of the right to pursue the complaint in question provided it meets the normal requirements for legally binding contracts at common law, that is:

- there has been a valid offer and acceptance;
- consideration (such as compensation) has been provided for the agreement;
- there is an intention to create legal relations between the parties; and
- a party's consent to the agreement is not rendered void by reason of duress, undue influence, misrepresentation or mistake.

---

7   See Employment Rights Act (ERA) 1996 s203, Sex Discrimination Act (SDA) 1975 s77, Race Relations Act (RRA) 1976 s72, Disability Discrimination Act (DDA) 1995 s9. Trade Union and Labour Relations (Consolidation) Act (TULRCA) 1992 s228, Working Time Regulations (WTR) 1998 reg 35, National Minimum Wage Act (NMWA) 1998 s49, Transnational Information and Consultation of Employees (TICE) Regulations 1999 reg 41, Part-time Workers (Prevention of Less Favourable Treatment) (PTW) Regulations 2000 reg 9, Fixed-term Employees (Prevention of Less Favourable Treatment) (FTE) Regulations 2002 reg 10, Employment Equality (Sexual Orientation) Regulations 2003 Sch 4, Employment Equality (Religion or Belief) Regulations 2003 Sch 4 part I.

Compromising statutory rights

13.10　Employment rights given by statute can be taken away only by statute and the protections provided apply until all questions of liability and remedy have been determined by the tribunal. Therefore, even where the question of liability has been determined and the issue of remedy has been adjourned to another day, an agreement between the parties will be void unless it conforms with one of the methods of compromising a claim provided by statute.[8]

13.11　There are, however, ways in which an employer can circumvent these protective measures, even in relation to the employee's statutory rights. Those acting for employees should not be surprised by the use of such tactical devices (particularly as part of a termination package) which give employers some guarantee against future claims without having to face the obstacles presented by the statutory means of settlement.

13.12　If an agreement is concluded with the employee which does not attempt to exclude the employee's right to go to a tribunal but does provide (for example) for the payment of a sum of money by way of an agreed settlement of all claims (including statutory claims) for compensation, the employee's subsequent claim to a tribunal may enable the employer to argue that the original agreement has been breached by the employee. This would not stop the employee continuing with the claim to the tribunal but may render it inadvisable to do so: he or she may lose the entitlement to receive the money promised under the original agreement. To give the employer greater certainty, this form of agreement may expressly provide that payment of the money is conditional on no legal proceedings (including tribunal proceedings) being commenced in relation to the (for example) dismissal, or for the money (or at least part of it) to be paid only after the relevant time limits for making a claim have expired. This does not breach the statutory provisions against contracting out, as it does not purport to stop the employee going to the tribunal but merely states that they will have to seek compensation via the tribunal and not under the terms of the agreement, if they choose to do so.

13.13　An employer who does not dismiss an employee but who invites him or her to resign on favourable terms may run the risk of a claim in the tribunal for constructive unfair dismissal. In *Billington v*

8　*Courage Take Home Trade Ltd v Keys* [1986] ICR 874; [1986] IRLR 427, EAT.

Michael Hunter & Sons Ltd,[9] an employee who was invited to resign made a claim to the tribunal that she had been constructively unfairly dismissed, arguing that such an invitation amounted to a vote of no confidence in her as an employee. The EAT held this to be a breach of the implied term of mutual trust and confidence but remitted the case to the tribunal to consider whether the employer had 'reasonable and proper cause' for asking the employee to resign.

13.14   Where an employee proceeds with a claim in the tribunal (assuming that no validly executed compromise agreement exists) after accepting a payment at the termination of employment, it is likely that this sum would be deducted from any compensatory award if he or she succeeded in a complaint. The question for the tribunal is whether it would be just and equitable to deduct the sum paid. Clearly if, for example, an employer has sought to put undue pressure on the employee to contract out of his or her rights, it would be difficult to see how that employer could contend that it would not be just and equitable to make any further award. Furthermore, even if the employer agreed to pay a sum equal to the statutory maximum, there is no guarantee that a further sum will not be awarded. The compensatory award is calculated by assessing the employee's loss from the date of the dismissal, less sums received from the employer and by way of mitigation. It is only after this calculation that the statutory ceiling is applied. If the employee's overall loss is very high, the *ex gratia* (voluntary) payment by the employer may do little to offset the compensatory award.

13.15   Sums paid by the employer voluntarily may also be taken to reduce any liability in respect of a redundancy payment or basic award, but only if it can be established that the payment made was clearly meant to represent settlement of this liability.[10] This will depend on the particular circumstances of each case. If a payment is intended to cover any liability for redundancy entitlement or for a basic award in an unfair dismissal claim, this should be made clear. An employer who makes a payment without expressly stating what that money is intended to cover risks having to make a further payment to cover a basic award in any subsequent tribunal proceedings.[11]

13.16   Alternatively, when an employer has already conceded liability (for

---

9   EAT/0578/03.
10 *Chelsea Football Club and Athletic Co Ltd v Heath* [1981] ICR 323; [1981] IRLR 73, EAT.
11 *Boorman v Allmakes Ltd* [1995] IRLR 553, CA.

example, by admitting that the dismissal was unfair) and has made an open offer to pay the maximum sum the tribunal could award pursuing a claim in the tribunal may result in an award of costs (expenses) being made against the employee concerned. Without a concession as to liability, however, a tribunal should not award costs against an employee simply because an open offer has been made of the maximum award possible.[12]

13.17   Thus, while such offers do not purport to restrict the employee's right to bring tribunal proceedings, pursuing a claim is rendered pointless and puts the employee at risk of costs.

Advisory, Conciliation and Arbitration Service

13.18   Advisory, Conciliation and Arbitration Service (ACAS) was established under the Employment Protection Act 1975, expressly to promote the improvement of industrial relations.[13] The secretary of state appoints the members of ACAS after consulting both employers' and workers' organisations.[14] ACAS is organised into regional offices: a list of addresses is set out in appendix D.

13.19   The primary function of ACAS is to conciliate in industrial disputes and the majority of its work falls outside the terms of this book. ACAS does, however, have express duties in individual employment disputes and plays an important role in conciliation in tribunal cases. ACAS also administers the unfair dismissal and flexible working arbitration schemes (see chapter 14).

The role of ACAS in tribunal claims

13.20   Conciliation officers may (and must if asked to do so by a party to a complaint) attempt to conciliate any complaints which could form the basis of a claim to a tribunal. They will only get involved in such cases *before* the presentation of a claim, however, if expressly asked to do so by one of the prospective parties.[15] ACAS cannot be used as a 'rubber-stamp' for agreements entered into between employers and employees.

---

12 *Telephone Information Services v Wilkinson* [1991] IRLR 148, EAT. See also *Kappel v Safeway Stores* [2003] IRLR 753, EAT.
13 See now Trade Unions and Labour Relations (Consolidation) Act (TULRCA) 1992 s209.
14 TULRCA 1992 s248.
15 Employment Tribunals Act (ETA) 1996 s18.

13.21   The July 1990 *ACAS Practice Direction* sets out three conditions which must be met before ACAS will agree to be involved in any conciliation process:

- the employee must have been dismissed, or received notice of dismissal (or ACAS has to be satisfied that the employee believes him or herself to have been constructively dismissed);
- the employee's employment rights must have been infringed; and
- the parties must not have agreed all the terms of the settlement, that is, there must remain some role for the services of ACAS.

13.22   Once a claim has been presented to the relevant regional office of employment tribunals, a conciliation officer is appointed by ACAS for all claims of:[16]

- unfair dismissal or failing to give reasons for dismissal;
- unlawful sex discrimination or breach of an equality clause under the Equal Pay Act (EqPA) 1970;
- unlawful racial discrimination;
- unauthorised deduction of wages;
- failing to make a redundancy payment;
- failing to give an itemised pay statement;
- failing to make a guaranteed payment;
- breach of contract;
- infringement of certain rights under Trade Unions and Labour Relations (Consolidation) Act (TULRCA) 1992;
- unlawful discrimination under the Disability Discrimination Act 1995;
- infringement of the National Minimum Wage Act 1998;
- breach of the Working Time Regulations (WT Regs) 1998;[17]
- breach of the Transnational Information and Consultation of Employees Regulations (TICE Regs) 1999;[18]
- breach of the Part-time Workers (Prevention of Less Favourable Treatment) Regulations (PTW Regs) 2000;[19]
- breach of right to make a flexible working request;
- subjecting an employee to a detriment on any of the grounds set out in ERA 1996 Part V;
- failing to permit time off on any of the grounds set out in ERA 1996 Part VI;

16 As set out in ETA 1996 s18(1).
17 SI No 1833.
18 SI No 3323.
19 SI No 1551.

- breaching an employee's right to suspension on medical grounds;
- breach of the FTE Regs 2002;
- breach of the Employment Equality (Sexual Orientation) Regulations 2003
- breach of the Employment Equality (Religion or Belief) Regulations 2003
- breach of the Merchant Shipping (Working Time: Inland Waterways) Regulations 2003

13.23   When a claim is presented to a tribunal under any of the above provisions, the secretary of the tribunals must send copies of all documents and notices relating to that claim to the conciliation officer concerned.[20] In most cases, the conciliation officer will contact the parties as a matter of course. If no such contact has been made, a party can find out which conciliation officer has been appointed to the case by contacting the relevant ACAS office (see appendix D).

13.24   The conciliation officer appointed to a claim presented to the tribunal under these provisions is under a duty to endeavour to promote a settlement between the parties before the determination of the claim by the tribunal. Under the 2004 Rules, the period of time for which the officer is under such a duty varies depending on the type of claim. A claim will fall into one of three conciliation categories:

- short conciliation period (7 weeks);
- standard conciliation period (13 weeks);
- no fixed conciliation period.

13.25   During a conciliation period, there can be no rule 26 Hearing of the claim, although pre-hearing reviews and case management discussions can take place. If a rule 26 Hearing is fixed to take place during a conciliation period, it must be postponed until after the end of the period.[21] If there is more than one respondent to the claim, there is a conciliation period in relation to each respondent.[22] The conciliation period commences on the date on which the secretary sends a copy of the claim to the respondent.[23]

---

20 2004 Rules r21.
21 2004 Rules r22(3).
22 2004 Rules r22(2).
23 2004 Rules r22(4).

Short conciliation period

13.26 The short conciliation period applies to claims which are deemed to be more straightforward. The list of claims to which this short period applies has been greatly extended from the early proposals, in particular by the inclusion of trade union related claims. It remains to be seen whether in practice conciliation will be achieved within such a short period of time in the majority of cases or a chairman will need to exercise his or her powers to extend the conciliation period into a standard one.[23a] The claims to which the short conciliation period applies are:[24]

- breach of contract;
- failure to pay wages/unauthorised deductions;
- right to a guarantee payment;
- right to time off for public duties;
- right to time off to look for work or arrange training;
- right to remuneration for time off to look for work or arrange training;
- right to time off for antenatal care;
- right to remuneration for time off for antenatal care;
- failure to pay remuneration while suspended for medical reasons;
- failure to pay remuneration while suspended on maternity grounds;
- failure to pay a redundancy payment;
- right not to suffer deductions of unauthorised subscriptions in respect of membership of a trade union;
- right to time off for carrying out trade union duties;
- failure to make payment for time off for carrying out trade union duties;
- right to time off for trade union activities;
- failure to pay remuneration under a protective award made as a result of a failure to consult in a collective redundancy situation;
- failure to pay compensation following failure to inform or consult on the transfer of an undertaking.

No fixed conciliation period

13.27 There is no fixed conciliation period in proceedings which include a discrimination claim, namely claims under the Equal Pay Act 1970,

23a 2004 Rules r22(8) and see also para 13.31 below.
24   2004 Rules r22(5).

Sex Discrimination Act 1975, Race Relations Act 1976, Disability Discrimination Act 1995, Employment Equality (Sexual Orientation) Regulations 2003[25] and the Employment Equality (Religion or Belief) Regulations 2003.[26] Neither is there a conciliation period for a claim of having been subjected to a detriment, dismissed or being selected for redundancy for making a protected disclosure.[27] There is also no fixed conciliation period in national security proceedings.[28]

Standard conciliation period

13.28   The standard conciliation period will apply to claims which do not fall into either of the above categories, for example, unfair dismissal.[29]

13.29   In unfair dismissal cases where the claimant has ceased to be employed by the employer, the conciliation officer has a specific duty to promote the reinstatement or re-engagement of a dismissed employee.[30] This obligation will only arise, however, if appropriate in the circumstances of any particular case. The officer is not under an absolute duty to promote reinstatement or re-engagement if it would clearly be futile to do so.[31] Even after the expiry of the standard conciliation period, there will be an ongoing duty to promote reinstatement or re-engagement whether the conciliation officer exercises his or her powers to promote settlement.

13.30   When a standard conciliation period applies, there will be a two week extension to the thirteen week period if ACAS informs the secretary to that effect prior to the expiry of the thirteen weeks. In order for ACAS to do so, the parties must agree to the extension, a party must have made a proposal for settling the claim which is under consideration and ACAS must consider it probable that settlement will be achieved within the further extended period.[32]

13.31   In a case to which a short conciliation period would apply, a chairman may, on considering the complexity of the proceedings, deem that a standard conciliation period would be more appropriate and make an order to that effect. The secretary must inform the parties and ACAS as soon as reasonably practicable of the making of

---

25   SI No 1661.
26   SI No 1660.
27   ERA 1996 ss 47B, 103A and 105(6A).
28   2004 Rules r22(1).
29   2004 Rules r22(6).
30   ETA 1996 s18(4).
31   *Moore v Duport Furniture Products Ltd* [1982] ICR 84; [1982] IRLR 31, HL.
32   2004 Rules r22(7).

such an order.[33] There appears to be no provision for the parties to object to such an extension although there should be room for objection if desired.

13.32   In particular circumstances, an otherwise fixed conciliation period may terminate on an earlier specified date. The relevant circumstances and the dates on which a conciliation period will terminate are:[34]

- default judgment in relation to liability and remedy has been issued against the relevant respondent (date on which judgment is signed);
- default judgment in relation to liability has been issued against the relevant respondent (14 days after judgment is signed);
- claim or response has been struck out (date on which the judgment to strike out is signed);
- claim is withdrawn (date of receipt of notice of withdrawal by the employment tribunal office);
- either party has informed ACAS in writing that they do not wish to proceed with attempting to conciliate proceedings (date on which ACAS sends notice to the parties and to the tribunal);
- when a settlement has been reached by way of compromise agreement including a compromise agreement to refer proceedings to arbitration (date on which the tribunal receives notice from both parties);
- when a settlement has been reached through a conciliation officer, including a settlement to refer the proceedings to arbitration (date of settlement);
- no response by a relevant respondent has been accepted in the proceedings and no default judgment has been issued against the respondent (14 days after the expiry of the time limit for presenting the response to the secretary).

13.33 When an order is made which re-establishes a respondent's right to respond to the claim, for example, if a default judgment is revoked, and, at the time the order is made, the conciliation period has expired or terminated early, the chairman or tribunal may order that a further conciliation period should apply.[35] If proceedings are stayed (in Scotland, sisted), any conciliation period is suspended. When the stay

---

33 2004 Rules r22(8).
34 2004 Rules r23(1).
35 2004 Rules r23(2).

comes to an end (or the sist is recalled), any unexpired portion of a conciliation period (or a default period of two weeks if greater) takes effect from that date.[36]

13.34 On the expiry or early termination of the fixed conciliation period, the conciliation officer is no longer under a duty to attempt to achieve conciliation of the dispute, but merely has the power to do so. This discretion is exercised by ACAS on the application of its own strict criteria. In discrimination cases to which no fixed conciliation period applies, the conciliation officer has an ongoing duty to seek resolution of the claim.

13.35 If the services of the conciliation officer are utilised, it is worth bearing in mind the following:

- the conciliation officer is independent and does not have the same relationship with a party as, for example, a lawyer or adviser;
- the conciliation officer is not an arbiter of tribunal cases and is not there to judge the merits of the case or to try to review the evidence;
- the conciliation officer will also be talking to the other side and will pass on information given, although he or she cannot be called to give evidence about a matter raised during negotiations if that was properly the subject of privilege and the communicator had not given permission;[37]
- any settlement reached with the help of a conciliation officer is still an agreement between the parties: the conciliation officer is not there to impose terms on the parties or even to recommend a particular settlement.

The effect of an agreement through ACAS

13.36 Before the presentation of a claim or at any point after the commencement of a claim, an agreement through the conciliation officer to forego the right to pursue a claim to the tribunal will be upheld in so far as it relates to the rights set out under ETA 1996 s18(1). However, a claimant will not be prevented from bringing another claim to the tribunal where the agreement does not specifically prevent the possibility of the next claim. An agreement 'in full and final settlement of all claims' will not suffice.[38] In other words, to ensure that the

36 2004 Rules r24.
37 ETA 1996 s18(7).
38 *Livingstone v Hepworth Refractories plc* [1992] ICR 287; [1992] IRLR 63, EAT.

agreement does dispose of all possible employment claims, it should expressly be stated to be in settlement of all claims, whether under ERA 1996, TULRCA 1992, SDA 1975, RRA 1976, DDA 1995, WT Regs 1998, National Minimum Wage Act (NMWA) 1998, TICE Regs 1999, PTW Regs 2000 and Fixed-term Employees (Prevention of Less Favourable Treatment) Regulations (FTE Regs) 2002, Employment Equality (Sexual Orientation) (EESO) Regulations 2003 and Employment Equality (Religion or Belief) (EERB) Regulations 2003 or EU law.

13.37   The words of a general exclusion can debar subsequent claims, provided that such claims were intended by the parties to have been excluded. Parties may even seek to include within the scope of the exclusion claims which do not fall within the jurisdiction of the tribunal, for example, personal injury claims. Unidentified claims, that is, those of which a claimant is ignorant, may be covered by a general exclusion but 'a long and . . . salutary line of authority shows that, in the absence of clear language, the court will be very slow to infer that a party intended to surrender rights and claims of which he was unaware and could not have been aware', per Lord Bingham in *Bank of Credit and Commerce International SA (in compulsory liquidation) v Ali*.[39] This case also serves as a reminder that the scope of general words of a release will depend on the context furnished by the surrounding circumstances in which the release was given (see Lord Nicholls). In that case the claimant was not precluded from pursuing a claim for stigma damages notwithstanding the 'general release' contained within his settlement agreement with BCCI.

13.38   The powers of conciliation officers in assisting in the settlement of tribunal claims have generally been construed liberally and the courts have demonstrated a reluctance to interfere with the actions of conciliation officers providing they have been carried out in good faith.[40]

13.39   Conciliation officers usually record agreements on a Form COT3, although this form does not have to be used for the parties to be bound by the agreement. Indeed, terms agreed in this way may still be binding on the parties even though they have not been reduced to writing at all.[41] Provided the conciliation officer has 'taken action' under ETA 1996 s18, the contract will be binding unless it is expressed to be part of the agreement that it should be recorded in a

39 [2001] UKHL 8; [2001] IRLR 292, HL.
40 *Hennessy v Craigmyle & Co Ltd and ACAS* [1986] ICR 461; [1986] IRLR 300, CA.
41 *Gilbert v Kembridge Fibres Ltd* [1984] ICR 188; [1984] IRLR 52, EAT.

particular document. Once a settlement has been achieved through a conciliation officer, it will be extremely difficult to challenge it later. It would probably require evidence that the conciliation officer acted in bad faith or adopted unfair methods in seeking to achieve a settlement before the agreement could be set aside.[42]

13.40   Any agreement entered into through the conciliation officer on behalf of a party by their adviser or representative will be binding on that party provided the adviser or representative has been held out as having authority to act on that party's behalf and no notice has been given to the contrary. The adviser or representative has ostensible authority to act as the party's agent for these purposes. If, in fact, that authority has not been given, the party will have a claim in the civil courts against the adviser or representative but will still be bound by the agreement apparently entered into on his or her behalf.

13.41   This principle applies to all types of adviser or representative, not just to qualified lawyers: in *Freeman v Sovereign Chicken Ltd*[43] the adviser was a Citizens' Advice (CA) worker who signed a COT3 in full and final settlement of the claimant's claims. The claimant later sought to lodge a further claim, arising from the same facts, but was prevented by law ('estopped') from asserting this because of the compromise agreement. His argument that the CA worker had not had his authority to compromise his claim was not successful, as the CA worker had ostensible authority to sign, and it did not matter that she did not have actual authority. Anyone acting for a party should make sure that they have express authority to enter into a particular agreement, checking that the client has seen the terms of the agreement and approved the wording of the settlement before it is finalised.

Compromise agreements and contracts

13.42   Another means by which parties (or potential parties) to tribunal claims can effectively agree to 'contract out' of their statutory employment rights is by entering into a compromise agreement or contract.[44] The term 'compromise agreement' is used in relation to

---

42   *Slack v Greenham (Plant Hire) Ltd* [1983] ICR 617; [1983] IRLR 271, EAT.
43   [1991] ICR 853; [1991] IRLR 408, EAT.
44   Under ERA 1996 s203(3) and (4), SDA 1975 s77, RRA 1976 s72, TULRCA 1992 s288(2A), DDA 1995 s9(2), WT Regs 1998 reg 35, NMWA 1998 s49, TICE Regs 1999 regs 40 and 41, PTW Regs 2000 reg 9, FTE Regs 2002, reg 10, EESO Regs 2003 Sch 4 and EERB Regs 2003 Sch 4.

claims under ERA 1996, WT Regs 1998, NMWA 1998, TICE Regs 1999. For those under SDA 1975, RRA 1976, TULRCA 1992, DDA 1995, EESO Regs 2003 and EERB Regs 2003 the appropriate term is 'compromise contract': there is no substantive difference between the two. A compromise agreement is narrowly defined and must comply with strict requirements if it is to be effective. The importance of satisfying the strict requirements was seen in *Riverside Health Authority v Chetty*[45] where the tribunal and Employment Appeal Tribunal (EAT) refused to strike out a claim in which the compromise agreement did not meet these requirements.

13.43 As one of the requirements is that the employee has received advice from a 'relevant independent adviser' before entering into the agreement, some claimants (who do not have access to such an adviser) will inevitably fall back on to the services of ACAS.

13.44 The compromise agreement procedure was really intended to assist those parties who knew precisely where they stood and wanted to enter into a binding agreement without subsequent claims in the tribunal. In such cases, ACAS had taken the view that it should not be used merely as a rubber stamp where agreement had already been reached and issued a practice direction in July 1990 to this effect.

13.45 To provide for cases which did not fall within the ACAS conditions, the compromise agreement exception to the prohibition on contracting out was provided by Trade Union Reform and Employment Rights Act 1993 s39.

13.46 Compromise agreements[46] may be made in order to prevent any proceedings being instituted or may relate to cases where proceedings have already been instituted. However, a compromise cannot seek to exclude potential complaints which have not yet arisen on the off chance that they might be raised – so the formula 'in full and final settlement of all claims that the claimant has or may have against the respondent, howsoever arising', should not be used.

13.47 A breach of contract claim brought under the Employment Tribunal (Extension of Jurisdiction) Order 1994[47] can be settled

---

45 EAT 1168/95, (unreported).
46 Relating to potential claims under ERA 1996, SDA 1975, RRA 1976, TULRCA 1992, DDA 1995, WT Regs 1998, NMWA 1998, TICE Regs 1999, PTW Regs 2000, FTE Regs 2002, EESO Regs 2003 and EERB Regs 2003.
47 SI No 1623, see appendix B.

without the use of a compromise agreement.[48] Such agreements are enforceable in the employment tribunal.[49]

Requirements of an effective compromise agreement

13.48   The conditions relating to such agreements are as follows:[50]

- the agreement must be in writing;
- the agreement must relate to the specific complaint;
- the employee must have received independent legal advice from an independent legal adviser (defined below) on the terms and effect of the proposed agreement and in particular its effect on his or her ability to pursue his or her rights before a tribunal;
- there must be in force, when the adviser gives the advice, a contract of insurance or an indemnity provided by the members of a professional body, covering the risk of a claim by the employee in respect of loss arising in consequence of taking the advice;
- the agreement must identify the adviser; and
- the agreement must state that the conditions regulating compromise agreements under the relevant Act are satisfied.[51]

13.49   Advice has to be given by a 'relevant independent adviser'[52] who is:

- a qualified lawyer (solicitor, barrister or advocate, or a person who is an 'authorised advocate' or 'authorised litigator' within the meaning of the Courts and Legal Services Act 1990);
- a trade union officer, employee or member, who is certified by the union as competent to give such advice, or who is authorised to do so on behalf of the union;
- a worker at an advice centre who is certified by the centre as competent to give such advice, or who is authorised to do so on behalf of the centre;
- a Fellow of the Institute of Legal Executives, employed by a solicitors' practice, if that person is supervised when giving advice by a solicitor who has a practising certificate in force.

---

48   See *Carter v Reiner Moritz Associates Ltd* [1997] ICR 881.
49   *Rock-It Cargo Limited v Green* [1997] IRLR 581.
50   See ERA 1996 s203(3).
51   *Lunt v Merseyside TEC Ltd* [1999] ICR 17, EAT – the agreement should specifically set out that the conditions regulating agreements under that statute for each statute relied on.
52   ERA 1996 s203(3A), SDA 1975 s77(4B), RRA 1976 s72(4B), TULRCA 1992 s288(4), DDA 1995 s9(4) and NMWA 1998 s49(5) as amended in all cases by the Compromise Agreements (Description of Person) Order 2004 SI No 754.

13.50 An adviser will not be 'independent', in relation to legal advice given to the employee (set out in ERA 1996 s203(3B)), if:

- the adviser is a lawyer who is acting in the matter for the employer or an associated employer;[53]
- the adviser is from a trade union or advice centre which is the employer, or an associated employer;
- in the case of an advice centre, the employee has to make payment for the advice received;
- in the case of a trade union or advice centre adviser, he or she is not certified or authorised to act on behalf of that organisation.
- in the case of a Fellow of the Institute of Legal Executives, if he or she is not supervised by a qualified solicitor.

13.51 The adviser must be covered by a 'contract of insurance, or an indemnity provided for members of a profession or professional body'. This makes it clear that the cover provided by the Solicitors' Indemnity Fund is sufficient to sign off on compromise agreements.

13.52 The requirement that the agreement must relate to a specific complaint means that this form of settlement cannot rule out all possible future claims and cannot exclude potential claims on the off chance that these might be raised at some point in the future. There is, therefore, no way of avoiding the difficulties which arose in *Livingstone v Hepworth Refractories plc*.[54] When the employee has raised a number of grievances in a claim or in a letter before claim, however, there seems no reason why one compromise agreement cannot deal with all those specific complaints raised which the parties have now agreed to settle. Each such complaint should be dealt with separately within the agreement and it should be clear that terms have been agreed by way of settlement under each head. If there is a settlement of a claim of unfair dismissal or application for flexible working on the basis that the complaint is to be subjected to arbitration, there must be a separate settlement of that aspect.

13.53 If a compromise agreement is entered into which meets these requirements, then the claims specified in it will have been effectively compromised and it can be relied on as overriding statutory rights.

---

53 See ERA 1996 s231 for the definition of an associated employer.
54 [1992] ICR 287; [1992] IRLR 63, EAT and see above.

Judgments by consent

13.54   Many agreements between parties take place at the door of the tribunal (either just before or during a tribunal hearing). While this
means that costs will already have been expended and tribunal time
wasted, it is an inevitable aspect of litigation: very often parties will
not have assessed the relative strengths of their cases until just before
the hearing, when they know, for example, which witnesses the other
side intends to call or the amount of losses claimed. There is also
something about the prospect of walking into a court or tribunal
which seems to focus minds and encourage parties to be more
favourably disposed to the idea of a settlement of the case.

13.55   Once the parties are at the tribunal, the requirements for a compromise agreement do not apply.[55] The protection is no longer needed
as any agreement must be effected by an order of the tribunal which
may decline to give it. It would be impracticable for a party in the
middle of a hearing, who was not represented by a qualified adviser,
to be unable to settle the claim just because the requirements of a
compromise agreement could not be fulfilled. One way of disposing
of the tribunal proceedings at that stage is for the claimant simply to
withdraw the complaint. The claimant has a right to withdraw all or
part of the claim at any time.[56] Withdrawal of the claim has the effect
of bringing proceedings against the relevant respondent to an end.
When a claim has been withdrawn, a respondent may then make an
application for the proceedings against it to be dismissed. The effect
of granting such an application is that those proceedings cannot be
continued by the claimant, unless the decision to dismiss the claim is
successfully reviewed or appealed.[57]

13.56   This provision in the 2004 Rules makes it imperative for those
advising claimants to consider carefully the implications of withdrawing proceedings. When the agreement provides for the
respondent to do something, such as pay agreed sums, the better
course would be for the tribunal to order that the case be stayed until
a specified date (by when, for example, the claimant will be sure that
the respondent will have paid the sums agreed) when it will be dismissed as withdrawn by the claimant, with both parties having liberty to apply for the matter to be reinstated at any time before that
date. If a claimant is concerned about the respondent not complying

55   *Times Newspapers Ltd v Fitt* [1981] ICR 637, EAT.
56   2004 Rules r25(1).
57   2004 Rules r25(4).

with an agreement to pay a particular sum, it would be sensible to specify a period during which any cheque should have been received and cleared in the claimant's bank account. Tribunals are usually amenable to making an order in these terms and it provides a particularly useful safeguard where there is a risk that the respondent might become insolvent before the terms of the agreement are met – in such circumstances the claimant may need to reinstate proceedings before the tribunal in order to recover monies from the secretary of state. The fact that such an order specifies that the claim will be dismissed as withdrawn on a particular date gives administrative certainty to all concerned.

13.57   Alternatively, if parties to a tribunal case have come to a written agreement, the tribunal has the power to make an order or judgment in the terms of that agreement.[58]

13.58   A judgment or order 'by consent' can be expressed directly in the terms agreed between the parties, that is, that the respondent is ordered to pay the claimant a certain sum of money. This order will be recorded as a judgment or order of the tribunal and will be enforceable in the county court, or directly in Scotland once a certificate is obtained from the secretary. A judgment or order in this form, however, has a number of disadvantages: it can only include matters within the tribunal's jurisdiction – if a tribunal would not usually have the power to make a judgment or order in the terms sought, then the fact that the parties have agreed to it will not change the situation. Furthermore, if the agreement is for the payment of money by the respondent to the claimant and this is recorded as a judgment or order of the tribunal, the recoupment provisions apply, that is, money received by an employee in receipt of jobseeker's allowance or income support may be recouped from the sum agreed to be paid in the tribunal proceedings.

13.59   To avoid these problems, as indicated above, parties can instead ask the tribunal to make a judgment or order merely to stay (sist) or adjourn the proceedings on terms scheduled to the tribunal's judgment or order. This judgment can use the form of order used in civil courts known as a '*Tomlin* order': that is, that all further proceedings in the case be stayed on the terms scheduled to the order save for the purpose of carrying such terms into effect, with liberty to apply for that purpose. The form of words approved in civil courts generally is set out in CPR Part 40.6 and the related

58   2004 Rules r28(2).

practice directions. As the terms of the agreement are not actually part of the tribunal's judgment but are merely scheduled to it, they can include matters which are outside the tribunal's jurisdiction (such as the terms of a reference or a confidentiality clause) and payments of money will not attract the attention of the recoupment provisions.

13.60   If the proceedings are stayed or adjourned with liberty to apply, and where an employer defaults on the agreement, the employee can choose to reinstate the proceedings by applying to lift the stay, or to seek an order from the tribunal or the county court in the terms of the agreement (although the tribunal would only be able to make such an order in so far as the terms were within its powers). If there is no provision for liberty to apply, the employee would be restricted to reinstating the proceedings, by lifting the stay, or pursuing a claim for breach of the agreement in a civil court.

13.61   The right to reinstate proceedings in the tribunal can be extremely important for employees. Not only does it reinstate the threat of the hearing against the employer, with the costs and publicity implications that that entails; but it also means that where the employer has been found to be insolvent, the employee can still pursue a claim for a basic award or redundancy payment which can then be recovered from the secretary of state under the provisions relating to the protection of employees on an employer's insolvency.

13.62   When a party is represented in tribunal proceedings and the representative (whether a lawyer, adviser or lay representative) agrees to a judgment or order being made 'by consent', it will be assumed that the party concerned has *in fact* consented, even if the representative acted without taking proper instructions. The party's remedy, if any, lies against the representative.[59] Those acting for parties in the settlement of a case by these means should adopt the same cautious approach as when entering into an agreement through a conciliation officer or by any other means: it is the representative's duty to make sure that the individual is properly advised on the terms and effect of the agreement and that he or she does in fact consent to that compromise of the claim.

---

59   *Times Newspapers Ltd v Fitt* [1981] ICR 637, EAT.

Checklist: Settlement and conciliation

For employees:
- If an offer of settlement has been made, how does it compare to the value of the claim as it is likely to be assessed by a tribunal?
- Are there advantages in compromising the claim rather than going ahead with the rule 26 Hearing, that is, the provision of a reference (without subsequent retraction or amendment), avoidance of the recoupment provisions, saving of costs?
- Could acceptance of the offer mean that rights other than those pursued in the tribunal proceedings might be lost (for example, a personal injury claim, pension rights, etc)?
- If considering entering into a compromise agreement, do so only on taking *independent* advice.
- Make sure the mechanism by which you settle the claim meets your requirements – make sure you understand and are happy with the terms of any agreement and utilise any safeguards necessary, that is, for exempting certain claims from a general release or for staying proceedings in the tribunal to enable the terms of the agreement to be carried out.
- Before accepting any offer: if in doubt, get advice.

For employers:
- Is the employee willing and able (that is, independently advised by a qualified, insured independent adviser) to enter into a binding compromise agreement or contract? If so, can an agreement be reached which would avoid the risk of subsequent proceedings?
- If the employee is unwilling or unable to enter into any agreement but there is a risk of subsequent tribunal proceedings, consider making an offer which includes a concession of liability, without prejudice save as to costs.
- If any payment is to be made to the employee, consider whether it should be made in open correspondence or 'without prejudice'.
- If a payment is made to the employee, make it clear what that payment is intended to cover: if it includes an amount in respect of a possible basic award, this should be expressly stated.

- If tribunal proceedings are contemplated or have been commenced, consider utilising the services of ACAS and entering into an agreement through a conciliation officer, recorded on Form COT3.

For advisers:
- Is your client in a sufficiently well-informed position to assess the pros and cons of settlement properly?
- If advising the employee, do you meet the definition of a relevant independent adviser for the purposes of entering into a compromise contract or agreement?
- Has an ACAS conciliation officer been involved in seeking to reach a compromise of the claim?
- If an agreement has been reached, does your client understand the full implications of the terms of the agreement?
- Keep a record of any agreement reached, signed by your client and those acting for the other party.
- Pay attention to time limits (for payment of money, etc) set out in the agreement and consider restoring the claim in the tribunal if these are not met.
- If the recoupment provisions apply to your client, is the settlement recorded in such a way as to avoid recoupment?

ACAS arbitration schemes

Introduction

14.1 The Advisory, Conciliation and Arbitration Service (ACAS) arbitration scheme came into force in 2001 providing a voluntary alternative to the employment tribunal for the resolution of unfair dismissal disputes in the form of arbitration. The original scheme, which was used only a handful of times, was repealed and its contents re-enacted in a modified form with effect from 6 April 2004.[1] The 2004 arbitration scheme applies to Scotland as well as to England and Wales ('the unfair dismissal Scheme'). An arbitration scheme for Northern Ireland was brought into force in 2004.[2]

14.2 Further, an arbitration scheme ('the flexible working Scheme') applies to England, Wales and Scotland with effect from 1 October 2004,[3] replacing a similar earlier Scheme which applied only England and Wales for the resolution of disputes where the claimant alleges that the employer has failed to deal with an application to vary the terms and conditions of employment or has made a decision to reject the application based on incorrect facts.[4] The discussion in this chapter relates to both schemes unless indicated otherwise.

14.3 It is only if both parties agree to arbitrate under either scheme that this means of determining a dispute can be used. It applies to disputes involving an employer who resides or carries on business in England, Wales or Scotland. A code of practice supplements the unfair dismissal arbitration scheme. A decision to submit a dispute to arbitration is an important one for the claimant as he or she must waive the right to litigate the relevant claim as part of the arbitration process.

1 The scheme is made under Trade Unions and Labour Relations (Consolidation) Act (TULRCA) 1992 s212A, which implements Employment Rights (Dispute Resolution) Act 1998 s7. See ACAS Arbitration Scheme (Great Britain) Order 2004 SI No 753 at Appendix C.
2 Employment (Northern Ireland) Order 2003 (Commencement and Transitional Provisions) Order (Northern Ireland) 2004 SI No 150 implementing the Employment Rights (Dispute Resolution) (Northern Ireland) Order 1998 SI No 150.
3 ACAS (Flexible Working) Arbitration Scheme (Great Britain) Order 2004 SI No 2333.
4 See Employment Rights Act (ERA) 1996 ss80F – 80G and 80H for the basis of a complaint to an employment tribunal.

Terms of reference

14.4   The terms of reference given to the arbitrator in an unfair dismissal arbitration are shown below:

> In deciding whether the dismissal was fair or unfair, the arbitrator shall:
> (i)   have regard to the general principles of fairness and good conduct in employment relations (including, for example, principles referred to in any relevant ACAS 'Disciplinary and Grievance Procedures' Code of Practice or 'Discipline at Work' Handbook), instead of applying legal tests or rules (for example, court decisions or legislation);
> (ii)   apply EU Law.
> The arbitrator shall not decide the case by substituting what he or she would have done for the actions taken by the employer.
>
> If the Arbitrator finds the dismissal unfair, he or she shall determine the appropriate remedy under the terms of this scheme.

14.5   In deciding whether to uphold the flexible working claim, the arbitrator must:

> (i)   have regard to the relevant provisions of the Flexible Working (Procedural Requirements) Regulations 2002 and to any relevant ACAS Guidance;[5]
> (ii)   apply EU law.
> The arbitrator must not decide the case by substituting what he or she would have done for the actions taken by the employer. If the arbitrator upholds the claim, the arbitrator shall determine the appropriate remedy under the terms of the scheme.

Scope of the schemes

14.6   The *unfair dismissal scheme* applies only to complaints of unfair dismissal which allege contravention of the Employment Rights Act (ERA) 1996 Part X. Any associated claim which an employee may have, such as a discrimination claim, or breach of contract claim, must either be withdrawn or else referred to the ET, as the arbitrator is limited to dealing with the unfair dismissal issue only.

14.7   Before submitting a dispute to arbitration the parties must agree to waive jurisdictional issues, and a specific form set out in appendix

---

5   There is no such Guidance in place at the present time.

A to the scheme must be completed. The scheme is not designed for disputes raising jurisdictional issues such as whether the applicant was an employee, whether the necessary continuous service had been completed, whether a claim was submitted within the appropriate time limit. There is assumed to be no jurisdictional barrier to the claim. If such issues are raised during the course of the arbitration by the parties, the arbitrator will not deal with them. Furthermore, in agreeing to an arbitration, parties will be treated as having agreed that a dismissal has taken place.

14.8   The *flexible working scheme* applies only to claims which allege that the employer has failed to deal with an application by an employee for flexible working or has based the decision to refuse the application on incorrect facts.[6] A waiver of rights contained in Appendix A to the scheme must be signed in similar terms to the unfair dismissal waiver.

14.9   In either scheme of arbitration, the arbitrator is under a duty to act fairly and impartially, giving each party an opportunity to put their case, and to deal with the other's case, and also to avoid delay and expense so as to provide a fair means of access for the resolution of disputes.

14.10   The parties must comply 'without delay' (which is not defined) with any determination or direction of the arbitrator, and all procedures under the schemes are strictly confidential.

Access to the schemes

14.11   An agreement to submit a dispute to arbitration must:

- be in writing;
- concern an existing dispute;
- not seek to alter or vary any provision of the scheme;
- have been reached either:
  - where a conciliation officer has taken action under Employment Tribunals Act 1996 s18; or
  - through a compromise agreement where the conditions regulating such agreements under ERA 1996 are satisfied;
- be accompanied by a completed waiver form for each party.

14.12   When a dispute other than a claim of unfair dismissal or, as the case

6   ERA 1996 ss80G(1) and 80H(1)(b).

may be, a flexible working claim, is settled, and the unfair dismissal or flexible working claim is referred to arbitration, separate settlements must be reached in respect of the different types of claim.

14.13   Within *two weeks* of signing an arbitration agreement, ACAS must be notified of the agreement, and the following documents must be sent to the ACAS Arbitration Section:

- arbitration agreement;
- claim;
- response;
- waiver form.

14.14   If ACAS is not notified within the two-week period, it will only accept the referral if it is shown that it was not reasonably practicable to have submitted the referral within time. It is assumed that the interpretation given by tribunals when considering whether it was reasonably practicable to lodge an unfair dismissal or flexible working complaint on time will be applied by ACAS, since the definition arises from analogous legislation.

Withdrawal and settlement

14.15   An employee can withdraw a complaint at any stage of the arbitration process, provided the withdrawal is in writing. A withdrawal from the arbitration scheme is treated as a dismissal of the claim and the arbitrator must upon receipt of withdrawal issue an award dismissing the claim. An employer cannot unilaterally withdraw once it has entered into the arbitration agreement.

14.16   Parties are free to reach an agreement settling the dispute at any stage and, on receipt of a joint written request, the ACAS Arbitration Section will terminate the proceedings. If the parties want the form of words of settlement to be recorded, this can be done, but the arbitrator may only record the parties' wording and may not approve, interpret or ratify any settlement. Further, the arbitrator is not permitted to record any settlement beyond the scope of either scheme, the arbitration agreement between the parties and the reference which was initially accepted by ACAS.

14.17   If the agreement to settle the dispute in an unfair dismissal arbitration includes an agreement that one party, presumably the employer, is to pay a sum of money to the other, the arbitrator must (unless the parties agree otherwise) draft an award ordering payment of the agreed sum with interest at the agreed rate until the date of payment.

Appointment of arbitrator

14.18 The arbitrator will be selected from an ACAS arbitration panel. This is made up of people who have practical knowledge and experience of discipline and dismissal issues in the workplace,[7] appointed via an open recruitment exercise. Appointments are for an initial period of two years, but may be renewed at the discretion of ACAS. Payment is on the basis of time spent in connection with arbitral proceedings.

14.19 The parties have no choice of arbitrator. Following their selection, the arbitrator must state in writing any circumstances known to them which would give rise to any justifiable doubts about their impartiality, or confirm in writing that there are no such circumstances. The arbitrator is under a continuing duty to disclose to ACAS, who will forward to the parties, any relevant circumstances which may have arisen since appointment. If a party objects to an arbitrator, they must apply to the ACAS Arbitration Section setting out their grounds of objection. The only grounds of objection permissible are those set out in the Arbitration Act 1996 s24(1)(a) and (c), that is, justifiable doubts about impartiality or physical or mental incapability of conducting the proceedings. If ACAS refuses the application, a party may apply to the High Court, or to the Central London County Court. In a Scottish arbitration, on the other hand, it is only ACAS who may remove an arbitrator. ACAS is permitted to remove an arbitrator if both parties agree to it.

14.20 If an arbitrator needs to be replaced, because of death or because they cease to hold office for any reason, a further arbitrator will be appointed. The replacement will have complete discretion about whether, and if so to what extent, the previous proceedings should stand.

---

7 The definition in the flexible working scheme is that the panel is made up of those with practical knowledge and experience of employment issues in the workplace.

The hearing

14.21   A hearing must be held in every case, even if the parties have agreed to a purely written procedure. A hearing will be arranged by the arbitrator as soon as is reasonably practicable. In any event, the arbitrator must decide the date and venue within 28 days of the initial notification being sent to ACAS. The arbitrator has the discretion to expedite the hearing if a party makes an application to that effect. The arbitrator's discretion in an unfair dismissal arbitration exists if the tribunal has granted interim relief (see chapter 21) prior to the referral of the dispute to the arbitrator or if there are other relevant circumstances.

14.22   Any venue can be used, though it should not be 'partisan', such as the workplace, unless both parties agree. ACAS will meet the reasonable expense of hiring a venue if necessary. There is no provision for any expenses to be paid to those involved in arbitrations, other than in circumstances in which assistance is required from, for example, interpreters and signers. Loss of earnings are not payable, although a successful employee may recover reasonable travelling expenses and loss of earnings as part of an award made in his or her favour. Once the hearing date has been fixed, any request for it to be moved must be made in writing within 14 days of notification.

14.23   At least 14 days before the hearing each party must send to the ACAS Arbitration Section a statement of case together with supporting documentation and a list of the names and title/role of all those people who will attend the hearing, as witnesses or otherwise. The likely nature of 'supporting documentation' is explained in the schemes. As in tribunals, these are likely to include contracts of employment, time sheets and attendance records, performance appraisals, warning and dismissal letters (in unfair dismissal cases), notes of meetings to consider the flexible working application, written reasons for the refusal of the application (in flexible working cases) wage slips and P60s, though this is not an exhaustive list.

14.24   Parties must also be prepared to deal with the issue of remedy. This is of most importance in an unfair dismissal arbitration, as the parties must be in a position to deal with the practicability or otherwise of reinstatement or re-engagement, and provide details of jobseeker's allowance or income support received, along with details of all attempts to find work or otherwise mitigate losses arising from dismissal. Parties must in either type of arbitration supply details of any relevant awards of compensation made by a tribunal in connection with the subject matter of the claim, for example, where loss of earnings has been compensated as part of a discrimination claim.

14.25 The arbitrator has no power to compel the disclosure of documents, or the attendance of witnesses, but may draw adverse inferences from a party's failure to co-operate. If the arbitrator considers that there may be considerable differences between the parties over an issue, including the availability of documents or witnesses, he or she may call the parties to a preliminary hearing to deal with the matter or give procedural directions in correspondence. If a party fails to attend a hearing, it may take place in their absence or be adjourned. Any written submissions or documents already submitted by that party will be considered. If a matter is adjourned, but an employee fails to demonstrate sufficient cause for his or her non-attendance, the complaint may be dismissed.

14.26 During a hearing, no party or witness can be cross-examined by a party or representative and they do not give evidence on oath or affirmation. This means that the role of the arbitrator is to take the initiative to ascertain the facts. Strict rules of evidence will not apply.

EU law, human rights and devolution issues

14.27 Further provision is made where questions arise concerning EU law or the Human Rights Act (HRA) 1998, and, in unfair dismissal arbitrations, devolution issues. Here, the arbitrator has the power, on application of either party or on their own initiative, to require the appointment by ACAS of a legal adviser who will assist to the extent that the law is relevant to the resolution of the dispute. The parties may make submissions about the content of any advice offered by the legal adviser, following which the arbitrator will take all the information into account before determining the dispute.

Awards

14.28 The awards which can be made by the arbitrator are the same as those which can be made by a tribunal in unfair dismissal claims and in flexible working claims. As in the tribunal, reinstatement and re-engagement are to be considered before a monetary award. Monetary awards are calculated and can be enforced in the same way as tribunal awards.[8] The main difference is that the arbitrations are confidential.

14.29   It appears that the recoupment of benefit regime[9] does not apply to arbitration awards since they are not *tribunal* awards, and there is no parallel requirement on the arbitrator to make inquiries and record the data relating to benefit. There is no mention of the issue in the unfair dismissal scheme.

Challenges and appeals

14.30   There are very limited opportunities for parties to appeal against, or otherwise challenge, the result of an arbitration. There is no general right to appeal on either a point of law or fact, with the exception that points of EU law, matters under the HRA 1998 or devolution issues may be appealed. If there are no points under EU law, the HRA 1998 or on devolution issues, the only challenge which can be made is under Arbitration Act 1996 ss67–69, on grounds of substantive jurisdiction, serious irregularity or a question of law. If any party continues to take part in proceedings without making an objection about substantive jurisdiction, proceedings being conducted improperly or any failure to comply with the arbitration agreement or scheme, or any other irregularity, they will lose their right to object at a later time.

8   See paras 20.24–20.27.
9   Employment Protection (Recoupment of Jobseeker's Allowance and Income Support) Regulations 1996 SI No 2349.

Preparing for the hearing

Notice of the hearing

15.1 The President, Vice President or a Regional chairman fixes the date, time and place of the rule 26 Hearing. On their behalf the secretary to the tribunal must send to each party a notice of the rule 26 Hearing together with information and guidance as to procedure at the hearing. The notice of rule 26 Hearing must be sent to every party not less than 14 days before the date fixed for the rule 26 Hearing.[1] This means that the notice should have been placed in the post at least 14 days prior to the rule 26 Hearing, but there is no requirement that it should have been served 14 days in advance.[2] The notice of rule 26 Hearing must inform the parties of their opportunity to submit written representations and to advance oral argument at the hearing. The notes accompanying the notice of rule 26 Hearing are likely to continue to include advice on attendance, the possibility of the case not getting heard, witness statements, and a note to employers to be prepared to deal with the issue of reinstatement and expenses.

Listing

15.2 The tribunal office will make arrangements for the listing of the case according to the practice operated in that particular region. Sometimes, the parties are consulted or send their own views on the estimate of time needed. The length of time the case is likely to take to present and for the tribunal to reach a decision need to be carefully evaluated and reasons given. The time estimate should be sufficient for a judgment and oral reasons to be provided. It is better to be conservative, and give ample time; no one complains if the hearing ends before the scheduled day as floating cases can be called on and it is preferable to adjourning the case part-heard, with all parties coming back weeks or even months later.

15.3 It is necessary to check the availability of all witnesses and any representative, and then send the tribunal the estimate of length and dates to avoid.

1 See Employment Tribunals Rules of Procedure (2004 Rules) r14(4), contained in Employment Tribunals (Constitution and Rules of Procedure) Regulations 2004 SI No 1861 Sch 1.
2 Employment Tribunals (Constitution and Rules of Procedure) Regulations 2004 (2004 Regs) reg 15(5).

Preliminary points of law

15.4   An application to seek a pre-hearing review for the purposes of determining a preliminary matter relating to the proceedings[3] should already have been made by now. It would appear that such an application should in any event be made not less than 10 days in advance of the rule 26 Hearing, unless it is not reasonably practicable to do so or the chairman or tribunal considers it to be in the interests of justice for shorter notice to be allowed.[4]

Chairman sitting alone (without lay members)

15.5   Whether or not the rule 26 Hearing is conducted by a full tribunal or chairman is determined in accordance with Employment Tribunals Act (ETA) 1996 s4(1) and (2) (see para 1.22 above).[5] If either party wants the case to be heard by a full tribunal or by a chairman, and there is a discretion given to the chairman to decide this under the provisions of the ETA 1996, the preference should be made known to the tribunal, with reasons.

Hearing in public

15.6   The rule 26 Hearing of a claim must be in public unless the tribunal or chairman considers that the rule 26 Hearing or part of it should be conducted in private on any of the grounds set out in 2004 Rules r16. Reasons must be provided for such a decision. Further, if the proceedings are national security proceedings, the rule 26 Hearing will take place in private if a Minister of the Crown has directed to that effect[6] or a chairman or tribunal has made an order under 2004 Rules r54(2).[7] The tribunal is required to keep under review the appropriateness of any such order having been made. If a case involves

3   2004 Rules r11(1).
4   2004 Rules r11(2).
5   2004 Rules r26(2).
6   See 2004 Rules r54(1) and Sch 2 r9(1).
7   Note that if the hearing is to be in private in accordance with rule 16, a member of the Council on Tribunals (or in Scotland, a member of the Council on Tribunals or its Scottish Committee) may attend the hearing in that capacity. Such a person is not entitled to attend a hearing held in private in national security proceedings.

allegations of sexual misconduct, or is a disability discrimination case, restricted reporting orders protecting the identity of those involved can be sought at this stage under 2004 Rules r50.

Written representations

15.7 Written representations can be made to the tribunal. They should be presented to the employment tribunal office seven days before the hearing with copies to be sent to all other parties at the same time.[8]

Skeleton arguments

15.8 In practice the tribunal will welcome the presentation of written arguments in skeleton form, as is the requirement in the Employment Appeal Tribunal (EAT) in England and Wales and in appeal proceedings and judicial review proceedings in the civil courts.[9] A short summary of the issues in opening, or a skeleton argument and draft findings of fact presented in closing, are usually accepted gratefully. They save time and release the tribunal from making detailed notes on oral submissions. There is no need to send them in advance to the tribunal or the other side unless there is an agreement or direction to do so. If the tribunal orders written submissions to be produced by the parties it must ensure that the timetable set allows for sufficient time for them to be prepared and for them to be considered by the other side and the tribunal before oral submissions are made.[10]

Agreed facts

15.9 Some cases are heard without any live evidence being called because there is no dispute on the facts. Transfer of undertakings cases and wages protection claims might usefully centre on issues of law alone, so it might be worthwhile to draft a statement and send it to the other side to see if agreement is possible.

---

8 2004 Rules r14(5).
9 Practice Guide 1 of the Civil Procedure Rules (CPR), paras 58–60.
10 *Sinclaire Roche & Temperley v Heard* [2004] IRLR 763.

Witness statements

15.10   Each party should decide which witnesses it is likely to call and take detailed statements from them.

15.11   Evidence from non-expert witnesses is generally called for in the form of written statements. The booklet which will normally accompany the notice of rule 26 Hearing in England and Wales includes the following:

> Even if you have not been directed to prepare written statements for yourself and your witnesses, you may still do so for the purposes of the hearing. Such pre-prepared statements may help you and your witnesses to include all the matters which you consider important to your case. Normally the tribunal will allow witness statements to be taken as the main evidence of the witness. Statements can either be read by the witness at the hearing or the tribunal will read the statement itself. Either way, the witness may then be questioned by the other party and the tribunal. You are advised to bring six copies of any statement to the hearing including your own copy.

15.12   The statement should therefore be in a form which can be disclosed in full to the other side and to the tribunal. There is no general requirement to exchange or send it in advance, although this may be ordered by the tribunal under 2004 Rules r10(2)(s). It is becoming increasingly common for tribunals as part of their standard directions to parties to require the preparation of witness statements and this is likely to continue. A similar rule applies in Northern Ireland.

15.13   A party should also consider whether an expert is needed, for example, on whether work is of equal value in an equal pay case, or on the issue of whether an applicant is 'disabled' in claims under the Disability Discrimination Act 1995. Evidence given by an expert in the form of an opinion in the civil courts must be provided in advance of the trial, and there is now a presumption that oral evidence will not be given by that expert, unless the court gives permission.[11] The court has power under the CPR to direct that evidence shall be given by a single joint expert and there is a presumption that this is how evidence is to be given 'unless there is a good reason not to do so'.[12] The EAT in *DeKeyser Ltd v Wilson*[13] stated that the instruction of a joint

---

11   CPR 35.5 and see also the accompanying Practice Direction to Part 35.
12   CPR 35.7, PD28 para 3.9 (fast-track cases), PD29 para 4.10 (multi-track cases).
13   [2001] IRLR 324, EAT.

expert is the 'preferred course', going on to set out guidelines to be followed when drawing up joint instructions. There is no specific requirement for a report to be provided in advance at a tribunal[14] but if an expert witness is produced without prior notice or an indication of the nature of his or her evidence, an application for adjournment is likely to be granted and costs could be awarded against the party producing the expert evidence. In a case when expert evidence is likely to be required, there may well have been a case management discussion where the issue will have been canvassed and directions made by the chairman as to how expert evidence is to be adduced prior to the hearing.[15] It is obviously unsatisfactory for one party to be unprepared for the evidence of an expert. Without advance access to their own expert, the other side is unable properly to evaluate the evidence. For this reason, the issue should be raised in advance and the leave of the tribunal sought to put forward the relevant evidence.

Documents

15.14   Parties are encouraged to agree what documents are to be put before the tribunal. A chairman has a specific power to order a party to disclose documents to another.[16] The power to order that a bundle be provided should fall within the general discretion to make such orders as appear appropriate for the management of the claim, and this may be ordered by the tribunal.[17] In unfair dismissal cases the employer will usually open the case and the preparation of the index and paginated bundles will often fall to the respondent as it is more likely to be represented and to have the greater amount of materials to be put in the bundle. Both sides should have a clear idea of the relevant material and the best way to present it. Usually this will be in chronological order, but there may be separate issues, or separate claim forms, which justify discrete bundles or sections. A clear and easily understood format should be adopted.

15.15   If an application for the costs to be paid by the losing side is to be made, perhaps on the ground of being put to unnecessary

---

14 Note, however, that there is a specific requirement in equal value cases for disclosure of a party's expert report 28 days prior to the rule 26 Hearing (2004 Rules Sch 6 r11(2)).
15 See chapter 22 on the provisions in equal pay cases.
16 2004 Rules r10(2)(2).
17 2004 Rules r10(1).

preparation, a separate bundle should be prepared for this purpose to use at the end of the hearing (see para 18.43).

Authorities to be referred to

15.16   It is necessary to consider what law is relevant to the case. A list of cases to be referred to should be handed in to the clerk at the tribunal on the hearing day, and exchanged with the other side before that. It is helpful to the tribunal and to your own submissions if a bundle of photocopies is provided for each tribunal member so that they and the representatives can highlight the relevant passages.

15.16   Tribunals and the Employment Appeal Tribunal are not required to follow the practice which applies in all civil courts[18] of requiring advocates to cite only one authority for each proposition and to cite the proposition for which the case stands. As a matter of common sense, representatives should adopt this practice, unless there is a good reason for departing from it. Nor do they follow the practice of the Court of Appeal[19] in requiring cases to be cited in the *Industrial Cases Reports* (ICR) if there is a choice of law report in preference to the *Industrial Relations Law Reports* (IRLR) and other reports. The IRLR are provided free to all chairmen and are more readily available to lay and professional representatives. ICR is available in all tribunal offices, chairmen have online access to both along with *Harvey on Employment Law* and *IDS Brief,* with good search facilities. To maintain uniformity, it is sensible to use either IRLR or ICR consistently, unless a particular case happens only to have been reported in one.

15.18   The tribunal chairman (but not the lay members) will have the legislation, so if it is necessary to refer to several statutes and European directives, it will help the case to have these photocopied for all three members too so that they can follow the point being made in submissions.

Warning witnesses to attend

15.19   A representative on the record is responsible for ensuring that the client is warned of the rule 26 Hearing date, and that notice of the

18 [2000] 1 WLR 1001.
19 [1999] 1 WLR 1027.

rule 26 Hearing is given to witnesses. A witness should be sent the final version of his or her statement and asked to sign it. There is nothing wrong in all witnesses seeing each others' statements, and indeed it saves time if a witness can comment in his or her own statement on evidence in other statements, especially if both people were at the same meeting or saw the same events. This is not encouraged in Scotland or Northern Ireland, where witnesses do not know other witnesses' testimony, and are not permitted to sit in the tribunal hearing before they give their own evidence.

The Hearing

continued

Introduction

16.1 This chapter sets out the principal features of a tribunal hearing, and refers to the law relating to procedure, and advice on the best practice in conducting a hearing. It should be noted that a substantive a procedural hearing of a complaint should be referred to as the Hearing.[1] The use of 'hearing' in this chapter is used to denote any of the various types of hearing which may be conducted under the 2004 Rules and 'Hearing' has the meaning given to it in the 2004 Rules in rule 26.

16.2 The common law right of every person to have a fair hearing within a reasonable period of time by an independent and impartial tribunal is now *guaranteed* through the Human Rights Act (HRA) 1998, which incorporates the European Convention on Human Rights (ECHR) into UK law, and in particular ECHR article 6.

Administration

Arrangements at the tribunal

16.3 Most tribunal hearing centres have a reception check-in to enable parties and witnesses to register. It is important for all who are likely to be called as witnesses to register either personally or through their representative. This is because the list of witnesses is then seen by the tribunal who can quickly decide whether their knowledge of any witness might cause them to be excused ('recused') from hearing the case. Representatives will also find it useful to see the list of the other side's witnesses, especially when no statements have been given in advance.

16.4 In most hearing centres there are separate rooms for parties and witnesses for each side of the case, that is, claimants and respondents. This appears to be the only civil forum where separation is deemed necessary – the civil courts do not have separated waiting areas. In some centres, conference rooms are available free of charge on a first come, first served basis.

16.5 In some centres, rooms are available for members of the tribunal adjacent to the hearing rooms. This enables the members to enter

1 Employment Tribunals Rules of Procedure 2004 (2004 Rules) r26, contained in Employment Tribunals (Constitution and Rules of Procedure) Regulations 2004 (2004 Regs) SI No 1861 Sch 1.

and withdraw while the parties are in the room. In other centres, no facilities are available and so the tribunal is already seated on the bench when the parties are ushered in by the tribunal clerk. Whenever possible, it is useful for clients and witnesses to see the tribunal room's layout before the Hearing starts in order to feel comfortable.

16.6   While waiting for the case to come on, claimants are frequently asked if they are claiming jobseeker's allowance or income support and if so, to give the name of the office where they are registered and their national insurance number. This is in case an award of compensation is made and the recoupment of benefits provisions apply. At the same time the tribunal clerk will take a note of the full name and job title or position of each witness and establish whether the witness is to swear an oath and if so, on which holy text, or whether the witness will affirm.

Listing

16.7   Parties are warned in the booklet accompanying the notice of Hearing that the case may not start on time. This is because the policy of the tribunals is to overbook so that on any given day there will be a number of 'floaters' which will be slotted in as and when any of the cases are settled or disposed of. These floaters are not attached to any particular tribunal and will go to the first one which becomes available. If there is no reasonable prospect of the floater being reached, parties will be advised by the tribunal clerk. Another date will be fixed by a chairman prior to the parties leaving that day. Sometimes this decision is not reached until midday or occasionally even later if the tribunal hopes to be able to hear the case that day.

16.8   From time to time, a major mistake occurs in listing, for example, a party is not sent a notice of Hearing, or a tribunal is unavailable. In such circumstances it is possible to make a claim against the Department of Trade and Industry, which administers tribunals, although there is no guarantee that such claims will be met.

Documents

16.9   Copies of documents which will be referred to should be handed in to the tribunal clerk. This enables the tribunal to have a more detailed look at the documents in the few minutes available before the Hearing. In practice, tribunals do not see any documents in advance of the day of the Hearing. On the day, a small bundle is prepared of the

tribunal documents, that is, claim, response, relevant correspondence with the tribunal, orders made and directions given, but this is
all that will be available to the tribunal unless the parties themselves
provide a more detailed bundle. It is advantageous to hand in the
bundles of documents at once so that the tribunal can start reading
and get a picture of the case. In lengthy cases, the directions may
arrange for a 'reading day' on the first day listed to enable the tribunal
to read into the case. The parties may be required to prepare reading
lists to guide the tribunal's reading.

16.10   The witness statements referred to in chapter 15 should also be
handed in at the beginning of the Hearing.

Authorities to be referred to

16.11 A list of cases to be referred to or a bundle of photocopies of the law
reports should be handed in to the clerk and exchanged with the
other side. It is helpful to the tribunal and to your own submissions
if a bundle of photocopies is provided for each tribunal member.
Otherwise only the chairman will be provided with a copy by the
tribunal clerk, making it invidious for the lay members.

Procedure

16.12 By rule 14(2) of the 2004 Rules, tribunals are required to avoid formality in so far as it is appears appropriate to do so and are not bound
by rules of evidence in the same way as courts are. They must make
enquiries of advocates and witnesses so as to clarify the issues and
handle the proceedings justly, and are of course required to act in
accordance with the overriding objective.[2]

16.13   Despite the encouragement of informality, tribunals are usually
conducted very formally. The requirement that tribunals should
make enquiries entitles the tribunal to be more inquisitorial and
directive than the civil courts: indeed a tribunal has the power to call a
witness itself.[3] A chairman has wide powers under rule 10 to manage
the proceedings and is permitted, with certain exceptions, to exercise
those powers on his or her own initiative, with or without a hearing.
The chairman or tribunal is to conduct any hearing in such manner

2   2004 Regs reg 3.
3   2004 Rules r10(2)(c).

as is considered most appropriate for the clarification of the issues and generally for the just handling of the proceedings.[4]

Chairman and members

16.14　The cases in which a chairman can sit without lay members at a Hearing are contained in Employment Tribunals Act 1996 s4(3).[5] A chairman will also conduct case management discussions[6] and will in most instances conduct pre-hearing reviews.[7]

Challenge to composition of tribunal

16.15　Given the local composition of tribunals, it is inevitable from time to time that members will know parties or witnesses in a case they are about to hear. Any direct interest in the case would automatically exclude a member from sitting.[8] That constitutes bias in the technical sense of having a pecuniary or proprietary interest in the outcome of proceedings. In *Jones v DAS Legal Expenses Insurers*,[9] the fact that the chairman's husband had been instructed on occasions by the respondent was not sufficient for her to be treated as having such an interest. But objection can be made to the composition of the tribunal on far less tangible grounds, since it is important to avoid any possibility of a challenge during or after a tribunal Hearing. Emphasis is placed not only on bias being avoided, but also any appearance of bias. Guidance was provided in *Jones* to tribunal chairmen as to how to explain conflicts of interest to parties. A full explanation should be given, the options for future conduct of the Hearing should be explained and the parties given an opportunity to reflect on what they wish to do.

16.16　The members should be selected at random from the panels of people drawn from both sides of employment relations. In cases of

4　2004 Rules r14(3) and see paras 1.22–1.29 above.
5　2004 Rules r26(2).
6　2004 Rules r17(1).
7　2004 Rules r18.
8　*Porter v Magill* [2002] 2AC 357, HL; see also *R v Bow Street Stipendiary Magistrate ex p Pinochet Ugarte (No 2)* [2000] 1 AC 119; [1999] 1 All ER 557, HL; *Locabail (UK) Ltd v Bayfield Properties Ltd* [2000] QB 451; [2000] IRLR 96, CA; *Director General of Fair Trading v Proprietary Association of Great Britain* [2001] 1 WLR 700, CA; *Re Medicaments and Related Classes of Goods (No 2)* [2001] ICR 564, CA.
9　[2004] IRLR 218.

race discrimination, effect is given to an assurance given during debates on the Race Relations Act 1976 that there should be at least one member with special knowledge or experience of race relations in the employment field. A separate list of people so qualified is kept by the tribunals. The absence in a race discrimination case of such a person will not invalidate the proceedings, but administrative arrangements are generally made to ensure such a person sits.[10] A similar assurance was not given in debates on the Sex Discrimination Act 1975, but in practice administrative arrangements are usually made to ensure that members of both sexes sit on cases of sex discrimination and equal pay. No particular arrangements are made in cases involving other forms of discrimination such as disability or sexual orientation. There are particular panels of chairmen and lay members who are permitted to sit in cases involving issues of national security.[11]

16.17　　The most appropriate time to make an objection about the composition of the tribunal is before the Hearing starts, while it remains a potential problem and before it becomes an actual problem. In *Halford v Sharples*[12] a member had 'specialist' knowledge of personnel practices in police forces and was specifically chosen to sit on a claim of sex discrimination brought by a senior officer. The Employment Appeal Tribunal (EAT) decided the tribunal should be selected at random and not by reference to any specialist experience. The proper test is:

> Could the reasonable and disinterested observer present at the hearing . . . reasonably take the view . . . that the continued presence of the member was undesirable in that a party could reasonably feel that injustice might occur during the hearing?[13]

16.18　　Further, in *University College of Swansea v Cornelius*[14] a tribunal decision was overturned because one of the members was the mother-in-law of a person who had sat on an internal appeal.

16.19　　If a list of potential witnesses has been handed in at the outset, the tribunal can consider whether any person on the list is known to any member. The proper approach is for the chairman to draw this to the attention of the parties and invite comments. Generally speaking, any

---

10　*Habib v Elkington & Co Ltd* [1981] ICR 435; [1981] IRLR 344, EAT.
11　2004 Regs regs 10 and 11.
12　[1992] ICR 146, EAT.
13　[1992] ICR 146 per Wood J.
14　[1988] ICR 735.

objection which is not 'irresponsible, frivolous or wholly without content'[15] will be acted upon. If no objection is made once the possible conflict is pointed out, the case can go on; if objection is made, the tribunal should consider whether the member should stand down.

Absence of a member

16.20   If a conflict arises before or during the course of the Hearing, and a member stands down, or becomes indisposed, the Hearing cannot continue without consent of all parties.[16] If consent is given, a decision can be made by a member and a chairman together and if they disagree the chairman has a casting vote.[17] It is therefore imperative to weigh carefully the advantages of making an objection, since it may abort the proceedings. It is useful to know which panel (in shorthand known as TUC or CBI)[18] the member comes from. In the ET and EAT when a panel member is absent, this information must be given.[19] One of the longest cases ever before a tribunal was heard by a chairman and one member following the death of the other – the claims of unfair dismissal on the grounds of trade union activity raised by dockworker shop stewards lasted for 197 days, the member dying after seven days.[20]

16.21   Consent need not be obtained from a person who is debarred from participating, because he or she is no longer a party to the proceedings. Further, consent will not need to be sought from a respondent whose response has not been accepted or against whom default judgment has been issued.[21]

Hearing in public

16.22   The hearing of a claim must be in public.[22] A Hearing will however be conducted in private if a minister so directs on the grounds of

---

15   *Halford v Sharples* [1992] ICR 146, EAT.
16   2004 Regs reg 9(3).
17   2004 Rules r28(4).
18   Trades Union Congress and Confederation of British Industry, respectively.
19   *de Haney v Brent Mind* [2004] ICR 348, CA; *Raballah v BT plc* EAT/382/04.
20   *Port of London Authority v Payne* [1994] ICR 555; [1994] IRLR 9, CA.
21   See 2004 Rules r9 which sets out the limited part to be played by such a party to the proceedings.
22   2004 Rules r26(3).

national security[23] or a chairman or tribunal makes an order under 2004 Rules r54(2). If a direction is made by a minister, it cannot be challenged in the tribunal; the only way of making a challenge is by way of judicial review.[24] The chairman or tribunal has discretion to hear evidence and additionally under the 2004 Rules, representations in private[25] if these are likely to consist of information:

- involving breach of a statutory provision;[26]
- involving disclosure of information given to the witness in confidence;
- which would cause substantial injury to any undertaking, excluding matters relating to the effect on collective bargaining.

16.23 Where an application is to be made for a Hearing to be held in private, the application will be heard in public. There appears to be no requirement in the 2004 Rules for a full tribunal to hear the application.[27]

16.24 In *Storer v British Gas plc*[28] the Court of Appeal set aside the judgment of a chairman relating to jurisdiction, which had been reached following a Hearing which took place in his chambers due to the fact that there were no tribunal rooms available. As access to the chairman's chambers was only via a door secured by a push button coded lock, beyond a door marked private, there was an infringement of the rule requiring a Hearing to be in public. In the Court of Appeal the view of Henry LJ was that the employment tribunal rules do not provide for any 'chambers-type procedure' as in civil courts.

16.25 In England and Wales and Northern Ireland, witnesses are generally permitted to sit in the tribunal room before giving evidence, save that the tribunal may exclude from the Hearing any person who is to give evidence until such time as they are to give evidence if it considers it in the interests of justice to do so.[29] In Scotland those who may be called to give evidence remain outside the tribunal until they are called.

---

23 2004 Rules r54(1), 2004 Rules Sch 2 r9(1) and Employment Tribunals Act (ETA) 1996 s10.
24 *Fry v Foreign and Commonwealth Office* [1997] ICR 512, EAT.
25 2004 Rules r16.
26 See *XXX v YYY* [2004] IRLR 137 in which it was held that evidence may be given in private if to show the evidence would be an infringement of ECHR art 8 rights and thus of the tribunal's own obligations as a public authority under HRA 1998 s6.
27 2004 Rules r11.
28 [2000] IRLR 495, CA.
29 2004 Rules r27(4).

Allegations of sexual offences and sexual misconduct, and disability cases

16.26   Provisions in ETA 1996 s11 allow tribunals to restrict reporting of cases involving sexual misconduct. Sexual misconduct means:

> . . . the commission of a sexual offence, sexual harassment or other adverse conduct (of whatever nature) related to sex, and conduct is related to sex whether the relationship with sex lies in the character of the conduct or in its having reference to the sex or sexual orientation of the person at whom the conduct is directed.[30]

16.27   In such a case (and in cases under the Disability Discrimination Act 1995 involving evidence of a personal nature) the tribunal can, on the application of a party in writing or orally at a hearing, or of its own initiative, decide to make a full restricted reporting order.[31] All parties must be given an opportunity to advance oral argument at a pre-hearing review or at a Hearing before a decision is made.[32] Any person, other than a party, who has a legitimate interest in whether an order is made, can apply to a chairman or the tribunal to make representations. The right to make such an application is new to the 2004 Rules and is likely to be used by the media.

16.28   The 2004 Rules also grants the power to a chairman or tribunal to make a temporary restricted reporting order, either on the application of a party or of its own initiative.[33] A temporary order may be made without holding a hearing or sending a copy of the application to other parties, and is in effect an ex parte process for an order to be obtained at short notice. If a temporary order is made, the secretary to the tribunal informs the parties as soon as possible of the fact that the order has been made and of the right to have the order revoked or converted into a full order within 14 days of the temporary order having been made.[34] If no application is made for conversion into a full order, the restriction automatically lapses at the end of the period.[35]

16.29   The order specifies the person who may not be identified in reports of the case; the order should be no wider than is necessary to prevent identification of the 'persons affected', and the tribunal must

30   ETA 1996 s11(6).
31   2004 Rules r50(2).
32   2004 Rules r50(6).
33   2004 Rules r50(3).
34   2004 Rules r50(4).
35   2004 Rules r50(5).

take an 'individual by individual' approach, and not simply apply a blanket ban.[36] The EAT held in *Chief Constable of the West Yorkshire Police v A*[37] that if there is a liability Hearing followed by a remedies Hearing, the promulgation of the decision refers to the date on which the whole proceedings are at an end, after the decision as to remedy. The provisions of the 2004 Rules[38] makes it clear that a full restricted reporting order shall remain in force until both liability and remedy have been determined, being the date on which the judgment disposing of the claim is sent to the parties.

16.30   A restricted reporting order cannot be granted to prevent the identification of a body corporate.[39]

16.31   The Rules require a notice of the fact that a restricted reporting order has been made to be affixed to the door of the tribunal and to the list of cases on the notice board at the tribunal office.[40] The effect of such a notice is to provide a warning to all journalists in the hearing centre. Breach of a restricted reporting order exposes people who publish the identity of a person to a fine.[41] For newspapers and other media, liability rests on the proprietor and the editor, and in respect of broadcast programmes, the company providing the service and anybody fulfilling functions corresponding to an editor. A person publishing the identity in any other form is also liable. Ignorance and lack of suspicion of the existence of an order is a defence.[42]

16.32   In addition to a restricted reporting order, tribunals must take certain steps when a case involves allegations of the commission of a sexual *offence*. This is defined as offences specified in the Sexual Offences (Amendment) Acts 1976 and 1992 and the Criminal Procedure (Scotland) Act 1995 s274(2).[43] The tribunal office must omit from the register, or delete from it, any judgment, document or record of the proceedings available to the public which is 'likely to lead members of the public to identify any person affected by or making such an allegation'.[44] The (possibly unintended) effect of this is to restrain publication of identifying material until the judgment or

---

36   *Associated Newspapers Ltd v London (North) Industrial Tribunal* [1998] IRLR 569, QBD.
37   [2000] IRLR 465 at 468.
38   Rule 50(8) and (11).
39   *Leicester University v A* [1999] IRLR 352, EAT.
40   2004 Rules r50(8)(c).
41   ETA 1996 s11(2).
42   ETA 1996 s11(3).
43   ETA 1996 s11(6).
44   2004 Rules r49.

order is issued and then to permit publication of names which must, on the other hand, be omitted from or deleted from the official record.

Representation at the tribunal

16.33   There is no restriction on the kind of person who may represent a party at the proceedings and so representation by counsel, solicitor, trade union official, employer's association, voluntary worker, friend or anyone at all is permitted. This is an unqualified right,[45] so in *Bache v Essex CC*[46] when the tribunal dismissed a representative and directed a claimant to represent herself, the tribunal was held by the Court of Appeal to have acted outside its powers. On the facts of that case however, there would have been no difference in the outcome had this infringement not occurred, so the decision stood.

16.34   Any party is entitled to give evidence, call witnesses, question witnesses and address the tribunal,[47] subject to the chairman or tribunal's discretion to conduct hearings as they consider appropriate.[48]

16.35   A respondent who fails to comply with an order or practice direction may have its response struck out.[49] A respondent whose response has not been accepted or who has not responded to the claim at all and has had default judgment entered against it cannot take part in the proceedings. A respondent who has not responded to the claim can apply for an extension of time for presenting a response, but only within the time limit for presenting a response.[50] A respondent who has not made a response or whose response has not been accepted can:

- make an application to review a default judgment against it;
- make an application to review any judgment made by administrative error, in the party's absence or where the interests of justice require a review;
- be called as a witness by another person;
- be sent a copy of a default judgment or corrected version of some other document sent out by the tribunal.[51]

45   ETA 1996 s6.
46   [2000] IRLR 251, CA.
47   2004 Rules r27(2).
48   2004 Rules r14(3).
49   2004 Rules r18(7)(e).
50   2004 Rules r4(4).
51   2004 Rules r9 as amended.

16.36 If a party who has been given notice of the Hearing fails to attend or be represented, the tribunal has a wide range of powers. The claim may be dismissed or disposed of in the absence of that party or the Hearing may be adjourned.[52] However, if the claim is to be dismissed or disposed of, the tribunal must first consider any information in its possession which has been made available to it by the parties.[53] This would appear to include, as under the old rules, the claim, the response, any further information which a party has been ordered to provide and written representations which may have been sent to the tribunal in advance of the hearing.

16.37 In practice, some tribunal offices make inquiries to ensure that the claimant has had proper notice of the Hearing by making phone calls, for example, to his or her home and employer (although this is not a requirement and no assumption should be made that a tribunal will do this). The EAT in *Southwark LBC v Bartholomew*[54] was of the view that it was a requirement for tribunals to make such enquiries. However, a subsequent EAT, again presided over by Burton P, in *Cooke v Glenrose Fish Company*[55] reconsidered the decision in *Bartholomew* and stated that the tribunal should only *consider* making such enquiries, although it held that it is best practice to make such enquiries, and that, on the facts, such enquiries should have been made. Neither case makes reference to the earlier decision of the Court of Appeal in *Roberts v Skelmersdale College*,[56] in which a claim was struck out when the claimant failed to attend at the Hearing. The Court of Appeal held that where a claimant fails to attend, the tribunal has no duty of its own motion to investigate the claim or to satisfy itself that the respondent has a good defence to the claim. The tribunal has a wide discretion and, in a proper case, is entitled to exercise that discretion to dismiss the claim without having considered further the evidence and the merits of the claim.

16.38 It should be noted that in the EAT appeals, above, there was no obvious reason for the non-attendance, while in *Roberts*, the claimant had been corresponding with the tribunal and knew that he had not been granted an adjournment of the Hearing, of which he claimed not to have received official notice. If there is no obvious reason for non-attendance, and the tribunal in the normal course of events

52 2004 Rules r27(5).
53 2004 Rules r27(6).
54 [2004] ICR 358, EAT.
55 EAT 0064/04.
56 [2004] IRLR 69 CA.

expects the claimant to arrive, it is likely to allow some leeway to a claimant, and may take another case while waiting for the claimant to arrive. It will be reluctant to determine or dismiss the case in the absence of any explanation from the claimant, but the tribunal certainly has the power to do so and frequently regards it as inappropriate to make inquiries. If there is a good explanation for non-attendance, a judgment can be set aside on an application for a review under 2004 Rules r34(1)(b), and the EAT in *Cooke* appeared to suggest that a review should be successful if there was such a good reason, coupled with an award of costs (or a preparation time order) for the respondent who had been required to attend at the original Hearing. If the fault for non-attendance lies with the claimant's representative, it would seem that the appropriate award would be one for wasted costs against that representative.

Written representations

16.39   Written representations can be made to the tribunal. They should be sent seven days before the Hearing with copies to other parties, but the tribunal has power to consider them even if they have been submitted within seven days of the Hearing.[57] In practice the tribunal will welcome the presentation of written arguments in skeleton form.

16.40   The real purpose of the rule allowing for written submissions is not clear: they do not replace oral evidence, especially as the tribunal has power to call witnesses and ask questions.[58] In pre-hearing reviews, however, written representations are crucial.

Adjournment or postponement

16.41   The circumstances in which a stay, adjournment or postponement is ordered are dealt with in chapter 12. The tribunal has a very wide discretion to permit or refuse an adjournment or postponement and in addition has a discretion specifically in relation to costs or preparation time incurred or allowances paid as a result of the postponement or adjournment of a Hearing or pre-hearing review.[59]

---

57   2004 Rules r14(5).
58   2004 Rules rr10(2)(c) and 14(3).
59   2004 Rules rr 10(2)(m), 40(1) and 44(1).

The issue to be determined

16.42 In most cases the issue to be determined will be clear: unfair dismissal, unauthorised deductions, sex discrimination, etc. In unfair dismissal cases, for example, tribunals often prefer to take evidence and make a decision on liability before dealing with remedies. This practice (which did not apply in Scotland) is now firmly discouraged, since the parties are warned in the listing letter to allow for all the time needed for the tribunal to reach a decision on all issues including remedy. It is important at the outset that the tribunal should announce, having considered representations, what issue it is about to determine. If, rarely, liability and remedy are to be determined at a split Hearing, it should also be made clear by the tribunal whether or not evidence is to be heard relating to liability for contributory fault or other conduct under Employment Rights Act (ERA) 1996 ss122(2) and 123(6).[60]

16.43 It would be contrary to the rules of natural justice for a tribunal which had announced it was to deal with only one issue to make findings on more than one without giving the parties an opportunity to make representations and call further evidence, or to take into account authorities playing a significant and material part in reaching a judgment or order without inviting representations on them.[61] It will also be contrary to the rules of natural justice for a tribunal to make findings in relation to a matter not pleaded by the claimant.[62] If an announcement has not been made at the outset, it must be assumed that evidence should be called relating to mitigation, remedies, reinstatement, a *Polkey*[63] reduction and so on.

16.44 If remedies are to be dealt with after a finding, or evidence, on liability, it is important to ensure that a date is fixed for the resumed Hearing on remedies, should the tribunal make a finding in favour of the claimant. It is convenient for all issues of liability, that is, liability and contributory conduct, to be dealt with at a single Hearing, since the evidence will be more or less the same, and it will enable the parties to make headway on negotiating a settlement following a successful result for the claimant once it is known whether, and if so to what extent, the claimant contributed to the dismissal.

60 *Iggesund Converters Ltd v Lewis* [1984] ICR 544; [1984] IRLR 431, EAT.
61 *Albion Hotel (Freshwater) Ltd v Maia e Silva* [2002] IRLR 200.
62 *Chapman v Simon* [1994] IRLR 124.
63 *Polkey v EA Dayton Services Ltd* [1987] IRLR 503, HL.

16.45   Separate Hearings are usually convenient for testing the material factor defence in equal pay claims.

16.46   In constructive dismissal cases, it is usually *unhelpful* to separate the issue of breach of contract from the issue of unfair dismissal. Again, the evidence is likely to be coterminous so that the claimant will be producing evidence to show that the employer behaved so badly that there was a breach of contract, and the employer will produce material either denying the facts said to constitute a breach of contract or seeking to show it behaved fairly.

16.47   In these circumstances, not much is to be gained by splitting the legal issues from the factual issues under ERA 1996 ss95(1) and 98(4). Most tribunals hearing an application to separate these considerations will hear all the evidence and make determinations on dismissal, that is, repudiation under ERA 1996 s95, the reason for dismissal under ERA 1996 s98(1) and the reasonableness of the dismissal under ERA 1996 s98(4). If the tribunal finds there was no dismissal, it is useful (for any future appeal) to invite the tribunal before the end of the Hearing to make decisions on the alternative hypothesis that if there *was* a dismissal, whether it was fair or unfair.

Late amendment, new allegations, late disclosure

16.48   Disputes about documents should be resolved at the outset of the Hearing, as should any last minute amendments to the claim, response, answers given to written questions from the tribunal and additional information provided. Concessions should also be made at this stage. Of course, amendments and concessions can be made during the course of proceedings. They are usually made orally, and if necessary can be reduced into writing at the end of the day.

Who goes first?

16.49   The running order should normally depend on where the burden of proof lies. As a rule of thumb, first in, last out operates, so that the party who has to prove any particular issue goes first and finishes last, that is, gives evidence first and makes the last speech. Once the burden of proof falls on a party, that party has not only the duty but the right to go first.[64] In unfair dismissal cases the burden of proof lies initially on the employer: to show the reason for dismissal and that it falls within the categories of fair dismissal in ERA 1996 s98(1) and (2).[65] The practical effect is that the employer goes first.

16.50 If the dismissal is not admitted, the burden of proof is on the employee. This assertion will be made either in the response or at the outset of the Hearing. If the employer disputes that there has been a constructive dismissal and claims the employee resigned or retired, the burden of proof is on the employee who will go first.

16.51 The burden is on the employer when there is a challenge to the jurisdiction of the tribunal, for example, that the claimant is said not to have the one year's continuous service entitling him or her to bring a claim of unfair dismissal. This practice has been approved by the EAT in *Post Office Counters Ltd v Heavey*.[66] As the chairman or tribunal must conduct a hearing in the manner considered most appropriate for the clarification of the issues and for handling the proceedings justly, it can decide to ask the employee to go first.[67]

16.52 Certain practical factors affect the way in which tribunals make this decision. If the claimant is unrepresented and is making allegations of unfair dismissal in a general way, it is often useful for the claimant to go first, not least because the concept of 'putting your case' is difficult to grasp (it means ensuring that every part of the case is put first to an employer's witness). If the employer is represented by a solicitor or counsel, the tribunal often invites the lawyer to outline briefly the facts and legal issues before inviting the claimant to give evidence. In other jurisdiction cases, the burden is on the claimant, for example, to prove the claim was made in time. In yet other cases, where the burden lies will depend on who has the means of producing the evidence of, for example, illness, knowledge, mistake.

16.53 The burden will transfer from claimant to respondent in sex, race, disability, sexual orientation and religion or belief discrimination cases if the claimant proves facts from which the tribunal could conclude in the absence of an adequate explanation that the respondent has committed or it to be treated as having committed an act of discrimination, unless the respondent proves that he did not commit

---

64 *Gill v Harold Andrews Sheepbridge Ltd* [1974] ICR 294; [1974] IRLR 109, NIRC.
65 *Maund v Penwith DC* [1984] IRLR 24.
66 [1990] ICR 1; [1989] IRLR 513.
67 2004 Rules r14(3); *Hawker Siddeley Power Engineering Ltd v Rump* [1979] IRLR 425, EAT.

or should not be treated as having committed that act.[68] The claimant will still call his or her evidence first in order to establish the prima facie case from which discrimination could be inferred, and the respondent knows that when it calls its evidence it has to disprove that prima facie case.

16.54   Although in almost all unfair dismissal cases where the dismissal is admitted, the employer's evidence is taken first, there is logically no reason why this should be so when a dismissal for a particular reason is accepted by the claimant. For example, the claimant says she was dismissed, the reason given is dishonesty and the claimant accepts that that was the reason but argues that the facts do not disclose dishonesty or do not give grounds for a dismissal in the circumstances. Here the employer has discharged the burden of proving the reason and a potentially fair reason and therefore, there being no burden of proof under ERA 1996 s98(4), it is logical to allow the claimant to make her allegations first and then to hear the evidence relating to the employer's explanation.

16.55   In both discrimination and dismissal cases there can be a very real advantage to the claimant in going first which should be seized if at all possible. In lengthy dismissal cases where the respondent opens, the first the tribunal hears from the claimant is after several days of evidence given by managers painting a very negative picture of his or her behaviour. In discrimination cases, the claimant naturally wishes to establish at the outset the wrong done to him or her. If the tribunal allows an opening speech to be made, this is the ideal opportunity for a statement to be made. And of course the press is more likely to be in attendance at the start of a Hearing than halfway through.

16.56   In claims for redundancy payments there is a presumption that a dismissal is on account of redundancy.[69] Therefore, an employer who claims that the reason for dismissal was not redundancy would go first, the onus being on the employer to prove this.

16.57   In claims combining unfair dismissal and discrimination, we suggest that as between the duty of the employer to show a reason for a dismissal and the right of a claimant to open a discrimination case, priority should be given to the claimant's right so that he or she would open all aspects of the discrimination and dismissal cases.

68   SDA 1975 s63A; RRA 1976 s54A, DDA 1995 s17A, EESO Regs 2003 reg 29(2) and EERB Regs 2003 reg 29(2); see also the decisions of the EAT in *Barton v Investec Henderson Crosthwaite Securities Ltd* [2003] IRLR 332, *University of Huddersfield v Wolff* [2004] IRLR 534 and *Chamberlin Solicitors v Emokpae* [2004] IRLR 592.
69   ERA 1996 s163(2).

16.58　　In equal pay cases where a material factor defence is raised under Equal Pay Act 1970 s1(3), the burden is on the employer. However, the claimant is still required to show an employment relationship and establish the basic facts against which (it is contended by the employer) a material factor defence exists to a claim for equal pay. Again, on a purely practical basis, the claimant should be allowed to open his or her case and call evidence. Although the focus of attention will quickly shift to the employer's material factor defence, at least the claimant will have established elementary components in his or her claim and the tribunal will have heard from him or her. At least one major equal pay case went to the Court of Appeal, back to the tribunal, then was referred to an independent expert, and it was more than five years before any claimant gave evidence.[70]

The opening speech

16.59　There is a right to make an opening speech only in appeals against training levies, prohibition, improvement and non-discrimination notices.[71] Otherwise there is no formal right. Rule 27(2) of the 2004 Rules entitles a party 'to address the tribunal' but this does not require the address to be made at the start of the case. Furthermore, rule 27(2) of the 2004 Rules is subject to rule 14(3), which gives the tribunal a wide discretion as to the handling of the proceedings. In Scotland, opening speeches are never made, except for appeals (above). In England and Wales and Northern Ireland, a brief opening may be permitted, or alternatively the tribunal may canvas the issues with the parties at the outset of the Hearing. If there are several claimants, each should be given the same right to open, as should multiple respondents if they open. If a respondent employer opens a case, the claimant employee coming second does not in practice make an opening speech.

16.60　　The purpose of an opening speech is to make a brief impression on the tribunal and to give a summary of the principal issues of law and of where disputes of fact will lie, together with a statement of what the person opening the case hopes to achieve. An outline of the evidence to be called and the names of witnesses are often given, but is not necessary. It can be risky to embark on a lengthy exploration of the evidence to be called if the witness whose evidence has been

---

70　*Bromley v H & J Quick Ltd* [1988] ICR 623; [1988] IRLR 249, CA.
71　2004 Rules Schs 3–5.

described does not subsequently come up to proof. As a matter of practicality, it is important to direct the tribunal to the relevant statutes (not quite so necessary in respect of ERA 1996 s98) and the names and at least the principles of relevant authorities which should be borne in mind by the tribunal during the Hearing.

16.61   It is not necessary to explore the bundles of documents. These will have to be examined by the relevant witnesses in any event – for example, a letter written by the manager dismissing the claimant will be examined by the writer and the recipient when they give their evidence. The law should be described neutrally but there is nothing wrong in making tendentious statements on your case at this stage.

Conduct of the hearing

16.62   Within the scope of the tribunal's duty under 2004 Rules r14(2) and (3) to avoid formality and conduct the proceedings 'in such manner as it considers most appropriate for the clarification of the issues . . . and the just handling of the proceedings', the tribunal has a very wide discretion. The duty clearly envisages a 'hands-on' approach if a tribunal cares to take it. The following issues may well arise in a Hearing.

Natural justice: a fair hearing

16.63   The conduct of the Hearing is subject to the rules of procedure (but not the civil law of evidence) and the rules of natural justice. They are now crystallised in the jurisprudence under article 6 of the European Convention on Human Rights (ECHR), incorporated by the Human Rights Act (HRA) 1998. These are that each side should be given the opportunity to present its case through evidence and argument and to cross-examine the other's witnesses. A serious allegation, should be made in such a way that the accused person has the fullest opportunity to meet it, consider its implications and to answer it. There will not be a fair Hearing if the allegation arises for the first time at the Hearing.[72] A judgment or order should not be reached on any issue about which a party has not been given the opportunity to

---

72   *Panama v Hackney LBC* [2003] IRLR 278 CA in which it was held that the claimant had not been afforded a fair Hearing when an allegation of fraud emerged for the first time in the course of cross-examination.

present evidence and address arguments.[73] As Lord Bridge said in *Lloyd v McMahon*:[74]

> ... the so-called rules of natural justice are not engraved on tablets of stone ... [W]hat the requirements of fairness demand when any body, domestic, administrative or judicial, has to make a decision which will affect the rights of individuals depends on the character of the decision-making body, the kind of decision it has to make and the statutory or other framework in which it operates

And in *Wiseman v Borneman*[75] Lord Reid said:

> Natural justice requires that the procedure before any tribunal which is acting judicially should be fair in all the circumstances, and I would be sorry to see this fundamental general principle degenerate into a series of hard and fast rules.

The right to a fair hearing under ECHR article 6 does not include a right to legal representation where no criminal charge is involved.[76] Lack of means to pay for legal representation has been held not to be a breach of the principle of equality of arms.

Formality

16.64   In *Aberdeen Steak Houses v Ibrahim*[77] the EAT laid down its own summary of what was required of tribunals under the rules of natural justice:

> Over the years a number of cases have given guidance on the appropriate procedure and on rules of evidence . . .
> (a) Some decisions bear upon the party who should present its case first: *Gill v Harold Andrews Sheepbridge Ltd* [1974] ICR 294 and *Oxford v DHSS* [1977] ICR 884.
> (b) It is for the party and not the tribunal to decide the order in which he calls his witnesses: *Barnes v BPC (Business Forms) Ltd* [1975] ICR 390.
> (c) It is the duty of the parties to ensure that all relevant evidence is put before the tribunal and it is not for the tribunal themselves to do this: *Craig v British Railways (Scottish Region)* (1973)8 ITR 636;

73   *Laurie v Holloway* [1994] ICR 32, EAT.
74   [1987] AC 625 at 702.
75   [1971] AC 297 at 308.
76   See, for example, *R v Securities and Futures Authority Ltd and another ex p Fleurose* [2001] IRLR 764.
77   [1988] ICR 550 at 557 per Wood J; [1988] IRLR 420, EAT.

Derby City Council v Marshall [1979] ICR 731; *Mensah v East Hertfordshire NHS Trust* [1998] IRLR 531, CA.

(d) A tribunal should not allow a party to be taken by surprise by an allegation of dishonesty made at the last minute, but should adjourn and give directions: *Hotson v Wisbech Conservative Club* [1984] ICR 859.

(e) When a party specifically states that he will not be calling evidence, he will normally be bound by his statement: *Stokes v Hampstead Wine Co Ltd* [1979] IRLR 298.

(f) Tribunals cannot refuse to admit evidence which is admissible and probative of one or more issues: *Rosedale Mouldings Ltd v Sibley* [1980] ICR 816.

Nevertheless in the same case the tribunal eschewed informality in accordance with what is now 2004 Rules r14(3) and said:

It is possible for informality to go too far and it is important for parties appearing before any judicial body and for their legal advisers in preparing for trial to know the rules normally to be applied during the hearing. It is important there should be consistency . . . Total informality and absence of generally recognised rules of procedure and evidence can be counter-productive.

The application of these judgments would ensure that tribunals do behave quite formally.

Human rights

16.65   The tribunal also falls under an obligation to be 'Convention compliant' by virtue of the fact that it is a public authority within the definition contained in HRA 1998 s6. Further, it has an obligation to construe if possible the legislation which it is required to interpret in a manner consistent with the Convention rights of parties before it.[78]

16.66   In *X v Y*,[79] the Court of Appeal considered a claim brought by a development officer for a charity working with young offenders who alleged that he had been unfairly dismissed in a manner inconsistent with respect for private life under ECHR article 8 and in breach of the prohibition in article 14 on the grounds of sexual orientation. Six months prior to his dismissal, he had been arrested and cautioned for committing a sexual act in a public toilet with another man, as a result of which his name appeared on the Sex Offenders Register. He

78   HRA 1998 s3.
79   [2004] IRLR 625, CA.

deliberately withheld this information from his employers, although he later accepted that the information was relevant for them to know. He was dismissed for committing a significant criminal offence and for deliberately failing to disclose it.

16.67   The Court of Appeal by a majority dismissed his appeal on the ground that the conduct did not take place in his private life nor within the scope of the application of his right to respect for it. It held that a criminal offence is not a purely private matter. The caution was relevant to his employment and he should have disclosed it. Further, their Lordships unanimously approved guidance for tribunals in determining human rights issues, namely:

i.   Do the circumstances of the dismissal fall within the ambit of one or more Convention rights? If not, the right is not engaged and need not be considered.
ii. If a right is engaged, does the state have a positive obligation to secure enjoyment of that right between private persons?
iii. If the state has such an obligation, is the interference with the employee's Convention right by dismissal justified? If so, the tribunal can proceed to (v).
iv. If it does not, was there a permissible reason for the dismissal under ERA 1996 which does not involve unjustified interference with a Convention right? If there was not, the dismissal will be unfair for the absence of a permissible reason to justify it.
v.   If there was an obligation, is the dismissal fair, tested by the provisions of ERA 1996 s98, reading and giving effect to them under HRA 1998 s3 so as to be compatible with a Convention right.

Admissibility of evidence

Estoppel

16.68   Estoppel is a rule of evidence which prevents cases, or issues in cases, being litigated twice. It operates as a defence and can be raised in tribunal proceedings.[80] An issue decided by a tribunal between the same parties will prevent either of the parties reopening the issue in, for example, subsequent tribunal proceedings or county court proceedings.[81]

---

80 *Henderson v Henderson* [1843] Hare 100; *Munir v Jang Publications Ltd* [1989] ICR 1; [1989] IRLR 224, CA.
81 *Green v Hampshire CC* [1979] ICR 861 and *O'Laoire v Jackel International Ltd* [1990] ICR 197; [1991] IRLR 70, CA.

16.69   The rule can prevent the reopening of a single issue or a whole cause of action. However, the original decision must have been within the competence of the original tribunal and have been essential for the decision in that case. If not, the decision is treated as a comment made by the way and not binding on subsequent tribunals and courts. The rule can additionally prevent a claim being made at a later date if there have been earlier proceedings, and the claim could and should have been brought forward in those proceedings.[82]

16.70   A particular difficulty in this context is created by the fact that employment tribunals do not have the power for proceedings to be discontinued as opposed to being withdrawn, as is the case under the Civil Procedure Rules (CPR). If a claimant in a civil claim discontinues a claim, he or she may apply to the court for permission to make another claim against the same defendant where that later claim arises from the same or substantially the same facts as the discontinued claim.[83] Thus, discontinuance does not release the cause of action, but preserves the right to establish an untried claim on the merits in other proceedings. The Court of Appeal held in the case of *AKO v Rothschild Asset Management Limited and another*[84] that when a claim was dismissed by the employment tribunal on withdrawal by the claimant at a stage before the respondent had even entered a response to the claim, that claimant was not estopped from raising the same points in subsequent proceedings, where the surrounding circumstances disclosed that the claimant intended effectively to discontinue when withdrawing a claim. The Court of Appeal therefore distinguished this situation from *Barber v Staffordshire CC*[85] where a claimant who had lodged a claim in the employment tribunal, which was dismissed on withdrawal on the day of the Hearing, was estopped from launching further proceedings on the same factual basis. The case had been going on for six months, a response to the claim had been presented, directions given, and a tribunal of three members was presented with a compromise agreement in which the claimant withdrew her claim and the respondent undertook not to make any applications (the clear inference being a costs application). Thus in *Barber*, the claimant had decided to abandon her claim, and was treated as estopped from pursing a fresh claim

82   *Divine-Bortey v Brent LBC* [1998] ICR 886 CA.
83   CPR 38.7.
84   [2002] IRLR 348, CA.
85   [1996] IRLR 209, CA.

arising from the same facts. Despite the Court of Appeal's observations in *AKO*, no power to discontinue proceedings has been granted to tribunals in the 2004 Rules.[86]

Hearsay

16.71 A statement made by a person who is not a witness in proceedings, adduced for the purpose of establishing the truth of what that person said, is hearsay and would be admissible in a civil court to the extent permitted by the Civil Evidence Act 1995. Tribunals may, and frequently, do take hearsay evidence. It is quite proper, albeit tactically injudicious, to object to it being heard at the time, and to lay down a marker so that in a closing speech the tribunal can be asked to pay less attention to that evidence because it was not subject to cross-examination. However, it must be borne in mind that, since the 1995 Act, hearsay is generally let in, and objecting to it is generally pointless. Once in, it can be criticised as being of light weight, but that is different.

16.72 Quite often the issue before a tribunal is not the truth, but what was known to an employer at the time a decision to dismiss was made. So in *Coral Squash Clubs Ltd v Matthews*[87] it was held that it was quite proper, and indeed necessary, for hearsay evidence to be adduced before the tribunal about information given to the employer. It did not matter whether the information was correct or not; the central question was what material was available before the employer decided to dismiss. Clearly, if the information is unsatisfactory and requires further investigation, it will often be unreasonable for the employer to dismiss on that basis.

16.73 The short point about hearsay evidence is that anyone who has relevant evidence must be brought to the tribunal as a witness. The more important their evidence, the more necessary it is for them to be there. The booklet accompanying the notice of Hearing warns parties that it is 'rarely satisfactory' for signed statements to be relied upon in the absence of the makers of those statements, particularly where that evidence might be challenged, and that it is the responsibility of a party to ensure that witnesses attend a Hearing. If they are going to give evidence, hearsay evidence from another witness is unnecessary. If they are not going to give evidence, hearsay evidence is of limited weight. Objection at the moment of its being given is

---

86 See 2004 Rules r25 on the right to withdraw proceedings.
87 [1979] ICR 607; [1979] IRLR 390, EAT.

often counter-productive, but the point should be made when addressing the tribunal in a closing speech.

Material before and after the relevant event

16.74   As a general rule, events after the relevant date are immaterial, for example, after the date of dismissal in an unfair dismissal case.[88] In such a case the central question is the information available to the employer at the time of the dismissal.

16.75   In cases of discrimination, particularly when the claimant still works for the employer, events before and after the event giving rise to the claim may be introduced in evidence 'if logically probative of a relevant fact'. In *Chattopadhyay v Headmaster of Holloway School*,[89] for the purpose of proving racial discrimination, evidence was admissible of hostility to the claimant both before the relevant event and after it.

16.76   If what is alleged is a series of discriminatory acts, then all evidence within the relevant time period will be admissible. The tribunal must examine all allegations of incidents relied upon as evidentiary facts of discrimination in the matters complained of, and these facts can both pre-date and post-date the substantive complaints of discrimination. The tribunal is required to find primary facts about those allegations from which they will be asked to draw inferences and then look at the totality in order to consider whether it is legitimate to infer discrimination in relation to the complaints in the claim.[90] A claimant is permitted to present evidence of matters long-past which are not the allegations made in the claim but which the claimant alleges amount to less favourable treatment in order to raise the inference that the ground of less favourable treatment in relation to the claim is a prohibited one.[91]

Without prejudice communications

16.77   These should not be introduced in the proceedings in evidence-in-chief or cross-examination. If a party wants to protect their position

---

88   *Devis Ltd v Atkins* [1977] ICR 662; [1977] IRLR 314, HL.
89   [1982] ICR 132; [1981] IRLR 487, EAT.
90   *Qureshi v Victoria University of Manchester* [2001] ICR 863.
91   *Commissioner of Police of the Metropolis v Hendricks* [2003] ICR 530. Note, however, the Court of Appeal's guidance about the case management obligations of parties where allegations range over a lengthy period of time to keep the discrimination proceedings within reasonable bounds by concentrating on the most serious and most recent allegations.

on an offer to settle, they should mark the offer 'without prejudice except as to costs'. It can then be opened up once the decision has been made and the only argument is over costs, or costs after a good offer has been made and rejected.

Credibility and collateral matters

16.78   As Wood J said in *Aberdeen Steak Houses Ltd v Ibrahim*:[92]

> When in cross-examination questions go to credit only, the party cross-examining should be bound by the answers of the witness.

This means strictly that it is not possible to call evidence to contradict evidence given by a witness affecting to the witness' credibility. It is part of a rule which prevents the admission of collateral evidence as to character or disposition indicating (largely to create an aura of prejudice) that the witness on previous occasions did wrong and therefore is likely to have done so on the occasion in question.

16.79   In *Snowball v Gardner Merchant Ltd*,[93] a claimant complaining of persistent sex discrimination was cross-examined as to her propensity to talk to fellow employees freely about sexual matters. She denied this and it was anticipated that evidence would be called by the employers to show that she was lying. The EAT upheld the admissibility of this evidence. The claimant argued that her attitude was in any event irrelevant to the question of whether she had been sexually harassed, but the EAT held that such evidence was relevant to any injury or detriment she may have claimed. It was therefore admitted even though indirectly it went to her credit (as was its purpose).

16.80   The general rule, more likely to be enforced in the light of the rule relating to the non-disclosure of the identity of those affected by allegations of sexual misconduct, is that evidence given in cross-examination relating to credibility is binding on those doing the cross-examining, and no new evidence may be brought to contradict it. Furthermore, evidence of an alleged propensity to sexual permissiveness is not relevant, and is therefore collateral, to the central issue of liability for sexual harassment. It is also unlikely to stand up to the right to privacy in ECHR article 8.

---

92   [1988] ICR 550.
93   [1987] ICR 719; [1987] IRLR 397, EAT.

16.81   It follows that, as in criminal courts, evidence as to the bad character of a witness or party will seldom be admissible.[94]

Sworn evidence

16.82   Tribunals are required to ensure that parties and witnesses who attend the Hearing give evidence on oath or affirmation by 2004 Rules r27(3). This requirement will apply equally to cases where interpreters are used, who are required to take an oath or affirmation that they will interpret truthfully and faithfully what the witness says. The usual practice in the absence of a clerk is for the chairman to administer the oath or affirmation in accordance with the wishes of the witness. A supply of holy books is available in all tribunals, and staff have been instructed to pay particular attention to the respectful preservation and handling of them.

16.83   Interpreters can also be used to assist disabled parties and witnesses, and the tribunal may award fees or expenses to enable them to attend. An application should be made at an early stage to the tribunal.

Notes of evidence

16.84   There is no statutory requirement for the chairman or other members to take notes. However, it has been held that a clear note should be taken of the relevant evidence by the chairman which should be made available if directed by the EAT in an appeal alleging, for example, perversity.[95] The Tribunals and Inquiries Act 1992 s10, which regulates tribunals, requires the relevant tribunal to give reasons. Rule 30(1) of the 2004 Rules also specifies that a tribunal or chairman must give oral or written reasons for any judgment or order, although reasons need only be given for orders where a request is made for them before or at the hearing where the order is made. The giving of reasons is a requirement of a judicial body such as a tribunal under ECHR article 6. If the reasons cannot be traced to the evidence, or the agreed documents, the tribunal's judgment is perverse.

---

94 Although, in criminal courts, it is now the case that cross-examination as to a complainant's sexual history is not permitted without leave of the court, such leave only being granted when belief as to consent is in issue: Youth Justice and Criminal Evidence Act 1999 s41.

95 *Houston v Lightwater Farms Ltd* [1990] ICR 502; [1990] IRLR 469, EAT.

Witness statements

16.85   Evidence from non-expert witnesses is increasingly called for in the form of written statements.[96] This almost corresponds to the production of witness statements by exchange in the civil courts.[97] The practice in the tribunals is to encourage parties to exchange witness statements, and this may be the subject of an order by the chairman on a party's application or of his or her own initiative.

16.86   The witness statement itself is not evidence until it is adduced by the relevant witness. Practice varies from region to region but it is usual for a witness to read his or her own statement. He or she may be asked supplementary questions by the representative of the party for whom the evidence is given, but permission is required to do this. It is more likely to arise when this party's case is presented second, since the witness may need to deal with any conflicts which have emerged in the case thus far. Tribunals can be reluctant to permit lengthy supplementary questions when the evidence sought from the witness should have been included within the witness statement.[98]

16.87   Witness statements are a very powerful tool. Given proper attention, a witness' evidence can be honed to perfection by skilled advisers. Since they are not always exchanged in advance, it is difficult to cross-examine immediately on every line in the statement. Examination-in-chief in the traditional way, without handing in a statement, gives more time to absorb the material and prepare cross-examination in addition to that prepared in advance. Mutual exchange is now common practice when parties are represented at a tribunal. Sometimes the procedure is shortened even further – if there are no other people present in the tribunal apart from the parties and their witnesses, the tribunal itself may retire to read the witness statements. Even if members of the public are present, statements can be taken 'as read' if a copy is left on the clerk's table for the public to read.

16.88   Live evidence given by a person who has not presented a written statement cannot be excluded on that ground alone, and it will be a breach of the rules of natural justice and ECHR article 6 to refuse to hear it. The failure to prepare a witness statement can be relevant to costs, particularly if an adjournment is required to deal with matters

---

96 See 2004 Rules r10(2)(s).
97 See CPR 32.4.
98 See CPR 32.5 for the restrictive approach of the civil courts to oral supplementary evidence.

arising from the evidence given. It should be noted that witness statements will normally not be available when the witness is being called pursuant to a witness order issued by the tribunal.[99]

16.89　　Witnesses who provide a written statement for lawyers and other representatives should carefully read the statement, making alterations and corrections as appropriate, and sign it only if all of it is correct. One advantage of written statements is that the parties can see where the conflict lies if, before the Hearing, there has been an exchange of statements.

The sequence of evidence

Evidence-in-chief

16.90　On the assumption that the employer is opening the case, evidence-in-chief from the primary witness will be called first. If a witness statement exists, it should be read. Questions may be asked in non-leading form. The best answers are monosyllabic or at most one-liners. It is important that the witness gives evidence in relation to all matters about which he or she has any information. In particular, they should be asked about all documents in the bundle for which they are responsible, that is, those they have written, or, for example, if the personnel manager, documents relevant to the personnel function – procedure agreements, disciplinary codes and so on. Witnesses should also be asked about letters which they have received so that they can say what they did when they received them and what their reaction was to them. All relevant matters must be spoken to.[100] It is good practice for the paragraphs of the witness statements to cross-refer to the relevant pages of the bundle containing the documents referred to in the evidence.

16.91　　Leading questions, which suggest the answer to be given, must not be asked without the tribunal's (or the other side's) permission and should be confined to issues which are not in dispute between the parties.

Cross-examination

16.92　The (usually elusive) goal of cross-examination is the extraction of an admission on one of the main issues in favour of the party cross-

99　2004 Rules r10(2)(c).
100　*Aberdeen Steak Houses v Ibrahim* [1988] ICR 550; [1988] IRLR 420, EAT.

examining. Such admissions are quite rare and admissions as to motive may be of limited value. Even an admission that the employer did not behave fairly or reasonably is not conclusive of the issue; the tribunal will still have to make up its own mind irrespective of admissions made by a witness for one of the parties. That in a sense is a question of opinion. Admissions as to facts will however be important.

16.93   The more prosaic purpose of cross-examination is to ensure that all points of the claimant's case have been put to the respondent or vice versa. A witness cannot raise evidence about matters upon which they have not given the other side's witnesses an opportunity to comment. If such questions are raised, it is likely to invoke an application to recall a witness which will have the attendant disadvantage of reinforcing that witness' testimony by leaving in the mind of the tribunal the enduring image of the witness.

16.94   Cross-examination consists of asking leading questions and is *not* restricted to material which has been adduced in-chief. Questioning can be on any matter relevant to the issues to be decided, but a party does not have 'an absolute right to cross-examine come what may'; the issue being asked about must be 'of assistance' to the tribunal.[101] The tribunal can properly control a line of questioning which appears to it not to be relevant to the issues requiring its determination. Any document about which the witness has some relevant input can also be put in cross-examination.

Questions by the tribunal

16.95   The most appropriate time for this to occur is immediately following cross-examination, but practices vary. For example, some tribunals ask questions throughout the Hearing, while some remain silent until after re-examination. The advantage in having the tribunal ask questions immediately following cross-examination is that it cuts down on the number of opportunities given to the representatives to ask further questions and therefore saves time. If questions are asked at this stage, the tribunal ought, in accordance with the rules of natural justice, to allow an opportunity to cross-examine on any new matter arising out of their questions. Parties should pay careful attention to tribunal questions as they can be a useful indicator of how the tribunal views the case and as to which are the issues upon which

101 *Zurich Insurance Co v Gulson* [1998] IRLR 118, EAT.

it requires persuasion. A scrupulous tribunal will ask open (not leading) questions.

Re-examination

16.96   This ought to be strictly confined to matters which have been raised in cross-examination and in questions by the tribunal. If a document has been raised in cross-examination, the whole of the document can be the subject of re-examination. As before, questions must be in non-leading form. If you have forgotten to put a point, it is better to own up, seek permission from the tribunal to deal with the matter in re-examination, and offer the other side an opportunity to cross-examine on it.

Power of tribunal to call witnesses of its own initiative

16.97   Rule 10(2)(c) of the 2004 Rules states that a chairman may, on the application of either party or of his or her own motion, require the attendance of any person in Great Britain, either to give evidence or to produce documents or information. In *Clapson v British Airways*,[102] the EAT held that, in a case where the claimant decided not to give evidence, the tribunal was entitled to issue a witness order compelling him to do so. Furthermore, under 2004 Rules r14(3), the tribunal could then decide that both sides be permitted to cross-examine that witness. The EAT stated that the procedure in an employment tribunal was part inquisitorial and part adversarial; it is a procedure peculiar to itself and not equivalent to the Civil Procedure Rules followed in civil courts (where a judge cannot order that a person gives evidence).

Rulings during the course of the Hearing

16.98   Depending on the degree of intervention by the chairman, tribunals make rulings from time to time or throughout a Hearing. Parties are encouraged to move on in their questioning, to give more attention to certain points, or told that they 'need not be troubled by' a particular point. A chairman might openly reflect on what appear to the tribunal to be the essentials of the case. Most of this is done as directions without being the subject of a formal ruling. However, three situations may call for a ruling in the course of the Hearing.

102   [2001] IRLR 184, EAT.

Admissibility of evidence

16.99 If there is a dispute on the admissibility of evidence, with arguments addressed by both sides, the chairman should be asked to give a ruling. The ruling may be accompanied by reasons at the time or by an undertaking that the reasons will form part of the reasons in the judgment.

Half-time submission of no case to answer

16.100 After the presentation of the whole of one side's evidence, which means the closing of its case, it is sometimes possible to make a submission that there is no case to answer. The EAT has approved this practice for both simple unfair dismissal cases and for constructive dismissals.[103] The device is particularly appropriate where there is a burden of proof and the party with the burden has a very weak case, or where an essential component for liability is missing. Such submissions are, however, rare. In *Logan v Commissioners of Customs and Excise*,[104] the Court of Appeal cautioned tribunals against such submissions in the following terms:

> Submissions of no case to answer are dangerous to make and to allow. It should be rare for a submission of no case to answer to be made to an employment tribunal and more rare for the submission to succeed. The law was trenchantly and accurately summarised in *Clarke v Watford Borough Council* as follows: '(1) There is no inflexible rule of law and practice that a tribunal must always hear both sides, although that should normally be done. (2) The power to stop a case at 'half-time' must be exercised with caution. (3) It may be a complete waste of time to call upon the other party to give evidence in a hopeless case. (4) Even where the onus of proof lies on the claimant, as in discrimination cases, it will only be in exceptional or frivolous cases that it would be right to take such a course. (5) Where there is no burden of proof, as under section 98(4) of the Employment Rights Act, it will be difficult to envisage arguable cases where it is appropriate to terminate the proceedings at the end of the first party's case.' The fourth proposition applies not only in discrimination cases but also in cases of constructive dismissal.

16.101 The party making the submission is not required by the tribunal to make an 'election'. In other words, the party does not have to choose

---

103 *George A Palmer Ltd v Beeby* [1978] ICR 196; *Walker v Josiah Wedgwood & Sons Ltd* [1978] ICR 744; [1978] IRLR 105.
104 [2004] IRLR 63, CA.

between a submission and calling no evidence. If the submission fails, evidence can still be called. The only danger to representatives is that the submission should avoid a statement that no evidence will be called. This happened in *Stokes v Hampstead Wine Co Ltd*[105] and so when the submission was rejected, the tribunal refused to allow the party to call any evidence. There is thus no formal risk to the case except the inherent danger that in making the submission you draw attention to a weakness or missing component in the other side's case, which may be put right on cross-examination of your own witnesses.

16.102   It is dangerous to call no evidence if the submission has been rejected. The tribunal will have made clear that it needs further persuasion and probably more evidence before it makes a decision in that party's favour on the merits.

16.103   Because of the tripartite character of the tribunal, it is less likely than a court or a chairman sitting alone to accept such a submission. Tribunals generally prefer to have both sides give their evidence. This is particularly so when the party going first is not represented and the party going second is. Bear in mind that if you are of the view that the other party's case is so weak as to be misconceived (which should be the case if a submission of no case to answer is being considered) that an application for costs can be made at the end of the case in addition to or instead of a submission of no case to answer.

16.104   A middle road which often emerges is encouragement by the tribunal to the parties to 'consider their positions' and try and settle. This practice, if done subtly and without expressing a firm view, is encouraged by the EAT as a means of shortening cases. For example, having heard the employer's witnesses about the circumstances of a dismissal and the absence of a proper procedure to deal with it, there may be little the claimant needs to add for a finding of unfair dismissal to be made, at least on procedural grounds. If the tribunal takes the provisional view that the employer's case is hopeless when it is closed, there is no reason to give the employer the chance to improve its case by exposing the claimant to cross-examination.

Unfairness during the hearing

16.105 The conduct of the Hearing by the chairman or the interventions by members can be the subject of a complaint of bias, apparent bias or

105   [1979] IRLR 298, EAT.

unfairness. Indeed a complaint may be made under ECHR article 6. Bias in its strict sense of involvement by a member in the outcome of the case, and prior knowledge of members either of the subject matter of the case or of the witnesses, are grounds for complaint at the start. The proper objective test to apply to the conduct of a Hearing in determining whether there is apparent bias is to ascertain all the circumstances which have a bearing on the suggestion that the tribunal was biased and then ask whether those circumstances would lead a fair-minded and informed observer, having considered the facts, to consider that there was a real possibility that the tribunal was biased.[106]

16.106   Complaints of bias should be raised by way of appeal – parties are not expected to raise such matters during the course of the Hearing.[107] In *Simper*, an application was made criticising the chairman's biased comments at the end of the claimant's cross-examination and before an adjourned Hearing. In fact the case was remitted to a fresh tribunal, but it was stressed that the proper course is to wait until the case is concluded:

> Save in extraordinary circumstances, it cannot be right for a litigant, unhappy with what he believes to be the indications from the tribunal as to how the case is progressing, to apply, in the middle of the case, for a re-hearing before another tribunal.

16.107 This is because it is undesirable for the tribunal to have to adjudicate on its own bias.[108] As a matter of general practice, it has been held that a party who considers that there is a risk that the tribunal is biased against it should not decline to participate in the proceedings, but rather appeal the decision on the issue of bias thereafter if it wishes to do so.[109]

16.108   Although the test in complaints of bias is an objective one,[110] tribunal members frequently raise matters themselves if they consider that a party could take objection (see also para 16.19). A common

106 *Porter v Magill* [2002] 2 AC 357, HL.
107 *Peter Simper & Co Ltd v Cooke* [1986] IRLR 19, EAT, per Peter Gibson J.
108 *Simper* was affirmed by the Court of Appeal in *Bennett v Southwark LBC* [2002] ICR 881. In this case it was held that a tribunal had been wrong to recuse themselves and refuse to hear the case without giving the parties an opportunity to comment in circumstances where a black representative had made allegations that he would have been treated differently if white.
109 *Turner v Harada Ltd* [2001] EWCA Civ 599; LTL 6/4/01 upholding the approach in *Simper & Co Ltd v Cooke* [1986] IRLR 19, EAT.
110 See *Porter v Magill* [2002] 2 AC 357, HL.

sense approach was taken in the case of *Williams v HM Inspector of Taxes,* one of the cases heard with *Locabail (UK) Limited v Bayfield Properties Ltd,*[111] where the Court of Appeal held that the suggestion of there being apparent bias on the part of a tribunal chairman who had once worked for the Inland Revenue in a junior capacity 35 years before, was fanciful.

16.109　If the conduct of the tribunal does become unacceptable, it is worth bearing in mind the *EAT Practice Direction* of December 2002[112] which provides (at para 11) that full particulars of any complaint must be given in the notice of appeal, and affidavits must be sworn by the complainant or relevant witnesses and advisers. These will all be sent to the chairman, and possibly the lay members, for appropriate comments. See also chapter 23 on EAT appeals.

16.110　This means that a party will need to be ready to justify fully any allegation made. In practice, complaints are rare and successful complaints even rarer. The Practice Direction warns parties that the EAT recognises the obligation of tribunals to observe the overriding objective and their wide powers of case management and that appeals in respect of their conduct are the less likely to succeed. Parties are also warned that the unsuccessful pursuit of such allegations, particularly in respect of case management decisions, may put the party raising the allegation at risk of an order for costs.

16.111　The Court of Appeal considered bias in tribunal proceedings in the case of *Lodwick v Southwark LBC.*[113] The claimant had brought a complaint of unfair dismissal and breach of contract. The chairman before whom he appeared had previously criticised his conduct in another case in which the claimant had represented one of the parties and an award of costs had been made against his client. The claimant asked the chairman to recuse himself which he refused to do, on the basis that the tribunal had three members and it would be possible for the claimant to have a fair Hearing. The tribunal subsequently dismissed the claims and ordered the claimant to pay £4,000 worth of costs. Overturning the decision of the tribunal and the EAT, the Court of Appeal took the view that the tribunal ought to have considered whether a fair minded observer would have considered that there was a bias. The fact that the chairman was the only legally qualified member of the tribunal made his position an important one and any

---

111　[2000] QB 451; [2000] IRLR 96, CA.
112　See appendix B.
113　[2004] ICR 884, CA.

apparent bias on his part was not nullified by the presence of his two wing members.[114]

16.112 The fact that a tribunal has given a premature expression of concluded views or has manifested a closed mind prior to giving its final decision may give rise to a complaint of apparent bias. However, the tribunal is permitted to share preliminary views with the parties, provided that they are genuinely preliminary. A strongly worded view can be a provisional one, and there is no impropriety in a tribunal encouraging the settlement of proceedings.[115] However, tribunals are warned that, as a matter of good practice, the parties should be left in no doubt that such expressions of view are only provisional and that the tribunal remains open to persuasion.[116]

16.113 Complaints about the conduct of the Hearing which do not fall into the categories of bias or apparent bias, namely that there has been unfairness, should be raised forthwith. So, a complaint that a member is not paying attention or has fallen asleep should, as a general rule, be raised at once.[117]

16.114 However, this will not necessarily prevent an appeal. The Court of Appeal in *Stansbury v Datapulse plc*,[118] which involved an allegation by the claimant that one of the lay members had been drunk and asleep during the Hearing of his claim, were of the view that while it was desirable for matters to be mentioned at the Hearing, it would be 'unrealistic' not to recognise the difficulties in raising a complaint with the tribunal.[119] In such circumstances, the Court of Appeal recognised that the Employment Appeal Tribunal might have to assume the role of judge of fact in relation to the complaint and resolve any factual disputes but that the Appeal Tribunal would be entitled to ask whether, on the assumption that the allegations were established, that was sufficient to vitiate the fairness of the Hearing. On the facts, the Court of Appeal decided on the balance of probabilities that the allegations were made out and remitted the case for rehearing, notwithstanding the fact that the claimant's counsel had not raised the matter at the Hearing.

---

114 See the decision of the House of Lords in *Lawal v Northern Spirit* [2003] IRLR 538 regarding the importance of the role of the legally qualified EAT judge.
115 *Southwark LBC v Jiminez* [2003] ICR 1176.
116 [2003] ICR 1176 per Gibson LJ at p1191.
117 *Red Bank Manufacturing Co Ltd v Meadows* [1992] ICR 204; [1992] IRLR 209, EAT.
118 [2004] ICR 523, CA.
119 Note however that these comments are strictly obiter as recognised by Peter Gibson LJ at p531.

Recall of witnesses

16.115 If new material emerges during the evidence of the party giving evidence second, it is right to allow the recall of witnesses whose case was presented first. But it would not be right to allow a represented party to make an allegation in cross-examination which could have been dealt with in evidence-in-chief by his or her own witness, in order to have a second bite at the cherry. For example, in an unfair dismissal case with the employer giving evidence first, allegations relating to contributory fault must be made during that evidence and should not be put for the first time in cross-examination of the claimant.

16.116   Given the requirement to attempt informality, most tribunals would allow an application to recall the witness either because of the mistake by a representative or by an unrepresented party in not addressing the issue properly first time around, or because the interests of justice require it. It should be borne in mind that as a matter of weight, little would be attached to the recall of a witness to deal with a matter which could have been dealt with by evidence-in-chief; it rather gives the impression of second thoughts or a last-ditch attempt to win the case.

Closing speeches

16.117 According to the rule of 'first in, last out', which is usually followed in England and Wales , the party giving evidence second goes first with closing speeches. In Scotland, closing speeches generally follow the order in which the evidence in the case was led. This will be the party's first opportunity to address the tribunal and is the manifestation of the right to do so contained in rule 27(2) of the 2004 Rules. In a well-conducted case, any authorities either party relies on will have been notified to each other and to the tribunal at the outset, and may have been described briefly by the representative opening the case. A representative is obliged to produce and deal with all authorities relevant to the case, whether helpful or unhelpful to their own argument. In particular, you must not wait for the other side to cite an authority first and hope to be given the opportunity to reply to it.[120]

16.118   The closing speech summarises the main points of the evidence.

---

120 See *Sinclaire Roche & Temperley v Heard* [2004] IRLR 763 on written submissions, see also para 15.9 above.

Where there is a conflict, the tribunal should be invited to make findings of fact in accordance with the evidence as that party or their representative sees it. Submissions are made on the law. On some points the tribunal may interrupt and give a right to reply once it has heard the way the other side puts it. It will do this where, during the course of the Hearing, the argument may have become much more difficult for the other side to oppose.

16.119   A closing speech for the party which has the burden of proof comes last. Since this party may at least briefly have opened on the central issues of law, it is not so necessary to deal in detail with all the authorities. It is quite proper to ask the other side when reading passages from an authority to read out passages, in addition to those already read, so as to draw the tribunal's attention to parts of the case on which it is intended to rely, and avoid repetition when making the closing speech. Otherwise it is best to keep quiet.

16.120   At this stage it is permissible for the tribunal to indicate its likely finding on any particular point. It does so by 'not calling on' the representative to deal with any particular point. In other words if after hearing A's argument on a particular point, it is convinced of the facts and the legal arguments, it is unnecessary to ask for the point to be elaborated further by B's side. If a representative is stopped in his or her tracks in this way, it will be a breach of the rules of natural justice for the tribunal to find against their client on that point.

16.121   The other side is not usually entitled to say anything after the party going first has made a closing speech. Occasionally, where new points of law or new cases are referred to in the closing speech, the other side has a right to reply but it does require a careful application and a sympathetic tribunal. If A has been informed of the cases on which B intends to rely, the fact that they are raised for the first time in B's closing speech does not entitle A to come back in reply and have the last word. It should have dealt with them in its own closing speech.

Orders, judgments and reasons

Introduction

17.1 The decision of the tribunal must have formal characteristics. A chairman may issue the following types of decision on behalf of him/herself or of a tribunal:

(a) a default judgment;[1]

(b) a judgment, being a final determination of the proceedings or a particular issue in those proceedings, which may include an award of compensation, a declaration or recommendation and may also include orders for costs, preparation time or wasted costs;[2]

(c) an order in relation to interim matters which will direct a person to do or not to do something;[3]

(d) a decision not to accept a claim.[4]

17.2 A judgment, including an order for costs or preparation time is entered on the register.[5] Written reasons are also be entered in the register. The register is open to public inspection without charge at all reasonable hours.[6] Material in any judgment, document or record of proceedings which is likely to lead to the identification of people involved in an allegation of the commission of a sexual offence must be deleted and omitted from the register.[7] Reasons for judgments must also be omitted from the register in any case in which evidence has been heard in private and the tribunal or chairman so directs.[8]

17.3 At the end of a hearing, the chairman must either give the order or judgment or may reserve the decision to be given in writing at a later date. When judgment is reserved, a written judgment will be sent to the parties 'as soon as practicable', it must be accompanied by guidance notes on how to review or appeal the judgment.[9] The judgment must be signed by the chairman or, if he or she is unable to do so because of incapacity, by the regional chairman or Vice President

---

1 Employment Tribunals Rules of Procedure 2004 (2004 Rules) r8(1), contained in Employment Tribunals (Constitution and Rules of Procedure) Regulations 2004 (2004 Regs) Sch 1.

2 2004 Rules r28 (1)(a).

3 2004 Rules r28(1)(b).

4 2004 Rules r3(5).

5 2004 Regs reg 17(1).

6 2004 Regs reg 17(2)(b) and Sch 1 r32(1).

7 2004 Rules r49.

8 2004 Rules r32(2).

9 2004 Rules r29(2).

where the chairman has dealt with the proceedings alone, or by the other members of the tribunal.[9a] The judgment of the tribunal can be by a majority but if only two people constitute the tribunal, the chairman has a casting vote.[10]

17.4   When the judgment includes an award of compensation or a determination that one party is required to pay a sum to another (which does not include an order for costs, allowances, preparation time or wasted costs), it must include the amount payable. The amount stated in the judgment becomes payable forty-two days after the date on which the judgment was sent to the parties. This is when the time to appeal runs out. The time for appealing or requesting reasons runs from the date of judgment (see paras 23.27–23.28).

Reasons

17.5   It is important to note the distinction between cases where reasons must be given and, within those, where reasons must be given in writing. The principle is that there should be reasons, so the parties know why they have won or lost the case or the point in issue, but they do not always have to be given in writing. The chairman must give *written* reasons for a decision not to accept a claim. The tribunal *must* always give reasons for a judgment. The reasons may be oral or written. Similarly, it must give reason for an order, but only *if requested* by a party. There is, apparently, no requirement to given reasons for a default judgment,[11] but in practice short reasons ought to be given since it determines liability and remedy. Under European Convention on Human Rights (ECHR) article 6.1 reasons for such a judgment would be necessary.

17.6   Reasons can be given orally at the time of issuing the judgment or order or they can be reserved to be given in writing at a later date. If reasons are given orally, they will not be provided in writing unless a party requests them or they are requested by the Employment Appeal Tribunal (EAT). The request for reasons must be made before the hearing, at the hearing or, if the written judgment or order is sent to the parties thereafter, within 14 days of the date on which it was sent.

9a   2004 Rules r31. The person signing must also certify that the chairman is
       unable to sign.
10   2004 Rules r28(4).
11   2004 Rules r8.

17.7 When a tribunal reserves its reasons, those must be given in writing, since 2004 Rules r30(2) provides for reasons to be given orally, or 'reserved to be given in writing'. When reasons are given orally a party knows why it has won or lost and will request written reasons when an appeal is being contemplated. If an appeal is a possibility, it is advisable to request written reasons at the hearing. The 14 day limit under the 2004 Rules will have to be heeded in any event.[12]

17.8 The 2004 Rules r30(6) prescribe the information which must be contained in the written reasons for a judgment as follows:

(a) the issues which the tribunal or chairman has identified as being relevant to the claim;

(b) if some identified issues were not determined, what those issues were and why they were not determined;

(c) findings of fact relevant to the issues which have been determined;

(d) a concise statement of the applicable law;

(e) how the relevant findings of fact and applicable law have been applied in order to determine the issues; and

(f) where a judgment includes an award of compensation or a determination that one party make a payment to another, a table showing how the amount or sum has been calculated or a description of the manner in which it has been calculated.

17.9 It would be sensible for the same approach to be taken by chairmen when providing oral reasons for their tribunal judgments. Reasons should:

> . . . contain an outline of the story which has given rise to the complaint and a summary of the tribunal's basic factual conclusions and a statement of the reasons which have led them to reach the conclusion which they do on those basic facts. The parties are entitled to be told why they have won or lost. There should be sufficient account of the facts and of the reasoning to enable the EAT . . . to see whether any question of law arises; and it is highly desirable that the decision of an industrial tribunal should give guidance both to employers and trade unions as to practices which should or should not be adopted.[13]

17.10 It has been held by the Court of Appeal that, on an application to

12 See rule 30(3) and (5).
13 *Meek v City of Birmingham DC* [1987] IRLR 250, CA at 251 per Bingham LJ.

appeal when insufficient reasons have been given, a judge should refuse permission to appeal if the defect can be remedied by giving further reasons.[13a] The practice of remitting cases for further reasons to be given, having adjourned an appeal, has also been approved by the EAT.[14]

17.11   A mistake in the reasons relating to a fact such as a date or the name of a person should be pointed out (tactfully) inviting a correction. Leaving errors on the record is undesirable and encourages false hopes of an appeal. It can be corrected by the tribunal under 2004 Rules r37(1).

17.12   If both parties agree in writing on the terms of a judgment or order, the tribunal can make it in those terms.[14a] This power is not affected by provisions relating to compromise agreements (see chapter 13), since under this provision the case is disposed of by the tribunal rather than by the parties. Judgments by consent are dealt with at paras 13.54–13.62.

17.13   When making findings of fact where evidence is disputed, tribunals are not required to give detailed pros and cons for accepting or rejecting any witness's evidence. It is the conclusion (rather than the detailed reasoning) which must be ascertainable.[15] On disputed issues, the reasons should specify the conclusion drawn by the tribunal, (although if a decision cannot be made between two conflicting sets of evidence, the tribunal may find that the party which bears the burden of proof has failed to discharge it). The tribunal must make findings on evidential disputes central to the case.[16] When inferences are relied on, the primary facts giving rise to the inference should be set out.[17] Sir John Donaldson P in *Martin v MBS Fastenings (Glynwed) Distribution Ltd*[18] said: 'So far as the findings of fact are concerned, it is helpful to the parties to give some explanation for them but it is not obligatory.' Peter Gibson LJ giving judgment in *High Table Ltd v Horst*[19] stated that:

> . . . whilst the tribunal must consider all that is relevant it need only deal with the points which were seen to be in controversy relating to

13a *English v Emery Reimbold* [2003] IRLR 710, CA.
14 *Burns v Royal Mail Group plc* [2004] ICR 1103, EAT.
14a 2004 Rules r28(2).
15 *Levy v Marrable & Co Ltd* [1984] ICR 583, EAT.
16 *Comfort v Lord Chancellor's Department* LTL 16/3/04, CA.
17 *British Gas plc v Sharma* [1991] ICR 19; [1991] IRLR 101, EAT.
18 [1983] ICR 511; [1983] IRLR 198.
19 [1997] IRLR 513 at 518, CA.

those issues, and then only with the principal important controversial points.

17.14 Codes of practice must be taken into account if they are relevant, although as they lack statutory force they will not by themselves be determinative of the case. In *Lock v Cardiff Railway Co*,[20] the EAT held that tribunals should have regard to the ACAS Code on Disciplinary and Grievance Procedures as being the basis upon which an employer's conduct should be judged.[21] In cases under the Disability Discrimination Act 1995 the tribunal should, according to the EAT in *Goodwin v Patent Office*[22] always make explicit reference to any relevant provision of the guidance or code which has been taken into account in arriving at their decision.

17.15 If multiple complaints are heard together, the tribunal must decide each complaint, as to both liability and remedy, separately. So for example, complaints of both unfair dismissal and discrimination must be considered separately.[23]

17.16 Once a judgment has been made and registered, it can be changed to correct clerical mistakes and accidental slips and omissions only.[24] Otherwise a review under 2004 Rules rr33 and 34 is required. Before registration, the tribunal has limited powers. If it has announced no oral decision, it clearly has power to recall the parties to hear additional evidence and additional arguments. After it has announced an oral decision, with or without reasons, its powers are much more limited. In *Hanks v Ace High Productions Ltd*[25] it was held that the power did not extend to hearing further arguments 'when already a clear decision has been reached'; and yet in that very case the tribunal, which *did* allow further argument, had its decision upheld. There is a conflict of authorities on the power to recall a case after a decision and/or reasons have been given.

17.17 On the one hand, it is arguable that a judgment is not a judgment until it is signed by the chairman[26] but this rule expressly includes judgments issued orally, and tribunals have been overruled for giving a judgment and reasons orally and changing them in

---

20 [1998] IRLR 358, EAT.
21 See, however, *Beedell v West Ferry Printers Ltd* [2000] IRLR 650.
22 [1999] IRLR 4, EAT.
23 *British Sugar v Kirker* [1998] IRLR 624, EAT.
24 2004 Rules r37(1). This is akin to the 'slip rule' in civil proceedings: CPR 40.12.
25 [1978] ICR 1155; [1979] IRLR 32, EAT.
26 2004 Rules r29(1).

writing.[27] This was because the judgment was changed, rather than because it was doubted that the tribunal had the power to do so. Obviously the EAT and the Court of Appeal are more likely to intervene when a judgment has been changed, and that is the only case they are likely to be dealing with. There may be less scope for such changes now in any event that oral reasons can be given at hearing without any further reasons being provided at a later date. The better view is that the tribunal is not discharged from its duty as soon as it announces its oral decision but remains in charge of the case until promulgation of the judgment and reasons (when required). However, if it wishes to reconsider its decision, it must give the parties an opportunity to be heard.

---

27   *Arthur Guinness Son & Co (Great Britain) Ltd v Green* [1989] ICR 241; [1989] IRLR 288, EAT; *Lamont v Fry's Metals Ltd* [1985] ICR 566; [1985] IRLR 470, CA.

CHAPTER 18

Costs

Introduction

18.1   The costs of bringing a case to a tribunal should have been considered at an early stage.

18.2   Unlike in cases in the High Court and most cases in the county court, a party cannot expect to be awarded costs if they win, but neither will they generally have to pay the other side's costs if they lose. This fact can encourage parties to seek to keep costs down and to take a 'commercial view' in tribunal proceedings. It is also in keeping with the aim of ensuring that tribunals are not expensive to use and remain the forum of the parties and not their lawyers.

18.3   The reality is, however, that many parties will use lawyers or other advisers to assist them in their tribunal case and will incur costs in doing so. At all times it should be borne in mind that those costs will probably not be recoverable. Advisers should be careful to consider whether there is some way of meeting the costs of legal or other professional representation, for example, by use of the 'legal help' scheme (advice only, not representation, though assistance is now available from the Legal Aid Board in Scotland in limited cases)[1] by recourse to a trade union or other professional body or trade association, by using the assistance of bodies such as the Commission for Racial Equality, the Equal Opportunities Commission or the Disability Rights Commission, or by applying for assistance under the increasingly common provisions for legal expenses insurance in many home and vehicle insurance policies. Many consultants are prepared to offer services on a contingent fee basis, taking a percentage of any award of settlement. Some lawyers offer services on a conditional fee basis which under a 'funding arrangement' defined in CPR Part 43.2, for example, no win, no fee. Morison J in *R v Securities and Futures Authority Ltd and another ex p Fleurose*[2] commented, obiter, that a right to a fair trial under European Convention on Human Rights (ECHR) article 6 may include a right to the assistance of a lawyer if that is indispensable for effective access to court, for example, because of the complexity of the case. This raises the question of how such 'assistance' would be funded – there can at present be no representation through legal aid.

18.4   A threat to apply for costs can be a powerful weapon in tribunal

---

1   See appendix D for the address of the Scottish Legal Aid Board.
2   [2001] IRLR 764.

proceedings. The Employment Tribunals Rules of Procedure[3] (2004 Rules) give a power for tribunals to award up to £10,000 in costs without ordering a detailed assessment. Parties are now having to pay close attention at an early stage to the prospects of success and to the risk of an award of costs or preparation time being made against them.

Some definitions

18.5   The 2004 Rules deal with three separate forms of order. A *costs order* is known in Scotland as an *expenses order*. In this book the term costs order covers both. It can be made only when the receiving party is legally represented at the rule 26 Hearing or, if there is no Hearing, when the proceedings are determined.[4] It includes the legal costs and the allowances paid by the secretary of state for witnesses' allowances.[5] The definition of legal costs are those fees, charges, disbursements or expenses incurred by or on behalf of a party in the proceedings. Solicitors', counsel's and experts' fees, letter-writing, conferences and written advice, travelling time and hearing time are all within this description. The order is for the paying party to pay the costs to the receiving party.

18.6   An extension to a costs order is a *wasted costs order* under 2004 Rules r48. This is made against a legal *or other* representative who must pay the receiving party, which may be the representative's own client, some or all of their own legal costs.

18.7   Quite separate is a *preparation time order* under 2004 Rules r42 which may be made against any paying party in favour of a party who has not been legally represented at a Hearing or during the proceedings if they are determined without a Hearing. A *summary assessment* of costs is done by the tribunal. A *detailed assessment* is carried out by a costs judge in the county court (or for the EAT, in the High Court).[5a]

When costs can be awarded

18.8   There are five circumstances in which specific provision is made for costs orders. They are:

3   Contained in Employment Tribunals (Constitution and Rules of Procedure) Regulations 2004 (2004 Regs) Sch 1.
4   2004 Rules r38(2) and (5).
5   2004 Rules r38(1).
5a   CPR Part 43.3–43.4, see also paras 18.46–18.50 below.

- failure to accede or reply to a request for reinstatement;[6]
- unreasonable, etc, conduct (see below);[7]
- conduct leading to adjournment or postponement of a rule 26 Hearing or pre-hearing review;[8]
- failing to comply with an order or practice direction;[9]
- where a party has been ordered to pay a deposit as a condition of being permitted to continue to participate in the proceedings and the tribunal or chairman has found against that party.[10]

18.9   It should be noted that a costs order may be made against or in favour of a respondent who has not had a response accepted in the proceedings in relation to the conduct of any part which he has taken in the proceedings.[11]

Reinstatement and re-engagement

18.10   The only situation in which the tribunal has a duty to make a costs order is when, in an unfair dismissal complaint:

- the claimant has expressed a wish to be reinstated or re-engaged and has communicated that wish to the respondent at least seven days before the Hearing; and
- the Hearing has to be postponed or adjourned due to the respondent's failure, without special reason, to adduce reasonable evidence as to the availability of the job from which the claimant was dismissed or of comparable or suitable employment.

18.11   The power does not depend on the respondent having behaved in the ways provided for by 2004 Rules r40(3). The tribunal *must* make an order in the circumstances set out in 2004 Rules r39(1) for the costs incurred as a result of the postponement or adjournment, *unless* 'special reasons' are made out to excuse the respondent's failure to adduce the evidence required.

---

6 2004 Rules r39.
7 2004 Rules r40(3).
8 2004 Rules r40(1).
9 2004 Rules r40(4).
10 2004 Rules r47(1).
11 2004 rules r38(4).

Unreasonable, etc, conduct

18.12   Tribunals have power to order costs only in limited circumstances. In general, the duty on the tribunal to *consider* awarding costs will only arise when under 2004 Rules r40(3):

> .. in the opinion of the tribunal or a chairman . . . the paying party has in bringing the proceedings, or a party or a party's representative has, in conducting the proceedings, acted vexatiously, abusively, disruptively or otherwise unreasonably, or the bringing or conducting of the proceedings by the paying party has been misconceived . . .

18.13   Tribunals may warn parties in appropriate cases that they consider that they are at risk of having a costs order made against them should they persist in having the claim determined by the tribunal. The Court of Appeal in *Gee v Shell*[12] held that a claimant should only be given a costs warning when there was a 'real risk' of an order being made at the end of the Hearing. If an unjustified costs warning is made, or made in an unjustified manner, and the claimant withdrew the claim as a result, the claimant would be denied a fair hearing by being deprived of a Hearing at all. The critical question is whether the risk of a costs order being made was sufficiently high to justify the tribunal putting pressure on a claimant to withdraw. Tribunals must be particularly careful not to place unfair pressure on a litigant in person. It will be useful to consider the similar criteria for striking out (paras 11.18–11.28) and for costs in the EAT (para 23.72).

'Vexatiously'

18.14   This term was considered in *Marler Ltd v Robertson*,[13] where it was held that:

> . . . [i]f an employee brings a hopeless case not with any expectation of recovering compensation but out of spite to harass his employers or for some other improper motive, he acts vexatiously, and likewise abuses the procedure.

'Abusively, disruptively'

18.15   The power to consider costs in this regard applies when a party has been abusive during the course of a tribunal hearing or has sought to

12   [2003] IRLR 82, CA.
13   [1974] ICR 72, NIRC.

disrupt it. The behaviour of the party or his representative is to be considered. An order for costs made under this provision will be costs paid by the party and not his representative.[14] It remains to be seen however whether tribunals will in practice consider making a wasted costs order (see below) instead in respect of the abusive or disruptive conduct of the representative, which conduct might well be characterised as improper or unreasonable under 2004 Rules r48(3).

'Otherwise unreasonably'

18.16   This expression is wide. This separate categorisation suggests that 'otherwise unreasonably' is not to be read as merely another way of saying 'frivolously' or 'vexatiously' but refers to conduct of a different kind. Tribunal decisions suggest, however, that this kind of distinction is not a precise science, with many orders based on 'unreasonable conduct' which could also be considered as 'frivolous' or 'vexatious' within the *Marler* guidelines. In *Stein v Associated Dairies Ltd*,[15] costs were awarded because of the claimant's unreasonable behaviour in pursuing a claim where he ought to have known that he had no prospect of succeeding, knowing that another employee dismissed for the same offence on the same day had failed in his unfair dismissal claim.

18.17   The EAT in *Koppel v Safeway Stores*[16] held that it would not be unreasonable conduct of litigation of itself for a claimant to refuse to accept an offer in full and final settlement of claims and then to go on to lose in the tribunal. However, the existence of the offer could be a factor in determining whether it was appropriate to award costs against the claimant if the tribunal considered that the refusal of the offer was unreasonable.

18.18   In *McPherson v BNP Paribas*,[17] the Court of Appeal held that where a tribunal contemplates making a costs order against a claimant who has withdrawn his case late in the day, it is not considering whether the withdrawal of the claim itself is unreasonable. There is no power as in the CPR Part 38.6(1) which provides that a claimant who

14 In the context of a decision overturned by the Court of Appeal to strike out a claim because of alleged scandalous conduct amounting to an abuse of process on the part of a representative, see *Bennett v Southwark LBC* [2002] ICR 881; consideration must be given to what the representative might have said on his own behalf if given the opportunity to put right such conduct.

15 [1982] IRLR 447, EAT.

16 [2003] IRLR 753, EAT.

17 [2004] EWCA Civ 569; [2004] IRLR 558.

discontinues proceedings is liable for the costs which a defendant has incurred before notice of discontinuance was served. The tribunal must consider whether, in all the circumstances of the case, the claimant withdrawing the claim has conducted the proceedings unreasonably.

'Misconceived'

18.19   This is described in the interpretation regulation of the 2004 Regs as 'includ[ing] having no reasonable prospects of success'.[18] The definition is not exhaustive, although applications in practice are made on the basis that the paying party should have known that he or she could not succeed. It is clear that the addition of this test gives the tribunal a great deal of discretion when considering awarding costs. It is likely to cover scenarios that would previously have been termed frivolous, but also go beyond that. Guidance on the meaning of the term frivolous was given in *Marler*[19] where it was indicated that conduct would be frivolous if:

> ... the employee knows that there is no substance in his claim and that it is bound to fail, or if the claim is on the face of it so manifestly misconceived that it can have no prospect of success ...

Of course, what applies to the employee must equally be true of the employer (or other respondent) where the conduct of the response to a claim was misconceived.

Party who has paid a deposit

18.20   If a party who has been ordered under 2004 Rules r20 to pay a deposit as a condition of being permitted to continue proceedings (see para 11.9) goes on to have a finding made against them in respect of that matter in the judgment, the tribunal must consider whether to make a costs order on the ground that he or she conducted the proceedings unreasonably in persisting in having the matter determined. The tribunal can only consider making an order for costs on this basis where no other award of costs has been made against that party in the proceedings.[20]

18.21   The tribunal or chairman is not permitted to make a costs order on this ground unless it has considered the order made under rule 20

---

18   2004 Regs reg 2.
19   *Marler Ltd v Robertson* [1974] ICR 72, NIRC.
20   2004 Rules r47(1).

and determined that the grounds upon which it found against the party in its judgment were substantially the same as the grounds recorded in the order for considering that the party's contentions had little reasonable prospects of success. The amount of the deposit paid goes to discharging a party's liability to pay costs, and if the amount of the deposit is greater than the amount of the costs, the balance must be refunded to the paying party.[21]

Relationship between costs and the party's conduct

18.22 In *Health Development Agency v Parish*,[22] the EAT held that the conduct of a party prior to proceedings, or unrelated to proceedings cannot found an award of costs. It held that there must be a causal relationship between the conduct of the party in bringing or conducting proceedings and the costs which are awarded under 2004 Rules r40(3).

18.23 The Court of Appeal in *McPherson v BNP Paribas*[23] held however that there is no requirement that the costs incurred by the other party must be 'attributable to' the unreasonable conduct of the paying party in the absence of any such words in the rules. The tribunal should have regard to the nature, gravity and effect of the unreasonable conduct as factors relevant to the exercise of discretion but there is no requirement that a party making the application prove that specific unreasonable conduct has caused particular costs to be incurred. The decision in *McPherson* was made under the 2001 Rules, but is equally applicable to the 2004 Rules as the relevant definition is the same.

Costs against respondents

18.24 Costs may be awarded against respondents if they behave in a manner outlined above. In *Cartiers Superfoods Ltd v Laws*,[24] however, it was stated that 'great care' should be exercised by tribunals before making an award against a respondent as 'obviously, a respondent must be entitled to defend proceedings brought against him'. What may appear obvious after the tribunal's decision on liability is not necessarily to be treated as having been obvious to a party at an earlier stage.

21 2004 Rules r47(2).
22 [2004] IRLR 550, EAT.
23 [2004] EWCA Civ 569; [2004] IRLR 558.
24 [1978] IRLR 315.

18.25   The right to defend proceedings does not mean that the response can be conducted unreasonably, and a respondent guilty of such conduct is just as liable to face an order for costs as a claimant in similar circumstances.

18.26   An award of costs cannot, however, be made against a respondent in respect of the conduct leading to the dismissal or other act complained of. It is the behaviour of the respondent *as* respondent that is relevant, that is, how the employer reacts to the claimant's claim rather than its conduct before any complaint has been made.[25]

Relevant considerations for a costs order

18.27 The tribunal or chairman will consider whether the conduct complained of falls under one or more of the heads set out in 2004 Rules r40. If a costs order is being considered under rule 40(3) for unreasonable, etc, conduct, the tribunal or chairman must consider additionally whether it is 'appropriate' for an order to be made.[26] In all cases, the tribunal or chairman must then go on to consider what (if any) costs have been occurred and the paying party's ability to pay. The making of a costs order by reason of an adjournment or postponement requires that costs incurred *as a result* of such action are payable. The making of a costs order by reason of unreasonable, etc, conduct, or where a party paying a deposit has lost, or where there has been non-compliance with an order or practice direction, consideration will need to be given to the *effect* of the relevant conduct.[27]

18.28   In order to reverse the judgment of the Court of Appeal in *Kovacs v Queen Mary and Westfield College*,[28] which held that the ability of a party to pay was not to be taken into account, the tribunal is now expressly permitted (but not directed) to have regard to a party's ability to pay when considering whether to make a costs order at all or how much that order should be.[29] The same position applies when determining whether to make a preparation time award or for what sum.[30]

---

25 *Davidson v John Calder Publishers and another* [1985] IRLR 97; *Health Development Agency v Parrish* [2004] IRLR 550, EAT.
26 2004 Rules r40(2).
27 See *McPherson v BNP Paribas* [2004] EWCA Civ 569; [2004] IRLR 558.
28 [2002] IRLR 414, CA.
29 2004 Rules r41(2).
30 2004 Rules r45(3).

In-house lawyers and other representatives

18.29 The legal costs incurred in tribunal litigation by in-house lawyers are as much recoverable as are the costs incurred by employing independent solicitors.[31] However, a wasted costs order cannot be made against them (see para 18.35 below).

Contingency fees

18.30 Costs will not be ordered if the obligation of the party to pay an adviser or representative arises only if the tribunal should make a finding on liability or an order for costs in his or her favour. This would be an unlawful contingency arrangement. It is quite different from a conditional fee agreement.[32] The tribunal cannot order a respondent to pay a claimant in respect of sums that a party is not liable to pay to his or her adviser.[33]

Wasted costs

18.31 A further significant change in the 2004 Rules is the ability of the tribunal to make orders for costs in respect of the conduct of proceedings by representatives. It applies to legal *and other* representatives or any employee of such representative.[34]

18.32 In making a wasted costs order, the tribunal or chairman may disallow, or order the representative to meet, the whole or part of any costs of any party. The order may say that the representative must repay to his or her client costs that have already been paid. The representative may also be ordered to pay to the secretary of state any allowances paid to a witness for having attended the tribunal.[35]

18.33 The definition of wasted costs in 2004 Rules r48(3), which is taken from the Supreme Court Act 1981 s51(6), is those costs incurred by a party, who in accordance with 2004 Rules r48(5) may include a party who is not legally represented or the representative's own client:

---

31 *Wiggin Alloys Ltd v Jenkins* [1981] IRLR 275.
32 See CPR Part 43.2 and para 18.3.
33 *British Waterways Board v Norman* (1994) 26 HLR 233, DC.
34 2004 Rules r48(4).
35 2004 Rules r48(2).

(a) as a result of any improper, unreasonable or negligent act or omission on the part of a representative; or

(b) where, in light of an act or omission by that representative occurring after the costs were paid, the tribunal considers it unreasonable that a party should have incurred them.

18.34   A wasted costs order can only be made in respect of legal costs, and not in respect of preparation time, as it is only a legal or other representative who can be ordered to pay under such an order. The definition of representative excludes those 'not acting in pursuit of profit with regard to those proceedings'[36] and representatives who are employees of a party.[37] This therefore excludes from the peril of a wasted costs order all in-house representatives of public, private and voluntary sector organisations, even when the receiving party's representative is exposed to the risk of such orders. It also excludes representatives of voluntary bodies and associations such as trade unions, employers' associations and law centres. Those acting on a conditional fee arrangement are considered to be acting in pursuit of profit and thus fall within the scope of the rule.[38]

18.35   A representative must be given a reasonable opportunity to make oral or written representations as to the reasons why an order should not be made prior to making one. The tribunal or chairman may also have regard to the representative's ability to pay when considering whether to make an order or to how much that order should be.[39]

Preparation time orders

18.36   A significant introduction under the 2004 Rules is the power of the tribunal to make a *preparation time order* in favour of a party who has not incurred legal costs as such. The provision is designed to make allowance for the cost to unrepresented parties, or those represented by volunteers, and not-for-profit representatives, of litigating claims in the tribunal. This is likely to be welcomed by organisations such as Citizens' Advice, law centres, trade unions and the Free Representation Unit who cannot recover a costs order in favour of their clients as those clients do not incur legal costs.

36   2004 Rules r48(4).
37   2004 Rules r48(5).
38   2004 Rules r48(4).
39   2004 Rules r48(6).

18.37   Preparation time under the 2004 Rules means time spent by the party (or their employees) in carrying out preparatory work directly relating to the proceedings and by the receiving party's legal or other advisers relating to the conduct of the proceedings. It includes time up to, but not time spent at, a rule 26 Hearing. A tribunal or chairman may not make a preparation time order and a costs order in favour of the same party in the same proceedings.[40]

18.38   The grounds for making a preparation time order are exactly the same as those available to a tribunal or chairman in considering whether to award *costs*. The tribunal *must* make an order if the claimant has communicated to the respondent more than seven days before an unfair dismissal hearing a wish to be reinstated or re-engaged and the hearing has had to be postponed or adjourned because of the respondent's failure to adduce reasonable evidence as to the availability of the claimant's job or of comparable or suitable employment. The tribunal *may* make a preparation time order where it has adjourned or postponed, where there has been unreasonable, etc, conduct or where there has been non-compliance with an order or practice direction. The tribunal must also consider making a preparation time order where a party who has been ordered to pay a deposit goes on to lose his or her case.[41]

18.39   Provision is made under the 2004 Rules r45 as to how tribunals are to calculate the amount of preparation time. The tribunal is to make an assessment of the number of hours spent on preparation on the basis of:

(a) information on time spent provided by the party in whose favour an order is being made; and

(b) the tribunal or chairman's own assessment of what it considers to be a reasonable and proportionate amount of time to spend on preparatory work, having regard to matters such as the complexity of the proceedings, the number of witnesses and the documents required.

18.40   The tribunal is directed to calculate the amount of the award by applying the rate of £25 an hour to each hour of preparation time allowed, subject to revision upward by £1 on 6 April 2006 and annually thereafter. As noted above, the ability of a party to pay may be relevant to the decision to make an award or to the amount to be awarded.

40 2004 Rules r46(1).
41 2004 Rules rr43, 44 and 47.

When the application should be made

18.41   The 2004 Rules rr38 and 42 provide that an application for a costs order or preparation time order must be made no later than 28 days from the date upon which judgment determining the claim was issued. This requirement may only be waived by a tribunal or chairman when it is considered that it is in the interests of justice to do so.

How to make the application

18.42   Many applications for costs in tribunals fail because of inadequate preparation. If, in advance of the rule 26 Hearing, it seems likely that such an application will be made, it is important to ensure that all relevant documentation, including correspondence and evidence in relation to the costs claimed, is put together in an easily readable form – a separate costs bundle if necessary. Consideration will also need to be given by unrepresented parties and not-for-profit representatives to the time spent by them in preparing for a rule 26 Hearing so as to be in a position to make an application for a preparation time order.

18.43   The costs bundle will include correspondence relied on, such as pre-hearing warnings as to the vexatious or misconceived nature of the complaint or grounds of resistance and early attempts to put the other side on notice to an application for costs. The bundle may also include letters written 'without prejudice save as to costs' or which might show the unreasonable conduct of the party against whom the order is sought.

18.44   Ideally, a separate schedule giving a statement of those costs will also be made available to the tribunal, setting out the costs incurred at the different stages of the proceedings (see below). When the costs in question are significant, a schedule of costs should be served on the other side in advance of the application. When a party is faced with such an application and is taken by surprise by late service of a schedule of costs, they would have good grounds for objecting to a summary assessment of the award to be made by the tribunal without further time to consider the amounts claimed and prepare any representations necessary. If a party wants the tribunal to make this order, it should be prepared to submit details when making the application. It should set out in the form of a schedule the costs incurred at each stage, including both solicitor and counsel costs if appropriate. If there has been no time to prepare a schedule, a party should still be in a position to advance some figures and evidence relating to costs so that the tribunal can carry out the assessment. It is always good practice for the case file to be available at the hearing with an up-dated printout of the bill of costs included. If counsel has been instructed, the tribunal may wish to see the brief fee marked on the back sheet to the instructions or to be told what fee has been agreed. Although there is no separate provision in the 2004 Rules for the prior service of schedules of costs and no formula for summary assessment has been laid down, best practice would suggest that something akin to the procedure of the Civil Procedure Rules (CPR) is adopted where possible, that is, the schedule should be served on the other side not less than 24 hours before the relevant hearing and the heads of costs listed in CPR PD 44 should be separately listed and the relevant amounts shown.[42] Any schedule or statement of costs should be signed, since it is the warranty by a solicitor that the sums are due from the client and thus may be claimed as costs.

Amounts to be awarded

18.45   The tribunal may order the party or a representative against whom the award is made to pay:

- the costs of the receiving party or a payment in respect of his or her preparation time; and/or
- the allowances payable by the secretary of state to any party or witness for attendance at the tribunal, which includes the expenses of any party.[43]

In other words, the tribunal has power both to compensate another party in respect of costs incurred and to protect the public purse.

18.46   An order for costs can be made in one of three ways under 2004 Rules r41(1), that is, that one party must pay to the other:

- a specified sum not exceeding £10,000;

---

42 See *Health Development Agency v Parrish* [2004] IRLR 550, EAT which states that regard should be had to CPR principles.
43 2004 Rules rr 38(1) and 48(2). Note that such allowances may be included in a normal costs order or in a wasted costs order but not in making a preparation time order.

- a sum which has been agreed between the parties; or
- the whole or a specified part of the costs to be the subject of detailed assessment or, in Scotland, taxation.

18.47   If the costs to be awarded are less than £10,000 the tribunal may itself be able to carry out the assessment of how much should be paid or may order a detailed assessment. Anyone who wants an order for costs must be in a position to give the tribunal the material it needs.[45] Since there is no strict analogue in the CPR, the receiving party should ask the tribunal to say that the costs should be assessed as though it were a multi-track case (generally when the claim is for more than £15,000). If the case lasted for only one day and was worth less than £15,000, the assessment should be on the fast-track scale.

18.48   If the costs ordered are greater than £10,000, and no agreement can be reached, the tribunal will merely order an award for the whole or some proportion of the costs incurred (that is, those relating to a particular application or part of the claim) but will not specify any amount. The bill of costs claimed will then be subject to detailed assessment, which the tribunal will order to be on the appropriate county court scale depending on the nature of the claim, that is, on an indemnity basis or the standard basis, or in Scotland to be taxed in accordance the sheriff court table.[46]

18.49   Detailed assessment of costs is the process by which the bill of costs claimed by a party is considered by a district judge (or deputy district judge) of the county court, or a judge in Scotland.[47] If it is assumed, as will normally be the case, that costs will be assessed on the standard basis, the court will not allow costs which have been unreasonably incurred or unreasonable in amount to be recovered. The court will only allow costs which are proportionate to the matters in issue to be recovered, and will resolve any doubt as to whether costs were reasonably incurred or reasonable and proportionate in amount in favour of the paying party.[48] In other words, if the receiving party has run up legal costs which were unnecessary, or has paid over the odds, it will not be entitled to recover these from the paying party.

---

45   See CPR PD 44 which makes it the duty of parties and their legal representatives to assist the judge in assessing costs on a summary basis and that a party who intends to claim costs must prepare a written statement of the costs incurred, with a separate schedule itemising the various heads.

46   2004 Rules r41(1)(c).

47   Costs are dealt with in CPR Parts 43–48.

48   CPR 44.4.

If, looked at globally, the costs are disproportionate, each item must be proved to have been *necessary*. If the tribunal orders that costs should be assessed on an 'indemnity basis', it will be for the party against whom the order has been made to establish before the county court that the costs were unreasonably incurred or unreasonable in amount. The EAT in *Beynon v Scadden*[49] made it clear that ordering costs on an indemnity basis is not penal, rather it is compensatory, and that it does not amount to a double penalty to order that costs be paid on an indemnity basis in an appropriate case, even though there will normally have been a finding of some degree of unreasonable behaviour before a costs order is made. It appears therefore that if the paying party has been particularly unreasonable, the order can properly be that payment should be on the indemnity basis. An order for costs may be pejorative, but is not punitive.[50]

Allowances

18.50 The allowances paid by the secretary of state to parties and witnesses attending the tribunal (regardless of the outcome) cover loss of wages, travel costs and other expenses. They will rarely fully compensate a person for any loss of wages, and fixed scales are set out under each head.[51] They do not extend to the costs of professional representatives.

18.51 When a costs order is made under 2004 Rules rr38(1) or 48(1), it is open to the tribunal to order that the allowances are repaid to the secretary of state by a party against whom an order for costs has been made. In practice, tribunals rarely make such an order.

Giving reasons for a costs order

18.52 Reasons must be given for any costs or preparation time or wasted costs order, since they are exceptional and require explanation.[52] The reasons must be given in writing if a request is made to the secretary to the tribunal within 14 days of the order.[53] Specific provision is made

---

49 [1999] IRLR 700, EAT.
50 *Khan v University of Warwick* EAT/1223/02.
51 Employment Tribunal Act 1996 s5(3).
52 *English v Emery Reimbold* [2003] IRLR 710, CA.
53 2004 Rules rr38(10), 42(8), 48(9).

in 2004 Rules r48(9) that this time limit may not be extended if requesting reasons for having made a wasted costs order, which suggests that it may be extended when requesting reasons for having made an order for costs or a preparation time order.

CHAPTER 19

Review

Introduction

19.1 Underlying all proceedings of a judicial nature is the principle that there should be finality in litigation. This consideration of public policy gives rise to the general rule that tribunal judgments cannot be reopened or relitigated. You do not get two bites at the cherry.[1] Exceptions are provided in limited circumstances: when the tribunal has made an error of law the judgment can be *appealed* to the Employment Appeal Tribunal (EAT) (see chapter 23), and when specific grounds exist, there is a power to *review* a tribunal's judgment.

19.2 A tribunal's power of review is unusual in judicial proceedings and has been said to provide:

> . . . a useful corrective, designed to prevent any injustice being suffered as a result of the very considerable relaxation of the rules of evidence and procedure which, in the interests of informality and an absence of legalism, is encouraged at . . . tribunal hearings.[2]

19.3 This does not mean that the power is to be invoked by any party aggrieved at a tribunal judgment seeking a rehearing of the case: the power is 'not intended to provide parties with the opportunity of a rehearing at which the same evidence can be rehearsed with different emphasis, or further evidence adduced which was available before'.[3]

Clerical mistakes

19.4 Purely clerical mistakes or errors arising from an accidental slip or omission in any order, judgment, decision or reasons may be corrected at any time by the chairman, regional chairman, Vice President or President by certificate.[4]

19.5 This power to correct small errors may be exercised at any time and is generally referred to as 'the slip rule'. It is limited to clerical slips, such as a reference to a limited company respondent as a 'plc' and arithmetical mistakes, and should not be confused with the power of review.

---

1   See, eg, *Morris v Griffiths* [1977] ICR 153 at 156 EAT, per Bristow J. See also *Asda Stores Ltd v Thompson (No 2)* [2004] IRLR 598.
2   Per Waite J in *Carryfast Ltd v Dawkins* EAT 290/83, unreported.
3   *Stevenson v Golden Wonder Ltd* [1977] IRLR 474, EAT.
4   Employment Tribunals Rules of Procedure 2004 (2004 Rules) r37(1), contained in Employment Tribunals (Constitution and Rules of Procedure) Regulations 2004 (2004 Regs) SI No 1861 Sch 1.

19.6   In practice, any slips are corrected and initialled by the chairman in manuscript on the original or a fresh document is issued, which is then sent together with the certificate of correction to the secretary to the tribunal so that the entry in the register can be altered.[5] The secretary will send a copy of the corrected entry to the parties and to any relevant court.

The power to review decisions

19.7   The limited power to review a decision lies in respect of only some of the types of decisions which can be made under the 2004 Rules.[6] The tribunal or chairman may review, either by application of a party or of their own initiative:

- a default judgment;
- a decision not to accept a claim, response or counterclaim;[7]
- a judgment[8] other than a default judgment, which can include the making of an order for costs, expenses, preparation time or wasted costs; and
- in respect of decisions under 2004 Regs Sch 4 r6(3) relating to the conduct of appeals against health and safety improvement and prohibition notices.

19.8   Other types of decision, including case management orders, cannot be the subject of review.[9] The proper course to follow is to apply to the tribunal for the order to be varied or revoked,[10] or, in an appropriate case, to appeal the decision to the Employment Appeal Tribunal.[10a] However, it should be noted that most orders will be a pure exercise of discretion or case management, and thus are unlikely to give valid grounds for an appeal. If an order is made after considering representations from only one party, the order is provisional and may be reconsidered by the tribunal on an application from another party.

---

5   2004 Rules r37(2).
6   2004 Rules rr33 and 34.
7   Note that only the party against whom the decision not to accept a claim or response can apply for review.
8   See 2004 Rules r28(1) for the definition of a 'judgment'.
9   2004 Rules r34(1).
10   2004 Rules r11(1).
10a Note that in relation to exercising case management powers, CPR principles are to be followed and orders should not be revised in the absence of a material change of circumstances when the application is made. *Goldman Sachs Services Ltd v Mantali* [2002] ICR 1251, EAT.

19.9 When a claim has been dismissed or struck out as a result of some error which gives rise to a ground for review, the claimant should apply for a review and not issue a further claim, even if still in time to do so. The issue of a further claim in these circumstances has been held to be vexatious, and may be struck out on that ground under 2004 Rules r18(7)(b).

19.10 No distinction is made between oral and written judgments: the power to review applies to them all. It appears that there is no requirement to obtain written reasons in order to make an application for review.

Review of default judgments

19.11 A claimant or respondent must make an application in writing to the tribunal to have a review of a default judgment within 14 days of the date on which the judgment was sent to the parties. The time limit may be extended by a chairman if he or she considers it just and equitable to do so.

19.12 An application for review must state the reasons why the default judgment should be varied or revoked. A respondent applying to have the default judgment reviewed must include with the application its proposed response to the claim and an application for an extension of the time limit for presenting the response, together with an explanation of the reasons for failing either to present a response in time or for making an application in time for an extension of time for presenting a response.[11]

19.13 A review of a default judgment must be conducted by a chairman in public, having sent a notice of the hearing and the application to all other parties. The chairman has the power to refuse the application, vary the judgment, revoke all or part of it or confirm the default judgment. If the whole claim was satisfied before judgment was issued or the claim has been settled, the judgment must be revoked. In other cases, the chairman may revoke or vary all or part of a default judgment if he or she considers that the respondent has a reasonable prospect of successfully responding to the claim or part of it.[12] The chairman in considering the application must have regard to whether there was good reason for the response not having been presented within the applicable time limit.[13]

11 2004 Rules r33(2).
12 2004 Rules r33(5) reflecting CPR13.2 and 13.3.
13 2004 Rules r33(6).

Review of other decisions

19.14   A decision other than a default judgment can be reviewed on the
following bases:[14]

- the decision was wrongly made as a result of an administrative
  error;
- a party did not receive notice of the proceedings leading to the
  decision;
- the decision was made in the absence of a party;
- new evidence has become available since the conclusion of the
  hearing to which the decision relates, providing that its existence
  could not have been reasonably known of or foreseen at that time;
  or
- the interests of justice require such a review.

It should be noted that if the application is being made to review a
decision not to accept a claim or response, it can only be on the first
and last grounds set out above.[15]

Administrative error

19.15   In practice, it is rare for a review to be based on this ground, as most
errors on the part of the administrative staff of tribunals would either
be capable of correction under the slip rule (2004 Rules r37(1) see
para 19.4 above) or would more appropriately be considered under
2004 Rules r34(3)(b) or (c), that is, failure to give proper notice of the
proceedings or reaching a decision in the absence of a party.

19.16   Furthermore, the mere fact that an administrative error has been
made will not be sufficient for a party to succeed on an application for
review on this ground: the power to review on this basis arises only
when a decision was *wrongly made as a result of* the error.

No notice of proceedings

19.17   Under 2004 Rules r14(4) the secretary to the tribunal is obliged to
send all parties a notice of any hearing other than a case management
discussion at least 14 days before the date fixed for that hearing.[16] By

---

14   2004 Rules r34(3).
15   2004 Rules r34(4).
16   Note that the rule means exactly that; the secretary must ensure that the notice is
     put in the post at least 14 days in advance but is not required to effect service 14
     days in advance (2004 Regs reg 15(5)).

2004 Rules r61(1) this notice is authorised to be sent by post, fax or other means of electronic communication or by personal delivery. By rule 61(2), where a notice has been given or sent by one of these means, it is deemed to have been received unless the contrary is proved. The 2004 Rules further provide for deemed dates of receipt, which mirror almost exactly the provisions of Civil Procedure Rules (CPR) 6 and are: within the ordinary course of post (letters), the same day (fax, etc) and the date of delivery (personal service). Note that the sending of a notice to the authorised representative of a party is deemed to be sending it to that party.[17]

19.18   This presumption that the notice has been effectively served by committing it to the post is difficult to rebut. It would not be sufficient for a party to claim that the document must have been intercepted after delivery by some third party or that it had been lost within some complicated corporate structure: parties are presumed to have made adequate arrangements for the receipt of their mail during the course of tribunal proceedings.[18] In the case of a limited company, service at the company's registered address is deemed to have been effected, even if no reply has been received.[19]

Absence of a party

19.19   This ground does not open the way for a party to choose not to attend a hearing and subsequently apply for a review of the decision on the ground of non-attendance. A party who makes the conscious choice not to appear at a tribunal hearing must take the consequences.[20] When a party has inadvertently failed to attend and the tribunal has not made any enquiries about his or her whereabouts on the day, the tribunal is expected to give sympathetic consideration to an application for review.[21]

19.20   A party wishing to apply for a review of a tribunal decision on this ground must demonstrate a genuine reason for the original absence, such as some unforeseen illness or accident. In *Morris v*

17   2004 Rules r61(4).
18   *Capital Foods Retail Ltd v Corrigan* [1993] IRLR 430; in the context of receiving an acknowledgement of a claim, the EAT held that a professional adviser has an obligation to employ some system of checking that replies which might reasonably be expected have been received.
19   *Migwain Ltd (in liquidation) v TGWU* [1979] ICR 597, EAT.
20   *Fforde v Black* EAT 68/80, unreported.
21   *Cooke v Glenrose Fish Company* EAT 0064/04.

Griffiths[22] the EAT overturned a tribunal decision since it, the EAT, found the respondent employer's explanation as to how he fell ill on the way to the tribunal hearing, and 'had been succoured by ... his sister who conveniently live[d] half way' was honest and gave grounds for allowing a review.

19.21   When an application is made under this head, much will depend on the view taken by the tribunal as to the credibility of the party concerned, so where the question arises whether the reason given is 'genuine', it has been stated that an oral hearing of the application for review is required.[23]

New evidence

19.22   This must have arisen since the conclusion of the rule 26 Hearing to which the judgment relates, provided that its existence could not have been reasonably known of or foreseen at the time of the Hearing. A party wishing to apply for a review under this head must show:

- some reasonable explanation for not having produced the evidence before the tribunal, that is, the new evidence was not available before the conclusion of the original rule 26 Hearing and its existence could not reasonably have been known of or foreseen at that time;
- the new evidence is apparently credible (although it may still be open to contradiction); and
- the new evidence would or might have some important effect on the original tribunal decision.[24]

19.23   These conditions are those applied by the civil courts generally for new evidence on appeal. It has been stressed by the EAT that merely because tribunals have less formal procedures than the High Court, applications to admit fresh evidence are no more likely to be favourably entertained as a matter of course.[25] The conditions have been strictly applied by tribunals. In *Flint v Eastern Electricity Board*,[26] the tribunal refused to review its decision by considering new medical evidence which could have been adduced by the employee at the

---

22   [1977] ICR 153, EAT.
23   See *Morris v Griffiths* [1977] ICR 153, EAT.
24   See *Bagga v Heavy Electricals (India) Ltd* [1972] ICR 118, NIRC; *Wileman v Minilec Engineering Ltd* [1988] ICR 318.
25   *Borden (UK) Ltd v Potter* [1986] ICR 647, EAT.
26   [1975] ICR 395; [1975] IRLR 277, QBD.

original rule 26 Hearing, although there was clearly much sympathy for the employee and the evidence was acknowledged to be genuine and to be relevant to the tribunal's decision.

19.24   A party may be unfairly confronted by evidence at the original tribunal Hearing. For example, if, after the respondent's case, the claimant gives evidence on matters which he or she has failed to put to the respondent, the respondent should apply for an adjournment at that stage to allow time to consider whether there might be evidence in rebuttal. It would be wrong to wait until after the tribunal decision and then seek to adduce evidence in rebuttal by way of review.[27] However, if the party taken by surprise is unrepresented, and the tribunal fails to draw attention to the possibility of an adjournment, an application for review under 2004 Rules r34(3)(d) may succeed.[28]

19.25   Even if the evidence was not previously available and could not reasonably have been foreseen, the application will fail unless it can be shown that the new evidence is both relevant and probative and is likely to have an important influence on the result of the case. In *Wileman v Minilec Engineering Ltd*[29] it was held that the claimant's subsequent behaviour in posing for a national newspaper in a 'flimsy costume' did not meet the test of relevance, and was unlikely to have any influence in determining her complaint of sexual harassment.

19.26   In other cases, however, evidence of matters which have taken place subsequent to the tribunal judgment has been held to be admissible under this rule. In *Help the Aged Housing Association (Scotland) Ltd v Vidler*[30] evidence of the claimant's subsequent employment was held to be admissible and led to a reduction in the compensation previously awarded. And in *Ladup Ltd v Barnes*[31] the EAT held that it was unjust not to allow a review where there has been a subsequent conviction in relation to the very matter (growing cannabis) for which the employee had been dismissed, when the tribunal had previously held that there had been no contributory fault. A judgment which was correct at the time of the Hearing may become unsound later. Yet in *Yorkshire Engineering and Welding Co Ltd v Burnham*[32] the National Industrial Relations Court (NIRC) held that a change in

27 *Douglas Water Miners Welfare Society Club v Grieve* EAT 487/ 84, unreported.
28 *Grieves v Coldshield Windows Ltd* EAT 218/82, unreported.
29 [1988] ICR 318; [1988] IRLR 144, EAT.
30 [1977] IRLR 104, EAT.
31 [1982] ICR 107; [1982] IRLR 7, EAT.
32 [1974] ICR 77; [1973] IRLR 316, NIRC.

circumstances of a less substantial nature was not sufficient to give rise to a ground for a review of the previous award of compensation. Furthermore, generally speaking, evidence which simply goes to the credibility of a witness will not be admitted unless it can be shown to be central to the main issue(s) of the case.

19.27   When applying for a review under 2004 Rules r34(3)(d), details should be given of the new evidence which is sought to be adduced, as well as the reason why it was not produced at the first hearing.[33]

Interests of justice

19.28   While this residual ground gives a wide discretion to tribunals, the discretion must be exercised judicially and with regard to the interests of *all* parties, and to the public interest in finality in litigation.[34] It has furthermore been stressed that the power to grant a review on this ground should be exercised cautiously.[35] The power should, however, be exercised consistently with the right to a fair trial under European Convention on Human Rights (ECHR) article 6(1).

19.29   Seeking a review in the interests of justice is not merely an alternative to the other grounds for review and a party will rarely succeed on this basis when the reasons for making the application have already been rejected under another head; there needs to be 'some special additional circumstance ... or mitigating factor',[36] which leads to the conclusion that justice does in fact require a review. In *General Council of British Shipping v Deria*[37] the EAT put the test even higher, as requiring 'exceptional circumstances' which relate not to wider matters such as the unusual nature of the case or the public importance attached to it, but to factors relating to the case itself. In *Deria*, the tribunal had allowed the application for a review of the original decision (based on grounds of new evidence and the interests of justice), as the case involved 'an issue of widespread public importance and related to a technical loophole in the Race Relations Act', matters which outweighed the public interest in finality in litigation. On appeal, the EAT reversed the tribunal's decision, holding that the approach taken had been wrong in principle.

---

33   *Vauxhall Motors Ltd v Henry* [1978] ITR 332, EAT.
34   See *Flint v Eastern Electricity Board* [1975] ICR 395; [1975] IRLR 277, QBD.
35   *Lindsay v Ironsides Ray & Vials* [1994] ICR 384, EAT, where it was held that the failings of a representative will not generally constitute grounds for review.
36   See *Flint v Eastern Electricity Board* [1975] ICR 395; [1975] IRLR 277, QBD.
37   [1985] ICR 198, EAT.

19.30   Cases which fall under 'interests of justice' alone have been divided into two categories: (1) those involving some procedural mishap, and (2) those where the tribunal's decision has been undermined by events occurring shortly thereafter.

Procedural mishaps

19.31   These include the following:

- when a party has not been given a fair opportunity to address the tribunal on a point of substance, for example, on the questions of remedy or mitigation of loss[38] (this would also be a ground of complaint under ECHR article 6(1));
- when a point affecting the tribunal's jurisdiction to hear the case was not raised at the original hearing;[39]
- when the claim was withdrawn at the original hearing due in part to a mistaken view of the law on the part of the tribunal chairman and in part to a failure to disclose all relevant documents;[40]
- when the tribunal has failed to draw to the attention of the parties an authority which has played an influential part in the judgment by significantly altering or affecting the way the issues were addressed, where a fair minded observer could say that the case was decided in a way that could not have been anticipated by a party with a reasonable knowledge of the law and procedure, provided that a material injustice resulted from the lack of opportunity to comment.[41]

19.32   Some procedural mishaps might involve the tribunal also correcting an error of law when reviewing the previous decision. This is not a bar to carrying out a review in such cases, even if the error of law is a major or substantial one: see *Trimble v Supertravel Ltd*,[42] where Browne-Wilkinson J stated that the determination of whether a case was suitable for review was whether there had been some procedural mishap. The distinction between 'major' and 'minor' errors did not assist in this regard. An application for review may even be the correct approach where a simple mistake has led to the tribunal failing to

38 *Trimble v Supertravel Ltd* [1982] ICR 440; [1982] IRLR 451, EAT.
39 *British Midland Airways Ltd v Lewis* [1978] ICR 782, EAT.
40 *Harber v North London Polytechnic* [1990] IRLR 198, CA.
41 *Stanley Cole (Wainfleet) Ltd v Sheridan* [2003] ICR 1449, CA; *Albion Hotel (Freshwater) Ltd v Maia e Silva* [2002] IRLR 200; *Nelson v Carillion Services* [2003] ICR 1256.
42 [1982] ICR 440; [1982] IRLR 451, EAT.

consider a question of jurisdiction, which can be raised at any stage of the proceedings, as in *British Midland Airways Ltd v Lewis*,[43] or failing to consider the award of interest on compensation in a discrimination case.

Subsequent events

19.33   Subsequent events which might give grounds for applying for a review of the original decision in the interests of justice include the following:

- where the compensatory award was made on forecasts as to earnings which subsequently are found to have been falsified by the claimant, as in *Yorkshire Engineering and Welding Co Ltd v Burnham*[44] (although in that case the application for a review failed);
- where a compensatory award has been made with no deduction for contributory fault, and the claimant is subsequently convicted: see *Ladup v Barnes*.[45]

The number of applications

19.34   Following the decision in *Goldman Sachs Services Ltd v Mantali*[46] an application for review should only be permissible once, and a material change in circumstances will be required for a subsequent application.

Application of party or on tribunal's own initiative

19.35   A review can be considered either on the application of a party or of the tribunal or of the chairman's own initiative.[47]

Parties

19.36   If one of the parties wishes to apply for a review, the application must be made to the Employment Tribunal Office within 14 days of the date on which the decision was sent to the parties.[48] The time limit

---

43 [1978] ICR 782, EAT.
44 [1974] ICR 77; [1973] IRLR 316, NIRC.
45 [1982] ICR 107; [1982] IRLR 7, EAT.
46 [2002] ICR 1251, EAT.
47 2004 Rules r34(1) and (5).
48 2004 Rules r35(1).

can be extended by a chairman on a just and equitable basis. The application must be in writing and must identify the grounds upon which the application is made. As a matter of practice, an application should also specify the grounds for contending that the decision of which a review is sought is wrong.[49] If the decision to be reviewed was made at a hearing, the application may be made orally at that hearing.

19.37　　The application to have a decision reviewed must be considered by the chairman of the tribunal who made the decision. If it is not practicable for that chairman to consider the application, it falls to be considered by a regional chairman or the Vice President, any chairman nominated by either of those persons or the President. There is no requirement that a hearing be held. If the person considering the application is of the view that no grounds for review have been established or that there are no reasonable prospects of the decision being varied or revoked, the application will be refused. The secretary to the tribunal will then inform the party who has made the application in writing of the decision and the reasons for it.[50]

19.38　　If a party seeks to review a decision on the basis that it did not receive notice of the proceedings and the decision was made in its absence, the EAT has held that it would be inappropriate for the question of whether the application has reasonable prospects of success to be considered by a chairman alone, but rather it should be considered by the full tribunal so that evidence can be taken.[51] There appears to be no statutory basis for this restriction on the rule, which predates the jurisdiction for chairmen to sit alone. The 2004 Rules contain no such requirement; on the contrary, it expressly states that an application can be sifted out by a chairman without an oral hearing, and the Department for Trade and Industry (DTI) Guidance Notes state that there is no requirement for a hearing. A party may wish in any event to ask for a hearing to consider its application, but there appears to be no obligation to accede to such a request.

The tribunal

19.39　If the application passes the preliminary consideration stage, the decision proceeds to be reviewed. Before the 2004 Rules, a chairman alone had no power to conduct a review. Now, where practicable, a review should be considered by the chairman or tribunal which made

---

49　*P J Drakard & Sons Ltd v Wilton* [1977] ICR 642, EAT.
50　2004 Rules r35(4).
51　See *P J Drakard & Sons Ltd v Wilton* [1977] ICR 642, EAT.

the decision under review. If it is not practicable, the regional chairman, the Vice President or the President will appoint another chairman or tribunal.[54] However, if the review is being sought of the tribunal's own initiative, the review must be carried out by the same tribunal or chairman, as only it knows why a review is being considered. If the tribunal or chairman is reviewing a decision of their own motion, a notice must be sent to each of the parties explaining in summary the grounds upon which and the reasons why it is proposed to review the decision. The parties are to be given the opportunity to give reasons why there should be no review. The notice of a decision to review of the tribunal's own motion must be sent before the expiry of 14 days from the date on which the original decision was sent to the parties.[55]

Hearing the application

19.40   The procedure at the hearing of the review will depend on the grounds on which the application is made; some explanation of the reason for applying for a review will be required and evidence may need to be called. For instance, in an application under 2004 Rules r34(3)(c) (decision made in a party's absence), once it has been established that the ground for the application has been made out, evidence which would have been adduced at the original hearing will need to be called to demonstrate that the original decision was wrong.[56] In an application under 2004 Rules r34(3)(d) (new evidence has become available), evidence may first need to be given to establish why the existence of the evidence could not reasonably have been known or foreseen at the time of the original hearing. Then the tribunal may allow the evidence itself to be adduced and go on to consider its effect.

19.41   When evidence is called, any party resisting the application for review will have the opportunity to test that evidence, by way of cross-examination or by calling further evidence in rebuttal. The review hearing also gives both parties the opportunity to make oral submissions.

54   2004 Rules r36(1).
55   2004 Rules r36(2).
56   *Hancock v Middleton* [1982] ICR 416, EAT.

Review and appeal

19.42 The hearing of an application for a review can continue even if the decision is also under appeal to the EAT. In practice, the grounds of appeal and the grounds for review may differ in nature and there may be no difficulty in allowing the two procedures to run in tandem. The EAT may itself suggest a review and will usually stay (sist) an appeal pending a review.[57]

19.43 The distinction between grounds suitable for appeal and grounds suitable for review were considered by the EAT in *Trimble v Supertravel Ltd*,[58] where Browne-Wilkinson P stated:

> We do not think it is appropriate for a . . . tribunal to review their decision simply because it is said there was an error of law on its face. If the matter had been ventilated and properly argued, then errors of law of that kind fall to be corrected by this appeal tribunal. If, on the other hand, due to an oversight or to some procedural occurrence one or other party can with substance say that he has not had a fair opportunity to present his argument on a point of substance, then that is a procedural shortcoming in the proceedings before the tribunal which, in our view, can correctly be dealt with by a review . . . however important the point of law or fact may be. In essence, the review procedure enables errors occurring in the course of the proceedings to be corrected but would not normally be appropriate when the proceedings had given both parties a fair opportunity to present their case and the decision had been reached in the light of all relevant argument.

19.44 As the tribunal or chairman has the power to review its decision of their own initiative, a further complication may arise where a party has entered an appeal against the decision. Although the tribunal obviously considers the case to be suitable for a review, if the grounds overlap with those which form the basis of the appeal, the *Blackpole Furniture* case[59] indicates that the tribunal should consult the registrar of the EAT before proceeding with the question of review, and the appeal will be stayed.

19.45 When new evidence has become available, the appropriate course is for the party seeking to adduce this evidence to apply for a review under 2004 Rules r34(3)(d) rather than seeking to do so on appeal. Indeed, when an appeal was pursued in order to adduce new

---

57 See para 23.39 below.
58 [1982] ICR 440; [1982] IRLR 451, EAT.
59 *Blackpole Furniture Ltd v Sullivan* [1978] ICR 558, EAT.

evidence, costs were awarded against the unsuccessful appellant for bringing an unnecessary appeal since the proper course is to apply for a review.[60]

Revocation or variation of the original decision

19.46   On reviewing a decision, a tribunal or chairman may confirm, vary or revoke the original decision. If the decision is revoked, the tribunal will order the decision to be taken again. The 2004 Rules do not specify whether the matter should be considered again by the same or a differently constituted tribunal. If the original decision was made at a hearing, a new hearing must be held, but the new decision can be taken in the absence of the parties if the original decision was made by a chairman without a hearing.[61]

19.47   The power to vary a decision includes the power to replace the previous decision completely if appropriate:

> [T]he tribunal can . . . decide that at the original hearing the decision it came to was wrong, and the right answer is so obvious that it can go straight to that right answer . . . [62]

Furthermore, the subsequent decision may replace the original completely, even though the application for review was directed only at one aspect of the decision:

> . . . a litigant who asks a tribunal to review its decision cannot pick and choose between which parts of the decision he wishes to have reviewed. If an application is made for a review and is acceded to, then the tribunal is free to review the whole of its decision.[63]

19.48   In such cases, however, the tribunal is bound to give the parties proper warning of the potentially wider consequences than envisaged by the application for review, and to allow them adequate opportunity to be heard fully on all points potentially in issue. In *Estorffe v Smith*[64] the case was remitted to allow the parties opportunity to be heard on issues again 'at large' before the tribunal, although this was not initially envisaged in the review application.

---

60   *Green & Symons Ltd v Shickell and another* EAT 528/83 (unreported); *William P Harrower Ltd v Hogg* EAT 215/78 (unreported).
61   2004 Rules r36(3).
62   *Stonehill Furniture Ltd v Phillippo* [1983] ICR 556, EAT.
63   *Estorffe v Smith* [1973] ITR 627, NIRC.
64   [1973] ITR 627, NIRC.

Checklist: Review of decisions

- Is there a judgment or decision or default judgment in respect of which an application for review might be made?
- If there is no judgment or decision but only an order, is it possible to make an application to vary or revoke that order or should an appeal be pursued?
- If review is being sought of a default judgment, does the respondent have mandatory grounds for seeking review or alternatively is there a reasonable prospect of successfully defending the claim?
- If the review is not being sought of a default judgment, does the party's grievance with the original decision properly fall within the limited grounds on which an application can be considered?
- If the grievance relates to a technical error in the decision, might this properly be corrected by use of the 'slip rule'?
- Is an application for review the proper course, or would an appeal be more appropriate?
- If an application for a review is made at the same time as an appeal is in progress, should the appeal continue or be stayed pending the outcome of the review?
- Is an application for review still in time or will the tribunal need also to be asked to consider extending time under 2004 Rules r35(1)? If the latter, what is the reason for the late application?
- In making the review application, detailed grounds should be presented in writing setting out both the specific ground on which the application is made and demonstrating why the original decision is wrong on the merits in the light of these grounds.
- In making an application for reviewing a default judgment, the respondent must include its proposed response to the claim together with the review application, an application for an extension of time for presenting the response and an explanation for not presenting a response in time.
- When an application is made under 2004 Rules r34(3)(a), (b) or (c), sufficient detail should be given to demonstrate that the application is not merely technical in nature.
- When an application is made under 2004 Rules r34(3)(d), a full

description of the new evidence should be provided, demonstrating how it is relevant and probative and likely to have an important effect on the original decision.

• The application should ask for the opportunity to be heard on the question of whether or not there should be a review as well as at any actual review.

• If the review is allowed and the tribunal indicates that it is likely to revoke the original decision, consider whether representations should be made as to whether the rehearing should be before the same or a differently constituted tribunal.

CHAPTER 20

Enforcement

Introduction

20.1 Enforcement of awards by tribunals differs according to the nature of the award and the person in whose favour an award is made.

Non-monetary orders, and monetary aspects of non-monetary orders

20.2 Failure to comply with certain orders of a tribunal may lead to enforcement procedures in front of the tribunal itself. For example, non-compliance with a reinstatement or re-engagement order under Employment Rights Act (ERA)1996 s113 is enforced by the tribunal, which must award a higher sum by way of compensation.[1] Failure to comply with any monetary part of an ERA s113 order, for example for back pay, is enforced through ERA 1996 s117, and not as a separate 'decision' of the tribunal in the county or sheriff court. Imaginative exploitation of the reinstatement provisions following unfair dismissal was blocked in *O'Laoire v Jackel International Ltd.*[2] The upper limit on compensation awards is raised to enable a tribunal to award more by a reinstatement order than it could had it not ordered reinstatement.[3] But the award remains essentially a non-monetary award, that is, an order for reinstatement under ERA 1996 s113 rather than an award of compensation under ERA 1996 s118. The former is not, therefore, amenable to enforcement in the county or sheriff court (see para 20.4).

20.3 A similar provision applies to awards for failure to comply with an order following a finding of dismissal for trade union reasons under Trade Unions and Labour Relations (Consolidation) Act (TULRCA) 1992 s166. A declaration by a tribunal of an individual's right not to be excluded or expelled unlawfully from a union can be enforced by an application for compensation to the tribunal or, if the individual has not been admitted or readmitted to the union, by an application direct to the EAT to assess compensation.[4]

1   ERA 1996 s117.
2   [1990] ICR 197; [1990] IRLR 70, CA.
3   ERA 1996 s124(3).
4   TULRCA 1992 s176.

Monetary awards

20.4   In order to obtain enforcement of an award of compensation, damages or costs, the decision must be registered at the county court in England and Wales, but this is not necessary in Scotland, where a certificate can be obtained from the tribunal and enforced without going to the sheriff court first.[5] This machinery is not available for *monetary* parts of awards for reinstatement (see above). By this method, the enforcement machinery of the county court is brought into play for the purposes of a tribunal award of 'any sum payable in pursuance of a decision'.

20.5   Civil Procedure Rules (CPR) Part 70, supplemented by a comprehensive practice direction, describes the procedure in England and Wales. The claimant is to apply, without notice to the paying party, on Form N322A, with a statement of truth verifying the sum due and producing a copy of the decision registered at the Central Office, together with a court fee, currently £30.[6] There is no hearing and the form is dealt with by a court officer who issues the order and a time for payment. The sum will have been increased to include the fixed fee and fixed solicitor's costs. If unpaid thereafter, the paying party becomes a judgment debtor to the judgment creditor.

20.6   The sum is recoverable as though it were an order of the county court. In Scotland it can be enforced 'in like manner as an extract registered decree arbitral bearing a warrant for execution' issued by the sheriff court.[7] This means enforcement may be effected by a writ of *fien facias* (in the High Court) or warrant of execution (in the county court), a third party debt order, a charging order or stop notice, an attachment of earnings order (in the county court) or the appointment of a receiver.[8] If the debt on the order is for less than £600 the warrant of execution must stay in the county court. If it exceeds £600 it *may* be transferred to the High Court for enforcement by the sheriff, and if over £5,000 it *must* be so transferred.[9]

20.7   In all of these procedures there is provision under CPR Part 71 for examination of the debtor in court. Since no order is of any use unless the debtor has goods or assets, it is sometimes helpful to call the debtor to court with the relevant financial records to answer

5   Employment Tribunals Act (ETA) 1996 s15(1) and (2).
6   Civil Procedure Rules Sch 2; County Court Rules Order 25 r12.
7   ETA 1996 s15(2).
8   CPR PD 70.
9   County Courts Act 1984 Pts V, VI, as in Civil Procedure, Vol 2, 9A-667–739.

questions from the court about assets. This can be done for an individual or a company.

Interest

20.8   There are two provisions dealing with interest. Under the Employment Tribunals (Interest) Order 1990[10] interest becomes payable on tribunal awards 42 days from the date of the decision. The interest rate is that specified in relation to the Judgments Act 1838.[11] So from the end of the time limit for an appeal, interest runs at the specific rate. It is therefore important to ensure that the tribunal does wherever possible make an award, rather than adjourning the matter for the parties to attempt to settle.

20.9   Separate provision is made for interest under the sex, race, disability, equal pay, sexual orientation and religion or belief legislation[12] by the Employment Tribunals (Interest on Awards in Discrimination Cases) Regulations 1996.[13] Here the date from which interest begins to accrue is the date of the decision,[14] but if the award of the tribunal is paid by the respondent within 14 days of the decision, no award of interest is made. Interest runs in respect of an award for injury to feelings from the date of the discriminatory act for the whole of the period up to the date of the decision. For other monetary awards in a discrimination case interest runs from the 'mid-point date' (the date half way between the start of the act or acts of discrimination and the date of calculation) to the date of calculation. The rate of interest under the 1996 Regs is determined according to the Special Investment Account under the Court Fund Rules 1987, and in Scotland according to the Act of Sederunt (Interest in Sheriff Court Decrees or Extracts) Act 1975. Since 1 August 1999 this rate has been seven per cent.

---

10   SI No 479.
11   8 per cent since 1993.
12   But not the Part-time Workers (Prevention of Less Favourable Treatment) Regulations 2000 SI No 1551.
13   SI No 2803.
14   Employment Tribunals (Constitution and Rules of Procedure) Regulations (Amendment) 1996 (1996 Regs) SI No 1757 reg 8(1).

Rights after death

20.10   Certain employment provisions may be enforced on behalf of an employee who has died before or after the commencement of proceedings (that is, ERA 1996 Parts I (so far as it relates to itemised pay statements), III, V, VI (ss50–57 and 61–63), VII, VIII, IX (ss92 and 93) and X to XII, dealing with most employment protection rights including unfair dismissal and redundancy pay: see ERA 1996 s207). Enforcement of orders made on behalf of the personal representatives of a dead employee is regulated by the Employment Tribunals Awards (Enforcement in Cases of Death) Regulations 1976.[16] This provides for awards to be made in favour of the estate of an employee who has died. It is not necessary for the personal representative to obtain letters of administration or probate or (in Scotland) confirmation.[17] While there is no equivalent to ERA 1996 s206 in the discrimination legislation, claims can nevertheless be instituted or continued by virtue of Law Reform (Miscellaneous Provisions) Act 1934 s1(1).[18]

Insolvent employers

20.11   Commencement and maintenance of proceedings against insolvent respondents is dealt with at para 4.8 above. Some debts due are recoverable from the secretary of state, paid out of the National Insurance Fund, under ERA 1996 s167 (redundancy pay) and section 182 (some other payments). Otherwise, employees rank as preferential creditors to the extent of certain elements of back pay and holidays and collect debts according to their priority in a winding-up.

16   SI No 663.
17   ERA 1996 s206.
18   *Harris (personal representative of Andrews (deceased)) v Lewisham and Guy's Mental Health NHS Trust* [2000] IRLR 320, CA.

Special cases: interim relief

Introduction

21.1   Tribunals have additional powers to intervene at an early stage in dismissal cases arising under 10 different statutory provisions: those involving trade union membership or activities; campaigning for or against union recognition; employee representation on transfers, redundancies and working time; health and safety at work; pension fund trustees and whistle blowing. The trade union provisions are set out in the Trade Unions and Labour Relations (Consolidation) Act (TULRCA) 1992 s161, which permits an application to be made in respect of a dismissal under TULRCA 1992 s152 and the others are known as the 'specified reasons' under Employment Rights Act (ERA) 1996 s128. In this chapter they are referred to as 'trade union and other specified' reasons for interim relief. The powers are to grant temporary remedies pending the hearing of the case, requiring the employer to reinstate or re-engage, or if the employer is unwilling to do so, to provide for continuation of the contract of employment. This is felt to be an important safeguard of the rights of union members and activists and certain others and operates as a kind of injunction preserving the situation as it was before the dismissal, or at least allowing the employee to be treated as suspended rather than as dismissed. It will also have the important effect for an employee of requiring the employer to continue to pay his or her salary or wage until the tribunal Hearing.

Dismissal for trade union and other specified reasons

21.2   The right to claim interim relief is confined to cases of dismissal where the principal reason is alleged to be the claimant's involvement with an independent trade union or for the prescribed reasons set out in ERA 1996 s128. Such dismissals are automatically unfair if that reason for dismissal is made out. The right to interim relief arises only if the principal reason for dismissal is said to be that the claimant:[1]

---

1   See TULRCA 1992 ss152, 161 (union involvement) and Sch A1 para 161(2) (union recognition); ERA 1996 s128 together with s100(1)(a) and (b) (health and safety), s101A(d) (working time), s102(1) (pension fund trustees), s103 (employee representative or candidate) and s103A (protected disclosure).

- was or proposed to become a member of an independent trade union;
- took part or proposed to take part at an 'appropriate time'[2] in its activities;
- was *not* a member of any union or a particular union, or refused to join or proposed to refuse to join or remain in a union;
- acted or proposed to act in various ways with a view to obtaining or preventing recognition of a trade union;
- carried out or proposed to carry out activities in connection with preventing or reducing risks to health and safety at work, having been designated by the employer to do so;
- performed or proposed to perform the functions of a health and safety representative or a member of a safety committee;
- performed or proposed to perform functions as a workforce representative, or candidate, under the Working Time Regulations 1998[3] Sch 1;
- performed or proposed to perform functions as an occupational pension scheme trustee;
- performed or proposed to perform functions as an employee representative for the purposes of consultation under Transfer of Undertakings (Protection of Employment) Regulations (TUPE) 1981[4] or TULRCA 1992 s188 (mass redundancies);
- made a protected disclosure under the whistle blowing provisions of ERA 1996 s47B.

21.3   There are other forms of automatically unfair dismissal which are not eligible for interim relief, such as that the claimant was *selected for redundancy* for one of the above trade union reasons[5] or for one of the prescribed reasons set out above, was dismissed for refusing to work in dangerous conditions,[6] was a protected shop or betting shop worker,[7] had sought leave for family reasons,[8] had asserted a statutory right,[9] had taken action with regard to obtaining the national minimum wage,[10]

---

2   TULRCA 1992 s152(2).
3   SI No 1833.
4   SI No 1794.
5   TULRCA 1992 s153.
6   ERA 1996 s100(1)(c)–(e).
7   ERA 1996 s101.
8   ERA 1996 s99.
9   ERA 1996 s104.
10   ERA 1996 s104A.

a tax credit[11] or for seeking to enforce rights with regard to flexible working.[12]

Procedural steps

21.4   References to the statutory procedure described here are to dismissals for union involvement but the nature of the procedure applies equally to the other specified cases under ERA 1996 ss128–129.

21.5   The claim for interim relief is separate from the main claim of unfair dismissal but may be made on the same claim form, or on a different form at the same or a different time. It must be presented not later than seven days after the dismissal.[13] A claimant claiming infringement of union rights, rather than non-union or other specified rights, must also present a certificate signed by an official of his or her union authorised to give such a certificate, and the union must be independent. The official should say that:

- the claimant was or proposed to become a member of the union at the date of dismissal; and
- there appear to be reasonable grounds for supposing that the reason or principal reason for the dismissal was the one alleged, that is, union involvement.[14]

The certificate must deal with the reasonableness of the belief and not simply assert the opinion of the union official, although it is axiomatic that the official would consider his or her beliefs to be founded on reasonable grounds.[15]

The hearing

21.6   A claim for interim relief is one of the types of pre-hearing review which can be heard by a chairman only.[16] However, a party may make an application for a full tribunal to hear the application not less than

---

11   ERA 1996 s104B.
12   ERA 1996 s104C.
13   TULRCA 1992 s161, ERA 1996 s128.
14   TULRCA 1992 s162.
15   *Bradley v Edward Ryde & Sons* [1979] ICR 488, EAT.
16   Employment Tribunals Rules of Procedure 2004 (2004 Rules) r18(2), contained in Employment Tribunals (Constitution and Rules of Procedure) Regulations 2004 (2004 Regs) SI No 1861, Sch 1.

10 days before the date in which the pre-hearing review is due to take place or a chairman may issue an order that the pre-hearing review should be conducted by a full tribunal if he or she considers that substantive issues of fact are likely to be determined and that it would be desirable for a full tribunal to conduct the pre-hearing review.[17]

21.7   The tribunal is required to determine a claim for interim relief as soon as practicable after receiving the claim. This has three effects. First, the employer is to be given copies of the claim (and union certificate) and at least seven days' notice of the pre-hearing review. Provision is made in union cases for additional parties to be joined on three days' notice.[18] Secondly, the tribunal is not to exercise its ordinary powers to postpone the hearing unless 'it is satisfied that special circumstances justify' it. Thirdly, the tribunal is required to announce its findings at the hearing.[19] The intention is that a decision should be made as quickly as is practicable.

21.8   The central issue at the hearing is whether it appears likely that the tribunal hearing the full case will find that the claimant was unfairly dismissed for the alleged reason, that is, trade union or other specified reason. This is really a balance of probabilities rather than a higher test, but it must be more likely than not that the automatically unfair reason will be made out.[20] If some other reason emerges which will also lead to a finding of unfair dismissal, the tribunal is not entitled to make an interim relief order. Tribunals are cautious about making interim relief orders. If the employee fails to secure an interim relief order, but succeeds in making out the automatically unfair reason for dismissal at full rule 26 Hearing, he or she can claim loss of earnings from the date of dismissal to the date of Hearing. However, if an interim relief order is granted but the employee fails to make out the automatically unfair reason at full Hearing, there is no provision for the employer to reclaim the salary or wages paid to the employee under the interim relief order.

21.9   Frequently, no witnesses are called but a submission is made by the claimant's representative and documents and a chronology are referred to. Since the evidence is likely to be controversial and subject to lengthy cross-examination, it is often counter-productive to call witnesses: the main facets of the claimant's case will have been

---

17   2004 Rules r18(3).
18   TULRCA 1992 s162.
19   TULRCA 1992 s163, ERA 1996 s129(2).
20   *Taplin v C Shippam Ltd* [1978] ICR 1068; [1978] IRLR 450, EAT.

exposed. There will be few cases in which the evidence points squarely to a dismissal for an automatically unfair reason and the tribunal will normally be asked to draw inferences that the real reason is trade union involvement, etc. In the face of predicted long cross-examination, it is sometimes felt more useful to go straight to an expedited full tribunal Hearing. Nevertheless there are no rules as to the type of evidence adduced and in many cases brief evidence from the claimant or the union official is appropriate so as to give the tribunal evidence from which the inference can be drawn.

Remedies

21.10   It is assumed that the claimant wants reinstatement, so the tribunal must ask the respondent if it is willing to reinstate or re-engage on no less favourable terms and conditions of employment. If the respondent is willing to re-engage on different terms and conditions of employment in another job, the tribunal will decide whether any refusal by the claimant is reasonable. If the respondent refuses both, or the claimant reasonably refuses re-engagement, the tribunal must make an order for continuation of the contract of employment.[21] If the tribunal is of the opinion that the refusal is unreasonable, it will make no order.[22]

21.11   An order for the continuation of a contract of employment provides that specified rights, namely the benefits of the contract of employment, seniority and pensions, and continuity of employment under statute are preserved. The contract continues from the date of termination until determination or settlement of the claim, including the hearing of any appeal.[23] The tribunal specifies the amounts and dates of payment of wages.

21.12   Between the hearing and final determination or settlement of the claim, either party can apply (to any tribunal, not just the one which decided it) for a revocation or variation of the order on the ground of a relevant change in circumstances.[24] What might amount to a relevant

---

21   TULRCA 1992 s163(5)(a) and (6).
22   TULRCA s163(5)(a).
23   *Zucker v Astrid Jewels* [1978] ICR 1088; [1978] IRLR 385, EAT. The contract only continues for these purposes, so cannot, for example, be a contract which transfers under TUPE Regs 1981 – *Dowling v Mellic Haulage* [2004] UKEAT/0836/03.
24   TULRCA 1992 s165 and *British Coal Corporation v McGinty* [1988] IRLR 7, EAT.

change is not defined and appears to be widely drafted. The same urgent timescale is to be observed. There is no reason why the same tribunal should not deal with variations but it may be unfair for it to sit on interim relief and the full hearing, because it will already have expressed a view.[25]

21.13   The claimant may complain to a tribunal that the employer has not complied with the terms of an order for reinstatement or re-engagement. The tribunal may then order the continuation of the contract of employment *and* order compensation to be paid, having regard to the infringement of the claimant's right to be reinstated or re-engaged and to any loss suffered in consequence of the failure to comply. If a continuation of contract order is not complied with, a claimant may complain to the tribunal about the non-compliance and seek an order for payment of a specified sum of those wages not paid.[26]

25   See *British Coal Corporation v McGinty* [1988] IRLR 7, EAT.
26   TULRCA 1992 s166.

CHAPTER 22

Equal pay

Introduction

22.1 The procedures for claiming equal pay differ from other tribunal claims and merit a chapter of their own. Section references in this chapter are to the Equal Pay Act (EqPA) 1970 unless otherwise indicated.

22.2 Equal pay claims may be brought, by women or men,[1] on three grounds under the EqPA 1970 and the Treaty of Rome:

- the claimant claims to be employed on 'like work' with a comparator of the opposite sex;[2]
- the claimant claims to be employed on work 'rated as equivalent' to that of the chosen comparator under a job evaluation study (JES);[3]
- the claimant claims to be employed on work which is different but of equal value to that of the comparator.[4]

22.3 Each of the three grounds is in the alternative to the others. A claim whereby the woman claims to be employed on work of equal value is made where a woman is not employed on like work or work rated as equivalent. If a woman claims in the alternative that she is, say, doing work rated as equivalent or work of equal value, the claim that she is employed on work rated as equivalent falls to be determined first.

European law

22.4 A claimant may claim equal pay for the same work, or for work done on a job classified as equal, or for work which is of equal value, but nevertheless find that the EqPA 1970 gives no effective remedy. Article 141 of the Treaty of Rome ('the treaty') and Directive 75/117/EEC (the Equal Pay Directive), which has been held to facilitate article 141 (see *Jenkins* at para 22.7 below), can be relied on in the tribunal.[5]

22.5 Article 141 can be relied on directly only if it is clear and can be operated to give equal pay without recourse to national implementing

---

1 Although, for convenience, references in this text assume the claim to have been brought by a woman against a male comparator.
2 EqPA 1970 s1(2)(a).
3 EqPA 1970 s1(2)(b).
4 EqPA 1970 s1(2)(c).
5 *Secretary of State for Scotland and Greater Glasgow Health Board v Wright and Hannah* [1991] IRLR 187, EAT.

measures necessary to define discrimination.[6] In *Pickstone v Freemans plc*,[7] the Court of Appeal held that article 141 could be relied on directly in an equal value case where the discrimination is obvious on a direct comparison of the two types of work.[8] Because most equal value claims are not so obvious, and require some form of expert or at least experienced evaluator, it must still be doubted if article 141 may be directly enforced in many claims.[9] No enforcement procedure is specified in the treaty or the directive, so the UK's own procedures governing tribunals are operated.[10]

Procedures under the Equal Pay Act 1970

22.6   The procedure is designed to lead to a declaration that the woman's contract contains an equality clause, so that *any* term of her contract which is or becomes less favourable than his is to be treated as so modified so as not to be less favourable, or her contract is to be treated as including any contractual term which the man enjoys under his contract. A complaint may be presented to the tribunal that there has been a contravention of a term modified or included by virtue of an equality clause, and seeking arrears of remuneration or damages.[11] The claimant will be entitled to seek arrears or damages extending back over a six year period from the date on which the claim was presented.[12] The Act is modified to deal with claims of unequal treatment in relation to occupational pension schemes, where no damages but a declaration only, may be awarded.[12a]

22.7   The basis of a *like work* claim is that a woman is doing work which

6   *Worringham v Lloyds Bank* [1981] ICR 558, ECJ at 589; [1981] IRLR 178.
7   [1987] ICR 867; [1987] IRLR218, CA (affirmed on different grounds [1988] ICR 697; [1988] IRLR 357, HL).
8   [1987] ICR 867 per Purchas LJ at 895 and Nicholls LJ at 880.
9   See the view of Lord Oliver in [1988] ICR 697 at 723, strictly obiter and the only speech containing a reference to this problem.
10   *Pickstone v Freemans plc* [1987] ICR 867; [1987] IRLR 218, CA and *Livingstone v Hepworth Refractories plc* [1992] ICR 287; [1992] IRLR 63, EAT.
11   EqPA 1970 s2(1).
12   EqPA 1970 s2(5) as amended by the Equal Pay Act (Amendment) Regulations 2003 SI No 1656 following the decision of the House of Lords and ECJ in *Preston v Wolverhampton NHS Trust* [2001] ICR 216; [2001] IRLR 237, HL and *Preston (No 3)* [2004] ICR 993, EAT. If the case is a concealment and/or disability case, the arrears date from which equal pay can be claimed for six years is the date of the contravention of the legislation by the employer (EqPA 1970 s2ZB(4)).
12a   Occupational Pension Schemes (Equal Treatment) Regulations 1995 SI No 3183.

is the same as, or is of a broadly similar nature to, that of a man. A claim that the woman is doing work that has been *rated as equivalent* will be based on a job evaluation study (JES) that has been conducted by the employer and which gives equal rating to the jobs of the woman and her comparator. The procedure involved in bringing cases based on like work and on a JES is generally the same as that for other types of tribunal claims described in this book. Claims under the Treaty and the Equal Pay Directive, which facilitates implementation of the Treaty[13] are directly enforceable in the tribunal in respect of like work,[14] where the normal rules of procedure apply, including those relating to time limits as amended.[15]

22.8   In *equal value* cases, different (and more complex) rules apply, varying the procedure in a number of respects. These are known as the Employment Tribunals (Equal Value) Rules of Procedure and are contained in Schedule 6 of the 2004 Regs (see para 22.28 below).[16]

A comparable male worker

22.9   The claimant in each type of case has to show that a man is doing this work:

- in the same establishment for the same employer; *or*
- at a different establishment in Great Britain for the same employer where common terms and conditions of employment are observed.[17]

22.10   For practical purposes the claimant must cite a male comparator at an early stage, although the choice of comparator is hers alone.[18] It has been held that she need not prove the comparator is representative of a particular group of employees.[19] Difficulties may arise if a

13   *Jenkins v Kingsgate Ltd* [1981] ICR 592 at 614; [1981] IRLR 228, ECJ.
14   *Pickstone v Freemans plc* [1987] ICR 867; [1987] IRLR 218, CA.
15   *Livingstone v Hepworth Refractories plc* [1992] ICR 287; [1992] IRLR 63, EAT and see paras 22.16–22.27 below.
16   Employment Tribunals (Constitution and Rules of Procedure) Regulations 2004 (2004 Regs) SI No 1861.
17   EqPA 1970 s1(6) and *British Coal Corporation v Smith* [1994] ICR 810; [1994] IRLR 342, CA. Note that this definition excludes reliance on a comparator who remains employed by the woman's same employer at the same establishment where the woman's employment has been 'contracted out' – *Lawrence v Regent Office Care Ltd* [2002] IRLR 822; *Allanby v Accrington and Rossendale College* [2004] IRLR 224.
18   *Ainsworth v Glass Tubes and Components Ltd* [1977] ICR 347; [1977] IRLR 74, EAT.
19   *Thomas v National Coal Board* [1987] ICR 757; [1987] IRLR 451, EAT.

wholly anomalous comparator is chosen, since the respondent is likely to justify a material factor other than the difference of sex as the reason for the different pay under EqPA 1970 s1(3).

22.11   The combined effect of the EqPA 1970 and article 141 allows claims to be made with a comparator who is not working simultaneously with the claimant, for example, when she is appointed to replace him but on a lower salary.[20] However, it is not permissible, either under EqPA 1970 or article 141 to seek to rely on a comparator employed by the woman's previous employer. There must be comparison with someone who is or has been in the same employment as the woman claiming equal pay.[21]

22.12   Restricting inter-establishment claims to Great Britain and not the whole of the UK is probably open to a successful challenge that the Treaty and the Equal Pay Directive are not properly implemented in the UK because of the subdivision of the member state. Comparison is prevented as between establishments in Northern Ireland and Great Britain, even though Northern Ireland has its own equivalent legislation.

Burden of proof

22.13   This is initially on the claimant, who must show that she is employed on like work, work rated as equivalent or work of equal value with a comparable man. The employer will bear the burden of proving the existence of a JES under EqPA 1970 s2A(2) so as to defeat an equal value claim. It seems that the employer is under a duty to show that any pay structure or policy is not discriminatory when it is not transparent (that is, so as to enable a woman to see how her pay and others' is made up),[22] or where that structure or policy has the effect of placing women on average below men (that is, is indirectly discriminatory on the ground of sex).[23] If the claimant can show that the pay structure under which she claims an entitlement to pay equal to that of her comparator indirectly discriminates against women, the employer must not only show a genuine material factor justifying the pay differential but must also objectively justify the difference.

22.14   Although the Burden of Proof Directive covers equal pay, the

20   *Macarthys Ltd v Smith (No 2)* [1980] ICR 672; [1980] IRLR 209, CA.
21   *Allanby v Accrington and Rossendale College* [2004] IRLR 224.
22   *Handels-og Kontorfunktionaerernes Forbund i Danmark v Dansk Arbejdsgiverforening (acting for Danfoss)* [1991] ICR 74; [1989] IRLR 532, ECJ.
23   *Enderby v Frenchay Health Authority* [1994] ICR 112; [1993] IRLR 591, ECJ.

Sex Discrimination (Indirect Discrimination and Burden of Proof) Regulations 2001[24] do not amend the EqPA 1970 as the government took the view that it already falls to the employer to prove that there has been no sex discrimination if pay differs. In *Nelson v Carillion Services*,[25] the Court of Appeal held that, in an equal pay case where indirect sex discrimination is alleged, the burden of proving disproportionate adverse impact lies on the claimant. The claimant must provide the necessary statistics to show, on the balance of probabilities, a disproportionate impact, and thereby establish a prima facie case that she has suffered indirect discrimination. Until this is done, there is no further burden of explanation on the employer.

Questionnaires

22.15 The questionnaire procedure from sex, race and disability discrimination legislation applies to equal pay claims (see para 4.17).[26] The claimant may serve a questionnaire in the prescribed or similar form prior to bringing a claim to the tribunal or within 21 days (or such longer period as the tribunal may allow) of presenting a claim, and the respondent will have a period of eight weeks in which to reply. If the respondent deliberately and without reasonable excuse fails to reply or replies in a manner which is evasive or equivocal, the tribunal is permitted to draw such inferences from the failure as are just and equitable, which may include the drawing of the inference that the respondent has breached the equality clause of the woman's contract.[27] In common with the provisions in other discrimination legislation for questionnaires to be served, the tribunal cannot order the respondent to reply, or to provide additional information about a reply.

Time limits

22.16 Claims under the EqPA 1970 must be brought no later than six months from the relevant date. Prior to the Equal Pay Act 1970 (Amendment) Regulations 2003[28] (the 2003 Regs), this meant that no claim could be brought if the woman had not been in the

---

24 SI No 2660.
25 [2003] ICR 1256; [2003] IRLR 428.
26 EqPA 1970 s7B.
27 EqPA 1970 s7B(4).
28 SI No 1656.

employment within the six months preceding the reference. Importantly, the tribunal has no discretion at all to extend the time limit for bringing an equal pay claim. The woman must bring her claim within that time, or will be debarred from making her claim.

22.17   The 2003 Regs introduced a new section 2ZA(2) into the EqPA 1970, which defines four types of claim where the six-month rule is modified:

(i)   a concealment case;
(ii)   a disability case;
(iii) a stable employment case; and
(iv)   a standard case.

22.18   A *concealment case* is one where the employer has deliberately concealed from a woman any fact which is relevant to the contravention to which the proceedings relate, *and* without knowledge of which the women could not reasonably have been expected to institute proceedings, *and* the woman did not discover the relevant fact (the 'qualifying fact') until after the last day on which she was employed or the day on which her stable employment relationship ended. The claim must be presented within six months of the date on which the qualifying fact was discovered or could, with reasonable diligence, have been discovered. The case law on Limitation Act 1980 s33 relating to extending limitation for bringing personal injury claims is likely to be relevant to the exercise of this discretion.

22.19   A *disability case* is one where the woman was under a disability (that is, was a minor or of unsound mind which is much more limited than under Disability Discrimination Act 1995 s1) at any time during the six months after the date on which she ceased to be employed, her stable employment relationship ended or she discovered (or could with reasonable diligence have discovered) the qualifying fact deliberately concealed from her by the employer if that date was later than the last day of employment. Six months run from the day after the day on which the woman ceased to be under a disability.

22.20   A *stable employment case* is one in which the proceedings relate to a period during which a stable employment relationship subsists between the woman and the employer, even if the period includes any time after the ending of a contract of employment and there is no further contract of employment in force. Proceedings must be brought within six months of the last date of that relationship.

22.21   A *standard case*, unsurprisingly, is defined as a case which is not any of the other types of case, and proceedings must be brought within six months of the last date of employment.

Claims based on a job evaluation study

22.22   A JES is relevant under the EqPA 1970 in two different situations (as noted by Dillon LJ in *Bromley v H & J Quick Ltd*):[29]

- it can form the basis of a claim for equality based on EqPA 1970 s1(2)(b);
- it can defeat a claim for equal value without reference to an independent expert.

The claimant's claim for equal pay

22.23   In these circumstances, if the claimant and the comparator are not doing like work, the claimant can say under EqPA 1970 s1(5) that:

(a)   there has been a JES;
(b)   it was made using an evaluation of the demand of the job on the jobholder under headings such as effort, skill and decision (that is, decision-making);
(c)   it compared her job and the comparator's;
(d)   it rated the work as equivalent, or would have if the system had not given different values for men and women under the same headings; and
(e)   she has not been given equal pay.

22.24   By definition, the work of each will be different. A JES which meets the test in (b) is properly described as 'analytical', since it compares the components of different jobs by analysing the special features demanded in each job, by reference to several factors common to all the jobs evaluated.

22.25   A JES will not meet the test in (d) if gender bias has entered into the scheme, or its application. The Court of Appeal has approved the use of the booklet *Job Evaluation Schemes Free of Sex-Bias*[30] on the need to avoid such bias.[31]

---

29   [1988] ICR 623 at 627; [1988] IRLR 249, CA.
30   Equal Opportunities Commission, 1993.
31   See also *Aldridge v BT* [1989] ICR 790; [1990] IRLR 10, EAT.

The respondent's defence based on a job evaluation study

22.26   The 2003 Regs[32] removed the general 'no reasonable grounds' defence in EqPA 1970 s2A(1)(b) for equal value claims (below). In determining whether the claimant's work is of equal value to that of her chosen comparator, the tribunal must either proceed to determine the question of equal value or require an independent expert to prepare a report on the question.[33]

22.27   However, the specific JES defence has been retained. If the tribunal is being asked to determine whether the work of the claimant and her comparator is of equal value and their work has been given different values by a non-sexist, truly analytical JES, the tribunal 'shall' determine that their work is not of equal value.[34]

Equal value claims

22.28   The right to bring a complaint based on work of equal value was introduced after the European Court of Justice found in *Commission of the European Communities v United Kingdom*[35] that the UK government had failed to fulfil its obligations under European law. Special rules of procedure applicable to such claims are now to be found as the Employment Tribunals (Equal Value) Rules of Procedure (2004 Equal Value Rules), contained in 2004 Regs Sch 6.[36]

22.29   Practical experience of equal value claims indicates that, far from empowering workers to bring equal value complaints, the procedures introduced are open to abuse, and often delay removal of the inequality. Cases can take many years to complete: four years for Julie Hayward,[37] seven years for Sybil Bromley,[38] over a decade for Dr Pamela Enderby and her colleagues,[39] and the claimants in the coal industry cases waited some 15 years after presenting their claims

---

32 Equal Pay Act 1970 (Amendment) Regulations 2003 SI No 1656.
33 EqPA 1970 s2A(1).
34 EqPA 1970 s2A(2) and (2A).
35 [1982] ICR 578; [1982] IRLR 333, ECJ.
36 Note that 2001 Rules Sch 3 will continue to apply to cases commenced before 1 October 2004 where an independent expert's report has already been commissioned – 2004 Regs reg 20(7).
37 *Hayward v Cammell Laird Shipbuilders Ltd* [1988] ICR 464; [1988] IRLR 257, HL.
38 *Bromley v H & J Quick Ltd* [1988] ICR 623; [1988] IRLR 456, settled in 1993.
39 *Enderby and others v Frenchay Health Authority and Secretary of State for Health* [1991] IRLR 44, ICR 382, EAT; [1992] IRLR 15, CA; [1993] IRLR 591, ICR 112, ECJ; [1999] IRLR 155, EAT; [2000] IRLR 257, CA.

before the cases were settled.[40] All too often, claimants are put off by delay, cost and legal complexity.

22.30   The 2004 Equal Value Rules attempt to meet these criticisms by providing a new streamlined procedure for dealing with equal value claims. By virtue of providing what is described as an indicative time-table[41] for completing various stages of the procedure, it is intended that an equal value claim where an independent expert has not been instructed should take 25 weeks to proceed from presenting the claim to full hearing. Claims involving an independent expert should take 37 weeks to proceed from initiating the claim to full hearing. It remains to be seen whether these timetables will be achieved in practice, given the numerous pre-hearing reviews, split Hearings to deal with various issues and appeals which are a feature of many large scale equal value claims.

Procedural steps

22.31   The procedure in the 2004 Equal Value Rules is set out below. Although not specifically referred to in the 2004 Equal Value Rules, the Government's consultation paper *Towards Equal Pay*, states that much of the detail of the procedure is to be fleshed out in practice directions. The procedure is meant to be operated only by tribunals and chairmen specialising in equal pay cases. In addition to ordinary case management (see para 8.1 above) further powers are given to a tribunal or chairman by 2004 Regs Sch 6 r3(1) in relation to facts, documents, timescales, access and experts.

Completion of claim/response

22.32   Follow normal procedure. Multi-claimant cases might be best served by using 2004 Rules r1(7) to present a number of claims in one document. Note that the tribunal or chairman has the power, where proceedings have been joined, to order that lead claimants be identified.[42]

---

40 *Smith and others v British Coal Corporation* [1993] IRLR 308, EAT; [1994] IRLR 342, ICR 810, CA; [1996] 3 All ER 97, IRLR 404, ICR 515, HL.
41 See Annex to the 2004 Equal Value Rules.
42 2004 Equal Value Rules r3(1)(f).

Interim stages

Requests for further information and completion of the questionnaire

22.33   These are as in other tribunal claims, except that the claimant may now request an employer to answer questions with a view to helping her to decide whether to institute proceedings and, if she does so, to formulate and present her case in the most effective manner.[43] The claimant will seek to obtain information relevant to her belief that she has not received equal pay in accordance with the Equal Pay Act 1970.

Disclosure

22.34   Employers are often reluctant to make full disclosure in discrimination cases, claiming confidentiality. In *Nassé v Science Research Council*[44] however, the House of Lords recognised that the necessary information to support a claim of discrimination is almost always in the possession of the employer, who can be ordered to disclose documents. An employer can refuse only when there is some overriding public interest in maintaining the confidentiality of documents.[45] However, an employer who may be able to claim that the public interest is against disclosure of certain classes of document in its possession will not succeed on that ground in withholding *all* documents (see paras 10.24–10.33).[46] Note the additional power of the tribunal in managing equal value proceedings to require the parties to send copies of documents or provide information to the independent expert as well as to the other parties to the proceedings.[47]

Conciliation

22.35   Copies of equal pay claims are sent to the Advisory, Conciliation and Arbitration Service (ACAS) and a duty is imposed under Sex Discrimination Act (SDA) 1975 s64(1), to promote the settlement of the dispute if so requested or if there is a reasonable prospect of achieving a settlement (see para 13.27). A claim under the Equal Pay Act 1970 is one of the claims to which no fixed period of conciliation applies.[48]

---

43   EqPA 1970 s7B(2).
44   [1979] ICR 921; [1979] IRLR 465, HL.
45   *Halford v Sharples and others* [1992] ICR 583, CA.
46   *Commissioner of Metropolitan Police v Locker* [1993] ICR 440, EAT.
47   2004 Equal Value Rules r3(1)(c).
48   2004 Rules r22.

Stage 1 equal value hearing

22.36 Under the 2004 Equal Value Rules, the first obligation on the tribunal is to consider whether or not there is a dispute as to whether the work in issue is of equal value. If it considers that there is a dispute, the tribunal convenes a stage 1 equal value hearing.[49] Where a respondent is seeking to rely on a JES, the tribunal must determine whether the JES is unreliable because it is tainted by sex discrimination or for some other reason. If the tribunal is of the view that the JES is reliable, it must determine that the work of the claimant and her comparator is not of equal value and strike out the claim or whichever part of the claim relies on the JES.[50] This power to strike out is stated to be in addition to the general power of the tribunal contained in 2004 Rules r18(7) to strike out claims (see para 11.17). The tribunal must give a claimant notice prior to striking out a claim or part of it so that she has the opportunity to see whether the provisions of EqPA 1970 s2A(2A) apply. There is no requirement to send a notice to the claimant if she has been given the opportunity to make representations orally to the tribunal as to why such a judgment should not be issued.[51]

22.37 If the JES is found to be unreliable, or there is no JES, the tribunal then proceeds to determine the question of whether the claimant's work is of equal value itself or whether to require an independent expert to prepare a report with respect to that question. If a party makes an application, the tribunal can hear evidence and be addressed upon the issue of the genuine material factor (GMF) defence before making its decision.[52]

22.38 It is generally in the employer's interest to raise the GMF defence at this stage. A tribunal does not have to accede to the request. If it does so, and concludes that the defence is made out, then it must forthwith dismiss the claim.[53] On the other hand, if the tribunal does not hear the defence at this stage, the respondent can still raise it after the independent expert's report has been received.

22.39 An employer not wishing the tribunal to consider the question of a GMF defence at this stage would still be well-advised to raise the point at as early a stage as possible (preferably in the response). If an

---

49 Note that a stage 1 equal value hearing must be conducted by a full tribunal (2004 Rules r4(2)).
50 2004 Equal Value Rules r4(3)(a).
51 2004 Equal Value Rules r4(4).
52 2004 Equal Value Rules r4(5).
53 *Reed Packaging Ltd v Boozer and Everhurst* [1988] ICR 391; [1988] IRLR 333, EAT.

employer indicates at this stage that it does not intend to rely on any GMF defence, it may be barred from raising it subsequently.[54]

22.40   The tribunal is expected to make certain standard directions at this hearing, unless it considers it inappropriate to do so. The tribunal may add to, vary or omit any of the directions as it considers appropriate. The standard directions are contained in 2004 Equal Value Rules r5, and provide as follows:

1. the claimant is to disclose the name of the comparator relied upon or, if she cannot name him, information from which it is possible for the respondent to identify the comparator, and identify the period in relation to which she considers that her work and that of the comparator is to be compared (14 days from Stage 1 hearing);

2. the respondent must disclose the name of the comparator when it has information from which to identify that comparator (28 days from Stage 1 hearing);

3. the parties are to provide each other with written job descriptions for the claimant and any comparator. It is proposed in the government's consultation paper that a standard format of job description will be prescribed by practice direction. The parties must also identify to each other in writing the facts which they consider to be relevant to the question of equal value (28 days from Stage 1 hearing);

4. the respondent must grant access to his premises during any period specified by the tribunal or chairman in order that the claimant and her representative may interview any comparator;

5. the parties must present to the tribunal a joint agreed statement in writing of the claimant and comparator's job descriptions, the facts relevant to the issue of whether the work is of equal value and the facts on which the parties disagree, either because they disagree about the fact itself or they disagree about its relevance, with reasons for their disagreement (56 days from Stage 1 hearing);

6. the parties must also disclose to each other, to any independent or other expert and to the tribunal written statements of any facts on which they intend to rely in evidence at the rule 26 Hearing (at least 56 days prior to the hearing);

7. the parties must also present the tribunal with a statement of the facts and issues on which the parties agree and disagree, together

---

54 *Hayward v Cammell Laird Shipbuilders Ltd* [1985] ICR 71; [1984] IRLR 463, IT.

with reasons for disagreement (at least 28 days before rule 26 Hearing).

22.41 Although the fixing of a standard timetable for the provision of information is a sensible means of achieving early identification of the issues, those advising claimants will need to be alert to the importance of setting a realistic agenda and timetable. Information is often much more readily available to the respondent than to the claimant, and it may be more appropriate to require the respondent to produce the relevant job descriptions, for example, as it will have a more comprehensive knowledge of the demands of the posts.

22.42 If the tribunal decides that an independent expert is to be instructed, the parties will be required to copy to the expert all information which they are required by order to disclose or agree between each other. The tribunal will then, having regard to the indicative timetable, fix a date for a stage 2 equal value hearing (for cases involving an independent expert) or fix a date for a rule 26 Hearing (where no expert is to be instructed).[55]

Stage 2 equal value hearing

22.43 The primary purpose of the stage 2 hearing is the determination of the factual matrix relevant to the claim by a full tribunal. The tribunal must make a determination of those facts on which the parties cannot agree. The independent expert will be provided with the facts agreed by the parties and the facts determined by the tribunal (to be known as 'the facts relating to the question') for the purposes of preparing the report. These are then the relevant facts upon which the report must be based, unless the expert applies to the tribunal for the facts to be amended, supplemented or omitted.[56] This is an odd provision, as it appears to provide that the *expert* can determine the scope of the enquiry into the question of equal value. The Equal Value Rules do not specify whether the parties are to be informed of such an application, but it is our view that the interests of justice would require that the parties be informed and be given the opportunity to make representations on the disputed facts.

22.44 A tribunal or chairman has an additional power, if it is considered appropriate at any stage of the proceedings, to order an independent expert to assist the tribunal in establishing the facts on which the

---

55 2004 Equal Value Rules r4(e)–(f).
56 2004 Equal Value Rules r7(6).

expert may rely in preparing the report. This power can only be exercised where the tribunal has determined that it will require a report on the question from an independent expert.[57] The Equal Value Rules provide examples of circumstances in which the tribunal or chairman may make an order, which include:

- a party not being legally represented;
- parties being unable to reach agreement as required by an order of the tribunal or chairman;
- where it is considered that insufficient information may have been disclosed by a party which may impair the ability of the independent expert to prepare the report;
- where the tribunal or chairman considers that the involvement of the independent expert may promote fuller compliance with orders made by the tribunal or chairman.

A party is also permitted to make an application in accordance with 2004 Rules r11 for such an order to be made.

22.45   The 2004 Equal Value Rules r7(5) provides that the facts relating to the question, as defined above, will be the only facts on which the tribunal relies at the rule 26 Hearing. The tribunal has a specific discretion to refuse to hear evidence of facts at the Hearing which have not been disclosed to the other party as required by the rules unless it was not reasonably practicable for that party to comply.[58]

22.46   The tribunal will be required to make standard specified directions at the stage 2 equal value hearing, unless it considers it inappropriate to do so, or considers that the directions should be added to, varied or omitted. The standard directions are contained in 2004 Equal Value Rules r8, as follows:

(a) the independent expert prepare the report and send copies to the parties and the tribunal by a specified date;
(b) the independent expert to prepare the report on the basis of the facts relating to the question and no other facts, whether or not they relate to the question.

Other hearings

22.47   The 2004 Equal Value Rules r13(2) specifically states that the requirement to hold a stage 1 or stage 2 equal value hearing does not

---

57   2004 Equal Value Rules r6(1) and (2).
58   2004 Equal Value Rules rr 3(1)(b) and 9(3).

preclude the tribunal from holding other hearings as provided for in the 2004 Rules. Given the complexity of the legal issues which are often at stake in equal value hearings, it would seem that pre-hearing reviews to determine questions of law are likely to continue to be a feature of equal pay litigation and, it seems almost inevitably, appeals against decisions reached at such hearings.

The independent expert's report

22.48 The independent expert (IE) is a member of a panel designated as suitably qualified and independent by ACAS, although he or she cannot be a member or employee of ACAS.[59] Since 1990, members of the IE panel have adopted a self-denying ordinance for their non-statutory practices and will not accept instructions to advise, give evidence or represent anyone in a case where it is likely that an IE will be required to report.

22.49 When the expert is instructed, they must be informed by the secretary to the tribunal of their duties and powers in relation to the report. The IE is to be the tribunal's expert and has a number of duties arising from his or her role, as set out in 2004 Equal Value Rules r10. The IE has a duty to assist the tribunal in furthering the overriding objective and must comply with the requirements of the rules and any orders made in relation to the proceedings. The IE must also keep the tribunal informed of progress in preparing the report, if requested to do so, and must volunteer information about likely delays. There is an obligation on the IE to comply with the timetable imposed so far as is reasonably practicable. The IE must also ensure that he or she is available to attend hearings in the proceedings. He or she is permitted to make applications for orders or for a hearing to be held as if they were a party to the proceedings. The secretary to the tribunal must ensure that the IE is kept up to date as to the progress of proceedings by sending them notices and informing them of any hearing, application, order or judgment.[60]

22.50 The parties are expected to furnish the IE with the information which they are required to disclose or agree between each other.[61] Following the stage 2 equal value hearing, the IE will also be provided with those facts agreed by the parties and determined by the tribunal.[62] A new provision in the 2004 Equal Value Rules is that the

59 EqPA 1970 s2A(4).
60 2004 Equal Value Rules r13(1).
61 2004 Equal Value Rules r4(3)(d).
62 2004 Equal Value Rules r7(3).

respondent can be required to grant access to its premises in order to allow the IE to conduct interviews with persons who the IE believes are relevant to the preparation of the report.[63] This is in addition to the power to require the respondent to grant access to the claimant and her representative to interview comparators.[64] It is a sensible provision evidently aimed at ensuring that the tribunal should not be deterred by obstructive tactics from obtaining all the information relevant to the question.

22.51   The tribunal may, if it wishes to do so, withdraw the requirement on the IE to produce a report. No grounds are specified as to when it will be appropriate for the tribunal to do so; given the delays which will inevitably accompany such a decision, the power is likely to be used restrictively. If it decides to revoke the requirement, the tribunal is permitted to determine the question of equal value itself, or require a different IE to prepare a report.[65] The IE is to be given the opportunity to make representations as to whether or not he or she should continue to be instructed. No provision is made for the parties either to be given notice or the opportunity to make representations; it is submitted that good practice would indicate that this should happen. If another IE is to be instructed, the first IE will be expected to provide the tribunal with all the relevant documentation and work in progress in the IE's possession for use by the tribunal or another IE.[66]

22.52   The IE should provide his report by a date fixed by the tribunal at the stage 2 equal value hearing. When the report is made available to the parties, they will have an opportunity to put questions to the IE.[67] Unless the tribunal or chairman agrees otherwise, written questions must be submitted within 28 days of receipt of the report and can only be put once. Questions can only be directed at clarifying the factual basis of the report. They must be copied to all other parties in the proceedings at the same time as they are sent to the IE. The IE's answers to the questions are treated as part of his report.[68]

National security cases

22.53   The 2004 Equal Value Rules r14 provides a modified procedure for use in national security proceedings. If the tribunal in such a case

---

63   2004 Equal Value Rules r3(1)(d).
64   2004 Equal Value Rules r5(1)(c).
65   2004 Equal Value Rules r10(4).
66   EqPA 1970 s2A(5), 2004 Equal Value Rules r10(5).
67   2004 Equal Value Rules r12(1).
68   2004 Equal Value Rules r12(3) and (4).

requires an IE to prepare a report, a copy of that report will be sent to the tribunal but not to the parties. If written questions are put to the IE, the IE is required to send the answers to the tribunal but not to the parties.[69]

22.54   Before the secretary to the tribunal sends a copy of the report or answers by an IE to the parties, he or she is obliged to follow the procedure in 2004 Rules Sch 2 r10(2) and send a copy to the minister. The IE's report and answers are not entered on the register. The parties will receive a copy of the report or answers to written questions only where no direction has been made by a minister within the period of 28 days from which the secretary received the report or answers. This is a direction under 2004 Rules Sch 2 r10(3), where the minister considers it expedient in the interests of national security, that the parties shall be sent an edited report or answers, omitting information specified in the direction, or that they shall not receive the report or answers at all.[70]

The parties' own experts

22.55   Notwithstanding the appointment of an independent expert, the parties may still wish to call their own experts to opine on the question of equal value. The tribunal will restrict expert evidence to that which is reasonably required to resolve the proceedings, mirroring the position in civil proceedings contained in CPR Part 35. Any experts called by the parties are under the same duty as the independent expert to help the tribunal with matters within their expertise. The duty is specified to override the obligation to the party paying the expert.[71] The tribunal's permission is required to call an expert or put in evidence an expert's report. Further, parties are not to be permitted to put an expert report in evidence unless it has been disclosed to all other parties and the independent expert at least 28 days prior to the Hearing.[72]

22.56   If an independent expert has been instructed, the tribunal will not allow further expert evidence to be adduced unless the evidence is based on the facts relating to the question of equal value which the tribunal has identified as being relevant to the report prepared by the independent expert. Any expert report permitted by the tribunal must

69 2004 Equal Value Rules Part 2 r1(1).
70 2004 Equal Value Rules r14(3) and Sch 2 r10(3).
71 2004 Equal Value Rules r11(2).
72 2004 Equal Value Rules r11(3).

further be disclosed to all parties and the tribunal at the same time as the independent expert sends out his or her report. If an expert fails to comply with the Rules or with any direction or order made, the tribunal can order that the evidence of the expert shall not be admitted.[73]

22.57   Further, the 2004 Equal Value Rules r11(6) provides that the tribunal may, if it wishes to do so, order that a joint expert be called to give evidence on behalf of the parties, rather than each side relying on its own expert. The tribunal is enabled to select that expert if the parties cannot agree upon selection. It should only rarely be appropriate for this course to be followed, given that the tribunal can already call upon an independent expert if it wishes to have a 'non-partisan' expert report.

22.58   The parties can ask questions of each other's expert, as they can of the independent expert, and the replies are to be treated as part of that expert's report. If an expert instructed by another party fails to answer a question within 28 days the tribunal can order that the party instructing the expert may not rely on his evidence.[74]

22.59   The tribunal or chairman also has the power to order, where more than one expert is to give evidence in the proceedings, that the experts present to the tribunal a joint statement of matters which are agreed between them and those matters on which they disagree.[75]

The Hearing

22.60   At the Hearing, the report of the IE is to be admitted into evidence unless the tribunal determines that it is not based on the facts identified at the stage 2 hearing as relating to the question.[76] If the tribunal refuses to admit the report, it can proceed to determine the question itself or appoint another expert to produce a report.[77]

22.61   The report is only *evidence to be taken into account* by the tribunal in determining the issue of equal value; it is not conclusive, it does not change the burden of proof, and the tribunal is entitled to reach a different conclusion without necessarily being considered perverse.[78]

22.62   A tribunal may require the IE to attend the Hearing to give evi-

---

73   2004 Equal Value Rules r11(4)–(5).
74   2004 Equal Value Rules r12(5).
75   2004 Equal Value Rules r3(1)(e), see also CPR 35.12.
76   2004 Equal Value Rules r9(1).
77   2004 Equal Value Rules r9(2).
78   *Tennants Textile Colours Ltd v Todd* [1989] IRLR 3, NICA.

dence and be cross-examined by the parties.[79] It is not unique in tribunal proceedings for a witness to be called by the tribunal, it has the power to do so under 2004 Rules r10(2)(c).[80] In equal value proceedings, however, it is likely that one party will seek to uphold the IE's report (assuming it to favour one side rather than another), yet there is no rule of evidence preventing leading questions being asked for that purpose. In practical terms, therefore, a party can cross-examine a favourable expert.

22.63   Either party may apply to call an expert witness at the Hearing, and this witness will then be available for cross-examination and re-examination in the normal way.[81]

22.64   Other than in the provision for expert evidence, the conduct of the Hearing will be similar to that for tribunals generally. The Hearing can be solely for the purpose of determining the question of equal value or also include consideration of the EqPA 1970 s1(3) genuine material factor defence.

79 2004 Equal Value Rules r10(1)(g).
80 *Clapson v British Airways plc* [2001] IRLR 184, EAT.
81 2004 Equal Value Rules r11(3).

CHAPTER 23

Appeals

continued

Introduction

23.1   This chapter deals with the procedure for appealing from a tribunal to the Employment Appeal Tribunal (EAT). The EAT Rules 1993,[1] as amended by the EAT (Amendment) Rules 2001 and 2004,[2] and a Practice Direction (EAT PD)[3] regulate the EAT's procedure. In Northern Ireland, appeal lies to the Northern Ireland Court of Appeal, in practice by way of case stated.[4] Before 2002 the EAT and the employment tribunals (ETs) were heavily criticised in the Court of Appeal and the European Court of Human Rights for the delays, sometimes up to eight years, in the hearing of cases.[5] Following the introduction of the EAT PD and the 2004 amendment rules, the EAT has adopted a rigorous approach to case management, so that most cases were being heard within three months. The EAT PD is issued to all users, is on the EAT website and should be read closely with this chapter. There is an EAT users' group.

Constitution

23.2   The EAT's powers derive from Employment Tribunals Act (ETA) 1996 s20. It is almost exclusively an appellate tribunal. There are however exceptions. It can hear:

- Claims for compensation by members unjustifiably disciplined or expelled from a trade union, and individuals unlawfully excluded from membership of a union.[6] In each case the reference to the EAT follows a declaration in the individual's favour by a tribunal, and a failure by the union to rectify the unlawful conduct. This jurisdiction ceases on 6 April 2005.[6a]
- Appeals on questions of law from decisions of the certification officer relating to the certification and listing of a trade union or

---

1   SI No 2854.
2   SI Nos 1128 and 2256 respectively. See appendix B.
3   *Practice Direction (Employment Appeal Tribunal: Procedure)* see appendix B.
4   Industrial Tribunals Order 1996 SI No 1921.
5   *Somjee v United Kingdom* [2002] IRLR 886 *Tran v Greenwich Vietnam Community Project* [2002] ICR 1101, 117, paragraph 49 per Brooke LJ.
6   Trade Unions and Labour Relations (Consolidation) Act (TULRCA) 1992 ss67(2) and 176(2).
6a   Employment Relations Act (ERA) 2004 s34.

employers' association.[7] From 6 April 2005 only questions of law are 'appealable questions'.[7a]

- A complaint under Transnational Information and Consultation of Employees Regulations 1999 (TICE Regs 1999)[8] regs 20(1), 34 and 35 that an employer has failed to set up a European Works Council or information and consultation procedure. The EAT hears and determines the complaint itself, may make an order requiring steps to be taken, and in certain cases must order a penalty to be paid to the secretary of state.[9]

23.3 Ironically, appeals from tribunals to the EAT are an exception to the principal statutory rule, which is that appeals lie to the High Court under Tribunals and Inquiries Act 1992 s11 and Civil Procedure Rules (CPR) Sch 1 and Part 52; CPR PD52 para 16–18. Only a handful of cases have been heard in this manner since the EAT was founded in 1976, mainly concerning compensation for public servants on loss or diminution of pay, and health and safety notices. Otherwise, appeals from tribunals under all the employment protection and discrimination legislation and regulations go to the EAT.

23.4 Appeals on questions of law from a decision of the Central Arbitration Committee on a failure to provide information under TICE Regs 1999 regs 8 and 38(8) can be made to the EAT. Appeals on questions of law from decisions of the certification officer relating to the application of union funds for political objects;[10] amalgamations and transfers of engagements;[11] certain breaches of union rules[12] also go to the EAT.

23.5 The President of the EAT is a High Court judge nominated by the Lord Chancellor.[13] In practice, Presidents hold office for three years. Other judges, who must include one from the Court of Session, are nominated to a panel. They include judges of the High Court, circuit judges, other senior judicial office holders, and recorders who are all nominated to sit as temporary additional judges of the EAT.[14]

23.6 The appointed members of the EAT, widely referred to as the lay

---

7 TULRCA 1992 ss3 and 4.
7a ERA 2004 s51.
8 SI No 3323.
9 TICE Regs 1999 reg 21(4) and (6).
10 TULRCA 1992 s95.
11 TULRCA 1992 s104.
12 TULRCA 1992 s108C.
13 ETA 1996 s22.
14 ETA 1996 s24.

members, are appointed by the Queen on the recommendation of the Lord Chancellor and the secretary of state. They must have 'special knowledge or experience of industrial relations, either as representatives of employers or representatives of workers' and they join one of two panels. There is open recruitment, and there is some training. In practice, most members are active or retired trade union national officials and serving or retired directors of corporations or service organisations. This is the highest level in the UK legal system to which a non-lawyer can be appointed. A full description of their appointment and role was given by Lord Steyn in *Lawal v Northern Spirit Ltd*.[15] There it was held to be a breach of the right to an impartial tribunal for a part-time judge of the EAT to appear as counsel before a panel which included a lay member with whom he had sat judicially. The general administration of the EAT is the responsibility of the Employment Tribunal Service.

23.7   Appeals must be heard by a judge and one member from each panel, and occasionally by a judge and two members from each side.[16] If all the parties consent, a hearing may go ahead with a judge and one member[17] provided that the parties know from which panel the member is drawn.[18] On appeals from decisions made by a tribunal chairman sitting alone, the appeal is usually heard by a judge alone unless a judge decides it should be heard with members.[19] An appeal from a two or three person tribunal cannot be heard by a judge alone.

23.8   The EAT is a superior court of record,[20] which means it can punish for contempt and compel attendance of witnesses[21] so long as money is provided for them to come[22] in the same way as the High Court or Court of Session. Contempt of a tribunal can be dealt with by a reference to the Divisional Court by the tribunal,[23] since the tribunal is an 'inferior court'. But it seems the reference cannot be made to the EAT even if it is presided over by a judge of the Queen's Bench Division.

15 [2003] ICR 856; [2003] IRLR 538, HL.
16 ETA 1996 s28(2).
17 ETA 1996 s28(3).
18 *De Haney v Brent Mind* [2004] ICR 348, CA.
19 ETA 1996 s28(4).
20 ETA 1996 s20(3).
21 ETA s29(2).
22 EAT Rules r27(2).
23 *Peach Grey & Co (A Firm) v Sommers* [1995] ICR 549; [1995] IRLR 363, DC and see CPR Procedural Guide 12.6 D1–031; County Court Rules Order 29 and Rules of the Supreme Court Order 52.

23.9   The EAT sits year-round in London and Edinburgh, and for a week each year in Cardiff, but can sit anywhere in England, Wales and Scotland. Its decisions are binding on tribunals throughout Great Britain. In *Williams v Cowell*[24] an employee who spoke both Welsh and English claimed race discrimination as he was forced to speak English at work; his tribunal claim was heard in Welsh, in Wales, and was dismissed. He appealed against that decision and asked that either the EAT sit in Wales, or else if it sat in London, that it be conducted in Welsh. The Court of Appeal confirmed that the EAT acted contrary to neither the Welsh Language Act 1993 nor the Human Rights Act 1998, in refusing these requests. Judge LJ however added that 'it is much to be hoped that it will not be too long before the necessary administrative arrangements can be made to enable the EAT to sit in Wales on a regular basis'. It now does so.

23.10   The EAT is bound by the doctrine of precedent, so it must follow judgments of the Court of Appeal. It is not bound by judgments of the divisions of the High Court. It is not bound by a decision of the Court of Session (unless it is hearing a Scottish appeal), although the latter's construction of a statute is highly persuasive.[24a] Its decisions are not binding on tribunals in Northern Ireland but they are customarily followed. The EAT will usually follow a decision of another division of the EAT, whether sitting in England, Wales or Scotland unless there are exceptional circumstances, or previous inconsistent decisions. If exceptional circumstances exist, and a previous decision is considered to be plainly wrong, the EAT will now direct that it should no longer be followed by employment tribunals.[25] When there are conflicting decisions of the EAT and the second has considered all the arguments and not followed the first, the EAT previously took the approach of following the second unless it was convinced that it was certainly wrong.[26] However this approach is no longer considered to be correct, and the EAT will now consider the conflict, and try to resolve it in the interests of industrial harmony, giving guidance about which decision ought to be followed.[27]

23.11   There are unrestricted rights to appear as an advocate before the EAT:

---

24   [2000] ICR 85, CA.
24a *Caulfield v Marshalls Clay Products Ltd* [2004] IRLR 564, CA.
25   *Tsangacos v Amalgamated Chemicals Ltd* [1997] IRLR 4 at 5; [1977] ICR 154 at 157, EAT.
26   *Colchester Estates (Cardiff) v Carlton Industries plc* [1986] Ch 80.
27   *Digital Equipment Co Ltd v Clements (No 2)* [1997] IRLR 140 at 141, 146; [1997] ICR 237 at 239, 252, EAT.

> A person may appear ... in person or be represented by counsel or a solicitor or a representative of a trade union or an employer's association or any other person ... [28]

23.12 Legal Services Commission help (legal aid) is available for advice and representation at the EAT.[29]

Case management and the overriding objective

23.13 Like the employment tribunals, the EAT is subject to the overriding objective to deal with cases justly. This is found in EAT Rules 2004 r2A and EAT PD 1(4) and corresponds, so far as is appropriate, with the CPR. Dealing justly means aiming to ensure the parties are on an equal footing, that expense is saved, that the case is handled in a way which is proportionate to the importance and complexity of the issues, and that it is dealt with expeditiously and fairly. The parties must assist the EAT to further the objective.

23.14 The first practical application of the objective is found in the treatment of a Notice of Appeal. If it is in time and contains sufficient documents, it will be put before a judge to 'sift'. This means deciding what track the appeal should occupy and what case management directions should be given. Directions on the sift are provisional, and parties are always given the opportunity to apply to vary or discharge them within a fixed period.

Questions of law

23.15 With the exceptions in para 23.2 above an appeal to the EAT lies only on a question of law.[30] The EAT is jealous of its jurisdiction restricted to questions of law. When it strays outside that jurisdiction, the Court of Appeal and the Court of Session have trenchantly criticised it.[31] It must be borne in mind that any appeal is against the judgment or order of the tribunal, and not against its *reasons*.[32] The EAT, like other courts and appellate jurisdictions, will not hear academic or

---

28 ETA 1995 s28.
29 Civil Legal Aid (General) Regulations 1989 SI No 339; as amended by Community Legal Service (Funding) Order 2000 reg 149.
30 ETA 1996 s21 and TULRCA 1992 s291(2).
31 *Hereford and Worcester CC v Neale* [1986] ICR 471; [1986] IRLR 168, CA.
32 *Harrod v Ministry of Defence* [1981] ICR 8, EAT approved in *Riniker v UCL* [2001] EWCA Civ 597 para 25.

hypothetical cases.[33] This principle comes from ETA 1996 s21(1) which affords appeals, as of right and without permission, from the decision of a tribunal. The extension to questions 'arising in any proceedings' brings in appeals from directions and orders. It might appear to include challenges to anything happening in a tribunal, including an unfair procedure. But an appeal lies only if the appellant seeks to overturn the judgment or order. You cannot appeal a decision wholly in your favour on the ground that the reasons are questionable or the procedure unfair.[34]

Error of law

23.16 This is described as misdirection on the law, or misapplication or misunderstanding of the law.[35] If a tribunal fails to ask the right legal question, or fails to answer the correct statutory question, or misconstrues a statute or a contract, or does not follow binding authority in a higher court, there is an error of law.

Perversity

23.17 In order to run a case based on perversity, it is sometimes necessary to have the chairman's notes, or an agreement on the evidence which the tribunal heard, so that some note of the relevant part of the proceedings before the tribunal, as well as the documents, are all available to the EAT.[36] The EAT then has some material upon which it can decide that no reasonable tribunal properly considering this evidence and directing itself according to the law could have reached the decision which it did. Full particulars must be given (EAT PD para 7). This is a more stringent test than a complaint that the tribunal made a decision contrary to the weight of evidence or did not adequately consider an aspect of the evidence. In these latter cases, the tribunal is the judge of the facts, the inferences and the weight to be given to the evidence, and the EAT will not intervene.[37] It is usually described as the industrial jury. In *Stewart v Cleveland Guest (Engineering) Ltd*,[38] Mummery J described the task:

33 *Sun Life Assurance v Jervis* [1944] AC 111, HL.
34 *Lake v Lake* [1955] P 336, CA.
35 *British Telecommunications plc v Sheridan* [1990] IRLR 27, CA.
36 *Piggott Brothers & Co Ltd v Jackson* [1992] ICR 85; [1991] IRLR 309, CA.
37 *Hollister v National Farmers Union* [1979] ICR 542; [1979] IRLR 238, CA.
38 [1994] IRLR 440 at 443, EAT.

This tribunal should only interfere with the decision of the [employment] tribunal where the conclusion of that tribunal on the evidence before it is 'irrational', 'offends reason', 'is certainly wrong' or 'is very clearly wrong' or 'must be wrong' or 'is plainly wrong' or 'is not a permissible option' or 'is fundamentally wrong' or 'is outrageous' or 'makes absolutely no sense' or 'flies in the face of properly informed logic'.

In a later case, *Yeboah v Crofton*,[39] Mummery LJ held that a perversity appeal should succeed only when 'an overwhelming case' is made out that the tribunal reached a decision which no reasonable tribunal, on a proper appreciation of the evidence and the law, would have reached. This is now the standard.

No evidence

23.18　The absence of evidence for a finding is a specific ground of appeal, although it might well fall within the category of perversity.[40] It is an error of law for a tribunal to make a decision for which there is no evidence in support. However, provided there is *some* evidence dealing with the subject matter, the tribunal decision ought not to be interfered with. If evidence on the particular subject has been given and challenged, the tribunal is entitled to accept or reject that evidence. If the evidence is unchallenged, the tribunal ought to accept it, and if it makes a decision contrary to it, the decision will fall into the 'no evidence' category.

Wrong exercise of discretion

23.19　This could form a ground within perversity but it is mentioned here because the test is much more exacting for appeals on this basis. The wrong exercise of a discretion will rarely be capable of successful challenge.[41] It includes taking into account a factor which it was improper to take into account, failing to take account of a proper factor and the exercise of a discretion 'so far beyond what any reasonable tribunal or chairman could have decided . . .'[42]

---

39 [2002] IRLR 634 CA.
40 See *British Telecommunications plc v Sheridan* [1990] IRLR 27, CA.
41 *Bastick v James Lane Turf Accountants Ltd* [1979] ICR 778, EAT and *Carter v Credit Change Ltd* [1979] ICR 908; [1979] IRLR 361, CA.
42 Applying the principle found in *Associated Provincial Picture Houses Ltd v Wednesbury Corporation* [1948] IKB 223; [1947] 2 All ER 680, CA.

Appeals against case management decisions

23.20   These, too, might be regarded as appeals against the exercise of discretion but they are specifically mentioned in EAT PD para 11(6)(b) as putting unsuccessful appellants at the risk of costs. Because tribunals are given wide powers and duties of case management (for example, under 2004 Rules r10) 'appeals in respect of their conduct . . . pursuant to these provisions, are the less likely to succeed'. Assistance may be gained from the similar approach adopted in the Court of Appeal in dealing with permission to appeal where the court may take into account whether:

(1) the issue is of insufficient significance to justify the costs of an appeal;

(2) the procedural consequences of an appeal (eg, loss of trial date) outweigh the significance of the case management decision;

(3) it would be more convenient to determine the issue at or after trial.[43]

Complaints about the conduct of the hearing

23.21   Bias, apparent bias, improper conduct by the tribunal and procedural irregularity are all grounds for setting aside a decision of a tribunal (see para 16.63). EAT PD para 11 requires a specific complaint to be made with full particulars in the notice of appeal, and the allegations to be put in an affidavit, usually at the sift of the appeal. It is then referred to the tribunal criticised, with comments sought from the chairman and members. An affidavit or statement may also be sought from the other parties. A successful allegation of bias or apparent bias is an error of law because it is a breach of the rules of natural justice.

23.22   In *Facey v Midas Retail Security*,[44] Lindsay P, set out a detailed procedure to be adopted by the EAT in cases where allegations of bias are made against the members of a tribunal, dealing with circumstances in which tribunal members may be required to provide sworn evidence.[45] This procedure is now seen as a last resort, and has been adapted following the steps set out in EAT PD para 11:

---

43   CPR PD52 para 4.5.
44   [2000] IRLR 812, [2001] ICR 287, EAT approved *Stansbury v Datapulse plc* [2004] ICR 523 CA.
45   [2000] IRLR 812 at 819.

(i)   First, the steps outlined in the EAT Practice Direction para 11 will be taken and unsworn comments may then be taken from the tribunal.

(ii) The EAT may next require sworn witness statements (or further ones) from other persons.

(iii) The EAT may then invite, but cannot require, the chairman or other members of the employment tribunal to provide sworn written evidence-in-chief as to primary fact.

(iv) It will in a suitable case be possible, after such an invitation, for adverse inferences to be drawn from a member's failure without good reason to provide sworn written evidence-in-chief of primary fact.

(v)   If, notwithstanding the material already collected, including whatever has been collected by way of disclosure orders, the EAT is of the view that it will materially assist it, it may require the attendance of, for cross-examination, deponents excluding the chairman and members.

(vi) The EAT is not to hear or require a member's cross-examination; be it as to primary or secondary fact, even where the member in question has agreed to attend.

(vii) The EAT is not to require disclosure of documents from him or her.

The full extent of this procedure has very rarely been reached. The role of the EAT in this is to decide the facts, as to what happened, and then to decide what effect any unfairness had on the hearing. In *Stansbury v Datapulse plc*[46] the Court of Appeal held that the EAT had been wrong to see its role otherwise than as finding facts, in a case where at the employment tribunal one member had been drunk and asleep. The decision was set aside, notwithstanding the seemingly hopeless case of the appellant on the merits, and the fact that his employer had become insolvent.

Delay

23.23   A question of law arises when a tribunal has delayed giving its judgment for an unreasonable period of time. In *Kwamin v Abbey National plc*[47] the EAT gave guidance on the effect of delays in the tribunal

---

46 [2004] ICR 523, CA.
47 [2004] ICR 841, EAT also cited as *Birmingham CC v Mtize*.

system, against a background of a right to a hearing with judgment in public within a reasonable time under European Convention on Human Rights (ECHR) article 6. A delay of more than three and a half months from the last oral hearing, or the last written submission after a hearing, is culpable. A judgment will not be set aside simply because there has been culpable delay: the delay must have caused some defect in the judgment such as loss of accurate recollection of the evidence.

Academic appeals

23.24   There must be a live issue between the parties which requires decision by the EAT (see para 23.15). In *Ainsbury v Millington*,[48] Lord Bridge held that the courts 'decide disputes between the parties before them' and do not 'pronounce on abstract questions of law where there is no dispute to be resolved'. Yet he did allow for 'friendly actions' and where the proceedings were brought specifically as a test case. More recently, a greater acceptance has been found where an appeal raises a point of law which, although academic or hypothetical, is of general public interest.[49] If the employer has been found liable for unfair dismissal, has already paid compensation in full and has said in correspondence that it would not seek to recover anything from the employee, there is no live issue.[50] A respondent wishing to appeal must make the payment awarded subject to the appeal. Of course, there is nothing to stop an employer who succeeds in the EAT waiving the right to recover compensation already paid over.

Serving a notice of appeal

23.25   A notice of appeal must be lodged actually, or by electronic means, with the EAT substantially in accordance with the precedent set out in forms at the back of the EAT Rules. These are fairly simple and require the nature of the claim and the grounds on which criticism is made of the tribunal to be set out. The notice of appeal must be served with a copy of the claim, the response and the written record of the judgment or order of the employment tribunal which is subject

---

48   [1987] 1 WLR 379, HL.
49   *Don Pasquale v HM Customs and Excise* [1990] 1 WLR 1108, CA.
50   *IMI Yorkshire Imperial Ltd v Olender* [1982] ICR 69, EAT.

to appeal and the written reasons for the judgment or order or an explanation as to why none is included.[51]

23.26   Slightly different requirements are made in national security and other appeals.[52]

Time limits

23.27   The documents must be with the EAT within 42 days.[53] The 42 days begin to run from different dates. There is always a record of the ET judgment or order, saying what has been decided. If the appeal is against an *order*, time runs from the date of the order. If the appeal is against a *judgment*, it is important to know whether written reasons have been requested. If written reasons were not requested by a party at the hearing or in writing within 14 days *and* the reasons were not reserved, that is, the tribunal did not say at the hearing that reasons would be given later in writing, time runs from the date the judgment (without reasons) was sent.

23.28   When reasons have been given, time runs from the date the reasons were sent in three situations:

- written reasons for an ET judgment have been requested orally at the hearing;
- written reasons are requested in writing within 14 days of the date the judgment (without reasons) was sent;
- reasons were reserved to be given later in writing.

23.29   The Interpretation Act 1978 s7 (allowing for time spent in the postal system) does not apply to the relatively generous 42-day period in the EAT.[54]

23.30   It follows from the rules on counting time (chapter 3) that if the date of the judgment or order is a Wednesday you have until the end of business on Wednesday six weeks later to serve the notice on the EAT, and this is made clear by EAT PD para 1.9. The day ends at 4.00 pm for the purpose of doing any act required by the rules or directions.[55]

51 EAT Rules r3.
52 EAT Rules r3(3)–(6).
53 EAT Rules r3(3).
54 *Gdynia American Shipping Lines (London) Ltd v Chelminski* [2004] EWCA Civ 871. *Hammersmith and Fulham LBC v Ladejobi* [1999] ICR 673, EAT; *Sian v Abbey National plc* [2004] ICR 55, EAT. *Mock v Inland Revenue Commissioners* [1999] IRLR 785, EAT, *Kanapathiar v Harrow LBC* EAT/1281/02.
55 EAT Rules r37(1A).

If on that day the EAT is closed, such as for a public holiday or training day, there is an automatic extension to the next open day.[56] Since reasons must accompany the notice, you effectively have only 14 days following an oral judgment to apply for reasons in order to mount an appeal.[57] The rigour of this timetable is mitigated by the requirement to give an explanation for the fact that the judgment is not accompanied by the reasons. In many cases, the reasons will not arrive before the end of the 42 days, so it is satisfactory to show that they have been sought.

23.31   An application for an extension of time can be made[58] and the rules set out in *Marshall v Harland & Wolff Ltd*[59] will be applied to determine whether there is any justifiable excuse, what the length of the delay is, and the degree of prejudice caused to the other party. The EAT has a discretion to extend time under EAT Rules r37, EAT PD para 3(2). It should be borne in mind that it exercises its powers sparingly and that the test is even more strict than that applied by the Court of Appeal.[60] It is more reluctant to extend time for entering an appeal than for complying with an interim order, since the appellant has already had one chance to have a trial of the merits.[61]

23.32   No time scale is prescribed for the service of a respondent's answer and notice of cross-appeal by the rules but the judge sifting the notice of appeal, or the EAT at a preliminary hearing will give directions to a respondent, setting out the relevant timescale, which is usually 14 days, with a right to apply to vary it.

Preliminary matters

Interim applications: restricted reporting orders

23.33   By EAT Rules r20, the registrar considers interim applications and he or she must have regard to the overriding objective and to any restricted reporting order. A restricted reporting order can be made

---

56   EAT Rules r37(2).
57   *William Hill Organisation Ltd v Gavas* [1990] IRLR 488, CA.
58   EAT PD para 3(2).
59   [1972] ICR 97; [1972] IRLR 90.
60   *Aziz v Bethnal Green City Challenge Co Ltd* [2000] IRLR 111, CA, approving *United Arab Emirates v Abdelghafar* [1995] IRLR243, EAT.
61   *Costellow v Somerset CC* [1993] 1 WLR 256; [1993] 1 All ER 952, CA, applied in *Fire Brigades Union v Knowles* EAT 123/94 (unreported).

on the same lines as can be made by a tribunal[62] in cases involving sexual misconduct. Similarly, where a sexual offence is alleged, identifying material must be omitted from the register of the EAT. The discretion of the EAT to regulate its own procedure under ETA 1996 s30(1) has been widely construed: see *X v Commissioner of Police of the Metropolis*.[63] There are also provisions to conceal the identity of parties or witnesses if necessary in cases concerning national security.[64]

23.34   The registrar may decide the matter him or herself or put it to a judge, who may decide it or put the matter to a full appeal tribunal. But only a judge or the EAT may decide an application for a restricted reporting order in cases involving allegations of sexual misconduct or the commission of sexual offences, or disability discrimination.[65] The application is determined finally after consideration of the representations of the parties, or a hearing[66] but a temporary order may be made in advance of that.

23.35   An appeal lies from the registrar to a judge, who may decide it or refer it to a full appeal tribunal.[67] Notice of appeal must be given within five working days of the decision appealed from (PD para 1.9).

Restriction orders

23.36   A party can be debarred from proceeding if the time limit for presenting a respondent's answer has passed and also if the party fails to comply with any direction.[68] There is also a specific provision in ETA 1996 s33 precluding vexatious litigants from instituting or continuing proceedings (see para 11.27). An opportunity must be given before an order is made for the party to make representations. The effect of a restriction order is that permission is required for the continuation of any further proceedings. The application is made to the EAT by the Attorney General or the Lord Advocate (in Scotland). The first case in which the power under ETA 1996 s33 was used, was that of *Attorney General v Wheen*.[69] Mr Wheen had instituted 15 claims in the employment tribunal, for sex, race and disability

---

62 See EAT Rules r23.
63 [2003] ICR 1031.
64 EAT Rules 2001 r30A.
65 EAT Rules rr 23 and 23A.
66 EAT PD para 4.
67 EAT Rules r21.
68 EAT Rules r26.
69 [2000] IRLR 461, EAT; upheld [2001] IRLR 91, CA.

discrimination. The fact that he is a white, non-disabled man does not mean, of course that he could not be subject to discrimination, but each of his claims was without merit. Upholding the decision of the EAT, Judge LJ held:

> . . . the hallmark of a vexatious proceeding is that it (a) has little or no basis in law; (b) subjects the defendant to inconvenience, harassment and expense out of all proportion to any gain to the claimant (whatever his motive may be); and (c) involves an abuse of the court process. On the facts, that was the case here.

23.37   In *Attorney General v England*[70] the EAT showed a flexible approach when faced with applications under ETA 1996 s33, as it adjourned generally for a period of 12 months, an application to make a restriction order in circumstances in which Mr England, who was aged 64, said that he did not intend to institute any further proceedings.

Directions for hearings

Automatic directions

23.38   The EAT will give automatic directions at the sift stage,[71] or at a preliminary hearing[72] on its own initiative or on the application of a party. Characteristically these deal with issues to be raised, duration of the hearing, amendment of proceedings, consolidation and documentation.[73] The principal decisions for case management are taken on the papers lodged by the appellant at the sift stage by a judge in chambers. They are all provisional, in that the parties can within the specified period, usually 14 days, apply to vary them on showing grounds.[74]

Staying (sisting) the appeal

23.39   At the sift stage it is sometimes apparent that an alternative solution is available and a stay, or postponement, is ordered, always for a finite period, in order to enable some other step to be taken. This may be done to allow an application to be made to the employment tribunal for a review, if necessary out of time, of the decision where what is

---

70   EAT/367/00.
71   EAT PD para 9.
72   EAT Rules rr24 and 25.
73   EAT Rules r24(5).
74   *Reddington v Straker* [1994] ICR 172, EAT.

complained about relates to evidence or facts.[75] It is also often done when it is contended that the employment tribunal did not make a decision on an issue which was live before it, or it has made a decision but not given reasons, or occasionally adequate reasons, for it. This practice follows the recommendation of the Court of Appeal in all first appeal cases in *English v Emery Reimbold.*[76]

23.40 A stay may also be ordered to allow for the gathering of material necessary to decide how an allegation of bias or procedural irregularity should be heard.

23.41 Wherever a stay is ordered, or directions are given, there is an order setting out a time limit and describing the consequences of non-compliance within that time. It may result in the dismissal of the appeal or of a particular ground of appeal.[77]

23.42 The EAT has no express power to stay proceedings in the employment tribunal while an appeal is pending (see para 12.21). This often occurs where a remedy hearing follows an appeal being lodged in the EAT. This is a matter for the employment tribunal unless the EAT has identified an error of law in the employment tribunal's handling of an application to it to stay proceedings. Clear injustice to the litigant would point to the EAT expediting such an appeal.[78]

Case track directions

23.43 Some cases are held by a judge at the sift stage to raise an obviously arguable point of law and are listed for a full hearing on the merits. If an urgent issue is to be resolved, the case can be allocated to the fast track. But some cases are listed for preliminary hearing where the object is to see if a reasonably arguable point exists.

No reasonable grounds for appeal

23.44 In the 2004 Rules, a wider power is given to the EAT than had previously been exercised by the registrar to weed out cases where the notice disclosed no point of law. Now, by EAT Rules r3(7), a judge (or the registrar, but in practice this decision is made by a judge on the sift) may form the opinion that the notice, or any particular ground in

---

75 EAT PD para 9(5).
76 [2003] IRLR 710 applied in *Burns v Consignia* FN CHK 2004.
77 EAT PD para 9(2) and EAT Rules r26.
78 *Teinaz v Wandsworth LBC* [2002] ICR 1471, CA, para 20 and see paras 12.6–12.7 above.

it, (a) discloses no reasonable grounds for bringing the appeal of the particular ground; or (b) is an abuse of the EAT's process or is otherwise likely to obstruct the just disposal of proceedings. Brief reasons are given. So if the case, or part of it, does not disclose a reasonably arguable point, the judge can make a direction that it should proceed no further. This is the Rule 3 procedure.

23.45   In this case, an appeal is not registered and a notice is sent by the EAT indicating that no further action will be taken on the notice of appeal. In practice, the appeal is then dismissed. Cases falling within this rule are appeals where the only issue is one of fact, or where the legal point is settled or unarguable, or where there are unsubstantiated attacks on the employment tribunal.

23.46   The appellant then has two choices for further action. A fresh notice may be lodged within 28 days.[79] Then it goes back into the sift and the process is repeated, except that there is no further right to submit a second fresh notice. Alternatively, the appellant who is dissatisfied with the reasons given for the decision may apply within 28 days to have the matter heard by a judge. This is in open tribunal, without the attendance of the other parties and, although not fixed by a practice direction, it lasts no more than an hour. A judgment is given if the case is dismissed, wholly or in part. If the case is to be proceeded with, a judgment is sometimes given and directions are given for its further conduct, for example, at a preliminary or a full hearing.

A note of the evidence

23.47   A party seeking to raise a point of law but who cannot do this without a written note of some or all of the evidence must apply to the EAT in the notice of appeal. This includes an application for the preparation by the chairman of his or her notes of evidence. Running a case of perversity without any form of note of the evidence is likely to be impossible.[80] The EAT is reluctant to order the production of the chairman's notes of evidence and will not do so merely to allow the appellant to conduct a fishing expedition. In Scotland, the chairman's notes will not be supplied to parties for an appeal unless they show cause.

23.48   In England and Wales, before any order is made for notes, a

---

79 EAT Rules r3(8).
80 *Hampson v Department of Education and Science* [1988] ICR 278; [1988] IRLR 87, EAT and *Piggott Brothers & Co Ltd v Jackson* [1992] ICR 85; [1991] IRLR 309, CA and see para 23.15 above.

specific application must be made, citing the issues and the witnesses to which the notes are relevant, and the gist of the evidence.[81] An agreed note by the parties may be sufficient and it is the policy of the EAT to seek the production of a jointly agreed note without the necessity for the chairman's notes. If there is disagreement, the dispute can be resolved by the EAT and if not, and the chairman's notes are required, those notes prevail.[82] A specific challenge to the accuracy of the chairman's notes must be made in accordance with a procedure set out in *Dexine Rubber Co Ltd v Alker*,[83] that is, submission of a competing note to the chairman with an opportunity for the chairman to agree or disagree; if the chairman's note is not accepted by the party criticising it, but is accepted by the other side, the matter can be taken no further.

Fresh evidence

23.49 An appeal can be made on the ground that new evidence has become available since the tribunal hearing. As Sir John Donaldson P said:

> Such evidence will be admitted only if some reasonable explanation can be produced for its not having been put before the tribunal . . . and if the new evidence is credible and if it would or might have had a decisive effect upon the decision.[84]

These rules, now found in EAT PD para 8.2, are essentially those for appeals to the Court of Appeal, set out in *Ladd v Marshall*.[85]

23.50 An application must be made and it must set out the substance of the evidence.[86] If it involves a witness's evidence, it must by disclosed to the other parties and lodged at the EAT in the form of an affidavit. The other parties have 14 days to provide any representations in opposition to the admission of the fresh evidence. A decision whether to admit this material is made by the EAT on the papers or at a preliminary hearing.[87] The EAT will exercise its discretion in accordance with the above principles.

---

81 EAT PD para 7.
82 *Houston v Lightwater Farms Ltd* [1990] ICR 502; [1990] IRLR 469, EAT.
83 [1977] ICR 434, EAT.
84 *Bagga v Heavy Chemicals (India) Ltd* [1972] ICR 118, NIRC.
85 [1954] 1 WLR 1489; see *Wileman v Minilec Engineering Ltd* [1988] ICR 318; [1988] IRLR 144, EAT.
86 EAT PD para 8.
87 EAT PD para 8(4).

New points of law

23.51 In general, the EAT will not allow points to be taken on appeal which have not been raised at the tribunal; this is set out in the leading case of *Kumchyk v Derby CC*.[88] This may appear to be a harsh rule, particularly where parties are not represented by lawyers at a tribunal but are on appeal, where new points legitimately can be thought of and taken. The reasons for the EAT's reluctance are that it would be unable to decide the appeal without remitting the case to the tribunal to hear more evidence.[89] There is also a public policy interest in the finality of litigation. On a point of pure construction, which is simply a matter of law, the EAT can hear additional arguments and it then can make up its own mind on the construction without the necessity for additional evidence.

23.52   The EAT may hear new points which affect the jurisdiction of the tribunal, though contrary to earlier EAT suggestions, the Court of Appeal has held in *Glennie v Independent Magazines (UK) Ltd*,[90] that the EAT does not have an unfettered discretion to decide whether justice requires a new point to be allowed to be taken. Rather the principles set out in *Kumchyk*[91] should be applied. Thus, the EAT decisions of *Russell v Elmdon Freight Terminal Ltd*[92] and *Barber v Thames Television*[93] can no longer be followed.

23.53   An appellant should raise the issue in the Notice of Appeal. A respondent who contends that a new point has been raised should say so within 14 days and in the event of a dispute as to whether the point is really a new point, the chairman will be asked for comments and the EAT will decide the next step.[94]

Witnesses

23.54 It is very rare for the EAT to hear live evidence, though it has power to require attendance,[95] and sometime does so in cases of alleged bias or

88 [1978] ICR 116, EAT.
89 *Kumchyk v Derby CC* [1978] ICR 116, EAT; confirmed by CA in *Glennie v Independent Magazines (UK) Ltd* [1999] IRLR 719, and in *Mensah v East Hertfordshire NHS Trust* [1998] IRLR 531.
90 [1999] IRLR 719, CA.
91 *Kumchyk v Derby CC* [1978] ICR 1116, EAT.
92 [1989] ICR 629, EAT.
93 [1991] IRLR 236, EAT.
94 EAT PD para 8(5).
95 EAT Rules r27.

procedural irregularity if the protocol in *Facey v Midas Retail Security*[96] is followed.

Papers for the hearing

23.55 Since 2002 when the preparation of the papers for the hearing – bundles – was effectively privatised, it has been the responsibility of the parties, and ultimately the appellant, to prepare for the hearing. The documents must be confined to those necessary for the appeal and if they run to more than 100 pages, permission must be sought from the registrar.[97] The content of the core bundle is prescribed in EAT PD para 6.2 and must include in the correct order the relevant decisions and papers used at the employment tribunal. For all hearings the appellant must prepare four bundles (unless the appeal is to be heard by a judge alone, where only two are required) and for a full hearing the parties must co-operate in agreeing the bundles.[98]

Respondent's submissions and answer

23.56 At the sift stage a decision will be made about the first contribution of the respondent to the proceedings. If a preliminary hearing is ordered, the respondent is invited, or sometimes required, to lodge 'concise written submissions in response to the Notice of Appeal, dedicated to showing that there is no reasonable prospect of success for any appeal.' The point about this procedure is that it allows a respondent to challenge an appeal at an early stage without the necessity for full preparation and attendance. It alerts the EAT to what the respondent contends are obvious reasons for not allowing the appeal to go to a full hearing.

23.57 If the appeal goes to a full hearing, the respondent must lodge an answer within 14 days. If it includes a cross-appeal the respondent must apply for directions about how that is to be handled. In effect it is a new sift and the cross-appeal must meet the same standard as the appeal, otherwise it will be subject to a Rule 3 determination or sent to a preliminary hearing. In practice, most cross-appeals are heard at the full hearing, with an upward amendment of the estimate of the hearing time.

---

96 [2000] IRLR 812, EAT.
97 EAT PD para 6(3).
98 EAT PD para 6(2).

Time estimates

23.58   The hearing of an appeal at a preliminary hearing takes place for no more than one hour, including judgment and directions.[99] In practice, the same applies to a Rule 3 hearing. When a full hearing is ordered, the judge estimates the time needed, but this is of course open to applications by the parties if it is thought to be wrong. Cases are allocated according to the degree of complexity into one of four categories and this also gives an indication of the time needed.

Judge alone or with members

23.59   Employment Tribunals Act 1996 s28(4) requires an appeal to be heard by a judge alone if it was heard by a chairman alone, unless the judge decides it should go to a three-person panel. If the employment tribunal consisted of two or three people, the EAT must be three. This is made clear in the automatic directions.

Skeleton arguments, chronology and legal authorities

23.60   There is a requirement in England for skeleton arguments and a chronology to be prepared in advance and this will be in the automatic directions.[100] Professional representatives without one are usually given short shrift. They should be served on the EAT and exchanged with the other parties within the time specified before the hearing. On a practical note, this enables the argument to be sent with the relevant papers to the lay members of the EAT so they may read them before the hearing. There is clearly an advantage to an advocate in having a written skeleton argument served in good time. The process is also of considerable advantage to a litigant in person who can put their thoughts and best points down in writing at home, and so lessen the stress of advancing an oral argument in open court.

23.61   A list of authorities should also be sent before the hearing. Copies are available for all three members of the EAT, but it is very useful for the members and for the advocate presenting a case for photocopies to be provided of the relevant authorities so the members can mark their own versions as the argument unfolds. This will often be stipulated in the automatic directions and is anyway required for

99   EAT PD para 9.11.
100   EAT PD para 13.

authorities relied on which are not in the accessible law reports.[101] The EAT encourages parties to cite from the same law report, that is, *Industrial Cases Reports* (ICR) or *Industrial Relations Law Reports* (IRLR) for the same case.

23.62   It is the duty of the appellant to provide a chronology, which should be agreed with the other parties, and in more complex cases a list of the relevant actors and their roles or job-titles.

23.63   Each member of the EAT is supplied with a copy of the relevant legislation, currently in Butterworths *Employment Law Handbook*, for reference is often made to provisions other than those directly in play in an appeal.

The hearing

23.64   A Rule 3 hearing takes place with just the appellant present and with no previous input from the potential respondent. For a preliminary hearing, the respondent is usually invited to give concise submissions as to why the appeal raises no reasonable grounds and it may, at the discretion of the EAT, attend and be heard (see above). The purpose of the hearing is for the appellant to show cause why the appeal or a ground in it should be heard as a reasonably arguable point, or for some other compelling reason such as that a decision binding on the EAT should be reconsidered or there is incompatibility with the Human Rights Act 1998.[102]

23.65   If a reasonably arguable point is raised, the hearing will cease and the matter will be listed for full hearing on another date. The EAT will then make directions after considering any submissions from the appellant, and any already sent in by the respondent. If the appeal shows no reasonably arguable case, judgment will be given dismissing the appeal and this is a substantive judgment of the EAT. If some points are allowed and some dismissed, there is judgment on the latter. New bundles must be prepared and lodged.

23.66   When a full hearing is listed before the EAT, parties are usually consulted about appropriate dates. It is the practice of the listing officer to acknowledge the advantage to the parties and to the EAT of having those representatives who appeared at the employment

---

101   EAT PD para 14.2.
102   EAT PD para 9.7.

tribunal appear at the EAT, and to try to accommodate them. Cases are given fixed dates and do not run over from one day to the next, unless they are booked for more than one day. Parties are required to notify the EAT should the time estimate originally given change. Certain cases are put on the 'fast-track', that is, those which involve other applicants or appeals from interim decisions or where remedies are wasting.[104]

23.67　　Hearings are in public at a dedicated building, Audit House, Victoria Embankment, London where there are six courtrooms; or 52, Melville Street, Edinburgh, although the EAT occasionally sits in court buildings elsewhere.

Judgment

23.68　Judgment in England and Wales is usually given orally immediately following the argument and a retirement of the three members to consider it. It is tape-recorded. Unlike tribunals, the judgment of the EAT takes effect from the time it is given rather than the time it is published but the order giving effect to the judgment may provide that time runs from the date of the sealed order. At a preliminary hearing where the appeal, or a ground of it, is dismissed, no transcript is provided unless the appellant is absent or either party applies within 14 days. At a full hearing, no transcript is provided unless either party applies within 14 days, or the EAT decides to order one.[105]

23.69　　If the EAT does not give a judgment on the day, it reserves its judgment and hands it down either in written form on a day fixed later or it is given orally by the judge. It must usually be given within three and a half months of the last oral hearing or last written submission, in common with the duty on tribunals in *Kwamin v Abbey National plc*.[106] There is a transcript of every reserved judgment which, if not given orally, is available on the morning it is handed down. Often it is made available to representatives of all parties in advance on strict terms as to confidentiality. In such a case, the representatives may submit suggestions for typographical or similar corrections. Any application for costs or for permission to appeal must be made 48 hours before the judgment is handed down. This should

104　EAT PD para 9.20.
105　EAT PD para 18.
106　[2004] ICR 841 EAT.

allow for consultation between the three members and the result can be given on the day of the reserved judgment. In such cases, this procedure allows for the matters to be dealt with on the papers without the necessity for the parties or their representatives to attend.

23.70　　Sometimes a different judge hands down the judgment of the previous EAT, on its behalf. Majority decisions can be made: the lay members can incorporate their own words in the judgment given by the presiding judge or the decision can be given indirectly by the judge as part of the judgment. All transcribed full hearing and many preliminary hearing judgments now appear on the EAT website.[107]

Costs (expenses)

23.71　Three issues arise on costs (expenses in Scotland). When can they be ordered, how are they assessed and who can be ordered to pay? For this purpose, costs includes legal costs and expenses and reimbursement allowed to a litigant in person. In practice a costs order is rarely made in the EAT: less than 0.5 per cent of cases disposed of.[108] The considerations in chapter 18 also apply here.

When costs may be ordered

23.72　The EAT has power to award costs to be paid by the paying party to the receiving party.[109] An order can be made at any stage of the proceedings but an application for costs will not be considered if it is made later than 14 days after the disposal of the proceedings. Before making an order the paying party must be given the opportunity to contest it, either at the hearing or by notice given to it. If it is made, reasons must be given in writing if a request is made within 21 days of the order.[110]

23.73　　The power can be exercised under EAT Rules r34A in two different sorts of case. The first is when the EAT decides that 'proceedings brought by the paying party were unnecessary, improper, vexatious or misconceived or that there has been unreasonable delay or other unreasonable conduct in the bringing or conducting of proceedings

107　See appendix D.
108　EAT Consultation on Draft Revised Rules April 2004.
109　EAT Rules r34. EAT PD para 18.
110　EAT Rules r34.

by the paying party'.[111] The second is when the conduct falls within a
particular example for the exercise of the power. Three circumstances
are thus regarded as falling within rule 34A. These are when the
paying party has not complied with a direction of the EAT (this goes
hand in hand with other powers under EAT Rules r26); or has
amended a notice of appeal or respondent's answer; or caused an
adjournment. Under this rule, only a party can be ordered to pay.

23.74   In considering whether to award costs, the fact that a case has
been allowed through at a preliminary hearing is not a bar to arguing
that it is unnecessary.[112] Nor is the fact that it was sifted straight to a
full hearing. This is because the material available to the EAT hearing
a full hearing is so much greater than at earlier stages in the appeal,
and the other parties are likely to have had a bigger input by that time,
so that a case which first appeared reasonably arguable may turn out
to be unreasonably pursued.

Assessment of costs

23.75   The EAT can make three kinds of order. It can specify the sum; it can
order whatever sum is agreed between the parties; and it can order all
or part of the sum reached after a detailed assessment in the High
Court in accordance with the CPR Parts 43–51.[113] This means that the
principles in the CPR affect the awards here, bearing in mind that the
EAT is dealing with an appeal rather than a first instance case. These
include:

(a)   the conduct of the parties before, as well as during, the
      proceedings;

(b)   whether it was unreasonable for a party to raise, pursue or
      contest a particular issue;

(c)   the manner in which a party has pursued or defended the appeal
      or a particular issue;

(d)   whether a claimant who has succeeded, in whole or in part,
      exaggerated the claim;

(e)   any admissible offer to settle made by a party.

23.76   In all cases, it should make clear whether the award is on the standard or the more generous and unusual indemnity basis. As in the

---

111   See paras 18.12–18.28 for the meaning of these terms.
112   *Tesco Stores Ltd v Wilson* [2000] UKEAT 749_98_1201.
113   EAT Rules r34B.

CPR, a party seeking costs should provide a schedule of them in advance to the other party (EAT PD para 18). At the end of the oral hearing, when making an application for costs to be paid at all, the receiving party must justify the sums in the schedule if it seeks a summary assessment by the EAT. The EAT will look at the figures for fees charged and compare them with the schedules in Appendix I and II in CPR Part 48 which contains notes on the assessment of costs in the High Court. The range of hourly fees charged by solicitors in different parts of the country can be gauged and applied by reference to the level of experience of lawyer required to conduct the case. Counsel's fees are based on the years of experience since call to the Bar. After hearing both sides, and deciding that costs should be paid, the EAT will decide the appropriate level of lawyer, the level of fee and the amount of work properly incurred. It can discount some items claimed or reduce them by a percentage to reflect its view of the scale of them.

23.77 If summary assessment is not done on the day, or the matter is more complicated, the EAT can order a detailed assessment. This is done in the High Court by a costs judge. An appeal lies to a High Court Judge.[114] Permission is required.[115] If the High Court Judge refuses permission to appeal, the Court of Appeal has no jurisdiction to hear an appeal from that refusal.[116] Sometimes there is summary assessment on part, and an order for detailed assessment on the rest.

23.78 It is most important to bear in mind the change effected by the Employment Act 2002 s23 which permits the EAT to have regard to the paying party's ability to pay when considering the amount of the order.[117]

23.79 Special rules apply to litigants in person (in Scotland, party litigants) under EAT Rules r34D. By CPR Part 48.6 the costs allowed to a litigant in person will be for the same categories of work and disbursements as would have been allowed if the work had been done or the disbursements made by a legal representative on behalf of the litigant in person. A litigant in person who is able to prove financial loss, will be allowed the amount he or she can prove for time reasonably spent doing the work up to a certain limit. The limit is two-thirds of the amount which would be allowed if the litigant were represented legally. The exercise to be conducted is to work out the time

114 Access to Justice Act 1999 (Destination of Appeals) Order 2000 SI No 1071.
115 *Tanfern Ltd v Cameron-MacDonald* [2000] 1 WLR 1311, CA.
116 *Riniker v University College London* [2001] 1 WLR 13, CA.
117 EAT Rules r34B(2).

spent and the loss suffered doing the work, for example, the time off work without pay. Calculate the rate of a legal representative. If the former exceeds two-thirds of the latter, it is capped at that figure. If below two-thirds, the full amount is allowed. If the litigant cannot prove the loss, the hourly rate is deemed to be £25 an hour for each hour the EAT considers reasonable.

23.80   This limit does not apply to disbursements, that is, actual payments made for goods or services in the preparation for or attendance at the appeal. These also include payments to obtain legal advice, payment of wages of the litigant's employees *in relation to the proceedings* and other expenses.

23.81   Special rules also apply before a costs order may be made in favour of or against a party assisted by Legal Services Commission funding, under Access to Justice Act 1999 s11, still known widely as legal aid. Guidance notes published in the High Court set out the practice[118] and are explained in *R v Secretary of State for the Home Department ex p Gunn.*[119] These rules are different from the order usually sought at the end of a hearing for assessment of a funded party's costs, and which is not dependent on that party winning or any finding that costs should be paid, for they simply allow the funded party's lawyers to recover their fees (EAT PD para 34B(3)).

Who must pay

23.82   A party can be ordered to pay all or part of the costs. So can a party's representative when wasted costs have been incurred.[120] There is a definition of representative for this rule which is a legal *or other* representative or their employee, but not someone who is not acting in pursuit of profit with regard to the proceedings. Someone acting under a conditional fee agreement pursuant to Courts and Legal Services Act 1990 s58 is acting in pursuit of profit.

23.83   This definition therefore excludes all publicly funded representatives of public sector parties, voluntary sector representatives such as trade unions and law centres and not for profit employers' associations, and would logically exclude in-house representatives of all parties where no commercial relationship exists between the party and the representative in the carrying out of the representation.

---

118   See CPR Part 48.13.
119   [2001] EWCA Civ 891.
120   EAT Rules r34C.

23.84   The exposure of a representative occurs in different circumstances from those of a party under EAT Rules r34. The costs are those of any party, including the representative's own client and a party who is not legally represented. Wasted costs are incurred as a result of any improper, unreasonable or negligent act or omission on the part of the representative. When the act or omission occurs after the costs were incurred, and it is reasonable to expect the party to pay, a wasted costs order can also be made. The order may make the representative pay the other party, or repay his or her own client, or disallow any costs charged to the client.

23.85   The representative must be given an opportunity to make oral or written submissions before an order is made and written reasons will be given if a request is made within 14 days of the order. It is assumed that oral reasons will be given at any hearing, for costs is an unusual order requiring reasons. The client is entitled to notice of the proceedings and any order made.

The order

23.86 The EAT can make any order the tribunal below could have made.[121] It can remit the case for rehearing by the same or a different tribunal. It can also remit for the purpose of completing its statutory duty: *English v Emery Reimbold*.[122] On considering remission at final, rather than interim judgment, the EAT will look at proportionality, time, bias and mishandling as a guard against offering a second bite at the cherry.[123] It can substitute its own decision for that of the tribunal and will do so provided that no new evidence is required to be admitted and the EAT can tell what the tribunal decision would have been had it, for example, applied the law correctly to the material it had. If there is any doubt, the EAT should remit.[123a]

23.87   The EAT can make a reference to the European Court of Justice, although in practice it is reluctant to do so before giving permission to appeal to the Court of Appeal.

---

121   ETA1996 s34.
122   [2003] IRLR 710 applied in *Burns v Royal Mail Group plc* [2004] ICR 1103.
123   *Sinclaire, Roche & Temperley v Heard* [2003] UKEAT/0738/03.
123a *O'Kelly v Trusthouse Forte plc* [1983] ICR 728; [1983] IRLR 369, CA.

Settlement

23.88   If the parties want to settle an appeal or reach a consent order, the EAT follows the practice of the Court of Appeal. In principle it will not routinely allow appeals by consent but must first be assured of the grounds for setting aside a decision of an inferior tribunal.[124] In practice appeals are disposed of by consent where the parties agree in writing.[125] Sometimes, however, it is suggested that one of the parties should attend and explain the basis of the order sought, especially if settlement or withdrawal occurs shortly before the hearing date.[126]

23.89   The EAT may adjourn a case or take any step it considers appropriate if it thinks there is a reasonable prospect of an agreement by conciliation.[127]

Review and appeal

23.90   An appeal from the EAT lies to the Court of Appeal or Court of Session, but only on a question of law and only with permission ('leave') of the EAT or the appeal court.[128] An application for permission should be made at the EAT at the conclusion of the judgment, this being an essential requirement in England and Wales, and highly desirable in Scotland.[129] CPR Part 52.3 states that permission to appeal will be granted more sparingly for second appeals. Technically, this is not a second appeal as defined in Access to Justice Act 1999 s55 since permission is not required from the appeal court. In *Cooke v Secretary of State for Social Security*[130] the Court of Appeal considered the criteria for permission to appeal from the Social Security Commissioner and applied general policy guidelines. The ordinary court system 'should approach such cases with an appropriate degree of caution'. A specialist appeal tribunal will have a more comprehensive understanding of the principles within its jurisdiction than the courts as Hale LJ pointed out.[131]

---

124   *J Sainsbury plc v Moger* [1994] ICR 800, EAT.
125   EAT PD para 15.
126   *British Publishing Co Ltd v Fraser* [1987] ICR 517, EAT.
127   EAT Rules r36.
128   ETA1996 s37.
129   EAT PD para19.
130   [2002] 3 All ER 279, CA.
131   [2002] 3 All ER 279 at paras 15–18.

23.91   Permission will be given by the EAT if the appeal would raise an important point of principle or practice, or if there is some other compelling reason for the appeal court to hear it. This might arise if there is a new and difficult statutory provision, or there are conflicting judgments of the EAT, or the area of law is not within the mainstream of Employment Tribunal proceedings, such as bankruptcy.[132]

23.92   The EAT will not overrule or readily re-open a judgment.[133] The time for appealing to the Court of Appeal is two weeks or to the Court of Session is six weeks from the date on which the EAT order was 'sealed or otherwise perfected'.[134]

23.93   The EAT of its own initiative or a judge's, or on application made within 14 days of the decision, can review a decision. A decision can be reviewed when:[135]

- it was wrongly made as a result of an error on the part of the EAT;
- proper notice was not given to a party; or
- the interests of justice.

A judge alone may allow or refuse an application for review.[136] In addition, the EAT, a judge or a member can correct clerical mistakes caused by an accidental slip or omission. This is known as the slip rule.

---

132   See for example, *Grady v Home Office* [2003] ICR 753.
133   *Asda Stores Ltd v Thompson* EAT/0063/03.
134   CPR 52.4(2).
135   EAT Rules r33.
136   EAT Rules r33(4).

Appendices

APPENDIX A

Forms

Claim to an Employment Tribunal

Please read the **guidance notes** and the notes on this page carefully **before** filling in this form.

By law, you **must** provide the information marked with ✳ and, if it is relevant, the information marked with ● (see guidance on Pre-acceptance procedure).

You may find it helpful to take advice **before** filling in the form, particularly if your claim involves discrimination.

How to fill in this form

All claimants **must** fill in **sections 1, 2 and 3**. You then only need to fill in those sections of the form that apply to your case. For example:

For **unpaid wages**, fill in **sections 4 and 8**.

For **unfair dismissal**, fill in **sections 4 and 5**.

For **discrimination**, fill in **sections 4 and 6**.

For a **redundancy payment**, fill in **sections 4 and 7**.

For **unfair dismissal** and **discrimination**, fill in **sections 4, 5 and 6**.

For **unfair dismissal** and **unpaid wages**, fill in **sections 4, 5 and 8**.

Fill in **section 10** only if there is some information you wish to draw to the tribunal's attention and **section 11** only if you have appointed a representative to act on your behalf in dealing with your claim.

If this form sets out a claim by more than one claimant arising from the same set of facts, please give the names and addresses of additional claimants on a separate sheet or sheets of paper.

Please make sure that all the information you give is as accurate as possible.

Where there are tick boxes, please tick the one that applies.

If you fax the form, do not send a copy in the post.

ET1

1 Your details

1.1 Title: Mr ☐ Mrs ☐ Miss ☐ Ms ☐ Other

1.2* First name (or names):

1.3* Surname or family name:

1.4 Date of birth (date/month/year): / / Are you: male? ☐ female? ☐

1.5* Address:

Postcode

You do not need to answer 1.6 and 1.7 if you have appointed a representative (see section 11).

1.6 Phone number **(where we can contact you during normal working hours)**:

1.7 How would you prefer us to communicate with you? Post ☐ Fax ☐ E-mail ☐

Fax:

E-mail address:

2 Respondent's details

2.1* Give the name of your employer or the organisation or person you are complaining about (the respondent).

2.2* Address:

Postcode

2.3 If you worked at an address different from the one you have given at 2.2, please give the full address.

Postcode

2.4● If your complaint is against more than one respondent please give the names, addresses and postcodes of additional respondents.

3   Action before making a claim

3.1* Are you, or were you, an employee of the respondent?   Yes ☐   No ☐
If 'Yes', please now go straight to section 3.3.

3.2 Are you, or were you, a worker providing services to the respondent?   Yes ☐   No ☐
If 'Yes', please now go straight to section 4.
If 'No', please now go straight to section 6.

3.3● Is your claim, or part of it, about a dismissal by the respondent?   Yes ☐   No ☐
If 'No', please now go straight to section 3.5.

3.4● Is your claim about anything else, in addition to the dismissal?   Yes ☐   No ☐
If 'No', please now go straight to section 4.
If 'Yes', please answer questions 3.5 to 3.7 about the
non-dismissal aspects of your claim.

3.5● Have you put your complaint in writing to the respondent?

> Yes ☐   Please give the date you put it to them in writing.   /   /
> No ☐

If 'No', please now go straight to section 3.7.

3.6● Did you allow at least 28 days between the date you put your   Yes ☐   No ☐
complaint to the respondent and the date you sent us this claim?
If 'Yes', please now go straight to section 4.

3.7● Please explain why you did not put your complaint in writing to the respondent or,
if you did, why you did not allow at least 28 days before sending us your claim.
(In most cases, it is a legal requirement to take these procedural steps. Your claim
will not be accepted unless you give a valid reason why you did not have to meet
the requirement in your case. If you are not sure, you may want to get legal advice.)

4   Employment details

4.1   Please give the following dates if possible.

When your employment started   /   /

When your employment ended or will end   /   /

Is your employment continuing?   Yes ☐   No ☐

4.2   Please say what job you do or did.

4.3   How many hours do or did you work each week?   ....hours each week

4.4   How much are or were you paid?

Pay before tax   £   each

Normal take-home pay (including overtime, commission, bonuses and so on)   £   each

4.5   If your employment has ended, did you work (or were you paid for) a period of notice?   Yes ☐   No ☐

If 'Yes', how many weeks or months did you work or were you paid for?   ....weeks ....months

5   Unfair dismissal or constructive dismissal

Please fill in this section only if you believe you have been unfairly or constructively dismissed.

5.1 ● If you were dismissed by your employer, you should explain why you think your dismissal was unfair. If you resigned because of something your employer did or failed to do which made you feel you could no longer continue to work for them (constructive dismissal) you should explain what happened.

5   Unfair dismissal or constructive dismissal continued

5.1 continued

5.2   Were you in your employer's pension scheme?   Yes ☐   No ☐

5.3   If you received any other benefits from your employer, please give details.

5.4   Since leaving your employment have you got another job?   Yes ☐   No ☐
      If 'No', please now go straight to section 5.7.

5.5   Please say when you started (or will start) work.

5.6   Please say how much you are now earning (or will earn).   £   each

5.7   Please tick the box to say what you want if your case is successful:
      a   To get your old job back and compensation (reinstatement)   ☐
      b   To get another job with the same employer and compensation (re-engagement)   ☐
      c   Compensation only   ☐

6 Discrimination

Please fill in this section only if you believe you have been discriminated against.

6.1 Please tick the box or boxes to indicate what discrimination (including victimisation) you are complaining about:

Sex (including equal pay)	☐	Race	☐
Disability	☐	Religion or belief	☐
Sexual orientation	☐		

6.2 Please describe the incidents which you believe amounted to discrimination, the dates of these incidents and the people involved.

7 Redundancy payments

Please fill in this section only if you believe you are owed a redundancy payment.

7.1● Please explain why you believe you are entitled to this payment and set out the steps you have taken to get it.

8 Other payments you are owed

Please fill in this section only if you believe you are owed other payments.

8.1● Please tick the box or boxes to indicate that money is owed to you for:

unpaid wages? ☐
holiday pay? ☐
notice pay? ☐
other unpaid amounts? ☐

8.2 How much are you claiming?

Is this: before tax? ☐ after tax? ☐

8.3● Please explain why you believe you are entitled to this payment. If you have specified an amount, please set out how you have worked this out.

9   Other complaints

Please fill in this section only if you believe you have a complaint that is not covered elsewhere.

9.1● Please explain what you are complaining about and why.
     Please include any relevant dates.

10 Other information

10.1 Please do not send a covering letter with this form.
You should add any extra information you want us to know here.

11 Your representative

Please fill in this section only if you have appointed a representative. If you do fill this section in, we will in future only send correspondence to your representative and not to you.

11.1 Representative's name:

11.2 Name of the representative's organisation:

11.3 Address:

Postcode

11.4 Phone number:

11.5 Reference:

11.6 How would they prefer us to communicate with them?

Post ☐   Fax ☐   E-mail ☐
Fax:
E-mail address:

Please sign and date here

Signature: Date: /   /

Data Protection Act 1998. We will send a copy of this form to the respondent(s) and Acas. We will put some of the information you give us on this form onto a computer. This helps us to monitor progress and produce statistics.

Response to an Employment Tribunal claim

IN THE CLAIM OF:

Case number:
(please quote this in all correspondence)

This requires your immediate attention. If you want to resist the claim made against you, your completed form must reach the tribunal office within 28 days of the date of the attached letter. If you do not return the form by __/__/__ you may not be able to take part in the proceedings and a default judgment may be entered against you.

Please read the **guidance notes** and the notes on this page carefully **before** filling in this form.

By law, you **must** provide the information marked with ✳ and, if it is relevant, the information marked with ● (see guidance on Pre-acceptance procedure).

Please make sure that all the information you give is as accurate as possible.

Where there are tick boxes, please tick the one that applies.

If you fax the form, do not send a copy in the post.

ET3

1 Your details

1.1* Name of your organisation:

Contact name:

1.2* Address:

Postcode

You do not need to answer 1.3 and 1.4 if you have appointed a representative (see section 7).

1.3 Phone number:

1.4 How would you prefer us to communicate with you?

Post ☐　　　　Fax ☐　　　　E-mail ☐
Fax:
E-mail address:

2 Action before a claim

2.1 Is, or was, the claimant an employee?
If 'Yes', please now go straight to section 2.3.
Yes ☐　　No ☐

2.2 Is, or was, the claimant a worker providing services to you?
If 'Yes', please now go straight to section 3.
If 'No', please now go straight to section 5.
Yes ☐　　No ☐

2.3 If the claim, or part of it, is about a dismissal,
do you agree that the claimant was dismissed?
If 'Yes', please now go straight to section 2.6.
Yes ☐　　No ☐

2.4 If the claim includes something **other than** dismissal,
does it relate to an action you took on
grounds of the claimant's conduct or capability?
If 'Yes', please now go straight to section 2.6.
Yes ☐　　No ☐

2.5 Has the substance of this claim been raised by the claimant
in writing under a grievance procedure?
Yes ☐　　No ☐

2.6 If 'Yes', please explain below what stage you have reached in the dismissal and
disciplinary procedure or grievance procedure (whichever is applicable).
If 'No' and the claimant says they have raised a grievance with you in writing, please say
whether you received it and explain why you did not accept this as a grievance.

3 Employment details

3.1 Are the dates of employment given by the claimant correct?   Yes ☐   No ☐
If 'Yes', please now go straight to section 3.3.

3.2 If 'No', please give dates and say why you disagree with the dates given by the claimant.

When their employment started   /   /

When their employment ended or will end   /   /

Is their employment continuing?   Yes ☐   No ☐

I disagree with the dates for the following reasons.

3.3 Is the claimant's description of their job or job title correct?   Yes ☐   No ☐
If 'Yes', please now go straight to section 3.5.

3.4 If 'No', please give the details you believe to be correct below.

3.5 Is the information given by the claimant correct about being
paid for, or working, a period of notice?   Yes ☐   No ☐
If 'Yes', please now go straight to section 3.7.

3.6 If 'No', please give the details you believe to be correct below. If you gave them no notice or
didn't pay them instead of letting them work their notice, please explain what happened and why.

3.7 Are the claimant's hours of work correct?   Yes ☐   No ☐
If 'Yes', please now go straight to section 3.9.

3.8 If 'No', please enter the details you believe to be correct.   hours each week

3.9 Are the earnings details given by the claimant correct?   Yes ☐   No ☐
If 'Yes', please now go straight to section 4.

3.10 If 'No', please give the details you believe to be correct below.

Pay before tax   £   each

Normal take-home pay (including overtime,
commission, bonuses and so on)   £   each

4   Unfair dismissal or constructive dismissal

4.1   Are the details about pension and other benefits
given by the claimant correct?
If 'Yes', please now go straight to section 5.

Yes ☐   No ☐

4.2   If 'No', please give the details you believe to be correct below.

5   Response

5.1* Do you resist the claim?
If 'No', please now go straight to section 6.

Yes ☐   No ☐

5.2● If 'Yes', please set out in full the grounds on which you resist the claim.

6   Other information

6.1   Please do not send a covering letter with this form. You should add any extra information
      you want us to know here.

7   Your representative   If you have a representative, please fill in the following.

7.1   Representative's name:

7.2   Name of the representative's organisation:

7.3   Address:

      Postcode

7.4   Phone number:

7.5   Reference:

7.6   How would they prefer us to   Post ☐   Fax ☐   E-mail ☐
      communicate with them?   Fax:
                                         E-mail address:

Please sign and date here

Signature: Date: /   /

Data Protection Act 1998. We will send a copy of this form to the claimant and Acas. We will put some of the
information you give us on this form onto a computer. This helps us to monitor progress and produce statistics.

Statutes, Regulations and Practice Directions

Statutes, Regulations and Practice Directions

Tribunals and Inquiries Act 1992 ss1, 10, 11 and Sch 1

THE COUNCIL ON TRIBUNALS AND THEIR FUNCTIONS

The Council on Tribunals

1 (1) There shall continue to be a council entitled the Council on Tribunals (in this Act referred to as 'the Council')–

(a) to keep under review the constitution and working of the tribunals specified in Schedule 1 (being the tribunals constituted under or for the purposes of the statutory provisions specified in that Schedule) and, from time to time, to report on their constitution and working;

(b) to consider and report on such particular matters as may be referred to the Council under this Act with respect to tribunals other than the ordinary courts of law, whether or not specified in Schedule 1, or any such tribunal; and

(c) to consider and report on such matters as may be referred to the Council under this Act, or as the Council may determine to be of special importance, with respect to administrative procedures involving, or which may involve, the holding by or on behalf of a Minister of a statutory inquiry, or any such procedure.

(2) Nothing in this section authorises or requires the Council to deal with any matter with respect to which the Parliament of Northern Ireland had power to make laws.

JUDICIAL CONTROL OF TRIBUNALS, ETC

Reasons to be given for decisions of tribunals and Ministers

10 (1) Subject to the provisions of this section and of section 14, where–

(a) any tribunal specified in Schedule 1 gives any decision, or

(b) any Minister notifies any decision taken by him–

(i) after a statutory inquiry has been held by him or on his behalf, or

(ii) in a case in which a person concerned could (whether by objecting or otherwise) have required a statutory inquiry to be so held,

it shall be the duty of the tribunal or Minister to furnish a statement, either written or oral, of the reasons for the decision if requested, on or before the giving or notification of the decision, to state the reasons.

(2) The statement referred to in subsection (1) may be refused, or the specification of the reasons restricted, on grounds of national security.

(3) A tribunal or Minister may refuse to furnish a statement under subsection (1) to a person not primarily concerned with the decision if of the opinion that to furnish it would be contrary to the interests of any person primarily concerned.

(4) Subsection (1) does not apply to any decision taken by a Minister after the holding by him or on his behalf of an inquiry or hearing which is a statutory inquiry by virtue only of an order made under section 16(2) unless the order contains a direction that this section is to apply in relation to any inquiry or hearing to which the order applies.

(5) Subsection (1) does not apply–
  (a) to decisions in respect of which any statutory provision has effect, apart from this section, as to the giving of reasons,
  (b) to decisions of a Minister in connection with the preparation, making, approval, confirmation, or concurrence in regulations, rules or byelaws, or orders or schemes of a legislative and not executive character, or
  (ba) to decisions of the Pensions Compensation Board referred to in paragraph 35(h) of Schedule 1,
  (c) . . .

(6) Any statement of the reasons for a decision referred to in paragraph (a) or (b) of subsection (1), whether given in pursuance of that subsection or of any other statutory provision, shall be taken to form part of the decision and accordingly to be incorporated in the record.

(7) If, after consultation with the Council, it appears to the Lord Chancellor and the Secretary of State that it is expedient that–
  (a) decisions of any particular tribunal or any description of such decisions, or
  (b) any description of decisions of a Minister,
  should be excluded from the operation of subsection (1) on the ground that the subject-matter of such decisions, or the circumstances in which they are made, make the giving of reasons unnecessary or impracticable, the Lord Chancellor and the Secretary of State may by order direct that subsection (1) shall not apply to such decisions.

(8) Where an order relating to any decisions has been made under subsection (7), the Lord Chancellor and the Secretary of State may, by a subsequent order made after consultation with the Council, revoke or vary the earlier order so that subsection (1) applies to any of those decisions.

Appeals from certain tribunals

11 (1) Subject to subsection (2), if any party to proceedings before any tribunal specified in paragraph 8, 15(a) or (d), 16 . . . , 24, 26, 31, 33(b), 37, 40A, 40B, 44 or 45 of Schedule 1 is dissatisfied in point of law with a decision of the tribunal he may, according as rules of court may provide, either appeal from the tribunal to the High Court or require the tribunal to state and sign a case for the opinion of the High Court.

(2) This section shall not apply in relation to–

    (a) proceedings before employment tribunals which arise under or by virtue of any of the enactments mentioned in section 21(1) of the Employment Tribunals Act 1996; or

    (b) proceedings under section 20 of the Abolition of Feudal Tenure, etc (Scotland) Act 2000 (asp 5) (reallotment of real burden).

(3) Rules of court made with respect to all or any of the tribunals referred to in subsection (1) may provide for authorising or requiring a tribunal, in the course of proceedings before it, to state, in the form of a special case for the decision of the High Court, any question of law arising in the proceedings; and a decision of the High Court on a case stated by virtue of this subsection shall be deemed to be a judgment of the Court within the meaning of section 16 of the Supreme Court Act 1981 (jurisdiction of Court of Appeal to hear and determine appeals from judgments of the High Court).

(4) In relation to proceedings in the High Court or the Court of Appeal brought by virtue of this section, the power to make rules of court shall include power to make rules prescribing the powers of the High Court or the Court of Appeal with respect to–

    (a) the giving of any decision which might have been given by the tribunal;

    (b) the remitting of the matter with the opinion or direction of the court for re-hearing and determination by the tribunal;

    (c) the giving of directions to the tribunal;

    and different provisions may be made for different tribunals.

(5) An appeal to the Court of Appeal shall not be brought by virtue of this section except with the leave of the High Court or the Court of Appeal.

(6) Subsection (1) shall apply to a decision of the Secretary of State on an appeal under section 41 of the Consumer Credit Act 1974 from a determination of the Office of Fair Trading as it applies to a decision of any of the tribunals mentioned in that subsection, but with the substitution for the reference to a party to proceedings of a reference to any person who had a right to appeal to the Secretary of State (whether or not he has exercised that right); and accordingly references in subsections (1) and (4) to a tribunal shall be construed, in relation to such an appeal, as references to the Secretary of State.

(7) The following provisions shall have effect for the application of this section to Scotland–

    (a) in relation to any proceedings in Scotland of any of the tribunals referred to in the preceding provisions of this section, or on an appeal under section 41 of the Consumer Credit Act 1974 by a company registered in Scotland or by any other person whose principal or prospective principal place of business in the United Kingdom is in Scotland, this section shall have effect with the following modifications–

        (i) for references to the High Court or the Court of Appeal there shall be substituted references to the Court of Session,

        (ii) in subsection (3) for 'in the form of a special case for the decision of the High Court' there shall be substituted 'a case for the opinion of the Court of Session on' and the words from 'and a decision' to the end of the subsection shall be omitted, and

(iii) subsection (5) shall be omitted,

(b) this section shall apply, with the modifications specified in paragraph (a)–

(i) to proceedings before any such tribunal as is specified in paragraph 51, 56(b), 59 or 63 of Schedule 1, and

(ii) subject to paragraph (c) below, to proceedings before the Lands Tribunal for Scotland,

as it applies to proceedings before the tribunals referred to in subsection (1);

(c) subsection (1) shall not apply in relation to proceedings before the Lands Tribunal for Scotland which arise under section 1(3A) of the Lands Tribunal Act 1949 (jurisdiction of the tribunal in valuation matters);

(d) an appeal shall lie, with the leave of the Court of Session or the House of Lords, from any decision of the Court of Session under this section, and such leave may be given on such terms as to costs or otherwise as the Court of Session or the House of Lords may determine.

(8) In relation to any proceedings in Northern Ireland of any of the tribunals referred to in subsection (1) and in relation to a decision of the Secretary of State on an appeal under section 41 of the Consumer Credit Act 1974 by a company registered in Northern Ireland or by any other person whose principal or prospective principal place of business in the United Kingdom is in Northern Ireland, this section shall have effect with the following modifications–

(a) in subsection (3), for the words from the beginning to 'provide' there shall be substituted 'Rules may be made under section 55 of the Judicature (Northern Ireland) Act 1978 providing', and for 'section 16 of the Supreme Court Act 1981' there shall be substituted 'section 35 of the Judicature (Northern Ireland) Act 1978';

(b) in subsection (4), for 'the power to make rules of court shall include power to make rules' there shall be substituted 'rules may be made under section 55 of the Judicature (Northern Ireland) Act 1978';

(c) at the beginning of subsection (5), there shall be inserted 'Rules made under section 55 of the Judicature (Northern Ireland) Act 1978, relating to such proceedings as are mentioned in subsection (4), shall provide that the appeal shall be heard, or as the case may be, the decision of the High Court shall be given, by a single judge, but'.

(9) Her Majesty may by Order in Council direct that all or any of the provisions of this section, so far as it relates to proceedings in the Isle of Man or any of the Channel Islands of the tribunal specified in paragraph 45 of Schedule 1, shall extend to the Isle of Man or to any of the Channel Islands subject to such modifications as may be specified in the Order.

(10) In this section 'decision' includes any direction or order, and references to the giving of a decision shall be construed accordingly.

SCHEDULE 1: TRIBUNALS UNDER GENERAL SUPERVISION OF COUNCIL

Tribunals Under Direct Supervision of Council

. . .

Employment

16   The employment tribunals for England and Wales established under [section 1(1) of the Employment Tribunals Act 1996 (c 17).

. . .

Employment Tribunals Act 1996

PART I: EMPLOYMENT TRIBUNALS

INTRODUCTORY

Employment tribunals

1   (1) The Secretary of State may by regulations make provision for the establishment of tribunals to be known as employment tribunals.

(2) Regulations made wholly or partly under section 128(1) of the Employment Protection (Consolidation) Act 1978 and in force immediately before this Act comes into force shall, so far as made under that provision, continue to have effect (until revoked) as if made under subsection (1) . . .

JURISDICTION

Enactments conferring jurisdiction on employment tribunals

2   Employment tribunals shall exercise the jurisdiction conferred on them by or by virtue of this Act or any other Act, whether passed before or after this Act.

Power to confer further jurisdiction on employment tribunals

3   (1) The appropriate Minister may by order provide that proceedings in respect of–

(a) any claim to which this section applies, or

(b) any claim to which this section applies and which is of a description specified in the order,

may, subject to such exceptions (if any) as may be so specified, be brought before an employment tribunal.

(2) Subject to subsection (3), this section applies to–

(a) a claim for damages for breach of a contract of employment or other contract connected with employment,

(b) a claim for a sum due under such a contract, and

(c) a claim for the recovery of a sum in pursuance of any enactment relating to the terms or performance of such a contract,

if the claim is such that a court in England and Wales or Scotland would under the law for the time being in force have jurisdiction to hear and determine an action in respect of the claim.

(3) This section does not apply to a claim for damages, or for a sum due, in respect of personal injuries.

(4) Any jurisdiction conferred on an [employment tribunal] by virtue of this section in respect of any claim is exercisable concurrently with any court in England and Wales or in Scotland which has jurisdiction to hear and determine an action in respect of the claim.

(5) In this section–

'appropriate Minister', as respects a claim in respect of which an action could be heard and determined by a court in England and Wales, means the Lord Chancellor and, as respects a claim in respect of which an action could be heard and determined by a court in Scotland, means the Secretary of State, and

'personal injuries' includes any disease and any impairment of a person's physical or mental condition.

(6) In this section a reference to breach of a contract includes a reference to breach of–

(a) a term implied in a contract by or under any enactment or otherwise,

(b) a term of a contract as modified by or under any enactment or otherwise, and

(c) a term which, although not contained in a contract, is incorporated in the contract by another term of the contract.

MEMBERSHIP, ETC

Composition of a tribunal

4 (1) Subject to the following provisions of this section and to section 7(3A), proceedings before an employment tribunal shall be heard by–

(a) the person who, in accordance with regulations made under section 1(1), is the chairman, and

(b) two other members, or (with the consent of the parties) one other member, selected as the other members (or member) in accordance with regulations so made.

(2) Subject to subsection (5), the proceedings specified in subsection (3) shall be heard by the person mentioned in subsection (1)(a) alone.

(3) The proceedings referred to in subsection (2) are–

(a) proceedings on a complaint under section 68A, 87 or 192 of the Trade Union and Labour Relations (Consolidation) Act 1992 or on an application under section 161, 165 or 166 of [that Act,

(b) proceedings on a complaint under section 126 of the Pension Schemes Act 1993,

(c) proceedings on a reference under section 11, 163 or 170 of the Employment Rights Act 1996, on a complaint under section 23, 34 or 188 of [that Act, on a complaint under section 70(1) of that Act relating to section 64 of that Act, on an application under section 128, 131 or 132 of that Act or for an appointment under section 206(4) of that Act, (ca) proceedings on a complaint under regulation 11(5) of the Transfer of Undertakings (Protection of Employment) Regulations 1981,

(cc) proceedings on a complaint under section 11 of the National Minimum Wage Act 1998;

(cd) proceedings on an appeal under section 19 or 22 of the National Minimum Wage Act 1998;

(d) proceedings in respect of which an employment tribunal has jurisdiction by virtue of section 3 of this Act,

(e) proceedings in which the parties have given their written consent to the proceedings being heard in accordance with subsection (2) (whether or not they have subsequently withdrawn it),

(f) . . . and

(g) proceedings in which the person (or, where more than one, each of the persons) against whom the proceedings are brought does not, or has ceased to, contest the case.

(4) The Secretary of State may by order amend the provisions of subsection (3).

(5) Proceedings specified in subsection (3) shall be heard in accordance with subsection (1) if a person who, in accordance with regulations made under section 1(1), may be the chairman of an employment tribunal, having regard to—

(a) whether there is a likelihood of a dispute arising on the facts which makes it desirable for the proceedings to be heard in accordance with subsection (1),

(b) whether there is a likelihood of an issue of law arising which would make it desirable for the proceedings to be heard in accordance with subsection (2),

(c) any views of any of the parties as to whether or not the proceedings ought to be heard in accordance with either of those subsections, and

(d) whether there are other proceedings which might be heard concurrently but which are not proceedings specified in subsection (3),

decides at any stage of the proceedings that the proceedings are to be heard in accordance with subsection (1).

(6) Where (in accordance with the following provisions of this Part) the Secretary of State makes employment tribunal procedure regulations, the regulations may provide that any act which is required or authorised by the regulations to be done by an employment tribunal and is of a description specified by the regulations for the purposes of this subsection may be done by the person mentioned in subsection (1)(a) alone.

(6A) Subsection (6) in particular enables employment tribunal procedure regulations to provide that—

(a) the determination of proceedings in accordance with regulations under section 7(3A), (3B) or (3C)(a),

(b) the carrying-out of pre-hearing reviews in accordance with regulations under subsection (1) of section 9 (including the exercise of powers in connection with such reviews in accordance with regulations under paragraph (b) of that subsection), or

(c) the hearing and determination of a preliminary issue in accordance with regulations under section 9(4) (where it involves hearing witnesses other than the parties or their representatives as well as where, in accordance with regulations under section 7(3C)(b), it does not),

may be done by the person mentioned in subsection (1)(a) alone.

(6B) Employment tribunal procedure regulations may (subject to subsection (6C)) also provide that any act which–

(a) by virtue of subsection (6) may be done by the person mentioned in subsection (1)(a) alone, and

(b) is of a description specified by the regulations for the purposes of this subsection,

may be done by a person appointed as a legal officer in accordance with regulations under section 1(1); and any act so done shall be treated as done by an employment tribunal.

(6C) But regulations under subsection (6B) may not specify–

(a) the determination of any proceedings, other than proceedings in which the parties have agreed the terms of the determination or in which the person bringing the proceedings has given notice of the withdrawal of the case, or

(b) the carrying-out of pre-hearing reviews in accordance with regulations under section 9(1).

(7) . . .

Remuneration, fees and allowances

5   (1) The Secretary of State may pay to–

(a) the President of the Employment Tribunals (England and Wales),

(b) the President of the Employment Tribunals (Scotland), . . .

(c) any person who is a member on a full-time basis of a panel of chairmen of tribunals which is appointed in accordance with regulations made under section 1(1), and

(d) any person who is a legal officer appointed in accordance with such regulations,

such remuneration as he may with the consent of the Treasury determine.

(2) The Secretary of State may pay to–

(a) members of employment tribunals,

(b) any assessors appointed for the purposes of proceedings before employment tribunals, and

(c) any persons required for the purposes of section 2A(1)(b) of the Equal Pay Act 1970 to prepare reports,

such fees and allowances as he may with the consent of the Treasury determine.

(3) The Secretary of State may pay to any other persons such allowances as he may with the consent of the Treasury determine for the purposes of, or in connection with, their attendance at employment tribunals.

PROCEDURE

Conduct of hearings

6   (1) A person may appear before an [employment tribunal] in person or be represented by–

(a) counsel or a solicitor,

(b) a representative of a trade union or an employers' association, or

(c) any other person whom he desires to represent him.

(2) Part I of the Arbitration Act 1996 does not apply to any proceedings before an employment tribunal.

Employment tribunal procedure regulations

7 (1) The Secretary of State may by regulations ('employment tribunal procedure regulations') make such provision as appears to him to be necessary or expedient with respect to proceedings before employment tribunals.

(2) Proceedings before employment tribunals shall be instituted in accordance with employment tribunal procedure regulations.

(3) Employment tribunal procedure regulations may, in particular, include provision–

(a) for determining by which tribunal any proceedings are to be determined,

(b) for enabling an employment tribunal to hear and determine proceedings brought by virtue of section 3 concurrently with proceedings brought before the tribunal otherwise than by virtue of that section,

(c) for treating the Secretary of State (either generally or in such circumstances as may be prescribed by the regulations) as a party to any proceedings before an employment tribunal (where he would not otherwise be a party to them) and entitling him to appear and to be heard accordingly,

(d) for requiring persons to attend to give evidence and produce documents and for authorising the administration of oaths to witnesses,

(e) for enabling an employment tribunal, on the application of any party to the proceedings before it or of its own motion, to order–

   (i) in England and Wales, such discovery or inspection of documents, or the furnishing of such further particulars, as might be ordered by a county court on application by a party to proceedings before it, or

   (ii) in Scotland, such recovery or inspection of documents as might be ordered by a sheriff,

(f) for prescribing the procedure to be followed in any proceedings before an employment tribunal, including provision–

   (i) . . .

   (ia) for postponing fixing a time and place for a hearing, or postponing a time fixed for a hearing, for such period as may be determined in accordance with the regulations for the purpose of giving an opportunity for the proceedings to be settled by way of conciliation and withdrawn, and

   (ii) for enabling an employment tribunal to review its decisions, and revoke or vary its orders and awards, in such circumstances as may be determined in accordance with the regulations,

(g) for the appointment of one or more assessors for the purposes of any proceedings before an employment tribunal, where the proceedings are brought under an enactment which provides for one or more assessors to be appointed,

(h) for authorising an employment tribunal to require persons to furnish information and produce documents to a person required for the purposes of section 2A(1)(b) of the Equal Pay Act 1970 to prepare a report, and

(j) for the registration and proof of decisions, orders and awards of employment tribunals.

(3ZA) Employment tribunal procedure regulations may–

(a) authorise the Secretary of State to prescribe, or prescribe requirements in relation to, any form which is required by such regulations to be used for the purpose of instituting, or entering an appearance to, proceedings before employment tribunals,

(b) authorise the Secretary of State to prescribe requirements in relation to documents to be supplied with any such form, and

(c) make provision about the publication of anything prescribed under authority conferred by virtue of this subsection.

(3A) Employment tribunal procedure regulations may authorise the determination of proceedings without any hearing in such circumstances as the regulations may prescribe.

(3B) Employment tribunal procedure regulations may authorise the determination of proceedings without hearing anyone other than the person or persons by whom the proceedings are brought (or his or their representatives) where–

(a) the person (or, where more than one, each of the persons) against whom the proceedings are brought has done nothing to contest the case, or

(b) it appears from the application made by the person (or, where more than one, each of the persons) bringing the proceedings that he is not (or they are not) seeking any relief which an employment tribunal has power to give or that he is not (or they are not) entitled to any such relief.

(3C) Employment tribunal procedure regulations may authorise the determination of proceedings without hearing anyone other than the person or persons by whom, and the person or persons against whom, the proceedings are brought (or his or their representatives) where–

(a) an employment tribunal is on undisputed facts bound by the decision of a court in another case to dismiss the case of the person or persons by whom, or of the person or persons against whom, the proceedings are brought, or

(b) the proceedings relate only to a preliminary issue which may be heard and determined in accordance with regulations under section 9(4).

(4) A person who without reasonable excuse fails to comply with–

(a) any requirement imposed by virtue of subsection (3)(d) or (h), or

(b) any requirement with respect to the discovery, recovery or inspection of documents imposed by virtue of subsection (3)(e), or

(c) any requirement imposed by virtue of employment tribunal procedure regulations to give written answers for the purpose of facilitating the determination of proceedings as mentioned in subsection (3A), (3B) or (3C), is guilty of an offence and liable on summary conviction to a fine not exceeding level 3 on the standard scale.

(5) Subject to any regulations under section 11(1)(a), employment tribunal procedure regulations may include provision authorising or requiring an employment tribunal, in circumstances specified in the regulations, to send notice or a copy of–

   (a) any document specified in the regulations which relates to any proceedings before the tribunal, or

   (b) any decision, order or award of the tribunal,

to any government department or other person or body so specified.

(6) Where in accordance with [employment tribunal] procedure regulations an employment tribunal determines in the same proceedings–

   (a) a complaint presented under section 111 of the Employment Rights Act 1996, and

   (b) a question referred under section 163 of that Act,

subsection (2) of that section has no effect for the purposes of the proceedings in so far as they relate to the complaint under section 111.

Practice directions

7A (1) Employment tribunal procedure regulations may include provision–

   (a) enabling the President to make directions about the procedure of employment tribunals, including directions about the exercise by tribunals of powers under such regulations,

   (b) for securing compliance with such directions, and

   (c) about the publication of such directions.

(2) Employment tribunal procedure regulations may, instead of providing for any matter, refer to provision made or to be made about that matter by directions made by the President.

(3) In this section, references to the President are to a person appointed in accordance with regulations under section 1(1) as–

   (a) President of the Employment Tribunals (England and Wales), or

   (b) President of the Employment Tribunals (Scotland).

Procedure in contract cases

8 (1) Where in proceedings brought by virtue of section 3 an employment tribunal finds that the whole or part of a sum claimed in the proceedings is due, the tribunal shall order the respondent to the proceedings to pay the amount which it finds due.

(2) An order under section 3 may provide that an employment tribunal shall not in proceedings in respect of a claim, or a number of claims relating to the same contract, order the payment of an amount exceeding such sum as may be specified in the order as the maximum amount which an employment tribunal may order to be paid in relation to a claim or in relation to a contract.

(3) An order under section 3 may include provisions–

   (a) as to the manner in which and time within which proceedings are to be brought by virtue of that section, and

   (b) modifying any other enactment.

(4) An order under that section may make different provision in relation to proceedings in respect of different descriptions of claims.

Pre-hearing reviews and preliminary matters

9 (1) Employment tribunal procedure regulations may include provision–
   (a) for authorising the carrying-out by an employment tribunal of a preliminary consideration of any proceedings before it (a 'pre-hearing review'), and
   (b) for enabling such powers to be exercised in connection with a pre-hearing review as may be prescribed by the regulations.

(2) Such regulations may in particular include provision–
   (a) for authorising any tribunal carrying out a pre-hearing review under the regulations to make, in circumstances specified in the regulations, an order requiring a party to the proceedings in question, if he wishes to continue to participate in those proceedings, to pay a deposit of an amount not exceeding £500, and
   (b) for prescribing–
      (i)   the manner in which the amount of any such deposit is to be determined in any particular case,
      (ii) the consequences of non-payment of any such deposit, and
      (iii) the circumstances in which any such deposit, or any part of it, may be refunded to the party who paid it or be paid over to another party to the proceedings.

(2A) Regulations under subsection (1)(b), so far as relating to striking out, may not provide for striking out on a ground which does not apply outside a pre-hearing review.

(3) The Secretary of State may from time to time by order substitute for the sum specified in subsection (2)(a) such other sum as is specified in the order.

(4) Employment tribunal procedure regulations may also include provision for authorising an employment tribunal to hear and determine separately any preliminary issue of a description prescribed by the regulations which is raised by any case.

National security

(1) If on a complaint under–
   (a) section 146 of the Trade Union and Labour Relations (Consolidation) Act 1992 (detriment: trade union membership), or
   (b) section 111 of the Employment Rights Act 1996 (unfair dismissal),

   it is shown that the action complained of was taken for the purpose of safeguarding national security, the employment tribunal shall dismiss the complaint.

(2) Employment tribunal procedure regulations may make provision about the composition of the tribunal (including provision disapplying or modifying section 4) for the purposes of proceedings in relation to which–
   (a) a direction is given under subsection (3), or
   (b) an order is made under subsection (4).

(3) A direction may be given under this subsection by a Minister of the Crown if–
  (a) it relates to particular Crown employment proceedings, and
  (b) the Minister considers it expedient in the interests of national security.

(4) An order may be made under this subsection by the President or a Regional Chairman in relation to particular proceedings if he considers it expedient in the interests of national security.

(5) Employment tribunal procedure regulations may make provision enabling a Minister of the Crown, if he considers it expedient in the interests of national security–
  (a) to direct a tribunal to sit in private for all or part of particular Crown employment proceedings;
  (b) to direct a tribunal to exclude the applicant from all or part of particular Crown employment proceedings;
  (c) to direct a tribunal to exclude the applicant's representatives from all or part of particular Crown employment proceedings;
  (d) to direct a tribunal to take steps to conceal the identity of a particular witness in particular Crown employment proceedings;
  (e) to direct a tribunal to take steps to keep secret all or part of the reasons for its decision in particular Crown employment proceedings.

(6) Employment tribunal procedure regulations may enable a tribunal, if it considers it expedient in the interests of national security, to do anything of a kind which a tribunal can be required to do by direction under subsection (5)(a) to (e).

(7) In relation to cases where a person has been excluded by virtue of subsection (5)(b) or (c) or (6), employment tribunal procedure regulations may make provision–
  (a) for the appointment by the Attorney General, or by the Advocate General for Scotland, of a person to represent the interests of the applicant;
  (b) about the publication and registration of reasons for the tribunal's decision;
  (c) permitting an excluded person to make a statement to the tribunal before the commencement of the proceedings, or the part of the proceedings, from which he is excluded.

(8) Proceedings are Crown employment proceedings for the purposes of this section if the employment to which the complaint relates–
  (a) is Crown employment, or
  (b) is connected with the performance of functions on behalf of the Crown.

(9) The reference in subsection (4) to the President or a Regional Chairman is to a person appointed in accordance with regulations under section 1(1) as–
  (a) a Regional Chairman,
  (b) President of the Employment Tribunals (England and Wales), or
  (c) President of the Employment Tribunals (Scotland).

Confidential information

10A (1) Employment tribunal procedure regulations may enable an employment tribunal to sit in private for the purpose of hearing evidence from any person which in the opinion of the tribunal is likely to consist of–

(a) information which he could not disclose without contravening a prohibition imposed by or by virtue of any enactment,

(b) information which has been communicated to him in confidence or which he has otherwise obtained in consequence of the confidence reposed in him by another person, or

(c) information the disclosure of which would, for reasons other than its effect on negotiations with respect to any of the matters mentioned in section 178(2) of the Trade Union and Labour Relations (Consolidation) Act 1992, cause substantial injury to any undertaking of his or in which he works.

(2) The reference in subsection (1)(c) to any undertaking of a person or in which he works shall be construed–

(a) in relation to a person in Crown employment, as a reference to the national interest,

(b) in relation to a person who is a relevant member of the House of Lords staff, as a reference to the national interest or (if the case so requires) the interests of the House of Lords, and

(c) in relation to a person who is a relevant member of the House of Commons staff, as a reference to the national interest or (if the case so requires) the interests of the House of Commons.

Restriction of publicity in cases involving national security

10B (1) This section applies where a tribunal has been directed under section 10(5) or has determined under section 10(6)–

(a) to take steps to conceal the identity of a particular witness, or

(b) to take steps to keep secret all or part of the reasons for its decision.

(2) It is an offence to publish–

(a) anything likely to lead to the identification of the witness, or

(b) the reasons for the tribunal's decision or the part of its reasons which it is directed or has determined to keep secret.

(3) A person guilty of an offence under this section is liable on summary conviction to a fine not exceeding level 5 on the standard scale.

(4) Where a person is charged with an offence under this section it is a defence to prove that at the time of the alleged offence he was not aware, and neither suspected nor had reason to suspect, that the publication in question was of, or included, the matter in question.

(5) Where an offence under this section committed by a body corporate is proved to have been committed with the consent or connivance of, or to be attributable to any neglect on the part of–

(a) a director, manager, secretary or other similar officer of the body corporate, or

(b) a person purporting to act in any such capacity,

he as well as the body corporate is guilty of the offence and liable to be proceeded against and punished accordingly.

(6) A reference in this section to publication includes a reference to inclusion in a programme which is included in a programme service, within the meaning of the Broadcasting Act 1990.

Restriction of publicity in cases involving sexual misconduct

11 (1) Employment tribunal procedure regulations may include provision–

(a) for cases involving allegations of the commission of sexual offences, for securing that the registration or other making available of documents or decisions shall be so effected as to prevent the identification of any person affected by or making the allegation, and provision–

(b) for cases involving allegations of sexual misconduct, enabling an employment tribunal, on the application of any party to proceedings before it or of its own motion, to make a restricted reporting order having effect (if not revoked earlier) until the promulgation of the decision of the tribunal.

(2) If any identifying matter is published or included in a relevant programme in contravention of a restricted reporting order–

(a) in the case of publication in a newspaper or periodical, any proprietor, any editor and any publisher of the newspaper or periodical,

(b) in the case of publication in any other form, the person publishing the matter, and

(c) in the case of matter included in a relevant programme–

(i) any body corporate engaged in providing the service in which the programme is included, and

(ii) any person having functions in relation to the programme corresponding to those of an editor of a newspaper,

shall be guilty of an offence and liable on summary conviction to a fine not exceeding level 5 on the standard scale.

(3) Where a person is charged with an offence under subsection (2) it is a defence to prove that at the time of the alleged offence he was not aware, and neither suspected nor had reason to suspect, that the publication or programme in question was of, or included, the matter in question.

(4) Where an offence under subsection (2) committed by a body corporate is proved to have been committed with the consent or connivance of, or to be attributable to any neglect on the part of–

(a) a director, manager, secretary or other similar officer of the body corporate, or

(b) a person purporting to act in any such capacity,

he as well as the body corporate is guilty of the offence and liable to be proceeded against and punished accordingly.

(5) In relation to a body corporate whose affairs are managed by its members 'director', in subsection (4), means a member of the body corporate.

(6) In this section–

'identifying matter', in relation to a person, means any matter likely to lead members of the public to identify him as a person affected by, or as the person making, the allegation,

'relevant programme' has the same meaning as in the Sexual Offences (Amendment) Act 1992, 'restricted reporting order' means an order–

   (a) made in exercise of a power conferred by regulations made by virtue of this section, and

   (b) prohibiting the publication in Great Britain of identifying matter in a written publication available to the public or its inclusion in a relevant programme for reception in Great Britain,

'sexual misconduct' means the commission of a sexual offence, sexual harassment or other adverse conduct (of whatever nature) related to sex, and conduct is related to sex whether the relationship with sex lies in the character of the conduct or in its having reference to the sex or sexual orientation of the person at whom the conduct is directed,

'sexual offence' means any offence to which section 4 of the Sexual Offences (Amendment) Act 1976, the Sexual Offences (Amendment) Act 1992 or section 274(2) of the Criminal Procedure (Scotland) Act 1995 applies (offences under the Sexual Offences Act 1956, Part I of the Criminal Law (Consolidation) (Scotland) Act 1995 and certain other enactments), and

'written publication' has the same meaning as in the Sexual Offences (Amendment) Act 1992.

Restriction of publicity in disability cases

(1) This section applies to proceedings on a complaint under section 17A or 25(8) of the Disability Discrimination Act 1995 in which evidence of a personal nature is likely to be heard by the [employment tribunal] hearing the complaint.

(2) Employment tribunal procedure regulations may include provision in relation to proceedings to which this section applies for–

   (a) enabling an employment tribunal, on the application of the complainant or of its own motion, to make a restricted reporting order having effect (if not revoked earlier) until the promulgation of the decision of the tribunal, and

   (b) where a restricted reporting order is made in relation to a complaint which is being dealt with by the tribunal together with any other proceedings, enabling the tribunal to direct that the order is to apply also in relation to those other proceedings or such part of them as the tribunal may direct.

(3) If any identifying matter is published or included in a relevant programme in contravention of a restricted reporting order–

   (a) in the case of publication in a newspaper or periodical, any proprietor, any editor and any publisher of the newspaper or periodical,

   (b) in the case of publication in any other form, the person publishing the matter, and

   (c) in the case of matter included in a relevant programme–

      (i) any body corporate engaged in providing the service in which the programme is included, and

     (ii) any person having functions in relation to the programme corresponding to those of an editor of a newspaper, shall be guilty of an offence and liable on summary conviction to a fine not exceeding level 5 on the standard scale.

(4) Where a person is charged with an offence under subsection (3), it is a defence to prove that at the time of the alleged offence he was not aware, and neither suspected nor had reason to suspect, that the publication or programme in question was of, or included, the matter in question.

(5) Where an offence under subsection (3) committed by a body corporate is proved to have been committed with the consent or connivance of, or to be attributable to any neglect on the part of–

(a) a director, manager, secretary or other similar officer of the body corporate, or

(b) a person purporting to act in any such capacity,

he as well as the body corporate is guilty of the offence and liable to be proceeded against and punished accordingly.

(6) In relation to a body corporate whose affairs are managed by its members 'director', in subsection (5), means a member of the body corporate.

(7) In this section–

'evidence of a personal nature' means any evidence of a medical, or other intimate, nature which might reasonably be assumed to be likely to cause significant embarrassment to the complainant if reported,

'identifying matter' means any matter likely to lead members of the public to identify the complainant or such other persons (if any) as may be named in the order,

'promulgation' has such meaning as may be prescribed by regulations made by virtue of this section,

'relevant programme' means a programme included in a programme service, within the meaning of the Broadcasting Act 1990,

'restricted reporting order' means an order–

(a) made in exercise of a power conferred by regulations made by virtue of this section, and

(b) prohibiting the publication in Great Britain of identifying matter in a written publication available to the public or its inclusion in a relevant programme for reception in Great Britain, and

'written publication' includes a film, a sound track and any other record in permanent form but does not include an indictment or other document prepared for use in particular legal proceedings.

Costs and expenses

13 (1) Employment tribunal procedure regulations may include provision–

(a) for the award of costs or expenses;

(b) for the award of any allowances payable under section 5(2)(c) or (3).

(1A) Regulations under subsection (1) may include provision authorising an employment tribunal to have regard to a person's ability to pay when considering the making of an award against him under such regulations.

(1B) Employment tribunal procedure regulations may include provision for authorising an employment tribunal–

(a) to disallow all or part of the costs or expenses of a representative of a party to proceedings before it by reason of that representative's conduct of the proceedings;

(b) to order a representative of a party to proceedings before it to meet all or part of the costs or expenses incurred by a party by reason of the representative's conduct of the proceedings;

(c) to order a representative of a party to proceedings before it to meet all or part of any allowances payable by the Secretary of State under section 5(2)(c) or (3) by reason of the representative's conduct of the proceedings.

(1C) Employment tribunal procedure regulations may also include provision for taxing or otherwise settling the costs or expenses referred to in subsection (1)(a) or (1B)(b) (and, in particular in England and Wales, for enabling the amount of such costs to be assessed by way of detailed assessment in a county court).

(2) In relation to proceedings under section 111 of the Employment Rights Act 1996–

(a) where the employee has expressed a wish to be reinstated or re-engaged which has been communicated to the employer at least seven days before the hearing of the complaint, . . .

(b) . . . ,

employment tribunal procedure regulations shall include provision for requiring the employer to pay the costs or expenses of any postponement or adjournment of the hearing caused by his failure, without a special reason, to adduce reasonable evidence as to the availability of the job from which the complainant was dismissed . . . or of comparable or suitable employment.

Payments in respect of preparation time

13A (1) Employment tribunal procedure regulations may include provision for authorising an employment tribunal to order a party to proceedings before it to make a payment to any other party in respect of time spent in preparing that other party's case.

(2) Regulations under subsection (1) may include provision authorising an employment tribunal to have regard to a person's ability to pay when considering the making of an order against him under such regulations.

(3) If employment tribunal procedure regulations include–

(a) provision of the kind mentioned in subsection (1), and

(b) provision of the kind mentioned in section 13(1)(a),

they shall also include provision to prevent an employment tribunal exercising its powers under both kinds of provision in favour of the same person in the same proceedings.

Interest

14 (1) The Secretary of State may by order made with the approval of the Treasury provide that sums payable in pursuance of decisions of employment tribunals shall carry interest at such rate and between such times as may be prescribed by the order.

(2) Any interest due by virtue of such an order shall be recoverable as a sum payable in pursuance of the decision.

(3) The power conferred by subsection (1) includes power–

(a) to specify cases or circumstances in which interest is not payable,

(b) to provide that interest is payable only on sums exceeding a specified amount or falling between specified amounts,

(c) to make provision for the manner in which and the periods by reference to which interest is to be calculated and paid,

(d) to provide that any enactment–

(i)   does or does not apply in relation to interest payable by virtue of subsection (1), or

(ii) applies to it with such modifications as may be specified in the order,

(e) to make provision for cases where sums are payable in pursuance of decisions or awards made on appeal from employment tribunals,

(f) to make such incidental or supplemental provision as the Secretary of State considers necessary.

(4) In particular, an order under subsection (1) may provide that the rate of interest shall be the rate specified in section 17 of the Judgments Act 1838 as that enactment has effect from time to time.

Enforcement

15 (1) Any sum payable in pursuance of a decision of an [employment tribunal] in England and Wales which has been registered in accordance with employment tribunal procedure regulations shall, if a county court so orders, be recoverable by execution issued from the county court or otherwise as if it were payable under an order of that court.

(2) Any order for the payment of any sum made by an [employment tribunal] in Scotland (or any copy of such an order certified by the Secretary of the Tribunals) may be enforced as if it were an extract registered decree arbitral bearing a warrant for execution issued by the sheriff court of any sheriffdom in Scotland.

(3) In this section a reference to a decision or order of an employment tribunal–

(a) does not include a decision or order which, on being reviewed, has been revoked by the tribunal, and

(b) in relation to a decision or order which on being reviewed, has been varied by the tribunal shall be construed as a reference to the decision or order as so varied.

RECOUPMENT OF SOCIAL SECURITY BENEFITS

Power to provide for recoupment of benefits

16 (1) This section applies to payments which are the subject of proceedings before employment tribunals and which are–

(a) payments of wages or compensation for loss of wages,

(b) payments by employers to employees under sections 146 to 151, sections 168 to 173 or section 192 of the Trade Union and Labour Relations (Consolidation) Act 1992,

(c) payments by employers to employees under–

    (i)   Part III, V, VI or VII,
    (ii)   section 93, or
    (iii) Part X,
    of the Employment Rights Act 1996, or

(d) payments by employers to employees of a nature similar to, or for a purpose corresponding to the purpose of, payments within paragraph (b) or (c),

and to payments of remuneration under a protective award under section 189 of the Trade Union and Labour Relations (Consolidation) Act 1992.

(2) The Secretary of State may by regulations make with respect to payments to which this section applies provision for any or all of the purposes specified in subsection (3).

(3) The purposes referred to in subsection (2) are–

(a) enabling the Secretary of State to recover from an employer, by way of total or partial recoupment of jobseeker's allowance or income support–

    (i)   a sum not exceeding the amount of the prescribed element of the monetary award, or

    (ii)   in the case of a protective award, the amount of the remuneration,

(b) requiring or authorising an employment tribunal to order the payment of such a sum, by way of total or partial recoupment of either benefit, to the Secretary of State instead of to an employee, and

(c) requiring an employment tribunal to order the payment to an employee of only the excess of the prescribed element of the monetary award over the amount of any jobseeker's allowance or income support shown to the tribunal to have been paid to the employee and enabling the Secretary of State to recover from the employer, by way of total or partial recoupment of the benefit, a sum not exceeding that amount.

(4) Regulations under this section may be framed–

(a) so as to apply to all payments to which this section applies or to one or more classes of those payments, and

(b) so as to apply to both jobseeker's allowance and income support, or to only jobseeker's allowance or income support.

(5) Regulations under this section may–

(a) confer powers and impose duties on [employment tribunals] or . . . other persons,

(b) impose on an employer to whom a monetary award or protective award relates a duty–

    (i)   to furnish particulars connected with the award, and

    (ii)   to suspend payments in pursuance of the award during any period prescribed by the regulations,

(c) provide for an employer who pays a sum to the Secretary of State in pursuance of this section to be relieved from any liability to pay the sum to another person,

(cc) provide for the determination by the Secretary of State of any issue arising as to the total or partial recoupment in pursuance of the regulations of a jobseeker's allowance, unemployment benefit or income support,

(d) confer on an employee a right of appeal to an appeal tribunal constituted under Chapter I of Part I of the Social Security Act 1998 against any decision of the Secretary of State on any such issue, and

(e) provide for the proof in proceedings before employment tribunals (whether by certificate or in any other manner) of any amount of job-seeker's allowance or income support paid to an employee.

(6) Regulations under this section may make different provision for different cases.

Recoupment: further provisions

17 (1) Where in pursuance of any regulations under section 16 a sum has been recovered by or paid to the Secretary of State by way of total or partial recoupment of jobseeker's allowance or income support–

(a) no sum shall be recoverable under Part III or V of the Social Security Administration Act 1992, and

(b) no abatement, payment or reduction shall be made by reference to the jobseeker's allowance or income support recouped.

(2) Any amount found to have been duly recovered by or paid to the Secretary of State in pursuance of regulations under section 16 by way of total or partial recoupment of jobseeker's allowance shall be paid into the National Insurance Fund.

(3) In section 16–

'monetary award' means the amount which is awarded, or ordered to be paid, to the employee by the tribunal or would be so awarded or ordered apart from any provision of regulations under that section, and

'the prescribed element', in relation to any monetary award, means so much of that award as is attributable to such matters as may be prescribed by regulations under that section.

(4) In section 16 'income-based jobseeker's allowance' has the same meaning as in the Jobseekers Act 1995.

CONCILIATION

Conciliation

18 (1) This section applies in the case of employment tribunal proceedings and claims which could be the subject of employment tribunal proceedings–

(a) under–

(i)   section 2(1) of the Equal Pay Act 1970,

(ii) section 63 of the Sex Discrimination Act 1975, or

(iii) section 54 of the Race Relations Act 1976,

(b) arising out of a contravention, or alleged contravention, of section 64, 68, 86, 137, 138, 146, 168, 168A, 169, 170, 174, 188 or 190 of the Trade Union and Labour Relations (Consolidation) Act 1992,

(c) under section 17A or 25(8) of the Disability Discrimination Act 1995,

(d) under or arising out of a contravention, or alleged contravention, of section 8, 13, 15, 18(1), 21(1), 28, 80G(1), 80H(1)(b), 80(1), 92 or 135, or of Part V, VI, VII or X, of the Employment Rights Act 1996, (dd) under or by virtue of section 11, 18, 20(1)(a) or 24 of the National Minimum Wage Act 1998,

(e) which are proceedings in respect of which an employment tribunal has jurisdiction by virtue of section 3 of this Act, . . .

(f) under or arising out of a contravention, or alleged contravention, of a provision specified by an order under subsection (8)(b) as a provision to which this paragraph applies, . . .

(ff) under regulation 30 of the Working Time Regulations 1998, . . .

(g) under regulation 27 or 32 of the Transnational Information and Consultation of Employees Regulations 1999, . . .

(h) arising out of a contravention, or alleged contravention of regulation 5(1) or 7(2) of the Part-time Workers (Prevention of Less Favourable Treatment) Regulations 2000,

(i) arising out of a contravention, or alleged contravention of regulation 3 or 6(2) of the Fixed-term Employees (Prevention of Less Favourable Treatment) Regulations 2002, . . .

(j) under regulation 9 of those Regulations, . . .

(k) under regulation 28 of the Employment Equality (Sexual Orientation) Regulations 2003, . . .

(l) under regulation 28 of the Employment Equality (Religion or Belief) Regulations 2003,

(m) under regulation 18 of the Merchant Shipping (Working Time: Inland Waterways) Regulations 2003,

(n) under regulation 19 of the Fishing Vessels (Working Time: Sea-fishermen) Regulations 2004.

(2) Where an application has been presented to an employment tribunal, and a copy of it has been sent to a conciliation officer, it is the duty of the conciliation officer–

(a) if he is requested to do so by the person by whom and the person against whom the proceedings are brought, or

(b) if, in the absence of any such request, the conciliation officer considers that he could act under this subsection with a reasonable prospect of success,

to endeavour to promote a settlement of the proceedings without their being determined by an employment tribunal.

(2A) Where employment tribunal procedure regulations include provision postponing the fixing of a time and place for a hearing for the purpose of giving an opportunity for the proceedings to be settled by way of conciliation and withdrawn, subsection (2) shall have effect from the end of the postponement to confer a power on the conciliation officer, instead of imposing a duty.

(3) Where at any time–

(a) a person claims that action has been taken in respect of which proceedings could be brought by him before an employment tribunal, but

(b) before any application relating to that action has been presented by him a request is made to a conciliation officer (whether by that person or by the person against whom the proceedings could be instituted) to make his services available to them,

the conciliation officer shall act in accordance with subsection (2) as if an application had been presented to an employment tribunal.

(4) Where a person who has presented a complaint to an employment tribunal under section 111 of the Employment Rights Act 1996 has ceased to be employed by the employer against whom the complaint was made, the conciliation officer shall (for the purpose of promoting a settlement of the complaint in accordance with subsection (2)) in particular–

  (a) seek to promote the reinstatement or re-engagement of the complainant by the employer, or by a successor of the employer or by an associated employer, on terms appearing to the conciliation officer to be equitable, or

  (b) where the complainant does not wish to be reinstated or re-engaged, or where reinstatement or re-engagement is not practicable, and the parties desire the conciliation officer to act, seek to promote agreement between them as to a sum by way of compensation to be paid by the employer to the complainant.

(5) Where at any time–

  (a) a person claims that action has been taken in respect of which a complaint could be presented by him to an employment tribunal under section 111 of the Employment Rights Act 1996, but

  (b) before any complaint relating to that action has been presented by him a request is made to a conciliation officer (whether by that person or by the employer) to make his services available to them,

the conciliation officer shall act in accordance with subsection (4) as if a complaint had been presented to an employment tribunal under section 111.

(6) In proceeding under this section a conciliation officer shall, where appropriate, have regard to the desirability of encouraging the use of other procedures available for the settlement of grievances.

(7) Anything communicated to a conciliation officer in connection with the performance of his functions under this section shall not be admissible in evidence in any proceedings before an employment tribunal, except with the consent of the person who communicated it to that officer.

(8) The Secretary of State may by order–

  (a) direct that further provisions of the Employment Rights Act 1996 be added to the list in subsection (1)(d), or

  (b) specify a provision of any other Act as a provision to which subsection (1)(f) applies.

Conciliation procedure

19 (1) Employment tribunal procedure regulations shall include in relation to employment tribunal proceedings in the case of which any enactment makes provision for conciliation–

  (a) provisions requiring a copy of the application by which the proceedings are instituted, and a copy of any notice relating to it which is lodged by or on behalf of the person against whom the proceedings are brought, to be sent to a conciliation officer, and

(b) provisions securing that the applicant and the person against whom the proceedings are brought are notified that the services of a conciliation officer are available to them, . . .

(c) . . .

(2) If employment tribunal procedure regulations include provision postponing the fixing of a time and place for a hearing for the purpose of giving an opportunity for the proceedings to be settled by way of conciliation and withdrawn, they shall also include provision for the parties to proceedings to which the provision for postponement applies to be notified that the services of a conciliation officer may no longer be available to them after the end of the postponement.

PART II: THE EMPLOYMENT APPEAL TRIBUNAL
INTRODUCTORY

The Appeal Tribunal

20 (1) The Employment Appeal Tribunal ('the Appeal Tribunal') shall continue in existence.

(2) The Appeal Tribunal shall have a central office in London but may sit at any time and in any place in Great Britain.

(3) The Appeal Tribunal shall be a superior court of record and shall have an official seal which shall be judicially noticed.

(4) Subsection (2) is subject to regulation 34 of the Transnational Information and Consultation of Employees Regulations 1999.

JURISDICTION

Jurisdiction of Appeal Tribunal

21 (1) An appeal lies to the Appeal Tribunal on any question of law arising from any decision of, or arising in any proceedings before, an employment tribunal under or by virtue of–

(a) the Equal Pay Act 1970,

(b) the Sex Discrimination Act 1975,

(c) the Race Relations Act 1976,

(d) the Trade Union and Labour Relations (Consolidation) Act 1992,

(e) the Disability Discrimination Act 1995, . . .

(f) the Employment Rights Act 1996 . . .

(g) this Act,

(ga) the National Minimum Wage Act 1998,

(gb) the Employment Relations Act 1999,

(h) the Working Time Regulations 1998, . . .

(i) the Transnational Information and Consultation of Employees Regulations 1999 . . .

(j) the Part-time Workers (Prevention of Less Favourable Treatment) Regulations 2000 . . .

(k) the Fixed-term Employees (Prevention of Less Favourable Treatment) Regulations 2002 . . .

(l) the Employment Equality (Sexual Orientation) Regulations 2003 . . .

(m) the Employment Equality (Religion or Belief) Regulations 2003,

(n) the Merchant Shipping (Working Time: Inland Waterways) Regulations 2003,

(o) the Fishing Vessels (Working Time: Sea-fishermen) Regulations 2004.

(2) No appeal shall lie except to the Appeal Tribunal from any decision of an employment tribunal under or by virtue of the Acts listed or the Regulations referred to in subsection (1).

(3) Subsection (1) does not affect any provision contained in, or made under, any Act which provides for an appeal to lie to the Appeal Tribunal (whether from an [employment tribunal], the Certification Officer or any other person or body) otherwise than on a question to which that subsection applies.

(4) The Appeal Tribunal also has any jurisdiction in respect of matters other than appeals which is conferred on it by or under–

(a) the Trade Union and Labour Relations (Consolidation) Act 1992,

(b) this Act, or

(c) any other Act.

MEMBERSHIP, ETC

Membership of Appeal Tribunal

22 (1) The Appeal Tribunal shall consist of–

(a) such number of judges as may be nominated from time to time by the Lord Chancellor from the judges (other than the Lord Chancellor) of the High Court and the Court of Appeal,

(b) at least one judge of the Court of Session nominated from time to time by the Lord President of the Court of Session, and

(c) such number of other members as may be appointed from time to time by Her Majesty on the joint recommendation of the Lord Chancellor and the Secretary of State ('appointed Members').

(2) The appointed members shall be persons who appear to the Lord Chancellor and the Secretary of State to have special knowledge or experience of industrial relations either–

(a) as representatives of employers, or

(b) as representatives of workers (within the meaning of the Trade Union and Labour Relations (Consolidation) Act 1992).

(3) The Lord Chancellor shall, after consultation with the Lord President of the Court of Session, appoint one of the judges nominated under subsection (1) to be the President of the Appeal Tribunal.

(4) No judge shall be nominated a member of the Appeal Tribunal except with his consent.

Temporary membership

23 (1) At any time when–

(a) the office of President of the Appeal Tribunal is vacant, or

(b) the person holding that office is temporarily absent or otherwise unable to act as the President of the Appeal Tribunal,

the Lord Chancellor may nominate another judge nominated under section 22(1)(a) to act temporarily in his place.

(2) At any time when a judge of the Appeal Tribunal nominated under paragraph (a) or (b) of subsection (1) of section 22 is temporarily absent or otherwise unable to act as a member of the Appeal Tribunal–

(a) in the case of a judge nominated under paragraph (a) of that subsection, the Lord Chancellor may nominate another judge who is qualified to be nominated under that paragraph to act temporarily in his place, and

(b) in the case of a judge nominated under paragraph (b) of that subsection, the Lord President of the Court of Session may nominate another judge who is qualified to be nominated under that paragraph to act temporarily in his place.

(3) At any time when an appointed member of the Appeal Tribunal is temporarily absent or otherwise unable to act as a member of the Appeal Tribunal, the Lord Chancellor and the Secretary of State may jointly appoint a person appearing to them to have the qualifications for appointment as an appointed member to act temporarily in his place.

(4) A person nominated or appointed to act temporarily in place of the President or any other member of the Appeal Tribunal, when so acting, has all the functions of the person in whose place he acts.

(5) No judge shall be nominated to act temporarily as a member of the Appeal Tribunal except with his consent.

Temporary additional judicial membership

24 (1) At any time when it appears to the Lord Chancellor that it is expedient to do so in order to facilitate in England and Wales the disposal of business in the Appeal Tribunal, he may appoint a qualified person to be a temporary additional judge of the Appeal Tribunal during such period or on such occasions as the Lord Chancellor thinks fit.

(2) In subsection (1) 'qualified person' means a person who–

(a) is qualified for appointment as a judge of the High Court under section 10 of the Supreme Court Act 1981, or

(b) has held office as a judge of the High Court or the Court of Appeal.

(3) A person appointed to be a temporary additional judge of the Appeal Tribunal has all the functions of a judge nominated under section 22(1)(a).

Tenure of appointed members

25 (1) Subject to subsections (2) to (4), an appointed member shall hold and vacate office in accordance with the terms of his appointment.

(2) An appointed member–

(a) may at any time resign his membership by notice in writing addressed to the Lord Chancellor and the Secretary of State, and

(b) shall vacate his office on the day on which he attains the age of seventy.

(3) Subsection (2)(b) is subject to section 26(4) to (6) of the Judicial Pensions and Retirement Act 1993 (Lord Chancellor's power to authorise continuance of office up to the age of seventy-five).

(4) If the Lord Chancellor, after consultation with the Secretary of State, is satisfied that an appointed member–

(a) has been absent from sittings of the Appeal Tribunal for a period longer than six consecutive months without the permission of the President of the Appeal Tribunal,

(b) has become bankrupt or made an arrangement with his creditors, or has had his estate sequestrated or made a trust deed for behalf of his creditors or a composition contract,

(c) is incapacitated by physical or mental illness, or

(d) is otherwise unable or unfit to discharge the functions of a member,

the Lord Chancellor may declare his office as a member to be vacant and shall notify the declaration in such manner as the Lord Chancellor thinks fit; and when the Lord Chancellor does so, the office becomes vacant.

Staff

26 The Secretary of State may appoint such officers and servants of the Appeal Tribunal as he may determine, subject to the approval of the Minister for the Civil Service as to numbers and terms and conditions of service.

Remuneration, pensions and allowances

27 (1) The Secretary of State shall pay–

(a) the appointed members,

(b) any person appointed to act temporarily in the place of an appointed member, and

(c) the officers and servants of the Appeal Tribunal,

such remuneration and such travelling and other allowances as he may, with the relevant approval, determine; and for this purpose the relevant approval is that of the Treasury in the case of persons within paragraph (a) or (b) and the Minister for the Civil Service in the case of persons within paragraph (c).

(2) A person appointed to be a temporary additional judge of the Appeal Tribunal shall be paid such remuneration and allowances as the Lord Chancellor may, with the approval of the Treasury, determine.

(3) If the Secretary of State determines, with the approval of the Treasury, that this subsection applies in the case of an appointed member, the Secretary of State shall–

(a) pay such pension, allowance or gratuity to or in respect of that person on his retirement or death, or

(b) make to the member such payments towards the provision of a pension, allowance or gratuity for his retirement or death,

as the Secretary of State may, with the approval of the Treasury, determine.

(4) Where–

(a) a person ceases to be an appointed member otherwise than on his retirement or death, and

(b) it appears to the Secretary of State that there are special circumstances which make it right for him to receive compensation, the Secretary of State may make to him a payment of such amount as the Secretary of State may, with the approval of the Treasury, determine.

Composition of Appeal Tribunal

28 (1) The Appeal Tribunal may sit, in accordance with directions given by the President of the Appeal Tribunal, either as a single tribunal or in two or more divisions concurrently.

(2) Subject to subsections (3) to (5), proceedings before the Appeal Tribunal shall be heard by a judge and either two or four appointed members, so that in either case there is an equal number–

(a) of persons whose knowledge or experience of industrial relations is as representatives of employers, and

(b) of persons whose knowledge or experience of industrial relations is as representatives of workers.

(3) With the consent of the parties, proceedings before the Appeal Tribunal may be heard by a judge and one appointed member or by a judge and three appointed members.

(4) Proceedings on an appeal on a question arising from any decision of, or arising in any proceedings before, an employment tribunal consisting of the person mentioned in section 4(1)(a) alone shall be heard by a judge alone unless a judge directs that the proceedings shall be heard in accordance with subsections (2) and (3).

(5) . . .

PROCEDURE

Conduct of hearings

29 (1) A person may appear before the Appeal Tribunal in person or be represented by–

(a) counsel or a solicitor,

(b) a representative of a trade union or an employers' association, or

(c) any other person whom he desires to represent him.

(2) The Appeal Tribunal has in relation to–

(a) the attendance and examination of witnesses,

(b) the production and inspection of documents, and

(c) all other matters incidental to its jurisdiction,

the same powers, rights, privileges and authority (in England and Wales) as the High Court and (in Scotland) as the Court of Session.

Appeal Tribunal procedure rules

30 (1) The Lord Chancellor, after consultation with the Lord President of the Court of Session, shall make rules ('Appeal Tribunal procedure rules') with respect to proceedings before the Appeal Tribunal.

(2) Appeal Tribunal procedure rules may, in particular, include provision–

(a) with respect to the manner in which, and the time within which, an appeal may be brought,

(b) with respect to the manner in which any application or complaint to the Appeal Tribunal may be made,

(c) for requiring persons to attend to give evidence and produce documents and for authorising the administration of oaths to witnesses,

(d) for requiring or enabling the Appeal Tribunal to sit in private in circumstances in which an employment tribunal is required or empowered to sit in private by virtue of section 10A of this Act,

(e) . . .

(f) for interlocutory matters arising on any appeal or application to the Appeal Tribunal to be dealt with otherwise than in accordance with section 28(2) to (5) of this Act.

(2A) Appeal Tribunal procedure rules may make provision of a kind which may be made by employment tribunal procedure regulations under section 10(2), (5), (6) or (7).

(2B) For the purposes of subsection (2A)–

(a) the reference in section 10(2) to section 4 shall be treated as a reference to section 28, and

(b) the reference in section 10(4) to the President or a Regional Chairman shall be treated as a reference to a judge of the Appeal Tribunal.

(2C) Section 10B shall have effect in relation to a direction to or determination of the Appeal Tribunal as it has effect in relation to a direction to or determination of an employment tribunal.

(3) Subject to Appeal Tribunal procedure rules, the Appeal Tribunal has power to regulate its own procedure.

Restriction of publicity in cases involving sexual misconduct

31 (1) Appeal Tribunal procedure rules may, as respects proceedings to which this section applies, include provision–

(a) for cases involving allegations of the commission of sexual offences, for securing that the registration or other making available of documents or divisions shall be so effected as to prevent the identification of any person affected by or making the allegation, and

(b) for cases involving allegations of sexual misconduct, enabling the Appeal Tribunal, on the application of any party to the proceedings before it or of its own motion, to make a restricted reporting order having effect (if not revoked earlier) until the promulgation of the decision of the Appeal Tribunal.

(2) This section applies to–

(a) proceedings on an appeal against a decision of an employment tribunal to make, or not to make, a restricted reporting order, and

(b) proceedings on an appeal against any interlocutory decision of an employment tribunal in proceedings in which the employment tribunal has made a restricted reporting order which it has not revoked.

(3) If any identifying matter is published or included in a relevant programme in contravention of a restricted reporting order–

(a) in the case of publication in a newspaper or periodical, any proprietor, any editor and any publisher of the newspaper or periodical,

(b) in the case of publication in any other form, the person publishing the matter, and

(c) in the case of matter included in a relevant programme–

(i) any body corporate engaged in providing the service in which the programme is included, and

(ii) any person having functions in relation to the programme corresponding to those of an editor of a newspaper,

shall be guilty of an offence and liable on summary conviction to a fine not exceeding level 5 on the standard scale.

(4) Where a person is charged with an offence under subsection (3) it is a defence to prove that at the time of the alleged offence he was not aware, and neither suspected nor had reason to suspect, that the publication or programme in question was of, or included, the matter in question.

(5) Where an offence under subsection (3) committed by a body corporate is proved to have been committed with the consent or connivance of, or to be attributable to any neglect on the part of–

(a) a director, manager, secretary or other similar officer of the body corporate, or

(b) a person purporting to act in any such capacity,

he as well as the body corporate is guilty of the offence and liable to be proceeded against and punished accordingly.

(6) In relation to a body corporate whose affairs are managed by its members 'director', in subsection (5), means a member of the body corporate.

(7) 'Restricted reporting order' means–

(a) in subsections (1) and (3), an order–

(i) made in exercise of a power conferred by rules made by virtue of this section, and

(ii) prohibiting the publication in Great Britain of identifying matter in a written publication available to the public or its inclusion in a relevant programme for reception in Great Britain, and

(b) in subsection (2), an order which is a restricted reporting order for the purposes of section 11.

(8) In this section–

'identifying matter', in relation to a person, means any matter likely to lead members of the public to identify him as a person affected by, or as the person making, the allegation,

'relevant programme' has the same meaning as in the Sexual Offences (Amendment) Act 1992,

'sexual misconduct' means the commission of a sexual offence, sexual harassment or other adverse conduct (of whatever nature) related to sex, and conduct is related to sex whether the relationship with sex lies in the character of the conduct or in its having reference to the sex or sexual orientation of the person at whom the conduct is directed,

'sexual offence' means any offence to which section 4 of the Sexual Offences (Amendment) Act 1976, the Sexual Offences (Amendment) Act 1992 or section 274(2) of the Criminal Procedure (Scotland) Act

1995 applies (offences under the Sexual Offences Act 1956, Part I of the Criminal Law (Consolidation) (Scotland) Act 1995 and certain other enactments), and

'written publication' has the same meaning as in the Sexual Offences (Amendment) Act 1992.

Restriction of publicity in disability cases

32 (1) This section applies to proceedings–

(a) on an appeal against a decision of an employment tribunal to make, or not to make, a restricted reporting order, or

(b) on an appeal against any interlocutory decision of an employment tribunal in proceedings in which the employment tribunal has made a restricted reporting order which it has not revoked.

(2) Appeal Tribunal procedure rules may, as respects proceedings to which this section applies, include provision for–

(a) enabling the Appeal Tribunal, on the application of the complainant or of its own motion, to make a restricted reporting order having effect (if not revoked earlier) until the promulgation of the decision of the Appeal Tribunal, and

(b) where a restricted reporting order is made in relation to an appeal which is being dealt with by the Appeal Tribunal together with any other proceedings, enabling the Appeal Tribunal to direct that the order is to apply also in relation to those other proceedings or such part of them as the Appeal Tribunal may direct.

(3) If any identifying matter is published or included in a relevant programme in contravention of a restricted reporting order–

(a) in the case of publication in a newspaper or periodical, any proprietor, any editor and any publisher of the newspaper or periodical,

(b) in the case of publication in any other form, the person publishing the matter, and

(c) in the case of matter included in a relevant programme–

(i) any body corporate engaged in providing the service in which the programme is included, and

(ii) any person having functions in relation to the programme corresponding to those of an editor of a newspaper,

shall be guilty of an offence and liable on summary conviction to a fine not exceeding level 5 on the standard scale.

(4) Where a person is charged with an offence under subsection (3), it is a defence to prove that at the time of the alleged offence he was not aware, and neither suspected nor had reason to suspect, that the publication or programme in question was of, or included, the matter in question.

(5) Where an offence under subsection (3) committed by a body corporate is proved to have been committed with the consent or connivance of, or to be attributable to any neglect on the part of–

(a) a director, manager, secretary or other similar officer of the body corporate, or

(b) a person purporting to act in any such capacity,

he as well as the body corporate is guilty of the offence and liable to be proceeded against and punished accordingly.

(6) In relation to a body corporate whose affairs are managed by its members 'director', in subsection (5), means a member of the body corporate.

(7) 'Restricted reporting order' means–

> (a) in subsection (1), an order which is a restricted reporting order for the purposes of section 12, and
>
> (b) in subsections (2) and (3), an order–
>
> > (i) made in exercise of a power conferred by rules made by virtue of this section, and
> >
> > (ii) prohibiting the publication in Great Britain of identifying matter in a written publication available to the public or its inclusion in a relevant programme for reception in Great Britain.

(8) In this section–

'complainant' means the person who made the complaint to which the proceedings before the Appeal Tribunal relate,

'identifying matter' means any matter likely to lead members of the public to identify the complainant or such other persons (if any) as may be named in the order,

'promulgation' has such meaning as may be prescribed by rules made by virtue of this section,

'relevant programme' means a programme included in a programme service, within the meaning of the Broadcasting Act 1990, and

'written publication' includes a film, a sound track and any other record in permanent form but does not include an indictment or other document prepared for use in particular legal proceedings.

Restriction of vexatious proceedings

33 (1) If, on an application made by the Attorney General or the Lord Advocate under this section, the Appeal Tribunal is satisfied that a person has habitually and persistently and without any reasonable ground–

> (a) instituted vexatious proceedings, whether in an employment tribunal or before the Appeal Tribunal, and whether against the same person or against different persons, or
>
> (b) made vexatious applications in any proceedings, whether in an employment tribunal or before the Appeal Tribunal,

the Appeal Tribunal may, after hearing the person or giving him an opportunity of being heard, make a restriction of proceedings order.

(2) A 'restriction of proceedings order' is an order that–

> (a) no proceedings shall without the leave of the Appeal Tribunal be instituted in any employment tribunal or before the Appeal Tribunal by the person against whom the order is made,
>
> (b) any proceedings instituted by him in any employment tribunal or before the Appeal Tribunal before the making of the order shall not be continued by him without the leave of the Appeal Tribunal, and
>
> (c) no application (other than one for leave under this section) is to be made by him in any proceedings in any employment tribunal or before the Appeal Tribunal without the leave of the Appeal Tribunal.

(3) A restriction of proceedings order may provide that it is to cease to have effect at the end of a specified period, but otherwise it remains in force indefinitely.

(4) Leave for the institution or continuance of, or for the making of an application in, any proceedings in an employment tribunal or before the Appeal Tribunal by a person who is the subject of a restriction of proceedings order shall not be given unless the Appeal Tribunal is satisfied–
   (a) that the proceedings or application are not an abuse of the process of the tribunal in question, and
   (b) that there are reasonable grounds for the proceedings or application.

(5) A copy of a restriction of proceedings order shall be published in the London Gazette and the Edinburgh Gazette.

Costs and expenses

34 (1) Appeal Tribunal procedure rules may include provision for the award of costs or expenses.

(2) Rules under subsection (1) may include provision authorising the Appeal Tribunal to have regard to a person's ability to pay when considering the making of an award against him under such rules.

(3) Appeal Tribunal procedure rules may include provision for authorising the Appeal Tribunal–
   (a) to disallow all or part of the costs or expenses of a representative of a party to proceedings before it by reason of that representative's conduct of the proceedings;
   (b) to order a representative of a party to proceedings before it to meet all or part of the costs or expenses incurred by a party by reason of the representative's conduct of the proceedings.

(4) Appeal Tribunal procedure rules may also include provision for taxing or otherwise settling the costs or expenses referred to in subsection (1) or (3)(b) (and, in particular in England and Wales, for enabling the amount of such costs to be assessed by way of detailed assessment in the High Court).

DECISIONS AND FURTHER APPEALS

Powers of Appeal Tribunal

35 (1) For the purpose of disposing of an appeal, the Appeal Tribunal may–
   (a) exercise any of the powers of the body or officer from whom the appeal was brought, or
   (b) remit the case to that body or officer.

(2) Any decision or award of the Appeal Tribunal on an appeal has the same effect, and may be enforced in the same manner, as a decision or award of the body or officer from whom the appeal was brought.

   . . .

Appeals from Appeal Tribunal

37 (1) Subject to subsection (3), an appeal on any question of law lies from any decision or order of the Appeal Tribunal to the relevant appeal court with the leave of the Appeal Tribunal or of the relevant appeal court.

(2) In subsection (1) the 'relevant appeal court' means–

(a) in the case of proceedings in England and Wales, the Court of Appeal, and

(b) in the case of proceedings in Scotland, the Court of Session.

(3) No appeal lies from a decision of the Appeal Tribunal refusing leave for the institution or continuance of, or for the making of an application in, proceedings by a person who is the subject of a restriction of proceedings order made under section 33.

(4) This section is without prejudice to section 13 of the Administration of Justice Act 1960 (appeal in case of contempt of court).

PART III: SUPPLEMENTARY

CROWN EMPLOYMENT AND PARLIAMENTARY STAFF

Crown employment

38 (1) This Act has effect in relation to Crown employment and persons in Crown employment as it has effect in relation to other employment and other employees.

(2) In this Act 'Crown employment' means employment under or for the purposes of a government department or any officer or body exercising on behalf of the Crown functions conferred by a statutory provision.

(3) For the purposes of the application of this Act in relation to Crown employment in accordance with subsection (1)–

(a) references to an employee shall be construed as references to a person in Crown employment, and

(b) references to a contract of employment shall be construed as references to the terms of employment of a person in Crown employment.

(4) Subsection (1)–

(a) does not apply to service as a member of the naval, military or air forces of the Crown, but

(b) does apply to employment by an association established for the purposes of Part XI of the Reserve Forces Act 1996, Part VI of the Reserve Forces Act 1980.

Parliamentary staff

39 (1) This Act has effect in relation to employment as a relevant member of the House of Lords staff or a relevant member of the House of Commons staff as it has effect in relation to other employment.

(2) Nothing in any rule of law or the law or practice of Parliament prevents a relevant member of the House of Lords staff or a relevant member of the House of Commons staff from bringing before an employment tribunal proceedings of any description which could be brought before such a tri-

bunal by a person who is not a relevant member of the House of Lords staff or a relevant member of the House of Commons staff.

(3) For the purposes of the application of this Act in relation to a relevant member of the House of Commons staff–

    (a) references to an employee shall be construed as references to a relevant member of the House of Commons staff, and

    (b) references to a contract of employment shall be construed as including references to the terms of employment of a relevant member of the House of Commons staff.

(4) In this Act 'relevant member of the House of Lords staff' means any person who is employed under a contract of employment with the Corporate Officer of the House of Lords.

(5) In this Act 'relevant member of the House of Commons staff' has the same meaning as in section 195 of the Employment Rights Act 1996; and (subject to an Order in Council under subsection (12) of that section)–

    (a) subsections (6) and (7) of that section have effect for determining who is the employer of a relevant member of the House of Commons staff for the purposes of this Act, and

    (b) subsection (8) of that section applies in relation to proceedings brought by virtue of this section.

GENERAL

Power to amend Act

40 (1) The Secretary of State may by order–

    (a) provide that any provision of this Act to which this section applies and which is specified in the order shall not apply to persons, or to employments, of such classes as may be prescribed in the order, or

    (b) provide that any provision of this Act to which this section applies shall apply to persons or employments of such classes as may be prescribed in the order subject to such exceptions and modifications as may be so prescribed.

(2) This section applies to sections 3, 8, 16 and 17 and to section 18 so far as deriving from section 133 of the Employment Protection (Consolidation) Act 1978.

Orders, regulations and rules

41 (1) Any power conferred by this Act on a Minister of the Crown to make an order, and any power conferred by this Act to make regulations or rules, is exercisable by statutory instrument.

(2) No recommendation shall be made to Her Majesty to make an Order in Council under section 38(4), and no order shall be made under section 3, 4(4) or 40, unless a draft of the Order in Council or order has been laid before Parliament and approved by a resolution of each House of Parliament.

(3) A statutory instrument containing–

(a) an order made by a Minister of the Crown under any other provision of this Act except Part II of Schedule 2, or

(b) regulations or rules made under this Act,

is subject to annulment in pursuance of a resolution of either House of Parliament.

(4) Any power conferred by this Act which is exercisable by statutory instrument includes power to make such incidental, supplementary or transitional provision as appears to the Minister exercising the power to be necessary or expedient.

Interpretation

42 (1) In this Act–

'the Appeal Tribunal' means the Employment Appeal Tribunal,

'Appeal Tribunal procedure rules' shall be construed in accordance with section 30(1),

'appointed member' shall be construed in accordance with section 22(1)(c),

'conciliation officer' means an officer designated by the Advisory, Conciliation and Arbitration Service under section 211 of the Trade Union and Labour Relations (Consolidation) Act 1992,

'contract of employment' means a contract of service or apprenticeship, whether express or implied, and (if it is express) whether oral or in writing,

'employee' means an individual who has entered into or works under (or, where the employment has ceased, worked under) a contract of employment,

'employer', in relation to an employee, means the person by whom the employee is (or, where the employment has ceased, was) employed,

'employers' association' has the same meaning as in the Trade Union and Labour Relations (Consolidation) Act 1992,

'employment' means employment under a contract of employment and 'employed' shall be construed accordingly,

'employment tribunal procedure regulations' shall be construed in accordance with section 7(1),

'statutory provision' means a provision, whether of a general or a special nature, contained in, or in any document made or issued under, any Act, whether of a general or special nature,

'successor', in relation to the employer of an employee, means (subject to subsection (2)) a person who in consequence of a change occurring (whether by virtue of a sale or other disposition or by operation of law) in the ownership of the undertaking, or of the part of the undertaking, for the purposes of which the employee was employed, has become the owner of the undertaking or part, and

'trade union' has the meaning given by section 1 of the Trade Union and Labour Relations (Consolidation) Act 1992.

(2) The definition of 'successor' in subsection (1) has effect (subject to the necessary modifications) in relation to a case where–

(a) the person by whom an undertaking or part of an undertaking is owned immediately before a change is one of the persons by whom (whether as partners, trustees or otherwise) it is owned immediately after the change, or

(b) the persons by whom an undertaking or part of an undertaking is owned immediately before a change (whether as partners, trustees or otherwise) include the persons by whom, or include one or more of the persons by whom, it is owned immediately after the change,

as it has effect where the previous owner and the new owner are wholly different persons.

(3) For the purposes of this Act any two employers shall be treated as associated if–

(a) one is a company of which the other (directly or indirectly) has control, or

(b) both are companies of which a third person (directly or indirectly) has control;

and 'associated employer' shall be construed accordingly.

FINAL PROVISIONS

. . .

Commencement

46   This Act shall come into force at the end of the period of three months beginning with the day on which it is passed.

Extent

47   This Act does not extend to Northern Ireland.

Short title

48   This Act may be cited as the Employment Tribunals Act 1996.

SCHEDULE 2: TRANSITIONAL PROVISIONS, SAVINGS AND TRANSITORY PROVISIONS

Part I: Transitional Provisions and Savings

1   The substitution of this Act for the provisions repealed or revoked by this Act does not affect the continuity of the law.

2   Anything done, or having effect as done, (including the making of subordinate legislation) under or for the purposes of any provision repealed or revoked by this Act has effect as if done under or for the purposes of any corresponding provision of this Act.

3   Any reference (express or implied) in this Act or any other enactment, or in any instrument or document, to a provision of this Act is (so far as the context permits) to be read as (according to the context) being or including in relation to times, circumstances and purposes the commencement of this Act a reference to the corresponding provision repealed or revoked by this Act.

4 (1) Any reference (express or implied) in any enactment, or in any instrument or document, to a provision repealed or revoked by this Act is (so far as the context permits) to be read as (according to the context) being or including in relation to times, circumstances and purposes after the commencement of this Act a reference to the corresponding provision of this Act.

(2) In particular, where a power conferred by an Act is expressed to be exercisable in relation to enactments contained in Acts passed before or in the same Session as the Act conferring the power, the power is also exercisable in relation to provisions of this Act which reproduce such enactments.

5 Paragraphs 1 to 4 have effect in place of section 17(2) of the Interpretation Act 1978 (but are without prejudice to any other provision of that Act).

6 The repeal by the Act of section 130 of, and Schedule 10 to, the Employment Protection (Consolidation) Act 1978 (jurisdiction of referees under specified provisions to be exercised by employment tribunals) does not affect–

(a) the operation of those provisions in relation to any question which may arise after the commencement of this Act, or

(b) the continued operation of those provisions after the commencement of this Act in relation to any question which has arisen before that commencement.

Part II: Transitory Provisions

9 (1) If section 31 of the Trade Union Reform and Employment Rights Act 1993 has not come into force before the commencement of this Act, section 38 shall have effect until the relevant commencement date as if for subsection (4) there were substituted–

'(4) Subsection (1)–

(a) does not apply to service as a member of the naval, military or air forces of the Crown, but

(b) does apply to employment by an association established for the purposes of Part XI of the Reserve Forces Act 1996.'

(2) The reference in sub-paragraph (1) to the relevant commencement date is a reference–

(a) if an order has been made before the commencement of this Act appointing a day after that commencement as the day on which section 31 of the Trade Union Reform and Employment Rights Act 1993 is to come into force, to the day so appointed, and

(b) otherwise, to such day as the Secretary of State may by order appoint.

. . .

Employment Act 2002 ss29–33 and Schs 2, 3 and 4

STATUTORY PROCEDURES

Statutory dispute resolution procedures

29 (1) Schedule 2 (which sets out the statutory dispute resolution procedures) shall have effect.

(2) The Secretary of State may by order–
  (a) amend Schedule 2;
  (b) make provision for the Schedule to apply, with or without modifications, as if–
    (i) any individual of a description specified in the order who would not otherwise be an employee for the purposes of the Schedule were an employee for those purposes; and
    (ii) a person of a description specified in the order were, in the case of any such individual, the individual's employer for those purposes.

(3) Before making an order under this section, the Secretary of State must consult the Advisory, Conciliation and Arbitration Service.

Contracts of employment

30 (1) Every contract of employment shall have effect to require the employer and employee to comply, in relation to any matter to which a statutory procedure applies, with the requirements of the procedure.

(2) Subsection (1) shall have effect notwithstanding any agreement to the contrary, but does not affect so much of an agreement to follow a particular procedure as requires the employer or employee to comply with a requirement which is additional to, and not inconsistent with, the requirements of the statutory procedure.

(3) The Secretary of State may for the purpose of this section by regulations make provision about the application of the statutory procedures.

(4) In this section, 'contract of employment' has the same meaning as in the Employment Rights Act 1996.

Non-completion of statutory procedure: adjustment of awards

31 (1) This section applies to proceedings before an employment tribunal relating to a claim under any of the jurisdictions listed in Schedule 3 by an employee.

(2) If, in the case of proceedings to which this section applies, it appears to the employment tribunal that–
  (a) the claim to which the proceedings relate concerns a matter to which one of the statutory procedures applies,
  (b) the statutory procedure was not completed before the proceedings were begun, and
  (c) the non-completion of the statutory procedure was wholly or mainly attributable to failure by the employee–
    (i) to comply with a requirement of the procedure, or
    (ii) to exercise a right of appeal under it,
    it must, subject to subsection (4), reduce any award which it makes to the employee by 10 per cent, and may, if it considers it just and equitable in all the circumstances to do so, reduce it by a further amount, but not so as to make a total reduction of more than 50 per cent.

(3) If, in the case of proceedings to which this section applies, it appears to the employment tribunal that–
  (a) the claim to which the proceedings relate concerns a matter to which one of the statutory procedures applies,

(b) the statutory procedure was not completed before the proceedings were begun, and

(c) the non-completion of the statutory procedure was wholly or mainly attributable to failure by the employer to comply with a requirement of the procedure,

it must, subject to subsection (4), increase any award which it makes to the employee by 10 per cent and may, if it considers it just and equitable in all the circumstances to do so, increase it by a further amount, but not so as to make a total increase of more than 50 per cent.

(4) The duty under subsection (2) or (3) to make a reduction or increase of 10 per cent does not apply if there are exceptional circumstances which would make a reduction or increase of that percentage unjust or inequitable, in which case the tribunal may make no reduction or increase or a reduction or increase of such lesser percentage as it considers just and equitable in all the circumstances.

(5) Where an award falls to be adjusted under this section and under section 38, the adjustment under this section shall be made before the adjustment under that section.

(6) The Secretary of State may for the purposes of this section by regulations–

(a) make provision about the application of the statutory procedures;

(b) make provision about when a statutory procedure is to be taken to be completed;

(c) make provision about what constitutes compliance with a requirement of a statutory procedure;

(d) make provision about circumstances in which a person is to be treated as not subject to, or as having complied with, such a requirement;

(e) make provision for a statutory procedure to have effect in such circumstance as may be specified by the regulations with such modifications as may be so specified;

(f) make provision about when an employee is required to exercise a right of appeal under a statutory procedure.

(7) The Secretary of State may by order–

(a) amend Schedule 3 for the purpose of–

(i)   adding a jurisdiction to the list in that Schedule, or

(ii) removing a jurisdiction from that list;

(b) make provision, in relation to a jurisdiction listed in Schedule 3, for this section not to apply to proceedings relating to claims of a description specified in the order;

(c) make provision for this section to apply, with or without modifications, as if–

(i)   any individual of a description specified in the order who would not otherwise be an employee for the purposes of this section were an employee for those purposes, and

(ii) a person of a description specified in the order were, in the case of any such individual, the individual's employer for those purposes.

Complaints about grievances

32 (1) This section applies to the jurisdictions listed in Schedule 4.

(2) An employee shall not present a complaint to an employment tribunal under a jurisdiction to which this section applies if–
  (a) it concerns a matter in relation to which the requirement in paragraph 6 or 9 of Schedule 2 applies, and
  (b) the requirement has not been complied with.

(3) An employee shall not present a complaint to an employment tribunal under a jurisdiction to which this section applies if–
  (a) it concerns a matter in relation to which the requirement in paragraph 6 or 9 of Schedule 2 has been complied with, and
  (b) less than 28 days have passed since the day on which the requirement was complied with.

(4) An employee shall not present a complaint to an employment tribunal under a jurisdiction to which this section applies if–
  (a) it concerns a matter in relation to which the requirement in paragraph 6 or 9 of Schedule 2 has been complied with, and
  (b) the day on which the requirement was complied with was more than one month after the end of the original time limit for making the complaint.

(5) In such circumstances as the Secretary of State may specify by regulations, an employment tribunal may direct that subsection (4) shall not apply in relation to a particular matter.

(6) An employment tribunal shall be prevented from considering a complaint presented in breach of subsections (2) to (4), but only if–
  (a) the breach is apparent to the tribunal from the information supplied to it by the employee in connection with the bringing of the proceedings, or
  (b) the tribunal is satisfied of the breach as a result of his employer raising the issue of compliance with those provisions in accordance with regulations under section 7 of the Employment Tribunals Act 1996 (c 17) (employment tribunal procedure regulations).

(7) The Secretary of State may for the purposes of this section by regulations–
  (a) make provision about the application of the procedures set out in Part 2 of Schedule 2;
  (b) make provision about what constitutes compliance with paragraph 6 or 9 of that Schedule;
  (c) make provision about circumstances in which a person is to be treated as having complied with paragraph 6 or 9 of that Schedule;
  (d) make provision for paragraph 6 or 9 of that Schedule to have effect in such circumstances as may be specified by the regulations with such modifications as may be so specified.

(8) The Secretary of State may by order–
  (a) amend, repeal or replace any of subsections (2) to (4);
  (b) amend Schedule 4;
  (c) make provision for this section to apply, with or without modifications, as if–
    (i) any individual of a description specified in the order who would not

> otherwise be an employee for the purposes of this section were an employee for those purposes, and
>
> (ii) a person of a description specified in the order were, in the case of any such individual, the individual's employer for those purposes.

(9) Before making an order under subsection (8)(a), the Secretary of State must consult the Advisory, Conciliation and Arbitration Service.

(10)In its application to orders under subsection (8)(a), section 51(1)(b) includes power to amend this section.

Consequential adjustment of time limits

33 (1) The Secretary of State may, in relation to a jurisdiction listed in Schedule 3 or 4, by regulations make provision about the time limit for beginning proceedings in respect of a claim concerning a matter to which a statutory procedure applies.

(2) Regulations under this section may, in particular–

> (a) make provision extending, or authorising the extension of, the time for beginning proceedings,
>
> (b) make provision about the exercise of a discretion to extend the time for beginning proceedings, or
>
> (c) make provision treating proceedings begun out of time as begun within time.

. . .

SCHEDULE 2: STATUTORY DISPUTE RESOLUTION PROCEDURES

SECTION 29

PART 1: DISMISSAL AND DISCIPLINARY PROCEDURES

CHAPTER 1: STANDARD PROCEDURE

Step 1: statement of grounds for action and invitation to meeting

1 (1) The employer must set out in writing the employee's alleged conduct or characteristics, or other circumstances, which lead him to contemplate dismissing or taking disciplinary action against the employee.

(2) The employer must send the statement or a copy of it to the employee and invite the employee to attend a meeting to discuss the matter.

Step 2: meeting

2 (1) The meeting must take place before action is taken, except in the case where the disciplinary action consists of suspension.

(2) The meeting must not take place unless–

> (a) the employer has informed the employee what the basis was for including in the statement under paragraph 1(1) the ground or grounds given in it, and
>
> (b) the employee has had a reasonable opportunity to consider his response to that information.

(3) The employee must take all reasonable steps to attend the meeting.

(4) After the meeting, the employer must inform the employee of his decision and notify him of the right to appeal against the decision if he is not satisfied with it.

Step 3: appeal

3 (1) If the employee does wish to appeal, he must inform the employer.
   (2) If the employee informs the employer of his wish to appeal, the employer must invite him to attend a further meeting.
   (3) The employee must take all reasonable steps to attend the meeting.
   (4) The appeal meeting need not take place before the dismissal or disciplinary action takes effect.
   (5) After the appeal meeting, the employer must inform the employee of his final decision.

CHAPTER 2: MODIFIED PROCEDURE

Step 1: statement of grounds for action

4 The employer must—
   (a) set out in writing—
       (i)   the employee's alleged misconduct which has led to the dismissal,
       (ii) what the basis was for thinking at the time of the dismissal that the employee was guilty of the alleged misconduct, and
       (iii) the employee's right to appeal against dismissal, and
   (b) send the statement or a copy of it to the employee.

Step 2: appeal

5 (1) If the employee does wish to appeal, he must inform the employer.
   (2) If the employee informs the employer of his wish to appeal, the employer must invite him to attend a meeting.
   (3) The employee must take all reasonable steps to attend the meeting.
   (4) After the appeal meeting, the employer must inform the employee of his final decision.

PART 2: GRIEVANCE PROCEDURES

CHAPTER 1: STANDARD PROCEDURE

Step 1: statement of grievance

6 The employee must set out the grievance in writing and send the statement or a copy of it to the employer.

Step 2: meeting

7 (1) The employer must invite the employee to attend a meeting to discuss the grievance.
   (2) The meeting must not take place unless—
       (a) the employee has informed the employer what the basis for the grievance was when he made the statement under paragraph 6, and

   (b) the employer has had a reasonable opportunity to consider his response to that information.

(3) The employee must take all reasonable steps to attend the meeting.

(4) After the meeting, the employer must inform the employee of his decision as to his response to the grievance and notify him of the right to appeal against the decision if he is not satisfied with it.

Step 3: appeal

8 (1) If the employee does wish to appeal, he must inform the employer.

   (2) If the employee informs the employer of his wish to appeal, the employer must invite him to attend a further meeting.

   (3) The employee must take all reasonable steps to attend the meeting.

   (4) After the appeal meeting, the employer must inform the employee of his final decision.

CHAPTER 2: MODIFIED PROCEDURE

Step 1: statement of grievance

9   The employee must–

   (a) set out in writing–

      (i)   the grievance, and

      (ii) the basis for it, and

   (b) send the statement or a copy of it to the employer.

Step 2: response

10   The employer must set out his response in writing and send the statement or a copy of it to the employee.

PART 3: GENERAL REQUIREMENTS

Introductory

11   The following requirements apply to each of the procedures set out above (so far as applicable).

Timetable

12   Each step and action under the procedure must be taken without unreasonable delay.

Meetings

13 (1) Timing and location of meetings must be reasonable.

   (2) Meetings must be conducted in a manner that enables both employer and employee to explain their cases.

   (3) In the case of appeal meetings which are not the first meeting, the employer should, as far as is reasonably practicable, be represented by a more senior manager than attended the first meeting (unless the most senior manager attended that meeting).

PART 4: SUPPLEMENTARY

Status of meetings

14   A meeting held for the purposes of this Schedule is a hearing for the purposes of section 13(4) and (5) of the Employment Relations Act 1999 (c 26) (definition of 'disciplinary hearing' and 'grievance hearing' in relation to the right to be accompanied under section 10 of that Act).

Scope of grievance procedures

15 (1)   The procedures set out in Part 2 are only applicable to matters raised by an employee with his employer as a grievance.

(2)   Accordingly, those procedures are only applicable to the kind of disclosure dealt with in Part 4A of the Employment Rights Act 1996 (c 18) (protected disclosures of information) if information is disclosed by an employee to his employer in circumstances where–

(a)   the information relates to a matter which the employee could raise as a grievance with his employer, and

(b)   it is the intention of the employee that the disclosure should constitute the raising of the matter with his employer as a grievance.

SCHEDULE 3: TRIBUNAL JURISDICTIONS TO WHICH SECTION 31 APPLIES

Section 31

Section 2 of the Equal Pay Act 1970 (c 41) (equality clauses)

Section 63 of the Sex Discrimination Act 1975 (c 65) (discrimination in the employment field)

Section 54 of the Race Relations Act 1976 (c 74) (discrimination in the employment field)

Section 146 of the Trade Union and Labour Relations (Consolidation) Act 1992 (c 52) (detriment in relation to trade union membership and activities)

Paragraph 156 of Schedule A1 to that Act (detriment in relation to union recognition rights)

Section 17A of the Disability Discrimination Act 1995 (c 50) (discrimination in the employment field)

Section 23 of the Employment Rights Act 1996 (c 18) (unauthorised deductions and payments)

Section 48 of that Act (detriment in employment)

Section 111 of that Act (unfair dismissal)

Section 163 of that Act (redundancy payments)

Section 24 of the National Minimum Wage Act 1998 (c 39) (detriment in relation to national minimum wage)

. . .

The Employment Tribunal Extension of Jurisdiction (England and Wales) Order 1994 (SI 1994/1623) (breach of employment contract and termination)

The Employment Tribunal Extension of Jurisdiction (Scotland) Order 1994 (SI 1994/1624) (corresponding provision for Scotland)

Regulation 30 of the Working Time Regulations 1998 (SI 1998/1833) (breach of regulations)

Regulation 32 of the Transnational Information and Consultation of Employees Regulations 1999 (SI 1999/3323) (detriment relating to European Works Councils)

Regulation 28 of the Employment Equality (Sexual Orientation) Regulations 2003 (discrimination in the employment field)

Regulation 28 of the Employment Equality (Religion or Belief) Regulations 2003 (discrimination in the employment field)

SCHEDULE 4: TRIBUNAL JURISDICTIONS TO WHICH SECTION 32 APPLIES

Section 32

Section 2 of the Equal Pay Act 1970 (c 41) (equality clauses)

Section 63 of the Sex Discrimination Act 1975 (c 65) (discrimination in the employment field)

Section 54 of the Race Relations Act 1976 (c 74) (discrimination in the employment field)

Section 146 of the Trade Union and Labour Relations (Consolidation) Act 1992 (c 52) (detriment in relation to trade union membership and activities)

Paragraph 156 of Schedule A1 to that Act (detriment in relation to union recognition rights)

Section 17A of the Disability Discrimination Act 1995 (c 50) (discrimination in the employment field)

Section 23 of the Employment Rights Act 1996 (c 18) (unauthorised deductions and payments)

Section 48 of that Act (detriment in employment)

Section 111 of that Act (unfair dismissal)

Section 163 of that Act (redundancy payments)

Section 24 of the National Minimum Wage Act 1998 (c 39) (detriment in relation to national minimum wage)

. . .

Regulation 30 of the Working Time Regulations 1998 (SI No 1833) (breach of regulations)

Regulation 32 of the Transnational Information and Consultation of Employees Regulations 1999 (SI No 3323) (detriment relating to European Works Councils)

Regulation 28 of the Employment Equality (Sexual Orientation) Regulations 2003 SI No 1661 (discrimination in the employment field)

Regulation 28 of the Employment Equality (Religion or Belief) Regulations 2003 SI No 1660 (discrimination in the employment field)

Employment Tribunals Extension of Jurisdiction (England and Wales) Order 1994 SI No 1623

Citation, commencement and interpretation

1 (1) This Order may be cited as the Employment Tribunals Extension of Jurisdiction (England and Wales) Order 1994 and comes into force on the first day after it is made.

(2) In this Order–

'contract claim' means a claim in respect of which proceedings may be brought before an employment tribunal by virtue of article 3 or 4; . . .

. . .

Extension of jurisdiction

3 Proceedings may be brought before an employment tribunal in respect of a claim of an employee for the recovery of damages or any other sum (other than a claim for damages, or for a sum due, in respect of personal injuries) if–

(a) the claim is one to which section 131(2) of the 1978 Act applies and which a court in England and Wales would under the law for the time being in force have jurisdiction to hear and determine;

(b) the claim is not one to which article 5 applies; and

(c) the claim arises or is outstanding on the termination of the employee's employment.

4 Proceedings may be brought before an employment tribunal in respect of a claim of an employer for the recovery of damages or any other sum (other than a claim for damages, or for a sum due, in respect of personal injuries) if–

(a) the claim is one to which section 131(2) of the 1978 Act applies and which a court in England and Wales would under the law for the time being in force have jurisdiction to hear and determine;

(b) the claim is not one to which article 5 applies;

(c) the claim arises or is outstanding on the termination of the employment of the employee against whom it is made; and

(d) proceedings in respect of a claim of that employee have been brought before an employment tribunal by virtue of this Order.

5 This article applies to a claim for breach of a contractual term of any of the following descriptions–

(a) a term requiring the employer to provide living accommodation for the employee;

(b) a term imposing an obligation on the employer or the employee in connection with the provision of living accommodation;

(c) a term relating to intellectual property;

(d) a term imposing an obligation of confidence;

(e) a term which is a covenant in restraint of trade.

In this article, 'intellectual property' includes copyright, rights in performances, moral rights, design right, registered designs, patents and trade marks.

Manner in which proceedings may be brought

6   Proceedings on a contract claim may be brought before an employment tribunal by presenting a complaint to an employment tribunal.

Time within which proceedings may be brought

7   An employment tribunal shall not entertain a complaint in respect of an employee's contract claim unless it is presented–

(a) within the period of three months beginning with the effective date of termination of the contract giving rise to the claim, or

(b) where there is no effective date of termination, within the period of three months beginning with the last day upon which the employee worked in the employment which has terminated,

(ba) where the period within which a complaint must be presented in accordance with paragraph (a) or (b) is extended by regulation 15 of the Employment Act 2002 (Dispute Resolution) Regulations 2004, the period within which the complaint must be presented shall be the extended period rather than the period in paragraph (a) or (b), or

(c) where the tribunal is satisfied that it was not reasonably practicable for the complaint to be presented within whichever of those periods is applicable, within such further period as the tribunal considers reasonable.

8   An employment tribunal shall not entertain a complaint in respect of an employer's contract claim unless–

(a) it is presented at a time when there is before the tribunal a complaint in respect of a contract claim of a particular employee which has not been settled or withdrawn;

(b) it arises out of a contract with that employee; and

(c) it is presented–

    (i)   within the period of six weeks beginning with the day, or if more than one the last of the days, on which the employer (or other person who is the respondent party to the employee's contract claim) received from the tribunal a copy of an originating application in respect of a contract claim of that employee; or

    (ii) where the tribunal is satisfied that it was not reasonably practicable for the complaint to be presented within that period, within such further period as the tribunal considers reasonable.

Death and bankruptcy

9   (1) Where proceedings in respect of a contract claim have been brought before an employment tribunal and an employee or employer party to them dies before their conclusion, the proceedings shall not abate by reason of the death and the tribunal may, if it thinks it necessary in order to ensure that all

matters in dispute may be effectually and completely determined and adjudicated upon, order the personal representatives of the deceased party, or other persons whom the tribunal considers appropriate, to be made parties and the proceedings to be carried on as if they had been substituted for the deceased party.

(2) Where proceedings in respect of a contract claim have been brought before an employment tribunal and the employee or employer who is the applicant party to them becomes bankrupt before their conclusion, the proceedings shall not abate by reason of the bankruptcy and the tribunal may, if it thinks it necessary in order to ensure that all matters in dispute may be effectually and completely adjudicated upon, order the person in whom the interest of the bankrupt party has vested to be made a party and the proceedings to be carried on as if he had been substituted for the bankrupt party.

Limit on payment to be ordered

10　An employment tribunal shall not in proceedings in respect of a contract claim, or in respect of a number of contract claims relating to the same contract, order the payment of an amount exceeding £25,000.

Employment Tribunals Extension of Jurisdiction (Scotland) Order 1994 SI No 1624

Citation, commencement and interpretation

1　(1) This Order may be cited as the Employment Tribunals Extension of Jurisdiction (Scotland) Order 1994 and comes into force on the first day after it is made.

(2) In this Order–

'contract claim' means a claim in respect of which proceedings may be brought before an industrial tribunal by virtue of article 3 or 4; . . .

. . .

Extension of jurisdiction

3　Proceedings may be brought before an employment tribunal in respect of a claim of an employee for the recovery of damages or any other sum (other than a claim for damages, or for a sum due, in respect of personal injuries) if–

(a) the claim is one to which section 131(2) of the 1978 Act applies and which a court in Scotland would under the law for the time being in force have jurisdiction to hear and determine;

(b) the claim is not one to which article 5 applies; and

(c) the claim arises or is outstanding on the termination of the employee's employment.

4   Proceedings may be brought before an employment tribunal in respect of a claim of an employer for the recovery of damages or any other sum (other than a claim for damages, or for a sum due, in respect of personal injuries) if–

(a) the claim is one to which section 131(2) of the 1978 Act applies and which a court in Scotland would under the law for the time being in force have jurisdiction to hear and determine;

(b) the claim is not one to which article 5 applies;

(c) the claim arises or is outstanding on the termination of the employment of the employee against whom it is made; and

(d) proceedings in respect of a claim of that employee have been brought before an employment tribunal by virtue of this Order.

5   This article applies to a claim for breach of a contractual term of any of the following descriptions–

(a) a term requiring the employer to provide living accommodation for the employee;

(b) a term imposing an obligation on the employer or the employee in connection with the provision of living accommodation;

(c) a term relating to intellectual property;

(d) a term imposing an obligation of confidence;

(e) a term which is a covenant in restraint of trade.

In this article, 'intellectual property' includes copyright, rights in performances, moral rights, design right, registered designs, patents and trade marks.

Manner in which proceedings may be brought

6   Proceedings on a contract claim may be brought before an employment tribunal by presenting a complaint to an employment tribunal.

Time within which proceedings may be brought

7   An employment tribunal shall not entertain a complaint in respect of an employee's contract claim unless it is presented–

(a) within the period of three months beginning with the effective date of termination of the contract giving rise to the claim, or

(b) where there is no effective date of termination, within the period of three months beginning with the last day upon which the employee worked in the employment which has terminated, or

(ba) where the period within which a complaint must be presented in accordance with paragraph (a) or (b) is extended by regulation 15 of the Employment Act 2002 (Dispute Resolution) Regulations 2004, the period within which the complaint must be presented shall be the extended period rather than the period in paragraph (a) or (b), or

(c) where the tribunal is satisfied that it was not reasonably practicable for the complaint to be presented within whichever of those periods is applicable, within such further period as the tribunal considers reasonable.

8   An employment tribunal shall not entertain a complaint in respect of an employer's contract claim unless–

(a) it is presented at a time when there is before the tribunal a complaint in respect of a contract claim of a particular employee which has not been settled or withdrawn;

(b) it arises out of a contract with that employee; and

(c) it is presented–

   (i) within the period of six weeks beginning with the day, or if more than one the last of the days, on which the employer (or other person who is the respondent party to the employee's contract claim) received from the tribunal a copy of an originating application in respect of a contract claim of that employee; or

   (ii) where the tribunal is satisfied that it was not reasonably practicable for the complaint to be presented within that period, within such further periods as the tribunal considers reasonable.

Death and legal incapacity

9 Where proceedings in respect of a contract claim have been brought before an employment tribunal and an employee or employer party to them dies or comes under legal incapacity before the conclusion of the proceedings, the tribunal may order any person who represents that party or his estate to be made a party to the proceedings in place of the party who has died or come under legal incapacity and the proceedings to be carried on accordingly.

Limit on payment to be ordered

10 An employment tribunal shall not in proceedings in respect of a contract claim, or in respect of a number of contract claims relating to the same contract, order the payment of an amount exceeding £25,000.

Employment Tribunals (Constitution and Rules of Procedure) Regulations 2004 SI No 1861 (as amended)[1]

Citation, commencement and revocation

1 (1) These Regulations may be cited as the Employment Tribunals (Constitution and Rules of Procedure) Regulations 2004 and the Rules of Procedure contained in Schedules 1, 2, 3, 4, 5 and 6 to these Regulations may be referred to, respectively, as–

(a) the Employment Tribunals Rules of Procedure;

(b) the Employment Tribunals (National Security) Rules of Procedure;

(c) the Employment Tribunals (Levy Appeals) Rules of Procedure;

---

1 Amended by the Employment Tribunals (Constitution and Rules of Procedure) (Amendment) Regulations 2004 SI No 2351.

(d) the Employment Tribunals (Health and Safety – Appeals against Improvement and Prohibition Notices) Rules of Procedure;

(e) the Employment Tribunals (Non-Discrimination Notices Appeals) Rules of Procedure; and

(f) the Employment Tribunals (Equal Value) Rules of Procedure.

Interpretation

2   In these Regulations and in Schedules 1, 2, 3, 4, 5 and 6–

'ACAS' means the Advisory, Conciliation and Arbitration Service referred to in section 247 of TULR(C)A;

'appointing office holder' means, in England and Wales, the Lord Chancellor, and in Scotland, the Lord President;

'chairman' means the President or a member of the panel of chairmen appointed in accordance with regulation 8(3)(a), or, for the purposes of national security proceedings, a member of the panel referred to in regulation 10 selected in accordance with regulation 11(a), and in relation to particular proceedings it means the chairman to whom the proceedings have been referred by the President, Vice President or a Regional Chairman;

'compromise agreement' means an agreement to refrain from continuing proceedings where the agreement meets the conditions in section 203(3) of the Employment Rights Act;

'constructive dismissal' has the meaning set out in section 95(1)(c) of the Employment Rights Act;

'Disability Discrimination Act' means the Disability Discrimination Act 1995;

'electronic communication' has the meaning given to it by section 15(1) of the Electronic Communications Act 2000;

'Employment Act' means the Employment Act 2002;

'Employment Rights Act' means the Employment Rights Act 1996;

'Employment Tribunals Act' means the Employment Tribunals Act 1996;

'Employment Tribunal Office' means any office which has been established for any area in either England & Wales or Scotland specified by the President and which carries out administrative functions in support of functions being carried out by a tribunal or chairman, and in relation to particular proceedings it is the office notified to the parties in accordance with rule 61(3) of Schedule 1;

'enactment' includes an enactment comprised in, or in an instrument made under, an Act of the Scottish Parliament;

'Equal Pay Act' means the Equal Pay Act 1970;

'excluded person' means, in relation to any proceedings, a person who has been excluded from all or part of the proceedings by virtue of–

(a) a direction of a Minister of the Crown under rule 54(1)(b) or (c) of Schedule 1, or

(b) an order of the tribunal under rule 54(2)(a) read with 54(1)(b) or (c) of Schedule 1;

'hearing' means a case management discussion, pre-hearing review, review hearing or Hearing (as those terms are defined in Schedule 1) or a sitting of a chairman or a tribunal duly constituted for the purpose of receiving evidence, hearing addresses and witnesses or doing anything lawful to enable the chairman or tribunal to reach a decision on any question;

'legally represented' has the meaning set out in rule 38(5) of Schedule 1;

'Lord President' means the Lord President of the Court of Session;

'misconceived' includes having no reasonable prospect of success;

'national security proceedings' means proceedings in relation to which a direction is given under rule 54(1) of Schedule 1, or an order is made under rule 54(2) of that Schedule;

'old (England & Wales) regulations' means the Employment Tribunals (Constitution and Rules of Procedure) (Scotland) Regulations 2001;

'old (Scotland) regulations' means the Employment Tribunals (Constitution and Rules of Procedure) Regulations 2001;

'panel of chairmen' means a panel referred to in regulation 8(3)(a);

'President' means, in England and Wales, the person appointed or nominated by the Lord Chancellor to discharge for the time being the functions of the President of Employment Tribunals (England and Wales), and, in Scotland, the person appointed or nominated by the Lord President to discharge for the time being the functions of the President of Employment Tribunals (Scotland);

'Race Relations Act' means the Race Relations Act 1976;

'Regional Chairman' means a member of the panel of chairmen who has been appointed to the position of Regional Chairman in accordance with regulation 6 or who has been nominated to discharge the functions of a Regional Chairman in accordance with regulation 6;

'Register' means the Register of judgments and written reasons kept in accordance with regulation 17;

'Secretary' means a person for the time being appointed to act as the Secretary of employment tribunals either in England and Wales or in Scotland;

'Sex Discrimination Act' means the Sex Discrimination Act 1975;

'special advocate' means a person appointed in accordance with rule 8 of Schedule 2;

'tribunal' means an employment tribunal established in accordance with regulation 5, and in relation to any proceedings means the tribunal to which the proceedings have been referred by the President, Vice President or a Regional Chairman;

'TULR(C)A' means the Trade Union and Labour Relations (Consolidation) Act 1992;

'Vice President' means a person who has been appointed to the position of Vice President in accordance with regulation 7 or who has been nominated to discharge the functions of the Vice President in accordance with that regulation;

'writing' includes writing delivered by means of electronic communication.

Overriding objective

3   (1) The overriding objective of these regulations and the rules in Schedules 1, 2, 3, 4, 5 and 6 is to enable tribunals and chairmen to deal with cases justly.

   (2) Dealing with a case justly includes, so far as practicable–
   (a) ensuring that the parties are on an equal footing;
   (b) dealing with the case in ways which are proportionate to the complexity or importance of the issues;
   (c) ensuring that it is dealt with expeditiously and fairly; and
   (d) saving expense.

   (3) A tribunal or chairman shall seek to give effect to the overriding objective when it or he–
   (a) exercises any power given to it or him by these regulations or the rules in Schedules 1, 2, 3, 4, 5 and 6; or
   (b) interprets these regulations or any rule in Schedules 1, 2, 3, 4, 5 and 6.

   (4) The parties shall assist the tribunal or the chairman to further the over-riding objective.

President of Employment Tribunals

4   (1) There shall be a President of Employment Tribunals (England and Wales), responsible for the administration of justice by tribunals and chairmen in England and Wales, who shall be appointed by the Lord Chancellor and shall be a person described in paragraph (3).

   (2) There shall be a President of Employment Tribunals (Scotland), responsible for the administration of justice by tribunals and chairmen in Scotland, who shall be appointed by the Lord President and shall be a person described in paragraph (3).

   (3) A President shall be a person–
   (a) having a seven year general qualification within the meaning of section 71 of the Courts and Legal Services Act 1990;
   (b) being an advocate or solicitor admitted in Scotland of at least seven years standing; or
   (c) being a member of the Bar of Northern Ireland or solicitor of the Supreme Court of Northern Ireland of at least seven years standing.

   (4) A President may resign his office by notice in writing to the appointing office holder.

   (5) If the appointing office holder is satisfied that the President is incapacitated by infirmity of mind or body from discharging the duties of his office, or the President is adjudged to be bankrupt or makes a composition or arrangement with his creditors, the appointing office holder may revoke his appointment.

   (6) The functions of President under these Regulations may, if he is for any reason unable to act or during any vacancy in his office, be discharged by a person nominated for that purpose by the appointing office holder.

Establishment of employment tribunals

5   (1) Each President shall, in relation to that part of Great Britain for which he has responsibility, from time to time determine the number of tribunals to be established for the purposes of determining proceedings.

(2) The President, a Regional Chairman or the Vice President shall determine, in relation to the area specified in relation to him, at what times and in what places in that area tribunals and chairmen shall sit.

Regional Chairmen

6 (1) The Lord Chancellor may from time to time appoint Regional Chairmen from the panel of full-time chairmen and each Regional Chairman shall be responsible to the President (England and Wales) for the administration of justice by tribunals and chairmen in the area specified by the President (England and Wales) in relation to him.

(2) The President (England and Wales) or the Regional Chairman for an area may from time to time nominate a member of the panel of full time chairmen to discharge for the time being the functions of the Regional Chairman for that area.

Vice President

7 (1) The Lord President may from time to time appoint a Vice President from the panel of full time chairmen and the Vice President shall be responsible to the President (Scotland) for the administration of justice by tribunals and chairmen in Scotland.

(2) The President (Scotland) or the Vice President may from time to time nominate a member of the panel of full time chairmen to discharge for the time being the functions of the Vice President.

Panels of members of tribunals – general

8 (1) There shall be three panels of members of Employment Tribunals (England and Wales), as set out in paragraph (3).

(2) There shall be three panels of members of Employment Tribunals (Scotland), as set out in paragraph (3).

(3) The panels referred to in paragraphs (1) and (2) are–

(a) a panel of full-time and part-time chairmen appointed by the appointing office holder consisting of persons–

(i) having a seven year general qualification within the meaning of section 71 of the Courts and Legal Services Act 1990;

(ii) being an advocate or solicitor admitted in Scotland of at least seven years standing; or

(iii) being a member of the Bar of Northern Ireland or solicitor of the Supreme Court of Northern Ireland of at least seven years standing;

(b) a panel of persons appointed by the Secretary of State after consultation with such organisations or associations of organisations representative of employees as she sees fit; and

(c) a panel of persons appointed by the Secretary of State after consultation with such organisations or associations of organisations representative of employers as she sees fit.

(4) Members of the panels constituted under these Regulations shall hold and vacate office under the terms of the instrument under which they are

appointed but may resign their office by notice in writing, in the case of a member of the panel of chairmen, to the appointing office holder and, in any other case, to the Secretary of State; and any such member who ceases to hold office shall be eligible for reappointment.

(5) The President may establish further specialist panels of chairmen and persons referred to in paragraphs (3)(b) and (c) and may select persons from such specialist panels in order to deal with proceedings in which particular specialist knowledge would be beneficial.

Composition of tribunals – general

9 (1) For each hearing, the President, Vice President or the Regional Chairman shall select a chairman, who shall, subject to regulation 11, be a member of the panel of chairmen, and the President, Vice President or the Regional Chairman may select himself.

(2) In any proceedings which are to be determined by a tribunal comprising a chairman and two other members, the President, Regional Chairman or Vice President shall, subject to regulation 11, select one of those other members from the panel of persons appointed by the Secretary of State under regulation 8(3)(b) and the other from the panel of persons appointed under regulation 8(3)(c).

(3) In any proceedings which are to be determined by a tribunal whose composition is described in paragraph (2) or, as the case may be, regulation 11(b), those proceedings may, with the consent of the parties, be heard and determined in the absence of any one member other than the chairman.

(4) The President, Vice President, or a Regional Chairman may at any time select from the appropriate panel another person in substitution for the chairman or other member of the tribunal previously selected to hear any proceedings before a tribunal or chairman.

Panels of members of tribunals – national security proceedings

10 In relation to national security proceedings, the President shall–

(a) select a panel of persons from the panel of chairmen to act as chairmen in such cases; and

(b) select–

(i) a panel of persons from the panel referred to in regulation 8(3)(b) as persons suitable to act as members in such cases; and

(ii) a panel of persons from the panel referred to in regulation 8(3)(c) as persons suitable to act as members in such cases.

Composition of tribunals – national security proceedings

11 In relation to national security proceedings–

(a) the President, the Regional Chairman or the Vice President shall select a chairman, who shall be a member of the panel selected in accordance with regulation 10(a), and the President, Regional Chairman or Vice President may select himself; and

(b) in any such proceedings which are to be determined by a tribunal comprising a chairman and two other members, the President, Regional Chairman or Vice President shall select one of those other members from the panel selected in accordance with regulation 10(b)(i) and the other from the panel selected in accordance with regulation 10(b)(ii).

Modification of section 4 of the Employment Tribunals Act (national security proceedings)

12 (1) For the purposes of national security proceedings section 4 of the Employment Tribunals Act shall be modified as follows.

(2) In section 4(1)(a), for the words 'in accordance with regulations made under section 1(1)' substitute the words 'in accordance with regulation 11(a) of the Employment Tribunals (Constitution and Rules of Procedure) Regulations 2004'.

(3) In section 4(1)(b), for the words 'in accordance with regulations so made' substitute the words 'in accordance with regulation 11(b) of those Regulations'.

(4) In section 4(5), for the words 'in accordance with Regulations made under section 1(1)' substitute the words 'in accordance with regulation 10(a) of the Employment Tribunals (Constitution and Rules of Procedure) Regulations 2004'.

Practice directions

13 (1) The President may make practice directions about the procedure of employment tribunals in the area for which he is responsible, including practice directions about the exercise by tribunals or chairmen of powers under these Regulations or the Schedules to them.

(2) The power of the President to make practice directions under paragraph (1) includes power–

(a) to vary or revoke practice directions;

(b) to make different provision for different cases or different areas, including different provision for specific types of proceedings.

(3) The President shall publish a practice direction made under paragraph (1), and any revocation or variation of it, in such manner as he considers appropriate for bringing it to the attention of the persons to whom it is addressed.

Power to prescribe

14 (1) The Secretary of State may prescribe–

(a) one or more versions of a form, one of which shall be used by all claimants for the purpose of commencing proceedings in an employment tribunal ('claim form') except any claim or proceedings listed in paragraph (3);

(b) one or more versions of a form, one of which shall be used by all respondents to a claim for the purpose of responding to a claim before an employment tribunal ('response form') except respondents to a claim or proceedings listed in paragraph (3); and

(c) that the provision of certain information and answering of certain questions in a claim form or in a response form is mandatory in all proceedings save those listed in paragraph (3).

(2) The Secretary of State shall publish the forms and matters prescribed pursuant to paragraph (1) in such manner as she considers appropriate in order to bring them to the attention of potential claimants, respondents and their advisers.

(3) The proceedings referred to in paragraph (1) are–
   (a) those referred to an employment tribunal by a court;
   (b) proceedings to which any of Schedules 3 to 5 apply; or
   (c) proceedings brought under any of the following enactments–
      (i) sections 19, 20 or 22 of the National Minimum Wage Act 1998;
      (ii) section 11 of the Employment Rights Act where the proceedings are brought by the employer.

Calculation of time limits

15 (1) Any period of time for doing any act required or permitted to be done under any of the rules in Schedules 1, 2, 3, 4, 5 and 6 or under any decision, order or judgment of a tribunal or a chairman, shall be calculated in accordance with paragraphs (2) to (6).

(2) Where any act must or may be done within a certain number of days of or from an event, the date of that event shall not be included in the calculation. For example, a respondent is sent a copy of a claim on 1st October. He must present a response to the Employment Tribunal Office within 28 days of the date on which he was sent the copy. The last day for presentation of the response is 29th October.

(3) Where any act must or may be done not less than a certain number of days before or after an event, the date of that event shall not be included in the calculation. For example, if a party wishes to submit representations in writing for consideration by a tribunal at a hearing, he must submit them not less than 7 days before the hearing. If the hearing is fixed for 8th October, the representations must be submitted no later than 1st October.

(4) Where the tribunal or a chairman gives any decision, order or judgment which imposes a time limit for doing any act, the last date for compliance shall, wherever practicable, be expressed as a calendar date.

(5) In rule 14(4) of Schedule 1 the requirement to send the notice of hearing to the parties not less than 14 days before the date fixed for the hearing shall not be construed as a requirement for service of the notice to have been effected not less than 14 days before the hearing date, but as a requirement for the notice to have been placed in the post not less than 14 days before that date. For example, a hearing is fixed for 15th October. The last day on which the notice may be placed in the post is 1st October.

(6) Where any act must or may have been done within a certain number of days of a document being sent to a person by the Secretary, the date when the document was sent shall, unless the contrary is proved, be regarded as the date on the letter from the Secretary which accompanied the document. For example, a respondent must present his response to a claim to the Employment Tribunal Office within 28 days of the date on which he was sent a copy of the claim. If the letter from the Secretary sending him a copy of the claim is dated 1st October, the last day for presentation of the response is 29th October.

Application of Schedules 1–5 to proceedings

16 (1) Subject to paragraphs (2), (3) and (4), the rules in Schedule 1 shall apply in relation to all proceedings before an employment tribunal except where separate rules of procedure made under the provisions of any enactment are applicable.

(2) In proceedings to which the rules in Schedule 1 apply and in which any power conferred on the Minister, the tribunal or a chairman by rule 54 (national security proceedings) of Schedule 1 is exercised, Schedule 1 shall be modified in accordance with Schedule 2.

(3) The rules in Schedules 3, 4 and 5 shall apply to modify the rules in Schedule 1 in relation to proceedings which consist, respectively, in–

(a) an appeal by a person assessed to levy imposed under a levy order made under section 12 of the Industrial Training Act 1982;

(b) an appeal against an improvement or prohibition notice under section 24 of the Health and Safety at Work etc Act 1974; and

(c) an appeal against a non-discrimination notice under section 68 of the Sex Discrimination Act, section 59 of the Race Relations Act or paragraph 10 of Schedule 3 to the Disability Rights Commission Act 1999.

(4) In proceedings which involve an equal value claim (as defined in rule 2 of Schedule 6), Schedule 1 shall be modified in accordance with Schedule 6.

Register

17 (1) The Secretary shall maintain a Register which shall be open to the inspection of any person without charge at all reasonable hours.

(2) The Register shall contain a copy of all judgments and any written reasons issued by any tribunal or chairman which are required to be entered in the Register in accordance with the rules in Schedules 1 to 5.

(3) The Register, or any part of it, may be kept by means of a computer.

Proof of decisions of tribunals

18 The production in any proceedings in any court of a document purporting to be certified by the Secretary to be a true copy of an entry of a judgment in the Register shall, unless the contrary is proved, be sufficient evidence of the document and of the facts stated therein.

Jurisdiction of tribunals in Scotland and in England and Wales

19 (1) An employment tribunal in England or Wales shall only have jurisdiction to deal with proceedings (referred to as 'English and Welsh proceedings') where–

(a) the respondent or one of the respondents resides or carries on business in England and Wales;

(b) had the remedy been by way of action in the county court, the cause of action would have arisen wholly or partly in England and Wales;

(c) the proceedings are to determine a question which has been referred to the tribunal by a court in England and Wales; or

(d) in the case of proceedings to which Schedule 3, 4 or 5 applies, the proceedings relate to matters arising in England and Wales.

(2) An employment tribunal in Scotland shall only have jurisdiction to deal with proceedings (referred to as 'Scottish proceedings') where–
  (a) the respondent or one of the respondents resides or carries on business in Scotland;
  (b) the proceedings relate to a contract of employment the place of execution or performance of which is in Scotland;
  (c) the proceedings are to determine a question which has been referred to the tribunal by a sheriff in Scotland; or
  (d) in the case of proceedings to which Schedule 3, 4 or 5 applies, the proceedings relate to matters arising in Scotland.

Transitional provisions

20 (1) These Regulations and Schedules 1 to 6 to them shall apply in relation to all proceedings to which they relate where those proceedings were commenced on or after 1 October 2004.

(2) These Regulations and Schedules 1 and 2 to them (with the exception of rules 1 to 3 and 38 to 48 of Schedule 1) shall apply to proceedings–
  (a) which were commenced prior to 1 October 2004; and
  (b) to which Schedule 1 to either the old (England & Wales) regulations or the old (Scotland) regulations applied;

provided that a copy of the originating application was not sent to the respondent prior to 1 October 2004.

(3) In relation to the proceedings described in paragraph (2), the following provisions of Schedule 1 to the old (England & Wales) regulations or the old (Scotland) regulations (as the case may be) shall continue to apply–
  (a) rule 1 (originating application);
  (b) rule 2 (action upon receipt of originating application) with the exception of paragraphs (2), (4) and (5) of that rule; and
  (c) rule 14 (costs).

(4) In relation to proceedings described in paragraph (2) but where a copy of the originating application was sent to the respondent prior to 1 October 2004, Schedules 1 and 2 to these Regulations shall apply with the exception of rules 1 to 9, 21 to 24, 33 and 38 to 48 of Schedule 1 and rules 2, 3 and 4 of Schedule 2.

(5) In relation to proceedings described in paragraph (4), the following provisions of the old (England & Wales) regulations or the old (Scotland) regulations (as the case may be) shall continue to apply–
  (a) in Schedule 1–
    (i)   rule 1 (originating application);
    (ii) rule 2 (action upon receipt of originating application) with the exception of paragraphs (2), (4) and (5) of that rule;
    (iii) rule 3 (appearance by respondent);
    (iv) rule 8 (national security);
    (v)   rule 14 (costs); and
  (b) rule 1 of Schedule 2.

(6) In relation to proceedings commenced prior to 1 October 2004 and to which Schedule 4, 5 or 6 to the old (England & Wales) regulations or the old

(Scotland) regulations (as the case may be) applied, the provisions of those schedules shall continue to apply to such proceedings.

(7) In relation to proceedings–

    (i)   which were commenced prior to 1 October 2004;

    (ii)   to which Schedule 3 to either the old (England & Wales) regulations or the old (Scotland) regulations applied; and

    (iii) in which the tribunal has not, prior to 1 October 2004, required a member of the panel of independent experts to prepare a report under section 2A(1)(b) of the Equal Pay Act;

these Regulations and rules 1 to 13 of Schedule 6, with the exception of rule 4(3)(a), shall apply.

(8) In relation to proceedings–

    (i)   which were commenced prior to 1 October 2004;

    (ii)   to which Schedule 3 to either the old (England & Wales) regulations or the old (Scotland) regulations applied; and

    (iii) in which the tribunal has, prior to 1 October 2004, required a member of the panel of independent experts to prepare a report under section 2A(1)(b) of the Equal Pay Act;

Schedule 3 to either the old (England & Wales) regulations or the old (Scotland) regulations (as the case may be) shall continue to apply.

(9) In relation to proceedings described in paragraph (8), the following rules of Schedule 6 shall also apply and shall take precedence over any conflicting provision in Schedule 3 to either the old (England & Wales) regulations or the old (Scotland) regulations, namely–

    –rules 3, 11(2), 11(4), 12, 13(1) and 13(3).

(10) Rule 14 of Schedule 6 shall apply to all proceedings to which, in accordance with this regulation, rule 10 of Schedule 2 applies.

SCHEDULE 1: THE EMPLOYMENT TRIBUNALS RULES OF PROCEDURE

HOW TO BRING A CLAIM

Starting a claim

1 (1) A claim shall be brought before an employment tribunal by the claimant presenting to an Employment Tribunal Office the details of the claim in writing. Those details must include all the relevant required information (subject to paragraph (5) of this rule and to rule 53 (Employment Agencies Act 1973)).

    (2) The claim may only be presented to an Employment Tribunal Office in England and Wales if it relates to English and Welsh proceedings (defined in regulation 19(1)). The claim may only be presented to an Employment Tribunal Office in Scotland if it relates to Scottish proceedings (defined in regulation 19(2)).

    (3) Unless it is a claim in proceedings described in regulation 14(3), a claim which is presented on or after 6 April 2005 must be presented on a claim

form which has been prescribed by the Secretary of State in accordance with regulation 14.

(4) Subject to paragraph (5) and to rule 53, the required information in relation to the claim is–

(a) each claimant's name;

(b) each claimant's address;

(c) the name of each person against whom the claim is made ('the respondent');

(d) each respondent's address;

(e) details of the claim;

(f) whether or not the claimant is or was an employee of the respondent;

(g) whether or not the claim includes a complaint that the respondent has dismissed the claimant or has contemplated doing so;

(h) whether or not the claimant has raised the subject matter of the claim with the respondent in writing at least 28 days prior to presenting the claim to an Employment Tribunal Office;

(i) if the claimant has not done as described in (h), why he has not done so.

(5) In the following circumstances the required information identified below is not required to be provided in relation to that claim–

(a) if the claimant is not or was not an employee of the respondent, the information in paragraphs (4)(g) to (i) is not required;

(b) if the claimant was an employee of the respondent and the claim consists only of a complaint that the respondent has dismissed the claimant or has contemplated doing so, the information in paragraphs (4)(h) and (i) is not required;

(c) if the claimant was an employee of the respondent and the claim does not relate to the claimant being dismissed or a contemplated dismissal by the respondent, and the claimant has raised the subject matter of the claim with the respondent as described in paragraph (4)(h), the information in paragraph (4)(i) is not required.

(6) References in this rule to being dismissed or a dismissal by the respondent do not include references to constructive dismissal.

(7) Two or more claimants may present their claims in the same document if their claims arise out of the same set of facts.

(8) When section 32 of the Employment Act applies to the claim or part of one and a chairman considers in accordance with subsection (6) of section 32 that there has been a breach of subsections (2) to (4) of that section, neither a chairman nor a tribunal shall consider the substance of the claim (or the relevant part of it) until such time as those subsections have been complied with in relation to the claim or the relevant part of it.

ACCEPTANCE OF CLAIM PROCEDURE

What the tribunal does after receiving the claim

2 (1) On receiving the claim the Secretary shall consider whether the claim or part of it should be accepted in accordance with rule 3. If a claim or part of

one is not accepted the tribunal shall not proceed to deal with any part which has not been accepted (unless it is accepted at a later date). If no part of a claim is accepted the claim shall not be copied to the respondent.

(2) If the Secretary accepts the claim or part of it, he shall–

(a) send a copy of the claim to each respondent and record in writing the date on which it was sent;

(b) inform the parties in writing of the case number of the claim (which must from then on be referred to in all correspondence relating to the claim) and the address to which notices and other communications to the Employment Tribunal Office must be sent;

(c) inform the respondent in writing about how to present a response to the claim, the time limit for doing so, what may happen if a response is not entered within the time limit and that the respondent has a right to receive a copy of any judgment disposing of the claim;

(d) when any enactment relevant to the claim provides for conciliation, notify the parties that the services of a conciliation officer are available to them;

(e) when rule 22 (fixed period for conciliation) applies, notify the parties of the date on which the conciliation officer's duty to conciliate ends and that after that date the services of a conciliation officer shall be available to them only in limited circumstances; and

(f) if only part of the claim has been accepted, inform the claimant and any respondent which parts of the claim have not been accepted and that the tribunal shall not proceed to deal with those parts unless they are accepted at a later date.

When the claim will not be accepted by the Secretary

3 (1) When a claim is required by rule 1(3) to be presented using a prescribed form, but the prescribed form has not been used, the Secretary shall not accept the claim and shall return it to the claimant with an explanation of why the claim has been rejected and provide a prescribed claim form.

(2) The Secretary shall not accept the claim (or a relevant part of one) if it is clear to him that one or more of the following circumstances applies–

(a) the claim does not include all the relevant required information;

(b) the tribunal does not have power to consider the claim (or that relevant part of it); or

(c) section 32 of the Employment Act (complaints about grievances) applies to the claim or part of it and the claim has been presented to the tribunal in breach of subsections (2) to (4) of section 32.

(3) If the Secretary decides not to accept a claim or part of one for any of the reasons in paragraph (2), he shall refer the claim together with a statement of his reasons for not accepting it to a chairman. The chairman shall decide in accordance with the criteria in paragraph (2) whether the claim or part of it should be accepted and allowed to proceed.

(4) If the chairman decides that the claim or part of one should be accepted he shall inform the Secretary in writing and the Secretary shall accept the relevant part of the claim and then proceed to deal with it in accordance with rule 2(2).

(5) If the chairman decides that the claim or part of it should not be accepted he shall record his decision together with the reasons for it in writing in a document signed by him. The Secretary shall as soon as is reasonably practicable inform the claimant of that decision and the reasons for it in writing together with information on how that decision may be reviewed or appealed.

(6) Where a claim or part of one has been presented to the tribunal in breach of subsections (2) to (4) of section 32 of the Employment Act, the Secretary shall notify the claimant of the time limit which applies to the claim or the part of it concerned and shall inform the claimant of the consequences of not complying with section 32 of that Act.

(7) Except for the purposes of paragraph (6) and (8) or any appeal to the Employment Appeal Tribunal, where a chairman has decided that a claim or part of one should not be accepted such a claim (or the relevant part of it) is to be treated as if it had not been received by the Secretary on that occasion.

(8) Any decision by a chairman not to accept a claim or part of one may be reviewed in accordance with rules 34 to 36. If the result of such review is that any parts of the claim should have been accepted, then paragraph (7) shall not apply to the relevant parts of that claim and the Secretary shall then accept such parts and proceed to deal with it as described in rule 2(2).

(9) A decision to accept or not to accept a claim or part of one shall not bind any future tribunal or chairman where any of the issues listed in paragraph (2) fall to be determined later in the proceedings.

(10) Except in rule 34 (review of other judgments and decisions), all references to a claim in the remainder of these rules are to be read as references to only the part of the claim which has been accepted.

RESPONSE

Responding to the claim

4 (1) If the respondent wishes to respond to the claim made against him he must present his response to the Employment Tribunal Office within 28 days of the date on which he was sent a copy of the claim. The response must include all the relevant required information. The time limit for the respondent to present his response may be extended in accordance with paragraph (4).

(2) Unless it is a response in proceedings described in regulation 14(3), any response presented on or after 6 April 2005 must be on a response form prescribed by the Secretary of State pursuant to regulation 14.

(3) The required information in relation to the response is–
(a) the respondent's full name;
(b) the respondent's address;
(c) whether or not the respondent wishes to resist the claim in whole or in part; and
(d) if the respondent wishes to so resist, on what grounds.

(4) The respondent may apply under rule 11 for an extension of the time limit

within which he is to present his response. The application must be presented to the Employment Tribunal Office within 28 days of the date on which the respondent was sent a copy of the claim (unless the application is made under rule 33(1)) and must explain why the respondent cannot comply with the time limit. Subject to rule 33, the chairman shall only extend the time within which a response may be presented if he is satisfied that it is just and equitable to do so.

(5) A single document may include the response to more than one claim if the relief claimed arises out of the same set of facts, provided that in respect of each of the claims to which the single response relates–
  (a) the respondent intends to resist all the claims and the grounds for doing so are the same in relation to each claim; or
  (b) the respondent does not intend to resist any of the claims.

(6) A single document may include the response of more than one respondent to a single claim provided that–
  (a) each respondent intends to resist the claim and the grounds for doing so are the same for each respondent; or
  (b) none of the respondents intends to resist the claim.

ACCEPTANCE OF RESPONSE PROCEDURE

What the tribunal does after receiving the response

5 (1) On receiving the response the Secretary shall consider whether the response should be accepted in accordance with rule 6. If the response is not accepted it shall be returned to the respondent and (subject to paragraphs (5) and (6) of rule 6) the claim shall be dealt with as if no response to the claim had been presented.

(2) If the Secretary accepts the response he shall send a copy of it to all other parties and record in writing the date on which he does so.

When the response will not be accepted by the Secretary

6 (1) Where a response is required to be presented using a prescribed form by rule 4(2), but the prescribed form has not been used, the Secretary shall not accept the response and shall return it to the respondent with an explanation of why the response has been rejected and provide a prescribed response form.

(2) The Secretary shall not accept the response if it is clear to him that any of the following circumstances apply–
  (a) the response does not include all the required information (defined in rule 4(3));
  (b) the response has not been presented within the relevant time limit.

(3) If the Secretary decides not to accept a response for either of the reasons in paragraph (2), he shall refer the response together with a statement of his reasons for not accepting the response to a chairman. The chairman shall decide in accordance with the criteria in paragraph (2) whether the response should be accepted.

(4) If the chairman decides that the response should be accepted he shall

inform the Secretary in writing and the Secretary shall accept the response and then deal with it in accordance with rule 5(2).

(5) If the chairman decides that the response should not be accepted he shall record his decision together with the reasons for it in writing in a document signed by him. The Secretary shall inform both the claimant and the respondent of that decision and the reasons for it. The Secretary shall also inform the respondent of the consequences for the respondent of that decision and how it may be reviewed or appealed.

(6) Any decision by a chairman not to accept a response may be reviewed in accordance with rules 34 to 36. If the result of such a review is that the response should have been accepted, then the Secretary shall accept the response and proceed to deal with the response as described in rule 5(2).

Counterclaims

7 (1) When a respondent wishes to present a claim against the claimant ('a counterclaim') in accordance with article 4 of the Employment Tribunals Extension of Jurisdiction (England and Wales) Order 1994, or as the case may be, article 4 of the Employment Tribunals Extension of Jurisdiction (Scotland) Order 1994, he must present the details of his counterclaim to the Employment Tribunal Office in writing. Those details must include–
(a) the respondent's name;
(b) the respondent's address;
(c) the name of each claimant whom the counterclaim is made against;
(d) the claimant's address;
(e) details of the counterclaim.

(2) A chairman may in relation to particular proceedings by order made under rule 10(1) establish the procedure which shall be followed by the respondent making the counterclaim and any claimant responding to the counterclaim.

(3) The President may by a practice direction made under regulation 13 make provision for the procedure which is to apply to counterclaims generally.

CONSEQUENCES OF A RESPONSE NOT BEING PRESENTED OR ACCEPTED

Default judgments

8 (1) In any proceedings if the relevant time limit for presenting a response has passed, a chairman may, in the circumstances listed in paragraph (2), issue a default judgment to determine the claim without a hearing if he considers it appropriate to do so.

(2) Those circumstances are when either–
(a) no response in those proceedings has been presented to the Employment Tribunal Office within the relevant time limit;
(b) a response has been so presented, but a decision has been made not to accept the response either by the Secretary under rule 6(1) or by a chairman under rule 6(3), and the Employment Tribunal Office has not received an application under rule 34 to have that decision reviewed; or
(c) a response has been accepted in those proceedings, but the respondent has stated in the response that he does not intend to resist the claim.

(3) A default judgment may determine liability only or it may determine liability and remedy. If a default judgment determines remedy it shall be such remedy as it appears to the chairman that the claimant is entitled to on the basis of the information before him.

(4) Any default judgment issued by a chairman under this rule shall be recorded in writing and shall be signed by him. The Secretary shall send a copy of that judgment to the parties, to ACAS, and, if the proceedings were referred to the tribunal by a court, to that court. The Secretary shall also inform the parties of their right to have the default judgment reviewed under rule 33. The Secretary shall put a copy of the default judgment on the Register (subject to rule 49 (sexual offences and the Register)).

(5) The claimant or respondent may apply to have the default judgment reviewed in accordance with rule 33.

(6) If the parties settle the proceedings (either by means of a compromise agreement (as defined in rule 23(2)) or through ACAS) before or on the date on which a default judgment in those proceedings is issued, the default judgment shall have no effect.

(7) When paragraph (6) applies, either party may apply under rule 33 to have the default judgment revoked.

Taking no further part in the proceedings

9 A respondent who has not presented a response to a claim or whose response has not been accepted shall not be entitled to take any part in the proceedings except to–

    (a) make an application under rule 33 (review of default judgments);

    (b) make an application under rule 35 (preliminary consideration of application for review) in respect of rule 34(3)(a), (b) or (e);

    (c) be called as a witness by another person; or

    (d) be sent a copy of a document or corrected entry in accordance with rule 8(4), 29(2) or 37;

and in these rules the word 'party' or 'respondent' includes a respondent only in relation to his entitlement to take such a part in the proceedings, and in relation to any such part which he takes.

CASE MANAGEMENT

General power to manage proceedings

10 (1) Subject to the following rules, the chairman may at any time either on the application of a party or on his own initiative make an order in relation to any matter which appears to him to be appropriate. Such orders may be any of those listed in paragraph (2) or such other orders as he thinks fit. Subject to the following rules, orders may be issued as a result of a chairman considering the papers before him in the absence of the parties, or at a hearing (see regulation 2 for the definition of 'hearing').

    (2) Examples of orders which may be made under paragraph (1) are orders–

        (a) as to the manner in which the proceedings are to be conducted, including any time limit to be observed;

(b) that a party provide additional information;

(c) requiring the attendance of any person in Great Britain either to give evidence or to produce documents or information;

(d) requiring any person in Great Britain to disclose documents or information to a party to allow a party to inspect such material as might be ordered by a County Court (or in Scotland, by a sheriff);

(e) extending any time limit, whether or not expired (subject to rules 4(4), 11(2), 25(5), 30(5), 33(1), 35(1), 38(7) and 42(5) of this Schedule, and to rule 3(4) of Schedule 2);

(f) requiring the provision of written answers to questions put by the tribunal or chairman;

(g) that, subject to rule 22(8), a short conciliation period be extended into a standard conciliation period;

(h) staying (in Scotland, sisting) the whole or part of any proceedings;

(i) that part of the proceedings be dealt with separately;

(j) that different claims be considered together;

(k) that any person who the chairman or tribunal considers may be liable for the remedy claimed should be made a respondent in the proceedings;

(l) dismissing the claim against a respondent who is no longer directly interested in the claim;

(m) postponing or adjourning any hearing;

(n) varying or revoking other orders;

(o) giving notice to the parties of a pre-hearing review or the Hearing;

(p) giving notice under rule 19;

(q) giving leave to amend a claim or response;

(r) that any person who the chairman or tribunal considers has an interest in the outcome of the proceedings may be joined as a party to the proceedings;

(s) that a witness statement be prepared or exchanged; or

(t) as to the use of experts or interpreters in the proceedings.

(3) An order may specify the time at or within which and the place at which any act is required to be done. An order may also impose conditions and it shall inform the parties of the potential consequences of non-compliance set out in rule 13.

(4) When a requirement has been imposed under paragraph (1) the person subject to the requirement may make an application under rule 11 (applications in proceedings) for the order to be varied or revoked.

(5) An order described in either paragraph (2)(d) which requires a person other than a party to grant disclosure or inspection of material may be made only when the disclosure sought is necessary in order to dispose fairly of the claim or to save expense.

(6) Any order containing a requirement described in either sub-paragraph (2)(c) or (d) shall state that under section 7(4) of the Employment Tribunals Act, any person who without reasonable excuse fails to comply with the requirement shall be liable on summary conviction to a fine, and the document shall also state the amount of the maximum fine.

(7) An order as described in paragraph (2)(j) may be made only if all relevant parties have been given notice that such an order may be made and they have been given the opportunity to make oral or written representations as to why such an order should or should not be made.

(8) Any order made under this rule shall be recorded in writing and signed by the chairman and the Secretary shall inform all parties to the proceedings of any order made as soon as is reasonably practicable.

Applications in proceedings

11 (1) At any stage of the proceedings a party may apply for an order to be issued, varied or revoked or for a case management discussion or pre-hearing review to be held.

(2) An application for an order must be made not less than 10 days before the date of the hearing at which it is to be considered (if any) unless it is not reasonably practicable to do so, or the chairman or tribunal considers it in the interests of justice that shorter notice be allowed. The application must (unless a chairman orders otherwise) be in writing to the Employment Tribunal Office and include the case number for the proceedings and the reasons for the request. If the application is for a case management discussion or a pre-hearing review to be held, it must identify any orders sought.

(3) An application for an order must include an explanation of how the order would assist the tribunal or chairman in dealing with the proceedings efficiently and fairly.

(4) When a party is legally represented in relation to the application (except where the application is for a witness order described in rule 10(2)(c) only), that party or his representative must, at the same time as the application is sent to the Employment Tribunal Office, provide all other parties with the following information in writing–
   (a) details of the application and the reasons why it is sought;
   (b) notification that any objection to the application must be sent to the Employment Tribunal Office within 7 days of receiving the application, or before the date of the hearing (whichever date is the earlier);
   (c) that any objection to the application must be copied to both the Employment Tribunal Office and all other parties;
   and the party or his representative must confirm in writing to the Employment Tribunal Office that this rule has been complied with.

(5) Where a party is not legally represented in relation to the application, the Secretary shall inform all other parties of the matters listed in paragraphs (4)(a) to (c).

(6) A chairman may refuse a party's application and if he does so the Secretary shall inform the parties in writing of such refusal unless the application is refused at a hearing.

Chairman acting on his own initiative

12 (1) Subject to paragraph (2) and to rules 10(7) and 18(7), a chairman may make an order on his own initiative with or without hearing the parties or giving them an opportunity to make written or oral representations. He may also decide to hold a case management discussion or pre-hearing review on his own initiative.

(2) Where a chairman makes an order without giving the parties the opportunity to make representations–

  (a) the Secretary must send to the party affected by such order a copy of the order and a statement explaining the right to make an application under paragraph (2)(b); and

  (b) a party affected by the order may apply to have it varied or revoked.

(3) An application under paragraph (2)(b) must (subject to rule 10(2)(e)) be made before the time at which, or the expiry of the period within which, the order was to be complied with. Such an application must (unless a chairman orders otherwise) be made in writing to an Employment Tribunal Office and it must include the reasons for the application. Paragraphs (4) and (5) of rule 11 apply in relation to informing the other parties of the application.

Compliance with orders and practice directions

13 (1) If a party does not comply with an order made under these rules, under rule 8 of Schedule 3, rule 7 of Schedule 4 or a practice direction, a chairman or tribunal–

  (a) may make an order in respect of costs or preparation time under rules 38 to 46; or

  (b) may (subject to paragraph (2) and rule 19) at a pre-hearing review or a Hearing make an order to strike out the whole or part of the claim or, as the case may be, the response and, where appropriate, order that a respondent be debarred from responding to the claim altogether.

(2) An order may also provide that unless the order is complied with, the claim or, as the case may be, the response shall be struck out on the date of non-compliance without further consideration of the proceedings or the need to give notice under rule 19 or hold a pre-hearing review or Hearing.

(3) Chairmen and tribunals shall comply with any practice directions issued under regulation 13.

DIFFERENT TYPES OF HEARING

Hearings – general

14 (1) A chairman or a tribunal (depending on the relevant rule) may hold the following types of hearing–

  (a) a case management discussion under rule 17;

  (b) a pre-hearing review under rule 18;

  (c) a Hearing under rule 26; or

  (d) a review hearing under rule 33 or 36.

(2) So far as it appears appropriate to do so, the chairman or tribunal shall seek to avoid formality in his or its proceedings and shall not be bound by any enactment or rule of law relating to the admissibility of evidence in proceedings before the courts.

(3) The chairman or tribunal (as the case may be) shall make such enquiries of persons appearing before him or it and of witnesses as he or it considers

appropriate and shall otherwise conduct the hearing in such manner as he or it considers most appropriate for the clarification of the issues and generally for the just handling of the proceedings.

(4) Unless the parties agree to shorter notice, the Secretary shall send notice of any hearing (other than a case management discussion) to every party not less than 14 days before the date fixed for the hearing and shall inform them that they have the opportunity to submit written representations and to advance oral argument. The Secretary shall give the parties reasonable notice before a case management discussion is held.

(5) If a party wishes to submit written representations for consideration at a hearing (other than a case management discussion) he shall present them to the Employment Tribunal Office not less than 7 days before the hearing and shall at the same time send a copy to all other parties.

(6) The tribunal or chairman may, if it or he considers it appropriate, consider representations in writing which have been submitted otherwise than in accordance with paragraph (5).

Use of electronic communications

15 (1) A hearing (other than those mentioned in sub-paragraphs (c) and (d) of rule 14(1)) may be conducted by use of electronic communications provided that the chairman or tribunal conducting the hearing considers it just and equitable to do so.

(2) Where a hearing is required by these rules to be held in public and it is to be conducted by use of electronic communications in accordance with this rule then, subject to rule 16, it must be held in a place to which the public has access and using equipment so that the public is able to hear all parties to the communication.

Hearings which may be held in private

16 (1) A hearing or part of one may be conducted in private for the purpose of hearing from any person evidence or representations which in the opinion of the tribunal or chairman is likely to consist of information–

(a) which he could not disclose without contravening a prohibition imposed by or by virtue of any enactment;

(b) which has been communicated to him in confidence, or which he has otherwise obtained in consequence of the confidence placed in him by another person; or

(c) the disclosure of which would, for reasons other than its effect on negotiations with respect to any of the matters mentioned in section 178(2) of TULR(C)A, cause substantial injury to any undertaking of his or any undertaking in which he works.

(2) Where a tribunal or chairman decides to hold a hearing or part of one in private, it or he shall give reasons for doing so. A member of the Council on Tribunals (in Scotland, a member of the Council on Tribunals or its Scottish Committee) shall be entitled to attend any Hearing or pre-hearing review taking place in private in his capacity as a member.

CASE MANAGEMENT DISCUSSIONS

Conduct of case management discussions

17 (1) Case management discussions are interim hearings and may deal with matters of procedure and management of the proceedings and they may be held in private. Case management discussions shall be conducted by a chairman.

(2) Any determination of a person's civil rights or obligations shall not be dealt with in a case management discussion. The matters listed in rule 10(2) are examples of matters which may be dealt with at case management discussions. Orders and judgments listed in rule 18(7) may not be made at a case management discussion.

PRE-HEARING REVIEWS

Conduct of pre-hearing reviews

18 (1) Pre-hearing reviews are interim hearings and shall be conducted by a chairman unless the circumstances in paragraph (3) are applicable. Subject to rule 16, they shall take place in public.

(2) At a pre-hearing review the chairman may carry out a preliminary consideration of the proceedings and he may–

(a) determine any interim or preliminary matter relating to the proceedings;

(b) issue any order in accordance with rule 10 or do anything else which may be done at a case management discussion;

(c) order that a deposit be paid in accordance with rule 20 without hearing evidence;

(d) consider any oral or written representations or evidence;

(e) deal with an application for interim relief made under section 161 of TULR(C)A or section 128 of the Employment Rights Act.

(3) Pre-hearing reviews shall be conducted by a tribunal composed in accordance with section 4(1) and (2) of the Employment Tribunals Act if–

(a) a party has made a request in writing not less than 10 days before the date on which the pre-hearing review is due to take place that the pre-hearing review be conducted by a tribunal instead of a chairman; and

(b) a chairman considers that one or more substantive issues of fact are likely to be determined at the pre-hearing review, that it would be desirable for the pre-hearing review to be conducted by a tribunal and he has issued an order that the pre-hearing review be conducted by a tribunal.

(4) If an order is made under paragraph (3), any reference to a chairman in relation to a pre-hearing review shall be read as a reference to a tribunal.

(5) Notwithstanding the preliminary or interim nature of a pre-hearing review, at a pre-hearing review the chairman may give judgment on any preliminary issue of substance relating to the proceedings. Judgments or orders made at a pre-hearing review may result in the proceedings being struck out or dismissed or otherwise determined with the result that a Hearing is no longer necessary in those proceedings.

(6) Before a judgment or order listed in paragraph (7) is made, notice must be given in accordance with rule 19. The judgments or order listed in paragraph (7) must be made at a pre-hearing review or a Hearing if one of the parties has so requested. If no such request has been made such judgments or order may be made in the absence of the parties.

(7) Subject to paragraph (6), a chairman or tribunal may make a judgment or order–

    (a) as to the entitlement of any party to bring or contest particular proceedings;

    (b) striking out or amending all or part of any claim or response on the grounds that it is scandalous, or vexatious or has no reasonable prospect of success;

    (c) striking out any claim or response (or part of one) on the grounds that the manner in which the proceedings have been conducted by or on behalf of the claimant or the respondent (as the case may be) has been scandalous, unreasonable or vexatious;

    (d) striking out a claim which has not been actively pursued;

    (e) striking out a claim or response (or part of one) for non-compliance with an order or practice direction;

    (f) striking out a claim where the chairman or tribunal considers that it is no longer possible to have a fair Hearing in those proceedings;

    (g) making a restricted reporting order (subject to rule 50).

(8) A claim or response or any part of one may be struck out under these rules only on the grounds stated in sub-paragraphs (7)(b) to (f).

(9) If at a pre-hearing review a requirement to pay a deposit under rule 20 has been considered, the chairman who conducted that pre-hearing review shall not be a member of the tribunal at the Hearing in relation to those proceedings.

Notice requirements

19 (1) Before a chairman or a tribunal makes a judgment or order described in rule 18(7), except where the order is one described in rule 13(2) or it is a temporary restricted reporting order made in accordance with rule 50, the Secretary shall send notice to the party against whom it is proposed that the order or judgment should be made. The notice shall inform him of the order or judgment to be considered and give him the opportunity to give reasons why the order or judgment should not be made. This paragraph shall not be taken to require the Secretary to send such notice to that party if that party has been given an opportunity to give reasons orally to the chairman or the tribunal as to why the order should not be made.

(2) Where a notice required by paragraph (1) is sent in relation to an order to strike out a claim which has not been actively pursued, unless the contrary is proved, the notice shall be treated as if it were received by the addressee if it has been sent to the address specified in the claim as the address to which notices are to be sent (or to any subsequent replacement for that address which has been notified to the Employment Tribunal Office).

PAYMENT OF A DEPOSIT

Requirement to pay a deposit in order to continue with proceedings

20 (1) At a pre-hearing review if a chairman considers that the contentions put forward by any party in relation to a matter required to be determined by a tribunal have little reasonable prospect of success, the chairman may make an order against that party requiring the party to pay a deposit of an amount not exceeding £500 as a condition of being permitted to continue to take part in the proceedings relating to that matter.

(2) No order shall be made under this rule unless the chairman has taken reasonable steps to ascertain the ability of the party against whom it is proposed to make the order to comply with such an order, and has taken account of any information so ascertained in determining the amount of the deposit.

(3) An order made under this rule, and the chairman's grounds for making such an order, shall be recorded in a document signed by the chairman. A copy of that document shall be sent to each of the parties and shall be accompanied by a note explaining that if the party against whom the order is made persists in making those contentions relating to the matter to which the order relates, he may have an award of costs or preparation time made against him and could lose his deposit.

(4) If a party against whom an order has been made does not pay the amount specified in the order to the Secretary either–
 (a) within the period of 21 days of the day on which the document recording the making of the order is sent to him; or
 (b) within such further period, not exceeding 14 days, as the chairman may allow in the light of representations made by that party within the period of 21 days;
 a chairman shall strike out the claim or response of that party or, as the case may be, the part of it to which the order relates.

(5) The deposit paid by a party under an order made under this rule shall be refunded to him in full except where rule 47 applies.

CONCILIATION

Documents to be sent to conciliators

21 In proceedings brought under the provisions of any enactment providing for conciliation, the Secretary shall send copies of all documents, orders, judgments, written reasons and notices to an ACAS conciliation officer except where the Secretary and ACAS have agreed otherwise.

Fixed period for conciliation

22 (1) This rule and rules 23 and 24 apply to all proceedings before a tribunal which are brought under any enactment which provides for conciliation except national security proceedings and proceedings which include a claim made under one or more of the following enactments–
 (a) the Equal Pay Act, section 2(1);

(b) the Sex Discrimination Act, Part II, section 63;

(c) the Race Relations Act, Part II, section 54;

(d) the Disability Discrimination Act, Part II, section 17A or 25(8);

(e) the Employment Equality (Sexual Orientation) Regulations 2003;

(f) the Employment Equality (Religion or Belief) Regulations 2003; and

(g) Employment Rights Act, sections 47B, 103A and 105(6A).

(2) In all proceedings to which this rule applies there shall be a conciliation period to give a time limited opportunity for the parties to reach an ACAS conciliated settlement (the 'conciliation period'). In proceedings in which there is more than one respondent there shall be a conciliation period in relation to each respondent.

(3) In any proceedings to which this rule applies a Hearing shall not take place during a conciliation period and where the time and place of a Hearing has been fixed to take place during a conciliation period, such Hearing shall be postponed until after the end of any conciliation period. The fixing of the time and place for the Hearing may take place during a conciliation period. Pre-hearing reviews and case management discussions may take place during a conciliation period.

(4) In relation to each respondent the conciliation period commences on the date on which the Secretary sends a copy of the claim to that respondent. The duration of the conciliation period shall be determined in accordance with the following paragraphs and rule 23.

(5) In any proceedings which consist of claims under any of the following enactments (but no other enactments) the conciliation period is seven weeks (the 'short conciliation period')–

(a) Employment Tribunals Act, section 3 (breach of contract);

(b) the following provisions of the Employment Rights Act –

   (i) sections 13 to 27 (failure to pay wages or an unauthorised deduction of wages);

   (ii) section 28 (right to a guarantee payment);

   (iii) section 50 (right to time off for public duties);

   (iv) section 52 (right to time off to look for work or arrange training);

   (v) section 53 (right to remuneration for time off under section 52);

   (vi) section 55 (right to time off for ante-natal care);

   (vii) section 56 (right to remuneration for time off under section 55);

   (viii) section 64 (failure to pay remuneration whilst suspended for medical reasons);

   (ix) section 68 (right to remuneration whilst suspended on maternity grounds);

   (x) sections 163 or 164 (failure to pay a redundancy payment);

(c) the following provisions of TULR(C)A –

   (i) section 68 (right not to suffer deduction of unauthorised subscriptions)

   (ii) section 168 (time off for carrying out trade union duties);

   (iii) section 169 (payment for time off under section 168);

   (iv) section 170 (time off for trade union activities);

   (v) section 192 (failure to pay remuneration under a protective award);

(d) regulation 11(5) of the Transfer of Undertakings (Protection of Employment) Regulations 1981 (failure to pay compensation following failure to inform or consult).

(6) In all other proceedings to which this rule applies the conciliation period is thirteen weeks (the 'standard conciliation period').

(7) In proceedings to which the standard conciliation period applies, that period shall be extended by a period of a further two weeks if ACAS notifies the Secretary in writing that all of the following circumstances apply before the expiry of the standard conciliation period–

(a) all parties to the proceedings agree to the extension of any relevant conciliation period;

(b) a proposal for settling the proceedings has been made by a party and is under consideration by the other parties to the proceedings; and

(c) ACAS considers it probable that the proceedings will be settled during the further extended conciliation period.

(8) A short conciliation period in any proceedings may, if that period has not already ended, be extended into a standard conciliation period if a chairman considers on the basis of the complexity of the proceedings that a standard conciliation period would be more appropriate. Where a chairman makes an order extending the conciliation period in such circumstances, the Secretary shall inform the parties to the proceedings and ACAS in writing as soon as is reasonably practicable.

Early termination of conciliation period

23 (1) Should one of the following circumstances arise during a conciliation period (be it short or standard) which relates to a particular respondent (referred to in this rule as the relevant respondent), that conciliation period shall terminate early on the relevant date specified (and if more than one circumstance or date listed below is applicable to any conciliation period, that conciliation period shall terminate on the earliest of those dates)–

(a) where a default judgment is issued against the relevant respondent which determines both liability and remedy, the date on which the default judgment is signed;

(b) where a default judgment is issued against the relevant respondent which determines liability only, the date which is 14 days after the date on which the default judgment is signed;

(c) where either the claim or the response entered by the relevant respondent is struck out, the date on which the judgment to strike out is signed;

(d) where the claim is withdrawn, the date of receipt by the Employment Tribunal Office of the notice of withdrawal;

(e) where the claimant or the relevant respondent has informed ACAS in writing that they do not wish to proceed with attempting to conciliate in relation to those proceedings, the date on which ACAS sends notice of such circumstances to the parties and to the Employment Tribunal Office;

(f) where the claimant and the relevant respondent have reached a settlement by way of a compromise agreement (including a compromise agreement to refer proceedings to arbitration), the date on which the Employment Tribunal Office receives notice from both of those parties to that effect;

(g) where the claimant and the relevant respondent have reached a settlement through a conciliation officer (including a settlement to refer the proceedings to arbitration), the date of the settlement;

(h) where no response presented by the relevant respondent has been accepted in the proceedings and no default judgment has been issued against that respondent, the date which is 14 days after the expiry of the time limit for presenting the response to the Secretary.

(2) Where a chairman or tribunal makes an order which re-establishes the relevant respondent's right to respond to the claim (for example, revoking a default judgment) and when that order is made, the conciliation period in relation to that respondent has terminated early under paragraph (1) or has otherwise expired, the chairman or tribunal may order that a further conciliation period shall apply in relation to that respondent if they consider it appropriate to do so.

(3) When an order is made under paragraph (2), the further conciliation period commences on the date of that order and the duration of that period shall be determined in accordance with paragraphs (5) to (8) of rule 22 and paragraph (1) of this rule as if the earlier conciliation period in relation to that respondent had not taken place.

Effect of staying or sisting proceedings on the conciliation period

24 Where during a conciliation period an order is made to stay (or in Scotland, sist) the proceedings, that order has the effect of suspending any conciliation period in those proceedings. Any unexpired portion of a conciliation period takes effect from the date on which the stay comes to an end (or in Scotland, the sist is recalled) and continues for the duration of the unexpired portion of that conciliation period or two weeks (whichever is the greater).

WITHDRAWAL OF PROCEEDINGS

Right to withdraw proceedings

25 (1) A claimant may withdraw all or part of his claim at any time – this may be done either orally at a hearing or in writing in accordance with paragraph (2).

(2) To withdraw a claim or part of one in writing the claimant must inform the Employment Tribunal Office of the claim or the parts of it which are to be withdrawn. Where there is more than one respondent the notification must specify against which respondents the claim is being withdrawn.

(3) The Secretary shall inform all other parties of the withdrawal. Withdrawal takes effect on the date on which the Employment Tribunal Office (in the case of written notifications) or the tribunal (in the case of oral notification) receives notice of it and where the whole claim is withdrawn, subject to paragraph (4), proceedings are brought to an end against the relevant

respondent on that date. Withdrawal does not affect proceedings as to costs, preparation time or wasted costs.

(4) Where a claim has been withdrawn, a respondent may make an application to have the proceedings against him dismissed. Such an application must be made by the respondent in writing to the Employment Tribunal Office within 28 days of the notice of the withdrawal being sent to the respondent. If the respondent's application is granted and the proceedings are dismissed those proceedings cannot be continued by the claimant (unless the decision to dismiss is successfully reviewed or appealed).

(5) The time limit in paragraph (4) may be extended by a chairman if he considers it just and equitable to do so.

THE HEARING

Hearings

26 (1) A Hearing is held for the purpose of determining outstanding procedural or substantive issues or disposing of the proceedings. In any proceedings there may be more than one Hearing and there may be different categories of Hearing, such as a Hearing on liability, remedies, costs (in Scotland, expenses) or preparation time.

(2) Any Hearing of a claim shall be heard by a tribunal composed in accordance with section 4(1) and (2) of the Employment Tribunals Act.

(3) Any Hearing of a claim shall take place in public, subject to rule 16.

What happens at the Hearing

27 (1) The President, Vice President or a Regional Chairman shall fix the date, time and place of the Hearing and the Secretary shall send to each party a notice of the Hearing together with information and guidance as to procedure at the Hearing.

(2) Subject to rule 14(3), at the Hearing a party shall be entitled to give evidence, to call witnesses, to question witnesses and to address the tribunal.

(3) The tribunal shall require parties and witnesses who attend the Hearing to give their evidence on oath or affirmation.

(4) The tribunal may exclude from the Hearing any person who is to appear as a witness in the proceedings until such time as they give evidence if it considers it in the interests of justice to do so.

(5) If a party fails to attend or to be represented (for the purpose of conducting the party's case at the Hearing) at the time and place fixed for the Hearing, the tribunal may dismiss or dispose of the proceedings in the absence of that party or may adjourn the Hearing to a later date.

(6) If the tribunal wishes to dismiss or dispose of proceedings in the circumstances described in paragraph (5), it shall first consider any information in its possession which has been made available to it by the parties.

(7) At a Hearing a tribunal may exercise any powers which may be exercised by a chairman under these rules.

ORDERS, JUDGMENTS AND REASONS

Orders and judgments

28 (1) Chairmen or tribunals may issue the following–

(a) a 'judgment', which is a final determination of the proceedings or of a particular issue in those proceedings; it may include an award of compensation, a declaration or recommendation and it may also include orders for costs, preparation time or wasted costs;

(b) an 'order', which may be issued in relation to interim matters and it will require a person to do or not to do something.

(2) If the parties agree in writing upon the terms of any order or judgment a chairman or tribunal may, if he or it thinks fit, make such order or judgment.

(3) At the end of a hearing the chairman (or, as the case may be, the tribunal) shall either issue any order or judgment orally or shall reserve the judgment or order to be given in writing at a later date.

(4) Where a tribunal is composed of three persons any order or judgment may be made or issued by a majority; and if a tribunal is composed of two persons only, the chairman has a second or casting vote.

Form and content of judgments

29 (1) When judgment is reserved a written judgment shall be sent to the parties as soon as practicable. All judgments (whether issued orally or in writing) shall be recorded in writing and signed by the chairman.

(2) The Secretary shall provide a copy of the judgment to each of the parties and, where the proceedings were referred to the tribunal by a court, to that court. The Secretary shall include guidance to the parties on how the judgment may be reviewed or appealed.

(3) Where the judgment includes an award of compensation or a determination that one party is required to pay a sum to another (excluding an order for costs, expenses, allowances, preparation time or wasted costs), the document shall also contain a statement of the amount of compensation awarded, or of the sum required to be paid.

Reasons

30 (1) A tribunal or chairman must give reasons (either oral or written) for any–

(a) judgment; or

(b) order, if a request for reasons is made before or at the hearing at which the order is made.

(2) Reasons may be given orally at the time of issuing the judgment or order or they may be reserved to be given in writing at a later date. If reasons are reserved, they shall be signed by the chairman and sent to the parties by the Secretary.

(3) Subject to paragraph 1, written reasons shall only be provided–

(a) in relation to judgments if requested by one of the parties within the time limit set out in paragraph (5); or

    (b) in relation to any judgment or order if requested by the Employment Appeal Tribunal at any time.

(4) When written reasons are provided, the Secretary shall send a copy of the reasons to all parties to the proceedings and record the date on which the reasons were sent. Written reasons shall be signed by the chairman.

(5) A request for written reasons for a judgment must be made by a party either orally at the hearing (if the judgment is issued at a hearing), or in writing within 14 days of the date on which the judgment was sent to the parties. This time limit may be extended by a chairman where he considers it just and equitable to do so.

(6) Written reasons for a judgment shall include the following information–

    (a) the issues which the tribunal or chairman has identified as being relevant to the claim;

    (b) if some identified issues were not determined, what those issues were and why they were not determined;

    (c) findings of fact relevant to the issues which have been determined;

    (d) a concise statement of the applicable law;

    (e) how the relevant findings of fact and applicable law have been applied in order to determine the issues; and

    (f) where the judgment includes an award of compensation or a determination that one party make a payment to the other, a table showing how the amount or sum has been calculated or a description of the manner in which it has been calculated.

Absence of chairman

31   Where it is not possible for a judgment, order or reasons to be signed by the chairman due to death, incapacity or absence–

    (a) if the chairman has dealt with the proceedings alone the document shall be signed by the Regional Chairman, Vice President or President when it is practicable for him to do so; and

    (b) if the proceedings have been dealt with by a tribunal composed of two or three persons, the document shall be signed by the other person or persons;

and any person who signs the document shall certify that the chairman is unable to sign.

The Register

32 (1) Subject to rule 49, the Secretary shall enter a copy of the following documents in the Register–

    (a) any judgment (including any costs, expenses, preparation time or wasted costs order); and

    (b) any written reasons provided in accordance with rule 30 in relation to any judgment.

(2) Written reasons for judgments shall be omitted from the Register in any case in which evidence has been heard in private and the tribunal or chairman so orders. In such a case the Secretary shall send the reasons to each of the parties and where there are proceedings before a superior court relating to the judgment in question, he shall send the reasons to that court, together

with a copy of the entry in the Register of the judgment to which the reasons relate.

POWER TO REVIEW JUDGMENTS AND DECISIONS

Review of default judgments

33 (1) A party may apply to have a default judgment against or in favour of him reviewed. An application must be made in writing and presented to the Employment Tribunal Office within 14 days of the date on which the default judgment was sent to the parties. The 14 day time limit may be extended by a chairman if he considers that it is just and equitable to do so.

(2) The application must state the reasons why the default judgment should be varied or revoked. When it is the respondent applying to have the default judgment reviewed, the application must include with it the respondent's proposed response to the claim, an application for an extension of the time limit for presenting the response and an explanation of why rules 4(1) and (4) were not complied with.

(3) A review of a default judgment shall be conducted by a chairman in public. Notice of the hearing and a copy of the application shall be sent by the Secretary to all other parties.

(4) The chairman may–
   (a) refuse the application for a review;
   (b) vary the default judgment;
   (c) revoke all or part of the default judgment;
   (d) confirm the default judgment;
   and all parties to the proceedings shall be informed by the Secretary in writing of the chairman's judgment on the application.

(5) A default judgment must be revoked if the whole of the claim was satisfied before the judgment was issued or if rule 8(6) applies. A chairman may revoke or vary all or part of a default judgment if the respondent has a reasonable prospect of successfully responding to the claim or part of it.

(6) In considering the application for a review of a default judgment the chairman must have regard to whether there was good reason for the response not having been presented within the applicable time limit.

(7) If the chairman decides that the default judgment should be varied or revoked and that the respondent should be allowed to respond to the claim the Secretary shall accept the response and proceed in accordance with rule 5(2).

Review of other judgments and decisions

34 (1) Parties may apply to have certain judgments and decisions made by a tribunal or a chairman reviewed under rules 34 to 36. Those judgments and decisions are–
   (a) a decision not to accept a claim, response or counterclaim;
   (b) a judgment (other than a default judgment but including an order for costs, expenses, preparation time or wasted costs); and

(c) a decision made under rule 6(3) of Schedule 4;

and references to 'decision' in rules 34 to 37 are references to the above judgments and decisions only. Other decisions or orders may not be reviewed under these rules.

(2) In relation to a decision not to accept a claim or response, only the party against whom the decision is made may apply to have the decision reviewed.

(3) Subject to paragraph (4), decisions may be reviewed on the following grounds only–
   (a) the decision was wrongly made as a result of an administrative error;
   (b) a party did not receive notice of the proceedings leading to the decision;
   (c) the decision was made in the absence of a party;
   (d) new evidence has become available since the conclusion of the hearing to which the decision relates, provided that its existence could not have been reasonably known of or foreseen at that time; or
   (e) the interests of justice require such a review.

(4) A decision not to accept a claim or response may only be reviewed on the grounds listed in paragraphs (3)(a) and (e).

(5) A tribunal or chairman may on its or his own initiative review a decision made by it or him on the grounds listed in paragraphs (3) or (4).

Preliminary consideration of application for review

35 (1) An application under rule 34 to have a decision reviewed must be made to the Employment Tribunal Office within 14 days of the date on which the decision was sent to the parties. The 14 day time limit may be extended by a chairman if he considers that it is just and equitable to do so.

(2) The application must be in writing and must identify the grounds of the application in accordance with rule 34(3), but if the decision to be reviewed was made at a hearing, an application may be made orally at that hearing.

(3) The application to have a decision reviewed shall be considered (without the need to hold a hearing) by the chairman of the tribunal which made the decision or, if that is not practicable, by –
   (a) a Regional Chairman or the Vice President;
   (b) any chairman nominated by a Regional Chairman or the Vice President; or
   (c) the President;
   and that person shall refuse the application if he considers that there are no grounds for the decision to be reviewed under rule 34(3) or there is no reasonable prospect of the decision being varied or revoked.

(4) If an application for a review is refused after such preliminary consideration the Secretary shall inform the party making the application in writing of the chairman's decision and his reasons for it. If the application for a review is not refused the decision shall be reviewed under rule 36.

The review

36 (1) When a party has applied for a review and the application has not been refused after the preliminary consideration above, the decision shall be reviewed by the chairman or tribunal who made the original decision. If

that is not practicable a different chairman or tribunal (as the case may be) shall be appointed by a Regional Chairman, the Vice President or the President.

(2) Where no application has been made by a party and the decision is being reviewed on the initiative of the tribunal or chairman, the review must be carried out by the same tribunal or chairman who made the original decision and–

  (a) a notice must be sent to each of the parties explaining in summary the grounds upon which it is proposed to review the decision and giving them an opportunity to give reasons why there should be no review; and

  (b) such notice must be sent before the expiry of 14 days from the date on which the original decision was sent to the parties.

(3) A tribunal or chairman who reviews a decision under paragraph (1) or (2) may confirm, vary or revoke the decision. If the decision is revoked, the tribunal or chairman must order the decision to be taken again. When an order is made that the original decision be taken again, if the original decision was taken by a chairman without a hearing, the new decision may be taken without hearing the parties and if the original decision was taken at a hearing, a new hearing must be held.

Correction of judgments, decisions or reasons

37 (1) Clerical mistakes in any order, judgment, decision or reasons, or errors arising in those documents from an accidental slip or omission, may at any time be corrected by certificate by the chairman, Regional Chairman, Vice President or President.

(2) If a document is corrected by certificate under paragraph (1), or if a decision is revoked or varied under rules 33 or 36 or altered in any way by order of a superior court, the Secretary shall alter any entry in the Register which is so affected to conform with the certificate or order and send a copy of any entry so altered to each of the parties and, if the proceedings have been referred to the tribunal by a court, to that court.

(3) Where a document omitted from the Register under rules 32 or 49 is corrected by certificate under this rule, the Secretary shall send a copy of the corrected document to the parties; and where there are proceedings before any superior court relating to the decision or reasons in question, he shall send a copy to that court together with a copy of the entry in the Register of the decision, if it has been altered under this rule.

(4) In Scotland, the references in paragraphs (2) and (3) to superior courts shall be read as referring to appellate courts.

COSTS ORDERS AND ORDERS FOR EXPENSES

General power to make costs and expenses orders

38 (1) Subject to paragraph (2) and in the circumstances listed in rules 39, 40 and 47 a tribunal or chairman may make an order ('a costs order') that–

  (a) a party ('the paying party') make a payment in respect of the costs incurred by another party ('the receiving party');

(b) the paying party pay to the Secretary of State, in whole or in part, any allowances (other than allowances paid to members of tribunals) paid by the Secretary of State under section 5(2) or (3) of the Employment Tribunals Act to any person for the purposes of, or in connection with, that person's attendance at the tribunal.

(2) A costs order may be made under rules 39, 40 and 47 only where the receiving party has been legally represented at the Hearing or, in proceedings which are determined without a Hearing, if the receiving party is legally represented when the proceedings are determined. If the receiving party has not been so legally represented a tribunal may make a preparation time order (subject to rules 42 to 45). (See rule 46 on the restriction on making a costs order and a preparation time order in the same proceedings.)

(3) For the purposes of these rules 'costs' shall mean fees, charges, disbursements or expenses incurred by or on behalf of a party, in relation to the proceedings. In Scotland all references to costs (except when used in the expression 'wasted costs') or costs orders shall be read as references to expenses or orders for expenses.

(4) A costs order may be made against or in favour of a respondent who has not had a response accepted in the proceedings in relation to the conduct of any part which he has taken in the proceedings.

(5) In these rules legally represented means having the assistance of a person (including where that person is the receiving party's employee) who—
   (a) has a general qualification within the meaning of section 71 of the Courts and Legal Services Act 1990;
   (b) is an advocate or solicitor in Scotland; or
   (c) is a member of the Bar of Northern Ireland or a solicitor of the Supreme Court of Northern Ireland.

(6) Any costs order made under rules 39, 40 or 47 shall be payable by the paying party and not his representative.

(7) A party may apply for a costs order to be made at any time during the proceedings. An application may be made at the end of a hearing, or in writing to the Employment Tribunal Office. An application for costs which is received by the Employment Tribunal Office later than 28 days from the issuing of the judgment determining the claim shall not be accepted or considered by a tribunal or chairman unless it or he considers that it is in the interests of justice to do so.

(8) In paragraph (7), the date of issuing of the judgment determining the claim shall be either—
   (a) the date of the Hearing if the judgment was issued orally; or
   (b) if the judgment was reserved, the date on which the written judgment was sent to the parties.

(9) No costs order shall be made unless the Secretary has sent notice to the party against whom the order may be made giving him the opportunity to give reasons why the order should not be made. This paragraph shall not be taken to require the Secretary to send notice to that party if the party has been given an opportunity to give reasons orally to the chairman or tribunal as to why the order should not be made.

(10) Where a tribunal or chairman makes a costs order it or he shall provide written reasons for doing so if a request for written reasons is made within 14 days of the date of the costs order. The Secretary shall send a copy of the written reasons to all parties to the proceedings.

When a costs or expenses order must be made

39 (1) Subject to rule 38(2), a tribunal must make a costs order against a respondent where in proceedings for unfair dismissal a Hearing has been postponed or adjourned and–
   (a) the claimant has expressed a wish to be reinstated or re-engaged which has been communicated to the respondent not less than 7 days before the Hearing; and
   (b) the postponement or adjournment of that Hearing has been caused by the respondent's failure, without a special reason, to adduce reasonable evidence as to the availability of the job from which the claimant was dismissed, or of comparable or suitable employment.

(2) A costs order made under paragraph (1) shall relate to any costs incurred as a result of the postponement or adjournment of the Hearing.

When a costs or expenses order may be made

40 (1) A tribunal or chairman may make a costs order when on the application of a party it has postponed the day or time fixed for or adjourned a Hearing or pre-hearing review. The costs order may be against or, as the case may require, in favour of that party as respects any costs incurred or any allowances paid as a result of the postponement or adjournment.

(2) A tribunal or chairman shall consider making a costs order against a paying party where, in the opinion of the tribunal or chairman (as the case may be), any of the circumstances in paragraph (3) apply. Having so considered, the tribunal or chairman may make a costs order against the paying party if it or he considers it appropriate to do so.

(3) The circumstances referred to in paragraph (2) are where the paying party has in bringing the proceedings, or he or his representative has in conducting the proceedings, acted vexatiously, abusively, disruptively or otherwise unreasonably, or the bringing or conducting of the proceedings by the paying party has been misconceived.

(4) A tribunal or chairman may make a costs order against a party who has not complied with an order or practice direction.

The amount of a costs or expenses order

41 (1) The amount of a costs order against the paying party shall be determined in any of the following ways–
   (a) the tribunal may specify the sum which the paying party must pay to the receiving party, provided that sum does not exceed £10,000;
   (b) the parties may agree on a sum to be paid by the paying party to the receiving party and if they do so the costs order shall be for the sum so agreed;
   (c) the tribunal may order the paying party to pay the receiving party the

whole or a specified part of the costs of the receiving party with the amount to be paid being determined by way of detailed assessment in a County Court in accordance with the Civil Procedure Rules 1998 or, in Scotland, as taxed according to such part of the table of fees prescribed for proceedings in the sheriff court as shall be directed by the order.

(2) The tribunal or chairman may have regard to the paying party's ability to pay when considering whether it or he shall make a costs order or how much that order should be.

(3) For the avoidance of doubt, the amount of a costs order made under paragraphs (1)(b) or (c) may exceed £10,000.

PREPARATION TIME ORDERS

General power to make preparation time orders

42 (1) Subject to paragraph (2) and in the circumstances described in rules 43, 44 and 47 a tribunal or chairman may make an order ('a preparation time order') that a party ('the paying party') make a payment in respect of the preparation time of another party ('the receiving party').

(2) A preparation time order may be made under rules 43, 44 or 47 only where the receiving party has not been legally represented at a Hearing or, in proceedings which are determined without a Hearing, if the receiving party has not been legally represented when the proceedings are determined. (See: rules 38 to 41 on when a costs order may be made; rule 38(5) for the definition of legally represented; and rule 46 on the restriction on making a costs order and a preparation time order in the same proceedings).

(3) For the purposes of these rules preparation time shall mean time spent by–
   (a) the receiving party or his employees carrying out preparatory work directly relating to the proceedings; and
   (b) the receiving party's legal or other advisers relating to the conduct of the proceedings;
   up to but not including time spent at any Hearing.

(4) A preparation time order may be made against a respondent who has not had a response accepted in the proceedings in relation to the conduct of any part which he has taken in the proceedings.

(5) A party may apply to the tribunal for a preparation time order to be made at any time during the proceedings. An application may be made at the end of a hearing or in writing to the Secretary. An application for preparation time which is received by the Employment Tribunal Office later than 28 days from the issuing of the judgment determining the claim shall not be accepted or considered by a tribunal or chairman unless they consider that it is in the interests of justice to do so.

(6) In paragraph (5) the date of issuing of the judgment determining the claim shall be either–
   (a) the date of the Hearing if the judgment was issued orally; or,
   (b) if the judgment was reserved, the date on which the written judgment was sent to the parties.

(7) No preparation time order shall be made unless the Secretary has sent notice to the party against whom the order may be made giving him the opportunity to give reasons why the order should not be made. This paragraph shall not be taken to require the Secretary to send notice to that party if the party has been given an opportunity to give reasons orally to the chairman or tribunal as to why the order should not be made.

(8) Where a tribunal or chairman makes a preparation time order it or he shall provide written reasons for doing so if a request for written reasons is made within 14 days of the date of the preparation time order. The Secretary shall send a copy of the written reasons to all parties to the proceedings.

When a preparation time order must be made

43 (1) Subject to rule 42(2), a tribunal must make a preparation time order against a respondent where in proceedings for unfair dismissal a Hearing has been postponed or adjourned and–

    (a) the claimant has expressed a wish to be reinstated or re-engaged which has been communicated to the respondent not less than 7 days before the Hearing; and

    (b) the postponement or adjournment of that Hearing has been caused by the respondent's failure, without a special reason, to adduce reasonable evidence as to the availability of the job from which the claimant was dismissed, or of comparable or suitable employment.

(2) A preparation time order made under paragraph (1) shall relate to any preparation time spent as a result of the postponement or adjournment of the Hearing.

When a preparation time order may be made

44 (1) A tribunal or chairman may make a preparation time order when on the application of a party it has postponed the day or time fixed for or adjourned a Hearing or a pre-hearing review. The preparation time order may be against or, as the case may require, in favour of that party as respects any preparation time spent as a result of the postponement or adjournment.

(2) A tribunal or chairman shall consider making a preparation time order against a party (the paying party) where, in the opinion of the tribunal or the chairman (as the case may be), any of the circumstances in paragraph (3) apply. Having so considered the tribunal or chairman may make a preparation time order against that party if it considers it appropriate to do so.

(3) The circumstances described in paragraph (2) are where the paying party has in bringing the proceedings, or he or his representative has in conducting the proceedings, acted vexatiously, abusively, disruptively or otherwise unreasonably, or the bringing or conducting of the proceedings by the paying party has been misconceived.

(4) A tribunal or chairman may make a preparation time order against a party who has not complied with an order or practice direction.

Calculation of a preparation time order

45 (1) In order to calculate the amount of preparation time the tribunal or chairman shall make an assessment of the number of hours spent on preparation time on the basis of–

(a) information on time spent provided by the receiving party; and

(b) the tribunal or chairman's own assessment of what it or he considers to be a reasonable and proportionate amount of time to spend on such preparatory work and with reference to, for example, matters such as the complexity of the proceedings, the number of witnesses and documentation required.

(2) Once the tribunal or chairman has assessed the number of hours spent on preparation time in accordance with paragraph (1), it or he shall calculate the amount of the award to be paid to the receiving party by applying an hourly rate of £25.00 to that figure (or such other figure calculated in accordance with paragraph (4)). No preparation time order made under these rules may exceed the sum of £10,000.

(3) The tribunal or chairman may have regard to the paying party's ability to pay when considering whether it or he shall make a preparation time order or how much that order should be.

(4) For the year commencing on 6th April 2006, the hourly rate of £25 shall be increased by the sum of £1.00 and for each subsequent year commencing on 6 April, the hourly rate for the previous year shall also be increased by the sum of £1.00.

Restriction on making costs or expenses orders and preparation time orders

46 (1) A tribunal or chairman may not make a preparation time order and a costs order in favour of the same party in the same proceedings. However where a preparation time order is made in favour of a party in proceedings, the tribunal or chairman may make a costs order in favour of another party or in favour of the Secretary of State under rule 38(1)(b) in the same proceedings.

(2) If a tribunal or a chairman wishes to make either a costs order or a preparation time order in proceedings, before the claim has been determined, it or he may make an order that either costs or preparation time be awarded to the receiving party. In such circumstances a tribunal or chairman may decide whether the award should be for costs or preparation time after the proceedings have been determined.

Costs, expenses or preparation time orders when a deposit has been taken

47 (1) When–

(a) a party has been ordered under rule 20 to pay a deposit as a condition of being permitted to continue to participate in proceedings relating to a matter;

(b) in respect of that matter, the tribunal or chairman has found against that party in its or his judgment; and

(c) no award of costs or preparation time has been made against that party arising out of the proceedings on the matter;

the tribunal or chairman shall consider whether to make a costs or preparation time order against that party on the ground that he conducted the proceedings relating to the matter unreasonably in persisting in having the matter determined; but the tribunal or chairman shall not make a costs or preparation time order on that ground unless it has considered the document recording the order under rule 20 and is of the opinion that the grounds which caused the tribunal or chairman to find against the party in its judgment were substantially the same as the grounds recorded in that document for considering that the contentions of the party had little reasonable prospect of success.

(2) When a costs or preparation time order is made against a party who has had an order under rule 20 made against him (whether the award arises out of the proceedings relating to the matter in respect of which the order was made or out of proceedings relating to any other matter considered with that matter), his deposit shall be paid in part or full settlement of the costs or preparation time order–

(a) when an order is made in favour of one party, to that party; and

(b) when orders are made in favour of more than one party, to all of them or any one or more of them as the tribunal or chairman thinks fit, and if to all or more than one, in such proportions as the tribunal or chairman considers appropriate;

and if the amount of the deposit exceeds the amount of the costs or preparation time order, the balance shall be refunded to the party who paid it.

WASTED COSTS ORDERS AGAINST REPRESENTATIVES

Personal liability of representatives for costs

48 (1) A tribunal or chairman may make a wasted costs order against a party's representative.

(2) In a wasted costs order the tribunal or chairman may–

(a) disallow, or order the representative of a party to meet the whole or part of any wasted costs of any party, including an order that the representative repay to his client any costs which have already been paid; and

(b) order the representative to pay to the Secretary of State, in whole or in part, any allowances (other than allowances paid to members of tribunals) paid by the Secretary of State under section 5(2) or (3) of the Employment Tribunals Act to any person for the purposes of, or in connection with, that person's attendance at the tribunal by reason of the representative's conduct of the proceedings.

(3) 'Wasted costs' means any costs incurred by a party–

(a) as a result of any improper, unreasonable or negligent act or omission on the part of any representative; or

(b) which, in the light of any such act or omission occurring after they were incurred, the tribunal considers it unreasonable to expect that party to pay.

(4) In this rule 'representative' means a party's legal or other representative or any employee of such representative, but it does not include a representative who is not acting in pursuit of profit with regard to those proceedings. A person is considered to be acting in pursuit of profit if he is acting on a conditional fee arrangement.

(5) A wasted costs order may be made in favour of a party whether or not that party is legally represented and such an order may also be made in favour of a representative's own client. A wasted costs order may not be made against a representative where that representative is an employee of a party.

(6) Before making a wasted costs order, the tribunal or chairman shall give the representative a reasonable opportunity to make oral or written representations as to reasons why such an order should not be made. The tribunal or chairman may also have regard to the representative's ability to pay when considering whether it shall make a wasted costs order or how much that order should be.

(7) When a tribunal or chairman makes a wasted costs order, it must specify in the order the amount to be disallowed or paid.

(8) The Secretary shall inform the representative's client in writing–
  (a) of any proceedings under this rule; or
  (b) of any order made under this rule against the party's representative.

(9) Where a tribunal or chairman makes a wasted costs order it or he shall provide written reasons for doing so if a request is made for written reasons within 14 days of the date of the wasted costs order. This 14 day time limit may not be extended under rule 10. The Secretary shall send a copy of the written reasons to all parties to the proceedings.

POWERS IN RELATION TO SPECIFIC TYPES OF PROCEEDINGS

Sexual offences and the Register

49   In any proceedings appearing to involve allegations of the commission of a sexual offence the tribunal, the chairman or the Secretary shall omit from the Register, or delete from the Register or any judgment, document or record of the proceedings, which is available to the public, any identifying matter which is likely to lead members of the public to identify any person affected by or making such an allegation.

Restricted reporting orders

50 (1) A restricted reporting order may be made in the following types of proceedings–
  (a) any case which involves allegations of sexual misconduct;
  (b) a complaint under section 17A or 25(8) of the Disability Discrimination Act in which evidence of a personal nature is likely to be heard by the tribunal or a chairman.

(2) A party (or where a complaint is made under the Disability Discrimination Act, the complainant) may apply for a restricted reporting order (either temporary or full) in writing to the Employment Tribunal Office, or orally at

a hearing, or the tribunal or chairman may make the order on its or his own initiative without any application having been made.

(3) A chairman or tribunal may make a temporary restricted reporting order without holding a hearing or sending a copy of the application to other parties.

(4) Where a temporary restricted reporting order has been made the Secretary shall inform all parties to the proceedings in writing as soon as possible of–
   (a) the fact that the order has been made; and
   (b) their right to apply to have the temporary restricted reporting order revoked or converted into a full restricted reporting order within 14 days of the temporary order having been made.

(5) If no application under paragraph (4)(b) is made within the 14 days, the temporary restricted reporting order shall lapse and cease to have any effect on the fifteenth day after the order was made. If such an application is made the temporary restricted reporting order shall continue to have effect until the pre-hearing review or Hearing at which the application is considered.

(6) All parties must be given an opportunity to advance oral argument at a pre-hearing review or a Hearing before a tribunal or chairman decides whether or not to make a full restricted reporting order (whether or not there was previously a temporary restricted reporting order in the proceedings).

(7) Any person may make an application to the chairman or tribunal to have a right to make representations before a full restricted reporting order is made. The chairman or tribunal shall allow such representations to be made where he or it considers that the applicant has a legitimate interest in whether or not the order is made.

(8) Where a tribunal or chairman makes a restricted reporting order–
   (a) it shall specify in the order the persons who may not be identified;
   (b) a full order shall remain in force until both liability and remedy have been determined in the proceedings unless it is revoked earlier; and
   (c) the Secretary shall ensure that a notice of the fact that a restricted reporting order has been made in relation to those proceedings is displayed on the notice board of the employment tribunal with any list of the proceedings taking place before the employment tribunal, and on the door of the room in which the proceedings affected by the order are taking place.

(9) Where a restricted reporting order has been made under this rule and that complaint is being dealt with together with any other proceedings, the tribunal or chairman may order that the restricted reporting order applies also in relation to those other proceedings or a part of them.

(10) A tribunal or chairman may revoke a restricted reporting order at any time.

(11) For the purposes of this rule liability and remedy are determined in the proceedings on the date recorded as being the date on which the judgment disposing of the claim was sent to the parties, and references to a restricted reporting order include references to both a temporary and a full restricted reporting order.

Proceedings involving the National Insurance Fund

51   The Secretary of State shall be entitled to appear as if she were a party and be heard at any hearing in relation to proceedings which may involve a payment out of the National Insurance Fund, and in that event she shall be treated for the purposes of these rules as if she were a party.

Collective agreements

52   Where a claim includes a complaint under section 6(4A) of the Sex Discrimination Act 1986 relating to a term of a collective agreement, the following persons, whether or not identified in the claim, shall be regarded as the persons against whom a remedy is claimed and shall be treated as respondents for the purposes of these rules, that is to say–

(a) the claimant's employer (or prospective employer); and

(b) every organisation of employers and organisation of workers, and every association of or representative of such organisations, which, if the terms were to be varied voluntarily, would be likely, in the opinion of a chairman, to negotiate the variation;

provided that such an organisation or association shall not be treated as a respondent if the chairman, having made such enquiries of the claimant and such other enquiries as he thinks fit, is of the opinion that it is not reasonably practicable to identify the organisation or association.

Employment Agencies Act 1973

53   In relation to any claim in respect of an application under section 3C of the Employment Agencies Act 1973 for the variation or revocation of a prohibition order, the Secretary of State shall be treated as the respondent in such proceedings for the purposes of these rules. In relation to such an application the claim does not need to include the name and address of the persons against whom the claim is being made.

National security proceedings

54 (1) A Minister of the Crown (whether or not he is a party to the proceedings) may, if he considers it expedient in the interests of national security, direct a tribunal or chairman by notice to the Secretary to–

(a) conduct proceedings in private for all or part of particular Crown employment proceedings;

(b) exclude the claimant from all or part of particular Crown employment proceedings;

(c) exclude the claimant's representative from all or part of particular Crown employment proceedings;

(d) take steps to conceal the identity of a particular witness in particular Crown employment proceedings.

(2) A tribunal or chairman may, if it or he considers it expedient in the interests of national security, by order–

(a) do anything which can be required by direction to be done under paragraph (1);

(b) order any person to whom any document (including any judgment or record of the proceedings) has been provided for the purposes of the proceedings not to disclose any such document or the content thereof–

    (i)   to any excluded person;

    (ii)   in any case in which a direction has been given under paragraph (1)(a) or an order has been made under paragraph (2)(a) read with paragraph (1)(a), to any person excluded from all or part of the proceedings by virtue of such direction or order; or

    (iii) in any case in which a Minister of the Crown has informed the Secretary in accordance with paragraph (3) that he wishes to address the tribunal or chairman with a view to an order being made under paragraph (2)(a) read with paragraph (1)(b) or (c), to any person who may be excluded from all or part of the proceedings by virtue of such an order, if an order is made, at any time before the tribunal or chairman decides whether or not to make such an order;

(c) take steps to keep secret all or part of the reasons for its judgment.

The tribunal or chairman (as the case may be) shall keep under review any order it or he has made under this paragraph.

(3) In any proceedings in which a Minister of the Crown considers that it would be appropriate for a tribunal or chairman to make an order as referred to in paragraph (2), he shall (whether or not he is a party to the proceedings) be entitled to appear before and to address the tribunal or chairman thereon. The Minister shall inform the Secretary by notice that he wishes to address the tribunal or chairman and the Secretary shall copy the notice to the parties.

(4) When exercising its or his functions, a tribunal or chairman shall ensure that information is not disclosed contrary to the interests of national security.

Dismissals in connection with industrial action

55 (1) In relation to a complaint under section 111 of the Employment Rights Act 1996 (unfair dismissal: complaints to employment tribunal) that a dismissal is unfair by virtue of section 238A of TULR(C)A (participation in official industrial action) a tribunal or chairman may adjourn the proceedings where civil proceedings have been brought until such time as interim proceedings arising out of the civil proceedings have been concluded.

(2) In this rule–

(a) 'civil proceedings' means legal proceedings brought by any person against another person in which it is to be determined whether an act of that other person, which induced the claimant to commit an act, or each of a series of acts, is by virtue of section 219 of TULR(C)A not actionable in tort or in delict; and

(b) the interim proceedings shall not be regarded as having concluded until all rights of appeal have been exhausted or the time for presenting any appeal in the course of the interim proceedings has expired.

Devolution issues

56 (1) In any proceedings in which a devolution issue within the definition of the term in paragraph 1 of Schedule 6 to the Scotland Act 1998 arises, the

Secretary shall as soon as reasonably practicable by notice inform the Advocate General for Scotland and the Lord Advocate thereof (unless they are a party to the proceedings) and shall at the same time–

(a) send a copy of the notice to the parties to the proceedings; and

(b) send the Advocate General for Scotland and the Lord Advocate a copy of the claim and the response.

(2) In any proceedings in which a devolution issue within the definition of the term in paragraph 1 of Schedule 8 to the Government of Wales Act 1998 arises, the Secretary shall as soon as reasonably practicable by notice inform the Attorney General and the National Assembly for Wales thereof (unless they are a party to the proceedings) and shall at the same time–

(a) send a copy of the notice to the parties to the proceedings; and

(b) send the Attorney General and the National Assembly for Wales a copy of the claim and the response.

(3) A person to whom notice is given in pursuance of paragraph (1) or (2) may within 14 days of receiving it, by notice to the Secretary, take part as a party in the proceedings, so far as they relate to the devolution issue. The Secretary shall send a copy of the notice to the other parties to the proceedings.

Transfer of proceedings between Scotland and England and Wales

57 (1) The President (England and Wales) or a Regional Chairman may at any time, with the consent of the President (Scotland), order any proceedings in England and Wales to be transferred to an Employment Tribunal Office in Scotland if it appears to him that the proceedings could be (in accordance with regulation 19), and would more conveniently be, determined in an employment tribunal located in Scotland.

(2) The President (Scotland) or the Vice President may at any time, with the consent of the President (England and Wales), order any proceedings in Scotland to be transferred to an Employment Tribunal Office in England and Wales if it appears to him that the proceedings could be (in accordance with regulation 19), and would more conveniently be, determined in an employment tribunal located in England or Wales.

(3) An order under paragraph (1) or (2) may be made by the President, Vice President or Regional Chairman without any application having been made by a party. A party may apply for an order under paragraph (1) or (2) in accordance with rule 11.

(4) Where proceedings have been transferred under this rule, they shall be treated as if in all respects they had been presented to the Secretary by the claimant.

References to the European Court of Justice

58　Where a tribunal or chairman makes an order referring a question to the European Court of Justice for a preliminary ruling under Article 234 of the Treaty establishing the European Community, the Secretary shall send a copy of the order to the Registrar of that Court.

Transfer of proceedings from a court

59 Where proceedings are referred to a tribunal by a court, these rules shall apply to them as if the proceedings had been sent to the Secretary by the claimant.

GENERAL PROVISIONS

Powers

60 (1) Subject to the provisions of these rules and any practice directions, a tribunal or chairman may regulate its or his own procedure.

(2) At a Hearing, or a pre-hearing review held in accordance with rule 18(3), a tribunal may make any order which a chairman has power to make under these rules, subject to compliance with any relevant notice or other procedural requirements.

(3) Any function of the Secretary may be performed by a person acting with the authority of the Secretary.

Notices, etc

61 (1) Any notice given or document sent under these rules shall (unless a chairman or tribunal orders otherwise) be in writing and may be given or sent–
  (a) by post;
  (b) by fax or other means of electronic communication; or
  (c) by personal delivery.

(2) Where a notice or document has been given or sent in accordance with paragraph (1), that notice or document shall, unless the contrary is proved, be taken to have been received by the party to whom it is addressed–
  (a) in the case of a notice or document given or sent by post, on the day on which the notice or document would be delivered in the ordinary course of post;
  (b) in the case of a notice or document transmitted by fax or other means of electronic communication, on the day on which the notice or document is transmitted;
  (c) in the case of a notice or document delivered in person, on the day on which the notice or document is delivered.

(3) All notices and documents required by these rules to be presented to the Secretary or an Employment Tribunal Office, other than a claim, shall be presented at the Employment Tribunal Office as notified by the Secretary to the parties.

(4) All notices and documents required or authorised by these rules to be sent or given to any person listed below may be sent to or delivered at–
  (a) in the case of a notice or document directed to the Secretary of State in proceedings to which she is not a party and which are brought under section 170 of the Employment Rights Act, the offices of the Redundancy Payments Directorate of the Insolvency Service at PO Box 203, 21 Bloomsbury Street, London WC1B 3QW, or such other office as may be notified by the Secretary of State;
  (b) in the case of any other notice or document directed to the Secretary of

State in proceedings to which she is not a party (or in respect of which she is treated as a party for the purposes of these rules by rule 51), the offices of the Department of Trade and Industry (Employment Relations Directorate) at 1 Victoria Street, London, SW1H 0ET, or such other office as be notified by the Secretary of State;

(c) in the case of a notice or document directed to the Attorney General under rule 56, the Attorney General's Chambers, 9 Buckingham Gate, London, SW1E 7JP;

(d) in the case of a notice or document directed to the National Assembly for Wales under rule 56, the Counsel General to the National Assembly for Wales, Crown Buildings, Cathays Park, Cardiff, CF10 3NQ;

(e) in the case of a notice or document directed to the Advocate General for Scotland under rule 56, the Office of the Solicitor to the Advocate General for Scotland, Victoria Quay, Edinburgh, EH6 6QQ;

(f) in the case of a notice or document directed to the Lord Advocate under rule 56, the Legal Secretariat to the Lord Advocate, 25 Chambers Street, Edinburgh, EH1 1LA;

(g) in the case of a notice or document directed to a court, the office of the clerk of the court;

(h) in the case of a notice or document directed to a party–
   (i)   the address specified in the claim or response to which notices and documents are to be sent, or in a notice under paragraph (5); or
   (ii) if no such address has been specified, or if a notice sent to such an address has been returned, to any other known address or place of business in the United Kingdom or, if the party is a corporate body, the body's registered or principal office in the United Kingdom, or, in any case, such address or place outside the United Kingdom as the President, Vice President or a Regional Chairman may allow;

(i) in the case of a notice or document directed to any person (other than a person specified in the foregoing provisions of this paragraph), his address or place of business in the United Kingdom or, if the person is a corporate body, the body's registered or principal office in the United Kingdom;

and a notice or document sent or given to the authorised representative of a party shall be taken to have been sent or given to that party.

(5) A party may at any time by notice to the Employment Tribunal Office and to the other party or parties (and, where appropriate, to the appropriate conciliation officer) change the address to which notices and documents are to be sent or transmitted.

(6) The President, Vice President or a Regional Chairman may order that there shall be substituted service in such manner as he may deem fit in any case he considers appropriate.

(7) In proceedings which may involve a payment out of the National Insurance Fund, the Secretary shall, where appropriate, send copies of all documents and notices to the Secretary of State whether or not she is a party.

(8) Copies of every document sent to the parties under rules 29, 30 or 32 shall be sent by the Secretary–

(a) in the case of proceedings under the Equal Pay Act, the Sex Discrimination Act or the Sex Discrimination Act 1986, to the Equal Opportunities Commission;

(b) in the case of proceedings under the Race Relations Act, to the Commission for Racial Equality; and

(c) in the case of proceedings under the Disability Discrimination Act, to the Disability Rights Commission.

SCHEDULE 2: THE EMPLOYMENT TRIBUNALS (NATIONAL SECURITY) RULES OF PROCEDURE

Application of Schedule 2

1   (1) The rules in this Schedule only apply to national security proceedings or proceedings where the right in rule 54(3) of Schedule 1 has been exercised.

(2) The rules in this Schedule modify the rules in Schedule 1 in relation to such proceedings. If there is conflict between the rules contained in this Schedule and those in any other Schedule to these Regulations, the rules in this Schedule shall prevail.

(3) Any reference in this Schedule to rule 54 is a reference to rule 54 in Schedule 1.

Notification of national security proceedings

2   When proceedings before an employment tribunal become national security proceedings the Secretary shall inform the parties of that fact in writing as soon as practicable.

Responding to a claim

3   (1) If before the expiry of the period for entering the response–

(a) a direction of a Minister of the Crown under rule 54(1)(b) (exclusion of claimant) applicable to this stage of the proceedings is given; or

(b) a Minister of the Crown has informed the Secretary in accordance with rule 54(3) that he wishes to address the tribunal or chairman with a view to the tribunal or chairman making an order under rule 54(2) applicable to this stage of the proceedings to exclude the claimant;

rule 4(3)(d) (grounds for the response) of Schedule 1 shall not apply and paragraphs (2) and (3) of this rule shall apply instead.

(2) In a case falling within paragraph (1)(b), if the tribunal or chairman decides not to make an order under rule 54(2), the respondent shall within 28 days of the decision present to the Employment Tribunal Office the written grounds on which he resists the claim. On receiving the written grounds the Secretary shall send a copy of them to all other parties and they shall be treated as part of the response.

(3) In a case falling within paragraph (1)(b) where the tribunal or chairman makes the order, or in a case falling within paragraph (1)(a), the respondent shall with 44 days of the direction or order being made, present to the Employment Tribunal Office (and, where applicable, to the special advocate) the written grounds on which he resists the claim and they shall be treated as part of the response.

(4) The time limits in paragraphs (2) and (3) may be extended if it is just and equitable to do so and if an application is presented to the Employment Tribunal Office before the expiry of the relevant time limit. The application must explain why the respondent cannot comply with the time limit.

Serving of documents by the Secretary

4 (1) The Secretary shall not send a copy of the response or grounds for the response to any person excluded from all or part of the proceedings by virtue of a direction or order given or made under rule 54.

(2) Where a Minister of the Crown has informed the Secretary in accordance with rule 54(3) that he wishes to address the tribunal or chairman with a view to an order being made under rule 54(2)(a) to exclude the claimant's representative from all or part of the proceedings, the Secretary shall not at any time before the tribunal or chairman has considered the Minister's representations, send a copy of the response or the grounds for the response to any person who may be excluded from all or part of the proceedings by such an order if it were made.

Default judgment

5 Rule 8(1) (default judgments) of Schedule 1 shall apply in relation to the time limit for presenting a response, but it shall not apply in relation to the time limits in paragraphs (2) and (3) of rule 3 in this Schedule.

Witness orders and disclosure of documents

6 (1) Where–
   (a) a Minister has issued a direction or the tribunal or a chairman has made an order under rule 54 to exclude a claimant or his representative from all or part of the proceedings; and
   (b) a chairman or the tribunal is considering whether to make, or has made, an order described in rule 10(2)(c) or (d) of Schedule 1 (requiring a person to attend and give evidence or to produce documents) or under rule 8 of Schedule 3 or rule 7 of Schedule 4;

a Minister of the Crown (whether or not he is a party to the proceedings) may make an application to the tribunal or chairman objecting to the imposition of a requirement described in rule 10(2)(c) or (d) of Schedule 1 or under Schedules 3 or 4. If such an order has been made the Minister may make an application to vary or set aside the order.

(2) The tribunal or chairman shall hear and determine the Minister's application in private and the Minister shall be entitled to address the tribunal or chairman. The application shall be made by notice to the Secretary and the Secretary shall give notice of the application to all parties.

Case management discussions and pre-hearing reviews

7 (1) Rule 14(4) (hearings – general) of Schedule 1 shall be modified in accordance with paragraph (2).

(2) In proceedings in which a special advocate has been appointed in respect of

the claimant, if the claimant has been excluded from a case management discussion or a pre-hearing review, at such a hearing the claimant shall not have the right to advance oral argument, but oral argument may be advanced on the claimant's behalf by the special advocate.

Special advocate

8 (1) In any proceedings in which there is an excluded person the tribunal or chairman shall inform the Attorney General (or in Scotland, the Advocate General) of the proceedings before it with a view to the Attorney General (or the Advocate General, in Scotland), if he thinks it fit to do so, appointing a special advocate to represent the interests of the claimant in respect of those parts of the proceedings from which–

(a) any representative of his is excluded;

(b) both he and his representative are excluded; or

(c) he is excluded, where he does not have a representative.

(2) A special advocate shall have a general qualification for the purposes of section 71 of the Courts and Legal Services Act 1990 or shall be an advocate or a solicitor admitted in Scotland.

(3) Where the excluded person is the claimant, he shall be permitted to make a statement to the tribunal or chairman before the commencement of the proceedings, or the part of the proceedings, from which he is excluded.

(4) Except in accordance with paragraphs (5) to (7), the special advocate may not communicate directly or indirectly with any person (including an excluded person)–

(a) (except in the case of the tribunal, chairman and the respondent) on any matter contained in the grounds for the response referred to in rule 3(3);

(b) (except in the case of a person who was present) on any matter discussed or referred to during any part of the proceedings in which the tribunal or chairman sat in private in accordance with a direction or an order given or made under rule 54.

(5) The special advocate may apply for orders from the tribunal or chairman authorising him to seek instructions from, or otherwise to communicate with, an excluded person–

(a) on any matter contained in the grounds for the response referred to in rule 3(3); or

(b) on any matter discussed or referred to during any part of the proceedings in which the tribunal or chairman sat in private in accordance with a direction or an order given or made under rule 54.

(6) An application under paragraph (5) shall be made in writing to the Employment Tribunal Office and shall include the title of the proceedings and the grounds for the application.

(7) The Secretary shall notify the Minister of an application under paragraph (5) and the Minister shall be entitled to address the tribunal or chairman on the application.

(8) In these rules and those in Schedule 1, in any case in which a special advocate has been appointed to represent the interests of the claimant in accordance with paragraph (1), any reference to a party shall (save in those references specified in paragraph (9)) include the special advocate.

(9) The following references to 'party' or 'parties' shall not include the special advocate–

(a) regulation 9(3);

(b) in Schedule 1, rule 2(2)(b), 9, 10(2)(r), 10(3), the first two references in rule 11(4), 11(5), 18(7), 20, 22, 23, 27(3), 27(5), 29(3), 30(6)(f), 33(1), 34(2), all references in rule 38 save that in 38(10), 39, 40, 41, all references in rule 42 save that in rule 42(8), 44 to 48, 51, 54(1), the first reference in rule 54(3), 56(3), 61(3), 61(4)(a) and (b), and 61(7);

(c) in Schedule 4, rule 5(b), 6(5) and 10; and

(d) in Schedule 5, rule 4(b).

Hearings

9 (1) Any hearing of or in connection with a claim shall, subject to any direction of a Minister of the Crown or order of a tribunal or chairman under rule 54 that all or part of the proceedings are to take place in private and subject to rule 16 of Schedule 1, take place in public.

(2) A member of the Council on Tribunals shall not be entitled to attend any hearing taking place in private in his capacity as member where the hearing is taking place in private under a direction of a Minister of the Crown or an order of a tribunal or chairman under rule 54.

(3) Subject to any direction of a Minister of the Crown or order of a tribunal or chairman under rule 54, a party shall be entitled to give evidence, to call witnesses, to question any witnesses and to address the tribunal at a Hearing.

Reasons in national security proceedings

10 (1) This rule applies to written reasons given under rule 30 of Schedule 1 for a judgment or order made by the tribunal or chairman in national security proceedings.

(2) Before the Secretary sends a copy of the written reasons ('the full written reasons') to any party, or enters them in the Register under rule 32 of Schedule 1, he shall send a copy of the full written reasons to the Minister.

(3) If the Minister considers it expedient in the interests of national security and he has given a direction or the tribunal or a chairman has made an order under rule 54 in those proceedings, the Minister may–

(a) direct the tribunal or chairman that the full written reasons shall not be disclosed to persons specified in the direction, and to prepare a further document ('the edited reasons') setting out the reasons for the judgment or order, but with the omission of such of the information as is specified in the direction;

(b) direct the tribunal or chairman that the full written reasons shall not be disclosed to persons specified in the direction, but that no further document setting out the tribunal or chairman's reasons should be prepared.

(4) Where the Minister has directed the tribunal or chairman in accordance with paragraph 3(a), the edited reasons shall be signed by the chairman and initialled in each place where an omission has been made.

(5) Where a direction has been made under paragraph (3)(a), the Secretary shall–
   (a) send a copy of the edited reasons referred to in paragraph (3)(a) to any person specified in the direction and to the persons listed in paragraph (7);
   (b) enter the edited reasons in the Register, but omit from the Register the full written reasons; and
   (c) send a copy of the full written reasons to the persons listed in paragraph (7).

(6) Where a direction has been made under paragraph (3)(b), the Secretary shall send a copy of the full written reasons to the persons listed in paragraph (7), but he shall not enter the full written reasons in the Register.

(7) The persons to whom full written reasons should be sent in accordance with paragraph (5) or (6) are–
   (a) the respondent;
   (b) the claimant or the claimant's representative if they were not specified in the direction made under paragraph (3);
   (c) if applicable, the special advocate;
   (d) where the proceedings were referred to the tribunal by a court, to that court; and
   (e) where there are proceedings before a superior court (or in Scotland, an appellate court) relating to the decision in question, to that court.

Correction of written reasons

11   Where written reasons (whether 'full' or 'edited') have been omitted from the Register in accordance with rule 10 and they are corrected by certificate under rule 37 of Schedule 1, the Secretary shall send a copy of the corrected reasons to the same persons who had been sent the reasons in accordance with rule 10.

Review of judgments or decisions

12   In rule 34(3) of Schedule 1 (review of other judgments and decisions), the reference in sub-paragraph (c) to decisions being made in the absence of a party does not include reference to decisions being made in the absence of a party where this is done in accordance with a direction given or an order made under rule 54.

SCHEDULE 3: THE EMPLOYMENT TRIBUNALS (LEVY APPEALS) RULES OF PROCEDURE

For use only in proceedings on levy appeals

Application of Schedule 1

1   Subject to rules 9 and 10 of this Schedule, Schedule 1 shall apply to levy appeals. The rules in this Schedule modify the rules in Schedule 1 in relation to levy appeals. If there is conflict between the rules contained in this Schedule and those in Schedule 1, the rules in this Schedule shall prevail.

Definitions

2   In this Schedule and in relation to proceedings to which this Schedule applies–

'Board' means in relation to an appeal the respondent industrial training board;

'Industrial Training Act' means the Industrial Training Act 1982;

'levy' means a levy imposed under section 11 of the Industrial Training Act;

'levy appeal' means an appeal against an assessment to a levy;

'respondent' means the Board.

Notice of Appeal

3   A person wishing to appeal an assessment to a levy (the appellant) shall do so by sending to the Board two copies of a notice of appeal which must be substantially in accordance with Form 1 in the Annex to this Schedule, and they must include the grounds of their appeal.

Action on receipt of appeal

4   (1)   Subject to rules 5 and 6, the Board shall, within 21 days of receiving the notice of appeal send the following documents to the Employment Tribunal Office–

(a) one copy of the notice of appeal;

(b) a copy of the assessment notice and of any notice by the Board allowing further time for appealing;

(c) a notice giving the Board's address for service under these rules where that address is different from the address specified in the assessment notice as the address for service of a notice of appeal; and

(d) any representations in writing relating to the appeal that the Board wishes to submit to the tribunal.

(2)   Failure to comply with any provision of this rule or rule 5 shall not make the appeal invalid.

Requests for further information

5   (1)   Subject to rule 6, this rule applies when, on receiving the notice of appeal, the Board considers that it requires further information on the appellant's grounds for the appeal and of any facts relevant to those grounds.

(2)   The Board shall send the appellant a notice specifying the further information required by the Board within 21 days of receiving the notice of appeal.

(3)   The appellant shall send the Board two copies of the further information within 21 days of receiving the notice requesting the information, or within such further period as the Board may allow.

(4)   Subject to paragraph (5), within 21 days of receiving the further information the Board shall send the following documents to the Employment Tribunal Office–

(a) the documents listed in rule 4(1);

(b) a copy of the notice requesting further information;

(c) any further information which has been provided to the Board; and

(d) any representations in writing regarding such information which the Board wishes to submit to the tribunal.

(5) If further information is not received by the Board within the time limit, the documents listed in sub-paragraphs (a) and (b) of paragraph (4) shall be sent by the Board to the Employment Tribunal Office–
   (a) within 50 days of the receipt of the notice of appeal by the Board; or
   (b) if the Board has allowed a further period of time for delivery of further particulars under paragraph (3), within 7 days of the end of that period.

Withdrawal of appeal or assessment

6 (1) The appellant may withdraw the notice of appeal by notice given to the Board at any time and in that event no further action shall be taken in relation to the appeal.

(2) When an assessment is withdrawn by the Board, it shall notify the Employment Tribunal Office and no further action shall be taken in relation to the appeal.

Entry of appeal

7 (1) The Secretary shall as soon as reasonably practicable after receiving from the Board the relevant documents in accordance with rule 4(1), 5(4) or 5(5)–
   (a) give notice to the appellant and to the Board of the case number of the appeal (which must from then on be referred to in all correspondence relating to the appeal) and of the address to which notices and other communications to the Employment Tribunal Office shall be sent;
   (b) give notice to the appellant of the Board's address for service; and
   (c) send to the appellant a copy of any representations in writing that the Board has submitted to the tribunal under rule 4 or 5.

Order for further information

8 (1) In any case in which the appellant has not sent to the Board further information which has been requested by the Board in accordance with rule 5, a chairman or tribunal may, on the application of the Board, by notice order the appellant to supply such further information as may be specified in the notice, and the appellant shall send two copies of such information to the Employment Tribunal Office within such time as the chairman or tribunal may direct.

(2) As soon as is reasonably practicable after receiving the further information from the appellant, the Secretary shall send a copy of the information to the Board.

(3) An order made under paragraph (1) shall be treated as an order made under rule 10 of Schedule 1 for the purposes of rule 13 of Schedule 1 (compliance with orders and practice directions).

Provisions of Schedule 1 which do not apply to levy appeals

9 The following rules in Schedule 1 shall not apply in relation to levy appeals: rules 1 to 9, 16(1)(c), 18(2)(c) and (e), 20 to 25, 33, 34(1)(a), 34(2), 34(4), 38(4), 39, 42(4), 43, 47, 49 to 53, 55, and paragraphs (4)(a), (7) and (8) of rule 61. All references in Schedule 1 to the rules listed in this rule shall have no effect in relation to a levy appeal.

Modification of Schedule 1

10 Schedule 1 shall be further modified in relation to levy appeals as follows–

(a) all references in Schedule 1 to a claim or claimant shall be read as references to a levy appeal or to an appellant in a levy appeal respectively and as the context may require; and

(b) in rule 61 (Notices, etc) after paragraph 4(i) insert–

'(j)   in the case of a notice of an appeal brought under the Industrial Training Act, the Board's address for service specified in the assessment notice;

(k)   in the case of any other document directed to the Board, the Board's address for service;'.

Annex

Form 1

Industrial Training Act 1982

Notice of Appeal Against an Assessment

TO:

*INDUSTRIAL TRAINING BOARD

....[ ]...

....

....

AND TO:

The Secretary of Tribunals (England and Wales) + (Scotland)

I/We +...of

....#..

....

hereby give notice that I / We + appeal to an employment tribunal under the Industrial Training Act 1982, section 12, against the assessment to the levy made by the above-mentioned industry training board on . . . . . 20 . . being the assessment numbered..

Grounds of appeal

The grounds of my / our + appeal are as follows:

Address for service

All communications regarding the appeal should be addressed to me / us + at ....#..

to my / our Solicitor(s) Agent(s)~,

.............................at....................................#...

Date..20..

Signed ....

*Insert name of the Board.

[ ] Insert the address of the Board.

+ Delete as relevant

Insert address applicable

~ If the notice is signed on behalf of the appellant, the signatory must state in what capacity or what authority he signs.

SCHEDULE 4: THE EMPLOYMENT TRIBUNALS (HEALTH AND SAFETY–APPEALS AGAINST IMPROVEMENT AND PROHIBITION NOTICES) RULES OF PROCEDURE

For use only in proceedings in an appeal against an improvement or prohibition notice

Application of Schedule 1

1   Subject to rules 11 and 12 of this Schedule, Schedule 1 shall apply to appeals against an improvement notice or a prohibition notice. The rules in this Schedule modify the rules in Schedule 1 in relation to such appeals. If there is conflict between the rules contained in this Schedule and those in Schedule 1, the rules in this Schedule shall prevail.

Definitions

2   In this Schedule and in relation to proceedings to which this Schedule applies–

'Health and Safety Act' means the Health and Safety at Work etc Act 1974;

'improvement notice' means a notice under section 21 of the Health and Safety Act;

'inspector' means a person appointed under section 19(1) of the Health and Safety Act;

'prohibition notice' means a notice under section 22 of the Health and Safety Act; and

'respondent' means the inspector who issued the improvement notice or prohibition notice which is the subject of the appeal.

Notice of appeal

3   A person wishing to appeal an improvement notice or a prohibition notice (the appellant) shall do so by sending to the Employment Tribunal Office of a notice of appeal which must include the following–

(a) the name and address of the appellant and, if different, an address to which he requires notices and documents relating to the appeal to be sent;

(b) the date of the improvement notice or prohibition notice appealed against and the address of the premises or the place concerned;

(c) the name and address of the respondent;

(d) details of the requirements or directions which are being appealed; and

(e) the grounds for the appeal.

Time limit for bringing appeal

4   (1) Subject to paragraph (2), the notice of appeal must be sent to the Employment Tribunal Office within 21 days from the date of the service on the appellant of the notice appealed against.

(2) A tribunal may extend the time mentioned above where it is satisfied, on an application made in writing to the Secretary either before or after the expiration of that time, that it is or was not reasonably practicable for an appeal to be brought within that time.

Action on receipt of appeal

5   On receiving the notice of appeal the Secretary shall–
   (a) send a copy of the notice of appeal to the respondent; and
   (b) inform the parties in writing of the case number of the appeal (which must from then on be referred to in all correspondence relating to the appeal) and of the address to which notices and other communications to the Employment Tribunal Office shall be sent.

Application for a direction suspending the operation of a prohibition notice

6   (1) When an appeal is brought against a prohibition notice, an application may be made by the appellant under section 24(3)(b) of the Health and Safety Act for a direction suspending the operation of the prohibition notice until the appeal is determined or withdrawn. The application must be presented to the Employment Tribunal Office in writing and shall include–
   (a) the case number of the appeal, or if there is no case number sufficient details to identify the appeal; and
   (b) the grounds on which the application is made.

   (2) The Secretary shall send a copy of the application to the respondent as soon as practicable after it has been received and shall inform the respondent that he has the opportunity to submit representations in writing if he so wishes, within a specified time but not less than 7 days.

   (3) The chairman shall consider the application and any representations submitted by the respondent, and may–
   (a) order that the application should not be determined separately from the full hearing of the appeal;
   (b) order that the operation of the prohibition notice be suspended until the appeal is determined or withdrawn;
   (c) dismiss the appellant's application; or
   (d) order that the application be determined at a Hearing (held in accordance with rule 26 of Schedule 1).

   (4) The chairman must give reasons for any decision made under paragraph (3) or made following a Hearing ordered under paragraph (3)(d).

   (5) A decision made under paragraph (3) or made following a Hearing ordered under paragraph (3)(d) shall be treated as a decision which may be reviewed upon the application of a party under rule 34 of Schedule 1.

General power to manage proceedings

7   (1) The chairman may at any time on the application of a party, make an order in relation to any matter which appears to him to be appropriate. Such orders may be those listed in rule 10(2) of Schedule 1 (subject to rule 11

below) or such other orders as he thinks fit. Subject to the case management rules in Schedule 1, orders may be issued as a result of a chairman considering the papers before him in the absence of the parties, or at a hearing (see regulation 2 for the definition of 'hearing').

(2) If the parties agree in writing upon the terms of any decision to be made by the tribunal or chairman, the chairman may, if he thinks fit, decide accordingly.

Appointment of an assessor

8   The President, Vice President or a Regional Chairman may, if he thinks fit, appoint in accordance with section 24(4) of the Health and Safety Act a person having special knowledge or experience in relation to the subject matter of the appeal to sit with the tribunal or chairman as an assessor.

Right to withdraw proceedings

9   (1) An appellant may withdraw all or part of the appeal at any time. This may be done either orally at a hearing or in writing in accordance with paragraph (2).

(2) To withdraw an appeal or part of one in writing the appellant must inform the Employment Tribunal Office in writing of the appeal or the parts of it which are to be withdrawn.

(3) The Secretary shall inform all other parties of the withdrawal. Withdrawal takes effect on the date on which the Employment Tribunal Office (in the case of written notifications) or the tribunal or chairman receives notice of it and where the whole appeal is withdrawn proceedings are brought to an end against the respondent on that date and the tribunal or chairman shall dismiss the appeal.

Costs and expenses

10   (1) A tribunal or chairman may make an order ('a costs order') that a party ('the paying party') make a payment in respect of the costs incurred by another party ('the receiving party').

(2) For the purposes of paragraph (1) 'costs' shall mean fees, charges, disbursements, expenses or remuneration incurred by or on behalf of a party in relation to the proceedings. In Scotland all references in this Schedule to costs or costs orders shall be read as references to expenses or orders for expenses.

(3) The amount of a costs order against the paying party can be determined in the following ways–

   (a) the tribunal may specify the sum which the party must pay to the receiving party, provided that sum does not exceed £10,000;

   (b) the parties may agree on a sum to be paid by the paying party to the receiving party and if they do so the costs order shall be for the sum so agreed;

   (c) the tribunal may order the paying party to pay the receiving party the whole or a specified part of the costs of the second party with the amount to be paid being determined by way of detailed assessment in a County

Court in accordance with the Civil Procedure Rules or, in Scotland, as taxed according to such part of the table of fees prescribed for proceedings in the sheriff court as shall be directed by the order.

(4) The tribunal or chairman shall have regard to the paying party's ability to pay when considering whether it or he shall make a costs order or how much that order should be.

(5) For the avoidance of doubt, the amount of a costs order made under either paragraph (4)(b) or (c) may exceed £10,000.

Provisions of Schedule 1 which do not apply to appeals against improvement notices or prohibition notices

11   The following rules in Schedule 1 shall not apply in relation to appeals against improvement and prohibition notices: rules 1 to 9, 10(1), 10(2)(g), (i), (k), (l) and (r), 12, 13, 16(1)(c), 18(2)(c) and (e), 18(8), 20 to 25, 29(3), 33, 34(1)(a), 34(2), 38 to 47, 49 to 53, 55, and 61(4)(a), (7) and (8). All references in Schedule 1 to the rules listed in this rule shall have no effect in relation to an appeal against an improvement notice or a prohibition notice.

Modification of Schedule 1

12   Schedule 1 shall be further modified so that all references in Schedule 1 to a claim shall be read as references to a notice of appeal or to an appeal against an improvement notice or a prohibition notice, as the context may require, and all references to the claimant shall be read as references to the appellant in such an appeal.

SCHEDULE 5: THE EMPLOYMENT TRIBUNALS (NON-DISCRIMINATION NOTICES APPEALS) RULES OF PROCEDURE

For use only in proceedings in an appeal against a non-discrimination notice

Application of Schedule 1

1   Subject to rules 5 and 6 of this Schedule, Schedule 1 shall apply to appeals against a non-discrimination notice. The rules in this Schedule modify the rules in Schedule 1 in relation to such appeals. If there is conflict between the rules contained in this Schedule and those in Schedule 1, the rules in this Schedule shall prevail.

Definitions

2   In this Schedule and in relation to proceedings to which this Schedule applies–

'appeal', unless the context requires otherwise, means an appeal referred to in section 68(1)(a) of the Sex Discrimination Act, in section 59(1)(a) of the Race Relations Act or, as the case may be, in paragraph 10(1) and (2)(a) of Schedule 3 to the Disability Rights Commission Act;

'Disability Rights Commission Act' means the Disability Rights Commission Act 1999;

'non-discrimination notice' means a notice under section 67 of the Sex Discrimination Act, under section 58 of the Race Relations Act or, as the case may be, under section 4 of the Disability Rights Commission Act; and

'respondent' means the Equal Opportunities Commission established under section 53 of the Sex Discrimination Act, the Commission for Racial Equality established under section 43 of the Race Relations Act or, as the case may be, the Disability Rights Commission established under section 1 of the Disability Rights Commission Act.

Notice of Appeal

3 A person wishing to appeal a non-discrimination notice (the appellant) shall do so by sending to the Employment Tribunal Office of a notice of appeal which must be in writing and must include the following–

(a) the name and address of the appellant and, if different, an address to which he requires notices and documents relating to the appeal to be sent;

(b) the date of the non-discrimination notice appealed against;

(c) the name and address of the respondent;

(d) details of the requirements which are being appealed; and

(e) the grounds for the appeal.

Action on receipt of appeal

4 On receiving the notice of appeal the Secretary shall–

(a) send a copy of the notice of appeal to the respondent; and

(b) inform the parties in writing of the case number of the appeal (which must from then on be referred to in all correspondence relating to the appeal) and of the address to which notices and other communications to the Employment Tribunal Office shall be sent.

Provisions of Schedule 1 which do not apply to appeals against non-discrimination notices

5 The following rules in Schedule 1 shall not apply in relation to appeals against a non-discrimination notice: rules 1 to 9, 16(1)(c), 18(2)(c) and (e), 20 to 24, 33, 34(1)(a), 34(2), 34(4), 38(4), 39, 42(4), 43, 47,49 to 53, 55, and paragraphs (4)(a), (7) and (8) of rule 61. All references in Schedule 1 to the rules listed in this rule shall have no effect in relation to an appeal against a non-discrimination notice.

Modification of Schedule 1

6 Schedule 1 shall be further modified so that all references in Schedule 1 to a claim shall be read as references to a notice of appeal or to an appeal against a non-discrimination notice, as the context may require, and all references to the claimant shall be read as references to the appellant in such an appeal.

SCHEDULE 6: THE EMPLOYMENT TRIBUNALS (EQUAL VALUE) RULES OF PROCEDURE

Regulation 16(4)

General

1   The rules in this Schedule shall only apply in proceedings involving an equal value claim and they modify and supplement the rules in Schedule 1. If there is conflict between Schedule 1 and this Schedule, the provisions of this Schedule shall prevail.

Interpretation

2   (1) In this Schedule and in relation to proceedings to which this Schedule applies–

'comparator' means the person of the opposite sex to the claimant in relation to whom the claimant claims that his work is of equal value as described in section 1(2)(c) of the Equal Pay Act;

'Equal Pay Act' means the Equal Pay Act 1970;

'equal value claim' means a claim by a claimant which rests upon entitlement to the benefit of an equality clause by virtue of the operation of section 1(2)(c) of the Equal Pay Act;

'the facts relating to the question' has the meaning in rule 7(3);

'independent expert' means a member of the panel of independent experts mentioned in section 2A(4) of the Equal Pay Act;

'indicative timetable' means the indicative timetable set out in the Annex to this Schedule;

'the question' means whether the claimant's work is of equal value to that of the comparator as described in section 1(2)(c) of the Equal Pay Act; and

'report' means a report required by a tribunal to be prepared by an independent expert, in accordance with section 2A(1)(b) of the Equal Pay Act.

(2) A reference in this Schedule to a rule, is a reference to a rule in this Schedule unless otherwise provided.

(3) A reference in this Schedule to 'these rules' is a reference to the rules in Schedules 1 and 6 unless otherwise provided.

General power to manage proceedings

3   (1) In addition to the power to make orders described in rule 10 of Schedule 1, the tribunal or chairman shall have power (subject to rules 4(3) and 7(4)) to make the following orders–

(a) the standard orders set out in rules 5 or 8, with such addition to, omission or variation of those orders (including specifically variations as to the periods within which actions are to be taken by the parties) as the chairman or tribunal considers is appropriate;

(b) that no new facts shall be admitted in evidence by the tribunal unless they have been disclosed to all other parties in writing before a date specified by the tribunal (unless it was not reasonably practicable for a party to have done so);

(c) that the parties may be required to send copies of documents or provide information to the other parties and to the independent expert;

(d) that the respondent is required to grant the independent expert access to his premises during a period specified by the tribunal or chairman in order for the independent expert to conduct interviews with persons identified as relevant by the independent expert;

(e) when more than one expert is to give evidence in the proceedings, that those experts present to the tribunal a joint statement of matters which are agreed between them and those matters on which they disagree;

(f) where proceedings have been joined, that lead claimants be identified.

(2) Any reference in Schedule 1 or 2 to an order made under rule 10 of Schedule 1 shall include reference to an order made in accordance with this Schedule.

Conduct of stage 1 equal value hearing

4 (1) When in an equal value claim there is a dispute as to whether any work is of equal value as mentioned in section 1(2)(c) of the Equal Pay Act, the tribunal shall conduct a 'stage 1 equal value hearing' in accordance with both this rule and the rules applicable to pre-hearing reviews in Schedule 1.

(2) Notwithstanding rule 18(1) and (3) of Schedule 1, a stage 1 equal value hearing shall be conducted by a tribunal composed in accordance with section 4(1) of the Employment Tribunals Act.

(3) At the stage 1 equal value hearing the tribunal shall–

(a) where section 2A(2) of the Equal Pay Act applies, strike out the claim (or the relevant part of it) if, in accordance with section 2A(2A) of that Act, the tribunal must determine that the work of the claimant and the comparator are not of equal value;

(b) decide, in accordance with section 2A(1) of the Equal Pay Act, either that–

(i)   the tribunal shall determine the question; or

(ii) it shall require a member of the panel of independent experts to prepare a report with respect to the question;

(c) subject to rule 5 and with regard to the indicative timetable, make the standard orders for the stage 1 equal value hearing as set out in rule 5;

(d) if the tribunal has decided to require an independent expert to prepare a report on the question, require the parties to copy to the independent expert all information which they are required by an order to disclose or agree between each other;

(e) if the tribunal has decided to require an independent expert to prepare a report on the question, fix a date for the stage 2 equal value hearing, having regard to the indicative timetable;

(f) if the tribunal has not decided to require an independent expert to prepare a report on the question, fix a date for the Hearing, having regard to the indicative timetable;

(g) consider whether any further orders are appropriate.

(4) Before a claim or part of one is struck out under paragraph (3)(a), the Secretary shall send notice to the claimant giving him the opportunity to make representations to the tribunal as to whether the evaluation contained in the study in question falls within paragraph (a) or (b) of section 2A(2A) of the Equal Pay Act. The Secretary shall not be required to send a notice under

this paragraph if the claimant has been given an opportunity to make such representations orally to the tribunal as to why such a judgment should not be issued.

(5) The tribunal may, on the application of a party, hear evidence upon and permit the parties to address it upon the issue contained in section 1(3) of the Equal Pay Act (defence of a genuine material factor) before determining whether to require an independent expert to prepare a report under paragraph (3)(b)(ii).

(6) When the Secretary gives notice to the parties of the stage 1 equal value hearing under rule 14(4) of Schedule 1, he shall also give the parties notice of the matters which the tribunal may and shall consider at that hearing which are described in paragraphs (3) and (5) of this rule and he shall give the parties notice of the standard orders in rule 5.

(7) The tribunal's power to strike out the claim or part of it under paragraph (3)(a) is in addition to powers to strike out a claim under rule 18(7) of Schedule 1.

Standard orders for stage 1 equal value hearing

5 (1) At a stage 1 equal value hearing a tribunal shall, unless it considers it inappropriate to do so and subject to paragraph (2), order that–

(a) before the end of the period of 14 days after the date of the stage 1 equal value hearing the claimant shall–

(i)   disclose in writing to the respondent the name of any comparator, or, if the claimant is not able to name the comparator he shall instead disclose such information as enables the comparator to be identified by the respondent; and

(ii) identify to the respondent in writing the period in relation to which he considers that the claimant's work and that of the comparator are to be compared;

(b) before the end of the period of 28 days after the date of the stage 1 equal value hearing–

(i)   where the claimant has not disclosed the name of the comparator to the respondent under sub-paragraph (a), if the respondent has been provided with sufficient detail to be able to identify the comparator, he shall disclose in writing the name of the comparator to the claimant;

(ii) the parties shall provide each other with written job descriptions for the claimant and any comparator;

(iii) the parties shall identify to each other in writing the facts which they consider to be relevant to the question;

(c) the respondent is required to grant access to the claimant and his representative (if any) to his premises during a period specified by the tribunal or chairman in order for him or them to interview any comparator;

(d) the parties shall before the end of the period of 56 days after the date of the stage 1 equal value hearing present to the tribunal a joint agreed statement in writing of the following matters–

      (i)   job descriptions for the claimant and any comparator;

      (ii) facts which both parties consider are relevant to the question;

      (iii) facts on which the parties disagree (as to the fact or as to the relevance to the question) and a summary of their reasons for disagreeing;

  (e) the parties shall, at least 56 days prior to the Hearing, disclose to each other, to any independent or other expert and to the tribunal written statements of any facts on which they intend to rely in evidence at the Hearing; and

  (f) the parties shall, at least 28 days prior to the Hearing, present to the tribunal a statement of facts and issues on which the parties are in agreement, a statement of facts and issues on which the parties disagree and a summary of their reasons for disagreeing.

(2) Any of the standard orders for the stage 1 equal value hearing may be added to, varied or omitted as the tribunal considers appropriate.

Involvement of independent expert in fact finding

6 (1) This rule applies only to proceedings in relation to which the tribunal has decided to require an independent expert to prepare a report on the question.

(2) In proceedings to which this rule applies a tribunal or chairman may if it or he considers it appropriate at any stage of the proceedings order an independent expert to assist the tribunal in establishing the facts on which the independent expert may rely in preparing his report.

(3) Examples of the circumstances in which the tribunal or chairman may make an order described in paragraph (2) may include–

  (a) a party not being legally represented;

  (b) the parties are unable to reach agreement as required by an order of the tribunal or chairman;

  (c) the tribunal or chairman considers that insufficient information may have been disclosed by a party and this may impair the ability of the independent expert to prepare a report on the question;

  (d) the tribunal or chairman considers that the involvement of the independent expert may promote fuller compliance with orders made by the tribunal or a chairman.

(4) A party to proceedings to which this rule applies may make an application under rule 11 of Schedule 1 for an order under paragraph (2).

Conduct of stage 2 equal value hearing

7 (1) This rule applies only to proceedings in relation to which the tribunal has decided to require an independent expert to prepare a report on the question. In such proceedings the tribunal shall conduct a 'stage 2 equal value hearing' in accordance with both this rule and the rules applicable to pre-hearing reviews in Schedule 1.

(2) Notwithstanding rule 18(1) and (3) of Schedule 1, a stage 2 equal value hearing shall be composed in accordance with section 4(1) of the Employment Tribunals Act.

(3) At the stage 2 equal value hearing the tribunal shall make a determination of facts on which the parties cannot agree which relate to the question and shall require the independent expert to prepare his report on the basis of facts which have (at any stage of the proceedings) either been agreed between the parties or determined by the tribunal (referred to as 'the facts relating to the question').

(4) At the stage 2 equal value hearing the tribunal shall–
   (a) Subject to rule 8 and having regard to the indicative timetable, make the standard orders for the stage 2 equal value hearing as set out in rule 8;
   (b) make any orders which it considers appropriate;
   (c) fix a date for the Hearing, having regard to the indicative timetable.

(5) Subject to paragraph (6), the facts relating to the question shall, in relation to the question, be the only facts on which the tribunal shall rely at the Hearing.

(6) At any stage of the proceedings the independent expert may make an application to the tribunal for the some or all of the facts relating to the question to be amended, supplemented or omitted.

(7) When the Secretary gives notice to the parties and to the independent expert of the stage 2 equal value hearing under rule 14(4) of Schedule 1, he shall also give the parties notice of the standard orders in rule 8 and draw the attention of the parties to paragraphs (4) and (5) of this rule.

Standard orders for stage 2 equal value hearing

8 (1) At a stage 2 equal value hearing a tribunal shall, unless it considers it inappropriate to do so and subject to paragraph (2), order that–
   (a) by a date specified by the tribunal (with regard to the indicative timetable) the independent expert shall prepare his report on the question and shall (subject to rule 14) have sent copies of it to the parties and to the tribunal; and
   (b) the independent expert shall prepare his report on the question on the basis of the facts relating to the question and no other facts which may or may not relate to the question.

(2) Any of the standard orders for the stage 2 equal value hearing may be added to, varied or omitted as the tribunal considers appropriate.

The Hearing

9 (1) In proceedings in relation to which an independent expert has prepared a report, unless the tribunal determines that the report is not based on the facts relating to the question, the report of the independent expert shall be admitted in evidence in those proceedings.

(2) If the tribunal does not admit the report of an independent expert in accordance with paragraph (1), it may determine the question itself or require another independent expert to prepare a report on the question.

(3) The tribunal may refuse to admit evidence of facts or hear argument as to issues which have not been disclosed to the other party as required by these rules or any order made under them, unless it was not reasonably practicable for the party to have so complied.

Duties and powers of the independent expert

10 (1) When a tribunal requires an independent expert to prepare a report with respect to the question or an order is made under rule 6(2), the Secretary shall inform that independent expert of the duties and powers he has under this rule.

(2) The independent expert shall have a duty to the tribunal to–

(a) assist it in furthering the overriding objective in regulation 3;

(b) comply with the requirements of these rules and any orders made by the tribunal or a chairman in relation to the proceedings;

(c) keep the tribunal informed of any delay in complying with any order in the proceedings with the exception of minor or insignificant delays in compliance;

(d) comply with any timetable imposed by the tribunal or chairman in so far as this is reasonably practicable;

(e) inform the tribunal or a chairman on request by it or him of progress in the preparation of the independent expert's report;

(f) prepare a report on the question based on the facts relating to the question and (subject to rule 14) send it to the tribunal and the parties;

(g) make himself available to attend hearings in the proceedings.

(3) The independent expert may make an application for any order or for a hearing to be held as if he were a party to the proceedings.

(4) At any stage of the proceedings the tribunal may, after giving the independent expert the opportunity to make representations, withdraw the requirement on the independent expert to prepare a report. If it does so, the tribunal may itself determine the question, or it may determine that a different independent expert should be required to prepare the report.

(5) When paragraph (4) applies the independent expert who is no longer required to prepare the report shall provide the tribunal with all documentation and work in progress relating to the proceedings by a date specified by the tribunal. Such documentation and work in progress must be in a form which the tribunal is able to use. Such documentation and work in progress may be used in relation to those proceedings by the tribunal or by another independent expert.

(6) When an independent expert has been required to prepare a report in proceedings the Secretary shall give the independent expert notice of all hearings, orders or judgments in those proceedings as if the independent expert were a party to those proceedings and when these rules require a party to provide information to another party, such information shall also be provided to the independent expert.

Use of expert evidence

11 (1) Expert evidence shall be restricted to that which, in the opinion of the tribunal, is reasonably required to resolve the proceedings.

(2) An expert shall have a duty to assist the tribunal on matters within his expertise. This duty overrides any obligation to the person from whom he has received instructions or by whom he is paid.

(3) No party may call an expert or put in evidence an expert's report without the

permission of the tribunal. No expert report shall be put in evidence unless it has been disclosed to all other parties and any independent expert at least 28 days prior to the Hearing.

(4) In proceedings in which an independent expert has been required to prepare a report on the question, the tribunal shall not admit evidence of another expert on the question unless such evidence is based on the facts relating to the question. Unless the tribunal considers it inappropriate to do so, any such expert report shall be disclosed to all parties and to the tribunal on the same date on which the independent expert is required to send his report to the parties and to the tribunal.

(5) If an expert (other than an independent expert) does not comply with these rules or an order made by the tribunal or a chairman, the tribunal may order that the evidence of that expert shall not be admitted.

(6) Where two or more parties wish to submit expert evidence on a particular issue, the tribunal may order that the evidence on that issue is to be given by one joint expert only. When such an order has been made, if the parties wishing to instruct the joint expert cannot agree who should be the expert, the tribunal may select the expert.

Written questions to experts

12 (1) When any expert (including an independent expert) has prepared a report, a party or any other expert (including an independent expert) involved in the proceedings may put written questions about the report to the expert who has prepared the report.

(2) Unless the tribunal or chairman agrees otherwise, written questions under paragraph (1)–
(a) may be put once only;
(b) must be put within 28 days of the date on which the parties were sent the report;
(c) must be for the purpose only of clarifying the factual basis of the report;
(d) must be copied to all other parties and experts involved in the proceedings at the same time as they are sent to the expert who prepared the report.

(3) When written questions have been put to an expert in accordance with paragraph (2) he shall answer those questions within 28 days of receiving them.

(4) An expert's answers to questions put in accordance with paragraph (2) shall be treated as part of the expert's report.

(5) Where a party has put a written question in accordance with this rule to an expert instructed by another party and the expert does not answer that question, or does not do so within 28 days, the tribunal may order that the party instructing the expert may not rely on the evidence of that expert.

Procedural matters

13 (1) In proceedings in which an independent expert has been required to prepare a report, the Secretary shall send him notices and inform him of any hearing, application, order or judgment in those proceedings as if he were a party to those proceedings.

(2) For the avoidance of doubt, any requirement in this Schedule to hold a stage 1 or a stage 2 equal value hearing does not preclude holding more than one of each of those types of hearing or other hearings from being held in accordance with Schedule 1.

(3) Any power conferred on a chairman in Schedule 1 may (subject to the provisions of this Schedule) be carried out by a tribunal or a chairman in relation to proceedings to which this Schedule applies.

National security proceedings

14 (1) In equal value cases which are also national security proceedings, if a tribunal has required an independent expert to prepare a report on the question, the independent expert shall send a copy of the report to the tribunal and shall not send it to the parties. In such proceedings if written questions have been put to the independent expert under rule 12, the independent expert shall send any answers to those questions to the tribunal and not to the parties.

(2) Before the Secretary sends to the parties a copy of a report or answers which have been sent to him by the independent expert under paragraph (1), he shall follow the procedure set out in rule 10 of Schedule 2 as if that rule referred to the independent expert's report or answers (as the case may be) instead of written reasons, except that the independent expert's report or answers shall not be entered on the Register.

(3) If the Minister does not give a direction under rule 10(3) of Schedule 2 within the period of 28 days from the date on which the Minister was sent the report or answers to written questions the Secretary shall send a copy of the independent expert's report or answers to written questions (as the case may be) to the parties.

ANNEX

The indicative timetable

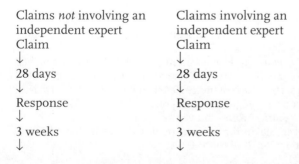

Claims *not* involving an independent expert
Claim
↓
28 days
↓
Response
↓
3 weeks
↓

Claims involving an independent expert
Claim
↓
28 days
↓
Response
↓
3 weeks
↓

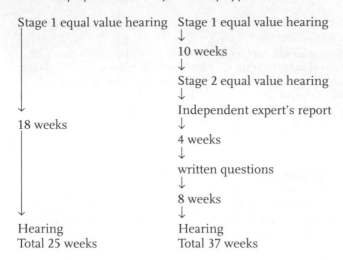

Stage 1 equal value hearing
↓
18 weeks
↓
Hearing
Total 25 weeks

Stage 1 equal value hearing
↓
10 weeks
↓
Stage 2 equal value hearing
↓
Independent expert's report
↓
4 weeks
↓
written questions
↓
8 weeks
↓
Hearing
Total 37 weeks

Employment Appeal Tribunal Rules 1993 SI No 2854 (as amended by the Employment Appeal Tribunal (Amendment) Rules 2001 and 2004)

Citation and commencement

1 (1) These Rules may be cited as the Employment Appeal Tribunal Rules 1993 and shall come into force on 16th December 1993.

  (2) . . .

Interpretation

2 (1) In these rules–

'the 1992 Act' means the Trade Union and Labour Relations (Consolidation) Act 1992;

'the 1996 Act' means the Employment Tribunals Act 1996;

'the 1999 Regulations' means the Transnational Information and Consultation of Employees Regulations 1999;

'the 2004 Regulations' means the European and Public Limited-Liability Company Regulations;

'the Appeal Tribunal' means the Employment Appeal Tribunal established under section 87 of the Employment Protection Act 1975 and continued in existence under section 20(1) of the 1996 Act and includes the President, a judge, a member or the Registrar acting on behalf of the Tribunal;

'the CAC' means the Central Arbitration Committee;

'the Certification Officer' means the person appointed to be the Certification Officer under section 254(2) of the 1992 Act;

'costs officer' means any officer of the Appeal Tribunal authorised by the President to assess costs or expenses;

'Crown employment proceedings' has the meaning given by section 10(8) of the 1996 Act;

'document' includes a document delivered by way of electronic communication;

'electronic communication' shall have the meaning given to it by section 15(1) of the Electronic Communications Act 2000;

'excluded person' means, in relation to any proceedings, a person who has been excluded from all or part of the proceedings by virtue of–

    (a) a direction of a Minister of the Crown under rule 30A(1)(b) or (c); or

    (b) an order of the Appeal Tribunal under rule 30A(2)(a) read with rule 30A(1)(b) or (c);

'judge' means a judge of the Appeal Tribunal nominated under section 22(1)(a) or (b) of the 1996 Act and includes a judge nominated under section 23(2) of, or a judge appointed under section 24(1) of, the 1996 Act to be a temporary additional judge of the Appeal Tribunal;

'legal representative' shall mean a person, including a person who is a party's employee, who–

    (a) has a general qualification within the meaning of the Courts and Legal Services Act 1990;

    (b) is an advocate or solicitor in Scotland; or

    (c) is a member of the Bar of Northern Ireland or a Solicitor of the Supreme Court of Northern Ireland.

'member' means a member of the Appeal Tribunal appointed under section 22(1)(c) of the 1996 Act and includes a member appointed under section 23(3) of the 1996 Act to act temporarily in the place of a member appointed under that section;

'national security proceedings' shall have the meaning given to it in regulation 2 of the Employment Tribunals (Constitution and Rules of Procedure) Regulations 2004;

'the President' means the judge appointed under section 22(3) of the 1996 Act to be President of the Appeal Tribunal and includes a judge nominated under section 23(1) of the 1996 Act to act temporarily in his place;

'the Registrar' means the person appointed to be Registrar of the Appeal Tribunal and includes any officer of the Tribunal authorised by the President to act on behalf of the Registrar;

'the Secretary of Employment Tribunals' means the person acting for the time being as the Secretary of the Central Office of the Employment Tribunals (England and Wales) or, as may be appropriate, of the Central Office of the Employment Tribunals (Scotland);

'special advocate' means a person appointed pursuant to rule 30A(4);

'writing' includes writing delivered by means of electronic communication.

(2) ...

(3) Any reference in these Rules to a person who was the claimant or, as the case may be, the respondent in the proceedings before an employment tribunal includes, where those proceedings are still continuing, a reference

to a person who is the claimant or, as the case may be, is the respondent in those proceedings.

Overriding objective

2A (1) The overriding objective of these Rules is to enable the Appeal Tribunal to deal with cases justly.

(2) Dealing with a case justly includes, so far as practicable–
   (a) ensuring that the parties are on an equal footing;
   (b) dealing with the case in ways which are proportionate to the importance and complexity of the issues;
   (c) ensuring that it is dealt with expeditiously and fairly; and
   (d) saving expense.

(3) The parties shall assist the Appeal Tribunal to further the overriding objective.

Institution of Appeal

3 (1) Every appeal to the Appeal Tribunal shall, subject to paragraphs (2) and (4), be instituted by serving on the Tribunal the following documents–
   (a) a notice of appeal in, or substantially in, accordance with Form 1, 1A or 2 in the Schedule to these rules;
   (b) in the case of an appeal from a judgment of an employment tribunal a copy of any claim and response in the proceedings before the employment tribunal or an explanation as to why none is included; and
   (c) in the case of an appeal from a judgment of an employment tribunal a copy of the written record of the judgment of the employment tribunal which is subject to appeal and the written reasons for the judgment, or an explanation as to why none is included;
   (d) in the case of an appeal made pursuant to regulation 38(8) of the 1999 Regulations or regulation 47(6) of the 2004 Regulations from a declaration or order of the CAC, a copy of that declaration or order; and
   (e) in the case of an appeal from an order of an employment tribunal a copy of the written record of the order of the employment tribunal which is subject to appeal and (if available) the written reasons for the order;
   (f) in the case of an appeal from a decision or order of the Certification Officer a copy of the decision or order of the Certification Officer which is subject to appeal and the written reasons for that decision or order.

(2) In an appeal from a judgment or order of the employment tribunal in relation to national security proceedings where the appellant was the claimant–
   (i) the appellant shall not be required by virtue of paragraph (1)(b) to serve on the Appeal Tribunal a copy of the response if the response was not disclosed to the appellant; and
   (ii) the appellant shall not be required by virtue of paragraph (1)(c) or (e) to serve on the Appeal Tribunal a copy of the written reasons for the judgment or order if the written reasons were not sent to the appellant but if a document containing edited reasons was sent to the appellant, he shall serve a copy of that document on the Appeal Tribunal.

(3) The period within which an appeal to the Appeal Tribunal may be instituted is—

(a) in the case of an appeal from a judgment of the employment tribunal—

    (i) where the written reasons for the judgment subject to appeal—

        (aa) were requested orally at the hearing before the employment tribunal or in writing within 14 days of the date on which the written record of the judgment was sent to the parties; or

        (bb) were reserved and given in writing by the employment tribunal

    42 days from the date on which the written reasons were sent to the parties;

    (ii) in an appeal from a judgment given in relation to national security proceedings, where there is a document containing edited reasons for the judgment subject to appeal, 42 days from the date on which that document was sent to the parties; or

    (iii) where the written reasons for the judgment subject to appeal—

        (aa) were not requested orally at the hearing before the employment tribunal or in writing within 14 days of the date on which the written record of the judgment was sent to the parties; and

        (bb) were not reserved and given in writing by the employment tribunal

    42 days from the date on which the written record of the judgment was sent to the parties;

(b) in the case of an appeal from an order of an employment tribunal, 42 days from the date of the order;

(c) in the case of an appeal from a decision of the Certification Officer, 42 days from the date on which the written record of that decision was sent to the appellant;

(d) in the case of an appeal from a declaration or order of the CAC under regulation 38(8) of the 1999 Regulations or regulation 47(6) of the 2004 Regulations, 42 days from the date on which the written notification of that declaration or order was sent to the appellant.

(4) In the case of an appeal from a judgment or order of the employment tribunal in relation to national security proceedings, the appellant shall not set out the grounds of appeal in his notice of appeal and shall not append to his notice of appeal the written reasons for the judgment of the tribunal.

(5) In an appeal from the employment tribunal in relation to national security proceedings in relation to which the appellant was the respondent in the proceedings before the employment tribunal, the appellant shall, within the period described in paragraph (3)(a), provide to the Appeal Tribunal a document setting out the grounds on which the appeal is brought.

(6) In an appeal from the employment tribunal in relation to national security proceedings in relation to which the appellant was the claimant in the proceedings before the employment tribunal—

(a) the appellant may, within the period described in paragraph (3)(a)(ii) or

(iii) or paragraph 3(b), whichever is applicable, provide to the Appeal Tribunal a document setting out the grounds on which the appeal is brought; and

(b) a special advocate appointed in respect of the appellant may, within the period described in paragraph 3(a)(ii) or (iii) or paragraph 3(b), whichever is applicable, or within 21 days of his appointment, whichever is later, provide to the Appeal Tribunal a document setting out the grounds on which the appeal is brought or providing supplementary grounds of appeal.

(7) Where it appears to a judge or the Registrar that a notice of appeal or a document provided under paragraph (5) or (6)–

(a) discloses no reasonable grounds for bringing the appeal; or

(b) is an abuse of the Appeal Tribunal's process or is otherwise likely to obstruct the just disposal of proceedings,

he shall notify the Appellant or special advocate accordingly informing him of the reasons for his opinion and, subject to paragraphs (8) and (10), no further action shall be taken on the notice of appeal or document provided under paragraph (5) or (6).

(7A) In paragraphs (7) and (10) reference to a notice of appeal or a document provided under paragraph (5) or (6) includes reference to part of a notice of appeal or document provided under paragraph (5) or (6).

(8) Where notification has been given under paragraph (7), the appellant or the special advocate, as the case may be, may serve a fresh notice of appeal, or a fresh document under paragraph (5) or (6), within the time remaining under paragraph (3) or (6) or within 28 days from the date on which the notification given under paragraph 7 was sent to him, whichever is the longer period.

(9) Where the appellant or the special advocate serves a fresh notice of appeal or a fresh document under paragraph (8), a judge or the Registrar shall consider such fresh notice of appeal or document with regard to jurisdiction as though it were an original notice of appeal lodged pursuant to paragraphs (1) and (3), or as though it were an original document provided pursuant to paragraph (5) or (6), as the case may be.

(10) Where notification has been given under paragraph (7) and within 28 days of the date the notification was sent, an appellant or special advocate expresses dissatisfaction in writing with the reasons given by the judge or Registrar for his opinion, he is entitled to have the matter heard before a judge who shall make a direction as to whether any further action should be taken on the notice of appeal or document under paragraph (5) or (6).

Service of notice of appeal

4 (1) On receipt of notice under rule 3, the Registrar shall seal the notice with the Appeal Tribunal's seal and shall serve a sealed copy on the appellant and on–

(a) every person who, in accordance with rule 5, is a respondent to the appeal; and

(b) the Secretary of Employment Tribunals in the case of an appeal from an employment tribunal; or

(c) the Certification Officer in the case of an appeal from any of his decisions; or

(d) the Secretary of State in the case of an appeal under ... Chapter II of Part IV of the 1992 Act or Part XI of the Employment Rights Act 1996 to which he is not a respondent; or

(e) the Chairman of the CAC in the case of an appeal from the CAC under regulation 38(8) of the 1999 Regulations or regulation 47(6) of the 2004 Regulations.

(2) On receipt of a document provided under rule 3(5)–

(a) the Registrar shall not send the document to a person in respect of whom a Minister of the Crown has informed the Registrar that he wishes to address the Appeal Tribunal in accordance with rule 30A(3) with a view to the Appeal Tribunal making an order applicable to this stage of the proceedings under rule 30A(2)(a) read with 30A(1)(b) or (c) (exclusion of a party or his representative), at any time before the Appeal Tribunal decides whether or not to make such an order; but if it decides not to make such an order, the Registrar shall, subject to sub-paragraph (b), send the document to such a person 14 days after the Appeal Tribunal's decision not to make the order; and

(b) the Registrar shall not send a copy of the document to an excluded person, but if a special advocate is appointed in respect of such a person, the Registrar shall send a copy of the document to the special advocate.

(3) On receipt of a document provided under rule 3(6)(a) or (b), the Registrar shall not send a copy of the document to an excluded person, but shall send a copy of the document to the respondent.

Respondents to appeals

5   The respondents to an appeal shall be–

(a) in the case of an appeal from an employment tribunal or of an appeal made pursuant to section 45D, 56A, 95, 104 or 108C of the 1992 Act from a decision of the Certification Officer, the parties (other than the appellant) to the proceedings before the employment tribunal or the Certification Officer;

(b) in the case of an appeal made pursuant to section 9 or 126 of the 1992 Act from a decision of the Certification Officer, that Officer

(c) in the case of an appeal made pursuant to regulation 38(8) of the 1999 Regulations or regulation 47(6) of the 2004 Regulations from a declaration or order of the CAC, the parties (other than the appellant) to the proceedings before the CAC.

Respondent's answer and notice of cross-appeal

6   (1) The Registrar shall, as soon as practicable, notify every respondent of the date appointed by the Appeal Tribunal by which any answer under this rule must be delivered.

(2) A respondent who wishes to resist an appeal shall subject to paragraph (6), and, within the time appointed under paragraph (1) of this rule, deliver to the Appeal Tribunal an answer in writing in, or substantially in, accordance with Form 3 in the Schedule to these Rules, setting out the grounds on

which he relies, so, however, that it shall be sufficient for a respondent to an appeal referred to in rule 5(a) or 5(c) who wishes to rely on any ground which is the same as a ground relied on by the employment tribunal, the Certification Officer or the CAC for making the judgment, decision, declaration or order appealed from to state that fact in his answer.

(3) A respondent who wishes to cross-appeal may subject to paragraph (6), do so by including in his answer a statement of the grounds of his cross-appeal, and in that event an appellant who wishes to resist the cross-appeal shall, within a time to be appointed by the Appeal Tribunal, deliver to the Tribunal a reply in writing setting out the grounds on which he relies.

(4) The Registrar shall serve a copy of every answer and reply to a cross-appeal on every party other than the party by whom it was delivered.

(5) Where the respondent does not wish to resist an appeal, the parties may deliver to the Appeal Tribunal an agreed draft of an order allowing the appeal and the Tribunal may, if it thinks it right to do so, make an order allowing the appeal in the terms agreed.

(6) In an appeal from the employment tribunal in relation to national security proceedings, the respondent shall not set out the grounds on which he relies in his answer to an appeal, nor include in his answer a statement of the grounds of any cross-appeal.

(7) In an appeal from the employment tribunal in relation to national security proceedings in relation to which the respondent was not the claimant in the proceedings before the employment tribunal, the respondent shall, within the time appointed under paragraph (1), provide to the Registrar a document, setting out the grounds on which he intends to resist the appeal, and may include in that document a statement of the grounds of any cross-appeal.

(8) In an appeal from the employment tribunal in relation to national security proceedings in relation to which the respondent was the claimant in the proceedings before the employment tribunal–

(a) the respondent may, within the time appointed under paragraph (1) provide to the Registrar a document, setting out the grounds on which he intends to resist the appeal, and may include in that document a statement of the grounds of any cross-appeal; and

(b) a special advocate appointed in respect of the respondent may, within the time appointed under paragraph (1), or within 21 days of his appointment, whichever is the later, provide to the Registrar a document, setting out the grounds, or the supplementary grounds, on which the respondent intends to resist the appeal, and may include in that document a statement of the grounds, or the supplementary grounds, of any cross-appeal.

(9) In an appeal from the employment tribunal in relation to national security proceedings, if the respondent, or any special advocate appointed in respect of a respondent, provides in the document containing grounds for resisting an appeal a statement of grounds of cross-appeal and the appellant wishes to resist the cross-appeal–

(a) where the appellant was not the claimant in the proceedings before the employment tribunal, the appellant shall within a time to be appointed by the Appeal Tribunal deliver to the Tribunal a reply in writing setting out the grounds on which he relies; and

(b) where the appellant was the claimant in the proceedings before the employment tribunal, the appellant, or any special advocate appointed in respect of him, may within a time to be appointed by the Appeal Tribunal deliver to the Tribunal a reply in writing setting out the grounds on which the appellant relies.

(10) Any document provided under paragraph (7) or (9)(a) shall be treated by the Registrar in accordance with rule 4(2), as though it were a document received under rule 3(5).

(11) Any document provided under paragraph (8) or (9)(b) shall be treated by the Registrar in accordance with rule 4(3), as though it were a document received under rule 3(6)(a) or (b).

(12) Where it appears to a judge or the Registrar that a statement of grounds of cross-appeal contained in respondent's answer or document provided under paragraph (7) or (8)–

(a) discloses no reasonable grounds for bringing the cross-appeal; or

(b) is an abuse of the Appeal Tribunal's process or is otherwise likely to obstruct the just disposal of proceedings,

he shall notify the appellant or special advocate accordingly informing him of the reasons for his opinion and, subject to paragraphs (14) and (16), no further action shall be taken on the statement of grounds of cross-appeal.

(13) In paragraphs (12) and (16) reference to a statement of grounds of cross-appeal includes reference to part of a statement of grounds of cross-appeal.

(14) Where notification has been given under paragraph (12), the respondent or special advocate, as the case may be, may serve a fresh statement of grounds of cross-appeal before the time appointed under paragraph (1) or within 28 days from the date on which the notification given under paragraph (12) was sent to him, whichever is the longer.

(15) Where the respondent or special advocate serves a fresh statement of grounds of cross-appeal, a judge or the Registrar shall consider such statement with regard to jurisdiction as though it was contained in the original Respondent's answer or document provided under (7) or (8).

(16) Where notification has been given under paragraph (12) and within 28 days of the date the notification was sent, a respondent or special advocate expresses dissatisfaction in writing with the reasons given by the judge or Registrar for his opinion, he is entitled to have the matter heard before a judge who shall make a direction as to whether any further action should be taken on the statement of grounds of cross-appeal.

Disposal of appeal

7 (1) The Registrar shall, as soon as practicable, give notice of the arrangements made by the Appeal Tribunal for hearing the appeal to–

(a) every party to the proceedings; and

(b) the Secretary of Employment Tribunals in the case of an appeal from an employment tribunal; or

(c) the Certification Officer in the case of an appeal from one of his decisions; or

(d) the Secretary of State in the case of an appeal under Part XI of the Employment Rights Act 1996 or Chapter II of Part IV of the 1992 Act to which he is not a respondent; or

(e) the Chairman of the CAC in the case of an appeal from a declaration or order of, or arising in any proceedings before, the CAC under regulation 38(8) of the 1999 Regulations or regulation 47(6) of the 2004 Regulations.

(2) Any such notice shall state the date appointed by the Appeal Tribunal by which any interim application must be made.

Application in respect of exclusion or expulsion from, or unjustifiable discipline by, a trade union

8 Every application under section 67 or 176 of the 1992 Act to the Appeal Tribunal for:

(a) an award of compensation for exclusion or expulsion from a trade union; or

(b) one or both of the following, that is to say–

   (i) an award of compensation for unjustifiable discipline;

   (ii) an order that the union pay to the claimant an amount equal to any sum which he has paid in pursuance of any such determination as is mentioned in section 64(2)(b) of the 1992 Act;

shall be made in writing in, or substantially in, accordance with Form 4 in the Schedule to these Rules and shall be served on the Appeal Tribunal together with a copy of the decision or order declaring that the claimant's complaint against the trade union was well-founded.

9 If on receipt of an application under rule 8(a) it becomes clear that at the time the application was made the claimant had been admitted or re-admitted to membership of the union against which the complaint was made, the Registrar shall forward the application to the Central Office of Employment Tribunals.

Service of application under rule 8

10 On receipt of an application under rule 8, the Registrar shall seal it with the Appeal Tribunal's seal and shall serve a sealed copy on the claimant and on the respondent trade union and the Secretary of Employment Tribunals.

Appearance by respondent trade union

11 (1) Subject to paragraph (2) of this rule, a respondent trade union wishing to resist an application under rule 8 shall within 14 days of receiving the sealed copy of the application enter an appearance in, or substantially in, accordance with Form 5 in the Schedule to these Rules and setting out the grounds on which the union relies.

(2) Paragraph (1) above shall not require a respondent trade union to enter an appearance where the application is before the Appeal Tribunal by virtue of having been transferred there by an employment tribunal and, prior to that

transfer, the respondent had entered an appearance to the proceedings before the employment tribunal.

12 On receipt of the notice of appearance under rule 11 the Registrar shall serve a copy of it on the claimant.

Application for restriction of proceedings order

13 Every application to the Appeal Tribunal by the Attorney General or the Lord Advocate under section 33 of the 1996 Act for a restriction of proceedings order shall be made in writing in, or substantially in, accordance with Form 6 in the Schedule to these Rules, accompanied by an affidavit in support, and shall be served on the Tribunal.

Service of application under rule 13

14 On receipt of an application under rule 13, the Registrar shall seal it with the Appeal Tribunal's seal and shall serve a sealed copy on the Attorney General or the Lord Advocate, as the case may be, on the Secretary of Employment Tribunals and on the person named in the application.

Appearance by person named in application under rule 13

15 A person named in an application under rule 13 who wishes to resist the application shall within 14 days of receiving the sealed copy of the application enter an appearance in, or substantially in, accordance with Form 7 in the Schedule to these Rules, accompanied by an affidavit in support.

16 On receipt of the notice of appearance under rule 15 the Registrar shall serve a copy of it on the Attorney General or the Lord Advocate, as the case may be.

Complaints under regulations 20 and 21 of the 1999 Regulations

16A Every complaint under regulation 20 or 21 of the 1999 Regulations shall be made by way of application in writing in, or substantially in, accordance with Form 4A in the Schedule to these Rules and shall be served on the Appeal Tribunal.

Applications under regulation 33(6) of the 2004 Regulations

16AA Every application under regulation 33(6) of the 2004 Regulations shall be made by way of application in writing in, or substantially in, accordance with Form 4B in the Schedule to these Rules and shall be served on the Appeal Tribunal together with a copy of the declaration referred to in regulation 33(4) of those Regulations, or an explanation as to why none is included.

Service of application under rule 16A

16B On receipt of an application under rule 16A or 16AA, the Registrar shall seal it with the Appeal Tribunal's seal and shall serve a sealed copy on the claimant and on the respondent.

Appearance by respondent

16C   A respondent wishing to resist an application under rule 16A or 16AA shall within 14 days of receiving the sealed copy of the application enter an appearance in, or substantially in, accordance with Form 5A in the Schedule to these Rules and setting out the grounds on which the respondent relies.

16D   On receipt of the notice of appearance under rule 16C the Registrar shall serve a copy of it on the claimant.

Disposal of application

17 (1) The Registrar shall, as soon as practicable, give notice to the parties to an application under rule 8, 13, 16A or 16AA of the arrangements made by the Appeal Tribunal for hearing the application.

(2) Any such notice shall state the date appointed by the Appeal Tribunal by which any interim application must be made.

Joinder of parties

18   The Appeal Tribunal may, on the application of any person or of its own motion, direct that any person not already a party to the proceedings be added as a party, or that any party to proceedings shall cease to be a party, and in either case may give such consequential directions as it considers necessary.

Interim applications

19 (1) An interim application may be made to the Appeal Tribunal by giving notice in writing specifying the direction or order sought.

(2) On receipt of a notice under paragraph (1) of this rule, the Registrar shall serve a copy on every other party to the proceedings who appears to him to be concerned in the matter to which the notice relates and shall notify the claimant and every such party of the arrangements made by the Appeal Tribunal for disposing of the application.

Disposal of interim applications

20 (1) Every interim application made to the Appeal Tribunal shall be considered in the first place by the Registrar who shall have regard to rule 2A (the overriding objective) and, where applicable, to rule 23(5).

(2) Subject to sub-paragraphs (3) and (4), every interim application shall be disposed of by the Registrar except that any matter which he thinks should properly be decided by the President or a judge shall be referred by him to the President or judge who may dispose of it himself or refer it in whole or part to the Appeal Tribunal as required to be constituted by section 28 of the 1996 Act or refer it back to the Registrar with such directions as he thinks fit.

(3) Every interim application for a restricted reporting order shall be disposed of by the President or a judge or, if he so directs, the application shall be referred to the Appeal Tribunal as required to be constituted by section 28 of the 1996 Act who shall dispose of it.

(4) Every interim application for permission to institute or continue or to make a claim or application in any proceedings before an employment tribunal or

the Appeal Tribunal, pursuant to section 33(4) of the 1996 Act, shall be disposed of by the President or a judge, or, if he so directs, the application shall be referred to the Appeal Tribunal as required to be constituted by section 28 of the 1996 Act who shall dispose of it.

Appeals from Registrar

21 (1) Where an application is disposed of by the Registrar in pursuance of rule 20(2) any party aggrieved by his decision may appeal to a judge and in that case . . . the judge may determine the appeal himself or refer it in whole or in part to the Appeal Tribunal as required to be constituted by section 28 of the 1996 Act.

(2) Notice of appeal under paragraph (1) of this rule may be given to the Appeal Tribunal, either orally or in writing, within five days of the decision appealed from and the Registrar shall notify every other party who appears to him to be concerned in the appeal and shall inform every such party and the appellant of the arrangements made by the Tribunal for disposing of the appeal.

Hearing of interim applications

22 (1) The Appeal Tribunal may, subject to any direction of a Minister of the Crown under rule 30A(1) or order of the Appeal Tribunal under rule 30A(2)(a) read with rule 30A(1), and, where applicable, to rule 23(6), sit either in private or in public for the hearing of any interim application.

(2) . . .

Cases involving allegations of sexual misconduct or the commission of sexual offences

23 (1) This rule applies to any proceedings to which section 31 of the 1996 Act applies.

(2) In any such proceedings where the appeal appears to involve allegations of the commission of a sexual offence, the Registrar shall omit from any register kept by the Appeal Tribunal, which is available to the public, or delete from any order, judgment or other document, which is available to the public, any identifying matter which is likely to lead members of the public to identify any person affected by or making such an allegation.

(3) In any proceedings to which this rule applies where the appeal involves allegations of sexual misconduct the Appeal Tribunal may at any time before promulgation of its decision either on the application of a party or of its own motion make a restricted reporting order having effect, if not revoked earlier by the Appeal Tribunal, until the promulgation of its decision.

(4) A restricted reporting order shall specify the persons who may not be identified.

(5) Subject to paragraph (5A) the Appeal Tribunal shall not make a full restricted reporting order unless it has given each party to the proceedings an opportunity to advance oral argument at a hearing, if they so wish.

(5A) The Appeal Tribunal may make a temporary restricted reporting order without a hearing.

(5B) Where a temporary restricted reporting order has been made the Registrar shall inform the parties to the proceedings in writing as soon as possible of:

(a) the fact that the order has been made; and

(b) their right to apply to have the temporary restricted reporting order revoked or converted into a full restricted reporting order within 14 days of the temporary order being made.

(5C) If no such application is made under subparagraph (5B)(b) within the 14 days, the temporary restricted reporting order shall lapse and cease to have any effect on the fifteenth day after it was made. When such an application is made the temporary restricted reporting order shall continue to have effect until the Hearing at which the application is considered.

(6) Any ... hearing shall, subject to any direction of a Minister of the Crown under rule 30A(1) or order of the Appeal Tribunal under rule 30A(2)(a) read with rule 30A(1), or unless the Appeal Tribunal decides for any of the reasons mentioned in rule 29(2) to sit in private to hear evidence, be held in public.

(7) The Appeal Tribunal may revoke a restricted reporting order at any time where it thinks fit.

(8) Where the Appeal Tribunal makes a restricted reporting order, the Registrar shall ensure that a notice of that fact is displayed on the notice board of the Appeal Tribunal at the office in which the proceedings in question are being dealt with, on the door of the room in which those proceedings are taking place and with any list of the proceedings taking place before the Appeal Tribunal.

(9) In this rule, 'promulgation of its decision' means the date recorded as being the date on which the Appeal Tribunal's order finally disposing of the appeal is sent to the parties.

Restricted reporting orders in disability cases

23A (1) This rule applies to proceedings to which section 32(1) of the 1996 Act applies.

(2) In proceedings to which this rule applies the Appeal Tribunal may, on the application of the complainant or of its own motion, make a restricted reporting order having effect, if not revoked earlier by the Appeal Tribunal, until the promulgation of its decision.

(3) Where the Appeal Tribunal makes a restricted reporting order under paragraph (2) of this rule in relation to an appeal which is being dealt with by the Appeal Tribunal together with any other proceedings, the Appeal Tribunal may direct that the order is to apply also in relation to those other proceedings or such part of them as it may direct.

(4) Paragraphs (5) to (9) of rule 23 apply in relation to the making of a restricted reporting order under this rule as they apply in relation to the making of a restricted reporting order under that rule.

Appointment for direction

24 (1) Where it appears to the Appeal Tribunal that the future conduct of any proceedings would thereby be facilitated, the Tribunal may (either of its own motion or on application) at any stage in the proceedings appoint a date for a meeting for directions as to their future conduct and thereupon the following provisions of this rule shall apply.

(2) The Registrar shall give to every party in the proceedings notice of the date appointed under paragraph (1) of this rule and any party applying for directions shall, if practicable, before that date give to the Appeal Tribunal particulars of any direction for which he asks.

(3) The Registrar shall take such steps as may be practicable to inform every party of any directions applied for by any other party.

(4) On the date appointed under paragraph (1) of this rule, the Appeal Tribunal shall consider every application for directions made by any party and any written representations relating to the application submitted to the Tribunal and shall give such directions as it thinks fit for the purpose of securing the just, expeditious and economical disposal of the proceedings, including, where appropriate, directions in pursuance of rule 36, for the purpose of ensuring that the parties are enabled to avail themselves of opportunities for conciliation.

(5) Without prejudice to the generality of paragraph (4) of this rule, the Appeal Tribunal may give such directions as it thinks fit as to–
  (a) the amendment of any notice, answer or other document;
  (b) the admission of any facts or documents;
  (c) the admission in evidence of any documents;
  (d) the mode in which evidence is to be given at the hearing;
  (e) the consolidation of the proceedings with any other proceedings pending before the Tribunal;
  (f) the place and date of the hearing.

(6) An application for further directions or for the variation of any directions already given may be made in accordance with rule 19.

Appeal Tribunal's power to give directions

25   The Appeal Tribunal may either of its own motion or on application, at any stage of the proceedings, give any party directions as to any steps to be taken by him in relation to the proceedings.

Default by parties

26   If a respondent to any proceedings fails to deliver an answer or, in the case of an application made under section 67 or 176 of the 1992 Act, section 33 of the 1996 Act, regulation 20 or 21 of the 1999 Regulations or regulation 33 of the 2004 Regulations, a notice of appearance within the time appointed under these Rules, or if any party fails to comply with an order or direction of the Appeal Tribunal, the Tribunal may order that he be debarred from taking any further part in the proceedings, or may make such other order as it thinks just.

Attendance of witnesses and production of documents

27 (1) The Appeal Tribunal may, on the application of any party, order any person to attend before the Tribunal as a witness or to produce any document.

  (1A) Where–
    (a) a Minister has at any stage issued a direction under rule 30A(1)(b) or (c) (exclusion of a party or his representative), or the Appeal Tribunal has at

any stage made an order under rule 30A(2)(a) read with rule 30A(1)(b) or (c); and

(b) the Appeal Tribunal is considering whether to impose, or has imposed, a requirement under paragraph (1) on any person,

the Minister (whether or not he is a party to the proceedings) may make an application to the Appeal Tribunal objecting to the imposition of a requirement under paragraph (1) or, where a requirement has been imposed, an application to vary or set aside the requirement, as the case may be. The Appeal Tribunal shall hear and determine the Minister's application in private and the Minister shall be entitled to address the Appeal Tribunal thereon. The application shall be made by notice to the Registrar and the Registrar shall give notice of the application to each party.

(2) No person to whom an order is directed under paragraph (1) of this rule shall be treated as having failed to obey that order unless at the time at which the order was served on him there was tendered to him a sufficient sum of money to cover his costs of attending before the Appeal Tribunal.

Oaths

28   The Appeal Tribunal may, either of its own motion or on application, require any evidence to be given on oath.

Oral hearings

29 (1) Subject to paragraph (2) of this rule and to any direction of a Minister of the Crown under rule 30A(1)(a) or order of the Appeal Tribunal under rule 30A(2)(a) read with rule 30A(1)(a), an oral hearing at which any proceedings before the Appeal Tribunal are finally disposed of shall take place in public before, where applicable, such members of the Tribunal as (section 28 of the 1996 Act) the President may nominate for the purpose.

(2) Notwithstanding paragraph (1), the Appeal Tribunal may sit in private for the purpose of hearing evidence from any person which in the opinion of the Tribunal is likely to consist of–

(a) information which he could not disclose without contravening a prohibition imposed by or by virtue of any enactment;

(b) information which has been communicated to him in confidence or which he has otherwise obtained in consequence of the confidence reposed in him by another person; or

(c) information the disclosure of which would, for reasons other than its effect on negotiations with respect to any of the matters mentioned in section 178(2) of the 1992 Act, cause substantial injury to any undertaking of his or in which he works.

Duty of Appeal Tribunal concerning disclosure of information

30   When exercising its functions, the Appeal Tribunal shall ensure that information is not disclosed contrary to the interests of national security.

Proceedings in cases concerning national security

30A (1) A Minister of the Crown (whether or not he is a party to the proceedings) may, if he considers it expedient in the interests of national security, direct the Appeal Tribunal by notice to the Registrar to–

    (a) sit in private for all or part of particular Crown employment proceedings;

    (b) exclude any party who was the claimant in the proceedings before the employment tribunal from all or part of particular Crown employment proceedings;

    (c) exclude the representatives of any party who was the claimant in the proceedings before the employment tribunal from all or part of particular Crown employment proceedings;

    (d) take steps to conceal the identity of a particular witness in particular Crown employment proceedings.

(2) The Appeal Tribunal may, if it considers it expedient in the interests of national security, by order–

    (a) do anything of a kind which the Appeal Tribunal can be required to do by direction under paragraph (1) of this rule;

    (b) direct any person to whom any document (including any decision or record of the proceedings) has been provided for the purposes of the proceedings not to disclose any such document or the content thereof–

        (i) to any excluded person;

        (ii) in any case in which a direction has been given under paragraph (1)(a) or an order has been made under paragraph (2)(a) read with paragraph (1)(a), to any person excluded from all or part of the proceedings by virtue of such direction or order; or

        (iii) in any case in which a Minister of the Crown has informed the Registrar in accordance with paragraph (3) that he wishes to address the Appeal Tribunal with a view to the Tribunal making an order under paragraph (2)(a) read with paragraph (1)(b) or (c), to any person who may be excluded from all or part of the proceedings by virtue of such an order, if an order is made, at any time before the Appeal Tribunal decides whether or not to make such an order;

    (c) take steps to keep secret all or part of the reasons for any order it makes.

The Appeal Tribunal shall keep under review any order it makes under this paragraph.

(3) In any proceedings in which a Minister of the Crown considers that it would be appropriate for the Appeal Tribunal to make an order as referred to in paragraph (2), he shall (whether or not he is a party to the proceedings) be entitled to appear before and to address the Appeal Tribunal thereon. The Minister shall inform the Registrar by notice that he wishes to address the Appeal Tribunal and the Registrar shall copy the notice to the parties.

(4) In any proceedings in which there is an excluded person, the Appeal Tribunal shall inform the Attorney General or, in the case of an appeal from an employment tribunal in Scotland, the Advocate General for Scotland, of the proceedings before it with a view to the Attorney General (or, as the case may be, the Advocate General), if he thinks it fit to do so, appointing a special advocate to represent the interests of the person who was the claimant in the proceedings before the employment tribunal in respect of those parts of the proceedings from which–

(a) any representative of his is excluded;

(b) both he and his representative are excluded; or

(c) he is excluded, where he does not have a representative.

(5) A special advocate shall have a general qualification within the meaning of section 71 of the Courts and Legal Services Act 1990, or, in the case of an appeal from an employment tribunal in Scotland, shall be–

(a) an advocate; or

(b) a solicitor who has by virtue of section 25A of the Solicitors (Scotland) Act 1980 rights of audience in the Court of Session or the High Court of Justiciary.

(6) Where the excluded person is a party to the proceedings, he shall be permitted to make a statement to the Appeal Tribunal before the commencement of the proceedings, or the part of the proceedings, from which he is excluded.

(7) Except in accordance with paragraphs (8) to (10), the special advocate may not communicate directly or indirectly with any person (including an excluded person)–

(a) (except in the case of the Appeal Tribunal or the party who was the respondent in the proceedings before the employment tribunal) on any matter contained in the documents referred to in rule 3(5), 3(6), 6(7) or 6(8)(b); or

(b) (except in the case of a person who was present) on any matter discussed or referred to during any part of the proceedings in which the Appeal Tribunal sat in private pursuant to a direction of the Minister under paragraph (1)(a) or an order of the Appeal Tribunal under paragraph (2)(a) read with paragraph (1)(a).

(8) The special advocate may apply for directions from the Appeal Tribunal authorising him to seek instructions from, or otherwise to communicate with, an excluded person–

(a) on any matter contained in the documents referred to in rule 3(5), 3(6), 6(7) or 6(8)(b); or

(b) on any matter discussed or referred to during any part of the proceedings in which the Appeal Tribunal sat in private as referred to in paragraph (7)(b).

(9) An application under paragraph (8) shall be made by presenting to the Registrar a notice of application, which shall state the title of the proceedings and set out the grounds of the application.

(10) The Registrar shall notify the Minister of an application for directions under paragraph (8) and the Minister shall be entitled to address the Appeal Tribunal on the application.

(11) In these rules, in any case in which a special advocate has been appointed in respect of a party, any reference to a party shall (save in those references specified in paragraph (12)) include the special advocate.

(12) The references mentioned in paragraph (11) are those in rules 5 and 18, the first and second references in rule 27(1A), paragraphs (1) and (6) of this rule, the first reference in paragraph (3) of this rule, rule 34(1), the reference in item 4 of Form 1, and in item 4 of Form 1A, in the Schedule to these Rules.

Drawing up, reasons for, and enforcement of orders

31 (1) Every order of the Appeal Tribunal shall be drawn up by the Registrar and a copy, sealed with the seal of the Tribunal, shall be served by the Registrar on every party to the proceedings to which it relates and–

   (a) in the case of an order disposing of an appeal from an employment tribunal or of an order under section 33 of the 1996 Act, on the Secretary of the Employment Tribunals; . . .

   (b) in the case of an order disposing of an appeal from the Certification Officer, on that Officer

   (c) in the case of an order imposing a penalty notice under regulation 20 or 21 of the 1999 Regulations or regulation 33 of the 2004 Regulations, on the Secretary of State; or

   (d) in the case of an order disposing of an appeal from the CAC made under regulation 38(8) of the 1999 Regulations, on the Chairman of the CAC.

(2) Subject to rule 31A, the Appeal Tribunal shall, on the application of any party made within 14 days after the making of an order finally disposing of any proceedings, give its reasons in writing for the order unless it was made after the delivery of a reasoned judgment.

(3) Subject to any order made by the Court of Appeal or Court of Session and to any directions given by the Appeal Tribunal, an appeal from the Tribunal shall not suspend the enforcement of any order made by it.

Reasons for orders in cases concerning national security

31A (1) Paragraphs (1) to (5) of this rule apply to the document setting out the reasons for the Appeal Tribunal's order prepared under rule 31(2) or any reasoned judgment of the Appeal Tribunal as referred to in rule 31(2), in any particular Crown employment proceedings in which a direction of a Minister of the Crown has been given under rule 30A(1)(a), (b) or (c) or an order of the Appeal Tribunal has been made under rule 30A(2)(a) read with rule 30A(1)(a), (b) or (c).

(2) Before the Appeal Tribunal gives its reasons in writing for any order or delivers any reasoned judgment, the Registrar shall send a copy of the reasons or judgment to the Minister.

(3) If the Minister considers it expedient in the interests of national security, he may–

   (a) direct the Appeal Tribunal that the document containing its reasons for any order or its reasoned judgment shall not be disclosed to any person who was excluded from all or part of the proceedings and to prepare a further document setting out the reasons for its order, or a further reasoned judgment, but with the omission of such reasons as are specified in the direction; or

   (b) direct the Appeal Tribunal that the document containing its reasons for any order or its reasoned judgment shall not be disclosed to any person who was excluded from all or part of the proceedings, but that no further document setting out the Appeal Tribunal's reasons for its order or further reasoned judgment should be prepared.

(4) Where the Minister has directed the Appeal Tribunal in accordance with

paragraph (3)(a), the document prepared pursuant to that direction shall be marked in each place where an omission has been made. The document may then be given by the Registrar to the parties.

(5) The Registrar shall send the document prepared pursuant to a direction of the Minister in accordance with paragraph (3)(a) and the full document without the omissions made pursuant to that direction–

    (a) to whichever of the appellant and the respondent was not the claimant in the proceedings before the employment tribunal;

    (b) if he was not an excluded person, to the person who was the claimant in the proceedings before the employment tribunal and, if he was not an excluded person, to his representative;

    (c) if applicable, to the special advocate; and

    (d) where there are proceedings before a superior court relating to the order in question, to that court.

(6) Where the Appeal Tribunal intends to take steps under rule 30A(2)(c) to keep secret all or part of the reasons for any order it makes, it shall send the full reasons for its order to the persons listed in sub-paragraphs (a) to (d) of paragraph (5), as appropriate.

Registration and proof of awards in respect of exclusion or expulsion from, or unjustifiable discipline by, a trade union

32 (1) This rule applies where an application has been made to the Appeal Tribunal under section 67 or 176 of the 1992 Act.

(2) Without prejudice to rule 31, where the Appeal Tribunal makes an order in respect of an application to which this rule applies, and that order–

    (a) makes an award of compensation, or

    (b) is or includes an order of the kind referred to in rule 8(b)(ii),

or both, the Registrar shall as soon as may be enter a copy of the order, sealed with the seal of the Tribunal, into a register kept by the Tribunal (in this rule referred to as 'the Register').

(3) The production in any proceedings in any court of a document, purporting to be certified by the Registrar to be a true copy of an entry in the Register of an order to which this rule applies shall, unless the contrary is proved, be sufficient evidence of the document and of the facts stated therein.

Review of decisions and correction of errors

33 (1) The Appeal Tribunal may, either of its own motion or on application, review any order made by it and may, on such review, revoke or vary that order on the grounds that–

    (a) the order was wrongly made as the result of an error on the part of the Tribunal or its staff;

    (b) a party did not receive proper notice of the proceedings leading to the order; or

    (c) the interests of justice require such review.

(2) An application under paragraph (1) above shall be made within 14 days of the date of the order.

(3) A clerical mistake in any order arising from an accidental slip or omission may at any time be corrected by, or on the authority of, a judge or member.

(4) The decision to grant or refuse an application for review may be made by a judge.

General power to make costs or expenses orders

34 (1) In the circumstances listed in rule 34A the Appeal Tribunal may make an order ('a costs order') that a party or a special advocate, ('the paying party') make a payment in respect of the costs incurred by another party or a special advocate ('the receiving party').

(2) For the purposes of these Rules 'costs' includes fees, charges, disbursements and expenses incurred by or on behalf of a party or special advocate in relation to the proceedings, including the reimbursement allowed to a litigant in person under rule 34D. In Scotland, all references to costs or costs orders (except in the expression 'wasted costs') shall be read as references to expenses or orders for expenses.

(3) A costs order may be made against or in favour of a respondent who has not had an answer accepted in the proceedings in relation to the conduct of any part which he has taken in the proceedings.

(4) A party or special advocate may apply to the Appeal Tribunal for a costs order to be made at any time during the proceedings. An application may also be made at the end of a hearing, or in writing to the Registrar within 14 days of the date on which the order of the Appeal Tribunal finally disposing of the proceedings was sent to the parties.

(5) No costs order shall be made unless the Registrar has sent notice to the party or special advocate against whom the order may be made giving him the opportunity to give reasons why the order should not be made. This paragraph shall not be taken to require the Registrar to send notice to the party or special advocate if the party or special advocate has been given an opportunity to give reasons orally to the Appeal Tribunal as to why the order should not be made.

(6) Where the Appeal Tribunal makes a costs order it shall provide written reasons for doing so if a request for written reasons is made within 21 days of the date of the costs order. The Registrar shall send a copy of the written reasons to all the parties to the proceedings.

When a costs or expenses order may be made

34A (1) Where it appears to the Appeal Tribunal that any proceedings brought by the paying party were unnecessary, improper, vexatious or misconceived or that there has been unreasonable delay or other unreasonable conduct in the bringing or conducting of proceedings by the paying party, the Appeal Tribunal may make a costs order against the paying party.

(2) The Appeal Tribunal may in particular make a costs order against the paying party when–
(a) he has not complied with a direction of the Appeal Tribunal;
(b) he has amended its notice of appeal, document provided under rule 3 sub-paragraphs (5) or (6), Respondent's answer or statement of grounds

of cross-appeal, or document provided under rule 6 sub-paragraphs (7) or (8); or

(c) he has caused an adjournment of proceedings.

(3) Nothing in paragraph (2) shall restrict the Appeal Tribunal's discretion to award costs under paragraph (1).

The amount of a costs or expenses order

34B (1) Subject to sub-paragraphs (2) and (3) the amount of a costs order against the paying party can be determined in the following ways–

(a) the Appeal Tribunal may specify the sum which the paying party must pay to the receiving party;

(b) the parties may agree on a sum to be paid by the paying party to the receiving party and if they do so the costs order shall be for the sum agreed; or

(c) the Appeal Tribunal may order the paying party to pay the receiving party the whole or a specified part of the costs of the receiving party with the amount to be paid being determined by way of detailed assessment in the High Court in accordance with the Civil Procedure Rules 1998 or in Scotland the Appeal Tribunal may direct that it be taxed by the Auditor of the Court of Session, from whose decision an appeal shall lie to a judge.

(2) The Appeal Tribunal may have regard to the paying party's ability to pay when considering the amount of a costs order.

(3) The costs of an assisted person in England and Wales shall be determined by detailed assessment in accordance with the Civil Procedure Rules.

Personal liability of representatives for costs

34C (1) The Appeal Tribunal may make a wasted costs order against a party's representative.

(2) In a wasted costs order the Appeal Tribunal may disallow or order the representative of a party to meet the whole or part of any wasted costs of any party, including an order that the representative repay to his client any costs which have already been paid.

(3) 'Wasted costs' means any costs incurred by a party (including the representative's own client and any party who does not have a legal representative)–

(a) as a result of any improper, unreasonable or negligent act or omission on the part of any representative; or

(b) which, in the light of any such act or omission occurring after they were incurred, the Appeal Tribunal considers it reasonable to expect that party to pay.

(4) In this rule 'representative' means a party's legal or other representative or any employee of such representative, but it does not include a representative who is not acting in pursuit of profit with regard to the proceedings. A person is considered to be acting in pursuit of profit if he is acting on a conditional fee arrangement.

(5) Before making a wasted costs order, the Appeal Tribunal shall give the representative a reasonable opportunity to make oral or written representations as to reasons why such an order should not be made. The Appeal

Tribunal may also have regard to the representative's ability to pay when considering whether it shall make a wasted costs order or how much that order should be.

(6) When the Appeal Tribunal makes a wasted costs order, it must specify in the order the amount to be disallowed or paid.

(7) The Registrar shall inform the representative's client in writing–
   (a) of any proceedings under this rule; or
   (b) of any order made under this rule against the party's representative.

(8) Where the Appeal Tribunal makes a wasted costs order it shall provide written reasons for doing so if a request is made for written reasons within 21 days of the date of the wasted costs order. The Registrar shall send a copy of the written reasons to all parties to the proceedings.

Litigants in person and party litigants

34D (1) This rule applies where the Appeal Tribunal makes a costs order in favour of a party who is a litigant in person.

(2) The costs allowed under this rule must not exceed, except in the case of a disbursement, two-thirds of the amount which would have been allowed if the litigant in person had been represented by a legal representative.

(3) The litigant in person shall be allowed–
   (a) costs for the same categories of–
      (i)   work; and
      (ii) disbursements,
   which would have been allowed if the work had been done or the disbursements had been made by a legal representative on the litigant in person's behalf;
   (b) the payments reasonably made by him for legal services relating to the conduct of the proceedings;
   (c) the costs of obtaining expert assistance in assessing the costs claim; and
   (d) other expenses incurred by him in relation to the proceedings.

(4) The amount of costs to be allowed to the litigant in person for any item of work claimed shall be–
   (a) where the litigant in person can prove financial loss, the amount that he can prove he had lost for the time reasonably spent on doing the work; or
   (b) where the litigant in person cannot prove financial loss, an amount for the time which the Tribunal considers reasonably spent on doing the work at the rate of £25.00 per hour;

(5) For the year commencing 6th April 2006 the hourly rate of £25.00 shall be increased by the sum of £1.00 and for each subsequent year commencing on 6 April, the hourly rate for the previous year shall also be increased by the sum of £1.00.

(6) A litigant in person who is allowed costs for attending at court to conduct his case is not entitled to a witness allowance in respect of such attendance in addition to those costs.

(7) For the purpose of this rule, a litigant in person includes–
   (a) a company or other corporation which is acting without a legal representative; and

(b) in England and Wales a barrister, solicitor, solicitor's employee or other authorised litigator (as defined in the Courts and Legal Services Act), who is acting for himself; and

(c) in Scotland, an advocate or solicitor who is acting for himself.

(8) In the application of this rule to Scotland, references to a litigant in person shall be read as references to a party litigant.

Service of documents

35 (1) Any notice or other document required or authorised by these Rules to be served on, or delivered to, any person may be sent to him by post to his address for service or, where no address for service has been given, to his registered office, principal place of business, head or main office or last known address, as the case may be, and any notice or other document required or authorised to be served on, or delivered to, the Appeal Tribunal may be sent by post or delivered to the Registrar–

(a) in the case of a notice instituting proceedings, at the central office or any other office of the Tribunal; or

(b) in any other case, at the office of the Tribunal in which the proceedings in question are being dealt with in accordance with rule 38(2).

(2) Any notice or other document required or authorised to be served on, or delivered to, an unincorporated body may be sent to its secretary, manager or other similar officer.

(3) Every document served by post shall be assumed, in the absence of evidence to the contrary, to have been delivered in the normal course of post.

(4) The Appeal Tribunal may inform itself in such manner as it thinks fit of the posting of any document by an officer of the Tribunal.

(5) The Appeal Tribunal may direct that service of any document be dispensed with or be effected otherwise than in the manner prescribed by these Rules.

Conciliation

36   Where at any stage of any proceedings it appears to the Appeal Tribunal that there is a reasonable prospect of agreement being reached between the parties or of disposal of the appeal or a part of it by consensual means, the Tribunal may take such steps as it thinks fit to enable the parties to avail themselves of any opportunities for conciliation, whether by adjourning any proceedings or otherwise.

Time

37 (1) The time prescribed by these Rules or by order of the Appeal Tribunal for doing any act may be extended (whether it has already expired or not) or abridged, and the date appointed for any purpose may be altered, by order of the Tribunal.

(1A) Where an act is required to be done on or before a particular day it shall be done by 4 pm on that day.

(2) Where the last day for the doing of any act falls on a day on which the appropriate office of the Tribunal is closed and by reason thereof the act

cannot be done on that day, it may be done on the next day on which that office is open.

(3) An application for an extension of the time prescribed for the doing of an act, including the institution of an appeal under rule 3, shall be heard and determined as an interim application under rule 20.

(4) An application for an extension of the time prescribed for the institution of an appeal under rule 3 shall not be heard until the notice of appeal has been served on the Appeal Tribunal.

Tribunal offices and allocation of business

38 (1) The central office and any other office of the Appeal Tribunal shall be open at such times as the President may direct.

(2) Any proceedings before the Tribunal may be dealt with at the central office or at such other office as the President may direct.

Non-compliance with, and waiver of, rules

39 (1) Failure to comply with any requirements of these Rules shall not invalidate any proceedings unless the Appeal Tribunal otherwise directs.

(2) The Tribunal may, if it considers that to do so would lead to the more expeditious or economical disposal of any proceedings or would otherwise be desirable in the interests of justice, dispense with the taking of any step required or authorised by these Rules, or may direct that any such steps be taken in some manner other than that prescribed by these Rules.

(3) The powers of the Tribunal under paragraph (2) extend to authorising the institution of an appeal notwithstanding that the period prescribed in rule 3(2) may not have commenced.

Transitional provisions

40 (1) Where, prior to 16th December 1993, an employment tribunal has given full written reasons for its decision or order, those reasons shall be treated as extended written reasons for the purposes of rule 3(1)(c) and rule 3(2) and for the purposes of Form 1 in the Schedule to these Rules.

(2) Anything validly done under or pursuant to the Employment Appeal Tribunal Rules 1980 shall be treated as having been done validly for the purposes of these Rules, whether or not what was done could have been done under or pursuant to these Rules.

SCHEDULE

Form 1

Notice of Appeal from Decision of Employment Tribunal

1 The appellant is (name a*nd address of appellant*).

2 Any communication relating to this appeal may be sent to the appellant at (*appellant's address for service, including telephone number if any*).

3 The appellant appeals from
(*here give particulars of the decision of the employment tribunal from which the appeal is brought including the date*).

4   The parties to the proceedings before the employment tribunal, other than the appellant, were (*names and addresses of other parties to the proceedings resulting in decision appealed from*).

5   A copy of the employment tribunal's written reasons are attached to this notice/the reason(s) why a copy of the employment tribunal's written reasons are not included are as follows (*here set out in paragraphs the reason(s) why no copy of the employment tribunal's written reasons is attached*).

6   The grounds upon which this appeal is brought are that the employment tribunal erred in law in that (*here set out in paragraphs the various grounds of appeal*).

Date

Signed

Form 1A

Notice of Appeal from the CAC Made Pursuant to Regulation 38(8) of the Transnational Information and Consultation of Employees Regulations 1999 or regulation 47(6) of the European Public Limited-Liability Company Regulations 2004

1   The appellant is (*name and address of appellant*).

2   Any communication relating to this appeal may be sent to the appellant at (*appellant's address for service, including telephone number if any*).

3   The appellant appeals from (*here give particulars of the decision, declaration or order of the CAC from which the appeal is brought including the date*).

4   The parties to the proceedings before the CAC, other than the appellant, were (*names and addresses of other parties to the proceedings resulting in decision appealed from*).

5   A copy of the CAC's decision, declaration or order appealed from is attached to this notice.

6   The grounds upon which this appeal is brought are that the CAC erred in law in that (*here set out in paragraphs the various grounds of appeal*).

Date

Signed

Form 2

Notice of Appeal from Decision of Certification Officer

1   The appellant is (*name and address of appellant*).

2   Any communication relating to this appeal may be sent to the appellant at (*appellant's address for service, including telephone number if any*).

3   The appellant appeals from
    (*here give particulars of the order or decision of the Certification Officer from which the appeal is brought*).

4   The appellant's grounds of appeal are:
    (*here state the grounds of appeal*).

5   A copy of the Certification Officer's decision is attached to this notice.

Date

Signed

Form 3

Respondent's Answer

1. The respondent is (*name and address of respondent*).

2. Any communication relating to this appeal may be sent to the respondent at (*respondent's address for service, including telephone number if any*).

3. The respondent intends to resist the appeal of (*here give the name of appellant*). The grounds on which the respondent will rely are (the grounds relied upon by the employment tribunal/Certification Officer for making the decision or order appealed from) (and) (the following grounds):
(*here set out any grounds which differ from those relied upon by the employment tribunal or Certification Officer, as the case may be*).

4. The respondent cross-appeals from
(*here give particulars of the decision appealed from*).

5. The respondent's grounds of appeal are:
(*here state the grounds of appeal*).
Date
Signed

Form 4

Application to the Employment Appeal Tribunal for Compensation for Exclusion or Expulsion from a Trade Union or for Compensation or an Order in respect of Unjustifiable Discipline

1. My name is
My address is

2. Any communication relating to this application may be sent to me at
(*state address for service, including telephone number, if any*).

3. My complaint against (*state the name and address of the trade union*) was declared to be well-founded by (*state tribunal*) on (*give date of decision or order*).

4. (*Where the application relates to exclusion or expulsion from a trade union*) I have not been admitted/re-admitted* to membership of the above-named trade union and hereby apply for compensation on the following grounds.
(*Where the application relates to unjustifiable discipline*) The determination infringing my right not to be unjustifiably disciplined has not been revoked./The trade union has failed to take all the steps necessary for securing the reversal of things done for the purpose of giving effect to the determination.*
(*Delete as appropriate)
Date
Signed
NB: A copy of the decision or order declaring the complaint against the trade union to be well-founded must be enclosed with this application.

Form 4A

Application under Regulation 20 or 21 of the Transnational Information and Consultation of Employees Regulations 1999

1   The claimant is (*name and address of claimant*).
2   Any communication relating to this application may be sent to the claimant at (*state address for service, including telephone number, if any*).
3   The application is made against (*state identity or, where applicable, identities of respondents*) who is/are, or is/are representative of, the central or local management/the European Works Council/one or more information and consultation representatives (*delete what does not apply*).
4   The address(es) of the respondent(s) is/are
5   My complaint against the respondent(s) is that it/they failed to comply with its/their obligations under regulation 20 or 21 of the Transnational Information and Consultation of Employees Regulations 1999 as follows (*give particulars, set out in paragraphs and making reference to the specific provisions in the 1999 Regulations alleged to have been breached*).
Date
Signed

Form 4B

Applications under Regulation 33 of the European Public Limited-Liability Company Regulations 2004

1   The applicant's name is (*name and address of applicant*)
2   Any communication relating to this application may be sent to the applicant at (*applicant's address for service, including telephone number if any*).
3   The application is made against (*state identity of respondent*)
4   The address of the respondent is
5   The Central Arbitration Committee made a declaration in my favour on [ ] (*insert date*) and I request the Employment Tribunal to issue a penalty notice in accordance with regulation 33 of the European Public Limited-Liability Company Regulations 2004.
Date
Signed

Form 5

Notice of appearance to Application to Employment Appeal Tribunal for Compensation for Exclusion or Expulsion from a Trade Union or for Compensation or an Order in respect of Unjustifiable Discipline

1   The respondent trade union is (*name and address of union*).
2   Any communication relating to this application may be sent to the respondent at (*respondent's address for service, including telephone number, if any*).
3   The respondent intends to resist the application of (*here give name of the claimant*).
The grounds on which the respondent will rely are as follows:
4   (*Where the application relates to exclusion or expulsion from the trade union, state whether or not the claimant had been admitted or re-admitted to membership on or before the date of application.*)
(*Where the application relates to unjustifiable discipline, state whether–*

(a) *the determination infringing the claimant's right not to be unjustifiably disciplined has been revoked; and*

(b) *the trade union has taken all the steps necessary for securing the reversal of anything done for the purpose of giving effect to the determination.*)

Date

Signed

Position in union

Form 5A

Notice of Appearance to the Employment Appeal Tribunal under Regulation 20 or 21 of the Transnational Information and Consultation of Employees Regulations 1999

1   The respondent is (*name and address of respondent*).

2   Any communication relating to this application may be sent to the respondent at (*respondent's address for service, including telephone number, if any*).

3   The respondent intends to resist the application of (*here give the name or description of the claimant*).

The grounds on which the respondent will rely are as follows: (*give particulars, set out in paragraphs and making reference to the specific provisions in the Transnational Information and Consultation of Employees Regulations 1999 alleged to have been breached*).

Date

Signed

Position in respondent company or undertaking:

(*Where appropriate give position in respondent central or local management or position held in relation to respondent Works Council*)

Form 6

Application to the Employment Appeal Tribunal Under Section 33 of the 1996 Act for a Restriction of Proceedings Order

1   The claimant is (*the Attorney General/Lord Advocate*).

2   Any communication relating to this application may be sent to the claimant at (*state address for service, including telephone number*).

3   The application is for a restriction of proceedings order to be made against (*state the name and address of the person against whom the order is sought*).

4   An affidavit in support of the application is attached.

Date

Signed

Form 7

Notice of appearance to Application to the Employment Appeal Tribunal under section 33 of the 1996 Act for a Restriction of Proceedings Order

1   The respondent is (*state name and address of respondent*).

2   Any communication relating to this application may be sent to the respondent at (*respondent's address for service, including telephone number, if any*).

3   The respondent intends to resist the application. An affidavit in support is attached to this notice.

Date

Signed

Employment Appeal Tribunal (Amendment) Rules 2004 SI No 2526 rr1 and 26[1]

Citation and commencement and interpretation

1   (1) These Rules may be cited as the Employment Appeal Tribunal (Amendment) Rules 2004 and shall come into force on 1st October 2004.

   (2) In these Rules, any reference to a rule or to the Schedule is a reference to a rule in, or to the Schedule to, the Employment Appeal Tribunal Rules 1993.

   . . .

Transitional provisions

26 (1) In any proceedings commenced in an employment tribunal prior to 1 October 2004–

   (a) the originating application and the notice of appearance shall be treated as the claim and response for the purposes of rule 3(1)(b);

   (b) where an employment tribunal has issued a written decision, that decision shall be treated as the written record of the judgment or order for the purposes of rule 3(1)(c); and

   (c) where an employment tribunal has issued extended reasons for its decision or order, those reasons shall be treated as written reasons for the judgment in rule 3(1)(c) and rule 3(3)(a).

   (2) In any proceedings commenced in the Appeal Tribunal prior to 1 October 2004 rule 34C shall not apply.

Employment Act 2002 (Dispute Resolution) Regulations 2004 SI No 752

Citation and Commencement

1   These Regulations may be cited as the Employment Act 2002 (Dispute Resolution) Regulations 2004 and shall come into force on 1st October 2004.

Interpretation

2   (1) In these Regulations–

   'the 1992 Act' means the Trade Union and Labour Relations (Consolidation) Act 1992;

---

1   Employment Appeal Tribunal (Amendment) Rules 2004 rr2–25 are incorporated into the Employment Appeal Tribunal Rules 1993 above.

'the 1996 Act' means the Employment Rights Act 1996;

'the 1999 Act' means the Employment Relations Act 1999;

'the 2002 Act' means the Employment Act 2002;

'action' means any act or omission;

'applicable statutory procedure' means the statutory procedure that applies in relation to a particular case by virtue of these Regulations;

'collective agreement' has the meaning given to it by section 178(1) of the 1992 Act;

'dismissal and disciplinary procedures' means the statutory procedures set out in Part 1 of Schedule 2;

'dismissed' has the meaning given to it in section 95(1)(a) and (b) of the 1996 Act;

'employers' association' has the meaning given to it by section 122 of the 1992 Act;

'grievance' means a complaint by an employee about action which his employer has taken or is contemplating taking in relation to him;

'grievance procedures' means the statutory procedures set out in Part 2 of Schedule 2;

'independent trade union' has the meaning given to it by section 5 of the 1992 Act;

'modified dismissal procedure' means the procedure set out in Chapter 2 of Part 1 of Schedule 2;

'modified grievance procedure' means the procedure set out in Chapter 2 of Part 2 of Schedule 2;

'non-completion' of a statutory procedure includes non-commencement of such a procedure except where the term is used in relation to the non-completion of an identified requirement of a procedure or to circumstances where a procedure has already been commenced;

'party' means the employer or the employee;

'relevant disciplinary action' means action, short of dismissal, which the employer asserts to be based wholly or mainly on the employee's conduct or capability, other than suspension on full pay or the issuing of warnings (whether oral or written);

'standard dismissal and disciplinary procedure' means the procedure set out in Chapter 1 of Part 1 of Schedule 2;

'standard grievance procedure' means the procedure set out in Chapter 1 of Part 2 of Schedule 2;

and a reference to a Schedule is a reference to a Schedule to the 2002 Act.

(2) In determining whether a meeting or written communication fulfils a requirement of Schedule 2, it is irrelevant whether the meeting or communication deals with any other matter (including a different matter required to be dealt with in a meeting or communication intended to fulfil a requirement of Schedule 2).

Application of dismissal and disciplinary procedures

3 (1) Subject to paragraph (2) and regulation 4, the standard dismissal and disciplinary procedure applies when an employer contemplates dismissing or taking relevant disciplinary action against an employee.

(2) Subject to regulation 4, the modified dismissal procedure applies in relation to a dismissal where–
   (a) the employer dismissed the employee by reason of his conduct without notice,
   (b) the dismissal occurred at the time the employer became aware of the conduct or immediately thereafter,
   (c) the employer was entitled, in the circumstances, to dismiss the employee by reason of his conduct without notice or any payment in lieu of notice, and
   (d) it was reasonable for the employer, in the circumstances, to dismiss the employee before enquiring into the circumstances in which the conduct took place,

but neither of the dismissal and disciplinary procedures applies in relation to such a dismissal where the employee presents a complaint relating to the dismissal to an employment tribunal at a time when the employer has not complied with paragraph 4 of Schedule 2.

Dismissals to which the dismissal and disciplinary procedures do not apply

4   (1) Neither of the dismissal and disciplinary procedures applies in relation to the dismissal of an employee where–
   (a) all the employees of a description or in a category to which the employee belongs are dismissed, provided that the employer offers to re-engage all the employees so dismissed either before or upon the termination of their contracts;
   (b) the dismissal is one of a number of dismissals in respect of which the duty in section 188 of the 1992 Act (duty of employer to consult representatives when proposing to dismiss as redundant a certain number of employees) applies;
   (c) at the time of the employee's dismissal he is taking part in–
      (i)   an unofficial strike or other unofficial industrial action, or
      (ii) a strike or other industrial action (being neither unofficial industrial action nor protected industrial action), unless the circumstances of the dismissal are such that, by virtue of section 238(2) of the 1992 Act, an employment tribunal is entitled to determine whether the dismissal was fair or unfair;
   (d) the reason (or, if more than one, the principal reason) for the dismissal is that the employee took protected industrial action and the dismissal would be regarded, by virtue of section 238A(2) of the 1992 Act, as unfair for the purposes of Part 10 of the 1996 Act;
   (e) the employer's business suddenly ceases to function, because of an event unforeseen by the employer, with the result that it is impractical for him to employ any employees;
   (f) the reason (or, if more than one principal reason) for the dismissal is that the employee could not continue to work in the position which he held without contravention (either on his part or on that of his employer) of a duty or restriction imposed by or under any enactment; or
   (g) the employee is one to whom a dismissal procedures agreement desig-

nated by an order under section 110 of the 1996 Act applies at the date of dismissal.

(2) For the purposes of paragraph (1)–

'unofficial' shall be construed in accordance with subsections (2) to (4) of section 237 of the 1992 Act;

'strike' has the meaning given to it by section 246 of the 1992 Act;

'protected industrial action' shall be construed in accordance with section 238A(1) of the 1992 Act;

and an employer shall be regarded as offering to re-engage an employee if that employer, a successor of that employer or an associated employer of that employer offers to re-engage the employee, either in the job which he held immediately before the date of dismissal or in a different job which would be suitable in his case.

Circumstances in which parties are treated as complying with the dismissal and disciplinary procedures

5 (1) Where–

(a) either of the dismissal and disciplinary procedures is the applicable statutory procedure in relation to a dismissal,

(b) the employee presents an application for interim relief to an employment tribunal pursuant to section 128 of the 1996 Act (interim relief pending determination of complaint) in relation to his dismissal, and

(c) at the time the application is presented, the requirements of paragraphs 1 and 2 or, as the case may be, paragraph 4 of Schedule 2 have been complied with but the requirements of paragraph 3 or 5 of Schedule 2 have not,

the parties shall be treated as having complied with the requirements of paragraph 3 or 5 of Schedule 2.

(2) Where either of the dismissal and disciplinary procedures is the applicable statutory procedure in relation to the dismissal of an employee or to relevant disciplinary action taken against an employee but–

(a) at the time of the dismissal or the taking of the action an appropriate procedure exists,

(b) the employee is entitled to appeal under that procedure against his dismissal or the relevant disciplinary action taken against him instead of appealing to his employer, and

(c) the employee has appealed under that procedure,

the parties shall be treated as having complied with the requirements of paragraph 3 or 5 of Schedule 2.

(3) For the purposes of paragraph (2) a procedure is appropriate if it–

(a) gives the employee an effective right of appeal against dismissal or disciplinary action taken against him, and

(b) operates by virtue of a collective agreement made between two or more employers or an employers' association and one or more independent trade unions.

Application of the grievance procedures

6 (1) The grievance procedures apply, in accordance with the paragraphs (2) to (7) of this regulation, in relation to any grievance about action by the employer that could form the basis of a complaint by an employee to an employment tribunal under a jurisdiction listed in Schedule 3 or 4, or could do so if the action took place.

(2) Subject to paragraphs (3) to (7), the standard grievance procedure applies in relation to any such grievance.

(3) Subject to paragraphs (4) to (7), the modified grievance procedure applies in relation to a grievance where–
   (a) the employee has ceased to be employed by the employer;
   (b) the employer–
      (i) was unaware of the grievance before the employment ceased, or
      (ii) was so aware but the standard grievance procedure was not commenced or was not completed before the last day of the employee's employment; and
   (c) the parties have agreed in writing in relation to the grievance, whether before, on or after that day, but after the employer became aware of the grievance, that the modified procedure should apply.

(4) Neither of the grievance procedures applies where–
   (a) the employee has ceased to be employed by the employer;
   (b) neither procedure has been commenced; and
   (c) since the employee ceased to be employed it has ceased to be reasonably practicable for him to comply with paragraph 6 or 9 of Schedule 2.

(5) Neither of the grievance procedures applies where the grievance is that the employer has dismissed or is contemplating dismissing the employee.

(6) Neither of the grievance procedures applies where the grievance is that the employer has taken or is contemplating taking relevant disciplinary action against the employee unless one of the reasons for the grievance is a reason mentioned in regulation 7(1).

(7) Neither of the grievance procedures applies where regulation 11(1) applies.

Circumstances in which parties are treated as complying with the grievance procedures

7 (1) Where the grievance is that the employer has taken or is contemplating taking relevant disciplinary action against the employee and one of the reasons for the grievance is–
   (a) that the relevant disciplinary action amounted to or, if it took place, would amount to unlawful discrimination, or
   (b) that the grounds on which the employer took the action or is contemplating taking it were or are unrelated to the grounds on which he asserted that he took the action or is asserting that he is contemplating taking it,
   the standard grievance procedure or, as the case may be, modified grievance procedure shall apply but the parties shall be treated as having complied with the applicable procedure if the employee complies with the requirement in paragraph (2).

(2) The requirement is that the employee must set out the grievance in a written statement and send the statement or a copy of it to the employer–
   (a) where either of the dismissal and disciplinary procedures is being fol-

lowed, before the meeting referred to in paragraph 3 or 5 (appeals under the dismissal and disciplinary procedures) of Schedule 2, or

(b) where neither of those procedures is being followed, before presenting any complaint arising out of the grievance to an employment tribunal.

(3) In paragraph (1)(a) 'unlawful discrimination' means an act or omission in respect of which a right of complaint lies to an employment tribunal under any of the following tribunal jurisdictions (specified in Schedules 3 and 4)–

section 2 of the Equal Pay Act 1970;

section 63 of the Sex Discrimination Act 1975;

section 54 of the Race Relations Act 1976;

section 17A of the Disability Discrimination Act 1995;

regulation 28 of the Employment Equality (Religion or Belief) Regulations 2003;

regulation 28 of the Employment Equality (Sexual Orientation) Regulations 2003.

8 (1) Where–

(a) the standard grievance procedure is the applicable statutory procedure,

(b) the employee has ceased to be employed by the employer,

(c) paragraph 6 of Schedule 2 has been complied with (whether before or after the end of his employment); and

(d) since the end of his employment it has ceased to be reasonably practicable for the employee, or his employer, to comply with the requirements of paragraph 7 or 8 of Schedule 2,

the parties shall be treated, subject to paragraph (2), as having complied with such of those paragraphs of Schedule 2 as have not been complied with.

(2) In a case where paragraph (1) applies and the requirements of paragraphs 7(1) to (3) of Schedule 2 have been complied with but the requirement in paragraph 7(4) of Schedule 2 has not, the employer shall be treated as having failed to comply with paragraph 7(4) unless he informs the employee in writing of his decision as to his response to the grievance.

9 (1) Where either of the grievance procedures is the applicable statutory procedure, the parties shall be treated as having complied with the requirements of the procedure if a person who is an appropriate representative of the employee having the grievance has–

(a) written to the employer setting out the grievance; and

(b) specified in writing to the employer (whether in setting out the grievance or otherwise) the names of at least two employees, of whom one is the employee having the grievance, as being the employees on behalf of whom he is raising the grievance.

(2) For the purposes of paragraph (1), a person is an appropriate representative if, at the time he writes to the employer setting out the grievance, he is–

(a) an official of an independent trade union recognised by the employer for the purposes of collective bargaining in respect of a description of employees that includes the employee having the grievance, or

(b) an employee of the employer who is an employee representative elected or appointed by employees consisting of or including employees of the same description as the employee having the grievance and who, having regard to the purposes for which and method by which he was elected or appointed, has the authority to represent employees of that description under an established procedure for resolving grievances agreed between employee representatives and the employer.

(3) For the purposes of paragraph (2)(a) the terms 'official', 'recognised' and 'collective bargaining' have the meanings given to them by, respectively, sections 119, 178(3) and 178(1) of the 1992 Act.

10 Where either of the grievance procedures is the applicable statutory procedure but–

(a) at the time the employee raises his grievance there is a procedure in operation, under a collective agreement made between two or more employers or an employers' association and one or more independent trade unions, that provides for employees of the employer to raise grievances about the behaviour of the employer and have them considered, and

(b) the employee is entitled to raise his grievance under that procedure and does so,

the parties shall be treated as having complied with the applicable statutory procedure.

General circumstances in which the statutory procedures do not apply or are treated as being complied with

11 (1) Where the circumstances specified in paragraph (3) apply and in consequence the employer or employee does not commence the procedure that would otherwise be the applicable statutory procedure (by complying with paragraph 1, 4, 6 or 9 of Schedule 2), the procedure does not apply.

(2) Where the applicable statutory procedure has been commenced, but the circumstances specified in paragraph (3) apply and in consequence a party does not comply with a subsequent requirement of the procedure, the parties shall be treated as having complied with the procedure.

(3) The circumstances referred to in paragraphs (1) and (2) are that–

(a) the party has reasonable grounds to believe that commencing the procedure or complying with the subsequent requirement would result in a significant threat to himself, his property, any other person or the property of any other person;

(b) the party has been subjected to harassment and has reasonable grounds to believe that commencing the procedure or complying with the subsequent requirement would result in his being subjected to further harassment; or

(c) it is not practicable for the party to commence the procedure or comply with the subsequent requirement within a reasonable period.

(4) In paragraph (3)(b), 'harassment' means conduct which has the purpose or effect of–

(a) violating the person's dignity, or

(b) creating an intimidating, hostile, degrading, humiliating or offensive environment for him, but conduct shall only be regarded as having that purpose or effect if, having regard to all the circumstances, including in particular the perception of the person who was the subject of the conduct, it should reasonably be considered as having that purpose or effect.

Failure to comply with the statutory procedures

12 (1) If either party fails to comply with a requirement of an applicable statutory procedure, including a general requirement contained in Part 3 of Schedule 2, then, subject to paragraph (2), the non-completion of the procedure shall be attributable to that party and neither party shall be under any obligation to comply with any further requirement of the procedure.

(2) Except as mentioned in paragraph (4), where the parties are to be treated as complying with the applicable statutory procedure, or any requirement of it, there is no failure to comply with the procedure or requirement.

(3) Notwithstanding that if regulation 11(1) applies the procedure that would otherwise be the applicable statutory procedure does not apply, where that regulation applies because the circumstances in sub-paragraph (a) or (b) of regulation 11(3) apply and it was the behaviour of one of the parties that resulted in those circumstances applying, that party shall be treated as if–

(a) the procedure had applied, and

(b) there had been a failure to comply with a requirement of the procedure that was attributable to him.

(4) In a case where regulation 11(2) applies in relation to a requirement of the applicable statutory procedure because the circumstances in sub-paragraph (a) or (b) of regulation 11(3) apply, and it was the behaviour of one of the parties that resulted in those circumstances applying, the fact that the requirement was not complied with shall be treated as being a failure, attributable to that party, to comply with a requirement of the procedure.

Failure to attend a meeting

13 (1) Without prejudice to regulation 11(2) and (3)(c), if it is not reasonably practicable for–

(a) the employee, or, if he is exercising his right under section 10 of the 1999 Act (right to be accompanied), his companion; or

(b) the employer,

to attend a meeting organised in accordance with the applicable statutory procedure for a reason which was not foreseeable when the meeting was arranged, the employee or, as the case may be, employer shall not be treated as having failed to comply with that requirement of the procedure.

(2) In the circumstances set out in paragraph (1), the employer shall continue to be under the duty in the applicable statutory procedure to invite the employee to attend a meeting and, where the employee is exercising his rights under section 10 of the 1999 Act and the employee proposes an alternative time under subsection (4) of that section, the employer shall be under a duty to invite the employee to attend a meeting at that time.

(3) The duty to invite the employee to attend a meeting referred to in paragraph

(2) shall cease if the employer has invited the employee to attend two meetings and paragraph (1) applied in relation to each of them.

(4) Where the duty in paragraph (2) has ceased as a result of paragraph (3), the parties shall be treated as having complied with the applicable statutory procedure.

Questions to obtain information not to constitute statement of grievance

14 (1) Where a person aggrieved questions a respondent under any of the provisions set out in paragraph (2), those questions shall not constitute a statement of grievance under paragraph 6 or 9 of Schedule 2.

(2) The provisions referred to in paragraph (1) are–
> section 7B of the Equal Pay Act 1970;
> section 74 of the Sex Discrimination Act 1975;
> section 65 of the Race Relations Act 1976;
> section 56 of the Disability Discrimination Act 1995;
> regulation 33 of the Employment Equality (Religion or Belief) Regulations 2003;
> regulation 33 of the Employment Equality (Sexual Orientation) Regulations 2003.

Extension of time limits

15 (1) Where a complaint is presented to an employment tribunal under a jurisdiction listed in Schedule 3 or 4 and–
(a) either of the dismissal and disciplinary procedures is the applicable statutory procedure and the circumstances specified in paragraph (2) apply; or
(b) either of the grievance procedures is the applicable statutory procedure and the circumstances specified in paragraph (3) apply;

the normal time limit for presenting the complaint is extended for a period of three months beginning with the day after the day on which it would otherwise have expired.

(2) The circumstances referred to in paragraph (1)(a) are that the employee presents a complaint to the tribunal after the expiry of the normal time limit for presenting the complaint but had reasonable grounds for believing, when that time limit expired, that a dismissal or disciplinary procedure, whether statutory or otherwise (including an appropriate procedure for the purposes of regulation 5(2)), was being followed in respect of matters that consisted of or included the substance of the tribunal complaint.

(3) The circumstances referred to in paragraph (1)(b) are that the employee presents a complaint to the tribunal–
(a) within the normal time limit for presenting the complaint but in circumstances in which section 32(2) or (3) of the 2002 Act does not permit him to do so; or
(b) after the expiry of the normal time limit for presenting the complaint, having complied with paragraph 6 or 9 of Schedule 2 in relation to his grievance within that normal time limit.

(4) For the purposes of paragraph (3) and section 32 of the 2002 Act the following acts shall be treated, in a case to which the specified regulation applies, as constituting compliance with paragraph 6 or 9 of Schedule 2–

(a) in a case to which regulation 7(1) applies, compliance by the employee with the requirement in regulation 7(2);

(b) in a case to which regulation 9(1) applies, compliance by the appropriate representative with the requirement in sub-paragraph (a) or (b) of that regulation, whichever is the later; and

(c) in a case to which regulation 10 applies, the raising of his grievance by the employee in accordance with the procedure referred to in that regulation.

(5) In this regulation 'the normal time limit' means–

(a) subject to sub-paragraph (b), the period within which a complaint under the relevant jurisdiction must be presented if there is to be no need for the tribunal, in order to be entitled to consider it to–

(i) exercise any discretion, or

(ii) make any determination as to whether it is required to consider the complaint, that the tribunal would have to exercise or make in order to consider a complaint presented outside that period; and

(b) in relation to claims brought under the Equal Pay Act 1970, the period ending on the date on or before which proceedings must be instituted in accordance with section 2(4) of that Act.

National security

16 Where it would not be possible to comply with an applicable statutory procedure without disclosing information the disclosure of which would be contrary to the interests of national security, nothing in these Regulations requires either party to comply with that procedure.

Amendments to secondary legislation

17 The statutory instruments referred to in this regulation shall be amended as follows–

(a) in the Sex Discrimination (Questions and Replies) Order 1975, for paragraph (a) of article 5 there shall be substituted–

'(a) where it was served before a complaint had been presented to a tribunal, if it was so served–

(i) within the period of three months beginning when the act complained of was done; or

(ii) where the period under section 76 of the Act within which proceedings must be brought is extended by regulation 15 of the Employment Act 2002 (Dispute Resolution) Regulations 2004, within that extended period;';

(b) in the Race Relations (Questions and Replies) Order 1977, for paragraph (a) of article 5 there shall be substituted–

'(a) where it was served before a complaint had been presented to a tribunal, if it was so served–

(i) within the period of three months beginning when the act complained of was done; or

(ii) where the period under section 68 of the Act within which proceedings must be brought is extended by regulation 15 of the Employment Act 2002 (Dispute Resolution) Regulations 2004, within that extended period;';

(c) in article 7 of the Employment Tribunals Extension of Jurisdiction (England and Wales) Order 1994, after paragraph (b) there shall be inserted–

'(ba) where the period within which a complaint must be presented in accordance with paragraph (a) or (b) is extended by regulation 15 of the Employment Act 2002 (Dispute Resolution) Regulations 2004, the period within which the complaint must be presented shall be the extended period rather than the period in paragraph (a) or (b).';

(d) in article 7 of the Employment Tribunals Extension of Jurisdiction (Scotland) Order 1994, after paragraph (b) there shall be inserted–

'(ba) where the period within which a complaint must be presented in accordance with paragraph (a) or (b) is extended by regulation 15 of the Employment Act 2002 (Dispute Resolution) Regulations 2004, the period within which the complaint must be presented shall be the extended period rather than the period in paragraph (a) or (b).';

(e) in regulation (2) of the Employment Protection (Continuity of Employment) Regulations 1996, the word 'or' at the end of paragraph (d) shall be omitted and after paragraph (e) there shall be inserted–

'or

(f) a decision taken arising out of the use of a statutory dispute resolution procedure contained in Schedule 2 to the Employment Act 2002 in a case where, in accordance with the Employment Act 2002 (Dispute Resolution) Regulations 2004, such a procedure applies.';

(f) in regulation 30(2)(b) of the Working Time Regulations 1998, after paragraph (2) there shall be inserted–

'(2A) Where the period within which a complaint must be presented in accordance with paragraph (2) is extended by regulation 15 of the Employment Act 2002 (Dispute Resolution) Regulations 2004, the period within which the complaint must be presented shall be the extended period rather than the period in paragraph (2).';

(g) in the Employment Equality (Religion or Belief) Regulations 2003–

(i)   for regulation 33(4)(a) there shall be substituted–
'where it was served before a complaint had been presented to a tribunal, if it was so served–

(i) within the period of three months beginning when the act complained of was done; or

(ii) where paragraph (1A) of regulation 34 applies, within the extended period;'; and

(ii)   in regulation 34, after paragraph (1) there shall be inserted–
'(1A) Where the period within which a complaint must be presented in accordance with paragraph (1) is extended by regulation 15 of the Employment Act 2002 (Dispute Resolution) Regulations 2004, the period within which the complaint must be presented shall be the extended period rather than the period in paragraph (1).'; and

(h) in the Employment Equality (Sexual Orientation) Regulations 2003–
  (i) for regulation 33(4)(a) there shall be substituted–
  'where it was served before a complaint had been presented to a tribunal, if it was so served–
(i) within the period of three months beginning when the act complained of was done; or
(ii) where paragraph (1A) of regulation 34 applies, within the extended period;'; and
  (ii) in regulation 34, after paragraph (1) there shall be inserted–
'(1A) Where the period within which a complaint must be presented in accordance with paragraph (1) is extended by regulation 15 of the Employment Act 2002 (Dispute Resolution) Regulations 2004, the period within which the complaint must be presented shall be the extended period rather than the period in paragraph (1).'.

Transitional Provisions

18 These Regulations shall apply–
  (a) in relation to dismissal and relevant disciplinary action, where the employer first contemplates dismissing or taking such action against the employee after these Regulations come into force; and
  (b) in relation to grievances, where the action about which the employee complains occurs or continues after these Regulations come into force,
but shall not apply in relation to a grievance where the action continues after these Regulations come into force if the employee has raised a grievance about the action with the employer before they come into force.

SCHEDULE 4: TRIBUNAL JURISDICTIONS TO WHICH SECTION 32 APPLIES

Section 32

Section 2 of the Equal Pay Act 1970 (c 41) (equality clauses)

Section 63 of the Sex Discrimination Act 1975 (c 65) (discrimination in the employment field)

Section 54 of the Race Relations Act 1976 (c 74) (discrimination in the employment field)

Section 146 of the Trade Union and Labour Relations (Consolidation) Act 1992 (c 52) (detriment in relation to trade union membership and activities)

Paragraph 156 of Schedule A1 to that Act (detriment in relation to union recognition rights)

Section 17A of the Disability Discrimination Act 1995 (c 50) (discrimination in the employment field)

Section 23 of the Employment Rights Act 1996 (c 18) (unauthorised deductions and payments)

Section 48 of that Act (detriment in employment)

Section 111 of that Act (unfair dismissal)

Section 163 of that Act (redundancy payments)

Section 24 of the National Minimum Wage Act 1998 (c 39) (detriment in relation to national minimum wage)

. . .

Regulation 30 of the Working Time Regulations 1998 (SI No 1833) (breach of regulations)

Regulation 32 of the Transnational Information and Consultation of Employees Regulations 1999 (SI No 3323) (detriment relating to European Works Councils)

Regulation 28 of the Employment Equality (Sexual Orientation) Regulations 2003 SI No 1661 (discrimination in the employment field)

Regulation 28 of the Employment Equality (Religion or Belief) Regulations 2003 SI No 1660 (discrimination in the employment field)

Employment Appeal Tribunal Practice Direction 2004

1   Introduction and Objective

1.1   This Practice Direction (PD) supersedes all previous Practice Directions. It comes into force on 1 December 2004.

1.2   The Employment Appeal Tribunal Rules 1993 (SI 1993/2854) as amended by the Employment Appeal Tribunal (Amendment) Rules 2001 (SI 2001/1128 and 2001/1476) and the Employment Appeal Tribunal Rules 2004 (SI 2004/2526) (the Rules) apply to all proceedings irrespective of when those proceedings were commenced.

1.3   By section 30(3) of the Employment Tribunals Act 1996 ('ETA 1996') the Employment Appeal Tribunal (the EAT) has power, subject to the Rules, to regulate its own procedure. In so doing, the EAT regards itself as subject in all its actions to the duties imposed by Rule 2A. It will seek to apply the overriding objective when it exercises any power given to it by the Rules or interprets any Rule or legal authority.

1.4   The overriding objective of this PD is to enable the EAT to deal with cases justly. Dealing with a case justly includes, so far as is practicable:

1.4.1   ensuring that the parties are on an equal footing;

1.4.2   saving expense;

1.4.3   dealing with the case in ways which are proportionate to the complexity and importance of the issues;

1.4.4   ensuring that it is dealt with expeditiously and fairly.

1.5   The parties are required to help the EAT to further the overriding objective.

1.6   Where the Rules do not otherwise provide, the following procedure will apply to all appeals to the EAT.

1.7   The provisions of this PD are subject to any specific Directions which the EAT may make in any particular case. Otherwise, the Directions set out below must be complied with in all appeals from Employment Tribunals. In national security appeals, and appeals from the Certification Officer and the

Central Arbitration Committee, the Rules set out the separate procedures to be followed and the EAT will normally give specific directions.

1.8   Where it is appropriate to the EAT's jurisdiction, procedure, unrestricted rights of representation and restricted costs regime, the EAT is guided by the Civil Procedure Rules. So, for example:

1.8.1   For the purpose of serving a valid Notice of Appeal under Rule 3 and para 3 below, when an Employment Tribunal decision is sent to parties on a Wednesday, that day does *not* count and the Notice of Appeal must arrive at the EAT on or before the Wednesday 6 weeks (ie, 42 days) later.

1.8.2   When a date is given for serving of a document or for doing some other act, the complete document must be received by the EAT or the relevant party by 4.00pm on that date. Any document received after 4.00pm will be deemed to be lodged on the next working day.

1.8.3   Except as provided in 1.8.4 below, all days count, but if a time limit expires on a day when the central office of the EAT, or the EAT office in Edinburgh (as appropriate), is closed, it is extended to the next working day.

1.8.4   Where the time limit is 5 days (eg, an appeal against a Registrar's order or direction), Saturdays, Sundays, Christmas Day, Good Friday and Bank Holidays do not count.

1.9   In this PD any reference to the date of an order shall mean the date stamped upon the relevant order by the EAT (the seal date).

1.10   The parties can expect the EAT normally to have read the documents (or the documents indicated in any essential reading list if permission is granted under para 6.3 below for an enlarged bundle) in advance of any hearing.

2   Institution of Appeal

2.1   The Notice of Appeal must be, or be substantially, in accordance with Form 1, (in the amended form annexed to this Practice Direction) or Forms 1A or 2 of the Schedule to the Rules and must identify the date of the judgment, decision or order being appealed. Copies of the judgment, decision or order appealed against and of the Employment Tribunal's written reasons, together with a copy of the Claim (ET1) and the Response (ET3) must be attached, or if not, a written explanation must be given. A Notice of Appeal without such documentation will not be validly lodged.

2.2   If the appellant has made an application to the Employment Tribunal for a review of its judgment or decision, a copy of such application should accompany the Notice of Appeal together with the judgment and written reasons of the Employment Tribunal in respect of that review application, or a statement, if such be the case, that a judgment is awaited. If any of these documents cannot be included, a written explanation must be given. The appellant should also attach (where relevant to the appeal) copies of any orders including case management orders made by the Employment Tribunal.

2.3   Where written reasons of the Employment Tribunal are not attached to the

Notice of Appeal, either (as set out in the written explanation) because a request for written reasons has been refused by the Employment Tribunal or for some other reason, an appellant must, when lodging the Notice of Appeal, apply in writing to the EAT to exercise its discretion to hear the appeal without written reasons or to exercise its power to request written reasons from the Employment Tribunal, setting out the full grounds of that application.

2.4   The Notice of Appeal must clearly identify the point(s) of law which form(s) the ground(s) of appeal from the judgement, decision or order of the Employment Tribunal to the EAT. It should also state the order which the appellant will ask the EAT to make at the hearing.

2.5   Rules 3(7)–(10) give a judge or the Registrar power to decide that no further action shall be taken in certain cases where it appears that the Notice of Appeal or any part of it (a) discloses no reasonable grounds for bringing the appeal, or (b) is an abuse of the Employment Appeal Tribunal's process or is otherwise likely to obstruct the just disposal of proceedings. The Rules specify the rights of the appellant and the procedure to be followed. The appellant can request an oral hearing before a judge to challenge the decision. If it appears to the judge or Registrar that a Notice of Appeal or an application gives insufficient grounds of, or lacks clarity in identifying, a point of law, the judge or Registrar may postpone any decision under Rule 3(7) pending the appellant's amplification or clarification of the Notice of Appeal or further information from the Employment Tribunal.

2.6   *Perversity Appeals:* an appellant may not state as a ground of appeal simply words to the effect that 'the judgment or order was contrary to the evidence,' or that 'there was no evidence to support the judgment or order', or that 'the judgment or order was one which no reasonable Tribunal could have reached and was perverse' unless the Notice of Appeal also sets out full particulars of the matters relied on in support of those general grounds.

2.7   A party cannot reserve a right to amend, alter or add, to a Notice of Appeal or a respondent's Answer. Any application for leave to amend must be made as soon as practicable and must be accompanied by a draft of the amended Notice of Appeal or amended Answer which makes clear the precise amendments for which permission is sought.

2.8   A respondent to the appeal who wishes to resist the appeal and/or to cross-appeal, but who has not delivered a respondent's Answer as directed by the Registrar, or otherwise ordered, may be precluded from taking part in the appeal unless permission is granted to serve an Answer out of time.

2.9   Where an application is made for leave to institute or continue relevant proceedings by a person who has been made the subject of a Restriction of Proceedings Order pursuant to s33 of ETA 1996, that application will be considered on paper by a judge, who may make an order granting, refusing or otherwise dealing with such application on paper.

3   Time for Instituting Appeals

3.1   The time within which an appeal must be instituted depends on whether the appeal is against a judgment or against an order or decision of the Employment Tribunal.

3.2   If the appeal is against an order or decision, the appeal must be instituted within 42 days of the date of the order or decision. The EAT will treat a Tribunal's refusal to make an order or decision as itself constituting an order or decision. The date of an order or decision is the date when the order or decision was sent to the parties, which is normally recorded on or in the order or decision.

3.3   If the appeal is against a judgment, the appeal must be instituted within 42 days from the date on which the written record of the judgment was sent to the parties. However in three situations the time for appealing against a judgment will be 42 days from the date when written reasons were sent to the parties. This will be the case *only* if (1) written reasons were requested orally at the hearing before the Tribunal or (2) written reasons were requested in writing within 14 days of the date on which the written record of the judgment was sent to the parties or (3) the Tribunal itself reserved its reasons and gave them subsequently in writing: such exception will *not* apply if the request to the Tribunal for written reasons is made out of time (whether or not such request is granted). The date of the written record and of the written reasons is the date when they are sent to the parties, which is normally recorded on or in the written record and the written reasons.

3.4   The time limits referred to in paras 3.1 to 3.3 above apply *even though* the question of remedy and assessment of compensation by the Employment Tribunal has been adjourned or has not been dealt with and *even though* an application has been made to the Employment Tribunal for a review.

3.5   An application for an extension of time for appealing cannot be considered until a Notice of Appeal in accordance with para 2.1 above has been lodged with the EAT.

3.6   Any application for an extension of time for appealing must be made as an interim application to the Registrar, who will normally determine the application after inviting and considering written representations from each side. An interim appeal lies from the Registrar's decision to a judge. Such an appeal must be notified to the EAT within 5 days of the date when the Registrar's decision was sent to the parties. [See para 4.3 below.]

3.7   In determining whether to extend the time for appealing, particular attention will be paid to whether any good excuse for the delay has been shown and to the guidance contained in the decisions of the EAT and the Court of Appeal, as summarised in *United Arab Emirates v Abdelghafar* [1995] ICR 65 and *Aziz v Bethnal Green City Challenge Co Ltd* [2000] IRLR 111.

3.8   It is not usually a good reason for late lodgement of a Notice of Appeal that an application for litigation support from public funds has been made, but not yet determined; or that support is being sought from, but has not yet been provided by, some other body, such as a trade union, employers' association or one of the equality Commissions.

3.9   In any case of doubt or difficulty, a Notice of Appeal should be lodged in time and an application made to the Registrar for directions.

4   Interim Applications

4.1   Interim Applications should be made in writing (no particular form is required) and will be initially referred to the Registrar who after considering the papers may deal with the case or refer it to a judge. The judge may dispose of it himself or refer it to a full EAT hearing. Parties are encouraged to make any such applications at a Preliminary Hearing (PH) or an Appointment for Directions if one is ordered (see paras 9.7–9.18 and 11.2 below).

4.2   Unless otherwise ordered, any application for extension of time will be considered and determined as though it were an interim application to the Registrar, who will normally determine the application after inviting and considering written representations from each side.

4.3   An interim appeal lies from the Registrar's decision to a judge. Such an appeal must be notified to the EAT within 5 days of the date when the Registrar's decision was sent to the parties.

5   The Right to Inspect The Register And Certain Documents And To Take Copies

5.1   Any document lodged in the Central Office of the EAT in London or in the EAT office in Edinburgh in any proceedings before the EAT shall be sealed with the seal of the EAT showing the date (and time, if received after 4.00pm) on which the document was lodged.

5.2   Particulars of the date of delivery at the Central Office of the EAT or in the EAT office in Edinburgh of any document for filing or lodgement together with the time, if received after 4.00pm, the date of the document and the title of the appeal of which the document forms part of the record shall be entered in the Register of Cases kept in the Central Office and in Edinburgh or in the file which forms part of the Register of Cases.

5.3   Any person shall be entitled during office hours by appointment to inspect and request a copy of any of the following documents filed or lodged in the Central Office or the EAT office in Edinburgh, namely:

    5.3.1   any Notice of Appeal or respondent's Answer or any copy thereof;

    5.3.2   any judgment or order given or made in court or any copy of such judgment or order; and

    5.3.3   with the permission of the EAT, which may be granted on an application, any other document.

5.4   A copying charge per page will be payable for those documents mentioned in para 5.3 above.

5.5   Nothing in this Direction shall be taken as preventing any party to an appeal from inspecting and requesting a copy of any document filed or lodged in the Central Office or the EAT office in Edinburgh before the commencement of the appeal, but made with a view to its commencement.

6   Papers for Use at the Hearing

6.1   It is the responsibility of the parties or their advisers (see paras 6.5 and 6.6 below) to prepare a core bundle of papers for use at any hearing. Ultimate responsibility lies with the appellant, following consultation with other parties. The bundle must include only those exhibits (*productions* in Scotland) and documents used before the Employment Tribunal which are considered to be necessary for the appeal. It is the duty of the parties or their advisers to ensure that only those documents are included which are (a) relevant to the point(s) of law raised in the appeal and (b) likely to be referred to at the hearing.

6.2   The documents in the core bundle should be numbered by item, then paginated continuously and indexed, in the following order:

6.2.1   Judgment or order appealed from and written reasons

6.2.2   Sealed Notice of Appeal

6.2.3   Respondent's Answer if a Full Hearing (FH), respondent's Submissions if a PH

6.2.4   ET1 Claim (and any Additional Information or Written Answers)

6.2.5   ET3 Response (and any Additional Information or Written Answers)

6.2.6   Questionnaire and Replies (discrimination and equal pay cases)

6.2.7   Relevant orders, judgments and written reasons of the Employment Tribunal

6.2.8   Relevant orders and judgments of the EAT

6.2.9   Affidavits and Employment Tribunal comments (where ordered)

6.2.10   Any documents agreed or ordered pursuant to para 7 below.

6.3   Other documents relevant to the particular hearing (for example the relevant particulars or contract of employment and any relevant procedures) referred to at the Employment Tribunal may follow in the core bundle, if the total pages do not exceed 100. No bundle containing more than 100 pages should be agreed or lodged without the permission of the Registrar or order of a judge which will not be granted without the provision of an essential reading list as soon as practicable thereafter. If permitted or ordered, further pages should follow, with consecutive pagination, in an additional bundle or bundles if appropriate.

6.4   All documents must be legible and unmarked.

6.5   **PH cases** (see para 9.5.2 below), **Appeals from Registrar's Order, Rule 3(10) hearings, Appointments for Directions:** the appellant must prepare and lodge 4 copies (2 copies if judge sitting alone) of the bundle as soon as possible after service of the Notice of Appeal and no later than 21 days from the seal date of the relevant order unless otherwise directed.

6.6   **FH cases** (see para 9.5.3 below): the parties must co-operate in agreeing a bundle of papers for the hearing. By no later than 35 days from the seal date of the relevant order, unless otherwise directed, the appellant is responsible for ensuring that 4 copies (2 copies if judge sitting alone) of a bundle agreed by the parties is lodged at the EAT. The EAT will not retain bundles from a case heard at a PH.

6.7   **Warned List and Fast Track FH cases:** the bundles should be lodged as soon as possible and (unless the hearing date is within 7 days) in any event within

7 days after the parties have been notified that the case is expedited or in the Warned List.

6.8   In the event of disagreement between the parties or difficulty in preparing the bundles, the Registrar may give appropriate directions, whether on application in writing (on notice) by one or more of the parties or of his/her own initiative.

7   Evidence Before the Employment Tribunal

7.1   An appellant who considers that a point of law raised in the Notice of Appeal cannot be argued without reference to evidence given (or not given) at the Employment Tribunal, the nature or substance of which does not, or does not sufficiently, appear from the written reasons, must ordinarily submit an application with the Notice of Appeal. The application is for the nature of such evidence (or lack of it) to be admitted, or if necessary for the relevant parts of the Chairman's notes of evidence to be produced. If such application is not so made, then it should be made:

7.1.1   if a PH is ordered, in the skeleton or written submissions lodged prior to such PH; or

7.1.2   if the case is listed for FH without a PH, then within 14 days of the seal date of the order so providing.

Any such application by a respondent to an appeal, must, if not made earlier, accompany the respondent's Answer.

7.2   The application must explain why such a matter is considered necessary in order to argue the point of law raised in the Notice of Appeal or respondent's Answer. The application must identify:

7.2.1   the issue(s) in the Notice of Appeal or respondent's Answer to which the matter is relevant;

7.2.2   the names of the witnesses whose evidence is considered relevant, alternatively the nature of the evidence the absence of which is considered relevant;

7.2.3   (if applicable) the part of the hearing when the evidence was given;

7.2.4   the gist of the evidence (or absence of evidence) alleged to be relevant; and

7.2.5   (if the party has a record), saying so and by whom and when it was made, or producing an extract from a witness statement given in writing at the hearing.

7.3   The application will be considered on the papers, or if appropriate at a PH, by the Registrar or a judge. The Registrar or a judge may give directions for written representations (if they have not already been lodged), or may determine the application, but will ordinarily make an order requiring the party who seeks to raise such a matter to give notice to the other party(ies) to the appeal/cross-appeal. The notice will require the other party(ies) to co-operate in agreeing, within 21 days (unless a shorter period is ordered), a statement or note of the relevant evidence, alternatively a statement that there was no such evidence. All parties are required to use their best endeavours to agree such a statement or note.

7.4   In the absence of such agreement within 21 days (or such shorter period as may be ordered) of the requirement, any party may make an application within 7 days thereafter to the EAT, for directions. The party must enclose all relevant correspondence and give notice to the other parties. The directions may include: the resolution of the disagreement on the papers or at a hearing; the administration by one party to the others of, or a request to the Chairman to respond to, a questionnaire; or, if the EAT is satisfied that such notes are necessary, a request that the Chairman produce his/her notes of evidence either in whole or in part.

7.5   If the EAT requests any documents from the Chairman, it will supply copies to the parties upon receipt.

7.6   In an appeal from an Employment Tribunal which ordered its proceedings to be tape recorded, the EAT will apply the principles above to any application for a transcript.

7.7   A note of evidence is not to be produced and supplied to the parties to enable the parties to embark on a 'fishing expedition' to establish grounds or additional grounds of appeal or because they have not kept their own notes of the evidence. If an application for such a note is found by the EAT to have been unreasonably made or if there is unreasonable lack of co-operation in agreeing a relevant note or statement, the party behaving unreasonably is at risk of being ordered to pay costs.

8   Fresh Evidence and New Points of Law

8.1   Where an application is made by a party to an appeal to put in, at the hearing of the appeal, any document which was not before the Employment Tribunal, and which has not been agreed in writing by the other parties, the application and a copy of the documents sought to be admitted should be lodged at the EAT with the Notice of Appeal or the respondent's Answer, as appropriate. The application and copy should be served on the other parties. The same principle applies to any oral evidence not given at the Employment Tribunal which is sought to be adduced on the appeal. The nature and substance of such evidence together with the date when the party first became aware of its existence must be disclosed in a document, where appropriate a witness statement from the relevant witness with signed statement of truth, which must be similarly lodged and served.

8.2   In exercising its discretion to admit any fresh evidence or new document, the EAT will apply the principles set out in *Ladd v Marshall* [1954] 1 WLR 1489, having regard to the overriding objective, ie:

8.2.1   the evidence could not have been obtained with reasonable diligence for use at the Employment Tribunal hearing;

8.2.2   it is relevant and would probably have had an important influence on the hearing;

8.2.3   it is apparently credible.

Accordingly the evidence and representations in support of the application must address these principles.

8.3   A party wishing to resist the application must, within 14 days of its being sent, submit any representations in response to the EAT and other parties.

8.4   The application will be considered by the Registrar or a judge on the papers (or, if appropriate, at a PH) who may determine the issue or give directions for a hearing or may seek comments from the Chairman. A copy of any comments received from the Chairman will be sent to all parties.

8.5   If a respondent intends to contend at the FH that the appellant has raised a point which was not argued below, the respondent shall so state:

8.5.1   if a PH has been ordered, in writing to the EAT and all parties, within 14 days of receiving the Notice of Appeal;

8.5.2   if the case is listed for a FH without a PH, in a respondent's Answer.

In the event of dispute the Chairman should be asked for his/her comments as to whether a particular legal argument was deployed.

9   Case Tracks and Directions: The Sift of Appeals

9.1   Consistent with the overriding objective, the EAT will seek to give directions for case management so that the case can be dealt with quickly, or better considered, and in the most effective and just way.

9.2   Applications and directions for case management will usually be dealt with on the papers ('the sift') by a judge, or by the Registrar with an appeal to a judge. Any party seeking directions must serve a copy on all parties. Directions may be given at any stage, before or after the registration of a Notice of Appeal. An order made will contain a time for compliance, which must be observed or be the subject of an application by any party to vary or discharge it, or to seek an extension of time. Otherwise, failure to comply with an order in time or at all may result in the EAT exercising its power under Rule 26 to strike out the appeal, cross-appeal or respondent's Answer or debar the party from taking any further part in the proceedings or to make any other order it thinks fit, including an award of costs.

9.3   Any application to vary or discharge an order, or to seek an extension of time, must be lodged at the EAT and served on the other parties within the time fixed for compliance. Such other parties must, if opposing the application and within 14 days (or such shorter period as may be ordered) of receiving it, submit their representations to the EAT and the other parties.

9.4   An application to amend a Notice of Appeal or respondent's Answer must include the text of the original document with any changes clearly marked and identifiable, for example with deletions struck through in red and the text of the amendment either written or underlined in red. Any subsequent amendments will have to be in a different identifiable colour.

9.5   Notices of Appeal are sifted by a judge or the Registrar so as to determine the most effective case management of the appeal. The sift will result in a decision as to which track the appeal will occupy, and directions will be given. There are 4 tracks:

9.5.1   Rule 3(7) cases [see para 9.6 below].

9.5.2   Preliminary Hearing (PH) cases [see paras 9.7–9.18 below].

9.5.3   Full Hearing (FH) cases [see para 9.19 below].

9.5.4   Fast Track Full Hearing (FTFH) cases [see paras 9.20–9.21 below].

The judge or Registrar may also stay (or *sist* in Scotland) the appeal for a period, normally 21 days pending the making or the conclusion of an application by the appellant to the Employment Tribunal (if necessary out of time) for a review or pending the response by the Employment Tribunal to an invitation from the judge or Regsitrar to clarify, supplement or give its written reasons.

Rule 3(7) cases (9.5.1)

9.6   The judge or Registrar, having considered the Notice of Appeal and, if appropriate, having obtained any additional information, may decide that it or any of the grounds contained in it disclose no reasonable grounds for bringing the appeal or are an abuse of the process or otherwise likely to obstruct the just disposal of the proceedings. Reasons will be sent and within 28 days the appellant may submit a fresh Notice of Appeal for further consideration or request an oral hearing before a judge. At that hearing the judge may confirm the earlier decision or order that the appeal proceeds to a Preliminary or Full Hearing. A hearing under Rule 3(10), including judgment and any directions, will normally last not more than one hour. A judge or Registrar may also follow the Rule 3(7) procedure, of his or her own initiative, or on application, at any later stage of the proceedings, if appropriate.

Preliminary Hearing cases (9.5.2)

9.7   The purpose of a PH is to determine whether:

9.7.1   the grounds in the Notice of Appeal raise a point of law which gives the appeal a reasonable prospect of success at a FH; or

9.7.2   for some other compelling reason the appeal should be heard, eg, that the appellant seeks a declaration of incompatibility under the Human Rights Act 1998; or to argue that a decision binding on the EAT should be considered by a higher court.

9.8   Prior to the PH there will be automatic directions. These include sending the Notice of Appeal to the respondent(s) to the appeal. The direction may order or in any event will enable the respondent(s) to lodge and serve, within 14 days of the seal date of the order (unless otherwise directed), concise written submissions in response to the Notice of Appeal, dedicated to showing that there is no reasonable prospect of success for all or any grounds of any appeal. Such submissions will be considered at the PH.

9.9   If the respondent to the appeal intends to serve a cross-appeal this must be accompanied by written submissions and must be lodged and served within 14 days of service of the Notice of Appeal. The respondent to the appeal must make clear whether it is intended to advance the cross-appeal:

9.9.1   in any event (an unconditional cross-appeal); or

9.9.2   only if the appellant succeeds (a conditional cross-appeal).

In either case the respondent is entitled to attend the PH, which will also amount to a PH of the cross-appeal, and make submissions.

9.10   All parties will be notified of the date fixed for the PH. In the normal case, unless ordered otherwise, only the appellant and/or a representative should attend to make submissions to the EAT on the issue whether the Notice of Appeal raises a point of law with a reasonable prospect of success:

9.10.1   Except where the respondent to the appeal makes a cross-appeal, or the EAT orders a hearing with all parties present, the respondent to the appeal is not required to attend the hearing and is not usually permitted to take part in it. But any written submissions as referred to in (8) above will be considered at the PH.

9.10.2   If the appellant does not attend, the appeal may nevertheless be dealt with as above on written submissions, and be wholly or in part dismissed or allowed to proceed.

9.11   The PH, including judgment and directions, will normally last no more than one hour.

9.12   The sift procedure will be applied to cross-appeals as well as appeals. If an appeal has been assigned to the FH track, without a PH, and the respondent includes a cross-appeal in the respondent's Answer, the respondent must immediately apply to the EAT in writing on notice to the appellant for directions on the papers as to whether the EAT considers that there should be a PH of the cross-appeal.

9.13   If satisfied that the appeal (and/or the cross-appeal) should be heard at a FH on all or some of the grounds of appeal, the EAT will give directions relating to, for example, a time estimate, any application for fresh evidence, a procedure in respect of matters of evidence before the Employment Tribunal not sufficiently appearing from the written reasons, the exchange and lodging of skeleton arguments and an appellant's Chronology, and bundles of documents and authorities.

9.14   Permission to amend a Notice of Appeal (or cross-appeal) may be granted:

9.14.1   *If the proposed amendment is produced at the hearing*, then, if such amendment has not previously been notified to the other parties, and the appeal (or cross-appeal) might not have been permitted to proceed but for the amendment, the opposing party(ies) will have the opportunity to apply on notice to vary or discharge the permission to proceed, and for consequential directions as to the hearing or disposal of the appeal or cross-appeal.

9.14.2   *If a draft amendment is not available at the PH*, an application for permission to amend, in writing on notice to the other party(ies) in accordance with para 9.4 above, will be permitted to be made within 14 days. Where, but for such proposed amendment, the appeal (or cross-appeal) may not have been permitted to proceed to a FH, provision may be made in the order on the PH for the appeal (or cross-appeal) to be dismissed if the application for permission to amend is not made. Where such an application is made and refused, provision will be made for any party to have liberty to apply, in writing on notice to the other party(ies), as to the hearing or disposal of the appeal.

9.15   If not satisfied that the appeal, or any particular ground of it, should go forward to a FH, the EAT at the PH will dismiss the appeal, wholly or in part, and give a judgment setting out the reasons for doing so.

9.16   If an appeal is permitted to go forward to a FH on all grounds, a reasoned judgment will not normally be given.

9.17   Parties who become aware that a similar point is raised in other proceedings at an Employment Tribunal or the EAT are encouraged to co-operate in bringing this to the attention of the Registrar so that consideration can be given to the most expedient way of dealing with the cases, in particular to the possibility of having two or more appeals heard together.

9.18   If an appeal is permitted to go forward to a Full Hearing, a listing category will be assigned, ie:

P (recommended to be heard in the President's list);

A (complex, and raising point(s) of law of public importance);

B (medium level);

C (involving legal principles which are well settled).

Full Hearing cases (9.5.3)

9.19   If a judge or the Registrar decides to list the case for a FH without a PH s/he will consider appropriate directions, relating for example to amendment, further information, any application for fresh evidence, a procedure in respect of matters of evidence at the Employment Tribunal not sufficiently appearing from the written reasons, allegations of bias, apparent bias or improper conduct, provisions for skeleton arguments, appellant's chronology and bundles of documents and of authorities, time estimates and listing category (as set out in para 9.18 above).

Fast Track Full Hearing cases (9.5.4)

9.20   FH cases are normally heard in the order in which they are received. However, there are times when it is expedient to hear an appeal as soon as it can be fitted into the list. Appeals placed in this Fast Track, at the discretion of a judge or the Registrar, will normally fall into the following cases:

9.20.1   appeals where the parties have made a reasoned case on the merits for an expedited hearing.

9.20.2   appeals against interim orders or decisions of an Employment Tribunal, particularly those which involve the taking of a step in the proceedings within a specified period, for example adjournments, further information, amendments, disclosure, witness orders;

9.20.3   appeals on the outcome of which other applications to the Employment Tribunal or the EAT or the civil courts depend;

9.20.4   appeals in which a reference to the European Court of Justice (ECJ), or a declaration of incompatibility under the Human Rights Act 1998, is sought;

9.20.5   appeals involving reinstatement, re-engagement, interim relief or a recommendation for action (discrimination cases).

9.21   Category C cases estimated to take two hours or less may also be allocated to the Fast Track.

10 Respondent's Answer And Directions

10.1 After the sift stage or a PH, at which a decision is made to permit the appeal to go forward to a FH, the EAT will send the Notice of Appeal, with any amendments which have been permitted, and any submissions or skeleton argument lodged by the appellant, to all parties who are respondents to the appeal. Within 14 days of the seal date of the order (unless otherwise directed), respondents must lodge at the EAT and serve on the other parties a respondent's Answer. If it contains a cross-appeal, the appellant must within 14 days of service (unless otherwise directed), lodge and serve a Reply.

10.2 After lodgement and service of the respondent's Answer and of any Reply to a cross-appeal, the Registrar may, where necessary, invite applications from the parties in writing, on notice to all other parties, for directions, and may give any appropriate directions on the papers or may fix a day when the parties should attend on an Appointment for Directions.

10.3 A judge may at any time, upon consideration of the papers or at a hearing, make an order requiring or recommending consideration by the parties or any of them of compromise, conciliation, mediation or, in particular, reference to ACAS.

11 Complaints about the Conduct of the Employment Tribunal Hearing

11.1 An appellant who intends to complain about the conduct of the Employment Tribunal (for example bias, apparent bias or improper conduct by the Chairman or lay members or any procedural irregularity at the hearing) must include in the Notice of Appeal full particulars of each complaint made.

11.2 An appeal which is wholly or in part based on such a complaint will be sifted by a judge or the Registrar as set out in para 9.5 above and this may result in a decision as to the appropriate track which the appeal will occupy. At the sift stage or before, the judge or Registrar may postpone a decision as to track, and direct that the appellant or a representative provide an affidavit setting out full particulars of all allegations of bias or misconduct relied upon. At the sift stage the Registrar may enquire of the party making the complaint whether it is intended to proceed with it.

11.3 If the appeal is allocated to the PH or FH track, the EAT may take the following steps prior to such hearing within a time-limit set out in the relevant order:

11.3.1 require the appellant or a representative to provide, if not already provided, an affidavit as set out in para 11.2 above;

11.3.2 require any party to give an affidavit or to obtain a witness statement from any person who has represented any of the parties at the Tribunal hearing, and any other person present at the Tribunal hearing or a relevant part of it, giving their account of the events set out in the affidavit of the appellant or the appellant's representative. For the above purpose, the EAT will provide copies of any affidavits received from or on behalf of the appellant to any other person from whom an account is sought;

11.3.3   seek comments, upon all affidavits or witness statements received, from the Chairman of the Employment Tribunal from which the appeal is brought and may seek such comments from the lay members of the Tribunal. For the above purpose, copies of all relevant documents will be provided by the EAT to the Chairman and, if appropriate, the lay members; such documents will include any affidavits and witness statements received, the Notice of Appeal and other relevant documents;

11.3.4   the EAT will on receipt supply to the parties copies of all affidavits, statements and comments received.

11.4   A respondent who intends to make such a complaint must include such particulars as set out in paras 11.1 and 11.2 above:

11.4.1   (in the event of a PH being ordered in respect of the appellant's appeal, in accordance with para 9.5.2 above) in the cross-appeal referred to in para 9.9 above, or, in the absence of a cross-appeal, in written submissions, as referred to in para 9.8 above;

11.4.2   (in the event of no PH being ordered, in accordance with para 9.5.3 above) in his respondent's Answer.

A similar procedure will then be followed as in para 11.3 above.

11.5   In every case which is permitted to go forward to a FH the EAT will give appropriate directions, ordinarily on the papers after notice to the appellant and respondent, as to the procedure to be adopted at, and material to be provided to, the FH; but such Directions may be given at the sift stage or at a PH.

11.6   Parties should note the following:

11.6.1   The EAT will not permit complaints of the kind mentioned above to be raised or developed at the hearing of the appeal unless this procedure has been followed.

11.6.2   The EAT recognises that Chairmen and Employment Tribunals are themselves obliged to observe the overriding objective and are given wide powers and duties of case management (see Employment Tribunal (Constitution and Rules of Procedure) Regulations 2004 (SI No 1861), so appeals in respect of their conduct of Employment Tribunals, which is in exercise of those powers and duties, are the less likely to succeed.

11.6.3   Unsuccessful pursuit of an allegation of bias or improper conduct, particularly in respect of case management decisions, may put the party raising it at risk of an order for costs.

12   Listing of Appeals

12.1   Estimate of Length of Hearing: the lay members of the EAT are part-time members. They attend when available on pre-arranged dates. They do not sit for continuous periods. Consequently appeals which run beyond their estimated length have to be adjourned part-heard (often with substantial delay) until a day on which the judge and members are all available. To avoid inconvenience to the parties and to the EAT, and to avoid additional delay and costs suffered as a result of adjournment of part-heard appeals, all parties are required to ensure that the estimates of length of hearing (allowing for the fact that the parties can expect the EAT to have pre-read the papers and for the giving of a judgment) are accurate when first given. Any change in such estimate, or disagreement with an estimate made by the EAT on a sift or at a PH, is to be notified immediately to the Listing Officer.

12.2   If the EAT concludes that the hearing is likely to exceed the estimate, or if for other reasons the hearing may not be concluded within the time available, it may seek to avoid such adjournment by placing the parties under appropriate time limits in order to complete the presentation of the submissions within the estimated or available time.

12.3   Subject to para 12.6 below a date will be fixed for a PH as soon as practicable after the sift (referred to in para 9.5 above) and for a FH as soon as practicable after the sift if no PH is ordered, or otherwise after the PH.

12.4   The Listing Officer will normally consult the parties on dates, and will accommodate reasonable requests if practicable, but is not bound to do so. Once the date is fixed, the appeal will be set down in the list. A party finding that the date which has been fixed causes serious difficulties may apply to the Listing Officer for it to be changed, having first notified all other parties entitled to appear on the date of their application and the reasons for it.

12.5   Parties receiving such an application must, as soon as possible and within 7 days, notify the Listing Officer of their views.

12.6   In addition to this fixed date procedure, a list ('the warned list') may be drawn up. Cases will be placed in such warned list at the discretion of the Listing Officer or maybe so placed by the direction of a judge or the Registrar. These will ordinarily be short cases, or cases where expedition has been ordered. Parties or their representatives will be notified that their case has been included in this list, and as much notice as possible will be given of the intention to list a case for hearing, when representations by way of objection from the parties will be considered by the Listing Officer and if necessary on appeal to the Registrar or a judge. The parties may apply on notice to all other parties for a fixed date for hearing.

12.7   Other cases may be put in the list by the Listing Officer with the consent of the parties at shorter notice: for example, where other cases have been settled or withdrawn or where it appears that they will take less time than originally estimated. Parties who wish their cases to be taken as soon as possible and at short notice should notify the Listing Officer. Representations by way of objection may be made by the parties to the Listing Officer and if necessary by appeal to a judge or the Registrar.

12.8   Each week an up-to-date list for the following week will be prepared, including any changes which have been made, in particular specifying cases which by then have been given fixed dates. The list appears on the EAT website.

13   Skeleton Arguments

(This part of the Practice Direction does not apply to an appeal heard in Scotland, unless otherwise directed by the EAT in Edinburgh)

13.1   Skeleton arguments must be provided by all parties in all hearings, unless the EAT is notified by a party or representative in writing that the Notice of Appeal or respondent's Answer or relevant application contains the full argument, or the EAT otherwise directs in a particular case. It is the practice of the EAT for all the members to read the papers in advance. A well-structured skeleton argument helps the members and the parties to focus on the point(s) of law required to be decided and so make the oral hearing more effective.

13.2   The skeleton argument should be concise and should identify and summarise the point(s) of law, the steps in the legal argument and the statutory provisions and authorities to be relied upon, identifying them by name, page and paragraph and stating the legal proposition sought to be derived from them. It is not, however, the purpose of the skeleton argument to argue the case on paper in detail. The parties can be referred to by name or as they appeared at the Employment Tribunal, ie, claimant (C) and respondent (R).

13.3   The skeleton argument should state the form of order which the party will ask the EAT to make at the hearing: for example, in the case of an appellant, whether the EAT will be asked to remit the whole or part of the case to the same or to a different Employment Tribunal, or whether the EAT will be asked to substitute a different decision for that of the Employment Tribunal.

13.4   The appellant's skeleton argument must be accompanied by a Chronology of events relevant to the appeal which, if possible, should be agreed by the parties. That will normally be taken as an uncontroversial document, unless corrected by another party or the EAT.

13.5   Unless impracticable, the skeleton argument should be prepared using the pagination in the index to the appeal bundle. In a case where a note of the evidence at the Employment Tribunal has been produced, the skeleton argument should identify the parts of the record to which that party wishes to refer.

13.6   Represented parties should give the instructions necessary for their representative to comply with this procedure within the time limits.

13.7   The fact that settlement negotiations are in progress in relation to the appeal does not excuse delay in lodging and exchanging skeleton arguments.

13.8   A skeleton argument may be lodged by the appellant with the Notice of Appeal or by the respondent with the respondent's Answer.

13.9   Skeleton arguments must (if not already so lodged):

13.9.1   be lodged at the EAT not less than 10 days (unless otherwise ordered) before the date fixed for the PH, appeal against Registrar's Order, Rule 3(10) hearing or Appointment for Directions; or, if the hearing is fixed at less than 7 days' notice, as soon as possible after the hearing date has been notified. In the event that the hearing has been ordered to be heard with all parties present, the skeleton arguments must also then be exchanged between the parties.

13.9.2   be lodged at the EAT, *and* exchanged between the parties, not less than 21 days before the FH.

13.9.3   in the case of warned list and fast track FH cases be lodged at the

EAT and exchanged between the parties as soon as possible and (unless the hearing date is less than 7 days later) in any event within 7 days after the parties have been notified that the case is expedited or in the warned list.

13.10   Failure to follow this procedure may lead to an adjournment of an appeal or to dismissal for non-compliance with the PD, and to an award of costs. The party in default may also be required to attend before the EAT to explain their failure. It will always mean that the defaulting party must immediately despatch any delayed skeleton argument to the EAT by hand or by fax or by email to londoneat@ets.gsi.gov.uk or, as appropriate, edinburgheat@ets.gsi.gov.uk and (unless notified by the EAT to the contrary) bring to the hearing sufficient copies (a minimum of six) of the skeleton argument and any authorities referred to. The EAT staff will not be responsible for supplying or copying these on the morning of the hearing.

14   Citation of Authorities

General

14.1   It is undesirable for parties to cite the same case from different sets of reports. The parties should, if practicable, agree which report will be used at the hearing. Where the Employment Tribunal has cited from a report it may be convenient to cite from the same report.

14.2   It is the responsibility of a party wishing to cite any authority to provide photocopies for the use of each member of the Tribunal and photocopies or at least a list for the other parties. All authorities should be bundled, indexed and incorporated in an agreed bundle.

14.3   Parties are advised not to cite an unnecessary number of authorities either in skeleton arguments or in oral argument at the hearing. It is of assistance to the EAT if parties could highlight or sideline passages relied on within the bundle of authorities.

14.4   It is unnecessary for a party citing a case in oral argument to read it in full to the EAT. Whenever a case is cited in a skeleton argument or in an oral argument it is helpful if the legal proposition for which it is cited is stated. References need only be made to the relevant passages in the report. If the formulation of the legal proposition based on the authority cited is not in dispute, further examination of the authority will often be unnecessary.

14.5   For decisions of the ECJ, the official report should be used where possible.

PH cases

14.6   If it is thought necessary to cite any authority at a PH, appeal against Registrar's Order, Rule 3(10) hearing or Appointment for Directions, 3 copies should be provided for the EAT (one copy if a judge is sitting alone), and additional copies for any other parties notified. All authorities should be bundled, indexed and incorporated in one agreed bundle.

14.7   The parties must co-operate in agreeing a list of authorities and must jointly or severally lodge a list and 3 bundles of copies (one copy if judge sitting alone) of such authorities at the EAT not less than 7 days before the FH, unless otherwise ordered.

15   Disposal of Appeals by Consent

15.1   An appellant who wishes to abandon or withdraw an appeal should notify the other parties and the EAT immediately. If a settlement is reached, the parties should inform the EAT as soon as possible. The appellant should submit to the EAT a letter signed by or on behalf of the appellant and signed also by or on behalf of the respondent, asking the EAT for permission to withdraw the appeal and to make a consent order in the form of an attached draft signed by or for both parties dismissing the appeal, together with any other agreed order.

15.2   If the other parties do not agree to the proposed order the EAT should be informed. Written submissions should be lodged at the EAT and served on the parties. Any outstanding issue may be determined on the papers by the EAT, particularly if it relates to costs, but the EAT may fix an oral hearing to determine the outstanding matters in dispute between the parties.

15.3   If the parties reach an agreement that the appeal should be allowed by consent, and that an order made by the Employment Tribunal should be reversed or varied or the matter remitted to the Employment Tribunal on the ground that the decision contains an error of law, it is usually necessary for the matter to be heard by the EAT to determine whether there is a good reason for making the proposed order. On notification by the parties, the EAT will decide whether the appeal can be dealt with on the papers or by a hearing at which one or more parties or their representatives should attend to argue the case for allowing the appeal and making the order that the parties wish the EAT to make.

15.4   If the application for permission to withdraw an appeal is made close to the hearing date the EAT may require the attendance of the appellant and/or a representative to explain the reasons for delay in making a decision not to pursue the appeal.

16   Appellant's Failure to Present a Response

16.1   If the appellant in a case did not present a Response (ET3) to the Employment Tribunal and did not apply to the Employment Tribunal for an extension of time for doing so, or applied for such an extension and was refused, the Notice of Appeal must include particulars directed to the following issues, namely whether:

16.1.1   there is a good excuse for failing to present a Response (ET3) and (if that be the case) for failing to apply for such an extension of time; and

16.1.2   there is a reasonably arguable defence to the Claim (ET1).

16.2   In order to satisfy the EAT on these issues, the appellant must lodge at the EAT, together with the Notice of Appeal, a witness statement explaining in detail the circumstances in which there has been a failure to serve a Response (ET3) in time or apply for such an extension of time, the reason for that failure and the facts and matters relied upon for contesting the Claim (ET1) on the merits. There should be exhibited to the witness statement all relevant documents and a completed draft Response (ET3).

17   Hearings

17.1   Where consent is to be obtained from the parties pursuant to s28(3) of the ETA 1996 to an appeal commencing or continuing to be heard by a judge together with only one lay member, the parties must, prior to the commencement or continuation of such hearing in front of a two-member court, themselves or by their representatives each sign a form containing the name of the one member remaining, and stating whether the member is a person falling within s28(1)(a) or (b) of the ETA 1996.

17.2   *Video and Telephone Hearings.* Facilities can be arranged for the purpose of holding short PHs or short Appointments for Directions by video or telephone link, upon the application (in writing) of an appellant or respondent who, or whose representative, has a relevant disability (supported by appropriate medical evidence). Such facilities will only be made available for a hearing at which the party or, if more than one party will take part, both or all parties is or are legally represented. An application that a hearing should be so held will be determined by a judge or the Registrar, and must be made well in advance of the date intended for the hearing, so that arrangements may be made. So far as concerns video conferencing facilities, they may not always be available, dependent on the location of the parties: as for telephone hearings or, especially, telephone conferencing facilities, consideration may need to be given as to payment by a party or parties of any additional expenditure resulting.

18   Handing Down of Judgments

(England and Wales)

18.1   When the EAT reserves judgment to a later date, the parties will be notified of the date when it is ready to be handed down. It is not necessary for a party or representative to attend unless it is intended to make an application, either for costs or for permission to appeal to the Court of Appeal (see paras 19 and 21 below), in which case notice of that fact, and, in the case of an intended application for costs, notice of the matters set out in para 19.3 below, should be given to the other party(ies) and to the EAT 48 hours before the date.

18.2   Copies of the judgment will be available to the parties or their representatives on the morning on which it is handed down or, if so directed by a judge, earlier to the parties' representatives in draft subject to terms as to confidentiality. Where a draft judgment has been provided in advance, any intended application for permission to appeal referred to in para 18.1 above must be accompanied by a draft Notice of Appeal.

18.3   The judgment will be pronounced without being read aloud, by the judge who presided or by another judge, on behalf of the EAT. The judge may deal with any application or may refer it to the judge and/or the Tribunal who heard the appeal, whether to deal with on the papers or at a further oral hearing on notice.

18.4 Transcripts of unreserved judgments at a PH, appeal against Regsitrar's Order, Appointments for Directions, Rule 3(10) hearing will not (save as below) be produced and provided to the parties:

    18.4.1 Where an appeal, or any ground of appeal, is dismissed in the presence of the appellant, no transcript of the judgment is produced unless, within 14 days of the seal date of the order, either party applies to the EAT for a transcript, or the EAT of its own initiative directs that a judgment be transcribed (in circumstances such as those set out in para 18.5.2 below).

    18.4.2 Where an appeal or any ground of appeal is dismissed in the absence of the appellant, a transcript will be supplied to the appellant.

    18.4.3 Where an appeal is allowed to forward to a PH or a FH, a judgment will not normally be delivered, but, if it is, the judge may order it to be transcribed, in which case a transcript is provided to the parties.

18.5 *Transcripts of unreserved judgments at a FH.* Where judgment is delivered at the hearing, no transcript will be produced and provided to the parties unless:

    18.5.1 either party applies for it to the EAT within 14 days of that hearing; or

    18.5.2 the EAT of its own initiative directs that the judgment be transcribed, eg where it is considered that a point of general importance arises or that the matter is to be remitted to, or otherwise continued before, the Employment Tribunal.

18.6 Where judgment at either a PH or a FH is reserved, and later handed down in writing, a copy is provided to all parties, and to recognised law reporters.

(Scotland)

18.7 Judgments are normally reserved in Scotland and will be handed down as soon as practicable thereafter on a provisional basis to both parties who will thereafter have a period of 14 days to make any representations with regard to expenses, leave to appeal or any other relevant matter. At the expiry of that period or after such representations have been dealt with, whichever shall be the later, an order will be issued to conform to the original judgment.

EAT Website

18.8 All FH judgments which are transcribed or handed down will be posted on the EAT website.

19 Costs (*Expenses* in Scotland)

19.1 In this PD 'costs' includes legal costs, expenses, allowances paid by the Secretary of State and payment in respect of time spent in preparing a case. Such costs may relate to interim applications or hearings or to a PH or FH.

19.2 An application for costs must be made either during or at the end of the relevant hearing, or in writing to the Registrar within 14 days of the seal date of the relevant order of the EAT or, in the case of a reserved judgment, as provided for in para 18.1 above.

19.3   The party seeking the order must state the legal ground on which the application is based and the facts on which it is based and, by a schedule or otherwise, show how the costs have been incurred. If the application is made in respect of only part of the proceedings, particulars must be given showing how the costs have been incurred on that specific part. If the party against whom the order is sought wishes the EAT to have regard to means and/or an alleged inability to pay, a witness statement giving particulars and exhibiting any documents must be served on the other party(ies) and lodged with the EAT: further directions may be required to be given by the EAT in such case.

19.4   Such application may be resolved by the EAT on the papers, provided that the opportunity has been given for representations in writing by all relevant parties, or the EAT may refer the matter for an oral hearing, and may assess the costs either on the papers or at an oral hearing, or refer the matter for detailed assessment.

19.5   *Wasted costs.* An application for a wasted costs order must be made in writing, setting out the nature of the case upon which the application is based and the best particulars of the costs sought to be recovered. Such application must be lodged with the EAT and served upon the party(ies) sought to be charged: further directions may be required to be given by the EAT in such case.

19.6   Where the EAT makes any costs order it shall provide written reasons for so doing if such order is made by decision on the papers. If such order is made at a hearing, then written reasons will be provided if a request is made at the hearing or within 21 days of the seal date of the costs order. The Registrar shall send a copy of the written reasons to all the parties to the proceedings.

20   Review

Where an application is made for a review of a judgment or order of the EAT, it can be considered on paper by a judge who may, if he or she heard the original appeal or made the original order alone, without lay members, make such order, granting, refusing, adjourning or otherwise dealing with such application, as he or she may think fit. If the original judgment or order was made by the judge together with lay members, then the judge may, pursuant to Rule 33, consider and refuse such application for review on the papers. If the judge does not refuse such application, he or she may make any relevant further order, but would not grant such application without notice to the opposing party and reference to the lay members, for consideration with them, either on paper or in open court.

21   Appeals from the EAT

Appeals heard in England and Wales

21.1   An application to the EAT for permission to appeal to the Court of Appeal must be made (unless the EAT otherwise orders) at the hearing or when a reserved judgment is handed down as provided in paras 18.1 and 18.2

above. If not made then, or if refused, or unless the EAT otherwise orders, any such applications must be made to the Court of Appeal within 14 days of the sealed order. An application for an extension of time for permission to appeal may be entertained by the EAT where a case is made out to the satisfaction of a judge or Registrar that there is a need to delay until after a transcript is received (expedited if appropriate). Applications for an extension of time for permission to appeal should however normally be made to the Court of Appeal.

21.2   The party seeking permission must state the point of law to be advanced and the grounds.

Appeals heard in Scotland

21.3   An application to the EAT for permission to appeal to the Court of Session must be made within 42 days of the date of the hearing where judgment is delivered at that hearing: if judgment is reserved, within 42 days of the date the transcript was sent to the parties.

21.4   The party seeking permission must state the point of law to be advanced and the grounds.

The Honourable Mr Justice Burton
President

9 December 2004

ANNEX

FORM 1

NOTICE OF APPEAL FROM DECISION OF EMPLOYMENT TRIBUNAL

1   The Appellant is (*name and address of the Appellant*):
2   Any communication relating to this appeal may be sent to the Appellant at (*Appellant's address for service, including telephone number if any*):
3   The Appellant appeals from (*here give particulars of the judgment, decision or order of the Employment Tribunal from which the appeal is brought including the location of the Employment Tribunal and the date*):
4   The parties to the proceedings before the Employment Tribunal, other than the Appellant, were (*names and addresses of other parties to the proceedings resulting in judgment, decision or order appealed from*):
5   Copies of:
   • the written record of the Employment Tribunal's judgment, decision or order and the Written Reasons of the Employment Tribunal
   • the Claim (ET1) and Response (ET3)
   or
   • an explanation as to why any of these documents are not included are attached to this notice.

[If relevant.]

[If the Appellant has made an application to the Employment Tribunal for a review of its judgment or decision, a copy of such application, together with the judgment and Written Reasons of the Employment Tribunal in respect of that review application, or a statement by or on behalf of the Appellant, if such be the case, that a judgment is awaited, is attached to this Notice. If any of these documents exist but cannot be included, then a written explanation must be given.]

6 The grounds upon which this appeal is brought are that the Employment Tribunal erred in law in that (*here set out in paragraphs the various grounds of appeal*):

Signed . . . . Date: . . . .

NB: The details entered on your Notice of Appeal must be legible and suitable for photocopying. The use of black ink or typescript is recommended.

ACAS Arbitration Scheme

ACAS Arbitration Scheme

ACAS Arbitration Scheme (Great Britain) Order 2004 SI No 753

Citation, commencement, interpretation and extent

1 (1) This Order may be cited as the ACAS Arbitration Scheme (Great Britain) Order 2004 and shall come into force on 6th April 2004.

   (2) In this Order–

   'the 1996 Act' means the Employment Rights Act 1996;

   'basic amount' means such part of an award of compensation made by an arbitrator as comprises the basic amount, determined in accordance with paragraphs 139 to 146 of the Scheme;

   'English/Welsh arbitration' means an arbitration under the Scheme, which the parties have agreed shall be determined under the laws of England and Wales;

   'the Scheme' means the arbitration scheme set out in the Schedule with the exception of paragraphs 52EW, 110EW, 183EW, 187EW, 194EW, 200EW, 205EW, 209EW, 212EW, 217EW, 223EW and 224EW thereof;

   'Scottish arbitration' means an arbitration under the Scheme, which the parties have agreed shall be determined according to the laws of Scotland.

   (3) This Order extends to Great Britain;

   (4) Paragraphs in the Schedule marked 'EW' apply only to English/Welsh arbitrations;

   (5) Paragraphs in the Schedule marked 'S' apply only to Scottish arbitrations;

   (6) Paragraphs in the Schedule not marked 'EW' or 'S' apply to both English/Welsh arbitrations and Scottish arbitrations.

Commencement of the Scheme

2 The Scheme shall come into effect on 6th April 2004.

Revocation

3 Subject to article 8, the ACAS Arbitration Scheme (England and Wales) Order 2001 is revoked.

Application of Part I of the Arbitration Act 1996

4 The provisions of Part I of the Arbitration Act 1996 referred to in the Schedule at paragraphs 52EW, 110EW, 183EW, 187EW, 194EW, 200EW, 205EW, 209EW, 212EW, 217EW, 223EW and 224EW and shown in italics shall, as

modified in those paragraphs, apply to English/Welsh arbitrations conducted in accordance with the Scheme.

5   (1) Section 46(1)(b) of the Arbitration Act 1996 shall apply to English/Welsh arbitrations conducted in accordance with the Scheme, subject to the following modification.

(2) For 'such other considerations as are agreed by them or determined by the tribunal' in section 46(1)(b) substitute 'the Terms of Reference in paragraph 17 of the arbitration scheme set out in the Schedule to the ACAS Arbitration Scheme (Great Britain) Order 2004'.

Enforcement of re-employment orders

6   (1) Employment tribunals shall enforce re-employment orders made in arbitrations conducted in accordance with the Scheme in accordance with section 117 of the 1996 Act (enforcement by award of compensation), modified as follows.

(2) In subsection (1)(a), subsection (3) and subsection (8), for the words 'section 113' substitute in each case 'paragraph 123(i) of the Scheme'.

(3) In subsection (2) for 'section 124' substitute 'section 124(1) and (5) and subsections (9) and (10)'.

(4) In subsection (3)(a) for the words 'sections 118 to 127A' substitute the words 'sections 118 to 123, section 124(1) and (5), sections 126 and 127A and subsections (9) and (11)'.

(5) After subsection (8) insert–

'(9) Section 124(1) shall not apply to compensation awarded, or to a compensatory award made, to a person in a case where the arbitrator finds the reason (or, if more than one, the principal reason) for the dismissal (or, in a redundancy case, for which the employee was selected for dismissal) to be a reason specified in any of the enactments mentioned in section 124(1)A.

(10) In the case of compensation awarded to a person under section 117(1) and (2), the limit imposed by section 124(1) may be exceeded to the extent necessary to enable the award fully to reflect the amount specified as payable under the arbitrator's award in accordance with paragraphs 131(i) or 134(iv) of the Scheme.

(11) Where–

(a) a compensatory award is an award under subsection (3)(a) of section 117, and

(b) an additional award falls to be made under subsection (3)(b) of that section, the limit imposed by section 124(1) on the compensatory award may be exceeded to the extent necessary to enable the aggregate of the compensatory award and additional awards fully to reflect the amount specified as payable under the arbitrator's award in accordance with paragraphs 131(i) or 134(iv) of the Scheme.

(12) In this section 'the Scheme' means the arbitration scheme set out in the Schedule to the ACAS Arbitration Scheme (Great Britain) Order 2004.'.

Awards of compensation

7 An award of a basic amount shall be treated as a basic award of compensation for unfair dismissal for the purposes of section 184(1)(d) of the 1996 Act (which specifies such an award as a debt which the Secretary of State must satisfy if the employer has become insolvent).

Transitional provision

8 (1) The Scheme has effect in any case where the appropriate date falls on or after 6th April 2004.

(2) In a case where the appropriate date falls before 6th April 2004, the arbitration scheme set out in the Schedule to the ACAS Arbitration Scheme (England and Wales) Order 2001 continues to apply.

(3) In this article, the 'appropriate date' means the date of the Arbitration Agreement. Where the parties sign the Arbitration Agreement on different dates, the appropriate date is the date of the first signature.

(4) In this article, 'Arbitration Agreement' means an agreement to submit the dispute to arbitration, as defined in paragraph 26 of the Scheme.

SCHEDULE: ACAS ARBITRATION SCHEME

I INTRODUCTION

1 The ACAS Arbitration Scheme ('the Scheme') is implemented pursuant to section 212A of the Trade Union and Labour Relations (Consolidation) Act 1992 ('the 1992 Act').

2 The Scheme provides a voluntary alternative to the employment tribunal for the resolution of unfair dismissal disputes, in the form of arbitration.

3 Resolution of disputes under the Scheme is intended to be confidential, informal, relatively fast and cost efficient. Procedures under the Scheme are non-legalistic, and far more flexible than the traditional model of the employment tribunal and the courts. For example (as explained in more detail below), the Scheme avoids the use of formal pleadings and formal witness and documentary procedures. Strict rules of evidence will not apply, and, as far as possible, instead of applying strict law or legal precedent, general principles of fairness and good conduct will be taken into account (including, for example, principles referred to in any relevant ACAS 'Disciplinary and Grievance Procedures' Code of Practice or 'Discipline and Grievances at Work' Handbook). Arbitral decisions ('awards') will be final, with very limited opportunities for parties to appeal or otherwise challenge the result.

4 The Scheme also caters for requirements imposed as a matter of law (eg, the Human Rights Act 1998, devolution issues, existing law in the field of arbitration and EC law).

5 The Scheme accommodates certain differences between the law of Scotland and the law of England and Wales relating to arbitrations generally. It does so by providing, to the extent necessary in order to accommodate those differences, separate provisions applicable to Scottish arbitrations on the one hand and to English or Welsh arbitrations on the other. For convenience, paragraphs that apply only to Scottish arbitrations are marked 'S' and

paragraphs that apply only to English or Welsh arbitrations are marked 'EW'.

II   THE ROLE OF ACAS

6   As more fully explained below, cases enter the Scheme by reference to ACAS, which appoints an arbitrator from a panel (see paragraphs 41 to 43 below) to determine the dispute. ACAS provides administrative assistance during the proceedings, and may scrutinise awards and refer any clerical or other similar errors back to the arbitrator. Disputes are determined, however, by arbitrators and not by ACAS.

Routing of communications

7   Unless in the course of a hearing, all communications between either party and the arbitrator shall be sent via the ACAS Arbitration Section.

8   Paragraph 218 below sets out the manner in which any document, notice or communication must be served on, or transmitted to, ACAS or the ACAS Arbitration Section.

III   TERMS AND ABBREVIATIONS

9   The term 'Employee' is used to denote the claimant (ie the former employee), including any person entitled to pursue a claim arising out of a contravention, or alleged contravention, of Part X of the Employment Rights Act 1996.

10   The term 'Employer' is used to denote the respondent.

11   The term 'EC law' means:
   (i)   any enactment in the domestic legislation of England and Wales or of Scotland giving effect to rights, powers, liabilities, obligations and restrictions from time to time created or arising by or under the Community Treaties, and
   (ii)   any such rights, powers, liabilities, obligations and restrictions, which are not given effect by any such enactment.

12   The term 'English/Welsh arbitration' means an arbitration under this Scheme, which the parties have agreed shall be an English/Welsh arbitration.

13   The term 'Scottish arbitration' means an arbitration under this Scheme, which the parties have agreed shall be a Scottish arbitration.

14   The term 'devolution issue' means a devolution issue as defined in paragraph 1 of Schedule 6 to the Scotland Act 1998 or a devolution issue as defined in paragraph 1 of Schedule 8 to the Government of Wales Act 1998.

15   With the exception of paragraphs 26(i) ('Requirements for entry into the Scheme'), 114EW ('Form of the award: English/Welsh arbitrations') and 117S ('Form of the award: Scottish arbitrations') below, references to anything being written or in writing include its being recorded by any means so as to be usable for subsequent reference.

IV APPLICATION OF THE SCHEME

16   Paragraphs 46EW, 47EW, 48EW, 49EW, 50EW, 51EW, 52EW, 53EW, 110EW, 114EW, 115EW, 116EW, 177EW, 181EW, 183EW, 187EW, 194EW, 200EW, 205EW, 209EW, 212EW, 217EW, 223EW, 224EW and 226EW below shall apply only to English/Welsh arbitrations. Paragraphs 54S, 55S, 56S, 57S, 58S, 59S, 111S, 112S, 117S, 118S, 119S, 178S, 182S, 184S, 188S, 189S, 190S, 191S, 192S, 193S, 195S, 196S, 197S, 198S, 199S, 201S, 202S, 203S, 204S, 206S, 207S, 208S, 210S, 211S, 213S, 225S and 227S below shall apply only to Scottish arbitrations.

V ARBITRATOR'S TERMS OF REFERENCE

17   Every agreement to refer a dispute to arbitration under this Scheme shall be taken to be an agreement that the arbitrator decide the dispute according to the following Terms of Reference:

In deciding whether the dismissal was fair or unfair, the arbitrator shall:

(i)   have regard to general principles of fairness and good conduct in employment relations (including, for example, principles referred to in any relevant ACAS 'Disciplinary and Grievance Procedures' Code of Practice or 'Discipline and Grievances at Work' Handbook), instead of applying legal tests or rules (eg, court decisions or legislation);

(ii) apply EC law.

The arbitrator shall not decide the case by substituting what he or she would have done for the actions taken by the Employer.

If the arbitrator finds the dismissal unfair, he or she shall determine the appropriate remedy under the terms of this Scheme.

VI SCOPE OF THE SCHEME

Cases that are covered by the Scheme

18   This Scheme only applies to cases of alleged unfair dismissal (ie disputes involving proceedings, or claims which could be the subject of proceedings, before an employment tribunal arising out of a contravention, or alleged contravention, of Part X of the Employment Rights Act 1996).

19   The Scheme does not extend to other kinds of claim which are often related to, or raised at the same time as, a claim of unfair dismissal. For example, sex discrimination cases, and claims for unpaid wages are not covered by the Scheme.

20   If a claim of unfair dismissal has been referred for resolution under the Scheme, any other claim, even if part of the same dispute, must be settled separately, or referred to the employment tribunal, or withdrawn. In the event that different aspects of the same dispute are being heard in the employment tribunal as well as under the Scheme, the arbitrator may decide, if appropriate or convenient, to postpone the arbitration proceedings pending a determination by the employment tribunal.

Waiver of Jurisdictional Issues

21 Because of its informal nature, the Scheme is not designed for disputes raising jurisdictional issues, such as for example:
- whether or not the Employee was employed by the Employer;
- whether or not the Employee had the necessary period of continuous service to bring the claim;
- whether or not time limits have expired and/or should be extended.

22 Accordingly, when agreeing to refer a dispute to arbitration under the Scheme, both parties will be taken to have accepted as a condition of the Scheme that no jurisdictional issue is in dispute between them. The arbitrator will not therefore deal with such issues during the arbitration process, even if they are raised by the parties, and the parties will be taken to have waived any rights in that regard.

23 In particular, in agreeing to arbitration under the Scheme, the parties will be treated as having agreed that a dismissal has taken place.

Inappropriate cases

24 The Scheme is not intended for disputes involving complex legal issues. Whilst such cases will be accepted for determination (subject to the Terms of Reference), parties are advised, where appropriate, to consider applying to the employment tribunal or settling their dispute by other means.

VII   ACCESS TO THE SCHEME

25 The Scheme is an entirely voluntary system of dispute resolution: it will only apply if parties have so agreed.

Requirements for entry into the Scheme

26 Any agreement to submit a dispute to arbitration under the Scheme must satisfy the following requirements (an 'Arbitration Agreement'):
- (i) the agreement of each party (which may be expressed in the same or in separate documents) must be in writing;
- (ii) the agreement must concern an existing dispute;
- (iii) the agreement must not seek to alter or vary any provision of the Scheme;
- (iv) the agreement must have been reached either:
  - (a) where a conciliation officer has taken action under section 18 of the Employment Tribunals Act 1996, or
  - (b) through a compromise agreement, where the conditions regulating such agreements under the Employment Rights Act 1996 are satisfied; and
- (v) the agreement must be accompanied by a completed Waiver Form for each party. Parties applying for English/Welsh arbitrations should complete Appendix A; parties applying for Scottish arbitrations should complete Appendix B.

27 Where an agreement fails to satisfy any one of these requirements or where the parties are unable to agree whether the arbitration should be an English/

Welsh arbitration or a Scottish arbitration, no valid reference to the Scheme will have been made, and the parties will have to settle their dispute by other means or have recourse to the employment tribunal.

28   Where:

(i)   a dispute concerning unfair dismissal claims as well as other claims has been referred to the employment tribunal, and

(ii)   the parties have agreed to settle the other claims and refer the unfair dismissal claim to arbitration under the Scheme,

a separate settlement must be reached referring the unfair dismissal claim to arbitration which satisfies all the requirements listed above (although it may form part of one overall settlement document).

Notification to ACAS of an Arbitration Agreement

29   All Arbitration Agreements must be notified to ACAS within two weeks of their conclusion, by either of the parties or their independent advisers or representatives, or an ACAS conciliator, sending a copy of the agreement and Waiver Forms, together with IT1 and IT3 forms if these have been completed, to the ACAS Arbitration Section.

30   For the purposes of the previous paragraph, an Arbitration Agreement is treated as 'concluded' on the date it is signed, or if signed by different people at different times, on the date of the last signature.

31   Where an Arbitration Agreement is not notified to ACAS within two weeks, ACAS will not arrange for the appointment of an arbitrator under the Scheme, unless notification within that time was not reasonably practicable. Any party seeking to notify ACAS of an Arbitration Agreement outside this period must explain in writing to the ACAS Arbitration Section the reason for the delay. ACAS shall appoint an arbitrator, in accordance with the appointment provisions below, to consider the explanation, and that arbitrator may seek the views of the other party, and may call both parties to a hearing to establish the reasons for the delay. The arbitrator shall then rule in an award on whether or not the agreement can be accepted for hearing under the Scheme.

32   Any such hearing and award will be governed by the provisions of this Scheme.

Consolidation of proceedings

33   Where all parties so agree in writing, ACAS may consolidate different arbitral proceedings under the Scheme.

VIII   SETTLEMENT AND WITHDRAWAL FROM THE SCHEME

Withdrawal by the Employee

34   At any stage of the arbitration process, once an Arbitration Agreement has been concluded and the reference has been accepted by ACAS, the party bringing the unfair dismissal claim may withdraw from the Scheme, provided that any such withdrawal is in writing. Such a withdrawal shall

constitute a dismissal of the claim and the arbitrator shall upon receipt of such withdrawal in writing issue an award dismissing the claim.

Withdrawal by the Employer

35   Once an Arbitration Agreement has been concluded and the reference has been accepted by ACAS, the party against whom a claim is brought cannot unilaterally withdraw from the Scheme.

Settlement

36   Parties are free to reach an agreement settling the dispute at any stage.

37   If such an agreement is reached:

(i)   upon the joint written request of the parties to the arbitrator or the ACAS Arbitration Section, the arbitrator (if appointed) or the ACAS Arbitration Section (if no arbitrator has been appointed) shall terminate the arbitration proceedings;

(ii)   if so requested by the parties, the arbitrator (if appointed) may record the settlement in the form of an agreed award.

38   An agreed award shall state that it is an award of the arbitrator by consent and shall have the same status and effect as any other award on the merits of the case.

39   If the agreement settling the dispute includes an agreement that one party (the 'paying party') shall pay a sum of money to the other (the 'receiving party') the arbitrator shall (unless the parties have agreed that the said agreement shall not be the subject of an award) draft an award ordaining the paying party to pay the agreed sum to the receiving party together (if the parties have agreed that interest shall run on the agreed sum) with interest thereon at such rate as the parties may have agreed and from such date or dates as the parties may have agreed until payment. The arbitrator shall send a copy of the said award in draft to each party and invite each party to confirm that the draft award accurately reflects the agreement between them. Upon receiving confirmation to that effect the arbitrator shall issue an award in the terms of the agreed draft.

40   Subject to paragraph 39, in rendering an agreed award, the arbitrator:

(i)   may only record the parties' agreed wording;

(ii)   may not approve, vary, transcribe, interpret or ratify a settlement in any way;

(iii)   may not record any settlement beyond the scope of the Scheme, the Arbitration Agreement or the reference to the Scheme as initially accepted by ACAS.

IX   APPOINTMENT OF AN ARBITRATOR

The ACAS Arbitration Panel

41   Arbitrators are selected to serve on the ACAS Arbitration Panel on the basis of their practical knowledge and experience of discipline and dismissal issues in the workplace. They are recruited through an open recruitment exercise, and appointed to the Panel on the basis of standard terms of appointment. It is a condition of their appointment that they exercise their duties in accordance with the terms of this Scheme. Each appointment is initially for a period of two years, although it may be renewed by ACAS, at the latter's discretion. Payment is made by ACAS on the basis of time spent in connection with arbitral proceedings.

Appointment to a case

42   Arbitral appointments are made exclusively by ACAS from the ACAS Arbitration Panel. Parties will have no choice of arbitrator.

43   Once ACAS has been notified of a valid Arbitration Agreement, it will select and appoint an arbitrator, and notify all parties of the name of the arbitrator so appointed.

Arbitrator's duty of disclosure

44   Immediately following selection (and before an appointment is confirmed by ACAS), every arbitrator shall disclose in writing to ACAS (to be forwarded to the parties) any circumstances known to him or her likely to give rise to any justifiable doubts as to his or her impartiality, or confirm in writing that there are no such circumstances.

45   Once appointed, and until the arbitration is concluded, every arbitrator shall be under a continuing duty forthwith to disclose to ACAS (to be forwarded to the parties) any such circumstances which may have arisen since appointment.

Removal of arbitrators: English/Welsh arbitrations

46EW   An arbitrator in an English/Welsh arbitration may only be removed by ACAS or the court (under the provisions in paragraphs 47EW to 53EW below).

47EW   Applications under the Scheme to remove an arbitrator on any of the grounds set out in sections 24(1)(a) and (c) of the Arbitration Act 1996, or on the basis that such removal has been agreed by both parties, shall be made in the first instance to ACAS (addressed to the ACAS Arbitration Section).

48EW   At the same time as an application is made to ACAS to remove an arbitrator a copy of the application shall be sent to the other party to the arbitration and to the arbitrator.

49EW   ACAS shall, following receipt of an application under paragraph 48EW, give the other party to the arbitration and the arbitrator such opportunity as ACAS in its sole discretion may consider appropriate to comment on the application.

50EW   ACAS may, after such procedures as ACAS in its sole discretion may consider appropriate, remove the arbitrator.

51EW   If ACAS refuses an application made under paragraph 47EW, a party may thereafter apply to the court.

52EW   Sections 24(1)(a) and (c), 24(2), 24(3), 24(5) and 24(6) of the Arbitration Act 1996 shall apply to arbitrations conducted in accordance with the Scheme, subject to the following modifications:

(i)   In subsection (1), for '(upon notice to the other parties, to the arbitrator concerned and to any other arbitrator) apply to the court' substitute '(upon notice to the other party, to the arbitrator concerned and to the Advisory, Conciliation and Arbitration Service ('ACAS')) apply to the High Court or Central London County Court'.

(ii) In subsection (2)–

    (a) omit 'If there is an arbitral or other institution or person vested by the parties with power to remove an arbitrator,'; and

    (b) for 'that institution or person' substitute 'ACAS'.

53EW The arbitrator may continue the proceedings and make an award while an application to ACAS (as well as the court) to remove him or her is pending.

Removal of arbitrators: Scottish arbitrations

54S An arbitrator in a Scottish arbitration may be removed by ACAS under the provisions in paragraphs 55S to 58S below.

55S An application under the Scheme to remove an arbitrator shall be made to ACAS (addressed to the ACAS Arbitration Section). At the same time as the application is sent to ACAS a copy of the application shall be sent to the other party to the arbitration and to the arbitrator.

56S ACAS shall, following receipt of an application under paragraph 55S give the other party to the arbitration and the arbitrator such opportunity as ACAS in its sole discretion may consider appropriate to comment on the application.

57S ACAS may, after such procedure as ACAS in its sole discretion may consider appropriate, remove the arbitrator if it is satisfied:

(i) that both parties to the arbitration agree that the arbitrator should be removed; or

(ii) that circumstances exist that give rise to justifiable doubts as to the impartiality of the arbitrator; or

(iii) that the arbitrator is physically or mentally incapable of conducting the proceedings or there are justifiable doubts as to his capacity to do so.

58S A decision of ACAS made under paragraph 57S shall be final.

59S The arbitrator may continue the proceedings and make an award while an application to ACAS to remove him or her is pending.

Death of an arbitrator

60 The authority of an arbitrator is personal and ceases on his or her death.

Replacement of arbitrators

61 Where an arbitrator ceases to hold office for any reason, he or she shall be replaced by ACAS in accordance with the appointment provisions above.

62 Once appointed, the replacement arbitrator shall determine whether and, if so, to what extent the previous proceedings should stand.

X   GENERAL DUTY OF THE ARBITRATOR

63 The arbitrator shall:

(i) act fairly and impartially as between the parties, giving each party a

> reasonable opportunity of putting his or her case and dealing with that of his or her opponent, and
>
> (ii) adopt procedures suitable to the circumstances of the particular case, avoiding unnecessary delay or expense, so as to provide a fair means for the resolution of the matters falling to be determined.

64 The arbitrator shall comply with the general duty (see paragraph 63 above) in conducting the arbitral proceedings, in his or her decisions on matters of procedure and evidence and in the exercise of all other powers conferred on him or her.

XI GENERAL DUTY OF THE PARTIES

65 The parties shall do all things necessary for the proper and expeditious conduct of the arbitral proceedings. This includes (without limitation) complying without delay with any determination of the arbitrator as to procedural or evidential matters, or with any order or directions of the arbitrator, and co-operating in the arrangement of any hearing.

XII CONFIDENTIALITY AND PRIVACY

66 Arbitrations, and all associated procedures under the Scheme, are strictly private and confidential. This rule does not prevent a party to the arbitration taking any step reasonably necessary for the purposes of any application to the court or enforcement of an award.

67 Hearings may only be attended by the arbitrator, the parties, their representatives, any interpreters, signers or communicators, witnesses and a legal adviser, if appointed. If the parties so agree, an ACAS official or arbitrator in training may also attend.

XIII ARRANGEMENTS FOR THE HEARING

Initial arrangements

68 A hearing must be held in every case, notwithstanding any agreement between the parties to a purely written procedure.

69 Once an arbitrator has been appointed by ACAS, a hearing shall be arranged as soon as reasonably practicable by him or her, with the administrative assistance of the ACAS Arbitration Section.

70 The arbitrator shall decide the date and venue for the hearing, in so far as an agreement cannot be reached with all parties within 28 days of the initial notification to ACAS of the Arbitration Agreement.

71 The ACAS Arbitration Section shall contact all parties with details of the date and venue for the hearing.

Expedited hearings

72 If:

(i) before the parties have agreed to refer a dispute to arbitration under the Scheme, an employment tribunal makes an order under interim relief provisions, or

(ii)   in the arbitrator's discretion, other relevant circumstances exist,

the arbitrator may expedite the hearing, on the application of any party.

Venue

73   Hearings may be held in any venue, provided that the hearing will only be held at the Employee's former workplace, or a similarly non-neutral venue, if all parties so agree.

74   Where premises have to be hired for a hearing, ACAS shall meet the reasonable costs of so doing.

Assistance

75   Where a party needs the services of an interpreter, signer or communicator at the hearing, ACAS should be so informed well in advance of the hearing. Where an arbitrator agrees that such assistance is required, ACAS shall meet the reasonable costs of providing this.

Travelling expenses/loss of earnings

76   Every party shall meet their own travelling expenses and those of their representatives and witnesses.

77   No loss of earnings are payable by ACAS to anyone involved in the arbitration. However, where an arbitrator rules that a dismissal was unfair, he or she may include in the calculation of any compensation a sum to cover reasonable travelling expenses and loss of earnings incurred by the Employee personally in attending the hearing.

Applications for postponements of, or different venues for, initial hearings

78   Any application for a postponement of, or a different venue for, an initial hearing must be made in writing, with reasons, to the arbitrator via the ACAS Arbitration Section within 14 days of the date of the letter notifying the hearing arrangements or, where this is not practicable, as soon as is reasonably practicable. Such applications will be determined by the arbitrator without an oral hearing after all parties have received a copy of the application and been given a reasonable opportunity to respond.

79   If the application is rejected, the initial hearing will be held on the original date and/or in the original venue.

80   This provision does not affect the arbitrator's general discretion (set out below) with respect to postponements after an initial hearing has been fixed, or with respect to other aspects of the procedure. In particular, procedural applications may be made to the arbitrator at the hearing itself.

XIV   NON-COMPLIANCE WITH PROCEDURE

81   If a party fails to comply with any aspect of the procedure set out in this Scheme, or any order or direction by the arbitrator, or fails to comply with the general duty in Part XI above, the arbitrator may (in addition to any other power set out in this Scheme):

(i)   adjourn any hearing, where it would be unfair on any party to proceed; and/or

(ii)   draw such adverse inferences from the act of non-compliance as the circumstances justify.

XV Outline of Procedure before the Hearing

82   Once a hearing has been fixed, the following procedure shall apply, subject to any direction by the arbitrator.

Written materials

83   At least 14 days before the date of the hearing, each party shall send to the ACAS Arbitration Section (for forwarding to the arbitrator and the other party) one copy of a written statement of case, together with:

(i)   any supporting documentation or other material to be relied upon at the hearing; and where appropriate

(ii)   a list of the names and title/role of all those people who will accompany each party to the hearing or be called as a witness.

84   Written statements of case should briefly set out the main particulars of each party's case, which can then be expanded upon if necessary at the hearing itself. The statement should include an explanation of the events which led up to the dismissal, including an account of the sequence and outcome of any relevant meetings, interviews or discussions. The parties should come to the hearing prepared to address the practicability of reinstatement or re-engagement, in so far as the Employee seeks such remedies.

85   Supporting documentation or other material may include (without limitation) copies of:

(i)   contracts of employment;

(ii)   letters of appointment;

(iii) written statement of particulars of employment;

(iv) time sheets and attendance records;

(v)   performance appraisal reports;

(vi) warning and dismissal letters;

(vii) written reasons for dismissal, where these have been given;

(viii) company handbooks, rules and procedures;

(ix) any information which will help the arbitrator to assess compensation, including (without limitation):

    (a) pay slips, P60s or wage records;

    (b) details of benefits paid to the Employee such as travelling expenses and free or subsidised accommodation;

    (c) guidance about, and (if available) actuarial assessments of, pension entitlements;

    (d) details of any welfare benefits received;

    (e) evidence of attempts to find other work, or otherwise mitigate the loss arising from the dismissal;

(x)   signed statements of any witnesses or outlines of evidence to be given by witnesses at the hearing.

86   The parties must also supply details of any relevant awards of compensation that may have been made by any other tribunal or court in connection with the subject matter of the claim.

87   Legible copies of documents must be supplied to ACAS even if they have already been supplied to an ACAS conciliator before the Arbitration Agreement was concluded.

88   No information on the conciliation process, if any, shall be disclosed by an ACAS conciliator to the arbitrator.

Submissions, evidence and witnesses not previously notified

89   Written statements of case and documentary or other material that have not been provided to the ACAS Arbitration Section prior to the hearing (in accordance with paragraph 83 above) may only be relied upon at the hearing with the arbitrator's permission.

90   All representatives and witnesses who have been listed as accompanying a party at the hearing should be present at the start of the hearing. Witnesses who have not been included in a list submitted to the ACAS Arbitration Section prior to the hearing may only be called with the arbitrator's permission.

Requests for documents

91   Any party may request the other party to produce copies of relevant documents which are not in the requesting party's possession, custody or control. Although the arbitrator has no power to compel a party to comply, the arbitrator may draw an adverse inference from a party's failure to comply with a reasonable request.

Requests for attendance of witnesses

92   Although the arbitrator has no power to compel the attendance of anybody at the hearing, the arbitrator may draw an adverse inference if an employer who is a party to the arbitration fails or refuses to allow current employees or other workers (who have relevant evidence to give) time off from work to attend the hearing, should such an employer be so requested.

Preliminary hearings and directions

93   Where the arbitrator believes that there may be considerable differences between the parties over any issue, including the availability or exchange of documents, or the availability of witnesses, the arbitrator may call the parties to a preliminary hearing to address such issues, or he or she may give procedural directions in correspondence.

94   In the course of a preliminary hearing or in correspondence, the arbitrator may express views on the desirability of information and/or evidence being available at the hearing.

XVI OUTLINE OF PROCEDURE AT THE HEARING

Arbitrator's overall discretion

95 Subject to the arbitrator's general duty (Part X above), and subject to the points set out below, the conduct of the hearing and all procedural and evidential matters (including applications for adjournments and changes in venue) shall be for the arbitrator to decide.

Language

96 The language of the proceedings shall be English, unless the Welsh language is applicable by virtue of the Welsh Language Act 1993 (as amended from time to time). Reference should be made to paragraph 75 above if the Welsh language is to be used.

Witnesses

97 No party or witness shall be cross-examined by a party or representative, or examined on oath or affirmation.

Examination by the arbitrator

98 The arbitrator shall have the right to address questions directly to either party or to anybody else attending the hearing, and to take the initiative in ascertaining the facts and (where applicable) the law.

Explanation of available remedies

99 In every case, the arbitrator shall:
(i) explain to the Employee what orders for reinstatement or re-engagement may be made in an award and under what circumstances these may be granted; and
(ii) ask the Employee whether he or she wishes the arbitrator to make such an award.

Representatives

100 The parties may be accompanied by any person chosen by them to help them to present their case at the hearing, although no special status will be accorded to legally qualified representatives. Each party is liable for any fees or expenses incurred by any representatives they appoint.

Strict rules of evidence

101 The arbitrator will not apply strict rules of evidence (or any other rules) as to the admissibility, relevance or weight of any material (oral, written or other) sought to be tendered on any matters of fact or opinion.

Interim relief

102 The arbitrator shall have no power to order provisional or interim relief, but may expedite the proceedings where appropriate.

Non-attendance at the hearing

103 If, without showing sufficient cause, a party fails to attend or be represented at a hearing, the arbitrator may:

    (i)   continue the hearing in that party's absence, and in such a case shall take into account any written submissions and documents that have already been submitted by that party; or

    (ii) adjourn the hearing.

104   In the case of the non-attendance of the Employee, if the arbitrator decides to adjourn the hearing, he or she may write to the Employee to request an explanation for the non-attendance. If the arbitrator decides that the Employee has not demonstrated sufficient cause for the non-attendance, he or she may rule in an award that the claim be treated as dismissed.

Post-hearing written materials

105   No further submissions or evidence will be accepted after the end of the substantive hearing without the arbitrator's permission, which will only be granted in exceptional circumstances. Where permission is granted, any material is to be sent to the ACAS Arbitration Section, to be forwarded to the arbitrator and all other parties.

XVII QUESTIONS OF EC LAW, DEVOLUTION ISSUES AND THE HUMAN RIGHTS ACT 1998

Appointment of legal adviser

106   The arbitrator shall have the power, on the application of any party or of his or her own motion, to require the appointment of a legal adviser to assist with respect to any issue of EC law or the Human Rights Act 1998 or any devolution issue that, in the arbitrator's view and subject to paragraph 17 above (Arbitrator's Terms of Reference), might be involved and relevant to the resolution of the dispute.

107   The legal adviser will be appointed by ACAS, to report to the arbitrator and the parties, and shall be subject to the duty of disclosure set out in paragraphs 44 and 45 above.

108   The arbitrator shall allow the legal adviser to attend the proceedings, and may order an adjournment and/or change in venue to facilitate this.

109   The parties shall be given a reasonable opportunity to comment on any information, opinion or advice offered by the legal adviser, following which the arbitrator shall take such information, opinion or advice into account in determining the dispute.

Court determination of preliminary points: English/Welsh arbitrations

110EW Section 45 of the Arbitration Act 1996 shall apply to English/Welsh arbitrations conducted in accordance with the Scheme, subject to the following modifications:

    (i)   in subsection (1)–

        (a) for 'Unless otherwise agreed by the parties, the court' substitute 'The High Court or Central London County Court';

        (b) for 'any question of law' substitute 'any question (a) of EC law, or (b) concerning the application of the Human Rights Act 1998, or (c) any devolution issue'; and

(c) omit 'An agreement to dispense with reasons for the tribunal's award shall be considered an agreement to exclude the court's jurisdiction under this section.';

(ii) omit sub-paragraph (i) from subsection (2)(b);

(iii) omit subsection (4); and

(iv) after subsection (6), insert–

'(7) In this section, 'EC law' means–

(a) any enactment in the domestic legislation of England and Wales giving effect to rights, powers, liabilities, obligations and restrictions from time to time created or arising by or under the Community Treaties, and

(b) any such rights, powers, liabilities, obligations and restrictions which are not given effect by any such enactment.

(8) In this section 'devolution issue' means a devolution issue as defined in paragraph 1 Schedule 6 to the Scotland Act 1998 or a devolution issue as defined in paragraph 1 Schedule 8 to the Government of Wales Act 1998.'.

Court determination of preliminary points: Scottish arbitrations

111S The arbitrator may make a reference to the Court of Session for determination as a preliminary point–

(i) of any question of EC law,

(ii) of any question concerning the application of the Human Rights Act 1998, or

(iii) of any devolution issue

which substantially affects the rights of one or more of the parties to the arbitration.

112S The arbitrator shall not make a reference under paragraph 111S unless:

(i) both parties have applied for or have agreed to the making of the reference; or

(ii) if an application for the reference has been made by one party and opposed by the other party, the arbitrator is satisfied that the application has been made without delay.

XVIII   AUTOMATIC UNFAIRNESS

113 In deciding whether the dismissal was fair or unfair, subject to paragraph 17 above (Arbitrator's Terms of Reference), the arbitrator shall have regard to:

(i) any provision of Part X of the Employment Rights Act 1996 (as amended from time to time) requiring a dismissal for a particular reason to be regarded as unfair, and

(ii) any other legislative provision requiring a dismissal for a particular reason to be regarded as unfair for the purpose of Part X of the Employment Rights Act 1996.

XIX   AWARDS

Form of the award: English/Welsh arbitrations

114EW The award in an English/Welsh arbitration shall be in writing, signed by the arbitrator.

115EW The award (unless it is an agreed award) shall:
- (i)   identify the reason (or, if more than one, the principal reason) for the dismissal (or, in a redundancy case, the reason for which the employee was selected for dismissal);
- (ii)   contain the main considerations which were taken into account in reaching the decision that the dismissal was fair or unfair;
- (iii)   state the decision(s) of the arbitrator;
- (iv)   state the remedy awarded, together with an explanation;
- (v)   state the date when it was made.

116EW If the award contains an order for the payment of money the award shall–
- (i)   order the Employer to pay the Employee the amount of the award of compensation; and
- (ii)   order the Employer to pay interest thereon in accordance with paragraph 186 of the Scheme.

Form of the award: Scottish arbitrations
117S   The award in a Scottish arbitration shall–
- (i)   be in writing;
- (ii)   state the date upon which it was made;
- (iii)   specify the arbitrator's order;
- (iv)   be signed by the arbitrator;
- (v)   be signed by a witness to the arbitrator's signature; and
- (vi)   specify the name and address of the witness.

118S   If the award contains an order for the payment of money the award shall–
- (i)   ordain the Employer to pay to the Employee the amount of the award of compensation; and
- (ii)   ordain the Employer to pay interest thereon in accordance with paragraph 186 of the Scheme.

119S   The arbitrator shall issue with his award (unless it is an agreed award) a Note, which shall–
- (i)   identify the reason (or, if more than one, the principal reason) for the dismissal (or, in a redundancy case, the reason for which the employee was selected for dismissal);
- (ii)   contain the main considerations which were taken into account in reaching the decision that the dismissal was fair or unfair;
- (iii)   state the decision(s) of the arbitrator;
- (iv)   state the remedy awarded, together with an explanation;
- (v)   state the date when the Note was issued; and
- (vi)   be signed by the arbitrator.

Awards on different issues
120   The arbitrator may make more than one award at different times on different aspects of the matters to be determined.

121   The arbitrator may, in particular, make an award relating:
- (i)   to an issue affecting the whole claim, or
- (ii)   to a part only of the claim submitted to him or her for decision.

122 If the arbitrator does so, he or she shall specify in his or her award the issue, or the claim or part of a claim, which is the subject matter of the award.

Remedies

123 In the event that the arbitrator finds that the dismissal was unfair:
   (i) if the Employee expresses such a wish, the arbitrator may make, in an award, an order for reinstatement or re-engagement (in accordance with the provisions below); or
   (ii) if no such order for reinstatement or re-engagement is made, the arbitrator shall make an award of compensation (calculated in accordance with the provisions below) to be paid by the Employer to the Employee.

124 In cases where the arbitrator finds that the dismissal was unfair by reason of the operation of EC law, the arbitrator shall in an English/Welsh arbitration apply the relevant provisions of English law and shall in a Scottish arbitration apply the relevant provisions of Scots law with respect to remedies for unfair dismissal, in so far as these may differ from Parts XX and XXI of the Scheme.

XX   AWARDS OF REINSTATEMENT OR RE-ENGAGEMENT

Definitions

125 An order for reinstatement (which must be in the form of an award) is an order that the Employer shall treat the Employee in all respects as if he or she had not been dismissed.

126 An order for re-engagement (which must be in the form of an award) is an order, on such terms as the arbitrator may decide, that the Employee be engaged by the Employer, or by a successor of the Employer or by an associated employer, in employment comparable to that from which he or she was dismissed or in other suitable employment.

Choice of remedy

127 In exercising his or her discretion with respect to the remedy to be awarded under paragraph 123(i) above, the arbitrator shall first consider whether to make an order for reinstatement, and in so doing shall take into account:
   (i) whether the Employee wishes to be reinstated;
   (ii) whether it is practicable for the Employer to comply with an order for reinstatement; and
   (iii) where the Employee caused or contributed to some extent to the dismissal, whether it would be just to order his or her reinstatement.

128 If the arbitrator decides not to make an order for reinstatement, he or she shall then consider whether to make an order for re-engagement and, if so, on what terms. In so doing, the arbitrator shall take into account:
   (i) any wish expressed by the Employee as to the nature of the order to be made;
   (ii) whether it is practicable for the Employer (or a successor or an associated employer) to comply with an order for re-engagement, and

(iii) where the Employee caused or contributed to some extent to the dismissal, whether it would be just to order his or her re-engagement and, if so, on what terms.

129   If ordering re-engagement, the arbitrator shall do so on terms which are, so far as is reasonably practicable, as favourable as an order for reinstatement (with the exception of cases where contributory fault has been taken into account under paragraph 127(iii) above).

Permanent replacements

130   Where in any case an Employer has engaged a permanent replacement for a dismissed Employee, the arbitrator shall not take that fact into account in determining, for the purposes of paragraphs 127(ii) and 128(ii) above, whether it is practicable to comply with an order for reinstatement or re-engagement. This does not apply, however, where the Employer shows:

(i) that it was not practicable for him or her to arrange for the dismissed Employee's work to be done without engaging a permanent replacement, or

(ii) that:

    (a) he or she engaged the replacement after the lapse of a reasonable period, without having heard from the dismissed Employee that he or she wished to be reinstated or re-engaged, and

    (b) when the Employer engaged the replacement it was no longer reasonable for him or her to arrange for the dismissed Employee's work to be done except by a permanent replacement.

Reinstatement

131   On making an order for reinstatement, the arbitrator shall specify:

(i) any amount payable by the Employer in respect of any benefit which the Employee might reasonably be expected to have had but for the dismissal (including arrears of pay) for the period between the date of termination of employment and the date of reinstatement,

(ii) any rights and privileges (including seniority and pension rights) which must be restored to the Employee, and

(iii) the date by which the order must be complied with.

132   If the Employee would have benefited from an improvement in his or her terms and conditions of employment had he or she not been dismissed, an order for reinstatement shall require him or her to be treated as if he or she had benefited from that improvement from the date on which he or she would have done so but for being dismissed.

133   In calculating for the purposes of paragraph 131(i) above any amount payable by the Employer, the arbitrator shall take into account, so as to reduce the Employer's liability, any sums received by the Employee in respect of the period between the date of termination of employment and the date of reinstatement by way of:

(i) wages in lieu of notice or ex gratia payments paid by the Employer, or

(ii) remuneration paid in respect of employment with another employer, and such other benefits as the arbitrator thinks appropriate in the circumstances.

Re-engagement

134 On making an order for re-engagement the arbitrator shall specify the terms on which re-engagement is to take place, including:
(i)   the identity of the employer,
(ii)   the nature of the employment,
(iii)   the remuneration for the employment,
(iv)   any amount payable by the employer in respect of any benefit which the Employee might reasonably be expected to have had but for the dismissal (including arrears of pay) for the period between the date of termination of employment and the date of re-engagement,
(v)   any rights and privileges (including seniority and pension rights) which must be restored to the Employee, and
(vi)   the date by which the order must be complied with.

135 In calculating, for the purposes of paragraph 131(iv) above, any amount payable by the Employer, the arbitrator shall take into account, so as to reduce the Employer's liability, any sums received by the Employee in respect of the period between the date of termination of employment and the date of re-engagement by way of:
(i)   wages in lieu of notice or ex gratia payments paid by the Employer, or
(ii)   remuneration paid in respect of employment with another employer,
and such other benefits as the arbitrator thinks appropriate in the circumstances.

Continuity of employment

136 The Employee's continuity of employment will be preserved in the same way as it would be under an award of the employment tribunal.

XXI   AWARDS OF COMPENSATION

137 When an arbitrator makes an award of compensation, instead of an award for reinstatement or re-engagement, such compensation shall consist of a basic amount and a compensatory amount.

138 Where paragraph 163 below applies, an award of compensation shall also include a supplementary amount.

The basic amount

139 Subject to the following provisions, the basic amount shall be calculated by:
(i)   determining the period, ending with the effective date of termination (see paragraph 140 below), during which the Employee has been continuously employed (see paragraph 141 below),
(ii)   reckoning backwards from the end of that period the number of years of employment falling within that period, and
(iii)   allowing the appropriate amount (see paragraph 142 below) for each of those years of employment.

140 As to the 'effective date of termination':

(i)   the 'effective date of termination' means:
   (a)   in relation to an Employee whose contract of employment is terminated by notice, whether given by his or her Employer or by the Employee, the date on which the notice expires;
   (b)   in relation to an Employee whose contract of employment is terminated without notice, the date on which the termination takes effect; and
   (c)   in relation to an Employee who is employed under a contract for a fixed term which expires without being renewed under the same contract, the date on which the term expires.
(ii) Where:
   (a)   the contract of employment is terminated by the Employer, and
   (b)   the notice required by section 86 of the Employment Rights Act 1996 (as amended from time to time) to be given by an Employer would, if duly given on the material date, expire on a date later than the effective date of termination (as defined in paragraph 140(i) above),
the later date is the effective date of termination.
(iii) In paragraph 140(ii)(b) above, 'the material date' means:
   (a)   the date when notice of termination was given by the Employer, or
   (b)   where no notice was given, the date when the contract of employment was terminated by the Employer.
(iv) Where:
   (a)   the contract of employment is terminated by the Employee, and
   (b)   the material date does not fall during a period of notice given by the Employer to terminate that contract, and
   (c)   had the contract been terminated not by the Employee but by notice given on the material date by the Employer, that notice would have been required by section 86 of the Employment Rights Act 1996 (as amended from time to time) to expire on a date later than the effective date of termination (as defined in paragraph 140(i) above),
   the later date is the effective date of termination.
(v)   In paragraph 140(iv) above, 'the material date' means:
   (a)   the date when notice of termination was given by the Employee, or
   (b)   where no notice was given, the date when the contract of employment was terminated by the Employee.

141   In determining 'continuous employment', the arbitrator shall have regard to Chapter I of Part XIV of the Employment Rights Act 1996 (as amended from time to time).

142   The 'appropriate amount' means:
(i)   one and a half weeks' pay for a year of employment in which the Employee was not below the age of forty-one,
(ii) one week's pay for a year of employment (not within sub-paragraph (i) above) in which he or she was not below the age of twenty-two, and
(iii) half a week's pay for a year of employment not within sub-paragraphs (i) or (ii) above.

143   In calculating the amount of a week's pay of an Employee, the arbitrator shall have regard to Chapter II of Part XIV of the Employment Rights Act 1996, as amended from time to time, or any other relevant statutory provision applicable to the calculation of a week's pay.

144   Where twenty years of employment have been reckoned under paragraph 139 above, no account shall be taken under that paragraph of any year of employment earlier than those twenty years.

145   Where the effective date of termination is after the sixty-fourth anniversary of the day of the Employee's birth, the amount arrived at under paragraphs 139, 142 and 144 above shall be reduced by the 'appropriate fraction' (see paragraph 146 below).

146   The 'appropriate fraction' means the fraction of which:

(i)   the numerator is the number of whole months reckoned from the sixty-fourth anniversary of the day of the Employee's birth in the period beginning with that anniversary and ending with the effective date of termination (see paragraph 140 above), and

(ii)   the denominator is twelve.

Minimum basic amounts in certain cases

147   A 'minimum basic amount' shall apply where the arbitrator has found that the dismissal was unfair, and where the reason (or, if more than one, the principal reason):

–   in a redundancy case (see paragraph 150(i) below), for selecting the Employee for dismissal, or

–   otherwise, for the dismissal

was one of the following:

Health and safety cases

(i)   having been designated by the Employer to carry out activities in connection with preventing or reducing risks to health and safety at work, the Employee carried out (or proposed to carry out) any such activities;

(ii)   being a representative of workers on matters of health and safety at work or a member of a safety committee:

(a)   in accordance with arrangements established under or by virtue of any enactment, or

(b)   by reason of being acknowledged as such by the Employer,

the Employee performed (or proposed to perform) any functions as such a representative or a member of such a committee;

Working time cases

(iii)   being:

(a)   a representative of members of the workforce for the purposes of Schedule 1 to the Working Time Regulations 1998 (as amended from time to time), or

(b)   a candidate in an election in which any person elected will, on being elected, be such a representative, performed (or proposed to perform) any functions or activities as such a representative or candidate;

Trustees of occupational pension schemes

(iv) being a trustee of a relevant occupational pension scheme which relates to his or her employment, the Employee performed (or proposed to perform) any functions as such a trustee;

Employee representatives

(v) being:
  (a) an employee representative for the purposes of Chapter II of Part IV of the Trade Union and Labour Relations (Consolidation) Act 1992 (redundancies) or Regulations 10 and 11 of the Transfer of Undertakings (Protection of Employment) Regulations 1981 (as amended from time to time), or
  (b) a candidate in an election in which any person elected will, on being elected, be such an employee representative,

performed (or proposed to perform) any functions or activities as such an employee representative or candidate;

(vi) the Employee took part in an election of employee representatives for the purposes of Chapter II of Part IV of the Trade Union and Labour Relations (Consolidation) Act 1992 (redundancies) or Regulations 10 and 11 of the Transfer of Undertakings (Protection of Employment) Regulations 1981 (as amended from time to time);

Union membership or activities

(vii) the Employee:
  (a) was, or proposed to become, a member of an independent trade union, or
  (b) had taken part, or proposed to take part, in the activities of an independent trade union at an appropriate time, or
  (c) was not a member of any trade union, or of a particular trade union, or of one of a number of particular trade unions, or had refused, or proposed to refuse, to become or remain a member.

(viii) for the purposes of paragraphs (vii) above to (xi) below, in defining the terms 'trade union' and 'independent trade union', the arbitrator shall have regard to sections 1 and 5 of the Trade Union and Labour Relations (Consolidation) Act 1992, as amended from time to time.

(ix) for the purposes of paragraph (vii)(b) above, an 'appropriate time' means:
  (a) a time outside the Employee's working hours, or
  (b) a time within his or her working hours at which, in accordance with arrangements agreed with or consent given by his or her employer, it is permissible for him or her to take part in the activities of a trade union;

and for this purpose 'working hours', in relation to an Employee, means any time when, in accordance with his or her contract of employment, he or she is required to be at work.

(x) where the reason, or one of the reasons, for the dismissal was:

(a) the Employee's refusal, or proposed refusal, to comply with a requirement (whether or not imposed by his or her contract of employment or in writing) that, in the event of his or her not being a member of any trade union, or of a particular trade union, or of one of a number of particular trade unions, he or she must make one or more payments, or

(b) his or her objection, or proposed objection, (however expressed) to the operation of a provision (whether or not forming part of his or her contract of employment or in writing) under which, in the event mentioned in paragraph (x)(a) above, his or her Employer is entitled to deduct one or more sums from the remuneration payable to him or her in respect of his or her employment,

the reason shall be treated as falling within paragraph (vii)(c) above.

(xi) references in paragraphs (vii) to (x) above to being, becoming or ceasing to remain a member of a trade union include references to being, becoming or ceasing to remain a member of a particular branch or section of that union or of one of a number of particular branches or sections of that trade union; and references to taking part in the activities of a trade union shall be similarly construed.

Other categories

(xii) where the reason or principal reason for the dismissal of the Employee qualifies under any other applicable legislative provision for a minimum basic award.

148 Before any reductions are taken into account under paragraphs 151 to 155 below ('Reductions to the basic amount'), the 'minimum basic amount' shall not be less than:

(i) in cases within paragraph 147(i), (ii), (iii), (iv), (v) and (vi) above, the amount provided for in section 120(1) of the Employment Rights Act 1996, as amended from time to time;

(ii) in cases within paragraph 147(vii) above, the amount provided for in section 156 of the Trade Union and Labour Relations (Consolidation) Act 1992, as amended from time to time;

(iii) in cases within paragraph 147(xii) above, the amount provided for in the relevant legislation.

Basic amount of two weeks' pay in certain cases

149 Where:

(i) the arbitrator finds that the reason (or, where there is more than one, the principal reason) for the dismissal of the Employee is that he or she was redundant and

(ii) the Employee:

(a) by virtue of section 138 of the Employment Rights Act 1996, as amended from time to time, is not regarded as dismissed for the purposes of Part XI of that Act, or

(b) by virtue of section 141 of that Act, as amended from time to time, is not, or (if he or she were otherwise entitled) would not be, entitled to a redundancy payment, the basic amount shall be two weeks' pay (for the definition of 'week's pay', see paragraph 143 above).

150 For the purposes of this Scheme:

(i) for the definition of 'redundancy', the arbitrator shall have regard to section 139 of the Employment Rights Act 1996, as amended from time to time;

(ii) for the definition of 'redundancy payment', the arbitrator shall have regard to Part XI of the Employment Rights Act 1996, as amended from time to time.

Reductions to the basic amount

151 Where the arbitrator finds that the Employee has unreasonably refused an offer by the Employer which (if accepted) would have the effect of reinstating the Employee in his or her employment in all respects as if he or she had not been dismissed, the arbitrator shall reduce or further reduce the basic amount to such extent as he or she considers just and equitable having regard to that finding.

152 Where the arbitrator considers that any conduct of the Employee before the dismissal (or, where the dismissal was with notice, before the notice was given) was such that it would be just and equitable to reduce or further reduce the basic amount to any extent, the arbitrator shall reduce or further reduce that amount accordingly. In assessing such conduct, the arbitrator shall disregard (if relevant) those matters set out in section 155 of the Trade Union and Labour Relations (Consolidation) Act 1992, as amended from time to time.

153 The preceding paragraph does not apply in a redundancy case (see paragraph 150(i) above) unless the reason for selecting the Employee for dismissal was one of those specified in paragraph 147 above ('Minimum basic amounts in certain cases'), and in such a case, the preceding paragraph applies only to so much of the basic amount as is payable because of paragraph 147 above.

154 Where the Employee has been awarded any amount in respect of the dismissal under a dismissal procedures agreement designated under section 110 of the Employment Rights Act 1996 (as amended from time to time), the arbitrator shall reduce or further reduce the amount of the basic award to such extent as he or she considers just and equitable having regard to that award.

155 The basic amount shall be reduced or further reduced by the amount of any payment made by the Employer to the Employee on the ground that the dismissal was by reason of redundancy (whether in pursuance of Part XI of the Employment Rights Act 1996, as amended from time to time, or otherwise).

The compensatory amount

156 Subject to the following provisions, the compensatory amount shall be such as the arbitrator considers just and equitable in all the circumstances having regard to the loss sustained by the Employee in consequence of the dismissal, in so far as that loss is attributable to action taken by the Employer.

157 The loss referred to in paragraph 156 above shall be taken to include:

(i) any expenses reasonably incurred by the Employee in consequence of the dismissal; and

(ii) subject to sub-paragraph (iii) below, loss of any benefit which he or she might reasonably be expected to have had but for the dismissal;

(iii) in respect of any loss of:

(a) any entitlement or potential entitlement to a payment on account of dismissal by reason of redundancy (whether in pursuance of Part XI of the Employment Rights Act 1996, as amended from time to time, or otherwise); or

(b) any expectation of such a payment

only the loss referable to the amount (if any) by which such a payment would have exceeded the basic amount in respect of the same dismissal (as calculated under the provisions set out above–but excluding any reductions under paragraphs 151 to 155 above ('Reductions to the basic amount')).

158 In ascertaining the loss referred to in paragraph 152 above, the arbitrator shall apply the principle that a person has a duty to mitigate his or her loss.

159 In determining, for the purposes of paragraph 152 above, how far any loss sustained by the Employee was attributable to action taken by the Employer, no account shall be taken of any pressure which by:

(i) calling, organising, procuring or financing a strike or other industrial action, or

(ii) threatening to do so,

was exercised on the Employer to dismiss the Employee; and that question shall be determined as if no such pressure had been exercised.

Reductions to the compensatory amount

160 Where the arbitrator finds that the dismissal was to any extent caused or contributed to by any conduct of the Employee, he or she shall reduce the compensatory amount by such proportion as he or she considers just and equitable having regard to that finding. In assessing such conduct, the arbitrator shall disregard (if relevant) those matters set out in section 155 of the Trade Union and Labour Relations (Consolidation) Act 1992, as amended from time to time.

161 If:

(i) any payment was made by the Employer to the Employee on the ground that the dismissal was by reason of redundancy (whether in pursuance of Part XI of the Employment Rights Act 1996, as amended from time to time, or otherwise); and

(ii) the amount of such a payment exceeds the basic amount that would have been payable under the provisions set out above (excluding for this purpose reductions on account of redundancy payments (see paragraph 150 above)),

that excess goes to reduce the compensatory amount.

Internal appeal procedures

162 Where an award of compensation is to be made, and the arbitrator finds that:

(i) the Employer provided a procedure for appealing against dismissal; and

(ii) the Employee was, at the time of the dismissal or within a reasonable period afterwards, given written notice stating that the Employer provided the procedure and including details of it; but

(iii) the Employee did not appeal against the dismissal under the procedure (otherwise than because the Employer prevented him or her from doing so),

the arbitrator shall reduce the compensatory amount included in an award of compensation by such amount (if any) as he or she considers just and equitable.

163 Where an award of compensation is to be made, and the arbitrator finds that:

(i) the Employer provided a procedure for appealing against dismissal; but

(ii) the Employer prevented the Employee from appealing against the dismissal under the procedure,

the award of compensation shall include a supplementary amount, being such amount (if any) as the arbitrator considers just and equitable.

164 In determining the amount of a reduction under paragraph 162 above or a supplementary amount under paragraph 163 above, the arbitrator shall have regard to all the circumstances of the case, including in particular the chances that an appeal under the procedure provided by the Employer would have been successful.

165 The amount of such a reduction or supplementary amount shall not exceed the amount of two weeks' pay (for the definition of 'week's pay', see paragraph 143 above).

Limits on the compensatory amount

166 With the exception of:

(i) cases falling within sections 100 or 105(3) (Health and Safety Cases) of the Employment Rights Act 1996, as amended from time to time; and

(ii) cases where the reason (or, if more than one, the principal reason):

    (a) in a redundancy case, for selecting the Employee for dismissal; or

    (b) otherwise for the dismissal,

was that the Employee made a protected disclosure (within the meaning of Part IVA of the Employment Rights Act 1996, as amended from time to time); and

(iii) cases falling within any other exception to the statutory limit,

no compensatory amount awarded by an arbitrator shall exceed the statutory limit provided for in section 124(1) of the Employment Rights Act 1996, as amended from time to time.

167 The limit referred to above applies to the amount which the arbitrator would award (apart from paragraph 166 above) in respect of the subject matter of the complaint, after taking into account:

(i) any payment made by the Employer to the Employee in respect of that matter, and

(ii) any reduction in the amount of the award required by any enactment or rule of law.

Double recovery

168 Where the same acts of the Employer are relied upon by the Employee:

(i) to ground a claim for unfair dismissal in arbitration as well as

(ii) to ground a claim in the employment tribunal for discrimination (under the Sex Discrimination Act 1975 and/or the Race Relations Act 1976 and/or the Disability Discrimination Act 1995, and/or any other relevant Act or subordinate legislation),

the arbitrator shall not award compensation in respect of any loss or other matter which is to be or has been taken into account by the employment tribunal in awarding compensation with respect to the discrimination claim.

In this regard, the arbitrator shall have regard to any information supplied by the parties under paragraph 86 above.

XXII   ISSUE OF AWARDS AND CONFIDENTIALITY

169 The arbitrator's award shall be sent by ACAS to both parties.

170 Subject to any steps which may be reasonably necessary for the purposes of any application to the Court or enforcement of the award, the award shall be confidential, and shall only be issued to the parties or to their nominated advisers or representatives. Awards will not be published by ACAS, or lodged with the employment tribunal by ACAS, although awards may be retained by ACAS for monitoring and evaluation purposes, and, from time to time, ACAS may publish general summary information concerning cases heard under the Scheme, without identifying any individual cases.

XXIII   CORRECTION OF AWARDS

Scrutiny of awards by ACAS

171 Before being sent to the parties, awards may be scrutinised by ACAS to check for clerical or computational mistakes, errors arising from accidental slips or omissions, ambiguities, or errors of form. Without affecting the arbitrator's liberty of decision, ACAS may refer the award back to the arbitrator (under the provisions below) in order to draw his or her attention to any such point.

Correction by the arbitrator

172 The arbitrator may, on his or her own initiative or on the application of a party or ACAS:

(i) correct the award so as to remove any clerical or computational mistake, or error arising from an accidental slip or omission, or to clarify or remove any ambiguity in the award, or

(ii) make an additional award in respect of any part of the claim which was presented to the arbitrator but was not dealt with in the award.

173   In so far as any such correction or additional award involves a new issue that was not previously before the parties, this power shall not be exercised without first affording the parties a reasonable opportunity to make written representations to the arbitrator.

174   Any application by a party for the exercise of this power must be made via the ACAS Arbitration Section within 28 days of the date the award was despatched to the applying party by ACAS.

175   Any correction of the award shall be made within 28 days of the date the application was received by the arbitrator or, where the correction is made by the arbitrator on his or her own initiative, within 28 days of the date of the award.

176   Any additional award shall be made within 56 days of the date of the original award.

177EW Any additional award in an English/Welsh arbitration shall so far as relevant comply with paragraphs 114EW, 115EW and 116EW.

178S Any additional award in a Scottish arbitration shall so far as relevant comply with paragraphs 117S and 118S. Any correction to an award shall be issued on a memorandum of correction which shall:
(i)   specify the correction;
(ii) be signed by the arbitrator;
(iii) be signed by a witness to the arbitrator's signature;
(iv) state the name and address of the witness; and
(v)   state the date upon which it was signed by the arbitrator.

179   Any correction of the award shall form part of the award.

XXIV EFFECT OF AWARDS, ENFORCEMENT AND INTEREST

Effect of awards

180   Awards made by arbitrators under this Scheme are final and binding both on the parties and on any persons claiming through or under them.

181EW This does not affect the right of a person to challenge an award under the provisions of the Arbitration Act 1996 as applied to this Scheme.

182S This does not affect the right of a person to challenge an award under Part XXV below.

Enforcement

183EW Section 66 of the Arbitration Act 1996 shall apply to English and Welsh arbitrations conducted in accordance with the Scheme, subject to the following modifications—
(i)   in subsection (1), for 'tribunal pursuant to an arbitration agreement' substitute 'arbitrator pursuant to the Scheme (except for an award of reinstatement or re-engagement)';
(ii) in subsection (3), for ' (see section 73)' substitute ' (see Part XXVI of the Scheme)'; and

(iii)   after subsection (4), insert–

'(5) In this section–

'the court' means the High Court or a county court; and

'the Scheme' means the arbitration scheme set out in the Schedule to the ACAS Arbitration Scheme (Great Britain) Order 2004.'.

184S   Any award requiring the payment of money which may be made in a Scottish arbitration under the Scheme may be registered for execution.

185   Awards of reinstatement or re-engagement will be enforced by the employment tribunal in accordance with section 117 of the Employment Rights Act 1996 (enforcement by award of compensation).

Interest

186   Awards of compensation that are not paid within 42 days of the date on which the award was despatched by ACAS to the Employer will attract interest on the same basis as for employment tribunal awards.

XXV   CHALLENGING THE AWARD

Challenges on grounds of substantive jurisdiction: English/Welsh arbitrations

187EW Section 67 of the Arbitration Act 1996 shall apply to English/Welsh arbitrations conducted in accordance with the Scheme, subject to the following modifications–

(i)   in subsection (1)–

(a)   for '(upon notice to the other parties and to the tribunal) apply to the court' substitute '(upon notice to the other party, to the arbitrator and to ACAS) apply to the High Court or the Central London County Court';

(b)   for '(see section 73)' substitute ' (see Part XXVI of the Scheme)'; and

(c)   after 'section 70(2) and (3)' insert 'as modified for the purposes of the Scheme'; and

(ii)   after subsection (1), insert–

'(1A)In this section–

'Arbitration Agreement' means an agreement to refer a dispute to arbitration in accordance with, and satisfying the requirements of, the Scheme'

'the Scheme' means the arbitration scheme set out in the Schedule to the ACAS Arbitration Scheme (Great Britain) Order 2004; and

'substantive jurisdiction' means any issue as to–

(a)   the validity of the Arbitration Agreement and the application of the Scheme to the dispute or difference in question;

(b)   the constitution of the arbitral tribunal; or

(c)   the matters which have been submitted to arbitration in accordance with the Arbitration Agreement.'.

Challenges on grounds of substantive jurisdiction: Scottish arbitrations

188S A party to a Scottish arbitration may appeal to the Court of Session–

(i) challenging any award of the arbitrator as to his or her substantive jurisdiction; or

(ii) on the ground that an award made by the arbitrator on the merits is of no effect, in whole or in part, because the arbitrator did not have substantive jurisdiction.

189S A party may lose the right to appeal under paragraph 188S in accordance with Part XXVI below.

190S Appeals under paragraph 188S are subject to the provisions of paragraphs 206S, 207S and 208S below.

191S For the purposes of paragraph 188S 'substantive jurisdiction' means any issue as to–

(i) the validity of the Arbitration Agreement and the application of the Scheme to the dispute or difference in question;

(ii) the constitution of the arbitral tribunal; or

(iii) the matters which have been submitted to arbitration in accordance with the Arbitration Agreement.

192S The arbitrator may continue the arbitral proceedings and make a further award while an appeal to the Court under paragraph 188S is pending in relation to an award of the arbitrator as to his substantive jurisdiction.

193S On an appeal under paragraph 188S the Court may (without prejudice to any other power which it may exercise or remedy which it may grant)–

(i) confirm the award;

(ii) vary the award;

(iii) declare the award to be of no effect in whole or in part; or

(iv) reduce the award in whole or in part.

Challenges for serious irregularity: English/Welsh arbitrations

194EW Section 68 of the Arbitration Act 1996 shall apply to English/Welsh arbitrations conducted in accordance with the Scheme, subject to the following modifications.

(i) in subsection (1)–

(a) for '(upon notice to the other parties and to the tribunal) apply to the court' substitute ' (upon notice to the other party, to the arbitrator and to ACAS) apply to the High Court or Central London County Court';

(b) for '(see section 73)' substitute ' (see Part XXVI of the Scheme)'; and

(c) after 'section 70(2) and (3)' insert 'as modified for the purposes of the Scheme';

(ii) in subsection (2)(a), for 'section 33 (general duty of tribunal)' substitute 'Part X of the Scheme (General Duty of the Arbitrator)';

(iii) in subsection (2)(b), after 'see section 67' insert 'as modified for the purposes of the Scheme';

(iv) in subsection (2)(c), for 'agreed by the parties' substitute 'as set out in the Scheme';

(v)   in subsection (2)(e), for 'any arbitral or other institution or person vested by the parties with powers in relation to the proceedings or the award' substitute 'ACAS';

(vi)   omit paragraph (h) from subsection (2);

(vii)   in subsection (2)(i), for 'any arbitral or other institution or person vested by the parties with powers in relation to the proceedings or the award' substitute 'ACAS';

(viii)   in subsection (3)(b) insert 'vary the award or' before 'set the award aside';

(ix)   in subsection (3), omit 'The court shall not exercise its power to set aside or to declare an award to be of no effect, in whole or in part, unless it is satisfied that it would be inappropriate to remit the matters in question to the tribunal for reconsideration.'; and

(x)   after subsection (4), insert–

'(5) In this section, 'the Scheme' means the arbitration scheme set out in the Schedule to the ACAS Arbitration Scheme (Great Britain) Order 2004.'.

Challenges for serious irregularity: Scottish arbitrations

195S   A party to a Scottish arbitration may appeal to the Court of Session against an award in the proceedings on the ground of serious irregularity affecting the arbitrator, the proceedings or the award.

196S   A party may lose the right to appeal under paragraph 195S above in accordance with Part XXVI below.

197S   Appeals under paragraph 195S are subject to the provisions of paragraphs 206S, 207S and 208S.

198S   For the purposes of paragraph 195S, 'serious irregularity' means an irregularity of one or more of the following kinds which the Court considers has caused or will cause substantial injustice to the appellant–

(i)   failure by the arbitrator to comply with Part X above (General Duty of Arbitrator);

(ii)   the arbitrator exceeding his or her powers (otherwise than by exceeding its substantive jurisdiction (as defined in paragraph 191S above));

(iii)   failure by the arbitrator to conduct the proceedings in accordance with the procedure set out in the Scheme;

(iv)   failure by the arbitrator to deal with all the issues put to him or her;

(v)   ACAS exceeding its powers;

(vi)   uncertainty or ambiguity as to the effect of the award;

(vii)   the award having been obtained by fraud or the way in which it was procured being contrary to public policy; or

(viii)   any irregularity in the conduct of the proceedings or in the award which is admitted by the arbitrator or ACAS.

199S   If there is shown to be serious irregularity affecting the arbitrator, the proceedings or the award, the Court may (without prejudice to any other power which it may exercise or remedy which it may grant)–

(i)   remit the award to the arbitrator, in whole or in part, for reconsideration,

(ii)   vary the award,

(iii)   declare the award to be of no effect in whole or in part, or

(iv)   reduce the award in whole or in part.

Appeals on questions of EC law and the Human Rights Act 1998: English/Welsh arbitrations

200EW Section 69 of the Arbitration Act 1996 shall apply to English/Welsh arbitrations conducted in accordance with the Scheme, subject to the following modifications–

(i)   In subsection (1):

    (a)   omit 'Unless otherwise agreed by the parties';

    (b)   for '(upon notice to the other parties and to the tribunal) appeal to the court' substitute ' (upon notice to the other party, to the arbitrator and to ACAS) appeal to the High Court or Central London County Court';

    (c)   for 'a question of law' substitute 'a question (a) of EC law, or (b) concerning the application of the Human Rights Act 1998 or (c) any devolution issue';

    (d)   omit 'An agreement to dispense with reasons for the tribunal's award shall be considered an agreement to exclude the court's jurisdiction under this section.';

(ii)   In subsection (2), after 'section 70(2) and (3)' insert 'as modified for the purposes of the Scheme';

(iii)   omit paragraph (b) from subsection (3);

(iv)   in subsection (3)(c), after the words 'on the basis of the findings of fact in the award' insert ', in so far as the question for appeal raises a point of EC law, the point is capable of serious argument, and in so far as the question for appeal does not raise a point of EC law';

(v)   in subsection (7), omit 'The court shall not exercise its power to set aside an award, in whole or in part, unless it is satisfied that it would be inappropriate to remit the matters in question to the tribunal for reconsideration.'; and

(vi)   after subsection (8), insert–

'(9) In this section–

'EC law' means–

    (a)   any enactment in the domestic legislation of England and Wales giving effect to rights, powers, liabilities, obligations and restrictions from time to time created or arising by or under the Community Treaties, and

    (b)   any such rights, powers, liabilities, obligations and restrictions which are not given effect by any such enactment;

'the Scheme' means the arbitration scheme set out in the Schedule to the ACAS Arbitration Scheme (Great Britain) Order 2004, and

'devolution issue' means a devolution issue as defined in paragraph 1 of Schedule 6 to the Scotland Act 1998 or a devolution issue as defined in paragraph 1 of Schedule 8 of the Government of Wales Act 1998.'

Appeals on questions of EC law, devolution issues and the Human Rights Act 1998: Scottish arbitrations

201S A party to a Scottish arbitration may appeal to the Court of Session:
  (i)   on a question of EC law,
  (ii) on a question concerning the application of the Human Rights Act 1998, or
  (iii) on a devolution issue

arising out of an award made in the arbitration.

202S An appeal shall not be brought under paragraph 201S except–
  (i) with the agreement of all the other parties to the proceedings; or
  (ii) with the leave of the Court.

203S Leave to appeal shall be given only if the Court is satisfied–
  (i)   that the determination of the question will substantially affect the rights of one or more of the parties;
  (ii) that on the basis of the findings of fact in the Note appended to the award, insofar as the question for appeal raises a point of EC law, the point is capable of serious argument, and insofar as the question for appeal does not raise a point of EC law:
    (a) the decision of the arbitrator on the question is obviously wrong, or
    (b) the question is one of general public importance and the decision of the arbitrator is at least open to serious doubt, and
  (iii) that, despite the agreement of the parties to resolve the matter by arbitration, it is just and proper in all the circumstances for the Court to determine the question.

204S On an appeal under paragraph 201S the Court may (without prejudice to any other power which it may exercise or remedy which it may grant)–
  (i)   confirm the award,
  (ii) vary the award,
  (iii) remit the award to the arbitrator, in whole or in part, for reconsideration in light of the Court's determination,
  (iv) declare the award to be of no effect in whole or in part,
  (v)   reduce the award in whole or in part, or
  (vi) recall the award in whole or in part.

Time limits and other procedural restrictions on challenges to awards: English/Welsh arbitrations

205EW Section 70 of the Arbitration Act 1996 shall apply to English/Welsh arbitrations conducted in accordance with the Scheme, subject to the following modifications–
  (i)   in subsection (1), after the words 'section 67, 68 or 69' insert the words '(as modified for the purposes of the Scheme)';
  (ii) omit paragraph (a) from subsection (2);
  (iii) in subsection (2)(b), for 'section 57 (correction of award or additional award)' substitute 'Part XXIII of the Scheme (Correction of Awards)';
  (iv) for subsection (3), for 'of the award or, if there has been any arbitral process of appeal or review, of the date when the applicant or appellant was notified of the result of that process' substitute 'the award was despatched to the applicant or appellant by ACAS, or if an application

for a correction or additional award under paragraph 172 has been made and declined, the date on which the arbitrator's decision was despatched to the applicant or appellant by ACAS';

(v)   omit subsection (5);

(vi) after subsection (8), insert–

'(9) In this section, 'the Scheme' means the arbitration scheme set out in the Schedule to the ACAS Arbitration Scheme (Great Britain) Order 2004.'

Time limits and procedural restrictions on challenges to awards: Scottish arbitrations

206S   An appeal under paragraphs 188S, 195S or 201S may not be brought if the appellant has not first exhausted any available recourse under Part XXIII of the Scheme (Correction of Awards).

207S   An appeal under paragraphs 188S, 195S or (where the parties have agreed under paragraph 202S(i)) 201S or an application for leave to appeal under paragraph 202S(ii) shall be lodged within 28 days of whichever is the later of:

(i)   the date on which the award was despatched to the appellant by ACAS;

(ii)   where, a correction or additional award has been made in accordance with Part XXIII above, the date on which a memorandum of correction or additional award under Part XXIII above was despatched to the appellant by ACAS; and

(iii) where a party has applied for a correction or additional award under paragraph 172 above but the arbitrator has declined to make any correction or additional award, the date on which intimation of the arbitrator's decision was despatched to the appellant by ACAS.

208S   If on an appeal under paragraphs 188S, 195S or 201S it appears to the Court that the award and the arbitrator's Note:

(i)   do not contain the arbitrator's reasons, or

(ii)   do not set out the arbitrator's reasons in sufficient detail to enable the Court properly to consider the application or appeal,

the Court may order the arbitrator to state the reasons for his or her award in sufficient detail for that purpose.

Common law challenges and saving

209EW Sections 81(1)(c) and 81(2) of the Arbitration Act 1996 shall apply to English/Welsh arbitrations conducted in accordance with the Scheme.

210S   Nothing in this Part of the Scheme shall be construed as excluding the operation of any rule of law as to the refusal of recognition or enforcement of an arbitral award in a Scottish arbitration on grounds of public policy.

Exclusion of stated case procedure

211S   Section 3 of the Administration of Justice (Scotland) Act 1972 shall not apply to any arbitration under the Scheme.

Challenge or appeal: effect of order of the court

212EW (1) Section 71 of the Arbitration Act 1996 shall apply to English/Welsh arbitrations conducted in accordance with the Scheme, subject to the following modifications–

(i) in subsection (1), after the words 'section 67, 68 and 69' insert the words '(as modified for the purposes of the Scheme)';

(ii) after subsection (3), insert–

'(3AIn this section, 'the Scheme' means the arbitration scheme set out in the Schedule to the ACAS Arbitration Scheme (Great Britain) Order 2004. and;'

(iii) omit subsection (4).

213S The following provisions have effect where the Court makes an order under paragraph 193S, 199S or 204S of the Scheme with respect to an award.

(i) Where the award is varied, the variation has effect as part of the arbitrator's award.

(ii) Where the award is remitted to the arbitrator in whole or in part for reconsideration the arbitrator shall make a fresh award in respect of the matters remitted within three months of the date of the order for remission or such longer or shorter period as the Court may direct.

XXVI LOSS OF RIGHT TO OBJECT

214 If a party to arbitral proceedings under this Scheme takes part, or continues to take part, in the proceedings without making, either forthwith or within such time as is allowed by the arbitrator or by any provision in this Scheme, any objection:

(i) in an English/Welsh arbitration, that the arbitrator lacks substantive jurisdiction as defined in paragraph 187EW, or in a Scottish arbitration that the arbitrator lacks substantive jurisdiction as defined in paragraph 191S, aside from any jurisdictional objection with respect to the circumstances of the dismissal, which will be waived in any event, as set out in paragraphs 21 to 23 above,

(ii) that the proceedings have been improperly conducted,

(iii) that there has been a failure to comply with the Arbitration Agreement or any provision of this Scheme, or

(iv) that there has been any other irregularity affecting the arbitrator or the proceedings,

he or she may not raise that objection later, before the arbitrator or the court, unless he or she shows that, at the time he or she took part or continued to take part in the proceedings, he or she did not know and could not with reasonable diligence have discovered the grounds for the objection.

XXVII IMMUNITY

215 An arbitrator under this Scheme is not liable for anything done or omitted in the discharge or purported discharge of his or her functions as arbitrator unless the act or omission is shown to have been in bad faith. This applies to a legal adviser appointed by ACAS as it applies to the arbitrator himself or herself.

216 ACAS, by reason of having appointed an arbitrator or nominated a legal adviser, is not liable for anything done or omitted by the arbitrator or legal adviser in the discharge or purported discharge of his or her functions.

XXVIII MISCELLANEOUS PROVISIONS

Requirements in connection with legal proceedings

217EW Sections 80(1), (2), (4), (5), (6) and (7) of the Arbitration Act 1996 shall apply to English/Welsh arbitrations conducted in accordance with the Scheme, subject to the following modification:

In subsection (1), for 'to the other parties to the arbitral proceedings, or to the tribunal' substitute 'to the other party to the arbitral proceedings, or to the arbitrator, or to ACAS'.

Service of documents and notices on ACAS or the ACAS Arbitration Section

218 Any notice or other document required or authorised to be given or served on ACAS or the ACAS Arbitration Section for the purposes of the arbitral proceedings shall be sent by pre-paid post to the address in the ACAS Guide to the Scheme

or transmitted by facsimile, addressed to the ACAS Arbitration Section, at the number stipulated in the ACAS Guide to the Scheme,

or by electronic mail, at the address stipulated in the ACAS Guide to the Scheme.

219 Paragraph 218 does not apply to the service of documents on the ACAS Arbitration Section for the purposes of legal proceedings.

Service of documents or notices on any other person or entity (other than ACAS or the ACAS Arbitration Section)

220 Any notice or other document required or authorised to be given or served on any person or entity (other than ACAS or the ACAS Arbitration Section) for the purposes of the arbitral proceedings may be served by any effective means.

221 If such a notice or other document is addressed, pre-paid and delivered by post:
   (i)   to the addressee's last known principal residence or, if he or she is or has been carrying on a trade, profession or business, his or her last known principal business address, or
   (ii) where the addressee is a body corporate, to the body's registered or principal office,
   it shall be treated as effectively served.

222 Paragraphs 220 and 221 do not apply to the service of documents for the purposes of legal proceedings, for which provision is made by rules of court.

Powers of court in relation to service of documents

223EW Section 77 of the Arbitration Act 1996 shall apply to English/Welsh arbitrations conducted in accordance with the Scheme, subject to the following modifications–
   (i)   in subsection (1), for 'in the manner agreed by the parties, or in accordance with provisions of section 76 having effect in default of agreement,' substitute 'in accordance with paragraphs 220 and 221';

(ii)   in subsection (2), for 'Unless otherwise agreed by the parties, the court' substitute 'The High Court or Central London County Court';

(iii)   in subsection (3), for 'Any party to the arbitration agreement may apply' substitute 'ACAS or any party to the Arbitration Agreement may apply'.

Reckoning periods of time

224EW Sections 78(2), (3), (4) and (5) of the Arbitration Act 1996 shall apply to English/Welsh arbitrations conducted in accordance with the Scheme, subject to the following modification to subsection (2) of that section.

(i)   omit 'If or to the extent that there is no such agreement,';

(ii)   after 'periods of time' insert 'provided for in any provision of this Part'.

225S Except as otherwise specified in the Scheme, periods of time shall in Scottish arbitrations be reckoned in accordance with the following provisions:

(i)   Where the act is required to be done within a specified period after or from a specified date, the period begins immediately after that date;

(ii)   Where the act is required to be done a specified number of clear days after a specified date, at least that number of days must intervene between the day on which the act is done and that date;

(iii) Where the period is a period of seven days or less which would include a Saturday, Sunday or a public holiday in the place where anything which has to be done within the period falls to be done, that day shall be excluded.

(iv) In relation to Scotland a 'public holiday' means a day which under the Banking and Financial Dealings Act 1971 is to be a bank holiday in Scotland and in relation to England and Wales or Northern Ireland a 'public holiday' means Christmas Day, Good Friday or a day which under the Banking and Financial Dealings Act 1971 is to be a bank holiday in England and Wales or Northern Ireland as the case may be.

XXIX GOVERNING LAW

226EW The seat of an English/Welsh arbitration shall be England and Wales. The arbitrator may nevertheless hold any meeting or hearing or do any act in relation to the arbitration outside England and Wales.

227S The seat of a Scottish arbitration shall be Scotland. The arbitrator may nevertheless hold any meeting or hearing or do any act in relation to the arbitration outside Scotland.

APPENDIX A: WAIVER OF RIGHTS

English/Welsh Arbitrations

The ACAS Arbitration Scheme ('the Scheme') is entirely voluntary. In agreeing to refer a dispute to arbitration under the Scheme, both parties agree to waive rights that they would otherwise have if, for example, they had referred their dispute to the employment tribunal. This follows from the informal nature of the Scheme, which is designed to be a confidential, relatively fast, cost-efficient and non-legalistic process.

As required by Part VII of the Scheme, as a confirmation of the parties' agreement to waive their rights, this form must be completed by each party and submitted to ACAS together with the agreement to arbitration.

A detailed description of the informal nature of arbitration under the Scheme, and the important differences between this and the employment tribunal, is contained in the ACAS Guide to the Scheme ('the ACAS Guide'), which should be read by each party before completing this form.

The Scheme is not intended for disputes involving complex legal issues, or questions of EC law. Parties to such disputes are strongly advised to consider applying to the employment tribunal, or settling their dispute by other means.

This form does not list all the differences between the Scheme and the employment tribunal, or all of the features of the Scheme to which each party agrees in referring their dispute to arbitration.

There are differences between the law of England and Wales on the one hand and the law of Scotland on the other. The Scheme accordingly makes separate provision for English/Welsh arbitrations and Scottish arbitrations. This form confirms the parties' agreement that the arbitration between them will be an English/Welsh arbitration.

I, ..., the Applicant / Respondent / Respondent's duly authorised representative [delete as appropriate] confirm my agreement to each of the following points:

1 Unlike proceedings in the employment tribunal, all proceedings under the Scheme, including all hearings, are conducted in private. There are no public hearings, and the final award will be confidential.

2 All arbitrators under the Scheme are appointed by ACAS from the ACAS Arbitration Panel (which is a panel of impartial, mainly non-lawyer, arbitrators appointed by ACAS on fixed, but renewable, terms). The appointment process and the ACAS Arbitration Panel are described in the Scheme and the ACAS Guide. Neither party will have any choice of arbitrator.

3 Proceedings under the Scheme are conducted differently from the employment tribunal. In particular:
   – arbitrators will conduct proceedings in an informal manner in all cases;
   – the attendance of witnesses and the production of documents cannot be compelled (although failure to co-operate may be taken into account by the arbitrator);
   – there will be no oaths or affirmations, and no cross-examination of witnesses by parties or their representatives;
   – the arbitrator will take the initiative in asking questions and ascertaining the facts (with the aim of ensuring that all relevant issues are considered), as well as hearing each side's arguments;
   – the arbitrator's decision will only contain the main considerations that have led to the result; it will not contain full or detailed reasons;
   – the arbitrator has no power to order interim relief.

4 Once parties have agreed to refer their dispute to arbitration in accordance with the Scheme, the parties cannot then return to the employment tribunal.

5   In deciding whether or not the dismissal was fair or unfair, the arbitrator shall have regard to general principles of fairness and good conduct in employment relations (including, for example, principles referred to in any relevant ACAS 'Disciplinary and Grievance Procedures' Code of Practice or 'Discipline and Grievances at Work' Handbook). Unlike the employment tribunal, the arbitrator will not apply strict legal tests or rules (eg, court decisions or legislation), with certain limited exceptions set out in the Scheme (see, eg, paragraph 17).

Similarly, in cases that do not involve EC law, the arbitrator will calculate compensation or award any other remedy in accordance with the terms of the Scheme, instead of applying strict legal tests or rules.

6   Unlike the employment tribunal, there is no right of appeal from awards of arbitrators under the Scheme (except for a limited right to appeal questions of EC law and, aside from procedural matters set out in the Scheme, questions concerning the Human Rights Act 1998 and devolution issues).

7   Unlike the employment tribunal, in agreeing to arbitration under the Scheme, parties agree that there is no jurisdictional argument, ie no reason why the claim cannot be heard and determined by the arbitrator. In particular, the arbitrator will assume that a dismissal has taken place, and will only consider whether or not this was unfair. This is explained further in the Scheme and in the ACAS Guide.

8   The arbitration shall be an English/Welsh arbitration

SIGNED: ....

DATED: ....

IN THE PRESENCE OF

Signature: ....

Full Name: ....

Position: ....

Address: ....

APPENDIX B: WAIVER OF RIGHTS

Scottish Arbitrations

The ACAS Arbitration Scheme ('the Scheme') is entirely voluntary. In agreeing to refer a dispute to arbitration under the Scheme, both parties agree to waive rights that they would otherwise have if, for example, they had referred their dispute to the employment tribunal. This follows from the informal nature of the Scheme, which is designed to be a confidential, relatively fast, cost-efficient and non-legalistic process.

As required by Part VII of the Scheme, as a confirmation of the parties' agreement to waive their rights, this form must be completed by each party and submitted to ACAS together with the agreement to arbitration.

A detailed description of the informal nature of arbitration under the Scheme, and the important differences between this and the employment tribunal, is contained in the ACAS Guide to the Scheme ('the ACAS Guide'), which should be read by each party before completing this form.

The Scheme is not intended for disputes involving complex legal issues, or questions of EC law. Parties to such disputes are strongly advised to consider applying to the employment tribunal, or settling their dispute by other means.

This form does not list all the differences between the Scheme and the employment tribunal, or all of the features of the Scheme to which each party agrees in referring their dispute to arbitration.

There are differences between the law of Scotland on the one hand and the law of England and Wales on the other. The Scheme accordingly makes separate provision for Scottish arbitrations and English/Welsh arbitrations. This form confirms the parties' agreement that the arbitration between them will be a Scottish arbitration and (as permitted in Scots law) that any award may be enforced by registration rather than by application to the Court.

I, ..., the Applicant / Respondent / Respondent's duly authorised representative [delete as appropriate] confirm my agreement to each of the following points:

1   Unlike proceedings in the employment tribunal, all proceedings under the Scheme, including all hearings, are conducted in private. There are no public hearings, and the final award will be confidential.

2   All arbitrators under the Scheme are appointed by ACAS from the ACAS Arbitration Panel (which is a panel of impartial, mainly non-lawyer, arbitrators appointed by ACAS on fixed, but renewable, terms). The appointment process and the ACAS Arbitration Panel are described in the Scheme and the ACAS Guide. Neither party will have any choice of arbitrator.

3   Proceedings under the Scheme are conducted differently from the employment tribunal. In particular:

– arbitrators will conduct proceedings in an informal manner in all cases;

– the attendance of witnesses and the production of documents cannot be compelled (although failure to co-operate may be taken into account by the arbitrator);

– there will be no oaths or affirmations, and no cross-examination of witnesses by parties or their representatives;

– the arbitrator will take the initiative in asking questions and ascertaining the facts (with the aim of ensuring that all relevant issues are considered), as well as hearing each side's arguments;

– the arbitrator's decision will only contain the main considerations that have led to the result; it will not contain full or detailed reasons;

– the arbitrator has no power to order interim relief.

4   Once parties have agreed to refer their dispute to arbitration in accordance with the Scheme, the parties cannot then return to the employment tribunal.

5   In deciding whether or not the dismissal was fair or unfair, the arbitrator shall have regard to general principles of fairness and good conduct in employment relations (including, for example, principles referred to in any relevant ACAS 'Disciplinary and Grievance Procedures' Code of Practice or 'Discipline and Grievances at Work' Handbook). Unlike the employment

tribunal, the arbitrator will not apply strict legal tests or rules (eg, court decisions or legislation), with certain limited exceptions set out in the Scheme (see, eg, paragraph 17).

Similarly, in cases that do not involve EC law, the arbitrator will calculate compensation or award any other remedy in accordance with the terms of the Scheme, instead of applying strict legal tests or rules.

6 Unlike the employment tribunal, there is no right of appeal from awards of arbitrators under the Scheme (except for a limited right to appeal questions of EC law and, aside from procedural matters set out in the Scheme, questions concerning the Human Rights Act 1998 and devolution issues. The provisions of section 3 of the Administration of Justice (Scotland) Act 1972 (which provides for arbitrators to state a case for the opinion of the Court of Session) shall not apply to this arbitration.

7 Unlike the employment tribunal, in agreeing to arbitration under the Scheme, parties agree that there is no jurisdictional argument, ie no reason why the claim cannot be heard and determined by the arbitrator. In particular, the arbitrator will assume that a dismissal has taken place, and will only consider whether or not this was unfair. This is explained further in the Scheme and in the ACAS Guide.

8 The arbitration shall be a Scottish arbitration.

9 The parties consent to registration for execution of any award requiring the payment of money which may be made under the Scheme.

SIGNED: ....

DATED: ....

IN THE PRESENCE OF

Signature: ....

Full Name: ....

Position: ....

Address: ....

ACAS (Flexible Working) Arbitration Scheme (Great Britain) Order 2004 SI No 2333

Citation, commencement, interpretation and extent

1 (1) This Order may be cited as the ACAS (Flexible Working) Arbitration Scheme (Great Britain) Order 2004 and shall come into force on 1st October 2004.

(2) In this Order–

'the 1996 Act' means the Employment Rights Act 1996;

'English/Welsh arbitration' means an arbitration under the Scheme which the parties have agreed shall be determined under the laws of England and Wales;

'the Scheme' means the arbitration scheme set out in the Schedule to this

Order, with the exception of paragraphs 52EW, 108EW, 135EW, 138EW, 145EW, 151EW, 156EW, 160EW, 163EW, 174EW and 175EW thereof;
'Scottish arbitration' means and arbitration under the Scheme which the parties have agreed shall be determined under the laws of Scotland.

(3) This Order extends to Great Britain.

(4) Paragraphs in the Schedule marked 'EW' apply only to English/Welsh arbitrations.

(5) Paragraphs in the Schedule marked 'S' apply only to Scottish arbitrations.

(6) Paragraphs in the Schedule not marked 'EW' or 'S' apply to both English/Welsh arbitrations and Scottish arbitrations.

Commencement of the Scheme

2   The Scheme shall come into effect on 1st October 2004.

Revocation

3   Subject to article 6, the ACAS (Flexible Working) Arbitration Scheme (England and Wales) Order 2003 is revoked.

Application of Part I of the Arbitration Act 1996

4   The provisions of Part I of the Arbitration Act 1996 referred to in paragraphs 52EW, 108EW, 135EW, 138EW, 145EW, 151EW, 156EW, 160EW, 163EW, 174EW and 175EW of the Schedule and shown in italics shall, as modified in those paragraphs, apply to English/Welsh arbitrations conducted in accordance with the Scheme.

5   (1) Section 46(1)(b) of the Arbitration Act 1996 shall apply to English/Welsh arbitrations conducted in accordance with the Scheme, subject to the following modification.

(2) For 'such other considerations as are agreed by them or determined by the tribunal' in section 46(1)(b) substitute 'the Terms of Reference in paragraph 18 of the arbitration scheme set out in the Schedule to the ACAS (Flexible Working) Arbitration Scheme (Great Britain) Order 2004'.

Transitional provision

6   (1) The Scheme has effect in any case where the appropriate date falls on or after 1st October 2004.

(2) In a case where the appropriate date falls before 1st October 2004, the arbitration scheme set out in the Schedule to the ACAS (Flexible Working) Arbitration Scheme (England and Wales) Order 2003 continues to apply.

(3) In this article – the
'appropriate date' means the date of signature of the Arbitration Agreement. Where the parties sign the Arbitration Agreement on different dates, the appropriate date is the date of the first signature.
'Arbitration Agreement' means an agreement to submit the dispute to arbitration, as defined in paragraph 26 of the Scheme.

SCHEDULE: ACAS (FLEXIBLE WORKING) ARBITRATION SCHEME

I Introduction

1 The ACAS (Flexible Working) Arbitration Scheme ('the Scheme') is implemented pursuant to section 212A of the Trades Union and Labour Relations (Consolidation) Act 1992.

2 The Scheme provides a voluntary alternative, in the form of arbitration, to the employment tribunal for the resolution of disputes arising out of an employee's application for a change in his terms and conditions of employment made under section 80F of the Employment Rights Act 1996.

3 Resolution of disputes under the Scheme is intended to be confidential, informal, relatively fast and cost efficient. Procedures under the Scheme are non-legalistic, and far more flexible than the traditional model of the employment tribunal and the courts. For example (as explained in more detail below), the Scheme avoids the use of formal pleadings and formal witness and documentary procedures; strict rules of evidence will not apply. Arbitral decisions ('awards') will be final, with very limited opportunities for parties to appeal or otherwise challenge the result.

4 The Scheme also caters for requirements imposed as a matter of law (eg, the Human Rights Act 1998, devolution issues, existing law in the field of arbitration and EC law).

5 The Scheme accommodates certain differences between the law of Scotland and the law of England and Wales relating to arbitrations generally. It does so by providing, to the extent necessary to accommodate those differences, separate provisions applicable to Scottish arbitrations on the one hand and to English or Welsh arbitrations on the other. For convenience, paragraphs that apply only to Scottish arbitrations are marked 'S' and paragraphs that apply only to English or Welsh arbitrations are marked 'EW'.

II THE ROLE OF ACAS

6 As more fully explained below, cases enter the Scheme by reference to ACAS, which appoints an arbitrator from a panel (see paragraphs 41–43 below) to determine the dispute. ACAS provides administrative assistance during the proceedings, and may scrutinise awards and refer any clerical or other similar errors back to the arbitrator. Disputes are determined, however, by arbitrators and not by ACAS.

Routing of communications

7 Unless in the course of a hearing, all communications between either party and the arbitrator shall be sent via the ACAS Arbitration Section.

8 Paragraph 169 below sets out the manner in which any document, notice or communication must be served on, or transmitted to, ACAS or the ACAS Arbitration Section.

III TERMS AND ABBREVIATIONS

9 The term 'Employee' is used to denote the claimant, including any person entitled to pursue a claim arising out of a contravention, or alleged contravention, of section 80G(1) or 80H(1)(b) of the 1996 Act (flexible working).

10　The term 'Employer' is used to denote the respondent.

11　The term 'devolution issue' means a devolution issue as defined in paragraph 1 of Schedule 6 to the Scotland Act 1998 or a devolution issue as defined in paragraph 1 of Schedule 8 to the Government of Wales Act 1998.

12　The term 'EC law' means:

(i)　any enactment in the domestic legislation of England and Wales or of Scotland giving effect to rights, powers, liabilities, obligations and restrictions from time to time created or arising by or under the Community Treaties, and

(ii)　any such rights, powers, liabilities, obligations and restrictions which are not given effect by any such enactment.

13　The term 'English/Welsh arbitration' means an arbitration under this Scheme which the parties have agreed shall be an English/Welsh arbitration.

14　The term 'Flexible Working Claim' means a claim by the Employee that his Employer has failed to deal with an application made under section 80F of the 1996 Act in accordance with section 80G(1) of that Act or that a decision by his Employer to reject the application was based on incorrect facts.

15　The term 'Scottish arbitration' means an arbitration under this Scheme which parties have agreed shall be a Scottish arbitration.

16　With the exception of paragraphs 26 ('Requirements for entry into the Scheme') 111EW ('Form of the award: English/Welsh arbitrations') and 114S ('Form of the award: Scottish arbitrations'), references to anything being written or in writing include its being recorded by any means so as to be usable for subsequent reference.

IV　**APPLICATION OF THE SCHEME**

17　Paragraphs 46EW, 47EW, 48EW, 49EW, 50EW, 51EW, 52EW, 53EW, 108EW, 111EW, 112EW, 113EW, 129EW, 135EW, 138EW, 145EW, 151EW, 156EW, 160EW, 163EW, 168EW, 174EW, 175EW and 177EW below shall apply only to English/Welsh arbitrations. Paragraphs 54S, 55S, 56S, 57S, 58S, 59S, 109S, 110S, 114S, 115S, 116S, 130S, 134S, 136S, 139S, 140S, 141S, 142S, 143S, 144S, 146S, 147S, 148S, 149S, 150S, 152S, 153S, 154S, 155S, 157S, 158S, 159S, 161S, 162S, 164S, 176S and 178S below shall apply only to Scottish arbitrations.

V　**ARBITRATOR'S TERMS OF REFERENCE**

18　Every agreement to refer a dispute to arbitration under this Scheme shall be taken to be an agreement that the arbitrator decide the dispute according to the following Terms of Reference:

In deciding whether to uphold the Flexible Working Claim the arbitrator shall:

－　have regard to relevant provisions of the Flexible Working (Procedural Requirements) Regulations 2002 and to any relevant ACAS Guidance;

－　apply EC law.

The arbitrator shall not decide the case by substituting what he or she would have done for the actions taken by the Employer.

If the arbitrator upholds the Flexible Working Claim, he or she shall determine the appropriate remedy under the terms of this Scheme.

VI SCOPE OF THE SCHEME

Cases that are covered by the Scheme

19 This Scheme only applies to disputes involving proceedings, or claims which could be the subject of proceedings, before an employment tribunal arising out of a contravention, or alleged contravention, of section 80G(1) or section 80H(1)(b) of the 1996 Act.

20 The Scheme does not extend to other kinds of claim which may be related to, or raised at the same time as, a Flexible Working Claim. For example, sex discrimination cases are not covered by the Scheme.

21 If a Flexible Working Claim has been referred for resolution under the Scheme, any other claim, even if part of the same dispute, must be settled separately, or referred to the employment tribunal, or withdrawn. In the event that different aspects of the same dispute are being heard in the employment tribunal as well as under the Scheme, the arbitrator may decide, if appropriate or convenient, to postpone the arbitration proceedings pending a determination by the employment tribunal.

Waiver of jurisdictional issues

22 Because of its informal nature, the Scheme is not designed for disputes raising jurisdictional issues, such as for example:
– whether or not the claimant is an employee of the Employer;
– whether or not the Employee had the necessary period of continuous service to bring the claim;
– whether or not time limits have expired and/or should be extended.

23 Accordingly, when agreeing to refer a dispute to arbitration under the Scheme, both parties will be taken to have accepted as a condition of the Scheme that no jurisdictional issue is in dispute between them. The arbitrator will not therefore deal with such issues during the arbitration process, even if they are raised by the parties, and the parties will be taken to have waived any rights in that regard.

Inappropriate cases

24 The Scheme is not intended for disputes involving complex legal issues. Whilst such cases will be accepted for determination (subject to the Terms of Reference), parties are advised, where appropriate, to consider applying to the employment tribunal or settling their dispute by other means.

VII ACCESS TO THE SCHEME

25 The Scheme is an entirely voluntary system of dispute resolution: it will only apply if parties have so agreed.

Requirements for entry into the Scheme

26   Any agreement to submit a dispute to arbitration under the Scheme must satisfy the following requirements (an 'Arbitration Agreement'):
   (i)   the agreement of each party (which may be expressed in the same or in separate documents) must be in writing;
   (ii)   the agreement must concern an existing dispute;
   (iii)   the agreement must not seek to alter or vary any provision of the Scheme;
   (iv)   the agreement must have been reached either:
       (a)   where a conciliation officer has taken action under section 18 of the Employment Tribunals Act 1996 or
       (b)   through a compromise agreement, where the conditions regulating such agreements under the 1996 Act are satisfied;
   (v)   the agreement must be accompanied by a completed Waiver Form for each party. Parties applying for English/Welsh arbitrations should complete Appendix A; parties applying for Scottish arbitrations should complete Appendix B.

27   Where an agreement fails to satisfy any one of these requirements or where the parties are unable to agree whether the arbitration should be an English/Welsh arbitration or a Scottish arbitration, no valid reference to the Scheme will have been made, and the parties will have to settle their dispute by other means or have recourse to the employment tribunal.

28   Where:
   (i)   a dispute concerning a Flexible Working Claim as well as other claims has been referred to the employment tribunal, and
   (ii)   the parties have agreed to settle the other claims and refer the Flexible Working Claim to arbitration under the Scheme,
   a separate settlement must be reached referring the Flexible Working Claim to arbitration which satisfies all the requirements listed above (although it may form part of one overall settlement document).

Notification to ACAS of an Arbitration Agreement

29   All Arbitration Agreements must be notified to ACAS within two weeks of their conclusion, by either of the parties or their independent advisers or representatives, or an ACAS conciliator, sending a copy of the agreement and Waiver Forms, together with IT1 and IT3 forms if these have been completed, to the ACAS Arbitration Section.

30   For the purposes of the previous paragraph, an Arbitration Agreement is treated as 'concluded' on the date it is signed, or if signed by different people at different times, on the date of the last signature.

31   Where an Arbitration Agreement is not notified to ACAS within two weeks, ACAS will not arrange for the appointment of an arbitrator under the Scheme, unless notification within that time was not reasonably practicable. Any party seeking to notify ACAS of an Arbitration Agreement outside this period must explain in writing to the ACAS Arbitration Section the reason for the delay. ACAS shall appoint an arbitrator, in accordance with the appointment provisions below, to consider the explanation, and that arbitra-

tor may seek the views of the other party, and may call both parties to a hearing to establish the reasons for the delay. The arbitrator shall then rule in an award on whether or not the agreement can be accepted for hearing under the Scheme.

32 Any such hearing and award will be governed by the provisions of this Scheme.

Consolidation of proceedings

33 Where all parties so agree in writing, ACAS may consolidate different arbitral proceedings under the Scheme.

VIII SETTLEMENT AND WITHDRAWAL FROM THE SCHEME

Withdrawal by the Employee

34 At any stage of the arbitration process, once an Arbitration Agreement has been concluded and the reference has been accepted by ACAS, the party bringing the Flexible Working Claim may withdraw from the Scheme, provided that any such withdrawal is in writing. Such a withdrawal shall constitute a dismissal of the claim and the arbitrator shall upon receipt of such withdrawal in writing issue an award dismissing the claim.

Withdrawal by the Employer

35 Once an Arbitration Agreement has been concluded and the reference has been accepted by ACAS, the party against whom a claim is brought cannot unilaterally withdraw from the Scheme.

Settlement

36 Parties are free to reach an agreement settling the dispute at any stage.

37 If such an agreement is reached:
   (i)   upon the joint written request of the parties to the arbitrator or the ACAS Arbitration Section, the arbitrator (if appointed) or the ACAS Arbitration Section (if no arbitrator has been appointed) shall terminate the arbitration proceedings;
   (ii) if so requested by the parties, the arbitrator (if appointed) may record the settlement in the form of an agreed award.

38 An agreed award shall state that it is an award of the arbitrator by consent and shall have the same status and effect as any other award on the merits of the case.

39 If the agreement settling the dispute includes an agreement that one party (the 'paying party') shall pay a sum of money to the other (the 'receiving party') the arbitrator shall (unless the parties have agreed that the said agreement shall not be the subject of an award) draft an award ordering the paying party to pay the agreed sum to the receiving party together (if the parties have agreed that interest shall run on the agreed sum) with interest thereon at such rate or rates as the parties may have agreed and from such date or dates as the parties may have agreed until payment. The arbitrator shall send a copy of the said award in draft to each party and invite each

party to confirm that the draft award accurately reflects the agreement between them. Upon receiving confirmation to that effect the arbitrator shall issue an award in terms of the agreed draft.

40   Subject to paragraph 39, in rendering an agreed award, the arbitrator:
(i)   may only record the parties' agreed wording;
(ii)   may not approve, vary, transcribe, interpret or ratify a settlement in any way;
(iii)   may not record any settlement beyond the scope of the Scheme, the Arbitration Agreement or the reference to the Scheme as initially accepted by ACAS.

IX   APPOINTMENT OF AN ARBITRATOR

The ACAS Arbitration Panel

41   Arbitrators are selected to serve on the ACAS Arbitration Panel on the basis of their practical knowledge and experience of employment issues in the workplace. They are recruited through an open recruitment exercise, and appointed to the Panel on the basis of standard terms of appointment. It is a condition of their appointment that they exercise their duties in accordance with the terms of this Scheme. Each appointment is initially for a period of two years, although it may be renewed by ACAS, at the latter's discretion. Payment is made by ACAS on the basis of time spent in connection with arbitral proceedings.

Appointment to a case

42   Arbitral appointments are made exclusively by ACAS from the ACAS Arbitration Panel. Parties will have no choice of arbitrator.

43   Once ACAS has been notified of a valid Arbitration Agreement, it will select and appoint an arbitrator, and notify all parties of the name of the arbitrator so appointed.

Arbitrator's duty of disclosure

44   Immediately following selection (and before an appointment is confirmed by ACAS), every arbitrator shall disclose in writing to ACAS (to be forwarded to the parties) any circumstances known to him or her likely to give rise to any justifiable doubts as to his or her impartiality, or confirm in writing that there are no such circumstances.

45   Once appointed, and until the arbitration is concluded, every arbitrator shall be under a continuing duty forthwith to disclose to ACAS (to be forwarded to the parties) any such circumstances which may have arisen since appointment.

Removal of arbitrators: English/Welsh arbitrations

46EW   An arbitrator in an English/Welsh arbitration may only be removed by ACAS or the court (under the provisions in paragraphs 47EW to 52EW below).

47EW   Applications under the Scheme to remove an arbitrator on any of the grounds set out in sections 24(1)(a) and (c) of the Arbitration Act 1996 or on the basis that such removal has been agreed by both parties, shall be made in the first instance to ACAS (addressed to the ACAS Arbitration Section).

48EW At the same time as an application is made to ACAS to remove an arbitrator a copy of the application shall be sent to the other party to the arbitration and to the arbitrator.

49EW ACAS shall, following receipt of an application under paragraph 47EW, give the other party to the arbitration and the arbitrator such opportunity as ACAS in its sole discretion may consider appropriate to comment on the application.

50EW ACAS may, after such procedures as ACAS in its sole discretion may consider appropriate, remove the arbitrator.

51EW If ACAS refuses an application made under paragraph 47EW, a party may thereafter apply to the court.

52EW Sections 24(1)(a) and (c), 24(2), 24(3), 24(5) and 24(6) of the Arbitration Act 1996 shall apply to English/Welsh arbitrations conducted in accordance with the Scheme, subject to the following modifications–

   (i)   In subsection (1) for '(upon notice to the other parties, to the arbitrator concerned and to any other arbitrator) apply to the court' substitute '(upon notice to the other party, to the arbitrator concerned and to the Advisory, Conciliation and Arbitration Service ('ACAS')) apply to the High Court or Central London County Court'.

   (ii) In subsection (2)–

      (a) omit 'If there is an arbitral or other institution or person vested by the parties with power to remove an arbitrator,';

      (b) for 'that institution or person' substitute 'ACAS'.

53EW The arbitrator may continue the proceedings and make an award while an application to ACAS (as well as the court) to remove him or her is pending.

Removal of arbitrators: Scottish arbitrations

54S An arbitrator in a Scottish arbitration may be removed by ACAS under the provisions in paragraphs 55S–58S below.

55S An application under the Scheme to remove an arbitrator shall be made to ACAS (addressed to the ACAS Arbitration Section). At the same time as the application is sent to ACAS a copy of the application shall be sent to the other party to the arbitration and to the arbitrator.

56S ACAS shall, following receipt of an application under paragraph 55S, give the other party to the arbitration and the arbitrator such opportunity as ACAS in its sole discretion may consider appropriate to comment on the application.

57S ACAS may, after such procedure as ACAS in its sole discretion may consider appropriate, remove the arbitrator if it is satisfied:

   (i)   that both parties to the arbitration agree that the arbitrator should be removed; or

   (ii) that circumstances exist that give rise to justifiable doubts as to the impartiality of the arbitration; or

   (iii) that the arbitrator is physically or mentally incapable of conducting the proceedings or there are justifiable doubts as to his or her capacity to do so.

58S   A decision of ACAS made under paragraph 57S shall be final.

59S   The arbitrator may continue the proceedings and make an award while an application to ACAS to remove him or her is pending.

Death of an arbitrator

60   The authority of an arbitrator is personal and ceases on his or her death.

Replacement of arbitrators

61   Where an arbitrator ceases to hold office for any reason, he or she shall be replaced by ACAS in accordance with the appointment provisions above.

62   Once appointed, the replacement arbitrator shall determine whether and, if so, to what extent the previous proceedings should stand.

X   GENERAL DUTY OF THE ARBITRATOR

63   The arbitrator shall–
  (i)   act fairly and impartially as between the parties, giving each party a reasonable opportunity of putting his or her case and dealing with that of his or her opponent, and
  (ii) adopt procedures suitable to the circumstances of the particular case, avoiding unnecessary delay or expense, so as to provide a fair means for the resolution of the matters falling to be determined.

64   The arbitrator shall comply with the general duty (see paragraph 63 above) in conducting the arbitral proceedings, in his or her decisions on matters of procedure and evidence and in the exercise of all other powers conferred on him or her.

XI   GENERAL DUTY OF THE PARTIES

65   The parties shall do all things necessary for the proper and expeditious conduct of the arbitral proceedings. This includes (without limitation) complying without delay with any determination of the arbitrator as to procedural or evidential matters, or with any order or directions of the arbitrator, and co-operating in the arrangement of any hearing.

XII   CONFIDENTIALITY AND PRIVACY

66   Arbitrations, and all associated procedures under the Scheme, are strictly private and confidential. This rule does not prevent a party to the arbitration taking any step reasonably necessary for the purpose of any application to the court or enforcement of an award.

67   Hearings may only be attended by the arbitrator, the parties, their representatives, any interpreters, witnesses and a legal adviser if appointed. If the parties so agree, an ACAS official or arbitrator in training may also attend.

XIII   ARRANGEMENTS FOR THE HEARING

Initial arrangements

68   A hearing must be held in every case, notwithstanding any agreement between the parties to a purely written procedure.

69   Once an arbitrator has been appointed by ACAS, a hearing shall be arranged as soon as reasonably practicable by him or her, with the administrative assistance of the ACAS Arbitration Section.

70   The arbitrator shall decide the date and venue for the hearing, in so far as an agreement cannot be reached with all parties within 28 days of the initial notification to ACAS of the Arbitration Agreement.

71   The ACAS Arbitration Section shall contact all parties with details of the date and venue for the hearing.

Expedited hearings

72   On the application of any party, the arbitrator may, at his or her discretion, expedite the hearing.

Venue

73   Hearings may be held in any venue, provided that the hearing will only be held at the Employee's workplace, or a similarly non-neutral venue, if all parties so agree.

74   Where premises have to be hired for a hearing, ACAS shall meet the reasonable costs of so doing.

Assistance

75   Where a party needs the services of an interpreter, signer or communicator at the hearing, ACAS should be so informed well in advance of the hearing. Where an arbitrator agrees that such assistance is required, ACAS shall meet the reasonable costs of providing this.

Travelling expenses/loss of earnings

76   Every party shall meet their own travelling expenses and those of their representatives and witnesses.

77   No loss of earnings are payable by ACAS to anyone involved in the arbitration. However, where an arbitrator upholds a Flexible Working Claim, he or she may include in the calculation of any compensation a sum to cover reasonable travelling expenses and loss of earnings incurred by the Employee personally in attending the hearing.

Applications for postponements of, or different venues for, initial hearings

78   Any application for a postponement of, or a different venue for, an initial hearing must be made in writing, with reasons, to the arbitrator via the ACAS Arbitration Section within 14 days of the date of the letter notifying the hearing arrangements or, where this is not practicable, as soon as is reasonably practicable. Such applications will be determined by the arbitrator without an oral hearing after all parties have received a copy of the application and been given a reasonable opportunity to respond.

79   If the application is rejected, the initial hearing will be held on the original date and/or in the original venue.

80   This provision does not affect the arbitrator's general discretion (set out below) with respect to postponements after an initial hearing has been fixed, or with respect to other aspects of the procedure. In particular, procedural applications may be made to the arbitrator at the hearing itself.

XIV   NON-COMPLIANCE WITH PROCEDURE

81   If a party fails to comply with any aspect of the procedure set out in this Scheme, or any order or direction by the arbitrator, or fails to comply with the general duty in Part XI above, the arbitrator may (in addition to any other power set out in this Scheme)–
  (i)   adjourn any hearing, where it would be unfair on any party to proceed; and/or
  (ii)   draw such adverse inferences from the act of non-compliance as the circumstances justify.

XV   OUTLINE OF PROCEDURE BEFORE THE HEARING

82   Once a hearing has been fixed, the following procedure shall apply, subject to any direction by the arbitrator.

Written materials

83   At least 14 days before the date of the hearing, each party shall send to the ACAS Arbitration Section (for forwarding to the arbitrator and the other party) one copy of a written statement of case, together with–
  (i)   any supporting documentation or other material to be relied upon at the hearing; and where appropriate
  (ii)   a list of the names and title/role of all those people who will accompany each party to the hearing or be called as a witness.

84   Written statements of case should briefly set out the main particulars of each party's case, which can then be expanded upon if necessary at the hearing itself. The statement should include an explanation of the events which led to the Flexible Working Claim being brought including an account of the outcome of any relevant meetings.

85   Supporting documentation or other material may include (without limitation) copies of–
  (i)   the Employee's application under section 80F of the 1996 Act;
  (ii)   contracts of employment;
  (iii) notes of meetings held between Employee and Employer to consider the application under section 80F;
  (iv)   letters of appointment;
  (v)   written statement of particulars of employment;
  (vi)   time sheets;
  (vii) written reasons for refusing the Employee's application under section 80F, where these have been given;
  (viii) company handbooks, rules and procedures;
  (ix)   any other written information which may assist the arbitrator in deciding the Flexible Working claim;

(x)   any information which will help the arbitrator to assess compensation, including (without limitation) pay slips, P60s or wage records;

(xi)   signed statements of any witnesses or outlines of evidence to be given by witnesses at the hearing.

86   The parties must also supply details of any relevant awards of compensation that may have been made by any other tribunal or court in connection with the subject matter of the claim.

87   Legible copies of documents must be supplied to ACAS even if they have already been supplied to an ACAS conciliator before the Arbitration Agreement was concluded.

88   No information on the conciliation process, if any, shall be disclosed by an ACAS conciliator to the arbitrator.

Submissions, evidence and witnesses not previously notified

89   Written statements of case and documentary or other material that have not been provided to the ACAS Arbitration Section prior to the hearing (in accordance with paragraph 83 above) may only be relied upon at the hearing with the arbitrator's permission.

90   All representatives and witnesses who have been listed as accompanying a party at the hearing should be present at the start of the hearing. Witnesses who have not been included in a list submitted to the ACAS Arbitration Section prior to the hearing may only be called with the arbitrator's permission.

Requests for documents

91   Any party may request the other party to produce copies of relevant documents which are not in the requesting party's possession, custody or control. Although the arbitrator has no power to compel a party to comply, the arbitrator may draw an adverse inference from a party's failure to comply with a reasonable request.

Requests for attendance of witnesses

92   Although the arbitrator has no power to compel the attendance of anybody at the hearing, the arbitrator may draw an adverse inference if an employer who is a party to the arbitration fails or refuses to allow current employees or other workers (who have relevant evidence to give) time off from work to attend the hearing, should such an employer be so requested.

Preliminary hearings and directions

93   Where the arbitrator believes that there may be considerable differences between the parties over any issue, including the availability or exchange of documents, or the availability of witnesses, the arbitrator may call the parties to a preliminary hearing to address such issues, or he or she may give procedural directions in correspondence.

94   In the course of a preliminary hearing or in correspondence, the arbitrator

may express views on the desirability of information and/or evidence being available at the hearing.

XVI   OUTLINE OF PROCEDURE AT THE HEARING

Arbitrator's overall discretion

95   Subject to the arbitrator's general duty (Part X above), and subject to the points set out below, the conduct of the hearing and all procedural and evidential matters (including applications for adjournments and changes in venue) shall be for the arbitrator to decide.

Language

96   The language of the proceedings shall be English, unless the Welsh language is applicable by virtue of the Welsh Language Act 1993 (as amended from time to time). Reference should be made to paragraph 75 above if the Welsh language is to be used.

Witnesses

97   No party or witness shall be cross-examined by a party or representative, or examined on oath or affirmation.

Examination by the arbitrator

98   The arbitrator shall have the right to address questions directly to either party or to anybody else attending the hearing, and to take the initiative in ascertaining the facts and (where applicable) the law.

Representatives

99   The parties may be accompanied by any person chosen by them to help them to present their case at the hearing, although no special status will be accorded to legally qualified representatives. Each party is liable for any fees or expenses incurred by any representatives they appoint.

Strict rules of evidence

100   The arbitrator will not apply strict rules of evidence (or any other rules) as to the admissibility, relevance or weight of any material (oral, written or other) sought to be tendered on any matters of fact or opinion.

Non-attendance at the hearing

101   If, without showing sufficient cause, a party fails to attend or be represented at a hearing, the arbitrator may–
   (i)   continue the hearing in that party's absence, and in such a case shall take into account any written submissions and documents that have already been submitted by that party; or
   (ii)   adjourn the hearing.
102   In the case of the non-attendance of the Employee, if the arbitrator decides to adjourn the hearing, he or she may write to the Employee to request an explanation for the non-attendance. If the arbitrator decides that the

Employee has not demonstrated sufficient cause for the non-attendance, he or she may rule in an award that the claim be treated as dismissed.

Post-hearing written materials

103 No further submissions or evidence will be accepted after the end of the substantive hearing without the arbitrator's permission, which will only be granted in exceptional circumstances. Where permission is granted, any material is to be sent to the ACAS Arbitration Section, to be forwarded to the arbitrator and all other parties.

XVII QUESTIONS OF EC LAW, THE HUMAN RIGHTS ACT 1998 AND DEVOLUTION ISSUES

Appointment of legal adviser

104 The arbitrator shall have the power, on the application of any party or of his or her own motion, to require the appointment of a legal adviser to assist with respect to any issue of EC law or the Human Rights Act 1998 or any devolution issue that, in the arbitrator's view and subject to paragraph 18 above (Arbitrator's Terms of Reference), might be involved and relevant to the resolution of the dispute.

105 The legal adviser will be appointed by ACAS, to report to the arbitrator and the parties, and shall be subject to the duty of disclosure set out in paragraphs 44 and 45 above.

106 The arbitrator shall allow the legal adviser to attend the proceedings, and may order an adjournment and/or change in venue to facilitate this.

107 The parties shall be given a reasonable opportunity to comment on any information, opinion or advice offered by the legal adviser, following which the arbitrator shall take such information, opinion or advice into account in determining the dispute.

Court determination of preliminary points: English/Welsh arbitrations

108EW Section 45 of the Arbitration Act 1996 shall apply to English/Welsh arbitrations conducted in accordance with the Scheme, subject to the following modifications.
  (i)   In subsection (1)–
        (a) for 'Unless otherwise agreed by the parties, the court' substitute 'The High Court or Central London County Court';
        (b) for 'any question of law' substitute 'any question (a) of EC law, or (b) concerning the application of the Human Rights Act 1998', or (c) any devolution issue;
        (c) omit 'An agreement to dispense with reasons for the tribunal's award shall be considered an agreement to exclude the court's jurisdiction under this section.'.
  (ii) Omit sub-paragraph (i) from subsection (2)(b);
  (iii) Omit subsection (4); and
  (iv) After subsection (6), insert–
'(7) In this section 'EC law' means–

(a) any enactment in the domestic legislation of England and Wales giving effect to rights, powers, liabilities, obligations and restrictions from time to time created or arising by or under the Community Treaties, and

(b) any such rights, powers, liabilities, obligations and restrictions which are not given effect by any such enactment.

(8) In this section 'devolution issue' means a evolution issue as defined in paragraph 1 of Schedule 6 of the Scotland Act 1998 or devolution issue as defined in paragraph 1 of Schedule 8 to the Government of Wales Act 1998.'

Court determination of preliminary points: Scottish arbitrations

109S The arbitrator may make a reference to the Court of Session for determination as a preliminary point–

(i)   of any question of EC law,

(ii) of any question concerning the application of the Human Rights Act 1998, or

(iii) of any devolution issue,

which substantially affects the rights of one or more of the parties to the arbitration.

110S The arbitrator shall not make a reference under paragraph 109S unless–

(i)   both parties have applied for or have agreed to the making of the reference; or

(ii) if an application for the reference has been made by one party and opposed by the other party, the arbitrator is satisfied that the application has been made without delay.

XVIII AWARDS

Form of the award: English/Welsh arbitrations

111EW The award in an English/Welsh arbitration shall be in writing, signed by the arbitrator.

112EW The award in an English/Welsh arbitration (unless it is an agreed award) shall–

(i)   state the decision(s) of the arbitrator;

(ii) contain the main considerations which were taken into account in reaching the decision(s);

(iii) where an award is made, state the remedy awarded, together with an explanation;

(iv) state the date when it was made.

113EW If the award contains an order for payment of money the award shall–

(i)   order the Employer to pay the Employee the amount of the award of compensation; and

(ii) order the Employer to pay interest thereon in accordance with paragraph 137 of the Scheme.

Form of the award: Scottish arbitrations

114S The award in a Scottish arbitration shall–
  (i) be in writing;
  (ii) state the date upon which it was made;
  (iii) specify the arbitrator's order;
  (iv) be signed by the arbitrator;
  (v) be signed by a witness to the arbitrator's signature; and
  (vi) specify the name and address of the witness.

115S If the award contains an order for the payment of money the award shall–
  (i) ordain the Employer to pay the Employee the amount of the award of compensation; and
  (ii) ordain the Employer to pay interest thereon in accordance with paragraph 137 of the Scheme.

116S The arbitrator shall issue with his award (unless it is an agreed award) a Note, which shall–
  (i) state the decision(s) of the arbitrator;
  (ii) contain the arbitrator's reasons for his decision;
  (iii) state any remedy or remedies awarded;
  (iv) contain the arbitrator's reasons for the award of any remedy;
  (v) state the date when the Note was issued; and
  (vi) be signed by the arbitrator.

Remedies

117 In the event that the arbitrator upholds the Employee's Flexible Working Claim, the arbitrator may make an award ordering–
  (i) the reconsideration of the application made under section 80F of the 1996 Act; and/or
  (ii) compensation (subject to the limits provided for below) to be paid by the Employer to the Employee.

XIX   AWARDS OF COMPENSATION

118 Subject to paragraph 119 below, when an arbitrator makes an award of compensation in respect of any contravention of section 80G(1) or 80H(1)(b) of the 1996 Act, whether or not in conjunction with an award for reconsideration, such compensation shall be such an amount, not exceeding 8 weeks' pay, as the arbitrator considers just and equitable in all the circumstances.

119 When an arbitrator makes an award of compensation in respect of breaches of Regulation 14(2) or (4) of the Flexible Working (Procedural Requirements) Regulations 2002 such compensation shall be such an amount, not exceeding 2 weeks' pay, as the arbitrator considers just and equitable in all the circumstances.

120 In calculating the amount of a week's pay of an Employee, the arbitrator shall have regard to Chapter II of Part 14 of the 1996 Act, as amended from time to time, or any other relevant statutory provision applicable to the calculation of a week's pay.

XX   ISSUE OF AWARDS AND CONFIDENTIALITY

121 The arbitrator's award shall be sent by ACAS to both parties.

122   Subject to any steps which may be reasonably necessary for the purposes of any application to the Court or enforcement of the award the award shall be confidential, and shall only be issued to the parties or to their nominated advisers or representatives. Awards will not be published by ACAS, or lodged with the employment tribunal by ACAS, although awards may be retained by ACAS for monitoring and evaluation purposes, and, from time to time, ACAS may publish general summary information concerning cases heard under the Scheme, without identifying any individual cases.

XXI   CORRECTION OF AWARDS

Scrutiny of awards by ACAS

123   Before being sent to the parties, awards may be scrutinised by ACAS to check for clerical or computational mistakes, errors arising from accidental slips or omissions, ambiguities, or errors of form. Without affecting the arbitrator's liberty of decision, ACAS may refer the award back to the arbitrator (under the provisions below) in order to draw his or her attention to any such point.

Correction by the arbitrator

124   The arbitrator may, on his or her own initiative or on the application of a party or ACAS–

    (i)   correct the award so as to remove any clerical or computational mistake, or error arising from an accidental slip or omission, or to clarify or remove any ambiguity in the award, or

    (ii)   make an additional award in respect of any part of the claim which was presented to the arbitrator but was not dealt with in the award.

125   In so far as any such correction or additional award involves a new issue that was not previously before the parties, this power shall not be exercised without first affording the parties a reasonable opportunity to make written representations to the arbitrator.

126   Any application by a party for the exercise of this power must be made via the ACAS Arbitration Section within 28 days of the date the award was despatched to the applying party by ACAS.

127   Any correction of the award shall be made within 28 days of the date the application was received by the arbitrator or, where the correction is made by the arbitrator on his or her own initiative, within 28 days of the date of the award.

128   Any additional award shall be made within 56 days of the date of the original award.

129EW Any additional award in an English/Welsh arbitration shall so far as relevant comply with paragraphs 111EW, 112EW and 113EW

130S   Any additional award in a Scottish arbitration shall so far as relevant comply with paragraphs 114S, 115S and 116S. Any correction to an award shall be issued on a memorandum of correction which shall–

    (i)   specify the correction;

    (ii)   be signed by the arbitrator;

(iii) be signed by a witness to the arbitrator's signature;

(iv) state the name and address of the witness; and

(v) state the date upon which it was signed by the arbitrator.

131 Any correction of the award shall form part of the award.

XXII EFFECT OF AWARDS, ENFORCEMENT AND INTEREST

Effect of awards

132 Awards made by arbitrators under this Scheme are final and binding both on the parties and on any persons claiming through or under them.

133 This does not affect the right of a person to challenge an award under the provisions of the Arbitration Act 1996 as applied to this Scheme.

134 This does not affect the right of a person to challenge an award under Part XXIII below.

Enforcement

135EW Section 66 of the Arbitration Act 1996 shall apply to English/Welsh arbitrations conducted in accordance with the Scheme, subject to the following modifications.

(i) In subsection (1) for 'tribunal pursuant to an arbitration agreement' substitute 'arbitrator pursuant to the Scheme'.

(ii) In subsection (3) for '(see section 73)' substitute '(see Part XXIV of the Scheme').

(iii) After subsection (4) insert–

'(5) In this section–

'the court' means the High Court or a county court; and

'the Scheme' means the arbitration scheme set out in the Schedule to the ACAS (Flexible Working) Arbitration Scheme (Great Britain) Order 2004.'

136S In a Scottish arbitration any award (including any additional award, any correction of an award or any variation to an award) requiring the payment of money may be registered for execution.

Interest

137 Awards of compensation that are not paid within 42 days of the date on which the award was despatched by ACAS to the Employer will attract interest on the same basis as for employment tribunal awards.

XXIII Challenging the Award

Challenges on grounds of substantive jurisdiction: English/Welsh arbitrations

138EW Section 67 of the Arbitration Act 1996 shall apply to English/Welsh arbitrations conducted in accordance with the Scheme, subject to the following modifications.

(i) In subsection (1)–

(a) for '(upon notice to the other parties and to the tribunal) apply to the court' substitute '(upon notice to the other party, to the arbitrator and to ACAS) apply to the High Court or the Central London County Court';

(b) for '(see section 73)' substitute '(see Part XXIV of the Scheme)'; and

(c) after 'section 70(2) and (3)' insert 'as modified for the purposes of the Scheme'.

(ii)   After subsection (1) insert–

'(1A) In this section–

'Arbitration Agreement' means an agreement to refer a dispute to arbitration in accordance with, and satisfying the requirements of, the Scheme;

'the Scheme' means the arbitration scheme set out in the Schedule to the ACAS (Flexible Working) Arbitration Scheme (Great Britain) Order 2004; and

'substantive jurisdiction' means any issue as to–

(a) the validity of the Arbitration Agreement and the application of the Scheme to the dispute or difference in question;

(b) the constitution of the arbitral tribunal; or

(c) the matters which have been submitted to arbitration in accordance with the Arbitration Agreement.'

Challenges on grounds of substantive jurisdiction: Scottish arbitrations

139S   A party to a Scottish arbitration may appeal to the Court of Session–

(i)   challenging any award of the arbitrator as to his or her substantive jurisdiction; or

(ii)   on the ground that an award made by the arbitrator on the merits is of no effect, in whole or in part, because the arbitrator did not have substantive jurisdiction.

140S   A party may lose the right to appeal under paragraph 139S in accordance with Part XXIV below.

141S   Appeals under paragraph 139S are subject to the provisions of paragraphs 157S, 158S and 159S below.

142S   For the purposes of paragraph 139S, 'substantive jurisdiction' means any issue as to–

(i)   the validity of the arbitration agreement and the application of the Scheme to the dispute or difference in question;

(ii)   the constitution of the arbitral tribunal; or

(iii)   the matters which have been submitted to arbitration in accordance with the Arbitration Agreement.

143S   The arbitrator may continue the arbitral proceedings and make a further award while an appeal to the Court under paragraph 139S is pending in relation to an award of the arbitrator as to his substantive jurisdiction.

144S   On the appeal under paragraph 139S the Court may (without prejudice to any other power which it may exercise or remedy which it may grant)–

(i)   confirm the award:

(ii) vary the award;

(iii) declare the award to be of no effect in whole or in part; or

(iv) reduce the award in whole or in part.

Challenges for serious irregularity: English/Welsh arbitrations

145EW Section 68 of the Arbitration Act 1996 shall apply to English/Welsh arbitrations conducted in accordance with the Scheme, subject to the following modifications.

(i)   In subsection (1)–

    (a) for '(upon notice to the other parties and to the tribunal) apply to the court' substitute '(upon notice to the other party, to the arbitrator and to ACAS) apply to the High Court or Central London County Court';

    (b) for '(see section 73)' substitute '(see Part XXIV of the Scheme)';

    (c) after 'section 70(2) and (3)' insert 'as modified for the purposes of the Scheme'.

(ii)   In subsection (2)–

    (a) in paragraph (a) for 'section 33 (general duty of tribunal)' substitute 'Part X of the Scheme (General Duty of the Arbitrator)';

    (b) in paragraph (b) after 'see section 67' insert 'as modified for the purposes of the Scheme'; and

    (c) in paragraph (c) for 'agreed by the parties' substitute 'as set out in the Scheme';

    (d) in paragraph (e) for 'any arbitral or other institution or person vested by the parties with powers in relation to the proceedings or the award' substitute 'ACAS';

    (e) omit paragraph (h);

    (f) in paragraph (i) for 'any arbitral or other institution or person vested by the parties with powers in relation to the proceedings or the award' substitute 'ACAS'.

(iii) In subsection (3)–

    (a) in paragraph (b) insert 'vary the award or' before 'set the award aside';

    (b) omit 'The court shall not exercise its power to set aside or to declare an award to be of no effect, in whole or in part, unless it is satisfied that it would be inappropriate to remit the matters in question to the tribunal for reconsideration.'.

(iv) After subsection (4) insert–

'(5) In this section, 'the Scheme' means the arbitration scheme set out in the Schedule to the ACAS (Flexible Working) Arbitration Scheme (Great Britain) Order 2004.'

Challenges for serious irregularity: Scottish arbitrations

146S A party to a Scottish arbitration may appeal to the Court of Session against an award in the proceedings on the ground of serious irregularity affecting the arbitrator, the proceedings or the award.

147S A party may lose the right to appeal under paragraph 146S above in accordance with section XXIV below.

148S Appeals under paragraph 146S are subject to the provisions of paragraphs 157S, 158S and 159S below.

149S For the purpose of paragraphs 146S 'serious irregularity' means an irregularity of one or more of the following kinds which the Court considers has caused or will cause substantial injustice to the appellant–
  (i)   failure by the arbitrator to comply with Part X above (General Duty of Arbitrator);
  (ii) the arbitrator exceeding his or her powers (otherwise than by exceeding his or her substantive jurisdiction as defined in paragraph 142S above);
  (iii) failure by the arbitrator to conduct the proceedings in accordance with the procedure set out in the Scheme;
  (iv) failure by the arbitrator to deal with all the issues put to him or her;
  (v)   ACAS exceeding its powers;
  (vi) uncertainty or ambiguity as to the effect of the award;
  (vii) the award having been obtained by fraud or the way in which it was procured being contrary to public policy; or
  (viii) any irregularity in the conduct of the proceedings or in the award which is admitted by the arbitrator or ACAS.

150S If there is shown to be serious irregularity affecting the arbitrator, the proceedings or the award, the Court may (without prejudice to any other power which it may exercise or remedy which it may grant)–
  (i)   remit the award to the arbitrator, in whole or in part, for reconsideration;
  (ii) vary the award;
  (iii) declare the award to be of no effect in whole or in part; or
  (iv) reduce the award in whole or in part.

Appeals on questions of EC law, the Human Rights Act 1998 and devolution issues: English/Welsh arbitrations

151EW Section 69 of the Arbitration Act 1996 shall apply to English/Welsh arbitrations conducted in accordance with the Scheme, subject to the following modifications.
  (i)   In subsection (1)–
    (a) omit 'Unless otherwise agreed by the parties';
    (b) for '(upon notice to the other parties and to the tribunal) appeal to the court' substitute '(upon notice to the other party, to the arbitrator and to ACAS) appeal to the High Court or Central London County Court';
    (c) for 'a question of law' substitute 'a question (a) of EC law, or (b) concerning the application of the Human Rights Act 1998, or (c) any devolution issue';
    (d) omit 'An agreement to dispense with reasons for the tribunal's award shall be considered an agreement to exclude the court's jurisdiction under this section'.

(ii) In subsection (2) after 'section 70(2) and (3)' insert 'as modified for the purposes of the Scheme'.

(iii) In subsection (3)–
   (a) omit paragraph (b);
   (b) in paragraph (c) after the words 'on the basis of the findings of fact in the award' insert, in so far as the question for appeal raises a point of EC law, the point is capable of serious argument, and in so far as the question for appeal does not raise a point of EC law'.

(iv) In subsection (7) omit 'The court shall not exercise its power to set aside an award, in whole or in part, unless it is satisfied that it would be inappropriate to remit the matters in question to the tribunal for reconsideration'.

(v) After subsection (8) insert–

'(9) In this section–

'EC law' means–
   (a) any enactment in the domestic legislation of England and Wales giving effect to rights, powers, liabilities, obligations and restrictions from time to time created or arising by or under the Community Treaties, and
   (b) any such rights, powers, liabilities, obligations and restrictions which are not given effect by any such enactment; and

'devolution issue' means a devolution issue as defined in paragraph 1 of Schedule 6 of the Scotland Act 1998 or a devolution issue as defined in paragraph 1 of Schedule 8 of the Government of Wales Act 1998; and

'the Scheme' means the arbitration scheme set out in the Schedule to the ACAS (Flexible Working) Arbitration Scheme (Great Britain) Order 2004.'

Appeals on questions of EC law, the Human Rights Act 1998 and devolution issues: Scottish arbitrations

152S A party to a Scottish arbitration may appeal to the Court of Session–
   (i) on a question of EC law,
   (ii) on a question concerning the application of the Human Rights Act 1998, or
   (iii) on a devolution issue

arising out of an award made in the arbitration.

153S An appeal shall not be brought under paragraph 152S except–
   (i) with the agreement of all the other parties to the proceedings; or
   (ii) with the leave of the Court.

154S Leave to appeal shall be given only if the Court is satisfied–
   (i) that the determination of the question will substantially affect the rights of one or more of the parties;
   (ii) that on the basis of the findings of fact in the Note issued with the award, insofar as the question for appeal raises a point of EC law, the point is capable of serious argument, and insofar as the question for appeal does not raise a point of EC law–
   (iii) the decision of the arbitrator on the question is obviously wrong, or

    (iv) the question is one of general public importance and the decision of the arbitrator is at least open to serious doubt, and

    (v) that, despite the agreement of the parties to resolve the matter by arbitration, it is just and proper in all circumstances for the Court to determine the question.

155S On an appeal under paragraph 152S the Court may (without prejudice to any other power which it may exercise or remedy which it may grant)–

    (i) confirm the award;

    (ii) vary the award;

    (iii) remit the award to the arbitrator, in whole or in part, for reconsideration in light of the Court's determination;

    (iv) declare the award to be of no effect in whole or in part;

    (v) reduce the award in whole or in part; or

    (vi) recall the award in whole or in part.

Time limits and other procedural restrictions on challenges to awards: English/Welsh arbitrations

156EW Section 70 of the Arbitration Act 1996 shall apply to English/Welsh arbitrations conducted in accordance with the Scheme, subject to the following modifications–

    (i) In subsection (1) after 'section 67, 68 or 69' insert '(as modified for the purposes of the Scheme)'.

    (ii) In subsection (2)–

        (a) omit paragraph (a);

        (b) in paragraph (b) for 'section 57 (correction of award or additional award)' substitute 'Part XXI of the Scheme (Correction of Awards)'.

    (iii) In subsection (3) for 'of the award or, if there has been any arbitral process of appeal or review, of the date when the applicant or appellant was notified of the result of that process' substitute 'the award was despatched to the applicant or appellant by ACAS or, if an application for a correction or additional award under paragraph 124 has been made and declined, the date on which the arbitrator's decision was despatched to the applicant or appellant by ACAS';

    (iv) Omit subsection (5).

    (v) After subsection (8) insert–

    '(9) In this section, 'the Scheme' means the arbitration scheme set out in the Schedule to the ACAS (Flexible Working) Arbitration Scheme (Great Britain) Order 2004.'

Time limits and other procedural restrictions on challenges to awards: Scottish Arbitrations

157S An appeal under paragraphs 139S, 146S or 152S may not be brought if the appellant has not first exhausted any available recourse under Part XXI of the Scheme (Correction of Awards).

158S An appeal under paragraphs 139S, 146S or (where parties have agreed under paragraph 153S(i)) 152S or an application for leave to appeal under paragraph 153S(ii) shall be lodged within 28 days of whichever is the later of–

(i) the date on which the award was despatched to the appellant by ACAS;

(ii) where a correction or additional award has been made in accordance with Part XXI above, the date on which a memorandum of correction or additional award under Part XXI above was despatched to the appellant by ACAS; and

(iii) where a party has applied for a correction or additional award under paragraph 124 above but the arbitrator has declined to make any correction or additional award, the date on which intimation of the arbitrator's decision was despatched to the appellant by ACAS.

159S If on an appeal under paragraph 139S, 146S or 152S it appears to the Court that the award and the arbitrator's Note

(i) do not contain the arbitrator's reasons, or

(ii) do not set out the arbitrator's reasons in sufficient detail to enable the court to properly consider the application or appeal,

the Court may order the arbitrator to state the reasons for his or her award in sufficient detail for that purpose.

Common law challenges and saving

160EW Sections 81(1)(c) and 81(2) of the Arbitration Act 1996 shall apply to English/Welsh arbitrations conducted in accordance with the Scheme.

161S Nothing in this Part of the Scheme shall be construed as excluding the operation of any rule of law as to the refusal of recognition or enforcement of an arbitral award in a Scottish arbitration on grounds of public policy.

Exclusion of stated case procedure

162S Section 3 of the Administration of Justice (Scotland) Act 1972 shall not apply to an arbitration under the scheme.

Challenge or appeal: effect of order of the Court

163EW Section 71 of the Arbitration Act 1996 shall apply to English/Welsh arbitrations conducted in accordance with the Scheme, subject to the following modifications–

(i) In subsection (1) after 'section 67, 68 and 69' insert '(as modified for the purposes of the Scheme)';

(ii) After subsection (3) insert–

'(3A) In this section, 'the Scheme' means the arbitration scheme set out in the Schedule to the ACAS (Flexible Working) Arbitration Scheme (Great Britain) Order 2004'

(iii) Omit subsection (4).

164S The following provisions have effect where the Court makes an order under paragraph 144S, 150S or 155S of the Scheme with respect to an award–

(i) where the award is varied, the variation has effect as part of the arbitrator's award;

(ii) where the award is remitted to the arbitrator in whole or in part for reconsideration the arbitrator shall make a fresh award in respect of the matters remitted within three months of the date of the order for remission or such longer or shorter period as the Court may direct.

XXIV   LOSS OF RIGHT TO OBJECT

165   If a party to arbitral proceedings under this Scheme takes part, or continues to take part, in the proceedings without making, either forthwith or within such time as is allowed by the arbitrator or by any provision in this Scheme, any objection–

(i)   in an English/Welsh arbitration that the arbitrator lacks substantive jurisdiction as defined in paragraph 138EW above or in a Scottish arbitration that the arbitrator lacks substantive jurisdiction as defined in paragraph 142S above;

(ii)   that the proceedings have been improperly conducted;

(iii)   that there has been a failure to comply with the Arbitration Agreement or any provision of this Scheme; or

(vi)   that there has been any other irregularity affecting the arbitrator or the proceedings;

he or she may not raise that objection later, before the arbitrator or the court, unless he or she shows that, at the time he or she took part or continued to take part in the proceedings, he or she did not know and could not with reasonable diligence have discovered the grounds for the objection.

XXV   IMMUNITY

166   An arbitrator under this Scheme is not liable for anything done or omitted in the discharge or purported discharge of his or her functions as arbitrator unless the act or omission is shown to have been in bad faith. This applies to a legal adviser appointed by ACAS as it applies to the arbitrator himself or herself.

167   ACAS, by reason of having appointed an arbitrator or nominated a legal adviser, is not liable for anything done or omitted by the arbitrator or legal adviser in the discharge or purported discharge of his or her functions.

XXVI   MISCELLANEOUS PROVISIONS

Requirements in connection with legal proceedings

168EW Sections 80(1), (2), (4), (5), (6) and (7) of the Arbitration Act 1996 shall apply to English/Welsh arbitrations conducted in accordance with the Scheme, subject to the following modification–

In subsection (1) for 'to the other parties to the arbitral proceedings, or to the tribunal' substitute 'to the other party to the arbitral proceedings, or to the arbitrator, or to ACAS'.

Service of documents and notices on ACAS or the ACAS Arbitration Section

169   Any notice or other document required or authorised to be given or served on ACAS or the ACAS Arbitration Section for the purposes of the arbitral proceedings shall be sent by pre-paid post to the address stipulated in the ACAS Guide to the Scheme.

or transmitted by facsimile, addressed to the ACAS Arbitration Section, at the number stipulated in the ACAS Guide to the Scheme,

or by electronic mail, at the address stipulated in the ACAS Guide to the Scheme.

170   Paragraph 169 does not apply to the service of documents on the ACAS Arbitration Section for the purposes of legal proceedings.

Service of documents or notices on any other person or entity (other than ACAS or the ACAS Arbitration Section)

171   Any notice or other document required or authorised to be given or served on any person or entity (other than ACAS or the ACAS Arbitration Section) for the purposes of the arbitral proceedings may be served by any effective means.

172   If such a notice or other document is addressed, pre-paid and delivered by post–
   (i)   to the addressee's last known principal residence or, if he or she is or has been carrying on a trade, profession or business, his or her last known principal business address, or
   (ii)   where the address is a body corporate, to the body's registered or principal office,

   it shall be treated as effectively served.

173   Paragraphs 171 and 172 (above) do not apply to the service of documents for the purposes of legal proceedings, for which provision is made by rules of court.

Powers of court in relation to service of documents: English/Welsh arbitrations

174EW Section 77 of the Arbitration Act 1996 shall apply to English/Welsh arbitrations conducted in accordance with the Scheme, subject to the following modifications.
   (i)   In subsection (1) omit 'in the manner agreed by the parties, or in accordance with provisions of section 76 having effect in default of agreement,';
   (ii)   In subsection (2) for 'Unless otherwise agreed by the parties, the court' substitute 'The High Court or Central London County Court'.
   (iii) In subsection (3) for 'Any party to the arbitration agreement may apply' substitute 'ACAS or any party to the Arbitration Agreement may apply'.

Reckoning periods of time

175EW Sections 78(2), (3), (4) and (5) of the Arbitration Act 1996 shall apply to English/Welsh arbitrations conducted in accordance with the Scheme, subject to the following modifications to subsection 2 of that section–
   (i)   omit 'If or to the extent that there is no such agreement,';
   (ii)   after 'periods of time' insert 'provided for in any provision of this Part'.

176S   Except as otherwise specified in the Scheme, periods of time shall in Scottish arbitrations be reckoned in accordance with the following provisions–

(i)   Where the act is required to be done within a specified period after or from a specified date, the period begins immediately after that date.

(ii)   Where an act is required to be done a specified number of clear days after a specified date, at least that number of days must intervene between the day on which the act is done and that date.

(iii)   Where the period is a period of seven days or less which would include a Saturday, Sunday or public holiday in the place where anything which has to be done within the period falls to be done, that day shall be excluded.

(iv)   In relation to Scotland a 'public holiday' means a day which under the Banking and Financial Dealings Act 1971 is to be a bank holiday in Scotland and in relation to England and Wales or Northern Ireland a 'public holiday' means Christmas Day, Good Friday or a day under which the Banking and Financial Dealings Act 1971 is to be a bank holiday in England and Wales or Northern Ireland as the case may be.

XXVII GOVERNING LAW, ETC

177EW The seat of an English/Welsh arbitration shall be in England and Wales. The arbitrator may nevertheless hold any meeting or hearing or do any act in relation to the arbitration outside England and Wales.

178S   The seat of a Scottish arbitration shall be Scotland. The arbitrator may nevertheless hold any meeting or hearing or do any act in relation to the arbitration outside Scotland.

APPENDIX A: WAIVER OF RIGHTS: ENGLISH/WELSH ARBITRATIONS

The ACAS Arbitration Scheme ('the Scheme') is entirely voluntary. In agreeing to refer a dispute to arbitration under the Scheme, both parties agree to waive rights that they would otherwise have if, for example, they had referred their dispute to the employment tribunal. This follows from the informal nature of the Scheme, which is designed to be a confidential, relatively fast, cost-efficient and non-legalistic process.

As required by Part VII of the Scheme, as a confirmation of the parties' agreement to waive their rights, this form must be completed by each party and submitted to ACAS together with the agreement to arbitration.

A detailed description of the informal nature of arbitration under the Scheme, and the important differences between this and the employment tribunal, is contained in the ACAS Guide to the Scheme, which should be read by each party before completing this form.

The Scheme is not intended for disputes involving complex legal issues, or questions of EC law. Parties to such disputes are strongly advised to consider applying to the employment tribunal, or settling their dispute by other means.

This form does not list all the differences between the Scheme and the employment tribunal, or all of the features of the Scheme to which each party agrees in referring their dispute to arbitration.

There are differences between the law of England and Wales on the one hand and the law of Scotland on the other. The Scheme accordingly makes separate provision for English/Welsh arbitrations and Scottish arbitrations. This form confirms the parties' agreement that the arbitration between them shall be an English/Welsh arbitration.

I, the Applicant / Respondent / Respondent's duly authorised representative [delete as appropriate] confirm my/the Respondent's agreement to each of the following points–

1   Unlike proceedings in the employment tribunal, all proceedings under the Scheme, including all hearings, are conducted in private. There are no public hearings, and the final award will be confidential.

2   All arbitrators under the Scheme are appointed by ACAS from the ACAS Arbitration Panel (which is a panel of impartial, mainly non-lawyer, arbitrators appointed by ACAS on fixed, but renewable, terms). The appointment process and the ACAS Arbitration Panel are described in the Scheme and the ACAS Guide. Neither party will have any choice of arbitrator.

3   Proceedings under the Scheme are conducted differently from the employment tribunal. In particular–
    – arbitrators will conduct proceedings in an informal manner in all cases;
    – the attendance of witnesses and the production of documents cannot be compelled (although failure to co-operate may be taken into account by the arbitrator);
    – there will be no oaths or affirmations, and no cross-examination of witnesses by parties or their representatives;
    – the arbitrator will take the initiative in asking questions and ascertaining the facts (with the aim of ensuring that all relevant issues are considered), as well as hearing each side's arguments;
    – the arbitrator's decision will only contain the main considerations that have led to the result; it will not contain full or detailed reasons.

4   Once parties have agreed to refer their dispute to arbitration in accordance with the Scheme, the parties cannot then return to the employment tribunal.

5   In deciding whether the employee's complaint that his Employer has failed to deal with an application under section 80F of the Employment Rights Act 1996 in accordance with section 80G(1) of that Act or that a decision by his Employer to reject the application was based on incorrect facts, the arbitrator shall have regard to the Flexible Working (Procedural Requirements) Regulations 2002, as well as any relevant ACAS guidance. Unlike the employment tribunal, the arbitrator will not apply strict rules of evidence.

6   Unlike the employment tribunal, there is no right of appeal from awards of arbitrators under the Scheme (except for a limited right to appeal questions of EC law and, aside from procedural matters set out in the Scheme, questions concerning the Human Rights Act 1998 and devolution issues).

7   Unlike the employment tribunal, in agreeing to arbitration under the

Scheme, parties agree that there is no jurisdictional argument, ie, no reason why the claim cannot be heard and determined by the arbitrator.

8   The arbitration shall be an English/Welsh arbitration.

SIGNED:

DATED:

IN THE PRESENCE OF

Signature:

Full Name:

Position:

Address:

APPENDIX B: WAIVER OF RIGHTS: SCOTTISH ARBITRATIONS

The ACAS Arbitration Scheme ('the Scheme') is entirely voluntary. In agreeing to refer a dispute to arbitration under the Scheme, both parties agree to waive rights that they would otherwise have if, for example, they had referred their dispute to the employment tribunal. This follows from the informal nature of the Scheme, which is designed to be a confidential, relatively fast, cost-efficient and non-legalistic process.

As required by Part VII of the Scheme, as a confirmation of the parties' agreement to waive their rights, this form must be completed by each party and submitted to ACAS together with the agreement to arbitration.

A detailed description of the informal nature of arbitration under the Scheme, and the important differences between this and the employment tribunal, is contained in the ACAS Guide to the Scheme, which should be read by each party before completing this form.

The Scheme is not intended for disputes involving complex legal issues, or questions of EC law. Parties to such disputes are strongly advised to consider applying to the employment tribunal, or settling their dispute by other means.

This form does not list all the differences between the Scheme and the employment tribunal, or all of the features of the Scheme to which each party agrees in referring their dispute to arbitration.

There are differences between the law of Scotland on the one hand and the law of England and Wales on the other. The Scheme accordingly makes separate provision for Scottish arbitrations and English/Welsh arbitrations. This form confirms the parties' agreement that the arbitration between them shall be an Scottish arbitration and (as permitted in Scots law) that any award may be enforced by registration.

I, ...the Applicant / Respondent / Respondent's representative duly authorised to sign on the Respondent's behalf [delete as appropriate] confirm my/the Respondent's agreement to each of the following points–

1   Unlike proceedings in the employment tribunal, all proceedings under the Scheme, including all hearings, are conducted in private. There are no public hearings, and the final award will be confidential.

2   All arbitrators under the Scheme are appointed by ACAS from the ACAS Arbitration Panel (which is a panel of impartial, mainly non-lawyer, arbitrators appointed by ACAS on fixed, but renewable, terms). The appointment

process and the ACAS Arbitration Panel are described in the Scheme and the ACAS Guide. Neither party will have any choice of arbitrator.

3   Proceedings under the Scheme are conducted differently from the employment tribunal. In particular–
   –   arbitrators will conduct proceedings in an informal manner in all cases;
   –   the attendance of witnesses and the production of documents cannot be compelled (although failure to co-operate may be taken into account by the arbitrator);
   –   there will be no oaths or affirmations, and no cross-examination of witnesses by parties or their representatives;
   –   the arbitrator will take the initiative in asking questions and ascertaining the facts (with the aim of ensuring that all relevant issues are considered), as well as hearing each side's arguments;
   –   the arbitrator's decision will only contain the main considerations that have led to the result; it will not contain full or detailed reasons.

4   Once parties have agreed to refer their dispute to arbitration in accordance with the Scheme, the parties cannot then return to the employment tribunal

5   In deciding whether the employee's complaint that his Employer has failed to deal with an application under section 80F of the Employment Rights Act 1996 in accordance with section 80G(1) of that Act or that a decision by his Employer to reject the application was based on incorrect facts, the arbitrator shall have regard to the Flexible Working (Procedural Requirements) Regulations 2002, as well as any relevant ACAS guidance. Unlike the employment tribunal, the arbitrator will not apply strict rules of evidence.

6   Unlike the employment tribunal, there is no right of appeal from awards of arbitrators under the Scheme (except for a limited right to appeal questions of EC law and, aside from procedural matters set out in the Scheme, questions concerning the Human Rights Act 1998) and devolution issues.

7   Unlike the employment tribunal, in agreeing to arbitration under the Scheme, parties agree that there is no jurisdictional argument, ie, no reason why the claim cannot be heard and determined by the arbitrator. The provisions of section 3 of the Administration of Justice (Scotland) Act 1972 (which provides for arbiters to state a case for the opinion of the Court of Session) shall not apply to this arbitration.

8   The party by or on behalf of whom this form is signed consents to registration for execution of the arbitration agreement, this waiver form and any award (including any additional award, any correction to an award and any variation of an award) requiring the payment of money which may be made in this arbitration.

9   The arbitration shall be a Scottish arbitration.
   SIGNED:
   DATED:
   IN THE PRESENCE OF
   Signature:
   Full Name:
   Position:
   Address:

Useful addresses

Useful addresses

EMPLOYMENT TRIBUNALS: ENGLAND AND WALES

Central office
Central Office of the
Employment Tribunals
19–29 Woburn Place
London WC1H 0LU
Tel: 020 7273 8575
Fax: 020 7273 8686

Employment Tribunal offices

Ashford
1st Floor Ashford House
County Square Shopping Centre
Ashford
Kent TN23 1YB
Tel: 01233 621346
Fax: 01233 624423

Bedford
8–10 Howard Street
Bedford MK40 3HS
Tel: 01234 351306
Fax: 01234 352315

Birmingham
1st Floor Phoenix House
1/3 Newhall Street
Birmingham B3 3NH
Tel: 0121 236 6051
Fax: 0121 236 6029

Bristol
The Crescent Centre
Temple Back
Bristol BS1 6EZ
Tel: 0117 929 8261
Fax: 0117 925 3452

Bury St Edmunds
100 Southgate Street
Bury St Edmunds
Suffolk IP33 2AQ
Tel: 01284 762171
Fax: 01284 706064

Norwich (hearing centre)
Elliot House
130 Ber Street
Norwich NR1 3TZ
Tel/Fax: as for Bury St Edmunds

Cardiff
2nd Floor Caradog House
1–6 St Andrews Place
Cardiff CF10 3BE
Tel: 029 2067 8100
Fax: 029 2022 5906

Exeter
2nd Floor Keble House
Southernhay Gardens
Exeter EX1 1NT
Tel: 01392 279665
Fax: 01392 430063

Leeds
4th Floor City Exchange
11 Albion Street
Leeds LS1 5ES
Tel: 0113 245 9741
Fax: 0113 242 8843

Hull (hearing centre)
Wilberforce Court
Alfred Gelder Street
Hull HU1 1YR
Tel/Fax: as for Leeds

Leicester
Kings Court
5A New Walk
Leicester LE1 6TE
Tel: 0116 255 0099
Fax: 0116 255 6099

Liverpool
1st Floor Cunard Building
Pier Head
Liverpool L3 1TS
Tel: 0151 236 9397
Fax: 0151 231 1484

London Central
19–29 Woburn Place
London WC1H 0LU
Tel: 020 7273 8575
Fax: 020 7273 8686
Fax: 020 8649 9470

London South
Montague Court
101 London Road
West Croydon CR0 2RF
Tel: 020 8667 9131

Manchester
Alexandra House
14–22 The Parsonage
Manchester M3 2JA
Tel: 0161 833 0581
Fax: 0161 832 0249

Newcastle
Quayside House
110 Quayside
Newcastle upon Tyne NE1 3DX
Tel: 0191 260 6900
Fax: 0191 222 1680

Thornaby (hearing centre)
Part Ground Floor
Christine House
4 Sorbonne Close
Thornaby-on-Tees
Cleveland TS17 6DA
Tel/Fax: as for Newcastle

Carlisle (hearing centre)
1st Floor Stockhund House
Castle Street
Carlisle
Cumbria
Tel/Fax: as for Newcastle

Nottingham
3rd Floor Byron House
2A Maid Marian Way
Nottingham NG1 6HS
Tel: 0115 947 5701
Fax: 0115 950 7612

Reading
5th Floor 30–31 Friar Street
Reading RG1 1DY
Tel: 0118 959 4917
Fax: 0118 956 8066

Sheffield
14 East Parade
Sheffield S1 2ET
Tel: 0114 276 0348
Fax: 0114 276 2551

Shrewsbury
Prospect House
Belle Vue Road
Shrewsbury SY3 7AR
Tel: 01743 358341
Fax: 01743 244186

Southampton
3rd Floor Duke's Keep
Marsh Lane
Southampton SO14 3EX
Tel: 023 8071 6400
Fax: 023 8063 5506

Brighton (hearing centre)
St James House
New England Street
Brighton BN1 4GQ
Tel: 01273 571488
Fax: 01273 623645

Stratford
44 The Broadway
Stratford
London E15 1XH
Tel: 020 8221 0921
Fax: 020 8221 0398

Watford
3rd Floor
Radius House
521 Clarendon Road
Watford
Herts WD1 1HU
Tel: 01923 281750
Fax: 01923 281781
www.employmenttribunals.gov.uk

EMPLOYMENT TRIBUNALS: SCOTLAND

Central office
Central Office of the
Employment Tribunals
Eagle Building
215 Bothwell Street
Glasgow G2 7TS
Tel: 0141 204 0730
Fax: 0141 204 0732

Employment Tribunal offices
Aberdeen
Mezzanine Floor
Atholl House
84–88 Guild Street
Aberdeen AB11 6LT
Tel: 01224 593137
Fax: 01224 593138

Dundee
13 Albert Square
Dundee DD1 1DD
Tel: 01382 221578
Fax: 01382 227136

Edinburgh
54–56 Melville Street
Edinburgh EH3 7HF
Tel: 0131 226 5584
Fax: 0131 220 6847

EMPLOYMENT APPEAL TRIBUNAL

Central Office
58 Victoria Embankment
London EC4Y 0DS
Tel: 020 7273 1040
Fax: 020 7273 1045
www.employmentappeals.gov.uk
londoneat@ets.gsi.gov.uk

Edinburgh Office
52 Melville Street
Edinburgh EH3 7HF
Tel: 0131 225 3963
Fax: 0131 220 6694
edinburgheat@ets.gsi.gov.uk

CENTRAL ARBITRATION COMMITTEE
Third Floor
Discovery House
28–42 Banner Street
London EC1Y 8EQ
Tel: 020 7251 9747
Fax: 020 7251 3114
E-mail: enquiries@cac.gov.uk
www.cac.gov.uk

ADVISORY, CONCILIATION AND ARBITRATION SERVICE
Midlands Region
West Midlands
Warwick House
6 Highfield Road
Edgbaston
Birmingham B15 3ED
Tel: 0121 456 5434

East Midlands
Lancaster House
10 Sherwood House
Nottingham NG7 6JE
Tel: 0115 985 8253

South Region
South West
The Waterfront
Welshback
Bristol BS1 4SB
Tel: 0117 906 5200
Fax: 0117 946 9501
Fax: 0117 946 9501

South East
Westminster House
125 Fleet Road
Fleet
Hampshire GU13 8PD
Tel: 01252 816650
Fax: 01252 811030

Yorkshire & Humber
The Cube
123 Albion Street
Leeds LS2 8ER
Tel: 0113 205 3800

North East Region
Cross House
Westgate Road
Newcastle upon Tyne
NE1 4XX
Tel: 0191 269 6000

North West Region
Commercial Union House
2–10 Albert Square
Manchester M60 8AD
Tel: 0161 833 8500

Pavilion 1
The Matchworks
Speke Road
Speke
Liverpool L19 2PH
Tel: 0151 728 5600

London, South and East of England
Euston Tower
286 Euston Road
London NW1 3JJ
Tel: 020 7396 0022

Ross House
Kempson Way
Suffolk Business Park
Bury St Edmunds
Suffolk IP32 7AR
Tel: 01284 774500

Suites 3–5 Business Centre
1–7 Commercial Road
Paddock Wood
Kent TN12 6EN
Tel: 01892 837273

Westminster House
125 Fleet Road
Fleet
Hants GU51 3QL
Tel: 01252 816650

Scotland
151 West George Street
Glasgow G2 7JJ
Tel: 0141 248 1400

Wales
3 Purbeck House
Lambourne Crescent
Llanishen
Cardiff CF14 7JR
Tel: 029 2076 2636

Head Office
Brandon House
180 Borough High Street
London SE1 1LW
Tel: 020 7210 3613
www.acas.org.uk

ACAS Helpline:
08457 47 47 47
08456 06 16 00 (textphone)

Equality Direct (confidential
advice service for small
businesses in equality):
08456 00 34 44

Advisory Service (formerly Race
and Equality Advisory Service):
08457 47 47 47

ACAS Equality Service (for
small to medium businesses in
Yorkshire & Humber only):
0113 205 3854
equalityservices@acas.org.uk

DEPARTMENT FOR TRADE AND INDUSTRY
www.dti.gov.uk

EQUAL OPPORTUNITIES COMMISSION
Arndale House
Arndale Centre
Manchester M4 3EQ
Tel: 0845 601 5901
Fax: 0161 838 1733
E-mail: info@eoc.org.uk
www.eoc.org.uk

COMMISSION FOR RACIAL EQUALITY
St Dunstan's House
201–211 Borough High Street
London SE1 1GZ
Tel: 020 7939 0000
Fax: 020 7939 0001
E-mail: info@cre.org.uk
www.cre.gov.uk

DISABILITY RIGHTS COMMISSION
Disability Rights Commission
Helpline
Freepost MID 02164
Stratford-upon-Avon
CV37 9BR
Tel: 08457 622 633
Fax: 08457 778 878
Textphone: 08457 622 644
www.drc.org.uk

FREE REPRESENTATION UNIT
6th Floor
289–293 High Holborn
London WC1V 7HZ
Tel: 0207 611 9555
Email:
admin@freerepresentationunit.org.uk

COMMUNITY LEGAL SERVICES
www.clsdirect.org.uk

LEGAL SERVICES COMMISSION
85 Gray's Inn Road
London WC1X 8TX
Tel: 020 7759 0000
www.legalservices.gov.uk

NORTHERN IRELAND LEGAL SERVICES COMMISSION
2nd Floor
Waterfront Plaza
8 Laganbank Road
Mays Meadow
Belfast BT1 3BN
Tel: 028 9024 6441
Fax: 028 9040 8990
www.nilsc.org.uk

SCOTTISH LEGAL AID BOARD
44 Drumsheugh Gardens
Edinburgh EH3 7SW
Tel: 0131 226 7061
Fax: 0131 225 5195
www.slab.org.uk

TRADES UNION CONGRESS
Congress House
Great Russell Street
London WC1 3LW
Tel: 020 7636 4030
Fax: 020 636 0632
www.tuc.org.uk

CITIZENS' ADVICE
Myddleton House
115–123 Pentonville Road
London N1 9LZ
Tel: 020 7833 2181
Fax: 020 7833 4371
www.nacab.org.uk

LAW CENTRES FEDERATION
Duchess House
18–19 Warren Street
London WC1P 5DP
Tel: 020 7387 8570
Fax: 020 7387 8368
www.lawcentres.org.uk

CERTIFICATION OFFICE FOR TRADE UNIONS AND EMPLOYERS' ASSOCIATIONS

Brandon House
180 Borough High Street
London SE1 1LW
Tel: 020 7210 3734
Fax: 020 7210 3612
www.certoffice.org

Index